W9-CGQ-969

THE OXFORD HANDBOOK OF

NEW RELIGIOUS MOVEMENTS

THE OXFORD HANDBOOK OF

NEW RELIGIOUS MOVEMENTS

Edited by

JAMES R. LEWIS

UNIVERSITY PRESS

2004

OXFORD
UNIVERSITY PRESS

Oxford   New York

Auckland   Bangkok   Buenos Aires   Cape Town   Chennai
Dar es Salaam   Delhi   Hong Kong   Istanbul   Karachi   Kolkata
Kuala Lumpur   Madrid   Melbourne   Mexico City   Mumbai   Nairobi
São Paulo   Shanghai   Taipei   Tokyo   Toronto

Copyright © 2004 by Oxford University Press, Inc.

Published by Oxford University Press, Inc.
198 Madison Avenue, New York, New York 10016

www.oup.com

Oxford is a registered trademark of Oxford University Press

Library of Congress Cataloging-in-Publication Data
The Oxford handbook of new religious movements / edited by James R. Lewis.
p.   cm.
Includes bibliographical references and index.
ISBN 0-19-514986-6
1. Cults. I. Lewis, James R.
BP603 .H36 2003
200'.9'04—dc21   2003002013

1 3 5 7 9 8 6 4 2

Printed in the United States of America
on acid-free paper

ACKNOWLEDGMENTS

....

As with all projects of this scope, so many people have assisted me in so many ways, large and small, that they cannot all be acknowledged here. I would, however, like briefly to acknowledge my more significant debts.

First, I would like to express my gratitude to my partner and wife, Evelyn. This volume was harder to finish than most, and it might never have reached completion without her support.

Second, thanks to Cynthia Read at Oxford University Press, who originally took interest in this project, and Theodore Calderara, who guided the compilation of this volume in its final stages.

Third and most important, I am indebted to my colleagues who contributed their time and expertise to this collection. Many of the contributors helped to found the new religious movements field. Among these, a special word of thanks to Gordon Melton and David Bromley.

Finally, as someone who takes every opportunity to interact with members of the groups he studies, I would also like to express my gratitude to the many informants and officials in various new religions I have studied firsthand.

CONTENTS

....

PART IV. NEO-PAGANS, UFOS, AND OTHER HETERODOXIES

CONTRIBUTORS

DICK ANTHONY is a research and forensic psychologist who specializes in research on the psychological concomitants of involvement in new religious movements. His research has been supported by United States government agencies such as the National Institute of Mental Health, the National Institute of Drug Abuse, and the National Endowment for the Humanities, and he has published its results in many articles and books. He also frequently testifies or serves as a trial consultant in cases involving allegations of coercive or harmful religious influence.

DAVID G. BROMLEY is Professor of Sociology at Virginia Commonwealth University. Among his recent books on religious movements are *Cults, Religion, and Violence* (2002), *Toward Reflexive Ethnography: Participating, Observing, Narrating* (2001), and *The Politics of Religious Apostasy: The Role of Apostates in the Transformation of Religious Movements* (1998). He is former president of the Association for the Sociology of Religion; founding editor of the annual series, Religion and the Social Order, sponsored by the Association for the Sociology of Religion; and former editor of *Journal for the Scientific Study of Religion*.

DOUGLAS E. COWAN is Assistant Professor of Religious Studies and Sociology at the University of Missouri–Kansas City. He is the author of *Bearing False Witness? An Introduction to the Christian Countercult* and *The Remnant Spirit: Conservative Reform in Mainline Protestantism*. He is also the coeditor (with Jeffrey K. Hadden) of *Religion on the Internet: Research Prospects and Promises* and (with Lorne L. Dawson) *Religion Online: Finding Faith on the Internet*.

SUSAN E. DARNELL manages a credit union in Gary, Indiana, and is a civil rights advocate journalist. She has worked with Anson Shupe on a number of projects, including *Bad Pastors: Clergy Misconduct in Modern America*.

LORNE L. DAWSON is Professor of Sociology and Chair of the Department of Religious Studies at the University of Waterloo in Canada. His research interests are the study of new religions, religion and the Internet, and questions of theory and method in the study of religion. He is the author of *Comprehending Cults* (1998) and the editor of *Cults and New Religious Movements* (2003) and *Religion Online* (2004) and has written many academic articles and chapters on these and other subjects.

ANDREAS GRÜNSCHLOß is Professor of Religious Studies at the University of Göttingen. His research focus is on New Religious Movements, Buddhism, systematic approaches in religious studies, syncretism, and interreligious hermeneutics. His publications include *Religionswissenschaft als Welt-Theologie: Wilfred Cantwell Smiths interreligiöse Hermeneutik* (1994); *Der eigene und der fremde Glaube: Studien zur interreligiösen Fremdwahrnehmung in Islam, Hinduismus, Buddhismus und Christentum* (1999); and contributions to academic journals, encyclopedias, and anthologies.

Until his passing, JEFFREY K. HADDEN was Professor of Sociology and Religious Studies at the University of Virginia. He was the founder of the Religious Movements Homepage Project, one of the most widely used resources for new religious movements on the Internet, and the author of several books, including *Prime Time Preachers, Televangelism: Power and Politics on God's Frontier*, and *The Gathering Storm in the Churches*.

OLAV HAMMER is Assistant Professor in Religious Studies at Amsterdam University. His research focuses on the application of various modes of critical theory in order to understand the processes of religious change and innovation. His publications include *Claiming Knowledge: Strategies of Claiming Knowledge from Theosophy to the New Age* (2001), a study of the construction of authority through religious discourse.

CHARLOTTE E. HARDMAN is an anthropologist, Senior Lecturer, and Alternate Head of the School of Arts and Cultures at Newcastle University, England. She is the coeditor (with Susan J. Palmer) of the book *Children in New Religions* and has written several articles on the anthropology of children, on children in new religions, and on Paganism. She is the author of the monograph *Other Worlds: Notions of Self and Emotion Among the Lohorung Rai*.

MASSIMO INTROVIGNE is the managing director of CESNUR, the Center for Studies on New Religions, an international research facility in Turin, Italy. He is the author or editor of thirty-two books on the history and sociology of religions (including the monumental *Enciclopedia delle religioni in Italia*) and of more than a hundred scholarly articles, published in several languages.

PHILIP JENKINS is Distinguished Professor of History and Religious Studies at Penn State University. He is the author of nineteen books, including *Mystics and Messiahs: Cults and New Religions in American History*, *The Next Christendom: The Rise of Global Christianity*, and *The New Anti-Catholicism: The Last Acceptable Prejudice*. He is currently completing a book about white appropriations of Native American spirituality.

R. GEORGE KIRKPATRICK is a scholar in the fields of sociological theory, collective behavior, and social movements. His notable studies have been of antipornography crusades, UFO religions, and American witches. He has taught with distinction for more than thirty years at San Diego State University.

RICHARD LANDES is Professor of Medieval History at Boston University. He is the director of the Center for Millennial Studies, and his work focuses on the relationships between elites and commoners, in particular the ways in which demotic religiosity, especially in its millennial forms, affects those relations. He is working on a multivolume work on the role of millennialism in the West, in which he argues that modernity is the unintended (and dynamic if deeply unstable) product of failed millennial movements.

JAMES R. LEWIS is an extensively published scholar of New Religious Movements and the New Age. His books include *The Encyclopedia of Cults, Sects, and New Religions, Legitimating New Religions*, and *Science and New Age Spirituality*. He currently teaches at the University of Wisconsin, Stevens Point.

J. GORDON MELTON is Director of the Institute for the Study of American Religions and a specialist in religion in the Department of Religious Studies at the University of California, Santa Barbara. He is a leading scholar of New Religious Movements and the author of such standard reference works as the *Encyclopedia of American Religions*.

SUSAN J. PALMER is an adjunct professor at Concordia University and a tenured professor at Dawson College, both in Montreal, Quebec. She has written over sixty articles on New Religious Movements and authored or edited eight books on New Religious Movements, including *Rael's UFO Religion: Racing and Cloning in the Age of Apocalypse*.

CHRISTOPHER PARTRIDGE is Senior Lecturer in Theology and Contemporary Religion at Chester College in Chester, England. He is the author of *UFO Religions* and editor of the forthcoming *Encyclopedia of New Religions*.

MICHAEL PYE is Professor of Religious Studies at Marburg University in Marburg, Germany. He was President of the International Association for the History of Religions (1995–2000) and is now an Honorary Life Member. His publications include *Ernst Troeltsch: Writings on Theology and Religion* (with Robert Morgan), *Skilful Means: A Concept in Mahayana Buddhism* (1978), *Emerging from Meditation* (1990), and the *Macmillan Dictionary of Religion* (1993), as well as many articles on various aspects of the study of religion, particularly Japanese religion.

SHELLEY TSIVIA RABINOVITCH holds a Ph.D. in religious studies, specializing in cultural anthropology, new religious movements, and First Nations studies. She has had numerous articles published in journals and is the coeditor, with James R. Lewis, of *The Encyclopedia of Modern Witchcraft and Neo-Paganism* (2002). She is a lecturer at the University of Ottawa.

síân lee reid is a lecturer in the Department of Sociology and Anthropology at Carleton University. Her research interests include sociology of religion, new religious movements, social theories of modernity and postmodernity, and reflexive narratives of the self. She holds a Ph.D. in sociology, an M.A. in religion, and a B.A. in English literature.

james t. richardson, J.D., Ph.D., is Professor of Sociology and Judicial Studies at the University of Nevada, Reno, where he directs the Grant Sawyer Center for Justice Studies as well as the Judicial Studies degree programs for trial judges. He is the author or coauthor of nearly two hundred articles and chapters, as well as seven books, including his latest, *Regulating Religion: Case Studies from around the Globe* (2003).

thomas robbins is a semi-retired sociologist of religion (Ph.D. from the University of North Carolina, 1974). He is the author of *Cults, Converts, and Charisma* (1988) and the coauthor of six collections of original papers, including *Millennium, Messiahs, and Mayhem* (1997) and *Misunderstanding Cults* (2001). He has published numerous articles, essays, and reviews in social science and religious studies journals.

mikael rothstein is Assistant Professor in the Department of History of Religions at the University of Copenhagen. He specializes in the study of new religions and is the author or editor of several books on the subject. He is a member of the board of the Research Network on New Religions (RENNER), based in Denmark, and Editor in Chief of *CHAOS*, a Danish-Norwegian journal on the history of religions.

john a. saliba has taught at the University of Detroit, Mercy, since 1970. He has been studying new religious movements since the late 1960s and has published two bibliographies and several books on the subject. His latest book is *Christian Responses to the New Age Movement*.

anson shupe is Professor of Sociology and Anthropology at the joint campus of Indiana University and Purdue University in Fort Wayne. He is the author of numerous professional articles and over two dozen books, including *Six Perspectives on New Religions, Born Again Politics and the Moral Majority,* and *Wealth and Power in American Zion*.

steven j. sutcliffe is Visiting Lecturer in the Department of Religious Studies at the University of Stirling, United Kingdom, where he was recently a research fellow in religion in contemporary Scotland. He has also taught in Religious Studies at the University of Sunderland and the Open University, both in the United Kingdom. He is the author of *Children of the New Age: A History of Spiritual Practices* (2003) and coeditor of *Beyond New Age: Exploring Alternative Spirituality*

(2000). He is currently guest editing a collection of papers on New Age studies for a special issue of the journal *Culture and Religion* (vol. 4, no. 1, 2003).

DIANA G. TUMMINIA teaches at California State University at Sacramento. She studied social psychology and ethnography at UCLA. Her publications address various topics in the sociology of religion, the psychology of belief, and excellence in teaching. Her expertise also extends into the areas of race and gender studies.

THE OXFORD HANDBOOK OF

NEW RELIGIOUS MOVEMENTS

OVERVIEW

JAMES R. LEWIS

ALTHOUGH new religions have often been the topic of journalistic stories, it is rare that the body of scholars who study them make the news. It was thus somewhat of a surprise when the annual meeting of the Center for Studies on New Religions (CESNUR), the premier international association of new religion scholars, was the subject of a feature article—"Oh, Gods!" by Toby Lester—in the February 2002 issue of the *Atlantic Monthly*. In his piece the author observed, among other things, that "the study of new religious movements—NRMs for short—has become a growth industry." In a similar vein, he also noted that "the NRM field is only a few decades old, but already it has made its mark" (p. 38).

The appearance of an article like "Oh, Gods!" is an indicator that the study of NRMs has achieved the status of a recognized academic specialty. This development is rather surprising when one considers that, as Gordon Melton notes in his contribution to the present volume, "in 1970 one could count the number of active researchers on new religions on one's hands." What accounts for the meteoric growth of this field of study? The short answer is that it arose in response to the cult controversy of the early 1970s, and it continued to grow in the wake of a series of headline-grabbing tragedies involving religious groups like the People's Temple and Heavens Gate. The long answer is somewhat more complicated.

As a field of scholarly endeavor, NRM studies actually emerged several decades earlier in Japan in the wake of the explosion of religious innovation following the Second World War. Even the name "new religions" is a direct translation of the expression *shin shukyo* that Japanese sociologists coined to refer to this phenomenon. Although the generation of new religious groups has been ongoing in Western countries (not to mention in the world as a whole) for millennia, the study of such groups and movements was the province of existing academic specializations in the West until the 1970s. Thus, to cite a few examples, the Pentecostal movement was studied as part of church history and phenomena like cargo cults were researched by anthropologists.

However, when a wave of nontraditional religiosity exploded out of the declining counterculture in the late 1960s and early 1970s, academics perceived it (correctly or incorrectly) as representing a different phenomenon from prior cycles of religious innovation. Not only did most of these new religions represent radical theological departures from the dominant Christian tradition, but—in contrast to movements like Pentecostalism—they also tended to recruit their adherents from the offspring of the middle class. Such characteristics caused these emergent religions to be regarded as categorical departures from the past, and they initially attracted scholars from a wide variety of disciplines. It was at this juncture that NRMs began to develop as a distinct field of scholarship in Western countries. And it should be noted that this development took place shortly *before* the cult controversy began to heat up. Two academic anthologies representative of this era are Glock and Bellah's *The New Religious Consciousness* (1976), and Needleman and Baker's *Understanding the New Religions* (1978). As reflected in many of the articles in these collections, the overall focus at the time was to attempt to assess the broader social significance of the newest wave of NRMs.

This academic landscape changed over the course of the seventies. By the latter part of the decade, it had become clear that new religions were *not* indicative of a broader social transformation—or at least not the kind of transformation observers had anticipated. In addition, issues raised by the cult controversy gradually came to dominate the field. Because social conflict is a bread-and-butter issue for sociology, more and more sociologists were drawn to the study of new religions. By the time of the Jonestown tragedy in 1978, NRMs was a recognized specialization within the sociology of religion.

It took much longer for new religions to achieve recognition as a legitimate specialization within religious studies. This was partially the result of the expansion of religious studies and its own quest for legitimacy within a mostly secular university system. During the early 1970s—when new religions were becoming a public issue—religious studies was busy establishing itself as an academic discipline. Most religion scholars were reluctant to further marginalize themselves by giving serious attention to what at the time seemed a transitory social phenomenon, and as a consequence they left the study of new religions to sociologists. Consequently, it was not until a series of major tragedies took place in the 1990s—specifically, the Branch Davidian debacle, the Solar Temple murder-suicides, the Aum Shinrikyō gas attack, and the Heaven's Gate suicides—that the field of NRMs was truly embraced by the religious studies establishment.

THE CULT CONTROVERSY

Although, as has already been indicated, the cult controversy was not responsible for initiating the new religions field, the development of this area of study almost immediately became tied to the controversy. From the beginning, most mainstream academic researchers rejected the popular stereotype of NRMs deceptively recruiting and "brainwashing" their members. Furthermore, almost all of the studies supporting the notion of "cultic mind control" were so obviously biased that mainstream social scientific journals routinely refused to publish them. Beginning in the mid-seventies, mainstream scholars steadily churned out studies directly relevant to this controversy. At present, a collection of academic books devoted to this controversy, plus books on new religions containing at least one full chapter addressing the controversy, would easily fill several standard library bookcases. This does not include the significant number of relevant articles published in academic journals.

The operative question new religion specialists have asked about mind control is this: How does one distinguish cultic brainwashing from other forms of social influence, such as advertising, military training, or even the normal socialization routines of public schools? Particularly in the 1970s, anti-cultists supported the notion that cult members were trapped in a kind of quasi-hypnotic trance, while others asserted that the ability of cult members to process certain kinds of information had "snapped" (Conway and Siegelman 1979). The problem with these and similar theories was that if cultic influences overrode the brain's ability to logically process information, then individuals suffering from cultic influences should perform poorly on I.Q. tests or, at the very least, should manifest pathological symptoms when they took standardized tests of mental health; yet when tested, they did not. In point of fact, such empirical studies often indicated that members of NRMs were actually smarter and healthier than the average member of mainstream society (e.g., Sowards, Walser, and Hoyle 1994).

Other kinds of studies also failed to support the view that new religions relied upon unusual forms of social influence to gain and retain members. For example, if NRMs possessed powerful techniques of mind control that effectively overrode a potential convert's free will, then everyone—or at least a large percentage of attendees—at recruiting seminars should be unable to avoid conversion. However, in her important study *The Making of a Moonie: Choice or Brainwashing?* (1984), Eileen Barker found that less than 10 percent of the people who visited centers run by the Unification Church—an organization many regard as the evil cult par excellence—eventually attended recruitment seminars. Of those who attended such seminars, less than 10 percent joined the Church (a net recruitment rate of under 1 percent). Furthermore, of those who joined, more than half dropped out within the first year of their membership. In another important study, *Radical*

Departures: Desperate Detours to Growing Up (1984), psychiatrist Saul Levine found that, out of a sample of over 800 people who had joined controversial religious groups, more than 90 percent dropped out within two years of membership—not the kind of statistics one would anticipate from groups wielding powerful techniques of mind control.

In these and other empirical studies, researchers asked further questions, such as, Given the lack of empirical support, where does the brainwashing notion come from? And, What is the more fundamental conflict that the cult stereotype obfuscates? The general conclusion of sociologists—as analyzed, for example, in David Bromley and Anson Shupe's *Strange Gods: The Great American Cult Scare* (1981)—was that the principal source of the controversy was a parent-child conflict in which parents failed to understand the religious choices of their adult children and attempted to reassert parental control by marshaling the forces of public opinion against the religious bodies to which their offspring had converted.

This core conflict was then exacerbated by irresponsible mass media that profited by printing and broadcasting exciting stories about weird cults that trapped their members and kept them in psychological bondage with exotic techniques of mind control. Also, once an industry was established that generated profits by "rescuing" entrapped cult members (via the practice of "deprogramming"), special interest groups emerged that had vested interests in promoting the most negative stereotypes of alternative religions. These special interest groups added further fuel to the parent-child conflict by scaring parents with lurid stories of what would happen to their adult child if they failed to have her or him deprogrammed. In this manner, many otherwise reasonable and well-meaning people were recruited into the controversy.

This, essentially, is the picture of the cult controversy that academic researchers have pieced together over the last three decades. Because of its vested interest in maintaining the conflict, the anti-cult movement was unresponsive to critical studies and proceeded with business as usual, as if these studies were nonexistent. Rather than responding directly to mainstream scholarship, anti-cultists instead conducted research on their own terms, creating alternative publications that featured pseudoscientific studies supporting the cult stereotype.

One of the consequences of this situation was that researchers found themselves forced to work in a highly politicized atmosphere. Articles on controversial religious groups published in specialized academic journals could directly impact people's lives, particularly when cited in legal briefs and judicial decisions. Thus, in contrast to academics who studied things like the mating habits of insects or the spectrum of light generated by distant galaxies, NRM specialists regularly found themselves the subjects of scrutiny and criticism.

Because mainstream new religion scholars have generally been critical of the cult stereotype (particularly the notion of cult mind control), they have, in turn, been criticized by those interested in perpetuating this stereotype. One counter-strategy commonly utilized by such interest groups is to refer to academicians whose research tends to undermine anti-cult ideology as "cult apologists," implying that they are in a conspiracy with—perhaps even covertly accepting money from—malevolent religious groups. The cult apologist accusation is a handy ideological tool because, in the hands of most anti-cultists, it is wielded as a tautology, immune to empirical disconfirmation. In other words, if a cult apologist is defined (usually implicitly) as any researcher producing scholarship critical of the cult stereotype, then anyone whose scholarship is critical of the cult stereotype is ipso facto a cult apologist. This strategy allows anti-cultists to reject any scholarship with which they disagree, saving them from the awkward necessity of taking it seriously.

Anti-cultists adhering to this rhetorical strategy sometimes make it appear that sinister pseudoreligious organizations regularly seek out scholars to legitimate their group and to attack their critics. One of the more absurd examples of this strategy can be found in the introduction to Michael Newton's *Raising Hell: An Encyclopedia of Devil Worship and Satanic Crime* (1993). Newton takes "liberal" academics to task for criticizing the notion of occult crime—referring to them as "cult apologists" (p. 2) as if they were mercenaries on the payroll of some grand underground satanic conspiracy, or, no less implausibly, as if their souls had been purchased by the Prince of Darkness himself.

In point of fact, only a few groups like the Unification Church—which for many years courted academicians, presumably because of its Confucian-derived understanding of the importance of scholars in society—have believed that academicians wielded this kind of power. The leaders of most other new religions have been far less naive about the social influence of scholars. Perhaps the only area where academic researchers have played a significant role in the cult controversy is in the debunking of mind-control notions and other aspects of the cult stereotype, making this the one area where academic specialists have entered the fray in support of NRMs. The fact that some of the most prominent scholars in the field have testified against the brainwashing thesis in relevant legislative hearings and legal cases has evoked the ire of anti-cultists and is the principal evidence for their contention that such academicians are "apologists."

BOUNDARY AND DISCIPLINARY ISSUES

In his contribution to the present volume, Gordon Melton has made the task of writing this introduction much easier by dealing with the history of the study of new religions and with some of the prominent issues in the NRM field. With the exception of a few areas of unavoidable overlap, I will try not to replicate his efforts.

One question I would like to address is why certain categories of new religions are studied while others are not. Like religious studies more generally, NRM studies is, as Melton points out, "defined by its subject matter rather than methodology." As a field significantly shaped by the cult conflict, the core of NRM studies is constituted by analyses of controversial new religions and analyses of the controversy itself. If everything related to these two topics was subtracted from the corpus of new religions scholarship, relatively little would be left. Like the emergent popularity of Islamic studies since the 9/11 attacks, NRM studies rose to prominence as a direct consequence of the public perception of certain religions as potential social threats. Thus, despite the regular expressions of dismay one sometimes overhears at academic conferences (e.g., as recorded by Lester, "I'm so damn sick of the cult/anti-cult debate, I could just puke!" [p. 41]), it is unlikely that this situation will change in the immediate future.

Because of this focus, it is appropriate to ask what this field of study might look like if not for the cult controversy. Certainly one of the major differences would be that existing scholarship would not be clustered around a couple dozen small groups. There have been more than a few major studies of groups such as the Unification Church that have a relatively small presence in Western countries. In contrast, there have been no monographs written about much larger—but less controversial—new religions like Eckankar. A more comprehensive approach that examined the many NRMs not locked in social conflict would likely provide a much different picture of the nature of these movements. Perhaps certain characteristics shared by the majority of new religions might have been warped or even missed as a consequence of focusing on the controversial groups.

Another issue is that NRM studies is in many ways a residual category. Although the designation "new religions" implies that all kinds of emergent religions are part of this field, in practice NRM scholars have tended to avoid studying movements perceived as the "turf" of other scholarly specialities. I have already mentioned that certain Christian new religious movements like Pentecostalism have for the most part been left to church historians, and that third world NRMs like cargo cults have been left to anthropologists. Similarly, although new religions researchers have occasionally examined black NRMs and Native American NRMs, the tendency has been to leave the study of these movements to scholars of black religions and scholars of Native American religions. And, finally, certain elite movements like the feminist spirituality movement have, with few exceptions, been left to other specialties, such as scholars of women's religion. Again, the problem with leaving out certain classes of new religions is that it potentially misses or obscures some of the more general traits of NRMs.

One final factor that has shaped the new religions field is that, because of the historical circumstances noted earlier, sociologists of religion were largely free to lay the foundations for the field of contemporary new religions. Sociology, however, views new religions as arising out of social forces; as a discipline, sociology does not consider religious experience as an independent motivating factor for the emergence of new religious forms. In recent years, as more and more religious studies academics have become involved in the study of new religions, the tendency has been to build upon these foundations uncritically. Little thought has been given to considering what this phenomenon might look like when viewed in terms of some of the other theoretical perspectives utilized in religious studies—such as perspectives that take religious experiences seriously as powerful, independent motivating factors. It should also be recalled that prior generations of scholars were seemingly *obsessed* with the issue of the beginnings of religion. This interest may have been misplaced, but it seems that the ruminations of our academic ancestors should be explored for potential insights into the process of the generation of new religious forms. On the other hand, perhaps studies of current new religions could throw light on such classic questions.

SURVEY OF CONTENTS

The collection's core chapters deal with issues that have consumed the most academic ink—conversion, the role of women, the brainwashing debate, millennialism, and so forth. Other chapters will deal with NRM subfields (e.g., Neopaganism and the New Age movement) that have come to be regarded as subspecialties. Yet another set of chapters will deal with new and emergent topics, such as the cultural significance of new religions and the use of myth in NRM studies.

As indicated by its title, J. Gordon Melton's "An Introduction to New Religions" provides a comprehensive introduction to NRM studies. Melton examines the emergence of this field of specialization from the disciplines of sociology and church history, emphasizing issues of classification and terminology. He concludes by offering a typology that focuses on each religious group's relationship with a specific religious tradition.

The remaining chapters have been organized into four sections. The chapters in section 1 examine the role that the related forces of modernization, science, and technology have played in contemporary new religions. Section 2 looks at NRM controversies from a number of different perspectives. The chapters in section 3 cover a variety of other topics, ranging from issues that have been core concerns for NRM studies such as conversion to newer issues such as the function of mythology in new religious movements. Finally, section 4 examines a series of subareas within NRM studies that have become identifiable subfields.

Part One

The focus of the first section is on the place of new religions in the modern world. In "Alternative Spiritualities, New Religions, and the Reenchantment of the West," Christopher Partridge weaves together a variety of different analyses indicating that earlier formulations of the secularization thesis were flawed. Although traditional religion is indeed on the decline in industrialized countries, new forms of deinstitutionalized spirituality have arisen to fill the void.

Similar to Partridge, Lorne Dawson's "The Sociocultural Significance of Modern New Religious Movements" criticizes approaches to NRMs that view them in terms of reactions to secularization or in terms of certain other understandings of modernity. Instead, he argues, one should draw from more nuanced understandings of the modern world, particularly Anthony Giddens's analysis of modernity/globalization. Giddens is, however, overly simplistic in his portrayal of religion, and Dawson suggests how globalization theory might be modified to be applicable to the interpretation of contemporary new religions.

One of the engines of modernity is empirical science. Traditional religions generally—though certainly not universally—tended to resist science because of its implicit critique of certain aspects of religion. This has not been the case with most new religions, which have developed various strategies for accommodating science and have even appropriated science's aura of legitimacy by claiming to be "scientific" in some way. In "Science and Religion in the New Religions," Mikael Rothstein discusses these strategies through a number of case studies of specific NRMs.

In the final chapter in the first section, "Virtually Religions: New Religious Movements and the World Wide Web," Douglas Cowan and Jeffrey Hadden examine the various ways in which the Internet has impacted NRMs, as well as the potential of this technology for impacting the generation of new religious forms. The Internet became a focus of interest to students of new religions as a result of the fear evoked in the wake of the Heaven's Gate suicides that dangerous groups could be recruiting via the World Wide Web, the conflict over the online publication of Scientology's esoteric teachings, and the use of the Internet by anti-cultists. The authors also explore the issue of online rituals through case studies of the Temple of Duality and of competing branches of the Hermetic Order of the Golden Dawn.

Part Two

The episodes of NRM-related violence in the mid-1990s that indirectly helped to establish new religions as a field of study also prompted NRM specialists to give greater attention to the issue of violence. In "Violence and New Religious Movements," David Bromley examines a number of general models that have been developed since the mid-nineties, models that have moved in the direction of taking into account the dynamics between NRMs and the social agencies with which they interact, and the potential for violent acts from either side. Bromley also outlines a number of theoretical and public policy issues that need to be addressed in the future.

Of the various dimensions of the "cult" controversy, the legal arena is the most significant in terms of its direct impact on the organizational functioning of NRMs. In "Legal Dimensions of New Religions," James Richardson provides a concise yet comprehensive overview of NRM-related legal developments in the U.S. and a survey of efforts to control new religions around the world. He also analyzes these developments in terms of the sociology of law and points out that an important factor fueling anti-NRM sentiment in at least some countries derives from antagonism to American cultural influence.

New religions became a major social issue as the direct result of the emergence of the anti-cult movement (ACM) as an organized countermovement. In "The North American Anti-Cult Movement: Vicissitudes of Success and Failure," Anson Shupe, David Bromley, and Susan Darnell examine the structure and development of the ACM from its *emergent stage* (late 1960s–1970s), though the *expansion/ consolidation stage* (1980s), to the *domestic accommodation/international expansion stage* (1990s–present). The authors discuss the ACM in terms of structure, economy, and alliance network—parameters that the authors argue is a productive way of analyzing any social movement.

As noted in both the Richardson and the Shupe et al. chapters, the North American anti-cult movement enjoyed considerable success exporting its peculiar ideology to Europe, particularly following the Solar Temple murder-suicides in the mid-1990s. In "Something Peculiar About France: Anti-Cult Campaigns in Western Europe and French Religious Exceptionalism," Massimo Introvigne begins by analyzing European attitudes toward NRMs in terms of two types of official reports issued by various nations. He then goes on to discuss France, which alone among European countries seems intent on abolishing all new religions.

Although the Satanism scare of the late 1980s and early 1990s did not involve an empirically existing new religion, it shared many themes with the cult controversy. Anti-cultists jumped on the Satanic Ritual Abuse (SRA) bandwagon as a way of promoting their own agenda, and NRM scholars spearheaded the academic analysis of the scare. In "Satanism and Ritual Abuse," Philip Jenkins presents a systematic survey of this phenomenon. Jenkins's discussion is especially strong in its analysis of the traditional folklore and literary sources for the SRA stereotype of a secretive network of diabolical Satanists.

Because the accusation of deceptive, manipulative recruitment has been at the core of the stereotype of new religions as organizations that "brainwash" their adherents, conversion has been a central issue in NRM scholarship for the past three decades. In "Conversion and 'Brainwashing' in New Religious Movements," Dick Anthony and Thomas Robbins revisit this issue, focusing on anti-cultism's implicit ideological assumptions and on the many empirical studies indicating that conversions to contemporary new religions result from garden-variety sociological and psychological factors rather than from esoteric "mind control" techniques.

Despite the obvious link between conversion/affiliation and apostasy/disaffiliation, the corresponding chapters have been placed in different sections because, while conversion has been an integral part of the cult controversy, deconversion has not. In the first part of "Leaving the Fold: Disaffiliating from New Religious Movements," David Bromley discusses a variety of factors precipitating disaffiliation and then analyzes the process in terms of a series of phases. In the second part of the chapter, Bromley indicates that in the future (1) a more integrated model of affiliation/disaffiliation needs to be constructed and (2) more attention needs to be given to different types of disaffiliation.

Part Three

In "Psychology and the New Religious Movements," John Saliba begins by contrasting psychology/psychiatry's traditional antagonism toward religion with the newer, more positive approach reflected in the fourth edition of the *Diagnostic and Statistical Manual of Mental Disorders* (1994). After a brief survey of relevant studies, he then explores the problems involved with psychological approaches to members of new religions through the example of studies of followers of Bhagwan Rajneesh. He concludes by outlining a series of unresolved issues regarding the psychology of NRM membership.

Although not all new religions are millenarian, many are. In "Millennialism," Richard Landes surveys millenarian movements and outlines a typology for classifying such groups. He concludes his chapter with a suggestive agenda for future research. One of the more significant aspects of Landes's discussion is the manner in which he sets his analysis of contemporary movements in the context of a broader analysis of historically prior movements and movements that have arisen in the so-called third world in response to the intrusion of colonial powers.

Mythology refers to sacred narratives that form the basis of a religion's worldview. In "Mythic Dimensions of New Religious Movements: Function, Reality

Construction, and Process," Diana Tumminia and George Kirkpatrick argue that, despite the significant body of theoretical work that has been carried out by anthropologists and others, the mythological dimension of new religions has been largely ignored. Using Unarius Society, feminist witchcraft, and the Movement of Spiritual Inner Awareness as examples, the authors observe that NRM myths are not fixed, but, rather, change in response to the ongoing process of reality construction taking place within such movements.

Observers have often noted that NRMs sometimes experiment with gender roles. The position of women in certain new religions has also been a focus of concern for critics. In "Women in New Religious Movements," Susan Palmer develops a typology of NRM sexual identity and points out that the actual arrangements within different new religions are often quite complex. To illustrate this complexity, she examines women's roles in the Osho Rajneesh group and in the Raelian movement.

In addition to the role of women, critics have also focused attention on the treatment of children in new religions—to such an extent that comparatively little has been written about children in NRMs not directly linked to the controversy. In "Children in New Religious Movements," Charlotte Hardman examines the body of literature arising out of the cult controversy. She then goes on to discuss the more general issue of the socialization and education of children in NRMs, pointing out that patterns of socialization vary widely and that much more research still needs to be done in this area.

Part Four

Two of the new religions that made world headlines in recent years were East Asian new religions—Falun Gong (China) and Aum Shinrikyo (Japan)—and an identifiable subfield of NRM studies is East Asian new religions. In "New Religions in East Asia," Michael Pye surveys East Asian new religions through a discussion of specific NRMs in China, Japan, Korea, and Vietnam. Without diminishing the uniqueness of each culture, these countries share a common cultural heritage from China which makes their attitudes toward new religions different from those of the West. However, like their counterparts in the West, East Asian NRMs embody a bewildering variety of ideals and opposing tendencies.

Another emergent subfield that has come into its own in recent years is the study of Western esotericism. Because this tradition incubated a number of more recent movements—from Neopaganism to the New Age—contemporary studies of esotericism overlap studies of these related phenomena. In "Esotericism in New Religious Movements," Olav Hammer articulates a concept of esotericism based on five characteristics—social formations, rituals, purported objectives, cognitive style, and relations to mainstream society. Hammer then analyzes a number of groups and movements—including, but not confined to, the Western tradition— exhibiting these characteristics.

In terms of both the movement's sheer size and the number of scholars and publications it has attracted, perhaps the most significant subfield to emerge out of NRM studies is New Age studies, though many observers object to the designation "New Age." In "The Dynamics of Alternative Spirituality: Seekers, Networks, and 'New Age,' " Steven Sutcliffe surveys the New Age milieu and its "quest culture." He also develops a critique of the adequacy of the 'New Age' label. Toward the end of his chapter, Sutcliffe offers a series of suggestions for future research.

For the most part, UFO religions were not taken seriously until after the Heavens Gate suicides in early 1997. Since that time, more and more scholarly attention has been given to UFO religions as well as to the religious motifs found in the more general ufological subculture. In "Waiting for the 'Big Beam': UFO Religions and 'Ufological' Themes in New Religious Movements," Andreas Gruenschloss discusses the historical emergence of this strain of spirituality out of modern esotericism, the millenarian aspect of ufological spirituality, the quest for a both a new science and a religious technology in UFO religions, and the religious significance of the "ancient astronaut" hypothesis which informs groups such as the Raelian movement.

The study of the Neo-Pagan movement has also begun to emerge as a distinctive subfield within NRM studies. In "Witches, Wiccans, and Neo-Pagans: A Review of Current Academic Treatments of Neo-Paganism," Shelley Rabinovitch and Sian Reid survey this area of study via a literature review of the primary books in the field. This survey leads into an analysis of the movement in terms of the ideas of three theorists of late modernity—Anthony Giddens, Michel Maffesoli, and Jürgen Habermas. These theorists are then brought to bear on a discussion of the issue of Neo-Pagan institutionalization, which is a hotly debated topic among movement participants. This latter discussion brings us full circle to the analysis of NRMs and modernity that was the focus of the initial chapters in section 1.

REFERENCES

American Psychiatric Association. 1994. *Diagnostic and Statistical Manual of Mental Disorders*. 4th ed. Washington, D.C.: American Psychiatric Association.
Barker, Eileen. 1984. *The Making of a Moonie: Choice or Brainwashing?* Oxford: Blackwell.

Bromley, David G., and Anson D. Shupe. 1981. *Strange Gods: The Great American Cult Scare.* Boston: Beacon.

Conway, Flo, and Jim Siegelman. 1979. *Snapping: America's Epidemic of Sudden Personality Change.* New York: Lippencott.

Glock, Charles Y., and Robert N. Bellah, eds. 1976. *The New Religious Consciousness.* Berkeley: University of California Press.

Lester, Toby. 2002. "Oh, Gods!" *The Atlantic Monthly* 289, no. 2 (February).

Levine, Saul. 1984. *Radical Departures: Desperate Detours to Growing Up.* New York: Harcourt Brace Jovanovitch.

Needleman, Jacob, and George Baker. 1978. *Understanding the New Religions.* New York: Seabury.

Newton, Michael. 1993. *Raising Hell: An Encyclopedia of Devil Worship and Satanic Crime.* New York: Avon Books.

Sowards, Bruce A., Michael J. Walser, and Rick H. Hoyle. 1994. "Personality and Intelligence Measurement of the Church Universal and Triumphant." In James R. Lewis and J. Gordon Melton, eds., *Church Universal and Triumphant in Scholarly Perspective.* Special Issue of *Syzygy: Journal of Alternative Religion and Culture.*

Wach, Joachim. 1958. *The Comparative Study of Religions.* New York: Columbia University Press.

CHAPTER 1

AN INTRODUCTION TO NEW RELIGIONS

J. GORDON MELTON

PERIODICALLY, the growing field of new religions studies pauses to survey the object of its concern. Unlike the major academic disciplines, it is a field more defined by its subject matter than by methodology. It is, in fact, self-consciously interdisciplinary and welcomes insights from a variety of methodological approaches, in spite of the obvious problems in communication such openness generates. This interdisciplinary approach has, however, also inhibited discussions of some of the basic theoretical questions posed by any attempt to define the subject(s) of interest in new religions studies. The variant emphases in the several disciplines lead to primary concerns being directed toward very different reference groups, as any survey of paper topics at recent gatherings of the American Academy of Religion (AAR) and the Society for the Scientific Study of Religion (SSSR) reveals. Additionally, at the AAR, questions have continually arisen concerning conflicting claims to hegemony over particular topics which seem to overlap with other fields such as Chinese religions (Yiguandao, Falun Gong), Japanese religions (Aum Shinrikyō), and Islamic studies (al-Qaeda).

This essay attempts to address some issues concerning what is or is not a "new religion." Some fuzziness at the boundaries of the field has grown out of its peculiar history, the field emerging as it did from the pre-1970 study of "cults." A different approach to the problem was adopted by European scholars who until recently operated without the joint categories of "sect" and "cult" that were implicit in North America throughout the twentieth century. In addition, the cult/

anti-cult controversy has had a unique (and some would say distorting) role in shaping the academic discussions on new religions.[1]

Below, I have attempted to integrate several lines of research and consideration of the new religions to reach a definition of this field of study of fringy religious phenomena. In doing so, I am suggesting that the field of new religions studies are concerned with a groups of religious bodies/movements that, though they do not share any particular set of attributes, have been assigned to the fringe of the dominant religious culture and secondarily by elements within the secular culture, and hence are a set of religious groups/movements that exist in a relatively contested space within society as a whole.

FROM CULT TO NEW RELIGION

New religions studies has its origins in the adoption of the term "cult" in the 1890s as an initial response to an awareness of an emerging religious pluralism in the United States,[2] and a brief review of the shifting understanding of "cult" provides some initial illumination to present questions concerning the boundaries of new religions studies. The emergence of new religions studies as a separate subdiscipline was occasioned by the sudden visibility of a new generation of new religions in the early 1970s and the controversy they generated.

The term "cult" was originally applied to groups such as Christian Science and Spiritualism, which were viewed as deviations from orthodox Christianity. A series of books written in the first half of the century employing such a definition would eventuate in the 1960s in the Christian countercult community, now embodied in several hundred organizations dedicated to refuting the "errors" of the "cults" and attempting to convert their members to Evangelical Christianity.[3] For Evangelical Christians, the issue with "cults" has been religious truth, which they believe is contained in the orthodox Christian tradition and which has been abandoned by the "cults." Decade by decade, they have placed a growing number of groups under the label "cult," though the appearance of so many Eastern religions has created its own problem, since they have been difficult to discuss as "Christian heresies."

In the 1950s, sociologists in America began to use Ernst Troeltsch as a starting point for a discussion of cults. In his *Social Teachings of the Christian Churches*,[4] Troeltsch attempted a history of European Christianity that was sociologically informed. Among other things, he tried to develop an understanding of the several types of Christian groups that were operating in Europe in the nineteenth century. In so doing he elaborated on the prior distinction of between the large inclusive "churches" (roughly equivalent to the state churches of most European countries) and the dissenting "sects" (such as the Baptists and Methodists), which tended to be more exclusive, as suggested by pioneering sociologist Max Weber.[5] Troeltsch also mentioned the mystical groups (by which he meant the small contemplative fellowships in the Roman Catholic orders). He drew no distinctions between those "sects" that would join the ecumenical community and attain some heightened respectability by, for example, joining the World Council of Churches (founded in 1948). Nor, as he was writing about Christianity, did he consider the social role of other European religious groups, most notably the Jewish synagogues.

In their dialogue with Troeltsch, American sociologists merged the older "cult" category from Christian countercult writings to create the now famous church-sect-cult tricotomy.[6] This effort led to the broad expansion in J. Milton Yinger's six types of religious groups—universal church, ecclesia, denomination, sect, established sect, and cult.[7] The first five of these categories also generally referred to Christian groups, with the last category being reserved for a set of leftover groups, including the only non-Christian groups Yinger mentioned. He did not consider the few substantial communities of Jews or Buddhists (Buddhist Churches of America), nor did he attempt to accommodate them in his set of categories.

While American Christianity was the basic reference point for the discussion of church and sect, sociologists did try to expand its usage to other societies and see the church-type as the dominant religious community of any culture. Such a dominant religious body, which may be Buddhist, Hindu, Islamic, etc., is seen as deeply integrated into any given society's social and economic structures, and demands only a nominal degree of regular participation and/or commitment. The sect, however, rises in protest against and offers competition to the dominant religious community(ies) while demanding a relatively high degree of participation and commitment. Over time, sects tended to become churches.

Prior to the 1970s, almost all groups that were receiving more than cursory scholarly attention could be seen as part of the church-sect continuum, and a significant amount of sociological attention would be paid to the movement from sect to church (or denomination). Meanwhile, "cult" remained a catchall term that included all the groups that did not fit easily as a church or sect, and Yinger's definition of a cult was adopted and used by sociologists.[8] Cults (and Yinger specifically referenced the Black Muslims and Spiritualism) were relatively small groups built around a charismatic leader. Cults were described as ephemeral, usually fragmenting after their founder/leader passed. They were more concerned with the problems of the individual than those of the society.

However, even as Yinger developed his understanding of cults, alternative directions were being offered. For example, Elmer T. Clark, a Methodist historian, had become interested in all the varieties of religious expression that he saw around him during the years of his doctoral work early in the twentieth century

and spent much of his leisure time in his thirties and forties visiting and corresponding with leaders in the many different groups, especially the Holiness and
Pentecostal churches in the American South. His influential *The Small Sects in
America* (1949)[9] classified all of the groups he had located according to their
dominant organizational thrust, thus finding sects that were pessimistic (or ad-
ventist), perfectionist (or subjectivist), charismatic (or pentecostal), communistic,
legalistic (or objectivist), egocentric (or New Thought), and esoteric (or mystical).

In a similar vein, British sociologist Bryan Wilson classified the sects according
to the path to salvation they outlined for their members; hence sects were classified as conversionist, revolutionist, introversionist, manipulationist, thamaturg-
ical, reformist, or utopian.[10] For our present purposes, the exact meaning of each
category for both Clark and Wilson is not as important as the fact that both
operated apart from the emerging distinction between sect and cult and hence
included discussions of groups that would later be seen as sects (Salvation Army,
Christadelphians) and those now considered cults (Christian Science, Jehovah's
Witnesses)[11] under the single rubric of sects. Clarke did find some leftover groups
(for example, the Self-Realization Fellowship, a Hindu group) that did not fit his
system. Wilson saw his categories as ideal types and had little interest in developing a classification system that would or could include all the groups then
operating in the United Kingdom.

As scholars in North America and Europe were absorbing Clark and Wilson
during the 1950s, a dynamic new scene was developing in Japan, where a century
of suppression of religious expression was followed by the introduction of religious freedom in 1945. Suddenly, a number of religious groups appeared as if out
of nowhere. Upon closer examination, some were seen to be older groups that
had assumed a low profile during the Meiji era, some were groups that had been
disbanded but were reformed after 1945, and some were brand new. Additionally,
new groups were being formed annually and by the 1960s the first English-
language texts appeared describing the *shin shukyo* or "new religions" of Japan.[12]

That term also came to be used to describe an equally dramatic phenomenon,
the emergence of so many unfamiliar alternative religions within the counterculture in the San Francisco Bay area at the end of the 1960s. Some of the groups
to which the term was applied were older groups that were gaining a new following, and some were relatively new, having arrived in the United States after World
War II and after changes in the law (1965) had made significant immigration from
Asia possible again. In 1970, Jacob Needleman, a philosopher by trade and an
adherent of the teachings of George I. Gurdjieff, authored *The New Religions*,[13]
with specific reference to Zen Buddhism, the followers of Meher Baba, Subud,
Transcendental Meditation, Krishnamurti, Tibetan Buddhism, and Gurdjieff,
among others. Unlike the purely descriptive work of the Japanese scholars, Needleman's work was both descriptive and normative, in that he invited readers to
consider not only the sociological and historical fact of the new religions and their

impact, but also the philosophical and theological questions about genuine religion and his hope that the new religions might inject the cosmic element back into American religion, an element he felt had been lost in the mainline Christian and Jewish communities. He would elaborate on these ideas in subsequent books.

Quite apart from Needleman's opinions, his designation of "new religions" would be adopted by a group of scholars operating in the Bay Area through the 1970s; by the end of the decade, the term "new religions" would virtually replace "cult" to describe all of those leftover groups that did not fit easily under the label of either church or sect.

The term "cult" did not die suddenly. It had become a cherished sociological category by which a set of religious phenomena could be bracketed on the path to discussions of more dominant, widespread, and significant social manifestations of religion. However, the emergence of the secular anti-cult movement, and with it the practice of deprogramming and the brainwashing ideologies that supported it, led many scholars concerned about the impact of anti-cultism on religious liberty to advocate the abandonment of the term. "New religion" or "new religious movement" (NRM), a term introduced from Japan, won out over other suggested terms such as "alternative religion" or "fringe religion."

While many scholars wanted to continue the use of the term "cult" in its narrow "scientific" sociological meaning, public discourse about cults as destructive brainwashing groups additionally encouraged the search for another more neutral term. At the same time, the public controversy over the "cults" was bringing many scholars into new religions studies. By the end of the 1970s the number of papers on the subject had risen significantly at the AAR, the SSSR, the Association for the Sociology of Religion, and their European counterparts. During the early and mid-1980s, those scholars who had studied new religions gave particular attention to the subject of brainwashing and the court testimony of some psychological professionals that cults brainwashed their members to the point that individual freedoms were overrun and suppressed. More than any other factor, this controversy attracted a number of scholars to the study of new religions and hastened its recognition as a meaningful subdiscipline within both religious studies and the sociology of religion. While in 1970 one could count the number of active researchers of new religions on one's hand, by the mid-1980s more than a hundred could be found; that number has steadily grown in the years since.

The brainwashing controversy,[14] while leading to the growth of the field, had its negative effects. A significant percentage of research on new religions was devoted to dealing with the controversy and with the small handful of new religions around which it was focused. The result was that the great majority of new religions were looked at only cursorily, that case studies of a single group (usually one of the most controversial groups) have predominated over comparative studies of a wide range of groups, and that those less controversial groups were little considered in developing overall understandings of the field. Also, as the great majority of scholars found brainwashing theory lacking and moved on to other concerns, those professionals who had supported brainwashing found themselves shut out and launched a new controversy as they began to direct personal attacks against the major new religions scholars whom they labeled "cult apologists."[15]

PARALLEL STUDIES

The interest in new religions generated by the cult controversy of the 1980s was paralleled by additional research that was to have some measurable affect on altering our view of new religions. First, in stages, Yinger's definition of cults was dismantled. That dismantling began with Geoffrey Nelson's work on the Spiritualist tradition, in which he pointed out that new religions were not one-generation phenomena.[16] A variety of subsequent work pointed out that the role of charismatic leaders[17] had been overestimated and that the other elements of the definition did not fit many of the prominent new religions of the 1970s and 1980s.

The dismantling of the working definition of cult/new religion left new religions scholars with little we could truly say about cults in general; there was no single characteristic or set of characteristics to which we could point that new religions shared (not even their newness). What they shared was what they lacked—they were not part of the religious establishment; their status and role in the culture was continually being contested; they were feared, disliked (even hated), and misunderstood by their neighbors; and they were viewed as being out of step with the general religious environment. Yinger had suggested that "cults are fairly close to the sect type." However, by the 1980s cults were seen as making a much more radical break with the dominant religious milieu. Sects may over time grow into churches. They differ from churches primarily over the level of strictness with which they attend to belief and practice. Cults, however, differ on substantive matters of belief and practice. Most are playing a very different religious game, and even those that operate within the larger Christian tradition dissent on such key issues that prevent them from attaining "church" status. To move along the sect-to-church continuum, they would have to alter very central elements of their belief structure or give up their religion altogether.[18]

A second line of research was being pursued by students of American religion, who began to document and quantify the many new and different religious bodies, both cults and sects, that were emerging in America. Periodically since the mid–nineteenth century, handbooks of denominations in America had been published. However, by the 1970s, this had become a challenging task. Through the early twentieth century, the U.S. Department of Commerce had published a very informative *Religious Census* each decade. However, that task was abandoned following the 1936 edition due to separation of church and state questions. Then, through the mid–twentieth century, one Lutheran Church–Missouri Synod scholar, F. E. Meyer, attempted to carry on, his results issuing forth in various editions of the *Religious Bodies of America*.[19] When Meyer died in the midst of a new edition, the task of completing his work was given to his colleague, theologian Arthur C. Piepkorn, who completed the last edition and then began a massive study that would be fully his own. The effort would consume the last years of his life—he died suddenly in 1973 as he was completing what would become a multivolume work. Unfortunately, only the three volumes covering his writing on Christian groups were ever published.[20]

It was during the 1970s that I stepped into this rather complex setting, and through the 1970s I began to try to make sense of the data that was being gathered on American religions (a task viewed by my major professor in graduate school as a waste of time) and produce a functional classification system of every religion operating in the United States. While Piepkorn, a theologian, had centered his evaluation on their belief systems, I wanted to combine the insights of various approaches in classifying the different groups utilizing not only theology, but also history, sociology, and anthropology (especially the work on revitalization groups). The result was the classification system that would be embodied in the successive editions of the *Encyclopedia of American Religions*.[21]

In creating this classification system,[22] I attempted to first identify major characteristics of a group which an ethnographer might want to consider in attempting to write about a group—its history and origin, its authority structures, its belief system, its ritual life, its dominant behavior patterns. Eventually I isolated some ten relevant characteristics.[23] After looking at the hundreds of groups that had been identified as existing in America in the 1970s, utilizing these characteristics, it became obvious that they fell into a rather small set of clusters. Within the Christian cluster, into which the majority of groups fit, denominational clusters were quite evident, with dissenting (sectarian) groups tending to keep the majority of their heritage while disagreeing with their parent body (churches) on relatively few points. Lutheran sectarian groups tended to look more like Lutheran "church" groups than, for example, Methodist sectarian groups. As large Pentecostal and Holiness groups moved along the sect-to-church continuum, they continued to resemble new Pentecostal and Holiness sects more than Presbyterian or Congregationalist churches.

Of particular relevance to this essay, when it came to those groups that had been at the center of the discussions of "cults" or "new religions," they also tended to resemble their parent groups more than each other. The International Society for Krishna Consciousness resembled other Hindu groups more than it resembled the Church of Scientology or the Church and school of Wicca. The Church Universal and Triumphant resembled other esoteric groups more than The Way International or a Zen Buddhist society. At the same time, Japanese scholars were finding that the Japanese new religions could also be fruitfully distinguished by their appropriation of a particular heritage, Shintoism, one of several Japanese Buddhist traditions or Japanese folk religions. The Asian-based new religions in America and Europe were an initial phase of a new missionary movement by Asian religions directed at the West, and even in the 1970s it was evident that they would not act like Yinger's "ephemeral" cults. New religions were serious religious activities and would have a long-term role in North America and Europe, much as Christianity was having in the places it had colonized in the nineteenth century.[24]

When the *Encyclopedia of American Religions* was created in the late 1970s, there was no separate section for new religions, nor has any been added in subsequent editions. This lack of need for a new religions section grew from the basic observation that almost all "new religions/cults" appear to have evolved from within a readily recognizable religious tradition and now exist as a variant within it. The few that did not fit had scarce information or self-consciously drew on two or more traditions in significant amounts (the Unification Church being the most notable current example).

Thus, almost all of the new religions operating in the West can be seen as more recent versions of an old religion. That is, they draw the majority of their belief, mode of organization, and spiritual practices from the parent tradition. In this regard we can recognize (in the West) some 12 to 15 major traditions—Christianity, Judaism, Buddhism, Hinduism, Islam, Jainism, Shintoism, Sikhism, Sant Mat, Taoism, Zoroastrianism, and Native American (and other ethnolinguistic religions). We can also recognize the various denominational families of Christianity, which take on added significance given the overwhelming dominance of Christianity in the West.[25]

Many of the new religions that were initially unfamiliar even to religious scholars came from the smaller of the world's religious tradition—often ignored or covered only cursorily in basic world religions classes—Shintoism, Taoism, Sikhism. Of particular interest is the Sant Mat or Radha Soami tradition of the Punjab, virtually unknown in the West prior to the 1970s. A basic knowledge of Sant Mat would have made such groups as the Divine Light Mission, ECKANKAR, and the Sant Bani Ashram more comprehensible as expressions of an older faith in a new context.

Possibly the least understood tradition has been Western Esotericm, the definition of which has been pursued in the last generation by scholars such as Antoine Faivre, Joscelyn Godwin, and Stillson Judah et al. Collectively, they have put together a picture of an alternative religious impulse in the West (often referred to as "occultism") that, while broken, has had a continuous presence at least since the second century C.E. and has grown steadily over the last four centuries. In the West, a large percentage of the "new" religions—Scientology, Wicca, New Age, and post–New Age groups—are recent additions to the Esoteric tradition.[26]

Interestingly enough, of the world's major religious traditions, the Western Esoteric tradition is possibly the least known by Western religious scholars, to a large extent as a result of its century of persecution by Christianity, followed by its dismissal as serious religion in more recent centuries. Any tracing of it could begin with ancient Gnosticism as a possible starting point and certainly include Neo-Platonism, Manicheanism (and Mandaeanism), the Albigensians/Cathars, Jewish Kabbalah, Alchemy, and Hermetics. It is to be noted that the modern revival of Esotericism can be traced to the same originating point as Protestantism, namely the University of Wittenberg at the beginning of the sixteenth century, where Martin Luther's Hebrew scholar Johann Rauchlin authored a book on the Christian Cabala. The more recent history is traced through the Rosicrucians, Speculative Freemasonry, Emanuel Swedenborg, Mesmer and the Magnetist movement, Templarism, Theosophy, and Ceremonial Magic to Theosophy and its many offshoots (Alice Bailey, I AM). The New Age movement and the many channeling groups have been the most recent expression of the Western Esoteric tradition.[27]

FROM RELIGIOUS FAMILY TRADITIONS TO NEW RELIGIONS

If we look at the major religious family traditions, some interesting patterns emerge. For example, within each tradition are those groups that dominate and control it (churches), those that dissent but within acceptable limits (sects), and those that diverge beyond those limits (new religions). From the perspective of the dominant group(s) within any given tradition, some groups are seen to differ to such an extent that they can no longer be recognized as fellow believers. Thus, if we go to Japan, the larger Buddhist groups have constituted the Japan Buddhist Federation. However, there are several hundred Buddhist "sects" in Japan. But among these Buddhist sects have been several groups that were largely shunned by the majority of Buddhists. The Sōka Gakkai and the Aum Shinrikyō, though for very different reasons, immediately come to mind. Through the 1960s and 1970s, the Sōka Gakkai engaged in some unacceptable behavior, especially high-pressure proselytizing, which led to its popular condemnation. As it began to grow spectacularly, much by the acquisition of members from other Buddhist groups, several books were written against it. And even before its commission of homicidal acts that has turned it into a pariah for everyone, Aum Shinrikyō had been viewed by the larger Buddhist community as something very different and foreign, a group inspired by Tibetan Vajrayana Buddhism rather than a variation on Japanese Mahayana Buddhism.

From the perspective of the dominant religious community—and most countries have a single religious tradition to which the majority of the population adhere—all of the representative groups of a particular "other" tradition may be defined as outsiders. Thus, in North America, almost all Western Esoteric groups are defined as cults. In India, Hindu leaders increasingly identify all Christian groups, even some of the older indigenous ones such as the St. Thomas Churches, as unwanted outsiders, the product of foreign influence. In Greece, all but the Greek Orthodox Church (including other Christian groups) have been listed as destructive cults. At the same time, the more pluralistic a culture becomes, the more open its leading religions become to broadening the definition of "legitimate" religious life.

Thus, from the perspective of the various religious traditions operating in the West, we might begin to build a definition of new religions as those religious groups that have been found, from the perspective of the dominant religious community (and in the West that is almost always a form of Christianity), to be not just different, but unacceptably different. At the same time, the list of groups that would be considered under the rubric of "new religions" would differ from country to country and always be under negotiation. For example, in the United States the United Methodist Church is one of the large dominant religious bodies. In Greece it was cited by the government as a destructive cult. Also, group status may change over time, and on occasion change quickly and radically. The Soka Gakkai, considered a new religion in Japan and widely attacked through the last half of the twentieth century, is now part of the religious establishment, as a result of the political party it founded becoming aligned at the end of the 1990s with the ruling coalition in the Japanese parliament. In the United States, the Worldwide Church of God changed its beliefs and practices and moved from cult status to membership in the National Association of Evangelicals (NAE).

Over the twentieth century, Pentecostals moved from being some of the most despised of religious groups to sect status to membership in the NAE. Under the leadership of Warith Deen Muhammad, the original Nation of Islam changed its beliefs and integrated into the mainstream of American Islam. At the same time, other groups have maintained their "unacceptable" beliefs and practices and continue to be condemned as cults—Theosophy, Spiritualism, Christian Science, Jehovah's Witnesses, Nation of Islam (Farrakhan), etc. A few groups, previously considered to be sects, have, by their actions, moved into the "cult" camp—the Branch Davidians being the most obvious example. The Peoples Temple, until the deaths in Guyana in 1978, had been a noted congregation in the large Christian

Church (Disciples of Christ), part of the dominant Protestant coalition in the United States, but has since become the epitome of a cult.

CHURCH? SECT? NEW RELIGION?

In most of the West, it is helpful to see different religious groups as falling into one of four types, and at this point I will hopefully begin to tie the discussion of religious traditions into the earlier discussion of church-sect-cult. First, we make note of the churches—those Christian denominations that form the religious establishment of the several Western countries. This category would include the Roman Catholic Church, the several Protestant state churches of Europe, the larger denominations in North America, and the member churches of the World Council of Churches and its affiliated national councils. Some of these member churches may be quite small in any given country (numbering members in the few thousands), but by their international associations they find themselves a part of the religious establishment.

With churches ("established religions" might be a better designation) we would also include those religious groups in non-Western countries that dominate the landscape in their own country—Hanafi Islam in Egypt, Wahhabi Islam in Bahrain, Shafiite Islam in Indonesia, Orthodox Judaism in Israel, Theravada Buddhism in Sri Lanka, or State Shinto and Shin Buddhism in Japan. The dominant established religion has the power to designate the boundaries of acceptable deviation in belief and practice and to identify those groups that fall outside those boundaries.

A second set of religious groups might best be termed "ethnic religions." Falling under this rubric in the West would be those groups that are not Christian but that serve a particular ethnic constituency. The most obvious examples are the several large Jewish synagogue associations, as well as Asian Buddhist and Hindu groups, Asian and Middle Eastern Muslim groups, and a variety of groups serving the smaller world religions—Sikhs, Zoroastrians, Jains, etc. In contrast, in countries where Islam predominates, many Christian minority groups assume a position as an "ethnic religion," for example, the Coptic Christians of Egypt or the Armenian Christians in Turkey. In these cases adherence to a unique form of Christianity and ethnicity are intimately interrelated.

Ethnic religions operate outside of the religious establishment and will not become churches, but they are seen by the establishment as somewhat analogous to them, especially as long as they continue to limit their activity to their own ethnic constituency. In many cases, ethnic religions are also separated from the dominant religious community linguistically. In most instances in the West, other than the older Jewish community, these ethnic religions serve communities that have taken up residence in the West since the end of World War II. In the Middle East, the ethnic Christians have been around for centuries, even predating Islam.

The sects make up a third set of groups. These are primarily Christian and Jewish groups that are seen as resembling the larger churches and the synagogue and mosque associations, but are perceived as stricter on matters of belief, more diligent in practice, and more fervent in worship. Sect groups are seen as existing along a spectrum of movement toward becoming a church, with new sects continually arising to protest the tendency of the older sects to adopt churchlike characteristics (less strict, less diligent, less fervent). In the West, many of the more churchlike sects are affiliated with the World Evangelical Alliance (formerly the World Evangelical Fellowship) and its associated national councils. Less churchlike sects may be associated with one of several fundamentalist associations or, in most cases, free from any ecumenical alignments at all. Churches view sects as different but at the same time affirm a filial relationship. Leaders in the more secularized churches, for example, often admire the sects for the depth of their member's commitment, the spirited worship, and the strength of their affirmation of a common tradition.

Throughout much of the Muslim world, many of the Sufi groups could be seen as Islamic sects (remembering that in part of West Africa they form a significantly large part of the religious establishment). In Japan, many of the smaller and newer Buddhist groups not affiliated with the Japan Buddhist Federation would be considered sect groups (as the term is used here). Within the Jewish community, the many Hassidic groups would qualify as sects.

When one has set aside the established religions, the ethnic religious groups, and the sects, those groups that remain are the new religions. While both ethnic religions and the sects have some recognized legitimacy in the eyes of the religious establishment, the new religions are yet to prove themselves. While they may be granted the minimal guarantees provided by laws on religious freedom, in most ways their status is under constant scrutiny and renegotiation. While the legitimate religious life of ethnic religions and sects is assumed, the "cults" are continually on the defensive to demonstrate that they are pursuing a genuinely religious existence and must periodically defend the authenticity of their spiritual practices.

New religions are thus primarily defined not by any characteristic(s) that they share, but by their relationship to the other forms of religious life represented by the dominant churches, the ethnic religions, and the sects. They are designated as in some measure unacceptable by the dominant churches, with some level of concurrence by the ethnic churches and sectarian groups. Secular organizations and government agencies that have become involved in the opposition to new religions have initially sought the sanction of established religious leaders as allies in their efforts.[28]

Within the ethnic traditions in the West, there may be some disagreement over whether or not a particular group within their tradition is a sect or a new religion. Thus most Hindus seem quite accepting of the International Society for Krishna Consciousness (defined as a cult by the dominant churches) but would tend to disagree concerning the status of the Ananda Marga Yoga Society. In the United States, the Satmar, a Jewish Hassidic group, is considered a Jewish sect, while Belgian authorities placed it on a list of questionable new religions.

In pointing out the role of the dominant, more established religions in the initial definition of those groups that could be considered new religions, I call attention to a lacuna in our understanding of new religions. This lacuna has developed as focus was placed upon the relatively small number of new religions that became the key targets of criticism in the 1970s by the cult awareness movement. Because of the concentration on the brainwashing controversy (the importance of which is undeniable), new religions scholars have tended to ignore the larger role assumed by the established religions and the sectarian churches in the long-term mobilization of support for anti-cult sentiments. This role initially became evident to me in the early 1980s when a rash of anti-cult initiatives were introduced into state legislatures. It became quite evident that the death of the proposed legislation was tied to the opposition of lobbyists representing the more established churches.

Those groups that are considered most unacceptable to the religious establishment, and by extension a range of secular and government agencies, have attained their status not because of any single characteristic or set of characteristics they share. However, there are a number of things a group may do that will cause it to be seen as unacceptable. Acquiring one or two of these negative characteristics is often sufficient by itself to define any religious community as an outsider group, but the more questionable attributes groups adopt the more likely it will be seen as unacceptable.

Topping the list of unacceptable attributes are differences on key beliefs with the religious establishment. In North America, the adoption of a Christian theology that dissents from traditional affirmations (Jehovah's Witnesses, Christian Science) or the adoption of a non-Christian religious ideology (Scientology, Tenrikyo) will quickly lead to a group being assigned outsider status. If that alternative belief system includes some unusual (including scientifically questionable or pseudoscientific) beliefs (ufology, mummification, channeling, magic) then the chances of been seen as different are heightened. Theological systems are immensely important in spotting outsider religions, as even the most secularized and established religions are still concerned with the promotion of a particular worldview and jealously guard it against competitors.

The adoption of a different belief system is by itself, of course, not sufficient for the assignment of outsider status. The ethnic churches have a very different worldview from the religious establishment, but they also have a high degree of acceptance. They are regularly invited to participate in interfaith dialogue. At the same time, some groups, which have a seemingly orthodox Christian theology (International Churches of Christ, Alamo Christian Foundation), have found themselves involved at the center of the cult controversy in the last generation.

Along with a different ideology, new religions invariably also adopt different behavior patterns—logical extensions of their beliefs—that are found to be unacceptable. In the West, few actions will get a group assigned to cult status as quickly as engaging in high-pressure proselytization, almost a prerequisite if a group is to have more than marginal growth in its first generation, especially if proselytizing efforts target older mainline religious groups (a practice known as "sheep stealing").[29] While most of the larger churches have gone through phases in which they used such tactics (and may continue to use them outside the West), the same tactics by other groups are deemed unacceptable. The door-to-door evangelism continued by the Latter-day Saints and Jehovah's Witnesses, although directly related to their persistent growth through the twentieth century, has kept them in a relatively high tension with their neighbors, in spite of these groups having some acceptance in other realms. The Jewish community, victimized by extreme evangelistic tactics from the Christian community in centuries past, is sensitive to any group attempting to proselytize within the Jewish community and has been concerned about the relatively high percentage of Jewish participation in the new religions.[30]

Other attributes of groups in the "new religion" category include the adoption of a different sexual ethic (which might include arranged marriages, polygamy, pedophilia, free love, or other minority sexual behavior); violent (homicide, suicide, brutality) or otherwise illegal (fraud, drug use) behavior; separatism; a communal life (which often includes separatism); a distinctive diet (veganism, macrobiotics) or medical restrictions (no doctors, no blood transfusions),[31] and the espousing of apocalyptic beliefs about the end of the world. Complaints against new religions may also concern conservative approaches to the role of women, a perceived foreignness, racial exclusiveness, or authoritarian leadership.[32]

The characteristics that lead to assignment as an outsider group will vary from culture to culture, of course. For example, some forms of Asian medicine would be quite mainstream in parts of the world, while their efficacy is continually questioned in the West. That is, relative to religious practice, what is considered "cultic" in one culture will have a quite different status in another. Also, especially in the West, practices that continue in an ethnic church may be tolerated and even lauded, while groups that advocate the same practice among Western members (for example, ayurveda or acupuncture) may find themselves condemned.

The religious scene in the last century has been in continual flux, and what is acceptable and/or tolerated belief and behavior for the dominant religions has shifted and expanded. At the same time, new religions change rapidly, especially those still in their first generation of life. Newly founded groups, which may adopt beliefs and practices that set them in a heightened tension level vis-à-vis the establishment, can significantly lower their tension by altering behavior with only minor adjustments to their belief system. Thus, The Family, which became known in the 1980s for creating a promiscuous sexual environment that allowed some pedophilia to occur, lowered its tension level considerably in the 1990s by its adoption of a more conventional sexual ethic that includes strong denunciations of such practices. The Unification Church lowered its tension level once it adopted more conventional methods of support and pulled members who were selling flowers off the streets.

CONCLUSION

This essay has offered a different way of defining the field of new religions studies by viewing the object of concern not as a group of religions that share particular attributes, but as a set of religions that have been assigned an outsider status by the dominant religious culture and then by elements within the secular culture; hence they are a set of religions that exist in a relatively contested space within society. Further, I have suggested that in understanding any particular new religion, it is helpful to locate it initially within its particular religious tradition and then to determine where it fits relative to the mainstream of that tradition, and secondly to determine its relation to whatever tradition is dominant in the particular country in which the group operates (recognizing that in countries such as France a nonreligious ideology may have a significant role in the process of labeling groups as religious outsiders).

Having placed the group on the religious landscape (relative to its own religious tradition and its relationship to the dominant religious community), we can then begin to look for the factors that led to its outsider status, always keeping in mind that those factors will be located both within the group (behavior/belief patterns) and in the larger society (level of religious tolerance, presence of cult-monitoring groups, etc.). From an overview of all the new religions that are operating in any location at any moment, we can then isolate for research purposes those new religions from different backgrounds that might share a particularly interesting attribute (eat a vegetarian diet, home school their children) or set of attributes. Recently, for example, scholars have isolated several new religions that have both been involved in violent incidents and adopted an apocalyptic worldview.[33]

Such an approach should direct those of us who study new religions to a greater concern for the relationships developed by new religions within the larger cultural scene and relative to various interested parties (other religious groups, legal authorities, cult-monitoring organizations, scholars, etc.).[34] It should also call attention to the unique complex of attributes (both ideological and behavioral) that any particular group adopts that allows it to be assigned cult status, while some seemingly similar groups are much more acceptable. Looking at such belief/behavior complexes should also assist us in understanding why some groups might adopt a particularly disastrous course of action, such as involvement in violence (homicide or suicide) or illegal activities (from polygamy to various financial schemes).

NOTES

1. This essay concerns an issue to which I have continually returned over the last twenty years. It has also been the subject of many conversations with colleagues whose insights have been integrated into my own thought over the years. To list those from whom I have learned would be, at this point, to list almost all who have worked in this field during this time, both those who thought I have found stimulating and from whom I have borrowed insights and those who have forced me to sharpen my ideas through their disagreement. I am however, especially grateful to Catherine Wessinger, Edward Irons, Massimo Introvigne, and David G. Bromley, who read earlier versions of this essay and offered a variety of helpful comments upon it.

2. See, for example, A. H. Barrington, *Anti-Christian Cults* (Milwaukee: Young Churchman, 1898).

3. On the Countercult movement, see Douglas E. Cowan, *Bearing False Witness? An Introduction to the Christian Countercult* (Westport, Conn.: Praeger, 2002).

4. *The Social Teachings of the Christian Churches*, trans. Olive Wyon, 2 vols. (London: George Allen & Unwin, 1931; originally published in German in 1911).

5. Cf. Max Weber, *The Protestant Ethic and the Spirit of Capitalism*, trans. Talcott Parsons (New York: Charles Scribner's Sons, 1958; originally published in German in 1904).

6. In tracing the creation of the church-sect-cult categories in America, see Gaius G. Atkins, *Modern Religious Cults and Movements* (New York: Fleming H. Revell, 1923); Louis R. Binder, *Modern Religious Cults and Society* (Boston: R. G. Badger, 1933); and Arthur Huff Fauset, *Black Gods of the Metropolis: Negro Religious Cults of the Urban North* (Philadelphia: University of Pennsylvania Press, 1944).

7. J. Milton Yinger, *Religion, Society and the Individual* (New York: Macmillan, 1957), 154–155.

8. See, for example, the recent discussion of church-sect-cult by sociologists Rodney Stark and William Sims Bainbridge in *A Theory of Religion* (New York, Peter Lang, 1987) and the insightful essay by Lorne Dawson, "Creating 'Cult' Typologies: Some Strategic Considerations," *Journal of Contemporary Religions* 12, no. 3 (October 1997): 363–382, a summary of which can be found in *Comprehending Cults: The Sociology of New Religious Movements* (New York: Oxford University Press, 1998). Both Stark and Dawson give

32 OXFORD HANDBOOK OF NEW RELIGIOUS MOVEMENTS

consideration to the different types of cults/new religions based upon the looseness of their organization, a consideration that goes beyond the topic of this essay.

9. Elmer T. Clark, *The Small Sects in America* (New York: Abingdon-Cokesbury, 1949).

10. See Wilson's various texts, including *Sects and Society* (Berkeley: University of California Press, 1961) and *Religious Sects: A Sociological Study* (London: Weidenfield and Nicolson, 1970).

11. A few of the more recent volumes to treat Jehovah's Witnesses and Christian Science as cults include Steven Hassan, *Releasing the Bonds: Empowering People to Think for Themselves* (Somerville, Mass.: Freedom of Mind Press, 2000); Linda S. Kramer, *The Religion That Kills: Christian Science, Abuse Neglect, and Mind Control* (Lafayette, La.: Huntington House Publishers, 2000); John Ankerberg and John Weldon, *Encyclopedia of Cults and New Religions* (Eugene, Ore.: Harvest House Publishers, 1999); and Philip Jenkins, *Mystics and Messiahs: Cults and New Religions in American History* (New York: Oxford University Press, 2000).

12. See Harry Thomsen, *The New Religions of Japan* (Rutland, Vt.: Charles E. Tuttle Company, 1963), and H. Neill McFarland, *The Rush Hour of the Gods* (New York: Macmillan, 1967). The process of the founding of new religions in Japan, of course, has continued unabated decade by decade to the present, shows no sign of slowing down, and has recently led to the designation of "new new religions," those groups whose founders and converts were born after 1945.

13. Jacob Needleman, *The New Religions* (New York: E. P. Dutton, 1970).

14. An overview of the brainwashing controversy was presented in my "Brainwashing and the Cults: The Rise and Fall of a Theory," in J. Gordon Melton and Massimo Introvigne, eds., *Gehirnwäsche und Secten: Interdisziplinäre Annäherungen* (Marburg, Germany: Dialogonal-Verlag, 2000). It is posted at http://www.cesnur.org/testi/melton.htm. Important items highlighting the controversy include Thomas Robbins and Dick Anthony, "The Limits of 'Coercive Persuasion' as an Explanation for Conversion to Authoritarian Sects," *Political Psychology* 2, no. 22 (Summer 1980): 22–37; James T. Richardson and David G. Bromley, eds., *The Brainwashing/Deprogramming Controversy* (Lewiston, N.Y.: Edwin Mellen Press, 1983); Dick Anthony, "Religious Movements and 'Brainwashing' Litigation: Evaluating Key Testimony," in Thomas Robbins and Dick Anthony, eds., *In Gods We Trust: New Patterns of Religious Pluralism in America*, 2nd ed. (New Brunswick, N.J.: Transaction Press, 1989): 295–344; and James T. Richardson, "A Social Psychological Critique of 'Brainwashing' Claims about Recruitment to New Religions," in David G. Bromley and Jeffrey K. Hadden, eds., *The Handbook of Cults and Sects in America: Religion and the Social Order*, vol. 3, part B (Greenwich, Conn.: JAI Press, 1993).

15. The term "cult apologist" was initially used in presentations at the annual meetings of the now defunct Cult Awareness Network in the early 1990s, following the rejection of brainwashing testimony in the courts. It was implicit in the court cases brought against two professional associations and a spectrum of new religions scholars by Margaret Singer, a psychotherapist most identified with the brainwashing hypothesis relative to new religions, and Richard Ofshe, a sociologist at the University of California, who had also testified on brainwashing in several court cases. Singer and Ofshe had been most effected by the negative court ruling on brainwashing testimony. Following the dismissal of their lawsuit, the term was picked up by representatives of the secular and

Christian movements opposing "cults" who opinions are primarily expressed in numerous Internet sites. It has most recently been raised as a matter of discussion in 1998 by sociologist Benjamin Zablocki, as part of his effort to revisit the brainwashing concept in his article "The Blacklisting of a Concept: The Strange History of the Brainwashing Conjecture in the Sociology of Religion," *Nova Religio: The Journal of Alternative and Emergent Religions* 1, no. 1 (October 1997). Zablocki's article resulted in a symposium discussion published as "Academic Integrity and the Study of New Religious Movements," *Nova Religio* 2, no. 1 (October 1988), and Benjamin Zablocki and Thomas Robbins, eds., *Misunderstanding Cults* (Toronto: University of Toronto Press, 2001).

16. Geoffrey K. Nelson, *Spiritualism and Society* (London: Routledge & Kegan Paul, 1969).

17. See, for example, J. Gordon Melton, "When Prophets Die: The Succession Crisis in New Religions," in *When Prophets Die: The Post Charismatic Fate of New Religious Movements*, ed. Timothy Miller (Albany: State University of New York Press, 1991): 1–12.

18. While unlikely, this is not entirely impossible, as was demonstrated in the 1990s when the Worldwide Church of God abandoned the whole set of its unique beliefs and adopted a mainline evangelical Christian perspective and joined the National Association of Evangelicals.

19. F. E. Meyer, *The Religious Bodies of America*, 4th ed. (St. Louis, Mo.: Concordia, 1961).

20. Arthur C. Piepkorn, *Profiles in Belief*, vols. 1–3 (San Francisco: Harper & Row, 1977–1979). The manuscript of his work, including his entries on the non-Christian groups, were eventually deposited in the library of the Graduate Theological Union in Berkeley, California.

21. J. Gordon Melton, *Encyclopedia of American Religions*, 6th ed. (Detroit: Gale Group, 1999).

22. A discussion of this classification system is found in J. Gordon Melton, *A Directory of Religious Bodies in the United States* (New York: Garland, 1977).

23. The ten characteristics were grouped under three headings: history (which included both the group's self-understanding of its own history and its history as presented by outside observers), its thought world (including both its overall belief system and any particular emphases such as glossolalia, sacramentalism, apocalyticism, etc.), and behavior patterns (including its approach to ethics, unique behavior patterns, worship format, organization, holidays celebrated, and distinctive spiritual practices).

24. In the long run, the acceptance of new religions as serious religious activity has proved a major underlying disagreement between the scholars studying new religions and the anti-cult critics. Critics have often tended to reduce new religions to centers of fraud, insincerity, and/or pathological deviance. Such groups are not seen as valid objects of study, nor would such groups be viewed as possibly making any contribution to the society as a whole. This basic difference can be seen, for example, in the various essays included in Michael D. Langone, *Recovery from Cults: Helps for Victims of Psychological and Spiritual Abuse* (New York: Norton, 1993).

25. Not to be forgotten, of course, are the groups of the religiously irreligious: that is, the groups of atheists, secular humanists, and agnostics who are not just irreligious or unconcerned with religion but who are vitally concerned with organizing and perpetuating a system of unbelief that parallels the religious traditions and assumes many of its functions. In countries like China and France, and to a lesser extent in other Western

nations, secular ideologies assume a controlling role relative to the designation of acceptable and unacceptable religions.

26. Cf. J. Stillson Judah, *The History and Philosophy of the Metaphysical Movements in America* (Philadelphia: Westminster Press, 1967); Antoine Faivre, *Theosophy, Imagination, Tradition: Studies in Western Esotericism* (Albany, N.Y.: State University of New York Press, 2000); and Joscelyn Godwin, *The Theosophical Enlightenment* (Albany: State University of New York Press, 1994). Possibly the most prominent sociological essay on the Esoteric community is Colin Campbell, "The Cult, the Cultic Milieu and Secularization," in *A Sociological Yearbook of Religion in Britain 5* (1972), 119–36. Campbell essay is most illuminating about the operation of the Esoteric world but quickly loses its application when applied to the larger world of new religions.

27. On the development of the esoteric tradition in the last generation see J. Gordon Melton, *Finding Enlightenment: Ramtha's School of Ancient Wisdom* (Hillsboro, Ore.: Beyond Words Publishing, 1998), especially pp. 31–44, and chapters 18–20 of J. Gordon Melton, *Encyclopedia of American Religions* (Detroit: Gale Group, 1999). A seventh edition of the encyclopedia appeared at the end of 2002.

28. Religious sanction to the secular cult awareness movement has been given by prominent spokespersons such as Catholic priest James LeBar, Jewish rabbi Maurice David, and Liberal Jewish executive James Rudin (who book attacking cults was published by a major Lutheran publishing house). Protestant church leaders who lent their support to the cult awareness movement include Ron Enroth, Paul R. Martin, and Richard L. Dowhower.

29. When they first appeared, both the International Churches of Christ and the Alamo Foundation were condemned for "sheep stealing," a practice that usually coincides with the adoption of a separatist relationship relative to one's own tradition. They were later also accused of "brainwashing" their members.

30. Cf. Annette Daum, ed., *Missionary and Cult Movements* (New York: Union of American Hebrew Congregations, 1977), and Natalie Isser and Lita Linzer Schwartz, *The History of Conversion and Contemporary Cults* (New York: Peter Lang, 1988).

31. Above and beyond medical restrictions, in the West there are a number of alternative medical practices that remain in contested space and are often associated with Oriental and New Age religious groups, including ayurveda, acupuncture, chiropractic, and naturopathy.

32. To this point in this essay, I have not raised the issue of brainwashing relative to developing a definition of new religions. Like most of my colleagues in new religion studies, I do not believe that a case for the existence of brainwashing (also called mind control, thought reform) has been made. Given the long history of attempts, I remain quite skeptical that such a case will ever be made. I have found that, in use, "brainwashing" has been a contrived attribute assigned to particular religions as a means of seeking government involvement (either through legislation or the courts) in the life of religious groups when they are engaging in minority but otherwise legal behavior. It has been my experience that saying that a group brainwashes its members most often says more about the individual opinions of the person speaking than the behavior of the group itself. While I favor government action against groups and their leadership when they break the law (especially when they commit acts of violence against members or others, engage in sexually coercive practices, or conduct fraudulent business dealings), I do not favor the intervention of legal authorities simply because they have adopted some-

behavior patterns (however intense) not commonly followed in the larger society nor personally acceptable to myself.

33. Cf. Catherine Wessinger, *How the Millennium Comes Violently: From Jonestown to Heaven's Gate* (New York: Seven Bridges Press, 2000); John R. Hall, Philip D. Schuyler, and Sylvaine Trinhet, *Apocalypse Observed: Religious Movements and Violence in North America, Europe, and Japan* (New York: Routledge, 2000); and David G. Bromley and J. Gordon Melton, eds., *Cults, Religion and Violence* (Cambridge: Cambridge University Press).

34. I am particularly indebted to my recent coauthor David Bromley for pushing me in this direction. Without the conversations and his insights concerning the violence issue, this essay could not have been completed.

PART I

MODERNIZATION AND NEW RELIGIONS

CHAPTER 2

ALTERNATIVE SPIRITUALITIES, NEW RELIGIONS, AND THE REENCHANTMENT OF THE WEST

CHRISTOPHER PARTRIDGE

"THE disenchantment of the world" (Max Weber), which can be traced back to the Protestant Reformation, is the result of a network of social and intellectual forces. More specifically, it is arguable that the emergence of particular rationality and individualism have led, on the one hand, to the erosion of religion as a communal phenomenon and, on the other hand, to the implausibility of many of its beliefs. While this secularizing process is deceptively complex, the essential idea is simple: "Modernization necessarily leads to a decline of religion, both in society and in the minds of individuals."[1] For Weber, the disenchantment of the world (*die Entzauberung der Welt*) is the process whereby magic and spiritual mystery is driven from the world, nature is managed rather than enchanted, the spiritual loses social significance, and institutions and laws do not depend on religion for their legitimation.

While not denying Western secularization, this chapter asks whether it is the *whole* story. Is the West witnessing a *thoroughgoing* erosion of belief in the supernatural? Is the loss of faith in otherworldly forces a linear, one-way, inevitable decline, or are there reasons to believe in the reemergence of religion in the West? On the other hand, if there is evidence indicating that the West is witnessing a gradual "sacralization," should we abandon notions of "secularization"? Or are we in the midst of a much more complex process in which accurate analysis demands that we take account of both secularization and sacralization, disenchantment and reenchantment?

While the current state of religion in the West is complicated and difficult to accurately map, and while simplistic analyses should be avoided, as the title indicates, overall I am persuaded that while disenchantment is ubiquitously apparent in the West, the forces of secularization have never quite been able to stifle the shoots of religion. Although traditional forms of institutional religion have been seriously damaged and do not seem to be able to arrest the process of erosion, cracks are appearing in the disenchanted landscape and new forms of significant spiritual life are emerging. As with all life, new conditions require evolution. Religion in the thin atmosphere of the modern West will necessarily evolve away from what we have become used to calling "religion." Moreover, as future generations of alternative spiritualities become established, rooted, and increasingly mainstream, they may prove more hardy and resistant to the disenchanting forces that their antecedents were ill equipped to deal with. (Of course, that is not to say that there will not be new antagonistic forces.) Indeed, as Cheris Shun-Ching Chan persuasively argues in her study of the Hong Kong group Lingsu Exo-Esoterics, Western reenchantment may be characterized by new hybrid forms of religion which are the result of a dialectical process of the sacralization of the secular and the secularization of sacred.[2]

THE DISENCHANTMENT OF THE WEST

Looking back over the past couple of centuries, it would seem overwhelmingly evident that religious beliefs, practices, and symbols are gradually being abandoned at all levels of modern society.[3] As Steve Bruce commented in 1996, "Sales of religious books have declined. The space given to church and spiritual matters in the popular press is now vestigial; only a sex scandal (for the tabloids) or a money scandal (for the broadsheets) will get the church out of a bottom corner on an inside page."[4] Whereas a more scientifically educated, cynical, and less credulous public is an important factor in the process of disenchantment, it is not the only or even the principal factor. To quote Bruce again, "Increasing knowledge and maturity cannot explain declining religion. There are too many examples of modern people believing the most dreadful nonsense to suppose that people change from one set of beliefs to another just because the second lot are better ideas."[5] Rather, the reasons for disenchantment are primarily social, not intellectual.[6] As noted above, secularization is intrinsically related to modernization, in that modern societies inhibit the growth of traditional, institutional religion. Central to societal modernization is the differentiation and specialization of social units. Commerce and industrialization have led to the division of labor and thereby to increasing societal fragmentation. Small, closely knit, family-based communities with the Church at the center, living under a protective "sacred canopy" (Berger), have been fatally eroded. Over the past few centuries religious authorities have lost their grip on the reins of economic power as the world of employment has been increasingly motivated by its own values. Gradually, education, economic production, health care, and a host of other activities have shifted from ecclesiastical control to specialized secular institutions. Consequently, religious influence has gradually weakened to the point that it is all but absent.

Central to this is, of course, the process of pluralization. Communities in which people operated with a shared religious worldview, a shared morality, and a shared identity, and within which an individual's material, intellectual, and spiritual sustenance was provided, are rapidly disappearing. "Kinship, politics, education, and employment all separate from an original unity and assume a dizzying variety of specialized forms. In the process, human society is transformed from a simple, homogenous collectivity into the pluralistic entities we know today."[7] Berger in particular has drawn attention to the fact that, unlike premodern communities in which a single religious worldview was dominant and permeated all areas of community life, in modern societies there are few shared values to which one can appeal and the beliefs an individual does hold cannot be taken for granted. The believer is constantly aware that a faith is a *chosen* worldview from a spectrum of available worldviews. The consequent popular relativism and the revision of traditional concepts of deity are further encouraged by contemporary consumer-centric cultures that are driven by an insistence on variety and individual choice. Hence, "by forcing people to do religion as a matter of personal choice rather than as fate, pluralism universalizes 'heresy.' A chosen religion is weaker than a religion of fate because we are aware that we chose the gods rather than the gods choosing us."[8] Religion is increasingly a private matter. It is not that religion disappears, but rather that it is relegated from the social to the private sphere—which is essentially what Weber had in mind when he referred to "disenchantment." For example, a palpable consequence of this overall secularizing, relativizing shift in modern democracies has been a series of laws that have repealed certain sanctions in order to ensure the equality of most forms of religious expression. Hence, in Britain, the 1951 repeal of the 1735 Witchcraft Act was not an attempt to promote witchcraft, but rather a logical step in a modern, secular democracy. There is no longer an acceptable rationale for defending the rights of one religious belief system over another. Since religion is simply a matter of personal preference, and since concepts of religious truth have been relativized (there being little empirical evidence to establish the validity of one choice over another, or indeed to establish the validity of any of the choices), there are few reasons to limit choice. As Bruce comments, "Modern society seeks to assimilate all citizens into the mass culture of free-wheeling choice where community commitments are notoriously difficult to maintain."[9]

Finally, "rationalization" is central to the secularization of modern societies, in that there is a "concern with routines and procedures, with predictability and order, with a search for ever-increasing efficiency."[10] Rationalization has therefore led both to increased bureaucracy and to an emphasis on process and organization. Everything can and should be done better, faster, cheaper, and more efficiently. Consequently, religious beliefs such as, for example, the value of petitionary prayer and divine providence are at odds with a culture that values predictability, order, routine, and immediate quantifiable returns. Many Westerners, including those with religious convictions, will implicitly or explicitly accept that there are better, more effective ways of getting through life than the traditionally religious ways. As such, secularization theorists point out that there seems to be relatively little left in the world for God to do. For example, in premodern societies immediate spiritual and moral connections would be made with tragic physical events, such as crop failure, and prayers of contrition would be offered. In the modern, industrial world, individuals instinctively seek a physical cause for a physical effect and, consequently, initially turn to physical remedies. Christians may pray for relief from a migraine, but few will not first avail themselves of the appropriate medication. Similarly, we can no longer accept that psychiatric disorders such as epilepsy and schizophrenia are the result of demonic possession. We know there are physical causes which can be very effectively controlled by the careful use of scientifically researched chemicals.

This then is the disenchanted world in which we live. The decline of the community, the proliferation of large, impersonal conurbations, the increasing fragmentation of modern life, the impact of multicultural and religiously plural societies, the growth of bureaucracy, the creeping rationalization, and the influence of scientific worldviews have together led to a situation in which religion is privatized, far less socially important, and far less plausible than it used to be in premodern communities. Certainly, a large question mark has been placed over the notion that there exists a single religious and ethical worldview which alone is true and, therefore, to which all good and reasonable people should assent.

New Religions, Alternative Spiritualities, and Western Disenchantment

Bearing the above in mind, what are we to make of the emergence of new religions and alternative spiritualities? Do they not present a rather large fly in the ointment, in that their proliferation is hardly a ringing endorsement of the demise of religion in the West? Some theorists have insisted that this is exactly what they are. At best they are manifestations of "pseudoenchantment."[11] For example, Bryan Wilson has argued that, rather than being evidence of the resurgence of religion, they are actually evidence of secularization.[12] New religious movements should not be regarded as revivals of a tradition, but rather

> they are more accurately regarded as adaptations of religion to new social circumstances. None of them is capable, given the radical nature of social change, of recreating the dying religions of the past. In their style and in their specific appeal they represent an accommodation to new conditions, and they incorporate many of the assumptions and facilities encouraged in the increasingly rationalised secular sphere. Thus it is that many new movements are themselves testimonies to secularization: they often utilise highly secular methods in evangelism, financing, publicity and mobilisation of adherents. Very commonly, the traditional symbolism, liturgy and aesthetic concern of traditional religion are abandoned for much more pragmatic attitudes and for systems of control, propaganda and even doctrinal consent which are closer to styles of secular enterprise than to traditional religious concerns.[13]

Similarly, Bruce has recently argued that New Age spiritualities are little more than the dying embers of religion in the concluding stages of the history of the secularization of the West.[14] Essentially, New Age and Pagan spiritualities provide privatized religion for disenchanted Westerners who want to hang on to the remnants of religious belief without inconveniencing themselves too much. Generally speaking, new forms of spirituality lack religious salience and function as weak substitutes for their dying predecessors. Western culture is increasingly characterized by forms of religion that do not claim absolute truth, do not require devotion to one religious leader, and do not insist on the authority of a single set of sacred writings, but rather encourage exploration, eclecticism, an understanding of the self as divine, and, consequently, often a belief in the final authority of the self.[15] In summary, Bruce is confident that the number of people interested in new religions and alternative spiritualities is relatively small,[16] "participation is shallow,"[17] and their beliefs lack ideological weight. His argument is that "because they are not embedded in large organisations or sustained by a long history ... many elements of the New Age are vulnerable to being co-opted by the cultural mainstream and trivialised by the mass media."[18] Indeed, as far as Bruce is concerned, as individualism and consumerism increase in the secular West, all forms of religion will become increasingly trivialized and subject to personal choice and whim.

There is much to commend in this assessment of the nature of the contemporary religious milieu. The disenchanted West has, as Olav Hammer has recently pointed out, "few generally accepted or imposed beliefs. Thus, those seeking religious answers will in a far greater measure be compelled to seek these out for themselves. The decline of religious monopoly in a secularized society may paradoxically lead to a proliferation of competing religious alternatives in a privatised spiritual market place."[19] Having said that, there are problems with this analysis of the situation. Indeed, some theorists are now arguing that this general model of secularization and, in particular, its interpretation of new religions is fundamentally mistaken. More significance needs to be accorded to the fact that, in line with the global trend of a gradual upsurge of religion, and along with streams of "fundamentalist" religion[20] (in particular, we might think of the increasing numbers of young Egyptians attracted to conservative forms of Islam, or the challenges made by Hindu "fundamentalists" to secularism in India, or indeed, the emergence of conservative Christianity in Latin America and sub-Saharan Africa),[21] there seems to be a subtle yet ubiquitous growth of new religions and alternative forms of spirituality in the West. Whether one accepts all their analyses or not, it is difficult to avoid the conclusion that the weight of evidence seems to favor the general thesis posited by Rodney Stark and William Sims Bainbridge. Essentially, their contention is that religion per se is so psychologically and socially bound up with the human condition that it is unlikely ever to disappear. Similarly, in a recent revision of his secularization thesis, Berger, after predicting that the world of the twenty-first century will be no less religious than it is today, asserts that "the religious impulse, the quest for meaning that transcends the restricted space of empirical existence in this world, has been a perennial feature of humanity . . . It would require something close to a mutation of the species to extinguish this impulse for good."[22] Hence, it is reasonable to conclude, as Stark and Bainbridge do, that if mainstream religion loses authority, new forms of religion will evolve to compensate. Consequently, any apparent disappearance of religion is illusory. It follows therefore that the secularization thesis as developed by Wilson and Bruce is flawed.[23] However, to accept this general position does not require the wholesale rejection of secularization. Stark and Bainbridge, for example, do not deny the existence of secularization, but rather understand it as part of a recurring process. The following statement is important:

> Secularization is nothing new . . . it is occurring constantly in all religious economies. Through secularization, sects are tamed and transformed into churches. Their initial otherworldliness is reduced and worldliness is accommodated. Secularization also eventually leads to the collapse of religious organizations as their extreme worldliness—their weak and vague conceptions of the supernatural—leaves them without the means to satisfy even the universal dimension of

religious commitment. Thus, we regard secularization as the primary dynamic of religious economies, a self-limiting process that engenders revival (sect formation) and innovation (cult formation).

The point is that those secularization theorists who regard new religions and alternative spiritualities as evidence of the ultimate demise of religion in the modern world fail to recognize that secularization is only a stage in a larger process, a stage which will be followed by the increasing significance of new religions. The process is, very briefly, as follows: churches/large religious institutions become ever more secular, liberal, diluted, and indistinct from their "worldly" contexts; consequently, they fail to meet the moral and spiritual needs/desires of their followers; revived breakaway groups (sects) or new, innovative forms of religion (cults) emerge; these grow larger and more established (e.g., sects become denominations); they, too, become gradually more secularized, and the long process continues.

In response to the argument that, relentlessly driven by modernization, secularization is a one-way process, accelerated and made all the more virulent and corrosive by the modern scientific worldview, Stark and Bainbridge again insist that religion will emerge as a dominant social and cultural force simply because science and secular worldviews in general are not able to satisfy fundamental human desires. More particularly, their argument is that naturalistic worldviews cannot offer the much-desired, large-scale rewards and "compensators" that religions offer (e.g., immortality/eternal life). The point is that, while religion cannot offer such rewards directly, it does offer attractive "compensators" which, while second best in comparison to direct rewards, are nevertheless very appealing.

> A compensator is the belief that a reward will only be obtained in the distant future or in some other context which cannot be immediately verified. . . . When we examine human desires, we see that people often seek rewards of such magnitude and apparent unavailability that *only by assuming the existence of an active supernatural can credible compensators be created.* . . . Some common human desires are so beyond direct, this-worldly satisfaction that only the gods can provide them. . . . So long as humans seek certain rewards of great magnitude that remain unavailable through direct actions, they will obtain credible compensators only from sources predicated on the supernatural. In this market, no purely naturalistic ideologies can compete. Systems of thought that reject the supernatural lack all means to credibly promise such rewards as eternal life in any fashion. Similarly, naturalistic philosophies can argue that statements such as "What is the meaning of life?" or "What is the purpose of the universe?" are meaningless utterances. But they cannot provide answers to these questions in the terms in which they are asked.[24]

Stark and Bainbridge thus define religions as "human organizations primarily engaged in providing general compensators based on supernatural assumptions."[25]

Bearing in mind the often mundane, self-centric, even body-centric nature of some contemporary "spiritualities," I would argue that though this particular understanding of the compensator thesis requires some modification, its central thrust is surely correct. That is to say, although perhaps a significant proportion of those involved in contemporary alternative spiritualities do not *belong* to a particular "new religion," "cult," or "sect," the point I want to make is simply that there will always be dissatisfaction with, and departure from, secularized worldviews and religions that dilute supernaturalism and thereby allow themselves to become internally secularized. As Christian theologian Vernon White comments, "The bracing world of modernity, with its own priests of rationality, liberated us from superstition. But it also left us a dull, one-dimensional, unconvincing world."[26] My point is simply that such a world will always be fertile soil for reenchantment. Unable to provide credible compensators, such internally secularized religions will decline and be replaced by new groups which either revive traditional compensators (sects) or develop new compensators (cults). This is why secularization is a "self-limiting process." Because the religious appetite is more or less constant, secularization will always be accompanied by the formation of sects, cults, or (as I think is increasingly going to be the case) networks of individuals (perhaps meeting only in the chat rooms of cyberspace) and small localized groups which are, in turn, the beginnings of new forms of supernaturalistic religion. Disenchantment is the precursor to reenchantment.[27]

New Religions, Alternative Spiritualities, and the Reenchantment of the West

Not only is spirituality being explored in some unexpected areas of Western life (such as the world of business),[28] but modern pluralized societies offer religious innovators an increasingly wide choice of beliefs and practices. Contemporary forms of spirituality may resemble traditional forms of Christianity or incorporate a range of beliefs informed by anything from the doctrines and practices of the world religions to ideas about UFOs. Hence, perhaps the first characteristic of contemporary reenchantment to note is that it is *not* a return to previous ways of being religious, but rather the emergence of new forms of spirituality and new ways of being religious. In other words, those who study contemporary religion in the West may need to reassess their definitions of religion and what it means to be religious.[29] Otherwise it would be easy to survey the religious landscape and, using inappropriate criteria, either fail to notice some central features or else misinterpret them as temporary outcrops or minor seasonal variations. As David Lyon has argued, "Secularization may be used to refer to the declining strength of some traditional religious group in a specific cultural milieu, but at the same time say nothing of the spiritualities or faiths that may be growing in popularity and influence. If we view religion in typically modern, institutional fashion, other religious realities may be missed."[30]

Evidence that the resurgence of religion in the West is taking a new trajectory is not difficult to find. For example, Michael York's recent study of alternative spirituality in Amsterdam, Aups, and Bath found that

> While the numbers involved with new forms of religiosity remain hard to identify precisely, we can at least recognize the ubiquity and growth of the diffuse religious consumer supermarket which demonstrates an increasingly vital presence in both urban Holland and rural France. These areas are witness to the spiritual ferment which is either a product of, or concomitant with, the decline of traditionally Western forms of religion and the growth of secularization as the acceptable form of public life. Change occurs against a background of ubiquitous experimentation and innovation with regard to spiritual practice— one which eschews dogma, conformity and belief and emphasises both individual autonomy and direct experience.[31]

Whether he understands the nature of secularization quite as I do is not clear, but his emphasis on nontraditional religious vitality within a secularized context is important—sacralization is taking place as "either a product of, or concomitant with," secularization.

Even in popular writing and the media, this nontraditional religious vitality is acknowledged. For example, a recent sympathetically written article on Wicca in America in a British teenagers' magazine makes the following interesting (if a little exaggerated) points: "Witchcraft, or Wicca, is the fastest growing 'religion' in the USA today. It is estimated that around a million and a half teenage Americans, often as young as thirteen, are practicing Wiccans. Television programs such as *Sabrina the Teenage Witch* and films like *The Craft* have sparked continent-wide interest in Witchcraft and awarded it the official Hollywood stamp of 'cool.' "[32] (It should be noted that a recent study has found that "while the earliest scholarly reports suggested that American witches predominantly were teenagers or very young adults, subsequent studies found that most of them were young to more middle-aged adults. . . . Our question about age produced the following results: 15.2 percent were 18 to 25; 26.7 percent were 26 to 33; 25 percent were 34–41; 20.1 percent were 41–48; 12 percent were 48 or older.")[33] This interest is, of course, not a new phenomenon. Nontraditional reenchantment has been a long time coming. In particular, over the past forty years or so there has been a sharp rise in not merely those tolerant of but also those taking a keen interest in new forms of spirituality and in what might loosely be termed "the occult." For example, the fact that the percentage of "occult" books published since 1930 has more than doubled[34] and, according to a recent report in the *Economist*, "sales of books about yoga and reiki . . . have exploded in the past 18 months"[35] is indicative of the steady increase of popular interest in alternative religiosity.[36] Similarly, Paul Heelas points out that not only have, for example, "New Age holidays . . . expanded rapidly during the last ten or so years," but "there is no reason to suppose that . . . spiritual economics will not continue to prosper. Since the 1960s, we have witnessed a clear pattern of growth."[37] Hence, Heelas quite rightly notes that while "it would be misleading in the extreme to conclude that everything going on beyond the frame of institutionalized worship is of great 'religious' (or spiritual, paranormal, etc.) significance . . . *many* more people are (somehow) 'religious' without going to church on anything approaching a regular basis than are attendees."[38] In other words, not only has "religious belief beyond church and chapel . . . become progressively more significant relative to numbers going to traditional institutions," but "it is possible to draw on statistics to argue that the numbers of those who have some kind of 'religion' without being involved in institutional worship has actually been increasing."[39]

Bearing the above in mind, it is no surprise to discover that, according to recent polls, while the numbers of people claiming belief in God or in heaven and hell are decreasing, once questions are asked about non-Judeo-Christian beliefs, or framed in a non-Judeo-Christian way, a different picture emerges, one which shows that growing numbers of people are becoming interested in "spirituality." Indeed, it is clear that while some people would not regard themselves as being "religious" (almost certainly because of the baggage that term carries), they do understand themselves to be "spiritual": "31 percent describe themselves as 'spiritual,' compared with only 27 percent who say they are 'religious.' "[40] Again, while the 1994 *British Social Attitudes* survey reports 48 percent agreeing that too often people believe in science and not enough in feelings and faith, in 1998 this had grown to 50 percent. Moreover, there are more people who hold recognizably religious beliefs than who want to describe themselves as either "religious" or "spiritual."[41] Similarly, while the numbers believing in "God as personal" are falling, those believing in "God as spirit," "universal spirit," or "life force" are rising.[42] Understandably this has led to reports claiming that "beyond the empty pews there is a spiritual revival. . . . Although the British are undoubtedly staying away from church, they are not abandoning spirituality."[43] The point I am making here is simply that, when exploring the contemporary alternative religious landscape in the West, account needs to be taken of those who may not belong to "new religious movements." As Eileen Barker points out, "There are people who might be horrified at the thought they could be in any way connected with a 'cult,' but who are, none the less, 'recipients,' even carriers, of ideas and practices that are borne by, if not always born in, NRMs."[44] Some may even carry recognizably "spiritual" ideas and practices that are not borne by or born in NRMs. It is important to think of new religion/spirituality (and the amorphous term "spirituality" has perhaps found a worthwhile, distinct use in this context)[45] apart from NRMs.

Interestingly, as I write this chapter, one of the main news stories in Britain concerns comments made by the Roman Catholic Archbishop of Westminster,

Cardinal Murphy-O'Connor, who told a conference of priests on 5 September 2001 that "Christianity was being pushed to the margins of society by New Age beliefs, the environmental movement, the occult and the free-market economy."[46] The reporting of his comments has been interesting. For example, Martin Wainwright of *The Guardian* writes:

> On three counts, the cardinal's analysis was refreshingly blunt. First, he is right to claim that Christianity no longer has any impact on the majority of British people's lives and the moral decisions they make. Second, Christianity's influence on modern culture and intellectual life is nonexistent. Third, a growing number of people now gain their "glimpses of the transcendent" from the loosely labelled New Age. . . . Cardinal Murphy-O'Connor is right. And he shows greater understanding than many of his fellow faith leaders in not equating this dramatic social development with secularization or "tacit atheism," as the Archbishop of Canterbury described it last year. In fact, opinion polls repeatedly show that around 70 percent claim they believe in God. And while we may no longer believe in eternal life, we do (curiously) believe in reincarnation. In the place of the church or synagogue, people are putting together their own patchwork of beliefs, practices and rituals which provide the meaning, consolation and experiences of the transcendent. This DIY [do it yourself] spirituality gains inspiration from Eastern traditions (from Buddhism and yoga to Sufism) and psychotherapy, but *it is now in the mainstream, no longer the preserve of New Age groupies.*[47]

While, as James Beckford has rightly warned, one should treat the often polarized and sensational media reports of new religions with caution,[48] this assessment is broadly supported by a recent analysis of British Gallup Poll data by Colin Campbell:

> Apparently straightforward evidence for secularization disguises the fact that this decline has been entirely at the expense of a Judaeo-Christian personal God. For when the question concerning belief "in a personal God" is distinguished from belief in "some sort of spirit or life-force," then virtually all of the falling off in belief in God over this period is accounted for by the fewer people who are prepared to state that they believe in a personal God. Such people now represent only about one-third of the population when, not so long ago, they constituted over half. By contrast that proportion prepared to admit belief in "some sort of spirit or life-force" has actually increased slightly in recent years. [Concerning the afterlife] that proportion of the population prepared to say that they believe in standard Christian beliefs concerning heaven and hell has declined considerably (so much so that both are now minority beliefs very much on a par with belief in the Loch Ness Monster or flying saucers). However, belief in reincarnation . . . has actually been going up. About one-fifth of Britons subscribe to this belief, which is even more marked among the young.[49]

This relative popularity of the non-Judeo-Christian belief in reincarnation[50] is interesting. Since the proportion of Hindus, Sikhs, or Buddhists in the West is relatively low (around 2 percent in Britain), it is significant, as Tony Walter points out, that surveys consistently discover that "around 20 per cent of the population of Western countries answer 'Yes' to the question 'Do you believe in reincarnation?' "[51] Indeed, some surveys indicate that a quarter of Europeans and North Americans do believe in reincarnation.[52] Quite simply, there has been a substantial increase "since the middle of the twentieth century when British surveys found figures of 4 per cent and 5 per cent."[53] Moreover, while it may be tempting to simply categorize Western believers in reincarnation as "New Agers," Helen Waterhouse has demonstrated that, while this may be true of some, many in fact operate within the mainstream of society and "appear to have derived their belief in reincarnation from outside the *cultic milieu* in which New Age religion operates and they hold their belief in reincarnation alongside more conventional and mainstream attitudes."[54] Consequently, it would seem that the claim that DIY spirituality is now in the mainstream, while perhaps a little exaggerated, is essentially sound. Spirituality is alive and well outside traditional and new religions in mainstream Western society.

Taking this line of thought a little further, an example of what I would understand to be "reenchantment" (i.e., alternative forms of spirituality which evolve, cease to remain purely private concerns, and start to "reenchant" the wider culture) is the way a typically modern, science-based profession such as medicine is now witnessing a rise of interest in what used to be called "New Age healing." Manuals such as the *Nurse's Handbook of Alternative and Complementary Therapies* (produced by medical professionals) are being published, and alternative medicine, holistic approaches to illness, and "the spiritual" are increasingly being explored and utilized. This is not surprising given the general public's rising levels of interest. For example, in his now famous study, David Eisenberg of the Harvard Medical School found that ordinary Americans were annually spending more than $13 billion on alternative therapies and that "an estimated one in three persons in the U.S. adult population used unconventional therapy in 1990."[55] As the *Nurse's Handbook* notes, "Andrew Weil and Deepak Chopra have become household names, and their books espousing the benefits of natural and Ayurvedic remedies sell by the millions."[56] While it would obviously be misleading to claim that all such consumers hold alternative spiritual worldviews, it is significant that, even in the areas of medicine and health, there seems to be a trend away from trusting *only* the conventional to experimentation with or trust in therapies and medicines which are not only unconventional, but are often supported by spiritual terminology and nonrational explanations. Many of the therapies, for example, have their roots in Eastern religious systems. As the *Nurse's Handbook* points out (in a way that suggests some verification of their value—which is in itself significant),[57] "many alternative therapies practiced today have been used since ancient times and come from the traditional healing practices of many cultures, primarily those of China and India. . . . The Indian principles of Ayurvedic medicine stem from the Vedas, the essential religious texts of Hinduism."[58] And, as one might expect in such a book, there are references, not simply to exercises and herbal remedies, but also to spiritual concepts and belief systems such as *qi* (or *chi*), *qigong, prana, meridians, chakras,* shamanism, prayer, Healing Touch, and *yin* and *yang*. All this and more in a nurse's handbook!

The point is simply that previously unusual spiritual beliefs and practices are being appreciated by and gradually absorbed into mainstream Western society. As Walter states regarding the belief in reincarnation, it is "not an exotic, fringe belief, but an idea that is being explored by a significant minority of otherwise conventional people."[59] This "deexotification" (if I can introduce another ugly term) of previously obscure and exotic beliefs is fundamental to and symptomatic of the process of reenchantment. While many of the particular new religions and alternative spiritualities may still be considered fringe concerns, increasingly their ideas and beliefs are becoming accepted as normal and incorporated into Western plausibility structures.

Secularization theory, as James Richardson has pointed out, "generally implies that religion is something of an anachronism in our differentiated and complex modern world. Anyone who believes is basically not 'with it' in the modern age . . . Rationality marches on and there is something odd about those who do not get in step, even if those discussing this inexorable process lament what they are describing."[60] However, we have seen that, in fact, the opposite is increasingly the case. The gap between religious "deviance" and "respectability" has considerably narrowed in recent years. Whether one thinks of spiritually informed environmentalism, the celebration of supposedly ancient traditions such as "Celtic Christianity,"[61] New Age retreats and holidays, the variety of religiously informed remedies and procedures, or spiritualities and practices from astrology to feng shui, these increasingly fail to raise eyebrows in the contemporary West. It is not simply that there is a lack of consensus about what is deviant, but rather that beliefs once considered deviant are now acceptable, even respectable. Consequently, those who do view such ideas as deviant and raise a wary eyebrow are viewed as outdated, out of touch, not "with it." As Campbell observes, the ideas of organizations which were "clearly 'fringe' or 'cultic' groups in the years immediately following the Second World War"—the response to which was "typically one of incredulity or ridicule"—are today "commonplace, having entered the mainstream of cultural thought and debate." He continues, "It is this shift which is significant; not so much the appearance of new beliefs, but rather the widespread acceptance of ones which formerly had been confirmed to a minority; a shift which, it appears, really dates from the 1960s, when they were espoused by that significant and influential minority who comprised the counter-culture."[62]

One form of spirituality worth mentioning briefly at this point is contemporary ecological spirituality. Not only is there an apparent skepticism regarding aspects of the scientific worldview, but, as Bron Taylor argues, "earth and nature-based spirituality is proliferating globally," and while those involved in counter-cultural environmentalist movements may be uncomfortable with the label "religion" (though, I suggest, not with the label "spirituality"), in fact many of the movements are essentially religious.[63] For example, while the 1994 *British Social Attitudes* survey reports that 60 percent agreed or strongly agreed that humans should respect nature because it was created by God, in 1998 this figure had risen to 62 percent (in Germany the 1998 figure was 74 percent, in Italy 84 percent, and in Ireland 90 percent).[64] Whether one thinks of the increasingly popular "creation spiritualities," the spiritual interpretations of the Gaia hypothesis, or deep ecology's shift from anthropocentrism to biocentrism, there has been a noticeable reenchantment of environmental concern.[65]

It should also be noted that, as Walter and Waterhouse have shown regarding reincarnation, Westerners tend to have detraditionalized, individualized understandings of the doctrine. In other words, the doctrine is enculturated or, to use the more managed and purposive Christian missiological term, inculturated.[66] Religious belief is always interpreted and shaped by particular contexts, always in the process of *becoming*. Hence, when, for example, Bryan Wilson comments that new spiritualities are "adaptations of religion to new social circumstances," or that "they often utilise highly secular methods in evangelism, financing, publicity and mobilisation of adherents," or that "very commonly, the traditional symbolism, liturgy and aesthetic concern of traditional religion are abandoned for much more pragmatic attitudes and for systems of control, propaganda and even doctrinal consent which are closer to styles of secular enterprise than to traditional religious concerns,"[67] he is doing little more than noting the strengths of what one would expect of an evolving religion in a Western context. Many new religions and spiritualities very effectively incarnate their theologies in contemporary Western culture. That they do so does not mean that they therefore trivialize religion and transform it into that which lacks depth and significance for its devotees. My own discussions with contemporary Pagans and New Agers suggest very much the opposite. The point is that, as supernaturalistic religions evolve, not only do they move away from traditional forms of religiosity which appear to offer little to those seeking an authentic spirituality, but they address concerns current in the cultures in which they are evolving (thus, in some cases, inspiring self-sacrificial, political, direct action), sometimes absorb myths which are popular in those cultures (UFOs, conspiracy theories, Gaia consciousness, etc.), utilize new practices, beliefs, ideas, and terms which are understood to more adequately meet spiritual needs, and promote these in effective new ways informed by their contexts. Hence, ideas such as reincarnation, feng shui, chakra, karma, prana, chi, nirvana, Brahman, yin and yang, tao, and meditation are not only entering mainstream Western thinking,[68] but they are being reinterpreted and owned by Westerners.

While disenchantment is part of an accurate interpretation of the Western landscape and for many years has been the dominant interpretation, it is time to move on and recognize the emergence of new realities. In many ways I would concur with Linda Woodhead, who notes that "the twentieth century has both confirmed and confounded the ideas of scholars who predicted widespread secularization. While it is true that some forms of traditional religion have declined, it is also true that the late modern West has witnessed the spread of a "luxuriant undergrowth" of religiosity."[69]

The Significance of Popular Culture

While I am wary of positing overly speculative theories, it would seem that popular culture is a key reenchanting factor which may have a far more influential role in the shaping and dissemination of contemporary thought than is often acknowledged. Indeed, a similar thesis was hinted at over a decade ago by Campbell and McIver in their examination of cultural sources of support for contemporary occultism.[70] The study demonstrates the integration of occultic worldviews within contemporary Western culture. By so doing the study goes some way to explaining why "ordinary" individuals in the West can develop a commitment to apparently obscure occult practices and beliefs. The point is that this is important when it comes to mapping the gradual shift from disenchantment to reenchantment.

Popular culture has a relationship with contemporary alternative religious thought that is both expressive and formative.[71] Whether musical, visual, or literary, popular culture is both an expression of the cultural milieu from which it emerges and formative of that culture, in that it contributes to the formation of worldviews and, in so doing, influences what people accept as plausible. Although not discussing religion, Elizabeth Traube nevertheless makes the relevant point that it matters little whether media professionals are concerned with the construction of subjectivities or with the simple telling of pleasurable stories, because the stories themselves "are vehicles for constructing subjectivities, and hence what stories are circulated is socially consequential."[72] My point is simply that, whatever is intended by the producers of popular culture, there is little doubt that people are developing religious and metaphysical ideas by reflecting on themes explored in literature, film, and video games[73]—which, in turn, reflect popular reenchantment and thus might be understood as part of a process of modern religious "deprivatization" (José Casanova). Moreover, it is not insignificant that producers of popular culture are increasingly interested in alternative religious and occult themes. As Campbell and McIver comment, "commercial interests dictate that the interests of the majority are catered for and hence the extensive treatment of occult themes is yet further testimony to a degree of popular occult commitment."[74]

While I am not claiming that this relationship with popular culture is a new development (for it clearly is not), the evidence seems to suggest that popular culture is both helping people to think through theological and metaphysical issues and also providing resources for the construction of alternative religious worldviews. Belief in astrology or in UFOs are good examples of popular commitment to such nonconventional, metaphysical themes.[75] For example, there is evidence of a close relationship between the fact that, as John Saliba has noted, Western popular culture encourages "the idea that space people and/or invaders exist"[76] and the fact that there are not only many people happy to entertain the existence of UFOs, but also many who are committed to notions of visitation, abduction, and related ideas. As Thomas Bullard comments, "Belief in UFOs was once an oddity, a badge of craziness in the routines of popular humour. But little by little this belief has become the norm, and nearly half of the population [of the U.S.] now affirms that UFOs are real."[77] In her intriguing book *Aliens in America: Conspiracy Cultures from Outerspace to Cyberspace*, Jodi Dean argues for the existence of a close two-way relationship between popular culture and seriously held conspiracy theories regarding alien abduction. This rise of interest in UFO mythology and alien abductions is not only reflected in programs such as *The X Files*; it is also stimulated and shaped by such programs: "*The X Files* capitalizes on and contributes to pop-cultural preoccupation with aliens." "Apparently, significant numbers of Americans are convinced. In June 1997, 17 percent of the respondents to a *Time*/CNN poll claimed to believe in abduction."[78] Similarly, Peter Knight's discussion of conspiracy culture notes that "more than a few *X-Files* viewers have come to take the show's conspiracy and fringe-science revelations as fact."[79] UFO mythology has not only begun to have a shaping effect on Western plausibility structures, but it is clear, that it has been an important source of inspiration for numerous occult/ metaphysical/New Age belief systems and that it is feeding into alternative spirituality more generally.[80]

As the connections between the occult and arts-based culture, particularly literature and film, are, as Campbell and McIver have argued, "obvious and indisputable," it is not surprising that some works of art should be treated as sacred narratives.[81] For example, in a recent conversation with one of the moderators of an occult Web site, the religious significance of certain films was explained to me. *The Matrix*, for example, is understood to be an "initiatic" film, in that it is believed to have been created (wittingly or unwittingly) with certain "trigger" symbols for "those who understand." As such, it is one of a group of recent films which can initiate a person into a more enlightened, spiritual understanding of reality. Hence, for such alternative religionists (many of whom may only meet with other believers *virtually* on the Internet—which is, needless to say, becoming increasingly important as a source of spiritual input), understandings of reality and plausibility structures are directly informed and/or supported by such films.

As for literature, while it would be wrong to make too much of children's fantasy stories such as J. K. Rowling's tales of Harry Potter, the significance of such literature on contemporary worldviews is worth mentioning. Campbell and McIver conclude their examination with the following important comments:

> No discussion of the sources of support for occultism would be complete with-out noting that there is at least one place where it has a secure and highly approved position within the culture of contemporary society, a place where it is not condemned but where it is heavily endorsed. This, of course, is in the context of the culture of childhood, which would be largely unrecognizable without the fairies, ghosts, alien beings and magical environments which are its stock-in-trade. Virtually all the themes of adult occultism are to be found in the books, plays and films aimed at children, although not, of course, in a fully elaborated form. Here the "rejected" knowledge of adults is presented as the "accepted" material for children, even if there is an attempt to do so within the framework of "a willing suspension of disbelief." . . . [This] necessarily means that almost all members of modern society are introduced to occult ma-terial at a tender age. Occultism is thus a central part of the world-view which they inherit and one which they must subsequently learn to reject. It would hardly be surprising if some fail to do so.[82]

The argument of this chapter has been that, for various reasons, increasing numbers of Westerners are indeed failing to do so. Many are finding such nar-ratives important spiritual resources. Hence, when it comes to thinking seriously about cosmologies and the construction of worldviews later in life, they have a store of terminological and conceptual basics on which to draw. "Fantasy does not necessarily misdirect people away from consciousness raising; it need not be an opiate, but can be the much needed catalyst for change."[83] Alan Garner's trilogy *The Wierdstone of Brisingamen, Elidor,* and *The Moon of Gomrath* (my own child-hood favorites) are, as Harvey notes, "among the books most frequently men-tioned as inspirations (and pleasures) by Pagans—who certainly contribute to their regular reprinting. Similarly, childhood pleasure in the adventures of Asterix the Gaul and his companions has prepared some contemporary Gallic Druids for their ritual 'roaring at the sky.' "[84]

A particularly interesting example of the direct influence of fantasy literature upon religions and worldviews[85] is the relationship that exists between Robert Heinlein's 1961 novel *Stranger in a Strange Land* and the establishment of the first Pagan group to obtain full state and federal recognition in America, the Church of All Worlds.[86] Taking its name from the fictional religious movement described in *Stranger in a Strange Land,* the group claims that "science fiction [is] 'the new mythology of our age' and an appropriate *religious* literature."[87] Another exam-ple—perhaps the supreme example—of canonized fantasy is J. R. R. Tolkien's magnum opus, *The Lord of the Rings,* which itself draws on the cosmology of Norse Paganism. It would be difficult to underestimate the significance of this work. "It is arguable," says Harvey, "that J. R. R. Tolkien's *Lord of the Rings* provided metaphorical binoculars through which the realm of Faerie became visible again . . . Tolkien gave back the words for those other-than-human persons glimpsed at twilight in the Greenwood, declared Faerie to be vital and necessary—and a whole generation grew up in an enchanted, richly inhabited world."[88] Elsewhere he observes that, while academic literature has been important in the construction of contemporary Paganism,

> Tolkien's *Lord of the Rings* and other fantasy writings are more frequently mentioned by Pagans. Fantasy reenchants the world for many people, allowing them to talk of elves, goblins, dragons, talking-trees, and magic. It also encourages contemplation of different ways of relating to the world. . . . It counters the rationality of modernity which denigrates the wisdoms of the body and subjectivity. Alongside Future Fiction, the genre explores new and archaic understandings of the world, and of ritual and myth, and attempts to find alternative ways of relating technology to the needs of today.[89]

Although, like C. S. Lewis, Tolkien was writing from a Christian perspective,[90] and although many of his themes are, strictly speaking, antithetical to the Pagan worldview, *The Lord of the Rings* has encouraged a host of Tolkienesque fantasy works which are written from an explicitly Pagan perspective. The point is, again, that particular concepts and cosmologies explored in popular culture are not merely expressions of contemporary interests and concerns, but they lead, first, to familiarization and fascination, and second, to the shaping of new plausibility structures and worldviews. Hence, while there is a complex network of reasons for the rising interest in alternative cosmologies, it seems clear that cult television programs such as *Buffy the Vampire Slayer*, and *Sabrina the Teenage Witch*, or films such as *The Craft* or *Star Wars*, or books such as Terry Pratchett's numerous volumes,[91] or the flood of fantasy video games, or the great variety of popular music inspired by Eastern, Pagan, and occult beliefs and practices,[92] are in some way contributing to the reenchantment of the West.

To follow this line of thought a little further, it is interesting to compare contemporary "horror films" and films of the same genre made from the 1930s to the 1970s.[93] Although there are still few films which wholeheartedly endorse the occult, there is a notable shift away from the unsympathetic treatments of Paganism as sinister, satanic, and dangerously deviant, to more positive portrayals of it as intriguing, sexually exciting, and darkly cool. Having said that, it should also be noted that portrayals of the occult as intriguing, mysterious, and not without an element of sexual appeal are not entirely new; these themes can be found in Gothic literature from Horace Walpole's *The Castle of Otranto* (1765) to Bram Stoker's portrayal of the iconic figure of a handsome, aristocratic vampire, the appeal of which seems perennial. However, earlier treatments of the occult tended to end with rational explanations for apparently supernatural events,[94] thereby reinforcing the rationalist, secularized worldview, or they were essentially moral tales warning against dabbling in the occult and demonstrating the power of the crucifix as a symbol for vanquishing evil (most obviously evident in the vampire stories), thereby reinforcing the Judeo-Christian worldview. Nowadays, the supernatural world is a fact, skeptical rationalists are made to eat their doubting words, occult powers can be used for good as well as evil, Paganism is seen as an environmentally friendly alternative to oppressive institutional religion, and the symbols of Christianity (particularly the crucifix) are shown to be impotent. (Interestingly, when it comes to the forces of evil, particularly vampires, while contemporary films are keen to make the point that on the one hand in the words of the vampire hunter in the film *Blade*, "crosses don't do squat," on the other hand, products of the natural world such as silver, sunlight, and garlic have a dramatic effect—their purity and goodness is swift in its destruction of all that is identified as "evil.") Again, while this is not in itself an argument, in the current context it is significant as an indication of nontraditional reenchantment.

As noted above, a recent article in a British teenagers' magazine made the exaggerated claim that not only is Wicca is the fastest growing religion in America, with an estimated 1.5 million teenage converts; it is also currently viewed as "cool." That it is cool is worth noting. Popular culture has shaped the thinking of certain sectors of Western society to such an extent that some forms of new supernaturalism are perceived to be cool. Certainly some Pagans are cautiously welcoming many of the increasingly sympathetic portrayals of their beliefs and mythologies in the visual and literary arts. Much of the emerging spirituality may be trivial, image oriented, and socially inconsequential, but some of it will not be.

The majority of alternative religionists are older (60 percent are between 35 and 54; 25 percent are over 55; and almost all of the remaining 15 percent are between 25 and 35), and this is to be expected. Is it surprising that many under the age of 25 would not be interested in attending workshops, lectures, exhibitions, and retreats run by those of an older generation? Is it surprising that they cannot afford to or do not want to spend their money on such activities? Having said that, my own impression of the average age of attendees at Pagan Federation conventions is that they are at the younger end of the spectrum.[95] The reason for this is not simply that many Pagan activities are free or inexpensive, but, I suggest, that the Pagan community is less 1960s oriented, more in tune with contemporary concerns, and—while it can slip into folk music, sandals, and woolly jumpers—generally has a strong relationship with popular culture and mythology. Moreover, there is enough evidence to suggest that, just as baby boomers of an earlier generation make up the majority of today's alternative religionists, so today's young people, while not directly involved in spiritual networks, are familiar with the religious ideas and will settle into some form of alternative religion in the future. While the form it will take is difficult to predict, bearing in mind that Internet user statistics indicate that the majority of users are aged under 35 (72.3 percent),[96] and that most of the sites surveyed by Lorne Dawson and Jenna Hennebry claimed that they respond to "several messages a day . . . one award-winning site claiming to receive 'about 100 messages a day,' "[97] it is clear that, as Dawson's and Hennebry's research concludes, "the new religious uses of the Internet are likely to exercise an increasingly determinant, if subtle, effect on the development of all religious life in the future."[98]

Liminality and Reenchantment

Those familiar with *The X Files* will know that in Fox Mulder's office there hangs a poster on which there is a photograph of a supposed UFO accompanied by the simple statement, "I want to believe." These words are indicative of what seems to be the liminal experience of many contemporary Westerners. In referring to the liminal stage, I am, of course, making use of the theories of the anthropologists Arnold van Gennep and, particularly, Victor Turner.[99] Many years prior to Turner, Van Gennep identified three phases in rites of passage: the "preliminal," the "liminal," and the "postliminal." The liminal, or the threshold phase, is the period during which a person passes from being an "outsider" to being an "insider," but during which s/he is neither one nor the other. For Turner, liminality is an extremely important, creative, and transformative period in which real and profound changes take place. During this period the old ways of thinking and the old plausibility structures are questioned and may even be torn down as new ones are adopted and created. Indeed, a rite of passage is essentially a journey from structure, through antistructure, and back to structure as one passes from one's old ways of thinking and behaving, through a transformative stage, to a new world of ideas and practices. This liminal period of adjustment and change, which can be very brief or extended indefinitely, is a period of uncertainty, questioning, and preparation.

While Turner's theories have not gone unchallenged, I do think that many Westerners find themselves in just such a creative, antistructural, liminal period as their worldviews are gradually sacralized. Intrigued by new concepts and novel practices and therapies, many are beginning to dip into a range of spiritual and quasi-spiritual worldviews. Unsatisfied by secular worldviews, unhappy with traditional forms of institutional religion, inspired by an increasingly reenchanted popular culture, but not yet certain of new ideas that seem strange and irrational to their secularized minds, they move from the preliminal stage of detached curiosity to a liminal "I want to believe" stage in which new worldviews are entertained and old certainties are seriously questioned. Understood in this way, it comes as little surprise to read Melanie McGrath's account of New Agers as

> suspicious . . . of the profanity of rationalism, and . . . a little afraid also of the pace and alienation of the times. Technology too had invaded and terrorized their spirits. The world, to them, seemed to be in the process of decline. They

felt overwhelmed by loss—the loss of intimacy, the loss of community, the loss of symbolism, the loss of belief. Disillusioned by conventional religion, which called into question their right and duty to think as individuals, horrified by the rise of Christian fundamentalism, they had decided to make their own way towards meaningfulness.[100]

That such people are carefully feeling their way into new systems of belief is supported by James Richardson's research into conversion: "Converts to new religions are active human beings seeking meaning and appropriate life-styles. Rational decisions are being made through which self-affirmation is occurring. This affirmation may involve a rejection of past beliefs and behaviours, but converts are not just 'running away.' They are involved in an active searching that quite often includes serious negotiations with a group concerning required beliefs and behaviours."[101] However, whether one thinks of new religions or simply private alternative spiritual worldviews, the point to note is that many Westerners are serious seekers whose life is shaped by a search for and commitment to the sacred. "People seem to be taking their religion seriously and, even in the modern world, representatives of the most affluent and well-educated generation in American history are *choosing to be religious.*"[102] While the insecure nature of new religious commitment may be obvious, and while much belief may be experimental and initially trivial, it needs to be understood within the wider context of a gradual, uneven reenchantment. This is a liminal period of unease and transition, the future of which is still unclear.

CONCLUSION

That secularization/disenchantment has reshaped Western societies cannot be denied. That said, it is myopic not to recognize the significance of the gradual and uneven emergence of personally and socially consequential new religions and alternative spiritualities. As Leonard Glick urges, "those of us who study people's responses to new religious ideas should not labour with the misconception that our world is one in which religion is disappearing. For, to the contrary, the evidence is that new religions are arising all the time, that people do not respond to new problems by abandoning religion but by developing a new religion on the ruins of the old."[103] It seems clear that religion/spirituality is able to sustain itself outside traditional institutions and indeed to thrive within a postmodern, Western consumer climate. That religion is reshaped and relocated (and, consequently, needs to be redefined—possibly as "spirituality") does not mean that it is thereby trivialized. New forms of religion/spirituality in which the tensions between the sacred and the secular, the spiritual and the rational, the divine and the mundane, the body and the soul are greatly reduced have taken root in the West. Reenchantment is not a modern reconstruction of the enchanted landscape of the past, but new growth in a secularized, globalized, technologically sophisticated, consumer-oriented landscape. As Lyon comments, "religious relationships and movements . . . are of increasing importance in today's modern world. Much secularization theory produced earlier in the twentieth century mistook the deregulation of religion for the decline of religion."[104] Whether one considers the increasing significance of the body, the importance of virtual communities and the symbolic, or the sacralization of popular culture, just as we are witnessing a revolution in the way twenty-first-century religion/spirituality is lived, so there will need to be a revolution in the way it is studied and understood.

NOTES

1. P. Berger, "The Desecularization of the World: A Global Overview," in *The Desecularization of the World: Resurgent Religion and World Politics*, ed. P. L. Berger (Grand Rapids, Mich.: Eerdmans, 2000), 2.

2. See C. Chan, "The Sacred-Secular Dialectics of the Reenchanted Religious Order: The Lungsu Exo-Esoterics in Hong Kong," *Journal of Contemporary Religion* 15 (2000): 45–63.

3. See N. D. De Graaf and A. Need, "Losing Faith: Is Britain Alone?" in *British Social Attitudes: The 17th Report*, ed. R. Jowell et al. (London: Sage, 2000), 119–136; A. Greeley, "Religion in Britain, Ireland and the U.S.A.," in *British Social Attitudes: The 9th Report*, ed. R. Jowell et al. (Aldershot: Dartmouth Publishing, 1992), 51–70.

4. S. Bruce, *Religion in the Modern World: From Cathedrals to Cults* (New York: Oxford University Press, 1996), 34.

5. Ibid., 38.

6. See B. Wilson, "Secularization: The Inherited Model," in *The Sacred in a Secular Age: Toward Revision in the Scientific Study of Religion*, ed. P. E. Hammond (Berkeley: University of California Press, 1985), 9–20.

7. R. W. Hefner, "Secularization and Citizenship in Muslim Indonesia," in *Religion, Modernity, and Postmodernity*, ed. P. Heelas (Oxford: Blackwell, 1998), 150.

8. S. Bruce, "Pluralism and Religious Vitality," in *Religion and Modernization: Historians Debate the Secularization Thesis*, ed. S. Bruce (Oxford: Oxford University Press, 1992), 170.

9. A. Walker, *Telling the Story: Gospel, Mission, and Culture* (London: SPCK, 1996), 6.

10. Bruce, *Religion in the Modern World*, 48–49.

11. See W. Swatos, "Enchantment and Disenchantment in Modernity: The Significance of 'Religion' as a Sociological Category," *Sociological Analysis* 44 (1983): 321–338.

12. See, for example, B. R. Wilson, *Contemporary Transformations of Religion* (New York: Oxford University Press, 1976).

13. B. R. Wilson, " 'Secularization': Religion in the Modern World," in *The World's Religions: The Study of Religion, Traditional and New Religions*, ed. S. Sutherland and P. Clarke (London: Routledge, 1988), 207.

14. See S. Bruce, "The New Age and Secularization," in *Beyond New Age: Exploring Alternative Spirituality*, ed. S. Sutcliffe and M. Bowman (Edinburgh: Edinburgh University Press, 2000), 220–236.

15. A particularly strident account of the significance of new religions and alternative spiritualities can be found in Gregory Baum's *Religion and the Rise of Scepticism* (New York: Harcourt, Brace and World, 1970), 186–197.

16. See S. Bruce, "Religion in Britain at the Close of the Twentieth Century: A Challenge to the Silver Lining Perspective," *Journal of Contemporary Religion* 11 (1996): 261–274.

17. Bruce, "The New Age and Secularization," 233.

18. Ibid., 234.

19. O. Hammer, *Claiming Knowledge: Strategies of Epistemology from Theosophy to the New Age* (Leiden: Brill, 2001), 31.

20. See C. Partridge, ed., *Fundamentalisms* (Carlisle: Paternoster Press, 2002).

21. See the essays in Berger, *The Desecularization of the World*.

22. Berger, "The Desecularization of the World: A Global Overview," 3.

23. See, for example, R. Stark and W. S. Bainbridge, *The Future of Religion: Secularization, Revival, and Cult Formation* (Berkeley: University of California Press, 1985); R. Stark, "Modernization, Secularization, and Mormon Success," in *In Gods We Trust: New Patterns of Religious Pluralism in America*, ed. T. Robbins and D. Anthony (New Brunswick: Transaction Publishers, 1991), 201–218; R. Stark, "Rationality," in *Guide to the Study of Religion*, ed. W. Braun and R. T. McCutcheon (London: Cassell, 2000), 239–258.

24. R. Stark and W. S. Bainbridge, *The Future of Religion*, 6–8 (emphasis in the original).

25. Ibid., 8.

26. V. White, "Re-enchanting the World: A Fresh Look at the God of Mystical Theology," *Theology* 103 (2000): 347.

27. "Disenchantment . . . has more than one cause. Reason expelled magic and God from ordinary events of nature and history. But it also ejected other methods of knowing, relegating them to marginal, specialist interests, outside the public domain. The far point of separation is now most obviously recognizable in what is called postmodernism: A world in which any number of private interpretations of reality is allowed, but none trusted to lay claim to a common public arena. . . . In a further twist, radical postmodernism sees reason itself as privatized, distorted by personal agendas. So *everything* is fragmented and unreliable, nothing can be commonly held. Which brings us full circle. It is a recipe for new superstition and magic. . . . No wonder we would like to re-enchant the world" (ibid., 349–350).

28. As Ewert Cousins comments, "The term *spirituality* is beginning to appear in contexts where traditionally it has been ignored or banned. In fact, it seems to be encompassing all life. For example, it is emerging in the world of business, where the classical dynamics of spirituality are being tapped. In June 2000, the Chancellor of the University of Massachusetts, David Scott, a physicist trained at Oxford University, organized a conference entitled 'Going Public with Spirituality in the Workplace, Higher Education and Business.' We may be in a new phase of the awakening of spirituality that encom-

passes all of life." Foreword to C. Erricker and J. Erricker, eds., *Contemporary Spiritualities: Social and Religious Contexts* (London: Continuum, 2001), xi. See also R. H. Roberts, *Religion, Theology and the Human Sciences* (Cambridge: Cambridge University Press, 2002), chap. 3; P. Heelas, "Cults for Capitalism? Self Religions, Magic and the Empowerment of Business," in *Religion and Power*, ed. P. Gee and J. Fulton (London: British Sociological Association, Sociology of Religion Study Group, 1991), 27–41; P. Heelas, "God's Company: New Age Ethics and the Bank of Credit and Commerce International," *Religion Today* 8 (1992): 1–4.

29. Surveys and discussions of trends in contemporary religion in the West focus on traditional institutional religion, particularly Trinitarian Christianity. Typical is Peter Brierley's "Religion," in *Twentieth-Century British Social Trends*, ed. A. H. Halsey and J. Webb (Basingstoke: Macmillan, 2000), 650–674. While brief mention is made of the percentage of occult books sold (which, significantly, has more than doubled since 1930), the percentage of people who believe in phenomena such as ghosts (which has, again, more than doubled since the 1940s), the percentage of people who believe in God as spirit (which has risen since the 1940s), rather than believing in God as personal (which has dramatically dropped) and the importance of "implicit religion" (667), there is no significant discussion of the implications of such beliefs. They are simply mentioned as interesting asides in a discussion of the overall downturn of traditionally Christian belief and practice.

30. D. Lyon, *Jesus in Disneyland: Religion in Postmodern Times* (Cambridge: Polity Press, 2000), 21.

31. M. York, "Alternative Spirituality in Europe: Amsterdam, Aups and Bath," in Sutcliffe and Bowman, *Beyond New Age*, 131.

32. Jane Brum, "Smells Like Teen Spirit," *Marie-Claire* (November 2000), 146.

33. D. L. Jorgensen and S. E. Russell, "American Neopaganism: The Participants' Social Identities," *Journal for the Scientific Study of Religion* 38 (1999): 330.

34. In 1930 occult books constituted 7 percent of religious books published. This gradually rose to 17 percent in 1990, dipped to 11 percent in 1995, and arose again to 15 percent in 2000. See Brierley, "Religion," 666–667.

35. "The Road Well Trodden: How to Succeed in Publishing," *The Economist* (19 May 2001), 35.

36. "Occult beliefs have increased dramatically in the United States during the last two decades. Far from being a 'fad,' preoccupation with the occult now forms a pervasive part of our culture. Garden-variety occultisms such as astrology and ESP have swelled. . . . Ouija boards overtook Monopoly as the nation's best-selling board game in 1967. . . . Occult beliefs are salient not only among the lay public, but also among college students, including those at some of our science oriented campuses. The occult trend shows no signs of diminishing." B. Singer and V. A. Benassi, "Occult Beliefs," in *Magic, Witchcraft and Religion: An Anthropological Study of the Supernatural*, 4th ed., ed. A. C. Lehmann and E. J. Myers (Mountain View: Mayfield Publishing Co., 1997), 384. The article first appeared in *American Scientist* 69 (1981): 49–55.

37. P. Heelas, "Prosperity and the New Age Movement: The Efficacy of Spiritual Economics," in *New Religious Movements: Challenge and Response*, ed. B. Wilson and J. Cresswell (London: Routledge, 1999), 71.

38. P. Heelas, "Expressive Spirituality and Humanistic Expressivism," in Sutcliffe and Bowman, *Beyond New Age*, 240.

39. For Heelas's calculations, which are based, interestingly, on the figures Bruce uses, see, Heelas, "Expressive Spirituality and Humanistic Expressivism," 240.

40. R. Brooks and C. Morgan, "Losing Our Religion," *Sunday Times* (15 April 2001), 13.

41. Andrew Greeley's discussion of belief in God in Britain highlights the importance of using the right words to ask the right question in the right way. People are clearly sensitive about how they are perceived when it comes to religious belief. Greeley, "Religion in Britain, Ireland and the U.S.A.," 66–68.

42. The Gallup Index of Leading Religious Indicators / Princeton Religion Research Index records the following: "Belief in God or a universal spirit: This percentage has been very high in the U.S. over the last six decades—consistently in the mid–90 percent range. However, considerably fewer (8 in 10) believe in a personal God, that is, a God who watches over humankind and answers prayers" (http://www.gallup.com/poll/releases/pr010329.asp [12 September 2001]). See also Brierley, "Religion," 663.

43. Brooks and Morgan, "Losing Our Religion," 13.

44. E. Barker, "New Religious Movements: Their Incidence and Significance," in Wilson and Cresswell, *New Religious Movements*, 19.

45. Paul Heelas has recently identified the shift discussed in this chapter as a shift from "religion" to "spirituality." See "The Spiritual Revolution: From 'Religion' to 'Spirituality,' " in *Religions in the Modern World: Traditions and Transformations*, ed. L. Woodhead, P. Fletcher, H. Kawanami, and D. Smith (London: Routledge, 2002), 357–377.

46. M. Wainwright, "Church Fears Modern Beliefs Are Undermining Traditional Values," *The Guardian* (7 September 2001), 3.

47. M. Wainwright, "Our Candid Cardinal: Empty Pews in an Age of DIY Spirituality," *The Guardian* (7 September 2001), 19 (emphasis mine).

48. J. Beckford, "The Mass Media and New Religious Movements," in Wilson and Cresswell, *New Religious Movements*, 103–119.

49. C. Campbell, "The Easternisation of the West," in Wilson and Cresswell, *New Religious Movements*, 36.

50. While some New Agers have sought to convince me that this is not the case and that Jesus actually taught reincarnation, and although such thoughtful Christians as Leslie Weatherhead and, more recently, Geddes MacGregor have seriously considered the doctrine, in the final analysis, it is difficult to disagree with John Whale's blunt conclusion that "there is not a shred of evidence for this doctrine of Karma or a series of Reincarnations in the New Testament" (55). See G. MacGregor, *Reincarnation in Christianity* (Wheaton: Theosophical Publishing House, 1978); "Is Reincarnation Compatible with Christian Faith?" in A. and J. Berger, *Reincarnation: Fact or Fable?* (Wellingborough: Aquarian Press, 1991), 89–98; L. Weatherhead, *The Christian Agnostic* (1965; reprint, London: Arthur James, 1989), chap. 14; J. S. Whale, *The Christian Answer to the Problem of Evil*, 4th ed. (1936; reprint, London: SCM, 1957), 53–55.

51. T. Walter, "Reincarnation, Modernity and Identity," *Sociology* 35 (2001): 21.

52. See Barker, "New Religious Movements," 19.

53. Walter, "Reincarnation, Modernity and Identity," 21.

54. H. Waterhouse, "Reincarnation Belief in Britain: New Age Orientation or Mainstream Option?" *Journal of Contemporary Religion* 14 (1999): 107; emphasis in original.

55. D. Eisenberg et al., "Unconventional Medicine in the United States: Prevalence, Costs, and Patterns of Use," *New England Journal of Medicine* 328 (1993): 251.

56. Springhouse Corporation, *Nurse's Handbook of Alternative and Complementary Therapies* (Springhouse: Springhouse Corporation, 1999), ix. See also D. Rankin-Box, *Nurse's Handbook of Complementary Therapies* (Edinburgh: Bailliere Tindall, Royal College of Nursing, 2001).

57. See my discussion of the significance of the premodern in alternative religious worldviews: "Truth, Authority and Epistemological Individualism in New Age Thought," *Journal of Contemporary Religion* 14 (1999): 87–88.

58. *Nurse's Handbook of Alternative and Complementary Therapies*, 3.

59. T. Walter, "Reincarnation, Modernity and Identity," *Sociology* 35 (2001), 22.

60. James T. Richardson, "Studies of Conversion: Secularization or Reenchantment?" in Hammond, *The Sacred in a Secular Age*, 107.

61. For an excellent, critical treatment of Celtic Christianity, ancient, modern, and postmodern, see D. E. Meek, *The Quest for Celtic Christianity* (Edinburgh: Handsel Press, 2000).

62. Campbell, "The Easternisation of the West," 37.

63. B. Taylor, "Earth and Nature-Based Spirituality (Part 1): From Deep Ecology to Radical Environmentalism," *Religion* 31 (2001): 175–193; "Earth and Nature-Based Spirituality (Part 2): From Earth First! and Bioregionalism to Scientific Paganism and the New Age," *Religion* 31 (2001): 225–245.

64. R. Dalton and R. Rohrschneider, "The Greening of Europe," in *British (and European) Social Attitudes: How Britain Differs: The 15th Report*, ed. R. Jowell et al. (Aldershot: Ashgate, 1998), 101–123; S. Witherspoon, "The Greening of Britain: Romance and Rationality," in *British Social Attitudes: The 11th Report*, ed. R. Jowell et al. (Aldershot: Dartmouth, 1994), 107–139.

65. For an interesting anthology see R. S. Gottlieb, *This Sacred Earth: Religion, Nature, Environment* (New York: Routledge, 1996). A helpful essay when seeking to understand the attraction of ecological spiritualities is Charlene Spretnak's "The Spiritual Dimension of Green Politics," in C. Spretnak and F. Capra, *Green Politics: The Global Promise* (London: Paladin, 1985), 230–258.

66. As an aspect of the process of contextualization, the concept of inculturation has been developed within contemporary Christian missiology. For an excellent overview of contemporary Christian missiological usage of contextualization and inculturation, see D. Bosch, *Transforming Mission: Paradigm Shifts in Theology of Mission* (Maryknoll: Orbis, 1991), 420–432, 447–457.

67. B. R. Wilson, " 'Secularization': Religion in the Modern World," in *The World's Religions: The Study of Religion, Traditional and New Religions*, ed. S. Sutherland and P. Clarke (London: Routledge, 1988), 207.

68. See Tony Walter's discussion of reincarnation in everyday conversation: "Reincarnation, Modernity and Identity," 26–27.

69. L. Woodhead, "The World's Parliament of Religions and the Rise of Alternative Spirituality," in *Reinventing Christianity: Nineteenth-Century Contexts*, ed. L. Woodhead (Aldershot: Ashgate, 2001), 81. See also D. Martin, *The Religious and the Secular: Studies in Secularization* (London: Routledge and Kegan Paul, 1969), 108; and Heelas, "Expressive Spirituality and Humanistic Expressivism," 239.

70. C. Campbell and S. McIver, "Cultural Sources of Support for Contemporary Occultism," *Social Compass* 34 (1987): 41–60.

71. R. Ohmann, ed., *Making and Selling Culture* (Hanover, 1996) is an interesting

volume discussing the extent "moviemakers, television and radio producers, advertising executives, and marketers merely reflect trends, beliefs and desires that already exist in our culture, and to what extent . . . they consciously shape our culture."

72. E. Traube, introduction to ibid., xvi.

73. It is significant that interactive video games in which fantasy worlds are explored, occult symbols deciphered, new ethical frameworks constructed, and supernatural powers utilized, are not only easily outstripping the sales of films and books, but also they are being discussed as important forms of art.

74. Campbell and McIver, "Cultural Sources of Support for Contemporary Occultism," 46.

75. See J. R. Lewis, ed., *UFOs and Popular Culture* (Santa Barbara: ABC-CLIO, 2000).

76. J. A. Saliba, "Religious Dimensions of UFO Phenomena," in *The Gods Have Landed: New Religions from Other Worlds*, ed. J. R. Lewis (New York: SUNY, 1995), 20.

77. T. E. Bullard, "Foreword: UFOs—Folklore of the Space Age," in Lewis, *UFOs and Popular Culture*, ix.

78. J. Dean, *Aliens in America: Conspiracy Cultures from Outerspace to Cyberspace* (Ithaca: Cornell University Press, 1998), 25, 30.

79. P. Knight, *Conspiracy Culture: From Kennedy to the X Files* (London: Routledge, 2000), 47.

80. See C. Partridge, ed., *UFO Religions* (London: Routledge, 2002); J. R. Lewis, ed., *UFOs and Popular Culture*; J. R. Lewis, ed., *The Gods Have Landed*; A. Grünschloβ, *Wenn die Götter landen . . . : Religiöse Dimensionen des UFO-Glaubens* (Berlin: EZW, 2000).

81. Campbell and McIver, "Cultural Sources of Support for Contemporary Occultism," 54.

82. Ibid., 58.

83. G. Harvey, "Fantasy in the Study of Religions: Paganism as Observed and Enhanced by Terry Pratchett," *Discus* 6 (2000): www.unimarburg.de/religionswissenschaft/journal/diskus.

84. Ibid.

85. According to Aidan Kelly, "The only authors who are coping with the complexity of modern reality are those who are *changing the way people perceive reality*, and these are authors who are tied in with science fiction." Quoted in M. Adler, *Drawing Down the Moon: Witches, Druids, Goddess-Worshippers, and Other Pagans in America Today* (Harmondsworth: Arkana, 1997), 285 (my emphasis).

86. The novel's influence is not limited to the Church of All Worlds. For example, certain words used by spiritually inspired environmental activists such as *grock* (meaning "understand") are taken directly from the *Stranger in a Strange Land*. See Taylor, "Earth and Nature-Based Spirituality (Part 1)," 232, 242.

87. Quoted in M. Adler, *Drawing Down the Moon*, 286 (my emphasis). The works of H. P. Lovecraft have also had a direct influence on certain groups, not least Satanist groups. The influence is explicit in the writings of Anton LaVey, the influential founder of the Church of Satan.

88. Harvey, "Fantasy in the Study of Religions."

89. G. Harvey, *Listening People, Speaking Earth: Contemporary Paganism* (London: Hurst, 1997), 181–182.

90. See C. Duriez, "The Theology of Fantasy in Lewis and Tolkien," *Themelios* 23 (1998): 35–51.

91. Again, see Harvey, "Fantasy in the Study of Religions."

92. Much contemporary "world music" explicitly religiously inspired, certain forms of rock music, "black metal" in particular, are (whether out of religious conviction or simply for the sake of rebellious imagery) inspired by occultic, sometimes Satanist, ideas, and much contemporary dance / "trance" music is Eastern and Pagan in orientation. An interesting collection of interviews with popular musicians about spirituality can be found in D. Ehrlich, *Inside the Music: Conversations with Contemporary Musicians about Spirituality, Creativity, and Consciousness* (Boston: Shambhala, 1997). For recent "music press" discussions of religious trends in popular music see P. Sutcliffe, "Go Forth and Rock," *Q* 40 (May 1998): 68–78; P. Wilding, "Lucifer Rising," *Classic Rock* 31 (September 2001): 52–59.

93. An early example would be the film the founder of the Church of Satan, Anton LaVey, described as "the best paid commercial for Satanism since the Inquisition," namely *Rosemary's Baby*. LaVey himself served as a consultant on the film as well as playing the role of Satan, who impregnated Rosemary (Mia Farrow). For an interesting interview with LaVey in which the film is mentioned, see L. Wright, "Sympathy for the Devil: It's Not Easy Being Evil in a World That's Gone to Hell," in Lehmann and Myers, *Magic, Witchcraft and Religion*, 393–404. The article first appeared in *Rolling Stone* (5 September 1991), 63–64, 66–68, 105–106.

94. While there are of course exceptions, it does seem to be the case that while the Enlightenment mind was fascinated with the occult, it was also dismissive of it. For example, Ann Radcliffe closed her novels with rational explanations for apparently supernatural events, and, as Gamer comments, while Walter Scott produced many works with occultic and supernatural themes, "he nevertheless moves from producing texts that celebrate black magic and the supernatural to debunking these same subjects in his critical writing—doing so with cool rationality in *Letters on Demonology and Witchcraft* (1830)." Michael Gamer, *Romanticism and the Gothic: Genre, Reception, and Canon Formation* (Cambridge: Cambridge University Press, 2000), 33.

95. See, for example, M. York, *The Emerging Network: A Sociology of the New Age and Neo-Pagan Movements* (Maryland: Rowan and Littlefield, 1995), 180.

96. L. L. Dawson and J. Hennebry, "New Religions and the Internet: Recruiting in Public Space," *Journal of Contemporary Religion* 14 (1999): 24. Interestingly, of all the areas supported by Oxford University's Computers in Teaching Initiative Centre, it received "more enquiries from the non-academic reader on the subject of religion than any other subject." M. Fraser, "Religion and Theology," in *Guide to Digital Resources for the Humanities* (Oxford: CTI Centre for Textual Studies, Humanities Computing Unit, University of Oxford, 2000), 167.

97. Dawson and Hennebry, "New Religions and the Internet," 25.

98. Ibid., 36. See also J. Zaleski, *The Soul of Cyberspace: How New Technology Is Changing Our Spiritual Lives* (New York: HarperEdge, 1997); G. Chryssides, "New Religions and the Internet," *Diskus* 4.2 (1996): http://www.unimarburg.de/religionswissenschaft/journal/diskus.

99. A. van Gennep, *The Rites of Passage*, trans. M. B. Vizedom and G. Cafee (Chicago: University of Chicago Press, 1960); V. Turner, *The Ritual Process: Structure and Anti-structure* (Ithaca: Cornell University Press, 1991).

100. M. McGrath, *Motel Nirvana: Dreaming of the New Age in the American Desert* (London: Flamingo, 1996), 226.

101. Richardson, "Studies of Conversion," 107–108.

102. Ibid., 109; emphasis in original.

103. Leonard Glick, quoted in ibid., 114.

104. D. Lyon, *Jesus in Disneyland*, 104.

CHAPTER 3

THE SOCIOCULTURAL SIGNIFICANCE OF MODERN NEW RELIGIOUS MOVEMENTS

LORNE L. DAWSON

EVERY article or book written on new religious movements implicitly assumes their sociocultural significance, and the volume of literature is substantial (see the overviews provided in Bromley and Hadden 1993 or Dawson 1998a). But outsiders to the field have often complained that the scholarly attention is not warranted, since so few people are involved in new religions in modern Western societies. Too much effort has been expended studying a statistically marginal phenomenon (e.g., Turner 1983). Yet the study of new religious movements has been a major aspect of the sociology of religion for decades, and popular and scholarly fascination with the topic continues. New religious movements (hereafter NRMs) have a symbolic and perhaps even an instrumental significance, it seems, that transcends the statistics. Why is this the case?

Only a few scholars have attempted to directly address the issue of the significance of NRMs, and I will not presume to offer a definitive explanation here. But the study of NRMs has reached a certain level of maturity, and it is time to adopt a more systematic and long-term perspective. Are the changes in the religious landscape associated with the emergence of so many NRMs, since the 1960s, indicative of greater things? Will the study of these groups lead to a better grasp of our collective religious and social future? There is no easy answer, but I will seek to clarify the parameters of the discussion and argue the advantages of taking a new tack.

For most sociologists of religion, I think, the cultural significance of NRMs stems from the role they play in the debate over secularization. A question lurks behind the scenes in the sociology of religion: Is the demise of religion imminent in the modern world? The analysis of NRMs raises this issue in a particularly graphic way. Committed to the intellectual ideals of the Enlightenment, sociologists of religion, like most other social scientists, wonder whether religion is even compatible with the social conditions of modernity (see Hadden 1987; Stark 1999). The existence of NRMs points to the ongoing birth of religiosity, of a rather extraordinary or radical kind, in a presumably secular age. So judgments of the significance of NRMs, in aggregate or as specific movements, tend to be linked to queries about the reality of secularization.

The dominant ways of conceiving the religious responses to modernity, however, are too restrictive. Religions tend to be categorized as either traditional in form and hence no longer relevant, or changed in ways that make them more relevant yet less truly religious. These interpretive options are plausible to a point. But the reality is more complex, especially with regard to NRMs. Another option exists, and this option abandons the grand abstractions of secularization theory, with its running contrast of the conditions of premodern (i.e., religious) and modern society (i.e., secular), in favor of investigating whether there is an elective affinity between NRMs and the known and changing religious sensibilities of contemporary Europeans and North Americans (Dawson 1998b, 2001). If there is an affinity of consequence, is it indicative of an even more fundamental correspondence between various NRMs and sweeping changes in the very structure of contemporary life? If so, we can imagine new religions that are adapted to modern social life and still intrinsically religious.

Several of the most direct attempts to address the sociocultural significance of NRMs have pursued similar lines of analysis (e.g., Hunter 1981; Wallis 1982; Robbins and Bromley 1992, 1993). They have tended, however, to remain tied to the restrictive interpretive options set in place by earlier thinkers preoccupied with the issue of secularization. In part this is because they lacked a sufficiently comprehensive and detailed understanding of the nature of the changes gripping late modern societies.

A corrective to this deficiency can be found in Anthony Giddens's influential analysis of the institutional and social psychological consequences of modernity (Giddens 1990, 1991, 1992). Giddens's well-known work is only beginning to be integrated into the study of religion (e.g., Mellor 1993, Beckford 1996, Walliss 2001), yet it provides one of the most insightful conceptualizations of the social changes shaping the operating environment of contemporary religions.

In the past I have argued that NRMs conforming to the new religious sensibilities of Western societies are more likely to succeed, and thus have an impact on the future forms of religious life (Dawson 1998b, 2001). In part, of course, these NRMs are a source of evidence for the supposition that people's' religious sensibilities are changing. Some NRMs are harbingers of things to come because they are among the actual agents of the social and cultural changes in question. The argument avoids being circular, if the changes are being driven by larger social forces and processes, as Giddens's analysis suggests. His understanding of the changed character of life in late or high modernity provides a better understanding of why the religious sensibilities of many people are shifting in the first place, and hence why certain styles of religiosity, embodied in many NRMs, are likely to persist, and perhaps even prosper.

Ironically, to use Giddens in this way I must make him abide by the wisdom of one of his own assumptions about the true character of modernity. While rebuking others for thinking of the contrast of premodern and modern societies in an overly dichotomized fashion, he tends to conceive of the relationship between religion and modernity in an equally dichotomized and unrealistic manner. In other words, he inconsistently accepts the limited conceptions of the nature and future of religion associated with the debate over secularization. He tends to think of religion in terms of the traditionalism of premodernity, discounting its future in the detraditionalized context of late modernity. His own analysis of modernity, however, clearly points to the social conditions facilitating a new and more complex understanding of the role of appropriately adapted forms of religion in the modern world.

REFOCUSING THE ANALYSIS

There is no obvious way to specify what we mean by the sociocultural significance of NRMs. Talk of "significance" is intrinsically elusive. In a methodological sense the study of NRMs is significant because they present a window of opportunity to empirically explore basic issues in the sociology of religion. Most notably, the public controversy surrounding contemporary NRMs has led to studies that have vastly improved our grasp of the nature and complexity of the processes of recruitment and conversion (e.g., Barker 1984, Snow and Machalek 1984, Richardson 1985, Dawson 1990, Rambo 1993). Less obviously, but as significantly, the study of NRMs has also prompted important advances in our understanding of religious innovation and group formation, religious change, and the structure and development of religious institutions (e.g., Gerlach and Hine 1970, Wallis 1974, 1977;

Stark and Bainbridge 1985, Lofland and Richardson 1984, Lucas 1995, Stark 1987, 1996). Similar claims could be made about other concerns, like the gendered character of religious preferences (e.g., Palmer 1994, Puttick 1997), the nature, emergence, operation, and liabilities of charismatic leadership (e.g., Feuerstein 1990, Bird 1993, Dawson 2002), and the roots of religious violence (e.g., Chidester 1988, Tabor and Gallagher 1995, Robbins and Anthony 1995, Dawson 1998a, Hall 2000). Of course there is nothing intrinsic to NRMs that makes them the only or even primary venue for exploring these kinds of issues. There are, however, certain advantages: (1) new religions often present analysts with smaller and more manageable forums for research; (2) they often provide unique chances to witness the beginnings of religious phenomena, or at any rate they often provide researchers with opportunities to observe phenomena free of the impact of tradition; and (3), they are more likely to present researchers with extremes of behavior and policy that are easier to measure and assess and then extrapolate to less extreme situations (on the model of scientific activity in many other fields, e.g., psychiatry, astronomy).

My use of the term "significance," however, hinges upon recognition of the ultimately "subjective," or I would prefer to say "hermeneutical," character of the social sciences, and my focus is more social structural and cultural. Is the study of NRMs significant for understanding other large social developments impinging on everyone in modern Western societies?

"All knowledge of cultural reality," Max Weber states (1949: 81), "is always knowledge from *particular points of view*" (emphasis in the original). Today this statement is an epistemological given. But we tend to forget, as Weber also argued, that the infinite array of data before us is only organized into meaningful and specific phenomena through the introduction of cultural presuppositions, presuppositions about the value of certain things. What has significance in this sense is worthy of study. In a lengthy analysis of this methodological a priori, Weber states (1949: 78): "A chaos of 'existential judgements' about countless individual events would be the only result of a serious attempt to analyse reality 'without presuppositions.' . . . Order is brought into this chaos only on the condition that in every case only a *part* of concrete reality is interesting and *significant* to us, because only it is related to the *cultural values* with which we approach reality."

At all points, I would argue, the study of NRMs has been motivated in some measure by the concern to see if the exotic and new expressions of religion scholars encountered were in some way reflective of changes in the very character of modern religious life (see e.g., Glock and Bellah 1976; Wilson 1976, 1982; Stone 1978; Campbell 1978, 1982; Wallis 1982; Westley 1983). The underlying "value" at stake is religion itself (no matter how irreligious sociologists tend to be), or more specifically the threat posed to religion—if only as a social phenomenon—by modernity.

This may not be readily apparent since the public controversy set off by the "cult scare" of the 1970s carried the field in other directions. In the face of the repressive efforts of the anti-cult movement the defense of "religious liberty" became a more specific prime mover for many academic studies of NRMs. Sociologists and other scholars of religion felt the need to correct the perceived distortions conveyed to the public by the media, at the prompting of the anti-cult movement (see Dawson 1998a; Robbins 2001). As legal cases multiplied in which the issues under dispute played a key role, a sense of urgency arose. In a more general sense the threat to the new religions was seen as an implicit threat to religious life in general. It was becoming increasingly difficult to differentiate between the supposed offenses or irrationalities of the new religions and the activities and beliefs of many more conventional expressions of religion. In the end the American courts began to think so as well, and they refused to entertain testimony on such central anti-cult suppositions as the "brainwashing" of cult converts (e.g., Richardson 1991; Anthony and Robbins 1992, Young and Griffiths 1992).

In recent years a resurgence of public hostility toward NRMs in Europe, Russia, China, and elsewhere has stimulated more research on NRMs. But, unlike some commentators (e.g., Zablocki and Robbins 2001), I do not think the cultural significance of NRMs rests primarily with this issue. In fact I think its importance in the past is easily exaggerated. But questions of church and state, as exemplified by the legal disputes involving cults, will continue to provide one context in which questions about the cultural significance of NRMs are raised (e.g., Wright 1995; Cote and Richardson 2001; Richardson and Introvigne 2001).

When scholars have occasionally turned more directly to the task of examining the sociocultural significance of NRMs, other issues have come to the fore, like their experimentation with alternative gender and sexual relations (e.g., Aidala 1985; Robbins and Bromley 1992, 1993; Davidman and Jacobs 1993; Palmer 1994; Dawson 2000), or their innovative economic resource mobilization mechanisms (e.g., Richardson 1988; Robbins and Bromley 1992). These analyses are important, and there are many other specific issues that warrant being explored by targeting NRMs as social indicators of broader currents of change (e.g., the links between NRMs and alternative healing practices; see McGuire 1985, 1993; Robbins and Bromley 1993).

Thomas Robbins and David Bromley (1992, 1993) have cogently argued that seeing NRMs as incubators of social experimentation has several advantages. First, it frees thought about the possible significance and meaning of these groups from the quagmire of contentious issues, and the distorting terms of reference, of the public and legal controversy over cults. Second, by demonstrating how contemporary movements are often reiterating and extending lines of social innovation associated with many of the new religions of the past (e.g., the Shakers, the Oneida Society, the Mormons, and Christian Scientists), it suggests that NRMs reflect and are contributing to a longer trajectory of social transformation. Third, by considering the presence of social experiments in several different NRMs simultaneously, and thus isolating larger patterns of innovation, the approach allows the significance of NRMs to be considered independently of the survival and continued growth of specific recent movements (Robbins and Bromley 1992: 21). The significance of any one movement or group of new religions is clearly linked to their "success" (i.e., their longevity, size, rate of growth, physical assets, etc.). Yet in the larger scheme of things, many failed religions may turn out, by accident or otherwise, to be of equal or greater significance as carriers of new paradigms of social relations or even conceptions of reality.

Any analysis of the significance of NRMs should retain these advantages. But it is extremely difficult to delineate just how or even if specific experiments in the esoteric culture of NRMs have had or will have an impact on social behavior of people in the larger exoteric culture. Moreover, the lines of causal analysis run both ways. NRMs are as much reflections of developments in the larger societies as they may on occasion be seedbeds of ideational and organizational innovation. Robbins and Bromley are sensitive to this problem and seek to ameliorate it by making specific comparisons between new and older religious movements. The longevity of the concerns addressed by these groups is indicative of their connection with larger social trends and cultural dilemmas. But we can go further now, I believe, and use resources like Giddens's theory of the consequences of modernity to postulate a more specific fit between new religious developments and structural changes in the very patterning context of daily life in late modernity. We must tread carefully, however, in pursuing this line of analysis.

The question of the significance of NRMs is raised, for example, by analyses of the factors affecting the relative success or failure of NRMs (e.g., Richardson, Stewart, and Simmonds 1979; Wilson 1987; Stark 1987, 1996; Stark and Iannaccone 1997). The primary focus in these studies is internal aspects of the various NRMs, their ideologies, leadership, organization, modes of recruitment, socialization, and so on. The analyses are premised often, though, on a broader set of judgments about the relative fit or continuity between the NRMs and important aspects of the surrounding societies. If a group is to succeed, its features must satisfy certain identifiable needs in that society. Plus they must strike an appropriate balance of differentiation from and similarity with the dominant ethos of the surrounding culture. Too little distinction and the group will not stand out sufficiently as a functional alternative to other ways of satisfying the needs in question in the society in question. Too much distinction and the group risks alienating potential recruits.

Likewise, analyses of why NRMs have emerged and proliferated in modern societies in the first place implicitly raise the significance issue. In this context again the focus is the fit between the groups and the larger societies, and the ways in which NRMs are meeting unrequited needs. Without elaborating here (see Dawson 1998a: 41–62), the needs specified are commonly about the provision of identity, community, and spirituality. As Thomas Robbins stipulates, the arguments all "tend to pinpoint some acute and distinctively modern dislocation which is said to be producing some mode of alienation, anomie or deprivation to which [people] are responding by searching for new structures of meaning and community" (1988: 60). In this manner discussions of the sociocultural signifi- cance of NRMs are commonly entwined with theories of relative deprivation, or compensation (e.g., Glock 1964; Bellah 1976; Tipton 1982; Anthony and Robbins 1982a, 1982b. Stark and Bainbridge 1985, 1996).

Many sociologists of religion find these approaches reductive and distasteful since they appear to discount the role of positive motivations in accounting for the appeal of NRMs (e.g., Hine 1974: 654, Wilson 1990: 195). It is difficult, however, to discuss the long-term significance of NRMs without invoking some neofunc- tionalist correlation of societal needs and religious compensations. Care must be taken, as Colin Campbell (1982) argues, to avoid slipping into the functionalist error of thinking that matching a social need with a possible religious response provides an "explanation" for the existence or success of NRMs. It is notoriously difficult to establish the causal link between the stated needs and the actual be- haviors of people, let alone their religious affiliations (see Gurney and Tierney 1982). The "needs" specified are too general in scope to explain why specific individuals join specific groups, when clearly many others are susceptible to the same need and choose not to seek a religious compensation. In other words, the conventional approach will not allow us to effectively discriminate between joiners and nonjoiners, and hence "explain" the emergence or relative success of a religion in a particular social and cultural context (see Dawson 1998a: 76).

It remains broadly plausible, though, to assume some link between needs and these groups. So what are we to do? Campbell suggests an important adjustment in our focus of attention (1982: 234):

> The question, which is most likely to lead to a better understanding of modern
> society as a whole, via an examination of the new religious movements, is not
> so much why people join as why they find their meaning-systems plausible.
> For only when this is the case can such movements actually be "available" to
> recruits and yet for this to be true such recruits must already be attuned to the
> particular movements' beliefs and values.

In the past I examined NRMs to see how they might be offering people something they wanted (Dawson 1998b). I delineated a set of six new religious sensibilities[1] present in many NRMs and expressed commonly by people interested in such groups. Then I postulated a plausible fit with the changing religious sensibilities of the larger society. My reading was from the groups to the society, though I lacked sufficient evidence of the matching changes in the larger society.

In this chapter, following Campbell, I am inverting the analysis. To under- stand why people may even be open to the siren call of some new religious groups, I will use Giddens's theories to understand (not "explain" per se) why the religious sensibilities of an ever-growing segment of modern Western societies may well be changing in ways congruent with the beliefs and practices of some NRMs. In other words, I am approaching the same nexus of religious systems and social preferences from the opposite direction, reading from the society back to the new religions.

It is time to heed the sage yet largely neglected advice of Campbell (1982: 235–236):

> Studies of new religious movements have typically focused upon their teach-
> ings, practices and patterns of authority and recruitment. Such a focus natu-
> rally leads to a better understanding of the movements themselves but it is
> doubtful if it is capable, by itself, of generating a satisfactory explanation of
> their origin and growth. This can only be achieved if attention is directed away
> from internal features toward the wider social and cultural environment. Al-
> though this fact is generally recognized and most studies of these movements
> include some reference to such postulated societal characteristics as seculariza-
> tion, alienation, or anomie, the link between these and the growth of the
> movements is either left unspecified or is sketched in the vaguest terms. . . .
>
> One of the principal reasons for this would appear to be the lack of a
> pertinent level of analysis intermediate between that of the movement itself
> (clearly the most convenient unit of study) and society at large. One necessary
> step in bridging this gap is to recognize that specific religious movements are
> themselves merely part of a larger and more diffuse phenomenon; one which
> can in turn be related to general social or cultural conditions.

Campbell's pertinent level of intermediate analysis can be found in Giddens's structural and institutional analysis of late modernity and its social psychological consequences.

But first we must consider how the debate over secularization has skewed the analysis of the significance of NRMs. We are compelled to do so because Giddens's own analysis of the place of religion in the late modern world is subject to the same distorting influence.

CIRCUMVENTING THE LEGACY
OF THE SECULARIZATION THESIS

Much of the literature addressing the significance of NRMs is explicitly or implicitly influenced by the understanding of the interpretive options laid out in
Peter Berger's seminal analysis of secularization (Berger 1967). Berger argues that
in the late twentieth century religions in the Western world were compelled to

adapt to two new realities of their social environment: privatization and pluralism. In the face of the extensive institutional differentiation of advanced capitalist societies, no religion can enjoy a monopoly of practice or social influence any longer. The "sacred canopy" of taken-for-granted assumptions about life and its meaning, and the corresponding social structures of society, have been replaced by a system of functional specialization, under the aegis of the historical forces of rationalization. Religion has become a matter of private concern and personal choice, and the number of choices available has grown exponentially in the absence of significant institutional restraints in a globalizing world. So religious traditions, "which previously could be authoritatively imposed, now [have] to be *marketed*" (Berger 1967: 138; emphasis in the original). Religions have become just one more product competing for the time, labor, and funds of ever busier and distracted consumers. To do so they must increasingly offer a product "consonant with the secularized consciousness" of the diverse, educated, and media-saturated populations of modern societies. But every struggle for competitive edge tends to relativize the truth of the message delivered in the face of so many alternatives.

In the end, Berger argues (1967: 153), contemporary religions face two options, neither of which bodes well for their long-term significance (relative to the great religions of the past):

> They can either accommodate themselves to the situation, play the pluralistic game of religious free enterprise, and come to terms as best they can with the plausibility problem by modifying their product in accordance with consumer demands. Or they can refuse to accommodate themselves, entrench themselves behind whatever socio-religious structures they can maintain or construct, and continue to profess the old objectivities as much as possible as if nothing had happened.

The same pessimistic diagnosis pervades the thought of the eminent British sociologist of religion, Bryan Wilson (e.g., 1976, 1988). Much like Berger, Wilson thinks that the macro-social changes associated with secularization have intrinsically limited the capacity of any NRM to ever significantly reverse the privatization of religion in the West. Why? Because in the last analysis he believes that most NRMs are largely the products of the modern societal system, rather than its opponents, and he implicitly equates privatization with the loss of significance.

New religious movements, whether in the Christian, Buddhist, or any other tradition, are not in the strict sense revivals of a tradition, they are more accurately regarded as adaptations of religion to new social circumstances. None of them is capable, given the radical nature of social change, of recreating the dying religions of the past. In their style and in their specific appeal they represent an accommodation to new conditions, and they incorporate many of the assumptions and facilities encouraged in the increasingly rationalized secular sphere. Thus it is that many new movements are themselves testimonies to secularization: they often utilize highly secular methods of evangelism, financing, publicity, and mobilization of adherents. Very commonly, the traditional symbolism, liturgy, and aesthetic concern of traditional religion are abandoned for much more pragmatic attitudes and for systems of control, accountancy, propaganda, and even doctrinal content which are closer to the styles of secular enterprise than to traditional religious concerns. The new religions do evidently indicate a continuing interest in—perhaps need for—spiritual solace and reassurance on the part of many individuals, but, in the West at least, they are also very much the creations of a secularized society (Wilson 1988: 965).

The proliferation of NRMs can be taken as evidence that the absolute secularization of our societies is unlikely. But NRMs emerge from this analysis as either mere remnants of religion, transformed and adapted to a reduced existence in a secular context, or fragmentary acts of protest against modernity surviving on the margins of society. Either way, we are left with the sense that their study can have little relevance for understanding the fate of the great secularizing mass of society. Every scholar who has turned his hand to the direct study of the significance of NRMs has sought in essence to refute this assumption, yet by first accepting the dichotomous analytic parameters established by Berger, Wilson, and others, they have unwittingly undermined their own efforts.

The Limitations of Previous Conceptions of the Significance of NRMs

This theoretical limitation is most blatant in James Davison Hunter's well-known attempt to delineate the significance of NRMs: "The New Religions: Demodernization and the Protest Against Modernity" (1981). Hunter relates the rise of NRMs and the New Christian Right of the 1970s and 1980s to a common problem: the anomic and alienating conditions of modern life. Calling on Berger's influential theories of religion and modernity (Berger 1967, Berger, Berger, and Kellner 1974), Hunter argues that the resurgence of all forms of religious life in a seemingly ever more secular context is a response to the root dilemma of "deinstitutionalization." Modernity, and the demise of the traditional social order, is commonly identified with the increased institutionalization of society. Massive bureaucracies are the order of the day in the "public" sphere of modern social life, in the realms of business, government, the law, education, health care, and even religion (e.g., the Catholic Church and other large Protestant denominations). Paradoxically, however, in the private sphere of life, the most emotionally significant aspects of people's lives are being deinstitutionalized. Patterns of courtship, marriage, child-rearing, sexuality, gender roles and relations, consumption, vocation, and spirituality have all become matters of choice, and for many people the choices are becoming bewildering. Anomie and uncertainty are the by-products of the new liberty unleashed, especially when lives are becoming increasingly impersonal and subject to the dictates of a strictly formal and functional rationality that cares little for idiosyncrasies. To the large bureaucracies people are increasingly interchangeable and expendable units. So one's identity hinges more on private choices. Yet these identities are becoming increasingly unstable and unreliable in the face of a plurality of ongoing and not easily understood choices.

New religions "resacralize" daily life by anchoring private activities and identities, and to some extent even public ones, in institutions conceived once again as reflections of the natural, cosmic, or divine order. Marriage, for example, is less likely to be followed by divorce, it is believed, if it is understood again as a religious and eternal commitment and not merely a personal act. Ambiguity and uncertainty are reduced and meaning increased by this "demodernizing" process, which accounts for the appeal of these new and relatively radical religious commitments.

Such a brief summary fails to do justice to the full texture of Hunter's deft application of Berger's ideas. All the same, two key points can be discerned. There is little sense in Hunter's analysis that the processes of modernization can be reversed, so the religious protest against modernity is ultimately futile and NRMs are marginal phenomena. Consequently, the sole significance of the emergence of NRMs is that they are "a sign that in some sectors of modern society, the strains of modernity have reached the limits of human tolerance, and are thus symbolic, at both the collective and social psychological levels, of the desire for relief and assuagement" (1981: 7). But actual relief from these hardships, it is implied, must come from elsewhere. So, in the end, NRMs are significant only as *symptoms* of a broader social malaise.

Roy Wallis (1982), like Hunter, proposes that NRMs "have developed in response to, and as attempts to grapple with the consequences of rationalization," or in other words modernity. More specifically, in "The New Religions as Social Indicators" he argues that they are a response to the consequent secularization of society, especially the loss of "transcendent values and absolute moral principles," as well as the alienation increasingly characteristic of public roles, the deinstitutionalization of the private sphere of life, and the attenuation of community (1982: 221–222). But, unlike Hunter, he argues that NRMs "*either* react against, *or* celebrate, major features of [modern] society" (1982: 216; emphasis in the original). In line with Weber's differentiation of sects and churches, Wallis distinguishes NRMs by their perspectives on society. There are at least two types of "cults": world-rejecting and world-affirming (see Wallis 1984, Dawson 1997). His description of world-rejecting NRMs bears a marked resemblance to Hunter's characterization of demodernizing religious movements. Both scholars see these groups as largely millennial, communal, totalistic, and introversionist in nature (e.g., the Children of God, Krishna Consciousness, the Unification Church). They are pictured as fashioning safe havens on the margins of society for the disillusioned yet still rebellious youth of the American counterculture of the 1960s and 1970s. These groups, Wallis says, "seem to offer much that the drop-outs and hippies had been trying to achieve: a stable, warm community; a rejection of worldly materialism, competition and achievement; a structured setting for the experience of ecstasy or mystical insight . . . [and those who joined them] were often willing to subordinate their autonomy for the benefits of this new way of life when it was offered" (1982: 226; see Bellah 1976 as well).

Other members of the same failed counterculture, however, chose to return to mainstream society, while maintaining an interest in the expressive values of their youth. They joined world-affirming NRMs promising to unlock their hidden human potential and offering training in esoteric techniques for relieving anxiety, increasing self-esteem and confidence, improving their health, and transforming their cognitive skills and sometimes even their acquisition of wealth (e.g., Scientology, est, Silva Mind Control, and dozens of other quasi-religious humanistic psychotherapies). These groups infuse a spiritual dimension of meaning into the busy lives of people with firm or growing attachments to the modern industrial world (1982: 228). Their beliefs and practices work to rationalize, justify, and further motivate the continued pursuit of achievement and material success, while offering compensations for the stresses of this life and mechanisms for coping with the guilt stimulated by indulging in the pleasures of this world or accepting its inequalities.

Hunter acknowledges the existence of such groups. But he seeks to discount their reality by forcing them into his demodernizing model. The real structure and the utopian ideals of organizations like Scientology, he argues, are "radically antimodern" (1981: 8). They may portray their beliefs and practices as being in line with modern science and technology, but in truth their teachings are largely metaphysical and their inner organization is increasingly segregated from society and totalistic. In these ways they are "at variance with the normal practice and assumptions of modern everyday life" (1981: 8).

But clearly in aspiration, language, daily activities, and involvements with the outside world, there are marked divergences between the religious practices of most Scientologists and the devotees of Krishna Consciousness. The latter group seems to fit Hunter's antimodern mould without much contention (though their use of modern technology poses problems). The former group can only be made to appear so with some interpretive finesse. In this or any other case, why should we give more interpretive weight to the similarities than the differences between these groups? Is it all a matter of perspective? Whatever is the case, more immediately the issue is the suspect adequacy of all such dichotomist interpretive frameworks, especially when they appear to continue to be informed by the assumptions of secularization theory.

When religions are more traditional in cast, as with Hunter's demodernizing or Wallis's world-rejecting NRMs, they are treated as unequivocally religious and yet invariably marginal, in a Western societal context. When religions, like Wallis's world-affirming groups, seem to deviate from past norms, primarily by being more private (i.e., subjective and segmented) and instrumental in practice, they are either explained away (Hunter) or treated as not fully religious (Wallis). World-affirming movements, Wallis suggests, "could perhaps more comfortably be called "quasi-religious" (1982: 220). Given the notorious difficulties of defining religion, independent of any specific historical tradition, it is understandable that this conceptual problem should arise. Either way, however, we are prevented from seriously entertaining the possibility that some NRMs may be genuinely religious and yet not be antimodern. Trapped in the implicit cognitive map of the secularization thesis, we are prevented from postulating a new religious reality that inherently challenges the assumptions of secularization theory.

At first glance the same pattern is displayed by Robbins and Bromley's "Social Experimentation and the Significance of American New Religions: A Focused Review Essay" (1992). A close reading of this excellent essay reveals, however, a few key differences. Robbins and Bromley frame their interpretation of NRMs as sites of social experimentation within a broader understanding of NRMs as responses to various structural conditions of modernity. They use James Hunter's (1981) analysis along with Bromley and Busching's (1988) contrast of premodern "covenantal" and modern "contractual" social relations to delineate the conditions they have in mind. Much like Berger and Hunter, Bromley and Busching depict NRMs as a reaction to the sociocultural shift from premodern "covenantal" relations to modern "contractual" relations.

The contrast is defined as follows (Robbins and Bromley 1992: 5, citing Bromley and Busching 1988: 16):

> Contractual social relations are those in which individuals coordinate their behavior through pledging themselves to specific reciprocal activity without pledging to one another's well-being. Covenantal social relations are those in which individuals coordinate their behavior by pledging themselves to one another's well being without pledging specific reciprocal activity. Thus contracts are articulated through the logic of calculative involvement and individual interest; covenants are articulated through a logic of moral involvement and unity.

In the modern world, contractualism is continuously expanding at the expense of covenantal forms of social relations.

Like Wallis, however, Robbins and Bromley recognize that the religious response to this shift "might take the form of either creating [new] premodern/ covenantal social forms or adapting to the requisites of modern/contractual social forms" (1992: 5). In the realm of sexual patterns and gender roles, for example, they note that the groups which largely precipitated the public controversy over cults (e.g., Unification Church, Children of God, Hare Krishna) were experimenting with ways to reinstate covenantal relations, "emphasizing communally regulated sexuality or creating patriarchal communities with very traditional conceptions of gender roles." But it must be appreciated, they stress, that other groups, such as feminist spirituality groups, are seeking "to empower women for equalitarian participation in the modern/contractual social order" (1992: 6). Unlike Wallis, however, there is little evidence in their essay that these latter groups are somehow less religious. In part this is because they have purposefully sought to separate the assessment of the sociocultural significance of NRMs from the debate over secularization. They have separated these issues in turn because they recognize that NRMs are not so much a reaction to the sheer decline of covenantal relations as the social psychological problems stemming from "the tension between contractual and convenantal forms of social relations" (1992: 4). This tension is "exacerbated by the expansion of contractualism. But ultimately it stems from the fact that the "contractual and covenantal spheres remain integrally related to one another"; tension is "generated by the simultaneous combination of the incompatibility and the integrality of the two social forms" (1992: 5).

Robbins and Bromley do not elaborate on what they mean by these claims. But their statement calls to mind Durkheim's seminal analysis of the abnormal forms of the division of labor (Durkheim 1964: 353–395). A measure of something like the collective conscience is essential to the maintenance of modern societies, to sustain the legitimacy and viability of even contractual relations, and to allow any society to successfully reproduce itself. It is difficult to imagine, for instance, a society in which socialization could proceed by way of contractual relations alone.

NRMs, then, are not all antimodern, nor are they simply antimodern or modern (see Dawson 1998a: 147). In imposing dichotomous analytical categories, scholars are distorting a more complex reality and implicitly perpetuating the myths of the secularization thesis. This in turn diminishes our capacity to discern the real play of social forces stimulating or at least facilitating the rise and spread of new forms of religious life. In this regard Robbins and Bromley's use of the contrast of covenantal and contractual relations is still too restrictive for our purposes. This dichotomous conceptual framework may lure us back into associating religion too exclusively with the traditional forms of social relations that the secularization paradigm says modernity is replacing (i.e., reinforcing the idea that religion and modernity are antithetical). Giddens's analysis of late modernity can serve as the midwife for a new paradigm capable of alerting us to a more

complex understanding of interface between religion and modernity. But, as indicated, his own allegiance to the old secularizationist paradigm—when explicitly
discussing the relationship of religion and modernity—must be broken for this
potential to be realized.

NRMs and the Social Conditions
of Late Modernity

Giddens's influential writings on the social conditions of late modernity offer
sociologists of religion a unique opportunity to reconfigure their notions of the
operating environment of contemporary religions (e.g., Giddens 1990, 1991, 1992,
1994, 2002). Saying this does not mean that I agree with every aspect of Giddens's
theorizing, but I think he presents a most plausible and fruitful account of the
conditions of life in contemporary Western societies. For introductory purposes,
the analysis in this chapter will be limited to issues raised by his first and perhaps
best-known book on this topic: *The Consequences of Modernity* (1990). Critical
reflection on his elaboration of these ideas in later works will have to await another essay, and even this delimited analysis is synoptic in nature.

   Giddens's argument can be broken into three parts: his diagnosis of the social-
structural conditions of "modernity"; his analysis of the social-psychological consequences of these conditions; and his conception of the different possible responses (social, cultural, and political) to these consequences.

Recasting the Conditions of Modernity

Giddens is not sympathetic to talk of postmodernity (1990: 2, 45–52). He prefers
to say that citizens of the advanced industrialized nations of the world are living
in a period in which the consequences of modernity are becoming radicalized and
universalized. Modernity, Giddens argues, cannot be equated simply with capitalism (Marx), industrialism (Durkheim), or rationalization (Weber), and previous analyses of the consequences of modernity, like Berger's, tend to be too reductive and unidimensional. Disentangling elements of social life affected by
modernity that he thinks other theorists have misleadingly conflated or ignored,
Giddens points to three dialectically related features of modern life that he believes
are more fundamental. The first feature is the separation and "distantiation" of
time and space. The second feature is the presence and effect of "disembedding"

mechanisms and processes. The third feature is the institutionalization of reflexivity.

Modernity is marked by technological and conceptual inventions that have separated time and space and rendered them "empty" or abstract. The invasive spread of chronological time and of methods of rapid and mass transportation and communication have opened the doors to change on a sweeping scale, as age-old restrictions of time and space are transcended on a daily basis. For growing numbers of individuals and groups, for example, space per se is no longer primarily, if not almost exclusively, envisioned in terms of any one particular place, and the patterning of social life can be imaginatively reconfigured, segmenting activities and identities and overriding the dictates of natural cycles and geographic barriers. This is in some respects also a consequence of the development and spread of disembedding mechanisms like "symbolic tokens" (e.g., money) and "expert systems" (e.g., meteorology, aeronautics, computer science) that have lifted social relations out of their traditional and set local contexts. Symbolic tokens and expert systems "provide 'guarantees' of expectations across distantiated time-space" (1990: 28). Each of these developments in turn has been facilitated by and has further stimulated the reflexive character of social life. Human life is reflexive. Individuals learn and develop by being reflexive. Such has more or less always been the case. But until recently reflexivity has been bounded by tradition, which is subject to its own reflexive change, but in gradual and measured ways. The universalization of reflexivity under conditions of rationalization has constitutively altered the very character of social practices.

> With the advent of modernity, reflexivity takes on a different character. It is introduced into the very basis of system reproduction, such that thought and action are constantly refracted back upon one another. The routinisation of daily life has no intrinsic connections with the past at all, save in so far as what "was done before" happens to coincide with what can be defended in a principled way in the light of incoming knowledge. (Giddens 1990: 38)

A future of possibilities has displaced the past as the guide of action and with the radicalization of reflexivity reason has turned on itself, calling the very possibility of certain knowledge into doubt (e.g., in postmodernist philosophy and constructionist studies of science). Yet the knowledge we have, as embodied by expert systems, is engaged in feedback loops with constant consequences for our daily existence. In discussing how the social sciences are "reflexively restructuring their subject matter," for example, Giddens comments that "marriage and the family would not be what they are today were they not thoroughly 'sociologised' and 'psychologised' " (1990: 43).

All of these developments fostered the processes of globalization and must be conceived as happening in a globalizing context. The conditions that mark modernity can not be confined to "societies" as units of analysis, though they may occur more readily or rapidly in one society or another. The complex relations of "local involvements" and "interactions across distance" are being stretched, Giddens stresses, as never before. Local culture is being transformed by distant events and developments, yet the very integration of the two is also prompting the intensification of localized sentiments—a process others call "glocalization." The global and the local are interlaced as never before.

The Social Psychological Consequences of Modernity

Building on Urlich Beck's innovative notion of the "risk society" (Beck 1992, originally in German in 1986), Giddens chooses to frame the social psychological consequences of living under the conditions of radicalized modernity in terms of a dialectic of "trust" and "risk." The central problematic of modern life is the creation and maintenance of trust in the "symbolic tokens" and even more importantly the "expert systems" that create and manipulate these tokens. It is trust in these key features of modernity that fills the gaps in knowledge between the local and the global, and between individuals and the complex social systems in which they are ensnared, and from which they benefit so greatly. As Giddens says (1990: 83–84; emphasis in the original):

> *The nature of modern institutions is deeply bound up with the mechanisms of trust in abstract systems*, especially trust in expert systems. In conditions of modernity, the future is always open, not just in terms of the ordinary contingency of things, but in terms of the reflexivity of knowledge in relation to which social practices are organized. This counterfactual, future-oriented character of modernity is largely structured by trust vested in abstract systems— which by its very nature is filtered by the trustworthiness of established expertise.

Creating trust is crucial to social order, as it always has been, but the modern societal need for trust happens in a new collective "environment of risk." Ironically, the very advancements in science and technology that have freed us from so many of the natural terrors visited upon our ancestors have also forced us to live with a heightened awareness of the potentially catastrophic risks facing humanity—many of which are in fact the products of the extension of human knowledge.

Giddens outlines the "specific risk profile of modernity" as follows (1990: 124–125). First, the "objective distribution of risks" has been altered in at least four ways in the modern world. Two of these ways have to do with the *scope* of risks. The risks have been globalized, both in terms of the intensity of the risks (e.g., nuclear holocaust or planetary ecological disasters) and the expanding number of contingent events that now can affect almost everyone on the planet. In two other ways the *types* of risk to which people are exposed have been altered. We are increasingly subject to risks stemming from our interventions into nature, our socialization of the material environment. Plus we have developed "*institutionalized risk environments* affecting the life-chances of millions: for example investment markets" (emphasis in the original). Second, the "perception of perceived risks" has been altered in at least three ways. There is an ever wider awareness of the risks to which humanity is subject, there is less confidence that the risks can be averted by supernatural or magical means, and people are increasingly aware of the limitations of expert systems to cope with the risks, even those of their own creation.

Stated in a slightly different way, the key difference between premodern and modern societies lies in two intimately related variables: the changed conditions of trust creation and the character of the risk exposure. In the contemporary context the creation of trust "is a matter of the calculation of benefit and risk in circumstances where expert knowledge does not just provide the calculus but actually *creates* (or reproduces) the universe of events, as a result of the continual reflexive implementation of that very knowledge." This means, in the context of globalization, "that no one can completely opt out of the abstract systems involved in modern institutions." Such is clearly the case with threats like nuclear war. "But it is true in a more thoroughgoing way of large tracts of day-to-day life, as it is lived by most of the population" (1990: 84).

Modern societies need to generate trust in their expert systems. This task is particularly crucial and problematic because of the new context of risk in which people are living. A key element that heightens the need for trust, in part because it enlarges the environment of risk, is the more radically reflexive character of modern consciousness and social institutions. The other key element is "a direct (although dialectical) connection between the globalising tendencies of modernity and . . . the transformation of intimacy in the context of day to day life" (Giddens 1990: 114). Globalizing processes have local consequences. Past students of modernity, like Berger and Wilson (building on Ferdinand Toennies and others), have tended to treat the connection in terms of a shift from communal social orders to more impersonal societal systems. Berger develops this orientation more specifically in terms of the theme of the "deinstitutionalization" of the private sphere (among other things). Giddens does not deny the validity of these insights. He just regrets the failure to carry the analysis down more squarely to the issues of daily life, and most particularly the tremendous emphasis he now sees people placing on their most intimate and emotional relationships. In fact the whole notion of "relationships" as an all-important concern is, Giddens argues, typically modern.

In part this emphasis stems from the fact that our personal relationships are a natural focal point for resolving the issues of trust. Trust in the social system must build on the most basic sense of ontological security imparted to us (or not imparted to us) in our childhood by our parents and other significant others. In a world of magnified trust demands, friendships and romantic relationships have taken on a new significance as extended forums for the creation and maintenance of ongoing ontological security.

But this forum of trust creation has been rendered significant and problematic by another dialectically related consequence of globalization (i.e., modernity): the turn inward to the self, or what Berger and others have called the increased "subjectivism" of social life. A preoccupation with personal identity, self-awareness, and fulfillment has become the natural counterbalance to the loss of real place in the distantiated space-time of a globalizing, risk-riddled, social world. This turn to the self is once again both a product of and contributor to the reflexivity of modernity. For the self is not a static entity, but rather a "reflexive project" of identity construction. The reflexive construction of self becomes the cultural medium through which the process of trust creation happens, and hence ironically an important source of societal stabilization, because the sense of self can only be constructed in the context of relationships characterized by a new social norm of "mutuality of self-disclosure." Trust depends on self-actualization in personal contexts that "can only be established by an 'opening out' of the self to the other" (Giddens 1990: 123–124).

Past social theorizing has committed two related errors in considering these developments. First, there has been a tendency to simply set off the impersonality of the abstract systems of modern society against the intimacies of personal life in traditional societies and to often lament the loss of the latter (e.g., Berger 1967. Berger, Berger, and Kellner 1974. Wilson 1982). Second, there has been a tendency, all the same, to castigate the modern preoccupation with self-development and expression as a form of socially destructive narcissism (e.g., Reiff 1968. Lasch 1979). Alternatively, Giddens asserts (1990: 124; emphasis in the original), "A *concern for self-fulfillment* . . . is not just a narcissistic defence against an externally threatening world, over which individuals have little control, but also in part a *positive appropriation* of circumstances in which globalised influences impinge upon everyday life." The reflexive project of self-construction, which happens primarily in the context of intimate relationships, has become the new hub of social concern in the late modern world, and for good reason. It is the primary forum for the generation of trust, the very experience of trust which derivatively makes the development, spread, and operation of the abstract systems of modernity possible. In a globalized world, there can be no turning back the clock, so there is little benefit, sociologically, in lamenting this change. The private sphere has been dialectically catapulted to an unprecedented significance (see Dawson 1998 as well).

Giddens denies, moreover, that this reflexive turn to the personal entails, by the same dialectical logic, any true turn away from the larger world or community. Christopher Lasch, for example, laments the modern preoccupation with well-being through exercise, diet, and spiritual regimens, charging that it is symptomatic of a retreat from the world into personal gratification. Taking issue with this pessimistic analysis, Giddens asks (1990: 123):

> Is the search for self-identity a form of somewhat pathetic narcissism, or is it, in some part at least, a subversive force in respect of modern institutions? Most of the debate about the issue has concentrated upon this question. . . . But . . . we should see that there is something awry in Lasch's statement. A "search for health and well-being" hardly sounds compatible with a "withdrawal of interest in the outside world." The benefits of exercise or dieting are not personal discoveries but came from the lay reception of expert knowledge, as does the appeal of therapy or psychiatry. The spiritual regimens in question may be an eclectic assemblage, but include religions and cults from around the world. The outside world not only enters in here; it is an outside world vastly more extensive in character than anyone would have had contact with in the premodern era.

Here and elsewhere religions, even new forms of religion, find their way into Giddens's analysis, and in ways that suggest a new and more positive understanding of the role of NRMs in contemporary life. The acknowledged privatization of religion, and the much-commented-upon preoccupation of new religions with issues of the private sphere, may not be indicative of a reduced significance for religion in the modern world. Rather they may be indicative of the systemic adaptation of religion to the realities of a globalizing modern culture as experienced by individuals. Giddens acknowledges the traditional role of religions in establishing trust (e.g., 1990: 103–104). But religion is not Giddens's concern and he does not heed the suggestive links in his own work between religion and the new focal point of trust creation. In fact religion plays little role in his discussion of the possible responses to the consequences of modernity because it is most often equated with premodern societal conditions, and in line with traditional secularization theory more or less factored out of his analysis (see, e.g., the chart on 102; Mellor 1996; Walliss 2001).

Responses to the Consequences of Modernity

In *The Consequences of Modernity* Giddens sketches a fourfold typology of possible responses to modernity: a life-orienting attitude of "pragmatic acceptance," "sustained optimism," "cynical pessimism," or "radical engagement." There is no opportunity here to assess the adequacy of this typology; moreover, that is not my point. Whatever the merits of Giddens's typology, it can serve a heuristic purpose in considering the sociocultural significance of NRMs.

The "pragmatic acceptance" response entails focusing on the practical accomplishment of day-to-day tasks, overcoming immediate problems, strategically participating in the world while recognizing that "much that goes on in the modern world is outside anyone's control." The psychological cost of this response is a certain numbness or ceaseless anxiety. But, Giddens stresses, pragmatic acceptance "is compatible with either an underlying feeling-tone of pessimism or with the nourishment of hope—which may coexist with it ambivalently" (1990: 135).

"Sustained optimism" amounts to "a continued faith in providential reason." Scientific, technological, or other reasonable solutions can be found for our problems, no matter how seemingly grave. But this response is also compatible, Giddens notes, with "certain types of religious ideals" (1990: 136).

"Cynical pessimism" combines a sort of fatalism, or "nostalgia for ways of life that are disappearing or a negative attitude toward what is to come" (1990: 137), with a black humor that introduces a measure of neutralizing detachment.

"Radical engagement" is just what it seems—a turn to mobilization and action to either reduce the impact of major problems or idealistically transcend them altogether. Hopeful action is the key to this response, not faith in reason or the supernatural.

Giddens only aligns religion explicitly with one of these responses: sustained optimism. But a moment's reflection suggests many other possibilities, given the range of contemporary expressions of religion. The association of religion with sustained optimism reflects, once again I suspect, Giddens's narrow identification of religion with a traditional and naive supernaturalism. In principle, however, each of these responses can be aligned with some mode of religious activity, even cynical pessimism, which may find some expression in the experimental forms of irreverent religious parody found on the Internet (Dawson and Hennebry 1999: 34–36), or some of the more postmodernist expressions of neo-paganism and the New Age movement. On whole religion is still closely associated, as Giddens asserts, with the provision of trust. So it is likely to continue to be identified with establishing the grounds for personal and collective hope in a sociocultural environment of risk. But in the pluralistic context of Western societies this can be done in many ways. There is no reason to exclude or belittle the possibility because its locus is now the reflexive process of personal identity formation, and not the legitimation of a collective and very public sacred canopy.

In a globalized context the personal takes on a collective significance. Trust may be created by immersion in the love of Krishna and all of the non-Western ritualized tradition that goes with it, combining a pessimism about the modern world of materialism and consumption with a transcendent engagement in more ultimate personal and human concerns. The trust in question is not so much about the expert systems of modernity, of course, as simply acquiring the level of ontological security required by some to live in a world of imminent and multifaceted risk. For others the trust may be created by strategically adapting to the world through a special appropriation of skills. This may come through the alternative, yet world-affirming, ideology and intensive auditing exercises of Scientology or the pragmatic worldview and daily chanting and mediation of Soka Gakkai (Dawson 2001). Here again, in ways yet to be delineated, modern individuals may be finding the transcendent, or at least quasi-transcendent, foundations for trust they need for a more satisfactory engagement with the conditions of modernity. The options are innumerable, but the elective fit with the socially structured needs of increasing numbers of people may be no less significant for all the plurality of the choices available and the privatized character of the process.

The analysis risks slipping with these comments, however, into the functionalists' assumptions that Campbell wisely warns against. In conclusion, then, let me offer four programmatic reasons for the further investigation of the possible sociocultural significance of NRMs in the light of Giddens's interesting diagnosis of the conditions of modernity, based on the broader notion of elective affinities.

Conclusion: Four Programmatic Suggestions

First, in agreement with Robbins and Bromley (1992), I think any approach to the study of the sociocultural significance of NRMs should be independent, in principle, from the limited terms of reference of the public controversy over cults, and from consideration of the survival or "success" of different NRMs. Like Robbins and Bromley, and Campbell as well, I favor adopting a more long-range perspective on the possible significance of NRMs, looking for links with a more extensive trajectory of societal changes. Few if any scholars have done so in a systematic way. One reason is probably the lack of a sufficiently broad, yet subtle and essentially simple theoretical framework. Berger's conception of the processes of deinstitutionalization was the best theoretical framework available for many years, but it is encumbered with the assumptions of secularization theory. Giddens's theory of late modernity, whatever its flaws, provides another and more comprehensive option, which can be used, with a bit of revision, to transcend the limited dualistic conception of the future of religion born of the secularizationist paradigm. Religions need not be conceived as either public in spirit, and thus truly religious but inevitably marginal in modern society, or private in nature, and thus less than truly religious but successfully accommodated to modernity. The fulfillment of this conceptual promise, however, hinges on developing the empirical links between the beliefs and practices of various new religions and the dialectic of trust and risk as embodied in the reflexive project of identity construction in specific NRMs and their host societies (see Dawson 2001).

Second, we must keep in mind that this approach entails more than simply finding new ways of matching perceived deprivations to perceived religious solutions. The negative cast of this dominant functionalist mode of analysis can be dissipated by considering the fully dialectical character of Giddens's phenomenology of modernity (1990: 137–149). Modernity, Giddens suggests, is a "juggernaut" that cannot be stopped. But it "is not an engine made up of integrated machinery." Rather it is one "in which there is a tensionful, contradictory, push-and-pull of different influences."

For example, on the one hand, modernity is an experience of "displacement" (or "disembedding"), but on the other hand it is also about "reembedding." In modernity we have the intersection of human "estrangement" from some experiences and situations, but we also have the introduction of new experiences and modes of "familiarity." Holding the realities of globalization in mind, Giddens states (1990: 140), "What happens is not simply that localised influences drain away into the more impersonalised relations of abstract systems. Instead, the very tissue of spatial experience alters, conjoining proximity and distance in ways that have few close parallels in prior ages." It is wrong to keep identifying modernity with just one side of the dialectic (and correspondingly, religion with the other). Using one of many concrete examples, Giddens notes, for instance (1990: 142), "The self-same processes that lead to the destruction of older city neighbourhoods and their replacement by towering office-blocks and skyscrapers often permit the gentrification of other areas and recreation of locality."

In like manner, in ways that can only be stated here, the processes that have rendered the modern world impersonal have also introduced a heightened demand and opportunity for intimacy. Every day we may have dealings with more strangers than our ancestors, but we are also systematically encouraged to invest in, and provided with the social structures to support, a range of intensely intimate ties far transcending those fostered by the familiarity of traditional village or rural life. We are awash in a sea of expertise as well, dependent as never before on abstract social systems. Yet we live in a world in which skills are being constantly developed and reappropriated by individuals. Much of the world is opaque to us, but knowledge is filtering back to us perpetually from the experts, and "no one can interact with abstract systems without mastering some of the rudiments of the principles upon which they are based" (1990: 144). Likewise, the "privativism" of modernity is intersected, Giddens proposes, by an expanded range of opportunities for "engagement" amid the "extraordinary interpolation of the local and the global." It is this more complex reality that should form the backdrop to discussions of the significance of NRMs. The question should be, How are different NRMs impacted by, or do they exemplify, these kinds of dialectical societal processes?

Third, additional and complimentary support can be found for doubting the tendency to relate the privatization of religion with its demise in the seminal writings of Roland Robertson on globalization (e.g., Robertson and Chirico 1985; Robertson 1992). Robertson argues that the seeming resurgence of religion in the modern world must be seen in the context of the processes of globalization as manifest at four levels: societies, selves, humanity, and the relations between societies. Specific NRMs may be understood, he suggests, in terms of how they relate to globalizing processes on one of these levels or through one of these loci. The new religious right in the United States (and perhaps elsewhere as well) can be understood primarily in terms of "the provision of a moral-religious definition of American-societal identity in a global context in which societal coherence becomes increasingly a matter of internal dispute and comparison with other societies" (Robertson and Chirico 1985: 40). Seemingly antimodern movements like Christian fundamentalism are essentially modern, from this perspective, because they are born in fact, if not in explicit self-awareness, out of a reflexive response to the processes of globalization. They are part of what he calls a new universal search for fundamentals to store up particularistic cultural identities in the face of the relativizing effects of globalization (1992: 164–181). Other NRMs, he suggests, but never systematically shows, have a similar point of origin relative to one or more of the other levels or loci of globalization.

Extending Robertson's logic, I have argued that NRMs like Vajradhatu/ Shambhala, Soka Gakkai, Scientology, and New Age channeling groups may be attempts to rethematize the self and humanity in the relativizing context of globalization.

> As is often stressed in the literature on NRMs, these kinds of NRMs are fixated on the promotion of new means of self-transformation congruent with their vision of a newly emergent humanity (e.g., Wallis 1977; Heelas 1996; Brown 1997; Hanegraaff 1996; Dawson and Eldershaw 1998). They are geared to both the immediate improvement of the quality of life for the individual, by changing people's subjective sense of their interactions with their environment, and the eventual birth of a global "new age," by identifying and stressing the importance of certain spiritual and psychological uniformities of [what Robertson calls] the "extrasocietal aspects of the self." (Dawson 1998c: 591)

Contrary to secularization theory, then, the sociocultural significance of NRMs may well lie in their very preoccupation with the reflexive development of the self. As both Robertson's theory of globalization and Giddens's theory of late modernity suggest, the so-called privatization of religion may well be emblematic of the progressive adaptation of religion to life in globalizing modern societies. The dialectic of trust and risk may help us to frame the social psychological struggles motivating this transformation of religiosity and the continued significance of religious experimentation and innovation.

Fourth and finally, let me end this chapter with a few comments that reflect where I might have begun, and indicate where any future discussion probably should begin. In the past I argued that the religious orientation of many of the people turning to NRMs is consonant with changes in the religious preferences of an expanding portion of North Americans and Europeans (Dawson 1998b; Lambert 1999). Both developments seem to reflect, I proposed, a shift in religious sensibilities that is rendering some forms of religion "more compatible with the new social order emerging around us, whether it is called advanced capitalism, late or high modernism, post-industrialism, or post-modernism" (Dawson 1998b: 141). I was able at the time to fill in some of the details of the change in sensibilities, but I said little about the social structural changes that either precipitated or at least facilitated these changed sensibilities.

The religious shift can be identified broadly in terms of six features. Most briefly, contemporary religious life is "marked by a pronounced . . . individualism," and an "emphasis . . . on experience and faith rather than doctrine and belief." The individualism in question entails putting a priority on both the needs and desires of the individual and turning inward to find the source of spiritual sustenance. This increased individualism and experiential orientation has resulted in the adoption of "a more pragmatic attitude to questions of religious authority and practice," and a remarkably more tolerant, even relativistic and syncretistic, approach to other religious worldviews and systems (Dawson 1998b: 138–139). Lastly, it is accompanied by a preference for greater organizational openness in religious groups and institutions (see Wuthnow 1998; Lambert 1999; and Roof 1999 for similar assessments). This means, as Yves Lambert and I have stressed in parallel yet different ways, that the new forms of religiosity favored in modernity tend to be this-worldly and parascientific in character (e.g., Scientology, the New Age Movement, and Eastern meditational/therapeutic groups like Vajradhatur/ Shambhala, Rajneesh/Osho Foundation, or Soka Gakkai).

This style of religiosity should be conceptualized with James Beckford's seminal proposal in mind (1992: 23; see also 1989: 171) that religion is becoming increasingly a "cultural resource" more than a social institution. The social structural transformations wrought by the emergence of advanced industrial societies have undermined the communal, familial, and organizational bases of religion. In Beckford's evocative phrase, "religion has come adrift from its former points of social anchorage" (1992: 22). In Giddens's terms of reference, religion is being disembedded. But this does not mean it is destined to disappear (a point argued by Beckford 1992; Robbins and Bromley 1992; and Dawson 1998b). On the contrary, Beckford asserts (1992: 23), "religious and spiritual forms of sentiment, belief and action have survived as relatively autonomous resources. They retain the capacity to symbolize, for example, ultimate meaning, infinite power, supreme indignation and sublime compassion" in unprecedented ways in diverse modern social contexts. Religion is being disembedded from its traditional home in the realms of group and social identity, and simultaneously reembedded, by the dialectical processes of global modernization, in the realms of personal and human identity. The social "place" of religion has been reconfigured, not lost altogether.

Giddens's interpretation of the social structural and social psychological dynamics of late modernity (only briefly surveyed here) may help us to better understand why religious "belief" is indeed persisting in the absence of "belonging" (Davie 1994, Bibby 1998). There is an apparent, though still yet to be systematically explored, affinity between the new religious sensibilities of large numbers of North Americans and Europeans (and perhaps others as well), the spiritual innovations and styles of many NRMs, and the structurally induced social psychological needs and preferences of people living in late modern societies. We may have a convergence of bodies of research, that is, that catapults the study of the sociocultural significance of NRMs beyond the restrictive confines of the options set by the secularization thesis. This leaves us to explain through more refined analysis why religion is relevant to only some late modern individuals. But the answer to that question probably goes to the heart of the appeal of religion in any age, in the past or the future.

NOTE

1. Preferences for more individualism, experientialism, pragmatism, syncretism and relativism, holism, and organizational openness.

REFERENCES

Aidala, Angela. 1985. "Social Change, Gender Roles, and New Religious Movements." *Sociological Analysis* 46 (3): 287–314.

Anthony, Dick, and Thomas Robbins. 1982a. "Contemporary Religious Ferment and Moral Ambiguity." In *New Religious Movements: A Perspective for Understanding Society,* ed. Eileen Barker, 243–263. New York: Edwin Mellen Press.

———. 1982b. "Spiritual Innovation and the Decline of American Civil Religion." In *Religion in America: Spirituality in a Secular Age,* ed. Mary Douglas and Steven Tipton, 229–248. Boston: Beacon Press.

———. 1992. "Law, Social Science and the 'Brainwashing' Exception to the First Amendment." *Behavioral Sciences and the Law* 10 (1): 5–27.

Barker, E. 1984. *The Making of a Moonie: Choice or Brainwashing.* Oxford: Blackwell.

Beck, Ulrich. 1992. *Risk Society: Towards a New Modernity.* London: Sage.

Beck, Ulrich, Anthony Giddens, and Scott Lash. 1994. *Reflexive Modernization.* Stanford, Calif.: Stanford University Press.

Beckford, James A. 1989. *Religion in Advanced Industrial Society.* London: Unwin Hyman.

————. 1992. "Religion, Modernity and Post-modernity." In *Religion: Contemporary Issues,* ed. Bryan Wilson, 11–23. London: Bellew Pub.

————. 1996. "Postmodernity, High Modernity and New Modernity: Three Concepts in Search of Religion." In *Postmodernity, Sociology and Religion,* ed. Kieran Flanagan and Peter C. Jupp, 30–47. New York: St. Martin's Press.

Bellah, Robert. 1976. "New Religious Consciousness and the Crisis of Modernity." In *The New Religious Consciousness,* ed. Charles Glock and Robert Bellah, 333–352. Berkeley: University of California Press.

Berger, Peter L. 1967. *The Sacred Canopy. Elements of a Sociological Theory of Religion.* New York: Doubleday.

Berger, Peter, Brigitte Berger, and Hansfried Kellner. 1974. *The Homeless Mind: Modernization and Consciousness.* New York: Vintage.

Bibby, Reginald W. 1993. *Unknown Gods. The Ongoing Story of Religion in Canada.* Toronto: Stoddart.

Bird, Fred S. 1993. "Charisma and Leadership in New Religious Movements." In *Religion and the Social Order, Vol. 3, Handbook on Cults and Sects in America, Part A,* ed. David G. Bromley and Jeffrey K. Hadden, 75–92. Greenwich, Conn.: JAI Press.

Bromley, David G., and Bruce C. Busching. 1988. "Understanding the Structure of Contractual and Covenantal Social Relations: Implications for the Sociology of Religion." *Sociological Analysis* 49 (supp.): 15–32.

Bromley, David G., and Jeffrey K. Hadden, eds. 1993. *The Handbook on Cults and Sects in America* (Religion and the Social Order, Vol. 3). Greenwich, Conn.: JAI Press.

Brown, Michael F. 1997. *The Channeling Zone: American Spirituality in an Anxious Age.* Cambridge, Mass.: Harvard University Press.

Campbell, Colin. 1978. "The Secret Religion of the Educated Classes." *Sociological Analysis* 39 (2): 146–156.

————. 1982. "Some Comments on the New Religious Movements, the New Spirituality, and Post-Industrial Society." In *New Religious Movements: A Perspective for Understanding Society,* ed. Eileen Barker, 232–242. New York: Edwin Mellen Press.

Chidester, David. 1988. *Salvation and Suicide: An Interpretation of Jim Jones, the Peoples Temple, and Jonestown.* Bloomington: Indiana University Press.

Cote, Pauline, and James T. Richardson. 2001. "Disciplined Litigation, Vigilant Ligitation, and Deformation: Dramatic Organization Changes in Jehovah's Witnesses." *Journal for the Scientific Study of Religion* 40 (1): 11–25.

Davidman, Lynn, and Janet Jacobs. 1993. "Feminist Perspectives on New Religious Movements." In *The Handbook on Cults and Sects in America* (Religion and the Social Order, Vol. 3), ed. David G. Bromley and Jeffrey K. Hadden, 173–190. Greenwich, Conn.: JAI Press.

Davie, Grace. 1994. *Religion in Britain since 1945: Believing without Belonging.* Oxford: Blackwell.

Dawson, Lorne L. 1990. "Self-Affirmation, Freedom, and Rationality: Theoretically Elaborating 'Active' Conversions." *Journal for the Scientific Study of Religion* 29: 141–163.

————. 1997. "Creating Cult Typologies: Some Strategic Considerations." *Journal of Contemporary Religion* 12 (3): 363–381.

————. 1998a. *Comprehending Cults: The Sociology of New Religious Movements.* New York: Oxford University Press.

————. 1998b. "Antimodernism, Modernism, and Postmodernism: Struggling with the

Cultural Significance of New Religious Movements." *Sociology of Religion* 59: 131–156.

———. 1998c. "The Cultural Significance of New Religious Movements and Globalization: A Theoretical Prolegomenon." *Journal for the Scientific Study of Religion* 37 (4): 580–595.

———. 2000. "Religious Cults and Sex." In *The Encyclopaedia of Criminology and Deviant Behavior,* ed. Clifford D. Bryant, 323–326. New York: Taylor and Francis.

———. 2001. "The Cultural Significance of New Religious Movements: The Case of Soka Gakkai." *Sociology of Religion* 63 (3): 337–364.

———. 2002. "Crises in Charismatic Legitimacy and Violent Behavior in New Religious Movements." In *Cults, Religion and Violence,* ed. David G. Bromley and J. Gordon Melton (forthcoming). Cambridge: Cambridge University Press.

Dawson, Lorne L., and Lynn Eldershaw. 1998. "Shambhala Warriorship: Investigating the Adaptations of Imported New Religious Movements." In *Les Societes devant le nouveau pluralisms religieux,* ed. B. Ouellet and R. Bergeron, 199–228. Montreal: Fides.

Dawson, Lorne L., and Jenna Hennebry. 1999. "New Religions and the Internet: Recruiting in a New Public Space." *Journal of Contemporary Religion* 14 (1): 17–39.

Durkheim, Emile. 1964. *The Division of Labour in Society.* New York: Free Press.

Eldershaw, Lynn, and Lorne L. Dawson. 1995. "Refugees in the Dharma: The Buddhist Church of Halifax as a Revitalization Movement." In *North American Religion,* vol. 4, ed. T. Robinson, 1–45. Waterloo, Ontario: Wilfrid Laurier University Press.

Feuerstein, Georg. 1990. *Holy Madness: The Shock Tactics and Radical Teachings of Crazy-Wise Adepts, Holy Fools, and Rascal Gurus.* New York: Penguin Books.

Gerlach, Luther P., and Virginia H. Hine. 1970. *People, Power, Change: Movements of Social Transformation.* Indianapolis: Bobbs-Merrill.

Giddens, Anthony. 1990. *The Consequences of Modernity.* Cambridge: Polity Press.

———. 1991. *Modernity and Self Identity: Self and Society in the Late Modern Age.* Cambridge: Polity Press.

———. 1992. *The Transformation of Intimacy.* Cambridge: Polity Press.

———. 1994. "Living in a Post-Traditional Society." In Ulrich Beck, Anthony Giddens, and Scott Lash, eds., *Reflexive Modernization.* Stanford, Calif: Stanford University Press.

———. 2002. *Runaway World: How Globalization Is Reshaping Our Lives.* London: Routledge.

Glock, Charles. 1964. "The Role of Deprivation in the Origin and Evolution of Religious Groups." In *Religion and Social Conflict,* ed. R. Lee and Martin Marty, 24–36. New York: Oxford University Press.

Glock, Charles, and Robert Bellah, eds. 1976. *The New Religious Consciousness.* Berkeley: University of California Press.

Gurney, Joan Neff, and Kathleen J. Tierney. 1982. "Relative Deprivation and Social Movements: A Critical Look at Twenty Years of Theory and Research." *Sociological Quarterly* 23 (4): 33–47.

Hadden, Jeffrey. 1987. "Towards Desacralizing Secularization Theory." *Social Forces* 65: 587–610.

Hall, John R. 2000. *Apocalypse Observed.* New York: Routledge.

Hanegraaff, Wouter J. 1996. *New Age Religion and Western Culture.* Leiden, The Netherlands: E. J. Brill.

Heelas, Paul. 1996. *The New Age Movement. The Celebration of the Self and the Sacraliza-tion of Modernity.* Oxford: Blackwell.

Hine, Virginia H. 1974. "The Deprivation and Disorganization Theories of Social Move-ments." In *Religious Movements in Contemporary America,* ed. I. Zarestsky and M. Leone, 646–661. Princeton, N.J.: Princeton University Press.

Hunter, James Davison. 1981. "The New Religions: Demodernization and the Protest Against Modernity." In *The Social Impact of the New Religious Movements,* ed. Bryan Wilson, 1–19. New York: Rose of Sharon Press.

Lambert, Yves. 1999. "Secularization or New Religious Paradigms?" *Sociology of Religion* 60 (3): 303–333.

Lasch, Christopher. 1979. *The Culture of Narcissism: American Life in an Age of Dimin-ishing Expectations.* New York: Warner Books.

Lofland, John, and James T. Richardson. 1984. "Religious Movements Organizations: El-emental Forms and Dynamics." In *Research in Social Movements, Conflict and Change,* ed. R. Ratcliff and L. Kriesberg, 29–51. Greenwich, Conn.: JAI Press.

Lucas, Phillip C. 1995. *The Odyssey of a New Religion.* Bloomington: Indiana University Press.

McGuire, Meredith B. 1985. *"Ritual Healing in Suburban America."* New Brunswick, N.J.: Rutgers University Press.

———. 1993. "Health and Healing in New Religious Movements." In *The Handbook on Cults and Sects in America* (Religion and the Social Order, Vol. 3), ed. David G. Bromley and Jeffrey K. Hadden, 139–155. Greenwich, Conn.: JAI Press.

Mellor, Phillip. 1993. "Reflexive Traditions: Anthony Giddens, High Modernity and the Contours of Contemporary Religiosity." *Religious Studies* 29: 111–127.

Palmer, Susan J. 1994. *Moon Sisters, Krishna Mothers, Rajneesh Lovers: Women's Roles in New Religions.* Syracuse, N.Y.: Syracuse University Press.

Puttick, Elizabeth. 1997. *Women in New Religions: Gender, Power and Sexuality.* New York: St. Martin's Press.

Rambo, Lewis. 1993. *Understanding Religious Conversion.* New Haven, Conn.: Yale Uni-versity Press.

Reiff, Philip. 1968. *The Triumph of the Therapeutic: Uses of Faith After Freud.* New York: Harper and Row.

Richardson, James T. 1985. "The Active vs. Passive Convert: Paradigm Conflict in Con-version/Recruitment Research." *Journal for the Scientific Study of Religion* 24 (2): 163–179.

———. 1991. "Cult/Brainwashing Cases and Freedom of Religion. *Journal of Church and State* 33 (1): 55–74.

———, ed. 1988. *Money and Power in New Religions.* Lewiston, N.Y.: Edwin Mellen Press.

Richardson, James T., and Massimo Introvigne. 2001. " 'Brainwashing' Theories in Euro-pean Parliamentary and Administrative Reports on 'Cults' and 'Sects.' " *Journal for the Scientific Study of Religion* 40 (2): 143–168.

Richardson, James T., Mary White Stewart, and Robert B. Simmonds. 1979. *Organized Miracles: A Study of a Contemporary Youth, Communal, Fundamentalist Organiza-tion.* New Brunswick, N.J.: Transaction.

Robbins, Thomas. 1988. *Cults, Converts, and Charisma.* London: Sage.

———. 2001. "Balance and Fairness in the Study of Alternative Religions." In *Misunder-*

standing Cults, ed. Benjamin Zablocki and Thomas Robbins, 71–98. Toronto: University of Toronto Press.

Robbins, Thomas, and Dick Anthony. 1995. "Sects and Violence: Factors Enhancing the Volatility of Marginal Religious Movements." In *Armageddon in Waco,* ed. Stuart Wright, 236–259. Chicago: University of Chicago Press.

Robbins, Thomas, and David G. Bromley. 1992. "Social Experimentation and the Significance of American New Religions: A Focused Review Essay." In *Research in the Social Scientific Study of Religion,* vol. 4, ed. Monty Lynn and David Moberg, 1–28. Greenwich, Conn.: JAI Press.

———. 1993. "What Have WE Learned About New Religions? New Religious Movements as Experiments." *Religious Studies Review* 19 (3): 209–216.

Robertson, Roland. 1992. *Globalization: Social Theory and Global Culture.* London: Sage.

Robertson, Roland, and Joanna Chirico. 1985. "Humanity, Globalization and Worldwide Religious Resurgence: A Theoretical Exploration." *Sociological Analysis* 46: 219–242.

Roof, Wade Clark. 1999. *Spiritual Marketplace: Baby Boomers and the Remaking of American Religion.* Princeton, N.J.: Princeton University Press.

Snow, David, and Richard Machalek. 1984. The Sociology of Conversion." In *Annual Review of Sociology,* ed. R. H. Turner and J. F. Short Jr., 167–190. Palo Alto, Calif.: Annual Reviews Inc.

Stark, Rodney. 1987. "How New Religious Movements Succeed: A Theoretical Model." In *The Future of New Religious Movements,* ed. David G. Bromley and Phillip E. Hammond, 11–29. Macon, Ga.: Mercer University Press.

———. 1996. "Why Religious Movements Succeed or Fail: A Revised General Model. *Journal of Contemporary Religion* 11: 133–146.

———. 1999. "Atheism, Faith, and the Social Scientific Study of Religion." *Journal of Contemporary Religion* 14 (1): 41–62.

Stark, Rodney, and William Sims Bainbridge. 1985. *The Future of Religion.* Berkeley: University of California Press.

———. 1996. *A Theory of Religion.* New Brunswick, N.J.: Rutgers University Press.

Stark, Rodney, and Laurence R. Innaccone. 1997. "Why the Jehovah's Witnesses Grow So Rapidly: A Theoretical Application." *Journal for the Contemporary Study of Religion* 12 (2): 133–157.

Stone, Donald. 1978. "New Religious Consciousness and Personal Religious Experience." *Sociological Analysis* 39: 123–134.

Tabor, James D., and Eugene V. Gallagher. 1995. *Why Waco?* Berkeley: University of California Press.

Tipton, Steven. 1982. *Getting Saved from the Sixties.* Berkeley: University of California Press.

Turner, Bryan S. 1983. *Religion and Social Theory.* London: Sage.

Wallis, Roy. 1974. "Ideology, Authority, and the Development of Cultic Movements." *Social Research* 41: 299–327.

———. 1977. *The Road to Total Freedom: A Sociological Analysis of Scientology.* New York: Columbia University Press.

———. 1982. "The New Religions as Social Indicators." In *New Religious Movements: A Perspective for Understanding Society,* ed. Eileen Barker, 216–231. New York: Edwin Mellen Press.

————. 1984. *The Elementary Forms of New Religious Life.* London: Routledge and Kegan Paul.

Walliss, John. 2001. "The Problem of Tradition in the Work of Anthony Giddens." *Culture and Religion* 2 (1): 81–98.

Weber, Max. 1949. *The Methodology of the Social Sciences.* Trans. and ed. Edward A. Shils and Henry A. Finch. New York: Free Press.

Westley, Frances. 1978. *The Complex Forms of the Religious Life.* Chico, Calif.: Scholars Press.

Wilson, Bryan R. 1976. *Contemporary Transformations of Religion.* Oxford: Clarendon Press.

————. 1982. *Religion in Sociological Perspective.* New York: Oxford University Press.

————. 1987. "Factors in the Failure of the New Religious Movements." In *The Future of New Religious Movements,* ed. David G. Bromley and Phillip E. Hammond, 30–45. Macon, Ga.: Mercer University Press.

————. 1988. "Secularization: Religion in the Modern World." In *The World's Religions,* ed. Stewart Sutherland et al., 953–966. London: Routledge.

————. 1990. *The Social Dimension of Sectarianism.* Oxford: Clarendon Press.

Wright, Stuart, ed. 1995. *Armageddon in Waco.* Chicago: University of Chicago Press.

Wuthnow, Robert. 1998. *After Heaven: Spirituality in America since the 1950s.* Berkeley: University of California Press.

Young, John L., and Ezra E. H. Griffiths. 1992. "A Critical Evaluation of Coercive Persuasion as Used in the Assessment of Cults." *Behavioral Sciences and the Law* 10: 89–101.

Zablocki, Benjamin, and Thomas Robbins. 2001. "Introduction: Finding a Middle Ground in a Polarized Scholarly Arena." In *Misunderstanding Cults,* ed. Benjamin Zablocki and Thomas Robbins, 3–31. Toronto: University of Toronto Press.

CHAPTER 4

SCIENCE AND RELIGION IN THE NEW RELIGIONS

MIKAEL ROTHSTEIN

IN a 1993 article, "New Religions, Science, and Secularization," sociologist of religion William S. Bainbridge concludes that the scientific community knows surprisingly little about what he terms scientistic cults. "Extensive scholarship is needed on these paradoxical groups," he says (Bainbridge 1993: 292). Unfortunately, this is still quite true even if most scholars probably would hesitate to proclaim the religions in question "paradoxical," and even if the scientific element in the belief systems of these groups only represents a part of their theological and mythological make-up. In general, our understanding of new religions and cultic groups has increased tremendously during the past decades, but much work needs to be done in order to fully understand how new belief systems develop, and, in this connection, how the relation between science and religion actually works in these movements. It is hardly enough to conclude that secularization, and thus the development of a thoroughly nonreligious worldview, is only a tendency and that religion is still alive and kicking.

In the following, reference will be made to a number of relevant scholarly contributions and a few suggestions for further research will be offered. The scholarly literature in this field of research is, however, surprisingly meager, even now some 10 years after Bainbridge's seminal article. Though many religious texts are easily available—some claiming to be scientific, others dissociating themselves from science—only a few in-depth studies of this phenomenon have appeared. Of course, historical studies on the relation between science and religion during the scientific community's formative period have been produced, and a great number of philosophical contributions discussing the relation between different kinds of knowledge have been published. However, usually the focal point is quite different from what is needed with respect to new religions.

A BRIEF OVERVIEW AND SOME EXAMPLES

Science and religion often collide. In the modern industrialized world where science has gained the highest momentum, this is especially apparent, not least in the case of new religions. However, the contemporary existence of two very different worldviews (stereotyped as "the scientific" and "the religious") does not mean that they function in isolated realms. It is true, of course, that some people deliberately avoid religion as an element in a secular lifestyle, and that others (presumably, very few) reject science altogether as ungodly and irrelevant. Nonetheless, for the vast majority, religion and science are two different modes of observing the world, two different ways of approaching existence that may well work together. Not every aspect of religion is based on irrational belief, and scientific speculation will often leave the safe harbor of rationality in order to explore and develop. Further, studies of human psychology reveal that quite different ways of understanding are usually simultaneously at work in the cognitive apparatus. Indeed "religion" and "science" are both human products created by the same kind of brains and bodies, even if the conditions for the two realms vary greatly.

The relation between science and religion, therefore, is not simply a question of pro and con. Rather, the science-religion debate is usually a question of how two very different epistemological systems are being balanced in complex psychological and social contexts. According to David J. Hess, this field can be described as a "boundary-work," a kind of negotiated cultural field where different groups and systems position themselves. "In short, scientific boundaries are recursive, nested, and multiple; there are scientificity layers that become clearer as one unfolds levels of skepticism and 'pseudoscientificity' both within and across discursive boundaries. Boundary-work, therefore, is going on in all directions, not just in the direction of orthodox science toward religion and 'pseudoscience' " (Hess 1993: 145–146).

This is not to say that science and religion go hand-in-hand with no difficulty or that they occupy parallel social or cognitive realms. On the contrary, quite often they certainly do not. What we need to observe is the impressive willingness and ability to seek some kind of understanding between science and religion on the part of most religious individuals, and thus, within most religious groups— not least the new religions of today's world. As pointed out by James Lewis, however, not only new religions of the present, but new religions since the beginning of the so-called modern era have consciously related to science and technology in their quest for explanations and practical solutions.

> This aspect of our cultural view of science shaped the various religious sects that incorporated "science" into their names. In sharp contrast to traditional religions, which emphasize salvation in the afterlife, the emphasis in these religions is on the improvement of this life. Groups within the Metaphysical (Christian Science-New Thought) tradition, for example, usually claim to have discovered spiritual "laws," which, if properly understood and applied, transform and improve the lives of ordinary individuals, much as technology has transformed society. (Lewis 2002: 3)

The notion of spiritual laws, Lewis explains, is taken directly from the "laws" of classical physics. As an example of how such groups "viewed themselves as investigating the mind or spirit in a practical, experimental way," Lewis quotes Ernest Holmes's classic New Thought text *Science of Mind* from 1926: "As soon as a law is discovered experiments are made with it, certain facts are proved to be true, and in this way a science is gradually formulated; for any science consists of the number of known facts about any given principle . . . This is true of the Science of Mind. No one has ever seen Mind or Spirit, but who could possibly doubt their existence?" (cited in Lewis 2002: 3).

In this connection, however, it is important to notice that "science"—not to mention the concept of "scientism"—is no single and therefore easily defined category. It is, for instance, important to distinguish between the self-confident scientism among academics in the scientific community and what Mikael Stenmark has dubbed "academic-external scientism" within the broader society. Considering the new religions, it is, no doubt, the last type that becomes relevant, even if "academic-internal scientism" occasionally occurs (Stenmark 1997). What we are dealing with is a popular nonexpert understanding of scientific method and results. This concept of "science" in the new religions, consequently, is not the same as the concept of "science" in science's traditional habitat.

In the following, however, it is not suggested that the new religions have been more successful than religions at large in establishing a working relationship with science. Very often, if not always, the religiously inclined use of science, in old as well as new religions, cannot live up to ordinary scientific standards. It is, as we shall see, religion, not science, which defines the standards in the interaction between the two systems in the modern context of the new religions: Science, in the scientific sense of the word, has been largely substituted by a mythological rendering of the same concept. The reason for this balance of power is quite obvious. Religion has the ability to transform science into something useful for its purpose, while science usually is deprived of the possibility of transforming religion into something scientifically meaningful.

The present situation is not new, although the religions in question are. Since the days of the Enlightenment and the breakthrough of philosophical humanism in opposition to religion, most religions in the Western world have been forced to justify their positions against science or, indeed, to seek some kind of understanding with science. In this respect, the new and emerging religions of contemporary Western society are challenged to the extreme. Science has become fundamental to virtually all walks of life, and it seems almost impossible to imagine new religions that do not engage in some kind of discussion or interaction with science and technology. The old religion-science debate wherein rationalism contested "myth and magic" has, in certain ways, been left behind. There is no longer an "either-or" situation. Rather, most new religions consider themselves scientifically based and it has become commonplace to include science in the mythological stew.

The reason behind this development seems quite obvious: No religion of the modern world will successfully be able to claim authority without some kind of scientific legitimization. In the words of theologian Derek Stanesby: "Today natural science rules as queen over all and is commonly accepted as the supreme source of all knowledge. The table has turned. Contemporary religious thinkers now tend to take the authority of science for granted and they try to match their theology to the prevailing western scientific tradition" (Stanesby 1985: 2).

However, when comparing the situation of presecularized society to that of today, a remarkable structural resemblance is noted. In the seventeenth century, when the foundation of modern science was laid, science had to justify itself through the theology and mythology of the religious establishment. Today, religion faces the same challenge: It very often has to justify itself through the dominant contemporary system of understanding that is science, or at least, to prove itself worthy of attention by arguing against science. Therefore, it is no surprise that modern religious movements will frequently align with science in different ways, by using scientific language, for instance, even if the content of the belief system is far from scientific (Ellwood and Partin 1988: 14), or by proclaiming some kind of balance between science and religion in this or that belief system.

Above all, it must be recognized that the relation between science and religion is primarily determined by the general power structures of the society in question. Where science occupies a dominant position (which is the case in the industrialized world), religion has to align with science to some degree, or at least to express an attitude toward science. Where science holds a more remote position, this is not a demand, and religion may develop with no scientific reference at all. A number of new religions such as the Baha'i faith, the Theosophical Society, TM, ISKCON, and others, provide good examples for the present. In every case, principles for the adaptation of scientific perspectives into religious systems are largely determined by religious standards.

Some Brief Examples

A number of principles espoused by Baha'is (attributed to the religion's founder Baha'u'llah), for instance, include "the harmony of science and religion." The idea is that "a well-educated religious community will be able, independently, to undertake intellectual enquiry and distinguish truth from error" and, for instance, evaluate scientific claims in light of religious belief. Thus, in accordance with Darwinism, Baha'is believe that species do evolve, but it is denied—quite contrary to scientific findings—that human beings evolve from a lower species (Chryssides 1999: 251). The adaptation of the scientific position is, it appears, limited to areas that are theologically acceptable. The outcome of the interaction between Baha'i theology and scientific positions on biological evolution, therefore, is determined by religious boundaries. It is not the result of negotiation between two equal adversaries.

Similarly, Theosophists will refer to the second paragraph in the Theosophical Society's bylaws as an important ideal that supports the true religious understanding of the world. Theosophists are inspired to "encourage studies in comparative religion, philosophy and science," but these principles will only apply to a certain extent. Indeed, the cofounder of the Theosophical Society, H. P. Blavatsky, was not unconditionally happy with science even if, in general, science is embraced in her teachings. In *The Secret Doctrine,* she wrote, "The divergence of scientific options is so great that no reliance can ever be placed upon scientific speculation," thus emphasizing that religion, not science, is at the heart of things (Hammer 2000: 22). This attempt to balance the religious use of science is rather important, not only to Theosophy, for the principal problems seem to be the same everywhere, even if the religions in question may vary considerably.

Trying to reinforce Unitarianism as a religion with popular appeal, in 1991 a group of Scandinavian Unitarians formulated 13 theses regarding their beliefs. One important paragraph reads (translated from the Danish): "We aim at harmony between religious, philosophical and scientific understandings" (Bovin 2000: 102). "Harmony" means that no single component (religion, philosophy, or science) should outweigh the others. This means that science is welcomed, but only so far as it is interpreted and used along religiously and philosophically relevant (and thus ideologically acceptable) paths. The harmony sought after by the Unitarians, consequently, presupposes that the different components (religion, philosophy, and science) can be balanced to form some kind of equilibrium. This means that religion should acknowledge a scientific challenge, but it certainly also implies a development the other way around. Thus, the principle question becomes: How much can science lend to religion without giving up being scientific?

More recent new religions with very different belief systems agree. According to George King, the founder of the Aetherius Society (a Theosophically based group with a special focus on Cosmic Masters on other planets), there are numerous indications that there is a "religious dimension to science" and that "the two [science and religion] no longer are separable" (King 1996: 19). The meaning is clear: No science can stand alone. It needs religion to make it meaningful. Conversely, no religion is meaningful if it is not "scientific," he claims. Introducing George King's religiously determined science, his close associate and disciple, Richard Lawrence, writes:

> After 1800 years of science accepting the Aristotelian concept that Planets were embedded in a crystalline sphere which moved in a uniform circular motion around the Earth, scientists such as Galileo, Newton and Kepler started to understand concepts of planetary motion, the laws of gravity and so on. Once their discoveries were accepted, so the religious and scientific establishments and the views of modern thinking people changed.
>
> The same could be, and I believe, will be true in the new millennium. Sir George King could be likened to Aristarchus of Samos in being centuries ahead of his time. As with Aristarchus, orthodoxy has rejected his views, but a change will come as it always does. The new millennium will see science and religion draw closer together and Spiritual Science, now being championed by Sir George and a few others, will eventually emerge as the established approach of the Aquarian Age. This time, however, it should not take 1,800 years. (King 1996: 17–18)

Transcendental Meditation (TM), which basically builds on Hindu monism, holds a similar position, even if the strategy and image of the organization is very different. The founder and leader of the group, Maharishi Mahesh Yogi, claimed in 1968 that everything he says will be scientifically verified as science matures (Rothstein 1996: 39). In this case, religion comes first, and it is believed that science will gradually reach the same epistemological level. When that happens, science apparently becomes bearer of the same knowledge as the Hindu sages. In fact, this means that science does not reveal anything new but merely confirms what, according to TM, was already known by the enlightened masters of a remote past, or by the secluded sages in the Himalayas of the present. The role of science is to reinforce what is already acknowledged in a strictly religious context.

Members of the Raelian religion see things differently, but their conception of science is nevertheless determined by the group's religious understanding. According to the prophet Rael's followers, he has been informed of everything he knows by a race of hyper-intelligent, scientifically advanced beings (known as the Elohim) from a distant planet. Fundamental to Rael's belief system is the notion that biblical religion, in fact, reflects a misconceived scientific project. Christian and Jewish theologians have not been able to interpret the texts correctly, but thanks to Rael's meeting with the Elohim, accurate knowledge is now available. They have explained to him how, due to a lack of intellectual understanding among humans, religious mystification came to cloud what was actually a scientific, highly technological project: the creation of life on Earth, including human life, by the Elohim. The Raelians do not dismiss "spirituality," but it is always emphasized that "the religious" must be understood through scientific rationality and that "the spiritual" basically is a materialistic category, a product of the physical mind.

What is celebrated and praised in the Raelian religion are creatures of a different race, but certainly biological entities, and the kind of fulfillment sought is primarily physical or material. To the Raelians, science is the way of the supreme beings, and therefore, in itself an attractive path. However, the science of the Elohim is not of this world. It is a mythological science—a science fiction—even if inspired by earthly, mundane science in a great many ways. "Science," in this situation, is a prefiguration of a science yet to come—a kind of extrapolation or projection of the science of the present into a mythological realm of the Elohim. In the words of Bryan Sentes and Susan Palmer, Raelianism "replaces the supernatural with the extraterrestrial and technological in order to demystify and demythologize [religion], simultaneously (if unconsciously) mythologizing and ideologizing science and technology" (Sentes and Palmer 2000: 86).

At other times, however, the concept of science is quite different. For instance, the International Society for Krishna Consciousness (ISKCON; also known as the Hare Krishna movement) dissociates itself from traditional science by claiming that science is, in fact, not scientific at all. *Real* science, it is claimed, is contained in the Vaisnava-Bhakti theology as laid out by the organization's founder, Bhaktivedanta Swami Prabhupada.

In fact, ISKCON forces us to play with words: The usual meaning of the word "science" is abandoned, and a new usage of the word is introduced. In speaking of a "higher-dimensional science," a *real* science, ISKCON wants to pave the way for a modern, yet literal, understanding of the Puranic cosmography and myths. For instance, one of ISKCON's leading intellectuals, Sadaputa dasa (Richard Thompson), has argued that scriptures talking about multiheaded gods or a flat earth are literally true, but that an understanding that transcends normal conceptions and the ordinary senses is presupposed on the part of the reader. His argumentation involves the notion of higher dimensions, and thus, a higher-dimensional science. His argumentation—religious argumentation—cannot, therefore, be advanced unless modern science is questioned at the same time. Linking his religiously based higher-dimensional science to the ordinary science, Sadaputa dasa says:

Modern cosmology may seem superior to its Vedic counterpart if we stick to the assumption that reality is limited to what ordinary human beings can perceive, using either their unaided senses or mechanical instruments. However, if the Vedic idea of higher realms of existence is even approximately correct, then it becomes clear that the modern scientific approach has caused us to focus our attention uselessly on relatively unimportant aspects of the universe. From this point of view, the technical sophistication of modern astrophysics appears more as an impediment to the attainment of knowledge than as an example of great scientific progress. (Thompson 1989: 21)

ISKCON maintains that science has not yet reached a genuine or true understanding of the universe, let alone a correct description. Compared to, for instance, TM's idea of science and scientific achievements, the difference is very clear. As it appears to TM, science has, in fact, reached, or is just about to reach, final truths and genuine cosmological descriptions. TM claims to prove what the physicists are assuming by offering the experience from "transcendental consciousness" as a means for empirical verification. ISKCON still awaits substantial scientific results and will undauntedly present the Vaisnava-Bhakti theology as the only fulfilling and comprehensive description and analysis of the universe. Only if science is willing to broaden its view and engage in close cooperation with higher-dimensional perspectives may it develop into something meaningful and truly useful, ISKCON asserts (Rothstein 1996: 132f).

Similarly, Christian groups such as the Jehovah's Witnesses and other maximalist organizations claim that science will never be correct or "true" as long as it is based on nonreligious method and theory. On the contrary, the starting point of any legitimate exploration of the world has to take the Christian dogmas into account.

In general, however, it is the science-embracing attitude that dominates the ideological and theological scene of the new religions (we shall return to some of the examples mentioned above later, including the science-rejecting perspective). A final perspective at the fringe of what we normally term religion, though, also needs to be mentioned: the secularist use of science within religion-like groups such as La Vey–inspired Satanism. According to James Lewis, the ideology of the Church of Satan is based on a secularist appropriation of modern science in the sense that it is essentially an "anti-theology" based in a secular "worldview" derived from natural science. Other groups, says Lewis, have "modeled their approach to spirituality after the methods of science" while La Vey's ideology, which programmatically counteracts Christianity, can, in itself, be understood as a secular product (Lewis 2002). This perspective, however, remains rare and typical only for ideological or semireligious groups that do not entertain notions of the supernatural.

In the remainder of this chapter, the relationship between science and religion in the new religions will be discussed within two different but associated frameworks: First, the meeting of religion and science is described and analyzed as an expression of syncretism, that is, as a merging of two different belief systems. Second, the deliberate integration of science and religion is discussed as a discourse strategy with clear missiological dimensions. Finally, a cognitively based explanation for the popularity of scientific religion is suggested.

Science and Religion: Syncretism

Syncretism is understood to be the process of two or more religious systems growing into one another, thus forming a new religious body of some kind, sometimes even new religious organizations. However, the nature of religious integration may vary significantly. On occasion, different belief systems are completely integrated into one another (one example is the Afro-Brazilian cults such as Macumba or Candomblé, which involve Catholicism and West African religion), while at other times, syncretism may constitute a religious partnership with no consistent merger (as with the relation between Shinto and Buddhism in Japan). Sometimes syncretism constitutes relations between complete wholes, but more often perhaps, relations are established between particular components in different religious systems and the ongoing construction of religious worldviews takes another turn. At other times, however, a religious body may consolidate itself by deliberately disregarding other religious constructions, thus fertilizing what is significant to itself while ignoring or counteracting foreign religious concepts and social systems. In doing so, however, the officially disregarded religious traditions are, in fact, being considered, and cultural and religious change will inevitably occur. Elsewhere, with reference to ISKCON, I have termed this process "negative syncretism" (Rothstein 1996).

Both possibilities are, as indicated earlier, seen in the new religions. Considering one well-known taxonomical principle regarding the new religions, this is no surprise at all. According to Roy Wallis's classic typology, new religions will typically position themselves in one of three possible sociological relations to the surrounding society: They may be "world affirming," "world rejecting," or "world accommodating" (Wallis 1984). By affirming or accommodating science, some new religions seek societal recognition of a sort, while others, by rejecting science, seek to occupy another sociological position. In any case, the construction of the new religion's belief system takes place in interaction with the surrounding society, which reminds us that the development of religious beliefs is highly influenced by the societal context of the religion in question. Even if questions of epistemology are at the heart of the science-religion relationship, social relations between the majority and various minorities is very often what triggers syncretistic developments.

The formative process of new religions almost inevitably includes syncretistic developments, and often science is one of the more significant components. The merging of religious and scientific systems may thus be understood along exactly the same lines, that is, as the merging of two or more religious systems. What should be expected, therefore, is the same kind of development—or at least similar developments—as we find when two different religious systems amalgamate. Science is neither religion nor a belief system, but science represents an epistemological framework with certain parallels to religious systems: Religion, as well as science, offers comprehensive descriptions and interpretations of the world. This is not the place, however, to discuss definitions of religion and science, even if the differences are important. All we need to stress here is that religious understandings of the world imply socially constructed superhuman agents, and scientific worldviews do not (Jensen and Rothstein 2000).

This also clarifies a crucial point, which (however similar in other respects) makes the merger of science and religion different from the merging of two religious systems: Religious systems that blend together may well support one another, but when science is embraced by religion the usual outcome is only relevant to religion. Put candidly, science rarely reaches out for religion, while religions in the modern world, to a considerable extent, have sought an alliance with science. This is probably true of all religions, but certainly not least the new religions or imported (and thus new in the local environment) religions. For instance, the well-known scholar of Buddhist traditions, Christmas Humphreys, speculated in 1968 that a particular Western form of Buddhism was to be expected sometime in the future. He did not suggest any specific kind but found it likely that the Buddhist doctrines would form some kind of unity with Western science: "There is no reason why it should not grow happily alongside, and even blend with the best of Western science, psychology and social science, and thus affect the ever changing field of Western thought. . . . Just what it will be we do not know, nor does it matter at the present time" (Humphreys 1968: 80 as quoted in Chryssides 1999: 223).

Humphreys turned out to be right. Obviously, no single Buddhist tradition has won the hearts of people in the West, but a number of different Buddhist schools, some of them quite new, have contributed to the present state of religious pluralism, and some of them are explicitly seeking to blend with science. George Chryssides, discussing matters pertaining to this question, also points to the fact that the Dalai Lama is a strong representative for the idea that Western science and philosophical Buddhism go hand-in-hand. In fact, some years ago the Dalai Lama made his position on this subject very clear: "If there is inconsistency between the sacred texts and modern science, the sacred books have to be rewritten" (Bang 1989: 202). (One should remember, though, that "modern science" is a very broad category and that the Dalai Lama probably would hesitate to acknowledge every contemporary scientific statement.)

As indicated above, the explanation for this development is obvious. Science has become a central element in the way modern humans think, and any religious system will build on, or at least relate to, already existing cultural resources, including intellectual resources. Consequently, the use of science in religious constructions is not simply a matter of missionary strategy, as is sometimes implied. Missionary endeavors may well be at work, but in a more general sense, science meets religion because they are brought together by creative religious minds or—conversely—science is rejected or transformed because religious minds find it unfit for a given religious project.

In the following, the susceptibility to syncretistic developments with science is briefly discussed with regard to two specific religions, TM and Scientology.

TM

How did TM's Advaita-Vedanta-based belief system become entangled with science in such an intimate way? From a sociological point of view, it has been suggested that science, at a certain time in the history of the TM movement, became an attractive partner. In earlier phases of the organization's development, other things had been in focus, but while attempting to accommodate the demands of modern Western society, TM embarked on a new journey and gradually changed its image. Leaving the hippie or countercultural period behind, TM was now seeking new social alliances. But perhaps another perspective is of more importance in order to understand why TM took such a decisive scientific turn: the basic structure of the TM belief system. As briefly mentioned above, TM builds upon a rather traditional Advaita-Vedanta ideology wherein impersonal divine forces (with *brahman* as the most important concept) rather than personal gods govern the universe. Together with ideas derived from Sankhya philosophy, TM's belief system—the Science of Creative Intelligence—relies on distinct and recognizable patterns of enumeration and methods of enquiry. With an emphasis on the equilibrium of the three *gunas*, the monistic idea that matter is one and that the evolution of a number of things out of that matter is understood as causation, it forms a *structural* parallel to modern scientific thinking. It is this structural coincidence that leaves TM with good opportunities for a syncretic development with science (as we shall see further below, this structural parallel also paves the way for a systematic discursive usage of science in TM's self-promoting strategies). As indicated previously, ISKCON's situation is precisely the opposite since the nucleus in Vaisnava-Bhakti theology is the notion of a very personal, very concrete physical god, the individual known as Krishna, which is structurally incompatible with the basics of modern scientific thinking (Rothstein 1996).

Scientology

The word "science" appears in the very name of the Church of Scientology, and indeed, this religion is, in many ways, based on notions and behavior derived from different scientific realms. Scientology considers itself to be scientific in the sense that all religious claims can be verified through experimentation, and it is believed that the *logos* of Scientology was derived through in-depth scientific methods. In this case, the experimentation is auditing therapy, a procedure that is basically ritual time travel back through the individual's former incarnations. The belief system of Scientology is heavily influenced by Freudian psychology, various inspirations from Eastern religions, and science fiction. The most important soteriological function, auditing, is carried out by means of an electronic device, the so-called E-meter, which is believed to register different kinds of problems that are preventing the *thetan* (a concept somewhat comparable to "soul") from evolving spiritually. At the same time, the founder and illuminated ideal of Scientology, L. Ron Hubbard, is portrayed as the ideal "scientist" or "researcher." He is believed to have "discovered the truth of the Scientology religion," much in the same way as scientists may discover truths about nature. As Scientologists see it, Hubbard never received revelations. Rather, through meticulous studies and thanks to his outstanding scientific genius, he found "the truth" himself. Consequently, the fact that this truth is presently available is the result of a scientific discovery on the part of the brightest and most important human being who has ever lived. This does not mean that Scientology is deprived of what is normally attributed to the category of religion (the cult of L. Ron Hubbard alone makes Scientology quite like a number of other religions). It simply reveals that Scientology, as a religion, was conceived during a period in modern Western history wherein technology and science were gaining more and more influence. In order to articulate Scientology's positions with some effect, Scientologists have embraced science and thus transformed science into something else—religion.

To some extent, Scientology actually grew out of science or at least a scientific ambition. From a historical point of view, Hubbard started out as the designer of a new psychotherapeutic system, *dianetics*, which he emphatically promoted as scientifically valid. Members of the general scientific community, though, felt differently, and Hubbard was forced from the conventional scientific path (Refslund Christensen, forthcoming). It is possible, therefore, that Scientology, as a soteriological religious system, owes its existence partly to this conflict with the conventional scientific community that made it impossible for Hubbard to continue as he originally intended. In fact, it may be the poor scientific standard of the alleged science of *dianetics* that led Hubbard to modify his system into a religion. Analyzing this process, historian of religions Dorthe Refslund Christensen has shown that the belief system of Scientology has become increasingly more self-referential, thus detaching itself from external influence. Scientific contributions normally refer to competing theories, and above all, empirical facts, but Scientology's frame of reference is almost exclusively the statements and positions of the organization (or belief system) itself.

This situation left Scientology in a very favorable position: While any scientific argument has to stand up to certain criteria, religious statements are, in principle, totally independent. Therefore, in Hubbard's case, leaving the realm of science in favor of the realm of religion made room for the further development of Scientology. The fact that Scientologists consider their religion scientifically valid has little to do with science and everything to do with religion. Science and religion have not formed a new synthesis. Rather, science has been changed into an integral part of religion. In this sense, the syncretistic belief system of Scientology represents no actual epistemological equilibrium. The merging of science and religion (including the pseudoscientific aspects of science fiction) turns out to be a religious venture.

Scientism as Discourse Strategy

Exploring the discursive mechanisms in New Age religion, historian of religions Olav Hammer sees the religious use of science as an important element in a strategy of legitimacy. Scientism, he says, is a mode of solving the dilemma between rational science and religion where "scientific inquiry—provided it is interpreted correctly—serves to prove the validity of the religious point of view." Thus, the scientific perspective is only one among several modes of solving the dilemma but probably the most convenient at this point in history. The absolute rejection of science on religious grounds has little to offer modern people, nor has the priority of "revelation" to meticulously established knowledge through experimentation. The "Two Worlds" approach, in which religion is seen as "wholly other" and thus utterly incommensurable with science (and, Hammer adds, therefore immune to attacks from it), also has its shortcomings in a cultural environment where both (science and religion) have something to say (Hammer 2001: 203).

In choosing the scientific position, the new religions try to benefit from religion as well as science. Discussing the Esoteric Tradition of Europe and the New Age movement that arose from it, Hammer sees the use of contemporary science primarily as a powerful source of legitimacy. Science cannot be escaped; therefore, rather than contest it, esotericists and partakers in the New Age vision embrace it by reinterpreting the concept for religious purposes. The scientistic understanding insists that science and "spirituality" are two sides of the same coin, and that good scientific arguments exist for accepting clairvoyance, healing, levitation, revelation, and many other traditional religious components. In doing so, says Hammer, the "intellectual and ethical import of science is judged against preexisting normative standards" (Hammer 2001: 203).

As we have already seen, in similar ways, the more institutionalized new religions have also used science as a way of attaining legitimacy. In each and every case, scientistic discourse is part and parcel of a religious project. One example among the many available is the discourse found among the residents of Damanhur, a gnostic-like movement near Turin, Italy. Along with several other components in this group's extremely diverse belief system, "the science of Selfica" is propagated as one of the more central features. In a book written by one of Damanhur's very enthusiastic supporters, Jeff Merrifield, Selfica is described thusly:

> Selfica is an ancient science based on the most basic form in our universe: the spiral. It was known to the Egyptians, the Celts and the Arabs, who used it up until the eighth century BC, and has been developed at Damanhur for over 20 years. It is the practical use of spirals and metals to concentrate and direct vital energies. The practical objects that are developed from this science are called Selfs. They are frequently constructed out of gold and silver, because these are the best conductors, but copper and brass are also used. (Merrifield 1998: 233)

Another Damanhur resident is quoted:

> Selfs are subtle beings. They have an existence. They have different forms because they have different functions. The simple ones, those that use metals, copper mostly, rather than alchemical liquids, range in function from amplifying the aura of a person to increasing the sensibility and perceptions, from regulating the immune system to helping the memory, or, for houses or motor vehicles, balancing the environment. (Merrifield 1998: 234)

It is obvious that the Damanhurians' "science of Selfica" is incompatible with the principles of conventional science. Nevertheless, it is precisely science that is used as the discursive path when the notion of Selfica is propagated. At the same time, the example reveals another typical feature of this kind of religious argumentation pointed to by Hammer: Credibility and legitimacy is aimed at by ascribing the religious knowledge (in this case the knowledge of the Selfica) to ancient times. By rooting religious representations in the remote past it attains an aura of "tradition" and "originality." In this way, the religious rhetoric among most new religions makes use of the oldest as well as the newest (science) and places the group itself at the mediating point. Being rooted in the oldest wisdom, and being in alignment with the most recent, gives the religion in question a favorable position in guiding people's lives.

But examples could be chosen from virtually any of the scientistically inclined new religions. One particularly good example is TM's institutionalized alignment with science, which was reinforced in the late 1980s and is still expanding. TM claims to be scientific in every way, but the organization's rhetoric will always place "Vedic science" above "modern science." However, as a discursive strategy, "modern science" will always be used in TM as the vehicle of "Vedic science" whenever the belief system is presented to people outside the organization's inner movement. An example: From the Maharishi International University (MIU) in Fairfield, Iowa, a journal was launched in 1987: *Modern Science and Vedic Science: An Interdisciplinary Journal Devoted to Research on the Unified Field of All Laws of Nature.* "The Unified Field" was, at that time, one among several "Grand Unification Theories" that claim all the natural forces (electromagnetism, weak interaction, strong interaction, and gravity) and particles of nature to be united in "Superunification," thus suggesting a basic unity in the cosmos. This idea that everything emerges from a common field, shares, as we have already seen, distinctive features with basic assumptions of the TM Advaita-Vedanta-related belief system. On the cover of one issue (Vol. 2, No. 1, 1988), the intention of the journal is described:

> Exploration of the Unified Field of all laws of nature is at the forefront of contemporary scientific research. This journal is devoted to research on the Unified Field and its applications for the benefit of mankind. It draws upon a new technology for investigating the Unified Field that combines the approach of modern science and ancient Vedic science as brought to light by Maharishi Mahesh Yogi. Modern science has arrived at an increasingly comprehensive and unified understanding of the laws of nature. Most recently, theoretical physics has identified a unified structure of natural law on the most fundamental distance scale of nature. In super-symmetric quantum field theories, this boundless and all-pervading "Unified Field" is described as the self-interacting, self-sufficient, and infinitely dynamic source of the physical world. All the force and matter fields that comprise the universe have their basis in it and sequentially emerge from it through a self-interacting dynamics by which this Unified Field gives rise to all diversity. In discovering the Unified Field, physics has glimpsed the unified structure of the entire universe.

In terms of discourse, the strictly religious is covered by the scientific. The actual reason for dealing with these questions is not directly addressed, but later in the same text it is revealed that "Maharishi has revitalized and reinterpreted [the ancient Vedic tradition] in the form of a modern systematic science [and] made available a technology . . . by which anyone can effectively investigate the Unified Field of all laws of nature on the level of direct experience of consciousness."

The terminology is still academic and scientific, but "the modern systematic science" remains an Advaita-Vedanta philosophy in the Shankara tradition, and the technology mentioned covers various types of traditional meditation rituals. This is not to say that the scientism of TM's belief system makes it less religious or less genuine. What is implied is simply that science is introduced more as a missionary device than is admitted by the organization. In general, scientism as a discursive strategy is one of the most typical features of TM and related religious movements; partly for missionary reasons, partly because modern religions need the support of science in order to appear trustworthy and rational to a modern audience.

A PSYCHOLOGICAL THEORY

Relating the use of science for religious purposes to the general cultural context is, of course, important. New religions in a modern context cannot escape the challenge of science, which means that the surrounding cultural milieu is of great significance. However, this does not necessarily explain why the religion-science cocktail seems to work quite well in many new religious groups. An entirely different approach, namely that of cognitive psychology, may suggest an additional explanation.

According to anthropologist Pascal Boyer, an important feature of religious ideas and experiences is that they entertain "counter-intuitive" elements. These elements transcend ordinary intuitive ontologies, that is, universally acknowledged ideas of the world and the categories that structure it. Transcending ordinary intuitive ontology, says Boyer, makes these elements excellent tools for thought and reasoning. Because such ideas are what Boyer calls "attention demanding," people are able to remember a myth or another type of sacred narrative or statement better than mundane or ordinary descriptions of "ordinary things." On the other hand, no religious system is entirely composed of counter-intuitive elements. On the contrary, according to Boyer, most religious systems will primarily rest upon an intuitive ontology of the world and the counter-intuitive or "supernatural" dimensions will, in fact, be few. Some kind of ontological balance is needed, and too strong of an emphasis on counter-intuitive representations may prove fatal for a religion's discourse.

The cognitive categories that structure the ideas of the world, whether shared collectively or upheld by an individual, cannot be too attention-demanding. However, it is precisely the attention-demanding, counter-intuitive elements that make dynamic meaning in specific situations possible. For example, the Christian narrative of Jesus' conviction and crucifixion displays no significant counter-intuitive dimensions, but decisive counter-intuitive elements are added in the subsequent myth of the resurrection (Boyer 1994a and 1994b). In terms of contemporary new religions, for instance, it is quite unchallenging to note that the Reverend Sun Myung Moon was born in Korea in 1920, but once we are told that he is the "Master of the Second Coming," and that his place of birth is the cosmic spot where God is fighting Satan most intensely, new and crucial dimensions are added to the story of this individual. Similarly, it is not at all strange to meet people who arrive in a vehicle from another place, but when the person is a Cosmic Master, the vehicle a flying saucer, and the other place the planet Venus, important counter-intuitive dimensions transform the otherwise normal situation into something special.

If the science-religion problem is analyzed according to Boyer's theory, it is possible to identify science as the necessary counterbalance to a belief system's strictly counter-intuitive elements. Arguably, scientific perspectives may often be unintelligible to the average person, but it is recognized that science aims at explaining the empirical world in naturalistic, rationalist, and nonsupernatural ways. But religion moves in very different ways. When religion is wrapped in science, as is the case of scientistic belief systems, an influx of "intuitive ontology" takes place in a predominantly counter-intuitive (i.e., mythological) belief system, and a balance is reached.

The myth of the UFOs and their occupants is a good example. To a certain extent, flying machines and creatures from distant places are understandable within scientific boundaries. However, at a certain point, flying machines and creatures may transcend what science can relate to. Their empirical status (they belong to the realm of myth) makes them irrelevant to science. The mythic "reality" of the alien crafts and their occupants, however, are given some kind of credibility because the narrative of UFOs systematically employs pseudoscientific terminology and pseudoscientific frames of reference.

CONCLUSION: MAKING SCIENCE SACRED

The examples above, including the psychological theory, not only show how religion is propagated through a scientistic strategy or discourse but also reveal how religion, not science, is in control. Scientistic religious groups, however, are not "paradoxical," as Bainbridge would have it. What they have accomplished is simply an expanded usage of a traditional religious strategy. Traditional religions are able to interpret any event, place, individual, object, or subject according to religious standards. Within the fabric of any given religion, everything in the world can be understood and measured along specific mythological or ritual paths. Scientistic religions have simply added the phenomenon of science to this capacity. By embracing science, which is basically a secular discourse, a number of new religions have overcome one of the paradoxes of the modern world, that is, the parallel existence of two mutually incongruous epistemological systems—science and religion.

It is quite obvious that the merging of science and religion in these examples only happens because religious people wish to pursue religious goals. Scientific perspectives that may question such religious interests are therefore noticeably absent in the scientistic belief systems. Science is not simply "science" to these groups. "Real science" is that which, one way or another, may support the specific religious claims and interests of the group in question. It is also worth noting that "the religious" is never made mundane in its meeting with science. To a certain extent, Sentes and Palmer are correct when they claim that "new religious movements arising within the context of the contemporary developed world, whose sources of revelation are extraterrestrial, spontaneously take their space-age deities to be merely natural or immanence rather than supernatural or transcendent, precisely because they exist within the horizon of our post-modern condition, i.e., within the horizon of the death of God" (Sentes and Palmer 2000: 86).

However, the *kind* of "immanence" or "naturalness" we find in such cases is far from what is normally understood to be "of this world." It would be more correct to say that the scientistic new religions have reversed the usual conceptualization in such a way that the extraordinary "out of this world" phenomena are being described and interpreted as natural and rational elements in human life. "The death of God" is a rumor but certainly not a fact, if, of course, "God" is taken to mean any notion of the supernatural.

The syncretistic process characteristic of the scientistic approach of new religions primarily transforms science and technology and bestows it with a new ontology, a new kind of meaning. It becomes sacred. This is perhaps the most important aspect of the science-religion problem pertaining to the new religions: The conspicuous ability to subject science to religious interpretation and use.

Perhaps *this* capacity on the part of the new religions is a significant feature of the dynamics of so-called postmodern culture. The religious revival need not be a counter strike against science, as for instance, the creationists' campaign against the theory of biological evolution. The new and emerging religious consciousness will probably more often overcome the challenge of science by enveloping scientific perspectives into a basically religious belief system. We should not ignore the possibility that scientists in the future, more often than at present, will have to defend their positions and argue against myth, miracle, and magic. A paradoxical helping hand offers itself in this connection: When the prophet Rael encountered the leader of the race of space beings that allegedly have created life on Earth in their laboratories, he was told that "humanity's objective is scientific progress" (Vorilhon 1986: 27).

REFERENCES

Bainbridge, William S. 1993. "New Religions, Science and Secularization." *Religion and Social Order* 3A: 277–92.

Bang, Jens M. 1989. "Naturvidenskab, tro og overtro." In *Vitenskap og Verdensbilder,* ed. Lars Gule and Henning Laugerud, 202–212. Bergen: Ariadne.

Bovin, Werner. 2000. *Unitarismen i Danmark og dens Forhistorie.* København: Unitarisk Forlag.

Boyer, Pascal. 1994a. "Cognitive Constraints on Cultural Representations: Natural Ontology and Religious Ideas." In *Mapping the Mind: Domain, Specificity and Culture,* ed. Lawrence A. Hirschfeld and Susan A. Gelman, 391–411. Cambridge: Cambridge University Press.

———. 1994b. The Naturalness of Religious Ideas. Berkeley: University of California Press.

Chryssides, George D. 1999. *Exploring New Religions.* London: Cassell.

Ellwood, Robert S., and Harry B. Partin. 1988. *Religious and Spiritual Groups in Modern America,* 2d ed. Englewood Cliffs, N.J.: Prentice-Hall.

Hammer, Olav. 2001. *Claiming Knowledge. Strategies for Epistemology from Theosophy to the New Age.* Leiden: Brill.

———. 2000. "Esoterisk naturvetenskap: Aspekter på scientismens historia." In *Gudars och gudinnors återkomst. Studier i nyreligiositet,* ed. Carl-Gustav Carlsson and Liselotte Frisk, 11–31. Umeå: Institutiuonen för Religionsvetenskap, Umeå Universitet.

Hess, David J. 1993. *Science in the New Age: The Paranormal, Its Defenders and Debunkers, and American Culture.* Madison: University of Wisconsin Press.

Humphreys, Christmas. 1968. *Sixty Years of Buddhism in England.* London: Buddhist Society.

Jensen, Tim, and Mikael Rothstein, eds. 2000. *Secular Theories in the Study of Religion: Current Perspectives.* Copenhagen: Museum Tusculanum Press.

King, George (with Richard Lawrence). 1996. *Contacts with Gods from Space: Pathway to the New Millennium.* Los Angeles, Calif.: Aetherius Society.

Lewis, James R. 2002. "Diabolical Authority: Anton La Vey, *The Satanic Bible* and the Satanist 'Tradition.' "*Marburg Journal of Religion* 7: 1.

Merrifield, Jeff. 1998. *Damanhur: The Real Dream.* London: Thorsons.

Refslund Christensen, Dorthe. Forthcoming. *Rethinking Scientology: Cognition and Representation in Religion, Therapy, and Soteriology.*

Rothstein, Mikael. 1996. "Belief Transformations. Some Aspects of the Relation between Science and Religion in Transcendental Meditation (TM) and the International Society for Krishna Consciousness (ISKCON)." *RENNER Studies on New Religions,* vol. 1. Åarhus: Aarhus University Press.

Sentes, Bryan, and Susan Palmer. 2000. "Presumed Immanent: The Raëlians, UFO Religions, and the Postmodern Condition." *Nova Religio* 4: 86–105.

Stanesby, Derek. 1985. *Science, Reason and Religion.* London: Routledge.

Stenmark, Mikael. 1997. "What Is Scientism?" *Religious Studies* 33 (1): 15–32.

Thompson, Richard (Sadaputa dasa). 1989. *Vedic Cosmography and Astronomy.* Los Angeles: Bhaktivedanta Book Trust.

Vorilhon, Claude. 1986. *The Message Given to Me by Extra-Terrestrials: They Took Me to Their Planet.* Tokyo: AOM.

Wallis, Roy. 1984. *The Elementary Forms of the New Religious Life.* London: Routledge & Kegan Paul.

CHAPTER 5

VIRTUALLY RELIGIOUS

New Religious Movements and the World Wide Web

DOUGLAS E. COWAN
JEFFREY K. HADDEN

E-SPACE AND THE CHANGING NATURE OF RELIGIOUS COMMUNITY

IN slightly more than a decade, the World Wide Web has developed into a communication and information metatechnology[1] that eclipses all forms of information dissemination heretofore available in human history. In that short span of time, the Web has developed its own specialized language, generated its own unique sets of social codes, and prompted lively discussions—both popular and academic—about ostensibly fixed notions of embodiment and disembodiment (cf. Collins 1996; Danet 1998; Dibbell 1996; Fisher 1997; Ito 1997; McRae 1997; O'Brien 1999). At the onset, this communication revolution developed in what appears now to be slow, tedious fashion. Soon, however, text-only messaging systems were replaced with wireless audio and video Internet access through infrared connections and personal digital assistants (PDAs).

The purpose of this essay is to explore how certain aspects of religious life have come to exist on the Internet—how they have both impacted and been impacted by the virtual reality of cyberspace. We begin with the simple observation that just as it is in the real world, *religion* is one of the most prominent and popular aspects of virtual reality. Religion on the Internet ranges from the tens of thousands of modest Web sites set up by local churches, synagogues, mosques, and temples, to sophisticated research sites such as the American Religion Data Archive (www.theARDA.com; cf. Finke, McKinney, and Bahr 2000), and from online religious rituals conducted in Internet chatrooms (see below) to elaborate commercial enterprises such as Beliefnet.com (also www.belief.net), a nondenominational religious information provider whose quarterly advertising billings are in the tens of millions (cf. Elliott 2000; Goldman 2000). The information disseminated across the World Wide Web is often of questionable reliability (cf. Cowan 2003; Donath 1999; Introvigne 2000; Knapp 1997; Tepper 1997), and we find no evidence to suggest that the nature of religious information is qualitatively different from other subject categories.

One of the important themes we will develop in this essay is the distinction between the Internet as a social structure used to communicate *about* religion, and the Internet as a locus for the development of new religious forms. As we and other scholars have noted, though (cf. Brasher 2001; Hadden and Cowan 2000a; Helland 2000), an important distinction needs to be drawn between *religion online* and *online religion*. In broad terms, we characterize *religion online* as the Internet provision of information about and services related to religious groups and traditions which are already established and operating offline. Religion online, for example, serves Internet navigators who want to learn about the organizational structure of the United Methodist Church (www.umc.org) or the doctrinal stance of Ahmadi Muslims (www.ahmadiyya.org); who want to shop online for religious paraphernalia ranging from Celtic crosses (www.celticattic.com) to Buddhist mala (www.mro.org); and who want to browse religious literature ranging from *The Book of Mormon* (www.scriptures.lds.org) to online Hadith in Arabic, with English, French, German, and Turkish translations (http://Hadith.al-islam.com/Bayan).

Online religion, on the other hand, uses the Internet to create an electronic space in which visitors can actually/virtually participate in religious liturgy, prayer, ritual, meditation, or other activity. Hindus, for example, can visit www.pujaroom.com for an online Durga puja. Virtual butter lamps frame an altar devoted to Kali, a wispy trail of incense just visible in the background. Flowers in full virtual bloom are gathered before the altar, flanked by a bell and an arti lamp. Devotees can click-and-drag flower blossoms to the Goddess's feet; clicking-and-dragging also moves the lamp for the arti ceremony; the altar bell is rung the same way, calling the virtual family to worship. Roman Catholic traditionalists, angry at the liturgical changes that have swept their church since Vatican II, can visit www.latinmass-ctm.org and download the complete Tridentine mass in either audio or video formats. While supporters regard an Internet mass as little different than masses which have been broadcast for decades over the radio or television— more sophisticated, perhaps, with greater options for interactivity, but essentially no different in kind (e.g., www.themass.com)—other Catholics maintain that the Church will never accept the validity of online sacraments.[2]

The founders of Beliefnet.com believe that the business of *religion online* represents a $40 billion per year market. For *online religion*, however, the central question remains: not unlike Memorex, is it virtual or is it actual? How is online participation in religious ritual or liturgy similar to these practices in real life? In what ways does it differ? How do the different technological and meta-technological factors associated with religious observance in cyberspace enhance or constrain the experience? Does the Internet offer unique opportunities for religious evolution, or merely more advanced versions of strategies already deployed? Are particular groups more likely to find the virtual environment more congenial to their religious vision, and perhaps less threatening than the real world?

With regard to this last question, we would like to suggest that there are, indeed, religious groups for whom the Internet is a more accommodating environment—for religious innovation, for an enhanced sense of control over one's religious life, and for the ability to contribute to the ongoing development of the tradition(s) in which that life is located. While it is highly unlikely that online religious observance will take the place of mass at one's local parish church, for certain new religious movements—especially those which are doctrinally, traditionally, and liturgically fluid—e-space presents an opportunity unparalleled in religious history.

In this chapter, following a review of the current research into new or controversial religious movements and the Internet, we would like to explore three aspects of the intersection between these movements and the constantly evolving virtual world: (a) the Internet as a medium for the emergence and evolution of new religions; (b) the Internet as a stage for the virtual practice of online religion; and (c) the Internet as a platform for conflict over religious lineage and authority.

Current Research

The growing literature on the relationship between religion and the Internet ranges across traditions, and from perspectives that vary from the academic to the evangelistic, and the celebratory to the admonitory (cf., for example, Brasher 2001; Brooke 1997; Bunt 2000a, 2000b; Careaga 1999; Careaga and Sweet 2001; Cobb 1998; Davis 1999; Dawson 2001a; Gold 1997; Groothuis 1997; Hadden and Cowan 2000b; Hammerman 2000; Kelly 1999a, 1999b; Kellner 1996; Lawrence

2000; Lucas 1998; Makkuni 1996; Moreau and O'Rear 2000; O'Leary 2000; Schroeder, Heather, and Lee 1998; Wilson 2000; Zaleski 1997). Literature that treats new and emergent religions specifically, however, as well as the Internet as a platform for countermovements against them, is more scarce. To date, scholarly contributions have been limited to a few journal articles, chapters in edited collections, and presentations at academic conferences (cf., for example, Chryssides 1996; Cowan 2000, 2001; 2003; Dawson 2001b; Dawson and Hennebry 1999; Green 2001; Hadden 2000; Introvigne 2000; Koenig 2001; Lippard and Jacobsen 1995; Mayer 2000a, 2000b; Peckham 1998; Robinson 1997; Robinson 2000; Urban 2000). While there are some exceptions (e.g., Green 2001; Hadden 2000; Koenig 2001; Robinson 2000), current scholarship has contained itself to investigating three principle areas: (a) the relationship between the Internet and the 1997 mass suicide of 39 members of Heaven's Gate; (b) the ongoing legal controversies surrounding the unauthorized Internet publication of esoteric Scientological teachings; and (c) the Internet as a low-cost venue for anticult and countercult propaganda.

Not surprisingly, on March 28, 1997, the *New York Times* carried ten separate articles on the Heaven's Gate suicides, three on the front page, and each of the ten linked by the header: "Death in a Cult." The articles covered story angles ranging from "The Theories" to "The Drugs," and "The Technology" to "The Town." In most, the group was referred to as "an obscure computer-related cult," a "computer-cult" populated (in the words of *Times* editorialists) by "wounded, foolish followers" who were "piped" to an early grave by Ti and Do (*New York Times*, March 29, 1997). Indeed, from the moment reports of the Heaven's Gate suicides appeared in mass media around the world, the connection was drawn between Marshall Herff Applewhite's UFO cult and the Internet. While the *New York Times* did say that "there is little evidence that the Net itself is acting as an instigator for cult behavior" (Markoff 1997), that qualification was followed almost immediately by the testimony of alleged cult "expert" Rick Ross, who opined that "the Internet has proven a powerful recruitment tool for cults," and that "Heaven's Gate was emblematic of a growing number of small, computer-connected cults that have flourished in the last decade" (Markoff 1997). A week later, in *Newsweek*'s "Blaming the Web," Tal Brooke, a Christian apologist with the California-based Spiritual Counterfeits Project, concurred with Ross's assessment. "I think the Net can be an effective cult recruiting tool," he said. "It's like fishing with a lure" (Levy 1997; cf. Brooke 1997). The argument seemed to be that because the Heaven's Gate group had owned computers, operated a moderately successful Web design company, and posted if not necessarily interacted online, the Web was guilty by association.

Defending the Internet, on the other hand, communications scholar Wendy Gale Robinson (1997) argues for its essential neutrality and declares that "the press acted irresponsibly by hastily pointing the finger at the Net although many factors influenced the decision of Applewhite and his followers to end their lives." She maintains that, far from glassy-eyed computer drones endlessly surfing the Web in search of cyber-experience lost to them in the outside world, those members of Heaven's Gate who did participate online were actually as alienated in virtual reality as they were in real life. Put simply, they were not good "Netizens." Their copious use of metatags and blanket distribution of group material "glutted search engines" (Robinson 1997) and separated them from those who advocated more responsible use of the Web. Media fear of cybercult conscription notwithstanding, Robinson concludes that "there is nothing in their literature and the interviews with surviving cult members to support the idea that they felt part of cyberculture or that the Internet was anything more than a digital bulletin board on which to affix their messages" (1997).

Following the line drawn by the mainstream media, however, historian Hugh Urban argues that Heaven's Gate was a "technological, on-line religion"; it was "very much a technologically based religion," whose members hoped to "ascend into a supra-material cyberspace world" (2000: 269, 270). Declaring that Heaven's Gate "was one of the first [religious sects] to emerge as a true religion of and for the computer age" (Urban 2000: 282), a claim belied somewhat by the actual history of the group, he contends that two principle dynamics render the Internet the perfect environment for the inception, incubation, and evolution of new religious movements. "First and most simply," he writes, "the Net is an ideal means of mass proselytization and rapid conversion—a missionary device which operates instantly, globally, and anonymously. Second, and more interesting, is the fact that the Internet, more than perhaps any other conventional medium, fosters the practice of religious syncretism and the blending of many different traditions drawn from radically different and seemingly contradictory sources" (Urban 2000: 283). Urban, however, specifies neither how the Net functions in this way (i.e., as "a missionary device"), nor how precisely it "fosters the process of religious syncretism," nor, finally, whether the Net played any real role in the development of Heaven's Gate's elaborate bricolage theology. Rather, following Baudrillard (principally 1983), he develops an impressionistic postmodern argument, locating the group (and ultimately explaining the suicides) within the context of a trialectic between science fiction, technological enchantment, and late capitalist angst.

Finally, sociologists Lorne Dawson and Jennifer Hennebry (1999) are careful to point out that what is not known about the group's life and death far and away exceeds that which is known, and they provide the most reasonable analysis of the Heaven's Gate event. In contrast to Robinson and Urban, they address the question of the Internet as a vehicle for recruitment directly, including the sociology of Internet culture, the process of recruitment and conversion to new religious movements, and the crucial intersection between the two that lies at the heart of concern over Heaven's Gate. First, and perhaps most significantly, Dawson and Hennebry point out that, despite media, industry, and devotee hyperbole, "the Internet is still only used, with any regularity, by a relatively small percentage of the population" (1999: 17). And, rather than any form of missionary interactivity, like the Web presence of many other religious groups, the Heaven's Gate site was devoted to religion online, "a way to advertise the groups and to deliver information about them cheaply" (Dawson and Hennebry 1999: 26). That is, the empirical evidence simply does not support the image of unsuspecting Internet navigators inexorably drawn into the virtual reality created as a trap by more mendacious Netizens. As we have noted elsewhere (Hadden and Cowan 2000a: 12), the often fragile technological nature of the Internet as it is currently constituted, "subject to the caprice of power supply, server fortitude, and operator error," weighs against its ability to function as a substantial mediator of long-term social construction.

Second, the popular stereotype of those considered "targets" for new religious movements, those who are "young, naïve and duped . . . social losers and marginal types seeking a safe haven from the real world" (Dawson and Hennebry 1999: 26)—a profile sustained by such commentators as Ross (Levy 1997), Brooke (1997), Davis (1999), and Zaleski (1997)—has been significantly challenged by two decades of scholarly investigation into the problem of NRM conversion. Synthesizing much of this research, Dawson and Hennebry declare that "first and foremost, the process of converting to an NRM is a social process. If the denizens of cyberspace tend in fact to be socially isolated, then it is unlikely that they will be recruited through the web or otherwise" (Dawson and Hennebry 1999: 28). Although they warn that "we must be careful not to underestimate what the future may hold," they conclude that, rather than virtually irresistible Internet proselytizing, "most new religions seem content to use the net in quite limited and conventional ways" (1999: 36).

Of these "quite limited and conventional ways," the provision of religious information online is the most common. Since it involves the least in terms of hardware, software, and technical expertise, this is hardly surprising. However, the second major intersection between the Internet and a new religious movement concerns precisely this provision—or, more precisely, what has been labeled the illegal provision of information. Briefly stated, in the early years of alt.religion.scientology, the main Usenet group for discussion of Scientology, Scientologists sought to counter criticism by overwhelming the newsgroup with messages, flooding bandwidth, and thus preventing other posts from getting through (Lippard and Jacobsen 1995). In 1994, however, material began appearing on the newsgroup that went significantly beyond criticism, and revealed hitherto secret Scientological teachings.[3] This time, rather than flood the newsgroup bandwidth, Scientologists allegedly responded with what Grossman (1995) called a war of "duelling cancelbots," and used specialized software to automatically eliminate targeted messages or message threads. In a number of instances, the cancelbots informed newsgroup participants that offending messages had been "CANCELLED BECAUSE OF COPYRIGHT INFRINGEMENT" (Grossman 1995; Lippard and Jacobsen 1995; Peckham 1998). Offline, the conflict escalated as well. In at least three instances, computer equipment and data were seized under warrant, and the owners were charged with copyright violations. Discussion of these events has occurred in the popular computer media (Grossman 1995; Lippard and Jacobsen 1995), law reviews (cf., for example, Benkler 1999; Lyons 2000), and scholarly journals and anthologies (Mayer 2000a, 2000b; Introvigne 2000; Peckham 1998).

While popular reports concentrate on reprising the situation from the perspective of the Internet industry, and legal analyses forms on the increasingly complicated business of intellectual property and its defense online, Peckham (1998) discusses the issue within the context of resource mobilization theory. Building on an analysis of movement/countermovement interaction, he argues that both sides in the dispute sought to deprive the other of the resources necessary to realize their objectives. By flooding the alt.religion.scientology bandwidth, Scientology denied its critics the ability to propagate criticism; by uploading sensitive or restricted Scientological material, critics deprived Scientology of its monopoly on that material. As a result of this, Peckham concludes that the Internet environment demands a reconceptualization of what constitutes "virtual resources," that is, "resources that have no intrinsic value and little meaning outside the context of on-line activity, yet are highly valued by Internet users" (Peckham 1998: 322). Of these, the most valuable are "bandwidth," "the total amount of information space available in particular forum," and "anonymity," the ability to "[access] bandwidth without revealing one's identity" (Peckham 1998: 322). While some theorists have postulated that the Internet is a research question/site without precedent, one which "necessitates an almost total overthrow of existing social theory" (Peckham 1998: 341), like Dawson and Hennebry, Peckham concludes that with suitable modification, current social theories can illuminate the virtual environment just as clearly as they do the actual.

If the Internet has not proved a particularly successful medium for the recruitment of significant numbers of converts to new religious movements, as Douglas Cowan (2001, 2003), Massimo Introvigne (2000), and Jean-François Mayer (2000b) have noted, it has shown remarkable development as a medium for the conduct of "information terrorism" (Introvigne 2000: 299), what Mayer has referred to as the "cyberspace propaganda wars" against NRMs (2000b: 250). While Introvigne and Mayer both discuss the issues of copyright infringement with which Scientology has had to contend, each also explores the related phenomenon of dedicated anticult Web sites—e-space information stalls designed specifically to demonize and disparage a wide variety of new religious movements, or to provide information and "exit resources" for interested or distressed visitors. Most often posted under the guise of "promoting or defending the truth," these sites divide along the conceptual boundaries of the secular anticult and evangelical Christian countercult (cf. Cowan forthcoming 2003b).[4] Victories online have been claimed by both sides in the e-space cult wars, but as Introvigne points out, these are "largely symbolic" (2000: 299) and "carrying on-line crusades off-line is a notoriously difficult exercise" (2000: 300). Cowan (2003) argues that, since the primary agenda of the Christian countercult is boundary maintenance—i.e., the ongoing reinforcement of the evangelical Christian worldview—the Internet provides a very effective environment for the propagation of material designed for no other purpose than the censure of religious traditions that differ from that worldview.

New Religions in E-Space

If the Internet is neither a particularly aggressive nor an especially viable mechanism for NRM recruitment—the claims and activities of Internet countermovements notwithstanding—what then does it offer these movements? Using examples drawn from the domains of Neopaganism and Western Esotericism, we would like to explore three aspects of this question, and suggest three concomitant avenues for further investigation: (a) the Internet as an environment conducive to the emergence and evolution of online religion; (b) the dramaturgical character of Internet participation in new religious movements; and (c), following the debate over copyrighted Scientological material, the diffusion and decay of religious authority as a product of information democratization on the Internet. We make no claim to an exhaustive survey of the ways in which new religious movements are participating in e-space; the fluid nature of the Internet renders any such claims self-defeating. Rather, we offer these examples as vignettes from which we might make some pertinent observations and draw some tentative conclusions.

EMERGENCE AND EVOLUTION: THE TEMPLE OF DUALITY

Sociologists of religion have recognized for many years the evolving individualism of religious practice in pluralistic contexts. Though secularization theory held sway for two decades, eventually it was admitted that society was not becoming less religious, but less *institutionally* religious (cf., for example, Bainbridge 1997; Hadden 1989; Stark 1999; Stark and Bainbridge 1987). Unconstrained by institutional mandate or overt social sanction, the rise of individually oriented spiritualities in a religiously plural context has led to an increase in nontraditional practices ranging from religious syncretisms such as "Bu-Jews" (Buddhist Jews) to religious innovations such as the Church of All Worlds (www.caw.org). And the Internet is proving a fertile environment for these forms of religious experimentation. Online, the construction of a "religious world" (in the Bergerian sense) is bounded only by the technology available to the creators, their relative facility with that technology, and the stock of religious knowledge and imagination they bring to the task.

"The Temple of Duality" (www.silverstormlavenderdawn.homestead.com), for example, is the online religious project of two Neopagans from Virginia. Still in its infancy, the Web site consists mostly of what Netizens term "shovelware"— the posting and reposting of basic information common to any number of similar Web sites. They hope to achieve something considerably more than that, however. "The Temple of Duality is our cyber version of what we would like to build," their Web site announces, "an interfaith church of Natural Spirituality." Unsatisfied with both the restrictions of the Christian Church, as well as what they regard as the overemphasis on the Goddess within many streams of Neopaganism, the couple are self-consciously constructing an eclectic religious tradition rooted in their own understanding of "balance." "We built our own tradition." In addition to pages devoted to such standard Neopagan fare as divination, magick, and the wheel of the year, the Temple of Duality also hosts online rituals through Yahoo.com's system of Internet chatrooms and e-mail groups.

Pragmatically speaking, while the ability of these Neopagans to accomplish their dream in real life is open to debate,[5] until the ready availability of Web site design programs and Internet server access that dream would have been confined even further, unavailable even in virtual reality. Another online religious service, however, has contributed to their conceptualization of the project. That is, both are "ordained High Priest and High Priestess in the Universal Life Church," "an ecumenical religious organization that recognizes all faiths as valid." Most important from the perspective of worldview construction and the legitimation of their religious enterprise, though, "the Universal Life Church made it possible for us to be legally recognized, praise be."

Founded by Kirby Hansen and headquartered in Modesto, California, the Universal Life Church is the most famous of the mail-order churches and claims to have ordained more than twenty million persons worldwide since 1959.[6] While it offers a wide variety of religious products and services, the advent of the Internet and the evolution of the Church's extensive Web site (www.ulc.org) has significantly increased the commercial scope of its most common product—distance ordination. After filling in fields for one's "TRUE Legal Name," as well as e-mail and mailing addresses, an "official certificate" of ordination in the ULC arrives by e-mail in about three minutes. Other e-mails follow, each detailing the benefits of ordination, as well as the various products available for purchase by the newly ordained minister. At $99, for example, "Ministry in a Box" contains Holy Land incense, Marriage and Renewal of Marriage Certificates, a Doctor of Divinity degree, a Sainthood Canonization document, wall and wallet credentials, and the "MINISTER'S MANUAL everyone has been asking about—the *real* kind, just like you always see being used in marriages on TV or in the movies." For $100, "serious students" can receive a "PhD in Religion"; a "Masters Degree" is available for $50. And, for $10 each, ULC offers a profusion of "special titles," including Lama, Rabbi, Soul Therapist, Iman, High Priest and High Priestess, Apostle of Humility, Saintly Healer, and Universal Philosopher of Absolute Reality.

Lest readers too quickly dismiss the ULC as simply a transparent religious scam, gone from the classified ads at the back of *Fate* magazine to the Java-script and Flash graphics of the World Wide Web, there is nothing in the Temple of Duality Web site to suggest that they are not entirely serious about their claims, their intent, or their belief that the ULC has conferred a measure of legitimacy upon their endeavors. Numerous others—from a group of Neopagans in New York who have gathered under the ULC banner to individuals such as Rev. Mike (ULC Bowling Green) and Rev. Kevin (Harmony ULC, "A Deist Reason Center")—now also advertise e-space variations on the Universal Life theme.[7] Indeed, ordained ULC members operate hundreds if not thousands of Web sites and at least four Web rings.

What is it about the Internet that facilitates this kind of religious innovation? Assuming that individuals such as the creators of the Temple of Duality *are* entirely serious, how does e-space support their ability to realize their particular religious vision? We would like to suggest three propositions in this regard: low-cost, flexibility, and low risk.

First, modest Web sites are relatively inexpensive to upload and operate. The Temple of Duality, as well as many of the ULC Web sites, exists on free server space provided as part of a basic Internet service package. As long as they remain within bandwidth limits and do not contravene any content restrictions set by the service provider, there is no charge to host the site. Instead, ISP charges are carried by commercial clients whose advertising "pop-ups" appear each time a page on the site is accessed. With no building to rent or maintain, no furniture or ritual paraphernalia to purchase, and no need to invest in, print materials, overhead shrinks to the monthly cost of the service package and whatever Web design program the operators choose. Print materials remain an option, of course, but they are no longer necessary to the administration of one's online religion. As the cost involved in such ventures decreases—the simple pleasure inherent in creating something like a Web site notwithstanding—the number of individuals or groups participating will increase.

Second, religious innovations that exist only or primarily in cyberspace are eminently flexible and allow for the constant reinvention of religious principles, doctrine, and practice. Syncretistic operators such as the Temple of Duality self-consciously draw on whatever spiritual resource, religious belief, or ritual practice they believe serves the needs of their particular brand of "Sheilaism."[8] If, for example, one of them comes across something which is deemed religiously valuable—whether from the *Tao te Ching*, the *Tibetan Book of the Dead*, or a *60 Minutes* report on New Age appropriation of Native American medicine wheels—within a few minutes the relevant pages on their Web site can be modified to incorporate this new insight into the evolving religious vision. No hard-copy books of doctrine need be updated; no denominational hierarchy need be consulted to approve the changes; no membership need be contacted and informed that the vision has changed. Thus, given the ease with which Internet content can be modified, religious innovation in virtual reality will be more fluid than such innovation could ever hope to be in real life.

Finally, the ephemeral metatechnology of the Internet presents a low-risk environment for religious innovation. If, for whatever reason, religious innovators no longer wish to market their religious wares online, their Web sites can be quickly decommissioned, with only the faintest of virtual footprints to testify to the fact that they existed at all. This was one of the strategies employed by some conservative Christians in the wake of the "failed failure" that was the Y2K crisis. Rather than admit that they had predicted an eschatological disaster that did not occur, they simply took their various Y2K links and Web sites offline and carried on as if nothing had happened (cf. Cowan forthcoming a). Similarly, if the costs of online religious innovation become greater than the benefits operators believe they receive, then these innovations will disappear. Thus, as a correlate of the online flexibility of new religious movements, while the aggregate number of online religious innovations may increase over time, significant individual fluctuations will occur within that aggregate. That is, as new e-space innovations emerge and decay, different Web sites will appear and regularly reconstitute the aggregate of virtual religion.

RITUAL PARTICIPATION IN CYBERSPACE:
ONLINE WICCAN RITUALS

Here is a snippet of online conversation that took place following a "Purification/ Protection Ritual" organized and orchestrated in cyberspace:

> MystikRose: *great job everyone . . . I could really feel and hear all of you . . .*
> Sinovess: I'm so glad . . . ok . . . feel teary . . . I'm so happy to have that experience with you ALL!
> ICPButterfly: I agree Wulf

Willow~Song: Mystik, I know!
celticwitan: Awesome job sin . . . you guys
Willow~Song: oh gosh Sin, now I'm teary
Sinovess: Everyone did an AMAZING job! EXCELLENT!

The ritual was organized by "Sinovess," the "High Priestess of Wicca East" and operator of the Online Wiccan Rituals Web site (http://go.to/OnlineWiccan Rituals). Following on-screen rubrics that described the various actions partici-pants were to take at different points in the ritual, Sinovess in North Carolina and co-presiders MystikRose (Indiana), Willow~Song, and ICPButterfly (Ari-zona) joined with three others Neopagans for the brief online ceremony. Each was asked to have some basic ritual items at hand—e.g., candles and incense—and was expected to follow along as the text of the ritual appeared on the screen. Because no one was in physical proximity to any other participant, they were guided to "imagine you are holding hands with the person next to you," and to repeat or respond to the various liturgical elements as they appeared. Just as it is in localized Neopagan rituals, the circle was cast, energy visualized and power raised, and a number of (in this case) Goddesses invoked. After a few minutes, the circle was opened, and Sinovess asked, "Is everyone back?"

Of greater interest than the ritual itself, which was by no means elaborate, is the exuberant online deconstruction that followed and the glimpse it gives us into the interpretation of this experience by the participants. "I was able to visualize every aspect," said "Celtica." "I could really feel and hear all of you," added MystikRose. "I could feel the energy as well," wrote Willow~Song, one of the co-presiders, "and got the distinct feeling I've been in circle with some of you before . . . long ago." While the others seemed content merely to chat about the event, Willow~Song, a 26-year-old woman also from Indiana, sought to connect the experience to deeper streams of Neopagan belief, such as shared past lives and common visions of ritual performance. "I have an odd question," she continued, "but when you guys were imagining us in a circle did anyone see stones around them?" "YES!!!!!!!!" replied Sinovess, adding as two others agreed, "STONES!!!!!! Like Stonehenge!" Gradually, other participants augmented this emerging, shared vision, adding trees, a "great big gigantic moon," and warmer temperatures. (The ritual took place January 16, 2002.)

Though critics might contest the authenticity of a ritual like this, experienced across thousands of miles, mediated through a metatechnology such as the Inter-net, and occurring principally in the imaginations of the participants, for these Neopagans, at least, "cyber-henge" seems a very hospitable environment and the experience no less real for its essential virtuality. We would like to suggest two reasons for this: the imaginative nature of Neopagan ritual itself, and the dram-aturgical character of the e-space environment.

First, since many Neopagans—particularly Wiccans who have been influenced by the teachings of writers such as Starhawk (1989) and Scott Cunningham

(1988)—regard the essence of ritual as the alteration of consciousness through the processes of imagination and visualization, physical proximity is arguably less important there than in a number of other religious traditions. Rather, it is the ability to *envision* the various aspects of the ritual that is central to its success. The "act of seeing with the mind, not the eye" is the foundational ritual technique in modern Wicca (Cunningham 1988: 82; cf. Collins 1996; Danet 1998; Davis 1995; Donath 1999; Grieve 1995; Ito 1997; McRae 1997). As such, since intention and practice are the key elements in successful visualization, there is no a priori reason to assume that it would not function as well at a shared distance as in a shared room—especially in the context of a supportive, online community such as the one gathered by Sinovess. Though only seven members participated in this particular event, further online rituals are planned to coincide with the regular festivals of the Neopagan year, and Sinovess hopes more Web site members will participate.

Second, since there is an explicitly theatrical element to ritual performance in general—especially ritual that involves the level of imagination demanded by online Neopaganism—dramaturgy (Goffman 1959, 1974) offers a useful analytic window into the experience. The two central concepts of the dramaturgical analogy are that, in everyday life, social actors play a variety of roles and stage manage their personal presentations in order to effect what Goffmann termed "impression management." More than 150 Neopagans have registered on Sinovess's site, nearly two-thirds of whom have posted a wide range of personal data, much of which contributes to the dramaturgical character of their participation.[9] An ideal environment for this kind of dramaturgy, the Internet offers a virtual stage on which actors can play any character or any number of characters. Switching roles is as easy as signing in to a chatroom with a new username and online profile.

In the context of this ritual, the organizing roles were those of a high priestess and her coven, the virtual stage set, as it were, according to the shared conceptions of North American Neopagans practicing in the Wiccan tradition. Online names— the endlessly mutable markers of identity in e-space—are all thoroughly Neopagan and serve not only to identify individual participants to each other, but also to describe what each regards as important aspects of their personality, spiritual practice, or attributes brought to the cyber-circle. "Wulfslaird," for example, is a 49-year-old rescue diver from Montana. A carving of a family of wolves forms the centerpiece of his personal altar. "Celtica" is a 51-year-old "Celtic Pagan" from Rhode Island. When the other children with whom she grew up wanted to be superheroes, she writes, "I wanted to be Merlin!" In many ways, the dramaturgical environment created through the confluence of the Internet and a supportive community of fellow travelers allows for the virtual fulfillment of that wish. It is important to recognize that this was a shared stage; though separated by thousands of miles, none of the participants understood themselves to be acting as Wiccan solitaries. If we give credence to their accounts of the event, their online ritual circle was no less real for the fact that it was envisioned imagistically and facilitated metatechnologically.

LINEAGE, LICENSE, AND THE PROBLEM OF AUTHORITY: THE HERMETIC ORDER OF THE GOLDEN DAWN

Finally, as we observed in the case of Scientology, the ability to create, upload, modify, and decommission one's own particular religious vision does present certain problems of lineage, license, and authority. In this section, we would like to examine this issue as exemplified in three online variants of the Hermetic Order of the Golden Dawn (HOGD). Grounded in the Western Hermetic Tradition and founded in the late nineteenth century by William Wynn Westcott, William Robert Woodman, and Samuel Liddell "MacGregor" Mathers, the HOGD was a system of ritual magic whose various lodges included, among other members, occultist Aleister Crowley, writer Arthur Edward Waite, and poets and Irish revolutionaries William Butler Yeats and Maude Gonne (cf. Gilbert 1997; Greer 1995; Howe 1972). In the early decades of the twentieth century, a variety of internecine conflicts resulted in the splintering of the HOGD and the emergence of a number of offshoots, including Crowley's Ordo Templi Orientis, Waite's Fellowship of the Rosy Cross, and the Stella Matutina (Morning Star) under Robert William Felkin. Though most of these were defunct by the time of the Second World War, as Gilbert notes (1997: 4), "the dead rituals live again," propagated by "a multitude of self-styled adepts," "warring bands of magicians who variously claim to be the heirs of the Golden Dawn." And it seems that e-space is one of the main battlegrounds in this war.

Claiming to be the "the official web site of the Hermetic Order of the Golden Dawn, the Ordo Rosae Rubeae et Aureae Crucis, R. R. et A. C., and the Rosicrucian Order of Alpha et Omega," the Authentic Hermetic Order of the Golden Dawn (www.golden-dawn.com) laments the fragmented nature of the HOGD tradition but seeks to reunite "the various initiatic strands of the fraternity and its egregore." Online conversation among adherents, adepts, and interested observers, however, reveals that its own claims to lineal authenticity do not go unchallenged. Among its particular appeals to that authenticity is the gift of the "personal magical accoutrements" of Israel Regardie, the controversial occultist who published the entire system of Golden Dawn teachings in the late 1930s. Apparently, these items were donated to the group by Regardie's former student and editor, Cris Monnastre. From the perspective of conflict over lineage and authenticity, however, the most important page on the Web site is entitled, simply, "Warning."

> Beware of organisations which do not perform initiations while candidates are physically present in legitimate Temples. "Initiation by Proxy," "Astral Initiation," and "Self-Initiation" are extremely dubious as well as potentially dangerous practices. While not explicitly claiming legitimacy, certain groups engaging in the aforementioned dubious initiatic practices have also been creating the misleading impression over the Internet that they possess initiatic or chartered affiliation through the Rosicrucian Order of Alpha et Omega. Let the public be aware that legitimate Temples of genuine lineal affiliations everywhere, including those of the Rosicrucian Order of Alpha et Omega, condemn the practices of "initiation by proxy" or of exclusively "astral initiation" as being ineffective, if not even fraudulent.

While it does not contain a similar warning, the Hermetic Order of the Golden Dawn (www.hermeticgoldendawn.org) concurs with the concerns around online recruitment, and declares unequivocally that their Web site is for information only. "This web page is not intended to be a vehicle for the recruitment of those individuals who are seeking initiation in a Golden Dawn temple," they write, "but rather as a resource for all students and practitioners of the Western Esoteric Tradition." Visitors who are sufficiently interested to pursue the matter further must make personal contact with the organization to request information.

Not so the Hermetic Order of the Morning Star International (www.golden-dawn.org), which appears to be the principal HOGD competitor with which both other groups are concerned. "A worldwide fraternity dedicated to preparing sincere people for true Adepthood," the Morning Star International too claims to be the "Foremost Guardians of the Golden Dawn System." Unlike the other two organizations, though, it does offer "astral initiation"—a ceremony at which the initiate is not present physically, but in which he or she participates through visualization—and extensive online membership information. A lengthy article describes the benefits of "astral initiation" and assures the prospective adherent of its efficacy. To access membership information over the Internet, visitors are first required to fill out a personal information form; without this, the site will not allow the membership pages to be viewed. Once submitted, however, the online membership material becomes available, all of which is organized to encourage visitors to purchase Morning Star International's correspondence lessons in ceremonial "magick."

For any organization that seeks to exercise centralized control over religious initiation, practice, or doctrine, the Internet presents two main problems for religious lineage and authority. First, unless the group is willing to litigate these issues in the manner of Scientology, in practical terms there is very little that they can do to stop the propagation and/or alteration of religious teachings. Given the fluid nature of the e-space environment and the ease with which material can be uploaded, changed, or deleted, navigating endlessly shifting cyber-currents in search of information offenders could easily drain the resources of new religious movements already operating under tenuous financial circumstances. As well, as in the case of these various contenders for the virtual HOGD throne, presumably any such litigation would be predicated on the demonstration of a legitimate claim to lineal authority in real life. Second, there is the possibility that religious teachings will degrade through Internet duplication, a decaying spiral of pedagogical reliability, as it were. Like a photocopy whose image deteriorates with repeated copying, information that is merely captured off one Web site, modified according to the inclinations and understanding of the new Web site operator, and then uploaded again risks an increasingly attenuated pedigree.

Concluding Remarks

In conclusion, we return to some of the questions with which we began. For many, perhaps even most religious traditions, the Internet will continue mainly to provide a venue for *religion online;* while some practitioners may find their way to *online religion*, real life will remain the environment in which liturgy, worship, prayer, and meditation take place. In terms of established religious traditions, institutional structure, the wide sweep of tradition, and the availability of the Internet only to a very small percentage of the global population all mitigate against any serious competition from the virtual world to religion in the real world.

In terms of religions whose traditional roots are more fluid, whether by historical accident or evolutionary design, cyberspace does present interesting opportunities for online religion—especially those new religious movements, like Neopaganism, whose ritual space is imaginatively constructed. If we are to credence the accounts above, and there appears little a priori reason not to, for some practitioners online ritual or liturgy is at least as powerful as that experienced in real life. Because the element of virtuality allows for a more developed sense of dramaturgy, it is perhaps even more powerful; the realities of life outside e-space need not intrude on the virtualities within. If, as Erik Davis (1995) asserts, "humanity has always lived within imaginative interfaces," then for an hour or so, metatechnologically, a 51-year-old woman from Rhode Island really can become "Merlin."

NOTES

1. Because "cyberspace" is not the real world of hardware and wiring, nor the command-and-control of software and programming, nor the communications that take place between Internet users, but something that exists in the interface and the liminal spaces between all three, we are suggesting the term "metatechnology" to describe this social reality. "Metatechnology" highlights the fact that the hardware, software, and Internet service provision are, perhaps, the least remarkable characteristics of the various developing e-space cultures. That these cultures require the existence of Internet technologies is not in dispute; they far exceed, however, the now commonplace electronics that make cyberspace possible. Also, while we recognize that there are subtle technical distinctions between the "Internet" (the Net) and the "World Wide Web" (the Web), for our purposes we will use them interchangeably.

2. The Pontifical Council for Social Communications has declared that "although the virtual reality of cyberspace cannot substitute for real interpersonal community, the incarnational reality of the sacraments and the liturgy, or the immediate and direct proclamation of the gospel, it can complement them, attract people to a fuller experience of the life of faith, and enrich the religious lives of users" (Foley 2002; cf. O'Leary 1996).

3. Scientological teachings are both exoteric and esoteric. Publicly available auditing procedures and personal use of the Dianetics material can bring one to the state of "clear," a point at which the "reactive mind" has been eliminated, and the individual is free from the constraints of automatic stimulus-response behavior. Beyond this, however, progression through the eight stages of "Operating Thetan" are esoteric teachings unavailable to the public at large (cf. Peckham 1998).

4. To put it broadly, the secular anticult operates from within the conceptual framework of the brainwashing hypothesis and seeks to effect the *extraction* of members from religious groups it considers dangerous or problematic. The Christian countercult, on the other hand, regards new religious movements as inherently problematic because of their rejection of evangelical Christian doctrine and operates to buttress belief in the superiority of the Christian worldview and, when possible, effect the migration of other religionists to evangelical Christianity (cf. Cowan 2003).

5. A review of available board of director records reveals that the Church of All Worlds, one of the oldest incorporated Neopagan churches in the U.S. and certainly one of the best-known, never operated at more than a subsistence level.

6. Miller (1995: 432) contends that the ULC was founded by Kirby Hansen in 1962, not 1959; cf. Ashmore 1977. Online information makes clear, however, that the Universal Life Church (www.ulc.org) is not to be confused with the Progressive Universal Life Church (www.pulc.com), which offers a similar range of products and services, but from which the ULC "dissolved . . . any and all ties" many years ago.

7. Not everyone takes the ULC ordination as seriously as these. One ordinand, at least, used his ULC credentials to form "The Church of the Profit$," whose main "tenet is Truth"—"You give me money and I keep it."

8. In *Habits of the Heart*, Bellah et al. (1985) coined the term "Sheilaism" to describe the religious hyperindividualism of one of their interviewees.

9. Of the 102 member profiles online at the time of writing, 78 were identified as female, 13 male, and 11 unknown. At OnlineWiccanRituals, the reported male average age was 40, though the reported time practicing Neopaganism varied from 33 years to 1 month. The female average age was 31, ranging from 13 (Virginia) to 62 (Texas); the average length of time in Neopagan practice was 7.5 years. While most member profiles who specified a location were drawn from the United States (75), participants were also reported from Australia (2), Canada (14), England (5), France (1), Italy (1), Puerto Rico (2), and Scotland (1).

REFERENCES

Ashmore, Lewis. 1977. *The Modesto Messiah: The Famous Mail-Order Minister*. Bakersfield, Calif.: Universal Press.

Bainbridge, William Sims. 1997. *The Sociology of Religious Movements*. New York: Routledge.

Baudrillard, Jean. 1983. *Simulations*. New York: Semiotext[e].

Bellah, Robert N. et al. 1985. *Habits of the Heart: Individualism and Commitment in American Life*. Berkeley and Los Angeles: University of California Press.

Benkler, Yochai. 1999. "Free as the Air to Common Use: First Amendment Constraints on Enclosure of the Public Domain." *New York University Law Review* 74: 354–446.

Brasher, Brenda. 2001. *Give Me That Online Religion*. San Francisco: Jossey-Bass.

Brooke, Tal. 1997. *Virtual Gods: The Seduction of Power and Pleasure in Cyberspace*. Eugene: Harvest House.

Bunt, Gary. 2000a. "Surfing Islam: Ayatollahs, Shayks and Hajjis on the Superhighway." In *Religion on the Internet: Research Prospects and Promises*, ed. Jeffrey K. Hadden and Douglas E. Cowan, 127–151. London: JAI/Elsevier Science.

———. 2000b. *Virtually Islamic: Computer-Mediated Communication and Cyber Islamic Environments*. Cardiff: University of Wales Press.

Careaga, Andrew. 1999. *E-vangelism: Sharing the Gospel in Cyberspace*. Lafayette, La.: Vital Issues Press.

Careaga, Andrew, and Leonard Sweet. 2001. *eMinistry: Connecting with the Net Generation*. Grand Rapids, Mich.: Kregel.

Chryssides, George D. 1996. "New Religions and the Internet." *Diskus: Web Edition* 4 (2); retrieved online from www.uni-marburg.de//religionswissenschaft/journal/diskus.

Cobb, Jennifer J. 1998. *Cybergrace: The Search for God in the Digital World*. New York: Crown.

Collins, Harry M. 1996. "Interaction without Society? What Avatars Can't Do." In *Internet Dreams: Archetypes, Myths, and Metaphors*, ed. Mark Stefik, 317–326. Cambridge: MIT Press.

Cowan, Douglas E. Forthcoming. "Confronting the Failed Failure: Y2K and Christian Eschatology in Light of the Passed Millennium."

———. 2000. "Religion, Rhetoric, and Scholarship: Managing Vested Interest in E-Space." In *Religion on the Internet: Research Prospects and Promises*, ed. Jeffrey K. Hadden and Douglas E. Cowan, 101–124. London: JAI/Elsevier Science.

————. 2001. "From Parchment to Pixels: The Christian Countercult on the Internet." Paper presented at the 2001 International Conference of CESNUR; retrieved online from www.cesnur.org/2001/london2001/cowan.htm.

————. 2002. "Exits and Migrations: Foregrounding the Christian Countercult." *Journal of Contemporary Religion.*

————. 2003. *Bearing False Witness? An Introduction to the Christian Countercult.* Westport, Conn.: Praeger.

Cunningham, Scott. 1988. *Wicca: A Guide for the Solitary Practitioner.* St. Paul: Llewellyn.

Danet, Brenda. 1998. "Text as Mask: Gender, Play, and Performance on the Internet." In *Cybersociety 2.0: Revisiting Computer-Mediated Communication and Community,* ed. Steven G. Jones, 129–158. Thousand Oaks, Calif.: Sage.

Davis, Erik. 1999. *Techgnosis: Myth, Magic, and Mysticism in the Age of Religion.* New York: Three Rivers Press.

Dawson, Lorne L. 2001a. "Cyberspace and Religious Life: Conceptualizing the Concerns and Consequences." Paper presented at the 2001 International Conference of CESNUR; retrieved from www.cesnur.org/2001/london2001/dawson.htm.

————. 2001b. "New Religions in Cyberspace: The Promise and the Perils of a New Public Space." *Council of Societies for the Study of Religion Bulletin* 30 (1): 3–9.

Dawson, Lorne L., and Jennifer Hennebry. 1999. "New Religions and the Internet: Recruiting in a New Public Space." *Journal of Contemporary Religion* 14 (1): 17–39.

Dibbell, Julian. 1996. "A Rape in Cyberspace: How an Evil Clown, a Haitian Trickster Spirit, Two Wizards, and a Cast of Dozens Turned a Database into a Society." In *Internet Dreams: Archetypes, Myths, and Metaphors,* ed. Mark Stefik, 293–315. Cambridge: MIT Press.

Donath, Judith S. 1999. "Identity and Deception in the Virtual Community." In *Communities in Cyberspace,* ed. Marc A. Smith and Peter Kollock, 29–59. New York: Routledge.

Elliott, Stuart. 2000. "The Media Business: Advertising." *New York Times,* February 29: C11.

Finke, Roger, Jennifer McKinney, and Matt Bahr. 2000. "Doing Research and Teaching with the American Religion Data Archive: Initial Efforts to Democratize Access to Data." In *Religion on the Internet: Research Prospects and Promises,* ed. Jeffrey K. Hadden and Douglas E. Cowan, 81–99. London: JAI/Elsevier Science.

Fisher, Jeffrey. 1997. "The Postmodern Paradiso: Dante, Cyberpunk, and the Technosophy of Cyberspace." In *Internet Culture,* ed. David Porter, 111–128. New York: Routledge.

Foley, John P. 2002. "The Church and the Internet." Pontifical Council for Social Communications; retrieved online from www.vatican.va/roman_curia/pontifical_councils/pccs.

Gilbert, R. A. 1997. *The Golden Dawn Scrapbook: The Rise and Fall of a Magical Order.* York Beach, Me.: Samuel Weiser.

Goffmann, Erving. 1959. *The Presentation of Self in Everyday Life.* Garden City: Doubleday.

————. 1974. *Frame Analysis: An Essay on the Organization of Experience.* Boston: Northeastern University Press.

Gold, Lauramaery. 1997. *Mormons on the Internet: Onine Resources for Latter-Day Saints.* Rocklin, Calif.: Prima.

Goldman, Ari L. 2000. "Figuring Our Whether E-Mammon Can Fit in the Temple." *New York Times,* June 7: H10.

Green, Dave. 2001. "Technoshamanism: Cyber-Sorcery and Schizophrenia." Paper presented at the 2001 International Conference of CESNUR; retrieved online from www.cesnur.org/2001/london2001/green.htm.

Greer, Mary K. 1995. *Women of the Golden Dawn: Rebels and Priestesses.* Rochester, Vt.: Park Street Press.

Grieve, Gregory Price. 1995. "Imagining a Virtual Religious Community: Neo-Pagans and the Internet." *Chicago Anthropology Exchange* 21: 87–118.

Groothuis, Douglas. 1997. *The Soul in Cyberspace.* Grand Rapids, Mich.: Baker Books.

Grossman, Wendy M. 1995. "alt.scientology.war." *Wired* 3 (12); retrieved online from www.wired.com/wired/archive/3.12/alt.scientology.war_pr.html.

Hadden, Jeffrey K. 1989. "Desacralizing Secularization Theory." In *Secularization and Fundamentalism Reconsidered,* ed. Jeffrey K. Hadden and Anson Shupe, 3–26. New York: Paragon House.

———. 2000. "Confessions of a Recovering Technophobe: A Brief History of the Religious Movements Homepage Project." In *Religion on the Internet: Research Prospects and Promises,* ed. Jeffrey K. Hadden and Douglas E. Cowan, 345–362. London: JAI/Elsevier Science.

Hadden, Jeffrey K., and Douglas E. Cowan. 2000a. "The Promised Land or Electronic Chaos? Toward Understanding Religion on the Internet." In *Religion on the Internet: Research Prospects and Promises,* ed. Jeffrey K. Hadden and Douglas E. Cowan, 3–21. London: JAI/Elsevier Science.

Hadden, Jeffrey K., and Douglas E. Cowan, eds. 2000b. *Religion on the Internet: Research Prospects and Promises.* Religion and the Social Order Vol. 8. London: JAI/Elsevier Science.

Hammerman, Joshua. 2000. *Thelordismyshepherd.Com: Seeking God in Cyberspace.* Deerfield Beach, Fla.: Simcha Press.

Helland, Chrisopher. 2000. "Online-Religion/Religion-Online and Virtual Communitas." In *Religion on the Internet: Research Prospects and Promises,* ed. Jeffrey K. Hadden and Douglas E. Cowan, 205–224. London: JAI/Elsevier Science.

Howe, Ellic. 1972. *The Magicians of the Golden Dawn: A Documentary History of a Magical Order, 1887–1923.* New York: Samuel Weiser.

Introvigne, Massimo. 2000. " 'So Many Evil Things': Anti-Cult Terrorism via the Internet." In *Religion on the Internet: Research Prospects and Promises,* ed. Jeffrey K. Hadden and Douglas E.Cowan, 277–306. London: JAI/Elsevier Science.

Ito, Mizuko. 1997. "Virtually Embodied: The Reality of Fantasy in a Multi-User Dungeon." In *Internet Culture,* ed. David Porter, 87–110. New York: Routledge.

Kellner, Mark A. 1996. *God on the Internet.* Foster City, Calif.: IDG Books.

Kelly, David. 1999a. "Digital Dharma." *The Middle Way: Journal of the Buddhist Society* 74 (1): 57–59.

———. 1999b. "Finding the Path on the Internet." *The Middle Way: Journal of the Buddhist Society* 74 (3): 185–87.

Knapp, James A. 1997. "Essayistic Messages: Internet Newsgroups as an Electronic Public Sphere." In *Internet Culture,* ed. David Porter, 181–197. New York: Routledge.

Koenig, P. R. 2001. "The Internet as Illustrating the McDonaldisation of Occult Culture." Paper presented at the 2001 International Conference of CESNUR; retrieved online from www.cesnur.org/2001/london2001/koenig.htm.

Lawrence, Bruce B. 2000. *The Complete Idiot's Guide to Religions Online.* Indianapolis: Alpha Books.

Levy, Steven. 1997. "Blaming the Web." *Newsweek,* April 7: 46.

Lippard, Jim, and Jeff Jacobsen. 1995. "Scientology v. the Internet: Free Speech and Copyright Infringement on the Information Super-Highway." *Skeptic* 3 (3): 35–41.

Lucas, Doug. 1998. "The Internet: Tentmaker's Coffeeshop for the Nineties." *International Journal of Frontier Missions* 15 (1): 29–31, 46.

Lyons, Theresa A. 2000. "Scientology or Censorship: You Decide: An Examination of the Church of Scientology, Its Recent Battles with Individual Internet Users and Service Providers, the Digital Millennium Copyright Act, and the Implications for Free Speech on the Web." *Rutgers Journal of Law and Religion* 2 (1); retrieved online from www-camlaw.rutgers.edu/publications/law-religion.

Makkuni, Ranjit. 1996. "Excerpt from 'The Electronic Capture and Dissemination of the Cultural Practice of Tibetan Thangka Painting.'" In *Internet Dreams: Archetypes, Myths, and Metaphors,* ed. Mark Stefik, 95–107. Cambridge: MIT Press.

Markoff, John. 1997. "Death in a Cult: The Technology." *New York Times,* March 28: A20.

Mayer, Jean-François. 2000a. "Les Nouveaux Mouvements Religieux a l'Heure d'Internet." *Cahiers de Littâerature Orale.* 47: 127–46.

———. 2000b. "Religious Movements and the Internet: The New Frontier of Cult Controversies." In *Religion on the Internet: Research Prospects and Promises,* ed. Jeffrey K. Hadden and Douglas E. Cowan, 249–276. London: JAI/Elsevier Science.

McRae, Shannon. 1997. "Flesh Made Word: Sex, Text and the Virtual Body." In *Internet Culture,* ed. David Porter, 73–86. New York: Routledge.

Miller, Timothy, ed. 1995. *America's Alternative Religions.* Albany: SUNY Press.

Moreau, A. Scott, and Mike O'Rear. 2000. "Doing Evangelism on the Internet." *Evangelical Missions Quarterly* 36 (2): 218–22.

O'Brien, Jodi. 1999. "Writing in the Body: Gender (Re)Production in Online Interaction." In *Communities in Cyberspace,* ed. Marc A. Smith and Peter Kollock, 76–104. New York: Routledge.

O'Leary, Stephen D. 1996. "Cyberspace as Sacred Space: Communicating Religion on Computer Networks." *Journal of the American Academy of Religion* 64 (4): 781–808.

———. 2002. "Religion in the Digital Age." *Online Journalism Review;* retrieved online from www.ojr.org/ojr/bunsiness/p1017965672.php.

Peckham, Michael. 1998. "New Dimensions of Social Movement/Countermovement Interaction: The Case of Scientology and Its Internet Critics." *Canadian Journal of Sociology/Cahiers Canadiens de Sociologie* 23 (4): 317–347.

Robinson, Bruce A. 2000. "Evolution of a Religious Web Site Devoted to Tolerance." In *Religion on the Internet: Research Prospects and Promises,* ed. Jeffrey K. Hadden and Douglas E. Cowan, 309–323. London: JAI/Elsevier Science.

Robinson, Wendy Gale. 1997. "Heaven's Gate: The End?" *Journal of Computer-Mediated Communication* 3 (3); retrieved online from http://jcmc.huji.ac.il/vol3/issue3/robinson.html.

Schroeder, Ralph, Noel Heather, and Raymond M. Lee. 1998. "The Sacred and the Virtual: Religion in Multi-User Virtual Reality." *Journal of Computer-Mediated Communication* 4 (2); retrieved online from http://jcmc.huji.ac.il/vol4/issue2/schroeder. html.

Starhawk. 1989. *The Spiral Dance: A Rebirth of the Ancient Religion of the Great Goddess.* 10th ann. ed. New York: Harper and Row.

Stark, Rodney. 1999. "Secularization, R.I.P." *Sociology of Religion* 60 (3): 249–273.

Stark, Rodney, and William Sims Bainbridge. 1985. *The Future of Religion: Secularization, Revival, and Cult Formation.* Berkeley and Los Angeles: University of California Press.

———. 1987. *A Theory of Religion.* New York: Routledge.

Tepper, Michele. 1997. "Usenet Communities and the Cultural Politics of Information." In *Internet Culture,* ed. David Porter, 23–38. New York: Routledge.

Urban, Hugh B. 2000. "The Devil at Heaven's Gate: Rethinking the Study of Religion in the Age of Cyber-Space." *Nova Religio* 3 (2): 269–302.

Wilson, Walter P. 2000. *The Internet Church.* Nashville: Word.

Zaleski, Jeff. 1997. *The Soul of Cyberspace: How New Technology Is Changing Our Spiritual Lives.* New York: HarperEdge.

PART II

SOCIAL CONFLICT

CHAPTER 6

VIOLENCE AND NEW RELIGIOUS MOVEMENTS

DAVID G. BROMLEY

As the study of new religious movements (NRMs) has developed as an area of specialization in the sociology of religion, a number of issues have been central foci of theory and research. These issues include the sociocultural conditions that generate new movements, the related processes of affiliation with and disaffiliation from movements, distinguishing characteristics of different types of new movements, the structure and dynamics of movement organization, movement success and failure, and societal responses to new movements. Over the last decade a new issue has been added to that agenda—the relationship between violence and NRMs. Violence logically connects to all of these prior issues in some way and is an issue of significance in its own right. However, it is also clear that scholars' disciplinary interests in understanding the patterning of violence has been influenced by events inside and outside of NRMs—radicalism and destabilization within some movements and governmental reaction to allegations of impending movement violence or in actual violent episodes.

Violence therefore is a topic of study in which scholarly and public policy issues intersect, given its importance as a social form and its potency as a label. There have been relatively few cases of collective violence of the kind we are examining. Prior to the 1990s only the Manson Family murders in 1969 and the Peoples Temple murder-suicides at Jonestown in 1978 would qualify as benchmark cases during the last half of the twentieth century. In this chapter I shall review research and theory on the four episodes of violence during the 1990s: the Branch

Davidians (Bromley and Silver 1995; Hall, Schuyler, and Trinh 2000; Wright 1995); Solar Temple (Hall and Schuyler 1997; Introvigne 1999; Mayer 1999); Aum Shin-rikyō (Lifton 1999; Reader 2000); and Heaven's Gate (Balch 1982, 1995; Balch and Taylor 2002).

The Branch Davidian community, which had been located just outside of Waco, Texas, for several decades, became involved in a gradually escalating confrontation with the state child welfare agency as well as federal law enforcement agencies during the early 1990s. On February 28, 1993, the U.S. Bureau of Alcohol, Tobacco, and Firearms (BATF) launched an armed raid on the Davidians' Mount Carmel compound. In the ensuing battle 4 federal agents and 5 Davidians were killed. A standoff then ensued until April 19 when a armed assault by FBI agents led to a conflagration that destroyed the compound buildings, causing the death of 74 Branch Davidians. The following year the Solar Temple was involved in a succession of murder-suicides. As the movement destabilized and became embroiled in legal difficulties, leaders determined that a "transit" to another planet was necessary. Beginning the first week in October 1994 there was a succession of episodes in Switzerland and Canada in which 52 Templars committed suicide or were murdered. In 1995 another 16 Templars were murdered or committed suicide in France. Finally, 5 Templars committed suicide in 1997 in Canada, apparently in an attempt to join their fellow members on the cosmic journey. The Japanese Aum Shinrikyō movement gradually moved in a more radical direction internally through the 1980s and by the early 1990s had begun murdering insiders believed to be disloyal and outsiders who might expose its crimes. An inner circle also began manufacturing nerve gas. The ultimate result was a nerve gas attack on subways in Tokyo on March 20, 1995. The attack killed 5 people and injured over 5,000. Finally, the 39 members of a small and reclusive UFO group, Heaven's Gate, engaged in a collective exit from earth beginning on March 22, 1997. The group had maintained an isolated existence since the early 1970s and gradually had become more detached from earthly existence. The group took the appearance of the Hale-Bopp comet as a sign that the moment had arrived for a collective exit that would take them to the life at the "Next Level" on another planet. In this chapter I shall place violence involving these four NRMs in historical and contemporary perspective, summarize current theorizing about the NRM-violence relationship, and connect current research findings to theoretical and public policy issues.

Definitions of the key terms, "new religious movements," "prophetic movements," and "violence" will be helpful in orienting this discussion. The term "new religious movements" identifies an important but difficult to demarcate set of religious entities, and there is not a uniform pattern of usage of the concept. Most often the term is used to designate groups that have appeared in Western societies since the mid-1960s, are nontraditional and nonimmigrant religious groups, have first-generation converts as their primary membership base, have attracted among

their converts higher-status young adults, have manifested social movement characteristics, have presented an anomalous profile with respect to traditional religious organization, and have proclaimed themselves to be engaged in spiritual
activity.

Our focus is on those NRMs that are prophetic in nature. The set of characteristics demarcating prophetic movements may be summarized for present purposes as denoting those movements that pose a fundamental challenge to the
established social order and hence are in high tension with it (Bromley 1997).
Prophetic movements may or may not be religious in nature, but religious movements constitute particularly important cases. These groups not only mount radical resistance to the dominant social order, they also sacralize that resistance. The
challenge these movements pose is therefore fundamental in nature as they
threaten the logic and organizational forms through which the dominant social
order is maintained. Since the prophetic movement-society tension level is high,
there is an increased, although not deterministic, potential for violence.

With respect to violence, we are concerned here with collective, relational acts
that are designed to or in fact do cause multiple deaths. To assert that violence
is relational means that it may be initiated or sustained by either movements or
control agencies and is rarely attributable to a single party. To focus on violence
that is collective in nature eliminates acts undertaken for personal motives. This
means that even if violent acts are committed by individuals, they are relevant
here only if undertaken in the name of the movement or control agent and the
violence is legitimated in terms of some organizational purpose. Collective violence may be internally or externally directed, and, in either event, it may or may
not reflect group consensus.

Violence and New Religions in Perspective

Given the radical stance of prophetic NRMs, it is not surprising that according
to conventional wisdom these groups are dangerously unstable and prone to be
involved in episodes of violence. However, this perspective typically is based on
questionable assumptions. It is important to challenge these assumptions since
they impede the identification of social factors that actually are significant in the
outbreak of violence.

One reason to be cautions about equating NRMs with the occurrence of
violence is that the number of movements has grown dramatically in recent de-

cades, creating the potential for more instances of movement-societal conflict. The long history and significance of nontraditional religious groups in the United States is well established (Moore 1986). Since most new groups survive, the overall number has continued to rise. The period beginning in 1965 was one of exceptional growth in NRMs; groups of Asian origin grew particularly rapidly as a result of a relaxation in immigration statutes. There are now at least two thousand religious groups in the United States, and more than half were founded after 1960 (Melton 1998). If the much larger number of movements that are quasi-religious in nature, such as New Age groups, is included, the total would be much larger (Melton, Lewis, and Kelly 1990; Greil and Robbins 1994). The few cases of violent episodes need to be interpreted in the context of the relatively large number and rapid growth of new movements.

A second problem is that it is unclear what constitutes a new movement or what it is about newness that may be problematic. In reality there are few truly new religions. Most movements labeled as "new" derive from or borrow major ideological and organizational elements from long-established religious traditions, as have the Hare Krishna from Bengali Hinduism, the Unification Church from Christianity, Aum Shinrikyō from Buddhism, and the Branch Davidians from Adventism. In short, the criteria for distinguishing newness are much more complex than can be conveyed through any simple dichotomy. The asserted connection between NRMs and violence rarely is based on a comparison between new and established religious traditions. Even a cursory examination of the extent of religiously inspired violence around the globe reveals the untenability of distinguishing new from old religions in terms of a connection to violence. For example, the most visible religious conflagrations around the globe currently include those between Protestants and Catholics in Northern Ireland, Israelis and Palestinians in the Middle East, and Muslims and Hindus in India. The duration, level, and societal implications of violence in each of these cases is qualitatively greater than any violence involving NRMs.

A third reason for skepticism about conventional wisdom is that the information on which the new religions-violence connection is based frequently has been unreliable former member accounts (Bromley 1998; Bromley, Shupe, and Ventimiglia 1979). For example, during the 1970s there were persistent but unsubstantiated reports with ominous undertones of "suicide training" in the Unification Church and allegations that The Way International and the International Society for Krishna Consciousness were arming themselves, presumptively for provocative action (Carroll and Bauer 1979). In recent years there has been a succession of news items in which religious groups were reported to be planning mass suicide. A highly publicized case involved the Chen Tao, a Taiwanese millennial group that was located in Garland, Texas, for a time and that has never exhibited violent proclivities (Szubin, Jensen, and Gregg 2000).

Finally, while a handful of cases in which movements have initiated violent incidents can be identified, the more likely scenario is that a new religion will be the target of violence or provocation. In most cases where movements have been the targets of violence they have responded by seeking reduction of tension or remedial action through the judicial system. For example, the Messianic Communities reacted to a predawn raid by dozens of armed state troopers during which all community children were taken into custody initially with redress through the courts and later with a program to reduce isolation and build bridges with the local community (Palmer 1999). Likewise, the response by The Family to dozens of raids by police and military personnel around the world on their homes and seizure of their children has been uniformly nonviolent and has resulted in legal exoneration in almost every case (Melton 1997). Finally, the growing tension between the Church Universal and Triumphant and federal authorities was defused when the church entered negotiations with authorities and ultimately reorganized the church.

In sum, the popular culture view that cultic groups are unstable and violence prone is based on stereotypical and faulty assumptions that have been disseminated through the media and by oppositional groups. Creating a category of putatively homogeneous groups that share a proclivity for violence is problematic on a number of counts. Precisely what distinguishes newer from older groups is not easily specified, and there is little evidence that new religions are more violence prone than their established counterparts, however those terms are defined. The number of violent episodes involving NRMs has been quite small, given the rapid growth in their numbers and their prophetic orientation. And the pattern of violent incidents reveals that NRMs have more often been the targets rather than the perpetrators of violence. It is important to challenge the simplistic logic underpinning the "dangerous and destructive cults" perspective in order to create the basis for more meaningful and sophisticated analysis.

THEORETICAL PERSPECTIVES

The recent series of episodes in which NRMs have become involved in collective violence has led to a theoretical project of identifying factors associated with violence episodes. This project has taken two directions. One is the analysis of single factors that have been widely thought to be related to violence, most notably charismatic leadership and millennial/apocalyptic organization. This part of the project is important because it has led to both a conceptual sharpening of those terms, which has improved their analytic utility, and a general concern about placing too much analytic weight on single factors. The other is general model building, in which a number of factors related to violence and interrelationships between them are specified. This component of the project leads toward building an integrated model that can be used to link apparently disparate cases as well as establishing the basis for analysis of future episodes.

LEADERSHIP AND ORGANIZATION

Groups with millennial/apocalyptic expectations have been proposed to be prone to violence due to their fiery rhetoric condemning the existing social order and separation from that order. Since many millennial groups regard themselves as the vanguard of the new order, there is a tendency to disregard the existing normative order. However, there does not appear to be any simple connection between millennialism and violence. Indeed, millennialism is an integral element of Western theologies and variants are found in a number of Christian traditions (Robbins 2002). One such strain of this thought, dispensationalism, is a key element of contemporary Christian fundamentalism, but fundamentalist groups have demonstrated no proclivity for violence. The nineteenth-century Millerite movement, which draws on this same tradition, provides another example. Following Miller's failed prophecies the movement splintered into numerous factions. Over a hundred churches, including the Seventh-day Adventists and the Jehovah's Witnesses, formed based on Miller's theology. The Adventists and Witnesses have maintained varying degrees of separation from conventional society, but they have manifested no tendency toward violence, although the Witnesses have been the targets of severe persecution and violence in many nations.

While millennialism as a general form may not be linked to violence, there have been several suggestions that specific types of millennialism may be so connected. Wessinger (1999a) has contrasted *progressive* and *catastrophic* millennialism. With progressive millennialism, transformation of the social order is gradual and humans play a role in fostering that transformation. Catastrophic millennialism deems the current social order as irrevocably corrupt, and total destruction of this order is necessary as the precursor to the building of a new, godly order. Conceiving of the world in dualistic terms, the damned and the elect, has a polarizing effect that heightens the level of hostility between movement and host social order. If the social order responds by initiating control mechanisms, then groups with catastrophic millennial ideologies may interpret such actions as the persecution that confirms their dire expectations. Robbins (2002) has pointed out the parallel between progressive and catastrophic millennialism and the traditional Christian notions of premillennialism and postmillennialism. He goes on to add the categories of pretribulationists and post-tribulationists, referring to whether the rapture of the faithful will occur before or after the time of tribulation. Robbins suggests that pretribulationists regard the moment of divine intervention as less imminent and are not as likely as post-tribulationists to be looking for signs of endtime persecution that they must endure. These specifications of elements of millennialism are helpful in moving toward a more theoretically useful concept. Even so, causally linking catastrophic millennialism with violence is problematic, however, as movements may evolve toward or away from a catastrophic position over time, particularly as tensions with the dominant social order intensify or diminish.

The other characteristics of NRMs typically linked to violence are type of organization and leadership, specifically totalistic organization and charismatic leadership. Many NRMs begin with a charismatic leader and small coterie of followers living communally (Stark 1991), and many established religious groups preserve both a measure of charismatic authority and sometimes what Kelley (1972) has termed "strong" (i.e., high-demand) organization. Therefore, it is problematic to assert a direct causal relationship between violence and either charismatic leadership or high-demand organization. Various characteristics of high-demand organizations are found throughout the social structure. Examples include therapy groups (London 1969), mental hospitals (Goffman 1961), prisons (Etzioni 1961), military training academies (Dornbush 1955), religious communities (Hillery 1969), and even corporations (Arnott 1999). Nonconventional organizations also exhibit high-demand qualities but not violent tendencies. The best-documented case is communes; the list of characteristics of successful communes closely parallels the attributes of high-demand organizations (Kanter 1972).

The relationship between charisma and deviance is likewise more complex than popularized depictions that highlight the outlandish and sometimes malevolent qualities of charismatic leaders and attribute all of a group's excesses to the leader. What is forgotten in these portrayals is the pervasiveness of limited charisma throughout the social structure. Many highly charismatic religious figures (Billy Graham, Oral Roberts, Martin Luther King) energize and mobilize their followers without resorting to violence. However, it is the more infamous figures, such as Jim Jones and Charles Manson, who tend to be evoked in critical treatments of NRMs. Further, while charismatic leaders typically play a decisive role in shaping religious movement organization and operation, there is considerable evidence that organizational lieutenants exert considerable influence in directing activity (Carter 1990; Maaga 1998).

If it is not simply the presence of charismatic authority that creates the potential for violence, then the question becomes what is it about charisma that may be problematic. Dawson provides a most insightful way of conceptualizing the issue as one of mismanagement of charismatic authority by both leader and followers. Mismanaging charismatic authority does not necessarily lead to violence, but it is likely to produce instability and volatility, which make extreme outcomes more likely. Following Weber (1964), Dawson notes that among the distinguishing features of charisma are a need for continual renewal and the absence of institutionalized constraints, which confronts charismatic leaders with a number of problems. As Dawson (2002: 86) puts it, "In dealing with these challenges, some leaders make choices that have the cumulative effect of fostering the social implosion of a group and hence violent behavior." Dawson delineates four specific problems.

Leaders must maintain their charismatic personas, which entails balancing the need for contact with members and recruits that replenishes charisma, with avoidance of an overexposure, which erodes the aura of mystery surrounding the leader. Many charismatic leaders choose to isolate themselves from adherents. This strategy means that leaders are likely to be surrounded by an inner circle of sycophants who do not provide meaningful feedback and that followers are unaware of and unable to respond to developments within leadership circles. Another problem is the degree of followers' identification with the leader. To the extent that there is a fusion of identities between leader and followers, attacks on the leader become attacks on the followers. Under these conditions there is particular hostility to apostates, and former members continue to harbor intense resentment against the group. When each side demonizes the other, conflict tactics on both sides may become increasingly more extreme. Charismatic leaders also confront tensions surrounding the routinization of their charisma. As groups grow, more bureaucratic forms of organization begin to take root, one of which is a rational-legal form of leadership. In confronting the challenge posed by the routinzation of charisma, leaders are likely to adopt a variety of strategies that destabilize the movement and leave followers more dependent on their personal authority. These strategies include abrupt changes in doctrines, escalating demands for sacrifice, creating crises that require intensified solidarity, eliminating dissent by followers, creating ever greater tests of follower loyalty, countering any potential rival leadership, and changing the location of the group to a more isolated location. Finally, charismatic leaders are constantly faced with the challenge of producing new successes to affirm their authority. One means used to renew or bolster authority is new prophetic utterances that may lead the group in a more radical direction.

Those scholars analyzing the relationship between high-demand organization, charismatic leadership, and violence generally both disavow single-factor theories and attempt to identify the conditions under which specific group characteristics become problematic. For example, Robbins (2002) has suggested that it is a combination of organizational and ideological factors that is most likely to produce movement volatility. Specifically, he suggests that totalistic organizations, in which adherents live communally with a charismatic leader in residence, engage in certain kinds of practices (such as adherents engaging in high-risk actions that move their commitment to very high levels) or are inhibited from communicating negative feedback to leaders (thereby undermining informed, balanced decision-making), may be more volatile.

GENERAL MODELS

There have been several attempts to frame general models of violent episodes involving NRMs. The cases that have received the most analytic attention include the Peoples Temple, Branch Davidians, Aum Shinrikyō, Solar Temple, and Heaven's Gate. All of the models include characteristics of the movement-society relationship, as well as characteristics of movements and institutions. However, to assert that violence is relational does not mean that violent outcomes are necessarily the product of movement and institutional actions in equal measure. Therefore, a major focus of these models is the balance of internal and external factors in producing outcomes. Here the models differ. Galanter's model emphasizes internal factors; the Hall, Schuyler, and Trinh model is weighted toward external factors; and Bromley's model leaves open the possibility of either internal or external precipitation.

Galanter's model emphasizes primarily internal factors. In his analysis of the Peoples Temple, Branch Davidians, Aum Shinrikyō, and Heaven's Gate, Galanter (1999: 179–184) argues that outbreaks of extreme cultic violence can be linked to four conditions: isolation, grandiosity and paranoia, absolute dominion, and government mismanagement. Isolation, whether produced through geographic separation or constant mobility, increases the likelihood of violence as it locks the group within it its own internally constructed definition of reality. By isolating itself, the group eliminates the corrective effects of external feedback. The probability of violence also is raised if the movement leader exhibits personality traits of "grandiosity" and "paranoia." Grandiosity, a need to maintain total control over adherents, generates paranoia, a fear that others will undermine the leader's total control. Those whom the leader fears may be seeking to usurp control may be external parties, such as government agencies, or movement insiders, such as disloyal members or rivals for power. Paranoia, in turn, motivates the leader to create a "siege mentality" within the group such that the group members expect imminent attack by their enemies. Absolute dominion refers to a process of "centripetal control" over adherents' thoughts and actions through close observation and regulation of members' daily lives. Finally, government mismanagement concerns governmental inaction in dealing with religious groups. Galanter advocates immediate legal action to counter illicit activity, coordination of intelligence information when groups are suspected of illegal activity, and education, particularly of young adults who may unwittingly be drawn into movements engaged in deviant activity. This model is somewhat distinctive in its focus primarily on factors internal to movements; the only external factor is government mismanagement, which refers to refers to a failure of agencies to exercise appropriate control as opposed to engaging in provocative or repressive actions.

By contrast, Hall, Schuyler, and Trinh (Hall and Schuyler 1998; Hall, Schuyler, and Trinh 2000) propose that extreme collective religious violence does not emanate from intrinsic qualities of NRMs but rather from the relationship between movement and social order. They do identify a set of specific movement characteristics that may dispose a group toward violent confrontation, characteristics that are found in several other analyses of NRM violence. These characteristics include an apocalyptic worldview, charismatic leadership, high levels of internal control, and intense internal solidarity that produces isolation from the surrounding society. However, Hall, Schuyler, and Trinh argue that these movement characteristics do not necessarily produce violence; rather, it is the interactive dynamics between religious movement and social order that is the critical factor. Based on their analysis of the Peoples Temple, Branch Davidians, Aum Shinrikyō, Solar Temple, and Heaven's Gate, Hall, Schuyler, and Trinh identify two apocalyptic scenarios. The first, the warring Apocalypse of religious conflict, entails an escalating confrontation between movement and a loose coalition among cultural opponents of the movement, media representatives, "who frame cult stories in terms of moral deviance," and "modern governments that have subsumed the 'religious' interest in enforcing cultural legitimacy into a state interest in monopolizing political legitimacy" (2000: 12). The second, the mystical Apocalypse of deathly transcendence, also involves external opposition, but opposition occurs at a lower level, at least from the perspective of outsiders. As the authors comment, "flight from external opposition can become a strong fixation within a group, even when real opponents are lacking, or ineffectual." In this solution, members choose the option of collective suicide to achieve an "other-worldly grace" (2000: 192). The Hall, Schuyler, and Trinh model thus is much more interactive in orientation than the Galanter model but does incorporate the kind of internal precipitating factors upon which Galanter focuses. The emphasis on cultural opponents, media, and governmental control creates a more externally centered source of violence precipitation.

Bromley (2002) develops a theory of what he terms "dramatic denouements," climactic moments "when a movement and some segment of the social order reach a juncture at which one or both conclude that the requisite conditions for maintaining their core identity and collective existence are being subverted and that such circumstances are intolerable. . . . Parties on one or both sides thereupon undertake a project of final reckoning under the aegis of a transcendent mandate to reverse their power positions and to restore what they avow to be appropriate moral order." Bromley's theory is sociohistorical in nature, as he argues that movement-society conflict builds through a series of stages: latent tension, nascent conflict, and intensified conflict. Dramatic denouements are most likely to occur during periods of intensified conflict when there is heightened mobilization and radicalization by both movements and oppositional groups, allies enter the conflict and produce coalitions, and parties on each side of the conflict begin to orient toward one another as "dangerous" rather than merely "troublesome." Dramatic denouements ensue when parties to the conflict polarize and the conflict relationship destabilizes. Polarized relationships yield a situation in which there is a combination of distance and connection between parties; both exist within the same social formation but are organized on fundamentally incompatible premises. Since the ideologies and organizations of the parties are contradictory, each becomes subversive to the other simply by its existence. A variety of factors foster polarization; these include threatening actions and symbolic designations by either side and internal radicalization that moves a party in a more extreme direction. The instability of polarized relationships can be accentuated by secrecy, organizational consolidation/fragmentation, and elimination of third parties. At this point the parties define one another as "subversive," which is a threat to their core identify and existence, and they launch projects of final reckoning intended to reverse power and moral relationships.

Bromley argues that the progression from latent tension to dramatic denouement is not inevitable, as there are three response options—contestive (disputation that creates conflict-oriented connections between parties, ranging from symbolic posturing to violent combat), accommodative (rapprochements by one or both sides, greater conformity by the movement, or greater tolerance by authorities), and retreatist (social or physical withdrawal by the movement or marginalization by the social order)—available at each dispute level. In fact, dramatic denouements are rare precisely because movement and/or societal agents typically elect accommodative or retreatist options over contestation. Where conflict does polarize and destabilize during a period of intensified conflict, however, the likelihood of a dramatic denouement is greatly augmented.

In dramatic denouements retreatist and contestive responses assume their most extreme forms, Exodus and Battle. Exodus involves an orchestrated, collective withdrawal from the social order that is being opposed. From the perspective of the party organizing an Exodus, the action is not a defeat. Rather the Exodus represents an assertion of moral superiority, a rejection of the existing social order, and a decisive separation from that order. By contrast, Battle is organized combat that represents an agreement by both parties that the conflict can only be resolved through force. The initiating party asserts its moral superiority, rejects a social order involving mutual existence or accommodation, and launches a coercive campaign to replace the present situation with its own vision of an appropriate social order. Each of the two responses thus constitutes a fundamental repudiation of continued mutual existence or at least existence in the same space.

The project of building a viable model linking NRMs to violent episodes remains very much a work-in-progress. All of the analyses conducted on contemporary episodes eschew single-factor explanations based on millennialism, high-demand organization, and charismatic leadership. At the same time, the analyses have all concluded that these factors are significant in understanding episodes of violence, that they require further theoretical specification, and that they must be incorporated into more general models. The general models, in turn, incorporate these and other factors and shift the emphasis toward an interactional relationship between movement and social order. The most promising models are those that leave open the possiblity of either movement or societal precipitation of violence.

Issues in Formulating Social Theory and Public Policy

The research that has been conducted to date on NRMs and violence has implications for both theory development and public policy formation. With respect to theoretical development, a key question is what issues need to be addressed in order to build upon the emerging corpus of work on existing theory and case studies. In the case of public policy, the central issue is how to connect academic theory and research to the concerns of legislative and law enforcement agencies.

Theoretical Issues

A number of issues need to be pursued to advance the model building on NRM-societal violence.

- There is emerging consensus among scholars studying violent episodes that they must be analyzed in interactional terms, even if the degree of provocation by parties varies in specific cases. One complex issue is assessing the degree of repression experienced by an NRM or the degree of resistance experienced by a control agency. Virtually all of the analyses of recent violent episodes rest on "objective" measures of repression and resistance. However, movements and control agencies may vary in their response to what appear to outsiders to be equivalent actions. In order to understand the escalation of violent encounters, it is necessary to incorporate means of measuring the subjective significance of acts to both parties to the conflict.

- Virtually all of the research to date on movement-control agency violence has focused on the movements. However, it is clear that control agencies are capable of provocative action that can escalate tension and precipitate conflict. The Branch Davidian episode provided compelling evidence on that point. Yet there are no case studies of control agency organization and operation; whatever analysis of control agencies exists typically consists of (often classified) documents produced by investigatory commissions. It is clear that the conditions under which control agencies radicalize and engender conflict escalation is poorly understood, but such an understanding is critical to the development of movement-social order violence modeling.

- Researchers studying NRMs have gained access primarily to rank-and-file members and low-level leaders. There is little research on the charismatic leaders of NRMs and, for the most part, of other top-tier leaders. As a result, research on NRMs consists of primary data on ordinary members and scattered, secondary reports on leadership. While the dominance of movements by charismatic leaders is overstated in popular accounts of NRMs, few would dispute that the charismatic leader in most instances is the single most influential individual in the movement. It is also the case that NRMs often experience power struggles at the upper levels and that organizational lieutenants may exercise considerable influence, sometimes without the knowledge of the charismatic leader. This appears to have been the case for both the Rajneesh and Peoples Temple movements (Carter 1990; Maaga 1998). Particularly since dramatic movement changes and violence initiatives are likely to emanate from top leadership levels, it is imperative that social scientists place higher priority on gaining access to the halls of power.

- Most of the research that has been conducted has focused on episodes where collective violence did occur. However, there are a number of instances—the Justus Freemen, Church Universal and Triumphant, and Rajneesh—in which confrontations that might have turned violent were resolved peacefully. Model building requires that these kinds of cases be incorporated into the analysis in order to specify the conditions under which conflict escalation does or does not occur.

- Model building requires dealing with a range of cases. All of the cases upon which current theory is based occurred in Western societies. Adequate theory requires incorporating cases occurring in non-Western contexts, such as the Movement for the Restoration of the Ten Commandments in Uganda. It will also be important to distinguish different types of movements. The violence committed by Christian Identity groups, for example, suggests a basic difference between movements that are organized militarily and those that assume a violent posture at some point in their developmental process.

Public Policy

There are number of public policy and law enforcement issues for which social science research on NRMs and violence can be informative.

- It is very likely that there will be future violent episodes involving NRMs. Religious movements historically have been both perpetrators and targets of violence, and the violence has involved conflicts between factions with movements, between rival religious groups, and between religious movements and control agencies. The relatively pacific relations among settled, established religions in many Western nations at the present time is misleading from a historical perspective. Not only are old patterns of religious conflict likely to be replicated at some point, but the number of new religious groups that potentially could come into conflict with their host social orders has increased dramatically in recent decades. At the same time, the number of incidents is likely to be small, and dealing with rare events always presents a challenge. However, there is now a substantial body of research on religious movements, as well as on violent episodes, upon which to draw. The incidents that occurred during the 1990s and the analysis of them can provide valuable perspective on dealing with future episodes. The most constructive posture for law enforcement agencies will be to treat events of the last decade as evidence of neither a predictable pattern of violence, which would lead to an overly aggressive posture, or idiosyncratic events, which would lead to dealing with future cases de novo and missing lessons learned from past events.
- Not only are new episodes of violence likely to occur at some point, but they also will be extremely difficult to anticipate both because they will be rare events and because there is little basis for determining which movements will be involved. Over the last several decades, the largest, most visible, and most maligned NRMs (e.g., The Family, Unificationist Movement, Church of Scientology, Hare Krishna) have not been violence prone. To the contrary, it is been relatively small and largely unknown groups (e.g., Heaven's Gate, Branch Davidians) that have been more likely candidates for violence. There are hundreds of such groups in Western nations and thousands around the globe (e.g., Movement for the Restoration of the Ten Commandments). The simple fact is that only a handful

of myriad new movements now in existence have been studied; virtually nothing is known about the vast majority. As a result, violent episodes are likely to be the occasion for the first public awareness of the group's existence, which was precisely the case in the Branch Davidian and Heaven's Gate episodes. The problem of identifying potentially violent situations is further complicated by the fact that new movements are prone to rapid, dramatic change that, at least in the initial stages, is not likely to be visible to outsiders. And so even accurate information on a movement at a particular moment in time may or may not have long-term utility. Both the Aum Shinrikyō and Rajneesh, for example, moved in a violent direction within a relatively short time period. Even insiders may be unaware of emerging violent proclivities. In the Aum case, for example, it is unlikely that more than a few dozen to a few hundred members had any clue about the plans that were being formulated by movement leaders. In the Rajneesh episode, it is apparent that both movement members and social scientists studying the movement ignored or repressed evidence that the group was rapidly becoming more radical and volatile (Goldman 2001). It is therefore questionable whether instances of violence can be anticipated in advance. This means that it is imperative to have in place general strategies for dealing with movement volatility that will produce the highest probability of nonviolent resolution of conflicts (Jensen and Hsieh 1999; Noesner 1999).

• Given the difficulty of anticipating cases of violence in advance and the limited information available, obtaining an accurate assessment of violence potential obviously is critical. As Barker (2002) has observed, there are a number of "cult-watching groups" with very different perspectives and missions. She distinguishes five types of groups: (1) cult-awareness groups; (2) counter-cult groups; (3) research-orientated groups; (4) human rights groups, and (5) cult-defender groups. In the recent cases of NRM violence, the cult-awareness and research-oriented groups have competed for influence with political and law enforcement officials. The former groups have gained more popular acceptance by disseminating "dangerous cult" imagery and relying almost exclusively on former movement members as an information base (Bromley 1998). In the Peoples Temple and Branch Davidian cases, for example, the media and control agencies were influenced by these groups, which served to escalate rather than diminish tensions (Wright 1995). The latter groups have attained greater professional acceptance by conducting primary research on what are more neutrally labeled "new religious movements." Religion scholars exercised more influence in the Justus Freemen standoff in Montana, which was resolved peacefully (Rosenfeld 1997; Wessinger 1999b). Each of the cult-watching groups possesses information that may be useful to policy makers and law enforcement officials. The most productive approach, therefore, is what Carter (1998) has termed "triangulation," in which information from various cult-watching groups and from current and former members is combined. What is vitally important is that those using diverse sources of information understand the utility and liabilities of those sources.

• Information about NRMs is only part of the problem, of course, as control agencies may also contribute to violence by either action or inaction. Determining the appropriate balance between restraint and intervention is therefore a key issue for control agencies. They may respond defensively to movement resistance given their self-understanding as representing legitimate authority and their interpretation of resistance as a direct challenge to their publicly authorized mission. In the case of the Branch Davidians, government agencies have been heavily criticized for escalating the violence and impeding a nonviolent solution to the confrontation (Wright 1999). Not only was the result unnecessary loss of life by both police officers and movement members, but the subsequent bombing of the Oklahoma City federal building has been directly linked to the federal agents' provocation in that incident. Control agencies may also be reluctant to intervene in cases involving religious groups in order to avoid threatening religious freedom. In the Aum case, for example, Japanese authorities have been castigated for failing to take action even after substantial, convincing evidence of Aum's hostile intent and activity had been amassed. One way to avoid either overreaction or underreaction is to maintain contacts with reliable, nonallied informants and avoid provocative agency actions. A model for this approach can be found in the Garland, Texas, police department's handling of Chen Tao, a millennial group that prophesied an impending apocalypse. The department responded by seeking accurate information from scholars studying the movement, screening out misinformation that was being circulated, initiating a "meaningful dialogue" with the group, and preparing contingency plans (Szubin, Jensen, Gregg 2000).

• A further complication in dealing with violent incidents is that, consistent with the process of globalization, many new movements organize internationally early in their histories. International organization presents a distinct challenge to policy makers and law enforcement officials since the implications of acts by a movement in one nation for other nations is not immediately obvious. One important finding from NRM research is that national wings of movements often possess distinctive culture and organization and may have very limited cohesiveness at the international level. In the case of the Unificationist Movement, for example, there a deep divisions between the Korean, Japanese, and American branches that are bridged by Reverend Moon's charismatic authority. But it is not at all clear that calls for concerted international action of a radical kind would draw the support of various national constituencies. By contrast, international coordination may occur as the sequence of murder-suicides committed by the Solar Temple in Switzerland, France, and Canada demonstrate. Policy makers and law enforcement officials need a much more sophisticated understanding of national differences in movement organization. They also need to recognize that international differences in control agency responses may have implications for movements. Provocation by control agencies in one nation could produce international violent episodes.

CONCLUSIONS

Theory and research on NRMs has become a major area of specialization in the study of religion over the last several decades. The series of violent episodes during the 1990, added the topic of religion and violence to the scholarly agenda. There have been a number of contributions to this developing project. It has been important to debunk popular assumptions and stereotypes about "dangerous and unstable cults" in order to refocus the scholarly and public debate in a more productive direction. Case studies of the major episodes have now been produced that provide a theoretical and information base for further inquiry. One significant development has been an analysis of factors widely thought to be connected to movement volatility—millennial doctrines, high-demand organization, and charismatic leadership. There is an emerging consensus that these factors are consequential in understanding movement volatility but that they need conceptual refinement and incorporation into more general models. The general models that have been developed to date move analysis in the direction of an interactional relationship between movement and social order that leaves open the possibility of greater or lesser violence provocation by either side. A number of theoretical and policy-related issues remain to be addressed. I have suggested that theoretical understanding will be advanced by a more adequate means of interpreting the subjective responses of parties in conflict, increasing knowledge of control agency dynamics and movement leadership processes, incorporating into the analysis episodes that were resolved prior to violent encounter, and distinguishing movements that are organized militarily from those that are not. With respect to public policy, I have argued that it is critical that policy makers learn from the series of violent episodes that have occurred, avoid an either overreactive or underreactive posture, identify and rely on credible sources of information, and deal with the implications of global NRM organization. Understanding rare and extreme events clearly poses a distinct theoretical challenge, and responding to them in the pressure of the moment constitutes a formidable test of societal principles and commitments. The project is a worthy one, however, for extreme cases and circumstances create stringent standards for theoretical models and public policy alike.

REFERENCES

Arnott, Dave. 1999. *Corporate Cults: The Insidious Lure of the All-Consuming Organization.* New York: American Management Association.

Balch, Robert. 1982. "Bo and Peep: A Case Study of the Origins of Messianic Leadership." In *Millennialism and Charisma* ed. Roy Wallis. Belfast, Northern Ireland: Queen's University Press.

————. 1995. "Waiting for the Ships: Disillusionment and the Revitalization of Faith in Bo and Peep's UFO Cult." In *The Gods Have Landed: New Religions from Other Worlds* ed. James Lewis. Albany: State University of New York Press.

Balch, Robert, and David Taylor. 2002. "Making Sense of the Heaven's Gate Suicides." In *Cults, Religion and Violence* ed. David G. Bromley and J. Gordon Melton. Cambridge: Cambridge University Press.

Barker, Eileen. 2002. "Watching for Violence: A Comparative Analysis of the Roles of Five Types of Cult-Watching Groups." In *Cults, Religion and Violence* ed. David G. Bromley and J. Gordon Melton. Cambridge: Cambridge University Press.

Bromley, David G. 1997. "Constructing Apocalypticism: Social and Cultural Elements of Radical Organization." In *Millennium, Messiah, and Mayhem* ed. Thomas Robbins and Susan Palmer. New York: Routledge.

————, ed. 1998. *The Politics of Religious Apostasy: The Role of Apostates in the Transformation of Religious Movements.* Westport, Conn.: Praeger.

————. 2002. "Dramatic Denouements." In *Cults, Religion and Violence* ed. David G. Bromley and J. Gordon Melton. Cambridge: Cambridge University Press.

Bromley, David G., Anson Shupe, and Joseph Ventimiglia. 1979. "Atrocity Tales, the Unification Church, and the Social Construction of Evil." *Journal of Communication* 29: 42–53.

Bromley, David G., and Edward Silver. 1995. "The Branch Davidians: A Social Profile and Organizational History." In *America's Alternative Religions* ed. Timothy Miller. Albany: State University of New York Press.

Bromley, David G., and J. Gordon Melton, eds. 2002. *Cults, Religion, and Violence.* Cambridge: Cambridge University Press.

Carroll, Jeffrey, and Bernard Bauer. 1979. "Suicide Training in the Moon Cult." *New West,* 29 January, 62–63.

Carter, Lewis. 1990. *Charisma and Control in Rajneeshpuram.* New York: Cambridge University Press.

————. 1998. "Carriers of Tales: On Assessing Credibility of Apostate and Other Outsider Accounts of Religious Practices." In *The Politics of Religious Apostasy: The Role of Apostates in the Transformation of Religious Movements* ed. David G. Bromley. Westport, Conn.: Praeger.

Dawson, Lorne. 2002. "Crises of Charismatic Legitimacy and Violent Behavior in New Religious Movements." In *Cults, Religion and Violence* ed. David G. Bromley and J. Gordon Melton. Cambridge: Cambridge University Press.

Dornbusch, Sanford. 1955. "The Military Academy as an Assimilating Institution." *Social Forces* 33: 316–321.

Etzioni, Amitai. 1961. *A Comparative Analysis of Complex Organizations: On Power, Involvement, and Their Correlates.* New York: Free Press of Glencoe.

Galanter, Marc. 1999. *Cults: Faith, Healing, and Coercion.* New York: Oxford University Press.

Goffman, Erving. 1961. *Asylums.* Garden City, N.J.: Doubleday.

Goldman, Marion. 2001. "The Ethnographer as a Holy Clown: Fieldwork, Disregard, and Danger." In *Toward Reflexive Ethnography: Participating, Observing, Narrating* ed. David G. Bromley and Lewis Carter. Oxford: Elsevier Science/JAI Press.

Greil, Arthur, and Thomas Robbins, eds. 1994. *Between Sacred and Secular: Research and Theory on Quasi-Religion.* Greenwich, Conn.: JAI Press and the Association for the Sociology of Religion.

Hall, John R., and Philip Schuyler. 1997. "The Mystical Apocalypse of the Solar Temple." In *Millennium, Messiahs, and Mayhem: Contemporary Apocalyptic Movements* ed. Thomas Robbins and Susan Palmer. New York: Routledge.

———. 1998. "Apostasy, Apocalypse, and Religious Violence." In *The Politics of Religious Apostasy* ed. David G. Bromley. Westport, Conn.: Praeger.

Hall, John R., with Philip Schuyler and Sylvaine Trinh. 2000. *Apocalypse Observed: Religious Movements, the Social Order, and Violence in North America, Europe, and Japan.* New York: Routledge.

Hillery, George. 1969. "The Convent: Community, Prison, or Task Force." *Journal for the Scientific Study of Religion* 8: 140–151.

Introvigne, Massimo. 1999. "The Magic of Death: The Suicide of the Solar Temple." In *Millennialism, Persecution, and Violence* ed. Catherine Wessinger. Syracuse, N.Y.: Syracuse University Press.

Jensen, C., and Y. Hsieh. 1999. "Law Enforcement and the Millennialist Vision: A Behavioral Approach." *FBI Law Enforcement Bulletin* 68: 1–8.

Kanter, Rosabeth. 1972. "Commitment and the Internal Organization of Millennial Movements." *American Behavioral Scientist* 16: 219–244.

Kelley, Dean. 1972. *Why Conservative Churches Are Growing: A Study in Sociology of Religion.* New York: Harper & Row.

Lifton, Robert. 1999. *Destroying the World to Save It.* New York: Holt.

London, Perry. 1969. *Behavior Control.* New York: Harper & Row.

Maaga, Mary. 1998. *Hearing the Voices of Jonestown.* Syracuse, N.Y.: Syracuse University Press.

Mayer, Jean Francios. 1999. "Our Terrestrial Journey Is Coming to an End: The Last Voyage of the Solar Temple." *Nova Religio: The Journal of Alternative and Emergent Religions* 2: 172–196.

Melton, J. Gordon. 1997. *The Family/The Children of God.* Salt Lake City: Signature Books.

————. 1998. *Encyclopedia of American Religions.* 6th ed. Detroit: Gale.

Melton, J. Gordon, James R. Lewis, and Aidan A. Kelly. 1990. *New Age Encyclopedia.* Detroit: Gale.

Moore, R. Laurence. 1986. *Religious Outsiders and the Making of America.* New York: Oxford University Press.

Noesner, Gary. 1999. "Negotiation Concepts for Commanders." *FBI Law Enforcement Bulletin* 68: 6–18.

Palmer, Susan J. 1999. "Frontiers and Families: The Children of Island Pond." In *Children in New Religions,* ed. Susan J. Palmer and Charlotte E. Hardman. New Brunswick, N.J.: Rutgers University Press.

Reader, Ian. 2000. *Religious Violence in Contemporary Japan: The Case of Aum Shinrikyô.* Richmond, Surrey, England: Curzon Press; Honolulu: University of Hawaii Press.

Richardson, James T. 2001. "Minority Religions and the Context of Violence: A Conflict/ Interactionist Perspective." *Terrorism and Political Violence* 13: 103–133.

Robbins, Thomas. 2002. "Sources of Volatility in Religious Movements." In *Cults, Religion and Violence* ed. David G. Bromley and J. Gordon Melton. Cambridge: Cambridge University Press.

Rosenfeld, Jean. 1991. "The Importance of the Analysis of Religion in Avoiding Violent Outcomes: The Justus Freemen Crisis." *Novo Religio: The Journal of Alternative and Emergent Religions* 1: 72–95.

Stark, Rodney. 1991. "Normal Revelations: A Rational Model of 'Mystical' Experiences." In *New Developments in Theory and Research* ed. David G. Bromley. Greenwich, Conn.: JAI Press and the Association for the Sociology of Religion.

Szubin, A., C. J. Jensen III, and R. Gregg. 2000. "Interacting with 'Cults': A Policing Model." *FBI Law Enforcement Bulletin* 69: 16–25.

Weber, Max. 1964. *The Theory of Social and Economic Organization.* Trans. A. M. Henderson and Talcott Parsons. New York: Free Press.

Wessinger, Catherine. 1999a. *How the Millennium Comes Violently.* Chappaqua, N.Y.: Seven Bridges Press.

————. 1999b. "Religious Studies Scholars, FBI Agents, and the Montana Freeman Standoff." *Nova Religio: The Journal of Alternative and Emergent Religions* 3: 36–44.

Wright, Stuart, ed. 1995. *Armageddon in Waco: Critical Perspectives on the Branch Davidian Conflict.* Chicago: University of Chicago Press.

————. 1999. "Anatomy of a Government Massacre: Abuses of Hostage-Barricade Protocols during the Waco Standoff." *Journal of Terrorism and Political Violence* 11: 39–68.

CHAPTER 7

LEGAL DIMENSIONS
OF NEW RELIGIONS

JAMES T. RICHARDSON

THE legal situation of new religions, sometimes pejoratively referred to as "cults and sects," can be analyzed from several different perspectives. One, favored by law reviews, would be a straightforward case law analysis focusing on case chronology and legal precedent, while basing the analysis on how the cases comport with major provisions of statutes and constitutional documents, or to significant concepts such as religious freedom. Such an approach, while of value, may not be as revealing as a more in-depth review from a sociological perspective. This review adopts a more sociological approach, applying some key variables from sociology and the sociology of law to the area of new religious movements (NRMs). It will focus on legal efforts to exert social control over new religions, especially involving court cases but also referencing some major legislative attempts to regulate of NRMs. Before dealing with these matters I will recount in broad terms efforts made to control NRMs within the U.S., where NRMs first came to the attention of the public and policy makers, but also other in countries where concern about NRMs developed somewhat later.

EARLY SOCIAL CONTROL EFFORTS
IN THE U.S.

Early efforts at social control of controversial new religions in the U.S. involved issues of consumer protection, with attempts in various states to define newer religions legislatively as a consumer good or service subject to regulation similar to consumer products. However, such efforts usually foundered because of problems defining what groups or activities were to be covered, or over issues of religious freedom and freedom of association (Richardson 1986; Guttman 1985; Flinn 1987).

Efforts to get the federal government to intervene by officially defining certain religious groups as unacceptable, and then acting on such designations, also were generally unsuccessful in the U.S., for reasons similar to those that led to the demise of state-level effort at legislative action.[1] This does not mean that all governmental entities in the U.S. were positively oriented toward NRMs. Indeed, there have been sporadic efforts to exert control over NRMs by state and local jurisdictions attempting to limit fund-raising, proselytizing efforts, or other activities. Also, certain federal agencies such as the Immigration and Naturalization Service have attempted to limit the ingress of foreign nationals associated with certain NRMs, or to remove foreign citizens who have come to this country as leaders of NRMs (see, e.g., Carter's 1990 discussion of the situation in Oregon concerning the Bhagwan Rajneesh and efforts to force him to leave).

Although these direct control efforts have often (but not always) suffered from enforcement of the religious freedom clause of the U.S. Constitution by the U.S. Supreme Court, there has also been a move by the U.S. Supreme Court to promote more of a European-style "management model" for minority faiths, including NRMs (Richardson 1995a; Regan 1986). Thus, particularly as demonstrated in the famous 1990 *Employment Division of Oregon v. Smith* case, religious freedom issues seem to have been relegated to a lesser position than has traditionally been the case in the U.S. The *Smith* ruling provoked a major reaction in the U.S. and led to passage in 1993 of the Religious Freedom Restoration Act (RFRA). This act forced governmental entities to demonstrate that there was a "compelling state interest" at stake any time a restriction on religious activity was being contemplated. The act also required governmental entities to show that there were no other less obtrusive alternatives available to accomplish the specific goal of a given law. However, RFRA was ruled unconstitutional five years later, thwarting this effort to reestablish religious freedom as a paramount value in the U.S. (Richardson 2000).

Much more successful in the U.S., at least initially, were efforts to define participation in religious groups as a mental health problem, thereby bringing the weight of the powerful mental health establishment to bear on the issue of controlling NRMs (Robbins, Anthony, and McCarthy 1983; Kilbourne and Richardson 1984; James 1986; Saliba 1993; Richardson 1991, 1993a, 1993b, 1995; Anthony 1990). The use of mental health constructs such as the pseudoscientific concepts "brainwashing" and "mind control" in early efforts at social control added a powerful weapon to the arsenal of those concerned about the development and spread of alternative religious experiences in the U.S. Given the heavy penetration of psychology and psychiatry into the American legal system (Faust and Ziskin 1988), it was just a matter of time before such concepts began to play a role in legal efforts to exert social control over the new religions. Indeed, it is arguable that the problematic constructs such as "brainwashing" were developed in the contemporary context with social control of controversial NRMs as their main purpose (Richardson and Kilbourne 1983).

Early efforts to apply such concepts were in "conservatorship" hearings designed to have the courts grant legal control over participants in some NRMs to parents of the participants, even though most participants were legally adults. Such hearings were often held in conjunction with "deprogrammings," in which parents attempted to gain legal approval for having their children who had chosen to participate in NRMs kidnapped and involved in a radical resocialization process. This use of conservatorships was allowed for a few years in the late 1960s and early 1970s, but it was eventually rejected by court decisions recognizing the problematic nature of applying laws designed to protect senile elderly people to obviously alert and functioning young people (LeMoult 1983; Bromley 1983). Thus, coercive deprogramming and conservatorships to justify them fell from favor and have diminished considerably within the U.S. However, deprogrammings have continued, sometimes in large numbers, in societies such as Japan, with notions of "brainwashing" and "mind control" being used there to justify such social control actions (Mickler 1994; Kurokawa 1999; Richardson and Edleman 2002).

Another major way that mental health constructs were used in social control was through the filing of private tort actions against specific NRMs, usually by disenchanted former members and their families. Mental health pseudoscientific theories relating to "brainwashing" and "mind control" were used to undergird tort claims such as "intentional infliction of emotional distress," "false imprisonment," and "fraud," with considerable success for a time (Anthony 1990, 1999; Richardson 1991, 1996; Anthony and Robbins 1992, 1998), Also, brainwashing/mind control ideas were quickly adopted as explanatory devices by a general public concerned about the rise of NRMs. These ideas became a major ideological justification for thousands of kidnapings and deprogrammings that have occurred (Shupe and Bromley 1980; Richardson and Kilbourne 1983; Robbins, Anthony, and McCarthy 1983). Thus, particularly in the U.S., with its constitutional protections of religious expression, self-help remedies (Black 1999) such as deprogrammings and civil court actions became the paramount method of attempts to exert control over alternative religious movements.[2]

The usual form of "brainwashed-based" civil action against an NRM and its leaders involved a suit filed by a former member, asking for money damages for actions the former member claimed were unfair or involved fraud of some sort, as was described above. Usually such cases were based on the claim that the person now suing was brainwashed into joining or under mind control while they remained a member. Some of these cases have resulted in quite large initial damage awards (Anthony 1990; Richardson 1991). Brainwashing has also sometimes been successfully used as a part of the defense when deprogrammers were sued in civil court for false imprisonment or assault, or when they were charged with kidnaping in a criminal action.[3] Some criminal defendants have attempted to use brainwashing claims as well as a part of their defense, saying that they broke a law because of their being brainwashed by the group of which they were a part. Such defenses have generally not been allowed in U.S. courts, however (Anthony and Robbins 1998).

"Brainwashing" evidence is very questionable from a scientific point of view (Ginsburg and Richardson 1998) and should seldom if ever be admitted as evidence. It fails important tests for expert evidence, including its lack of falsifiability (or "testability"), difficulties in ascertaining an "error rate" when designating individuals as brainwashed or not, and also a failure to meet usual requirements of general acceptance in relevant fields of inquiry for the theory involved in such claims. But such evidence was allowed with impunity for many years in the U.S. The fact that it was accepted seemed to demonstrate that the court was willing to allow it for reasons other than its scientific status.

Another somewhat successful tactic of control used with NRMs in the U.S. that became available as the movements grew older concerned children and accusations of child abuse. Most participants in the NRMs of the 1960s and 1970s initially were single young people. Some of those unmarried youths remained in the movements and married within them, thus forming families. In some instances large numbers of children resulted, particularly in groups whose ideology did not positively sanction birth control. Thus, some groups that were originally quite different, even radical, in their dress and behaviors found themselves having to deal with ordinary matters such as the care and feeding of large numbers of children. These groups tended to become more "domesticated" (Richardson 1985) through the pressures of having to care for their children (also see Barker 1995: 168–171). This was the case, for instance, with the Children of God (now known, interestingly, as The Family), which changed many of its former patterns of behavior under the pressures of child rearing (see Lewis and Melton 1994; Richardson 1994).[4]

Even as these groups with growing numbers of children were becoming more domesticated, they were also more vulnerable to social control efforts because of the presence of children in the groups. Palmer and Hardman (1999) present a number of reports of child-rearing issues that arise with newer religious groups, including one chapter (Richardson 1999b) describing a major shift from attempting to exert control over NRMs through "brainwashing" accusations to an approach based on accusations of child abuse, including sexual abuse. This chapter discusses the opportunities for social control offered by recently enacted statutes designed to stop child abuse, but it also notes serious problems associated with their application to NRMs, especially communal ones. For instance, most such laws were written to require specificity in terms of the time, place, and actions of identifiable individuals toward a given child, information that is difficult to discern in groups living an isolated life far from the eyes of teachers, social workers, and others.

Swantko (1999) describes the details of many battles the Twelve Tribes communal group has had with governmental authorities in several countries, including the U.S., but also in Canada, Germany, and France. Most of the problems involve issues such as custody battles between members and nonmembers, home schooling, and child abuse accusations because of the practice of corporal punishment. Her analysis shows that such difficulties are particularly severe in countries without constitutional protections for religion, and which have governments involved directly in the regulation of religious groups, sometimes assisted by private individuals or anti-cult groups which themselves may be receiving official governmental support.

SOCIAL CONTROL IN COUNTRIES OUTSIDE THE U.S.

As just indicated in the discussion of problems encountered by the Twelve Tribes group, in a number of countries federal action has been taken that allows the exertion of more control over minority faiths, especially ones that have young children involved. A consumer protection approach, while not particularly useful in the U.S., has been more successful in countries without formal constitutional protections for religious freedom or which have more paternalistic and protective approaches toward unconventional individual religious experiences. Beckford (1985: 242, 249–275) discusses the situation in a number of European countries, noting particularly the federal paternalism of Germany and France, compared to other European countries such as the United Kingdom. Richardson and Van Driel (1994) make comparisons between France, Germany, the U.K., and The Netherlands on the issue of control of NRMs, noting the much stronger tendencies to exert control in France and Germany than in other European countries.

Beckford (1985) and Richardson (1995d) have described how the pan-European parliamentary and judicial bodies of the European Union and the Council of Europe have dealt with minority faiths in legislative action and court decisions. There have been some efforts by the European Parliament and the Parliamentary Assembly of the Council of Europe to address perceived problems of NRMs in member countries. This has mainly taken the form of reports being developed and recommendations made that would result in more information on such groups being developed and shared. Richardson (1995d) also researched court decisions of the European Court of Human Rights (ECHR) and the European Court of Justice involving minority faiths, as has more recently Carolyn Evans with the ECHR (2001). This research demonstrates considerable deference being shown by such bodies to the actions of member countries, even as there has been some lip service paid to the idea of religious freedom. For example, even when religious freedom is honored in the rare court decision of the ECHR, it is usually done reluctantly, with a split vote and strong dissents urging the court to defer actions that would override a country's internal management of religious groups (also see Gunn 1996; Crumper 2001).

More recently, Fautre (1999) discusses the strong sentiments against certain minority religious groups in Belgium and measures taken to extend legal control over such groups. However, Deneaux (2002) has noted some significant shifts in governmental policy concerning NRMs in Belgium in recent years. Seiwert (1999) analyzes the political machinations in Germany associated with legislative efforts to exert control over "sects and cults," efforts that included the appointment of a high-level Enquete Commission to do a well-financed study of "New Religious and Ideological Communities and Psychogroups in the Federal Republic of Germany," a commission on which Seiwert was a member (Deutscher Bundestag, 1998). Introvigne (1999) examines in detail one particular religious group's difficulties with the French government after this group was included in an official parliamentary list of 174 "sects and cults" that were not to be considered real religions. Swantko (1999) describes the continuing problems experienced by Twelve Tribes groups in Germany and France on such issues as home schooling and accusations of child abuse.[5]

Richardson and Introvigne (2001) discuss the situation in several Western European countries, noting particularly major federal-level actions taken by France, Germany, and Belgium, but also pointing out the lack of major negative actions toward NRMs in countries such as Italy, Switzerland, and The Netherlands. Richardson and Introvigne were particularly focusing on the extent to which "brainwashing"-related ideas were being used to undergird policy development in Western European countries. They reported finding considerable evidence that this American ideological export was playing a prominent role in a number of these countries. (Also see Soper 2001; Robbins, 2001; and Introvigne and Richardson 2001, which were a part of the print symposium in the *Journal for the Scientific Study of Religion* 40[2], on the issue of why some Western European countries were taking such a punitive stance toward NRMs.)

Law professor Cole Durham (1999) has analyzed developments in a number of other European countries covered by the Organization for Security and Co-operation in Europe (OSCE), focusing on different problems that have developed for minority faiths, particularly in former Soviet Union countries, as onerous legal requirements are sometimes established for minority religions. Durham discusses proposed requirements (already in effect in some countries) that religious groups have large numbers of members before a group can be registered and gain legal status. Also, requirements that a group would be in existence for a number of years (such as 15 under the 1997 new law in Russia) before it can be registered by the state are criticized by Durham, as are requirements that religious groups conform to certain organizational forms. Other provisions of concern that make it difficult to register and function are also noted, as are provisions that allow governments to rather easily dissolve religious organizations.

Shterin and Richardson (2000) describe the evolution of federal actions toward minority faiths in Russia and the major influence of Western anti-cult ideas and organizations on those actions. In an earlier article Shterin and Richardson (1998) described how many local governmental entities in Russia ignored completely the guarantees in the constitution and statutes concerning freedom of religion, and instead exerted considerable control over minority religious groups, particularly those from the West. Later Shterin and Richardson (2002) described a major court case that played a role in the major changes which made the new 1997 national law in Russia much more restrictive. Edleman and Richardson (2002) have written about extremely punitive efforts by the Chinese government to exert legal control over or even to stamp out the Falun Gong. They note that the Chinese government, in its actions toward the Falun Gong, are not following the Chinese Constitution or relevant laws, and that new edicts concerning the Falun Gong have been developed in what appear to be extra-legal processes. Kisala and Mullins (2001) have examined the more measured federal reactions in Japan to the Aum Shinrikyō tragic episode, as have a number of scholars in a special issue of *SYZYGY: Journal of Alternative Religion and Culture* edited by James Lewis (1999). Richardson and Edleman (2002) have compared pre-Aum and post-Aum efforts at social control of NRMs, particularly the Unification Church, which has experienced thousands of deprogrammings over the past several decades in Japan, done often with the tacit approval of state authorities and involving ministers of Protestant denominations as deprogrammers.

In most other countries self-help remedies such as have occurred in the U.S. have generally not often been used, with Japan being a major exception, as noted. This "Japanese exceptionalism" that has seen deprogramming become a major activity of social control there may be a result of the confluence of two factors. One is the history of severe persecution of minority faiths prior to and during World War II, a history that makes many Japanese wary of the state becoming engaged in regulating religion. Also, as a result of the outcome of World War I, Japan was forced to accept a new constitution containing guarantees for religious freedom similar to those in the U.S. Constitution. However, there have been sporadic reports of deprogrammings in other countries, often carried out by visiting American deprogrammers. Indeed, a recent major motion picture dealing with deprogramming, *Holy Smoke*, was set in Australia, a country that has seen several such episodes of American-led deprogrammings. A few European countries also have seen deprogrammings occur, with justifications often based on brainwashing/mind control ideas spread from the U.S. to other parts of the globe (Beckford 1985: 199–203; Shupe and Bromley 1994; Richardson 1996).

One reason self-help remedies such as deprogramming and civil suits are not as popular in most other countries is that apparently they were not felt to be needed as much by citizens and policy makers. In some countries, NRMs are not viewed as a serious problem requiring either official attention or citizen self-help remedies. In some other countries where anti-cultist ideology has informed government policy (i.e., France, Belgium, Germany, and Russia) the state itself is empowered to take actions against NRMs, and this has relieved ordinary individual citizens of the need to engage in self-help solutions to felt problems concerning NRMs. This means fewer deprogrammings and civil law suits but more official actions by governmental agencies. Such actions include such things as official government studies of perceived problems associated with NRM participation, public information campaigns to inform the public of the "cult/sect menace," and official actions to control NRMs through statutory or administrative regulations of various kinds, or even to dissolve religious groups entirely. This latter point usually involves a process whereby the judiciary is asked to enforce provisions of a law that allows dissolution under certain conditions. Such a law was recently passed in France, even after much international attention focused on that country for considering such punitive measures (Richardson and Introvigne 2001).

EXPLANATIONS

A recent study focusing on the operation of *discretion* within legal systems (Richardson 2000) focused attention on evidentiary problems in court cases involving controversial religious groups. This research demonstrated the following provocative hypothesis:

Problems of quality of evidence arise in cases involving controversial groups or practices because courts may allow questionable evidence in such cases. Decisions are sometimes made to admit evidence that would not be admitted under other, more normal, circumstances. In addition, jurors (in societies using juries) are prone to accept questionable evidence when it supports biases and prejudices they hold about minority religious groups and alleged practices. (112)

It is also worth noting that decisions *not* to accept evidence that might be exculpatory in criminal cases or to shift liability in civil cases could also occur in cases involving controversial religious groups, with such decisions being made in ways that hinder the religious group in its effort to defend itself or be successful in litigation it had undertaken. Such problems of either accepting questionable evidence where its introduction might undercut a minority religious group, or refusing to accept evidence that could support such a group, can sometimes result in court decisions that can be characterized as discriminatory and not in the interest of social justice or religious freedom.

This hypothesis can be illustrated by examining several sorts of cases, including so-called "cult/brainwashing" cases, which have occurred in the U.S. and elsewhere, as discussed above. (See Richardson 1996 and Anthony 1999 for a discussion of the diffusion and use of this questionable concept in legal cases in countries outside the U.S.) Major cases involving controversial minority religious groups and alleged practices in Australia and New Zealand also demonstrate that courts were less interested in evidentiary quality than they were in other, more normative goals (Richardson 2000).

The major reason for such outcomes of "cult" cases seems related to the *normative function of the courts* (Richardson 2001a). This concept refers to the fact that in most contemporary societies the judicial system has some degree of ultimate authority and responsibility to determine what is acceptable behavior within a specific society. The judiciary performs this function by enforcing laws, which themselves have been established by a process that usually involves the interaction of executive and legislative authority within the society. Presumedly, the legal structure represents, to some degree, the values of a society which have been spelled out in specific laws; thus the process of applying the laws to a particular situation seems straightforward.

However, the application of specific laws to a given situation always involves considerable discretion on the part of those in positions of authority within a society. Decisions must be made about various aspects of any action that allegedly violates a law or accrues liability. And, in making such decisions, those in authority in the judicial system (judges and jurors, in societies having juries) may act in ways that are discriminatory toward unpopular or politically weak parties such as minority religious groups (see Pfeifer 1999 for reports of experimental evidence to support this claim). This is done, apparently, because those in authority think it their responsibility to be part of the process of exerting social control over individuals and groups defined as deviant by the norms and values of a given society. As judicial authorities act normatively, they may at the same time be discriminating against certain unpopular groups and thereby violate the religious freedom of participants in that group.

Discretion and discrimination in the operation of a judicial system can occur even in a situation that has a very strong judiciary, able to work its will on other societal institutions. What happens in such a situation depends on the personal values held by those in positions of power within the judicial system, and by the degree to which they are governed by binding legal provisions offering protection for unpopular religious groups and practices. Therefore, in societies with a strong and independent judiciary which also have, for instance, constitutional provisions guaranteeing religious freedom that are enforced by the judiciary, high degrees of religious freedom would be expected. But religious freedom concerns can become quite problematic when there is less judicial autonomy in a given country, coupled with a lack of legal provisions protecting such freedom or legal provisions in effect that actually are discriminatory on their face.[6] The worst possible situation would occur in situation with a weak judiciary, dominated by other institutional structures in society, no legal provisions offering protections for religious freedom for minority groups, and legal acceptance for treating unpopular groups in a discriminatory fashion. In such circumstances legal protections for minority religious groups would be weak, and indeed, one might expect to see the judicial system used as a major element of the weaponry of social control exerted against minority faiths by those in positions of authority in that country.

Why discretion often seems to operate in a discriminatory way toward minority religious groups requires explanation. The work of Donald Black (1976, 1999) on the "behavior of law" is helpful in developing an understanding of what occurs when unpopular religious groups get caught up in the machinations of a legal system. Black focuses on a few key concepts, including *status* and *intimacy* (the latter defined as "relational distance") as major explanatory variables in explaining how legal systems operate.

Status refers to a person's position in society, with Black suggesting that those higher in status in a given society use the legal system more, and more successfully, than those lower in the status hierarchy. Indeed, those higher in status even are able to construct the legal system more to their liking, to protect interests they hold dear.[7] It is nearly always the case that new and minority religious groups are lower in status than other religious groups (which may seek to use the legal system to protect their interests) and most others with whom the religious group interacts. In the case of NRMs in modern societies, their initial primary recruitment target of single young people led almost immediately to conflict with some of the parents of those young people. This in turn led to concern from those to whom the parents and friends of the recruit could turn for support, such as political figures who were asked to help exert control over recruitment activities of the NRMs.

In the U.S., as discussed above, getting the government to take direct action was usually difficult or unsuccessful because of constitutional provisions and a tradition of religious freedom (Richardson 1995b). As a result, self-help remedies developed, with the legal system being used to exert social control over controversial NRMs mainly via private civil actions and in other ways. "Brainwashing" claims became the initial ideological justification used in conservatorship hearings, for defense in legal cases involving charges against deprogrammers for kidnaping NRM members, and for civil actions by former members against some NRMs and their leaders. In most of these instances of use of the legal system to control NRMs, the NRMs did not prevail, at least initially. Eventually deprogramming was declared illegal in some key court cases, as violating the constitutional rights of adult NRM members (Bromley 1983; LeMoult 1983), and the pseudoscientific "brainwashing" concept was ruled not to be scientifically based and was thus inadmissable as evidence in the various types of "cult/brainwashing" cases.

Why the change in outcomes occurred in these sorts of cases in the U.S. requires some explanation, and it is here that Black's intimacy variable comes into play. Obviously NRMs, almost by definition, do not have intimate personal connections with powerful people in a given society where they develop, at least initially. There is considerable "relational distance" between most NRMs and those in positions of authority. Rod Stark, in his acclaimed *The Rise of Christianity* (1976), makes the important point that gaining adherents among relatively affluent women of the society contributed greatly to the rapid development, spread, and ultimate legitimacy of that NRM. However, he was talking about developments over the course of several hundred years, something that we are not able to assume with today's NRMs. Instead, we are left with a situation where NRMs are peopled by relatively low-status individuals (single, young, unemployed, or doing fairly menial labor) who have chosen to leave their usual social location and participate in something that many in society, including, quite importantly, many parents of NRM participants, do not value. NRM groups and their leaders usually do not have intimate ties with powerful people. Indeed, some of those with whom individual members have strong personal ties—their parents and friends—may be quite critical of participation in the NRM.

So a situation developed, and lasted for a number of years, where controversial NRMs had few friends in "high places," and some of them even developed "enemies" (some parents and friends) who could sometimes access those in high places, such as politicians and even judges. *Social repulsion* (Black, 1999: 144) was exhibited by many toward NRMs in their early history, with predictable effects in the legal arena.

When NRMs were involved in legal actions during this period, they usually lost, a situation that lasted for over two decades in the U.S. How did this situation change and develop into one where NRMs were able to themselves make use of the legal system to defend themselves and eventually win some crucial cases (Richardson 1998b)? And, relatedly, why has the situation in some countries outside the U.S. been slow to change in this regard, so that political and legal structures can still be used with impunity to exert control over NRM activities in some countries?

Black's theorizing is helpful in understanding the sometimes dramatic change that occurred with treatment of NRMs in the U.S. legal system. In simple terms, NRMs eventually were able to establish ties with important *third parties* (Black and Baumgartner 1999) who came to the defense of such groups, even if sometimes reluctantly. The NRMs were able to *attract* the attention and support of individuals and groups that would normally have had little interest in such groups. This occurred mainly because these third parties were interested in *ideas* that were being tested or ignored, through social control efforts being made toward NRMs. Thus, whereas originally NRMs had few high-status friends (and certainly not intimate ones in the sense meant by Black), they were able over time to establish important connections with some groups which became *partisans* for them within the legal system (Black 1999: 125).

What this means in simple terms is that more powerful groups within the U.S. came to be interested in the plight of NRMs that were being put upon by some parents and others involved in what is called by sociologists the "anti-cult movement" (Shupe and Bromley 1980). Thus the ACLU entered the fray quite early, with criticisms of deprogramming and the use of conservatorship laws to put a legal face on such actions by those wanting to control NRMs. The National Council of Churches also issued statements defending the right of adults to choose and practice the religion of their choice and decrying the use of deprogramming. Other groups, such as Americans for Separation for Church and State, entered the fray and issued statements defending the right of individuals to participate in NRMs, and the right of such groups to exist. Some of these groups even entered specific legal matters as parties or by furnishing legal advice and assistance to a few beleaguered NRMs.

The involvement of these significant third parties acting in a partisan way on behalf of unpopular NRMs forced those using the legal system as a device for social control of NRMs to recognize that doing so might be imperiling constitutional protections for freedom of religion and association. This countereffort by such significant third parties caught the attention of judges and others, and the U.S. legal system started being somewhat more responsive to NRMs' claims and defenses when they were involved in legal actions. This new situation in turn led to an increase in the odds of an NRM prevailing in a legal action, whether it was as a defendant in a civil action or when it was acting as a plaintiff in a legal action.

One important third-party group to NRMs has been scholars who study

NRMs, most of whom do not accept notions that people can be forced against their will to participate in such groups and their activities. The obvious ideological basis for such claims was offensive to a number of scholars whose fieldwork on various NRMs showed a clear volitional element when people chose to participate. Eventually a group of scholars, mostly sociologists of religion, but also some psychologists of religion and religious historians, became involved in some cases, giving advice and occasionally agreeing to offer rebuttal testimony to those who would propound "brainwashing"-based theories about why and how people participate in NRMs. Such involvement of scholars, offering scientifically based critiques of "brainwashing" testimony, led eventually to such testimony being disallowed in most U.S. courts for purposes of obtaining damages from NRMs by former members (Richardson 1991; Anthony 1990; Anthony and Robbins 1995; Ginsburg and Richardson 1998).

These scholars entering the legal arena on behalf of NRMs resulted in considerable controversy (Introvigne 1998; Robbins 1998; Richardson 1997, 1998a), and that controversy still rages within academic circles in the U.S. What is important for our purposes is not to detail the controversy, but to point out that *the conflict developed because some controversial NRMs were able to find important third parties to assist them in their legal battles.* Had these third parties not stepped forward there would have been no conflict, and the legal system within the U.S. would have continued to be used on occasion as an instrument of social control over unpopular NRMs. Such is still the case in some other countries, where basic legal protections or traditions of religious freedom do not exist (or are weak), and where potential high-status third parties might be hindered from becoming involved in such issues on behalf of minority faiths.

This seems to be particularly the case, for instance, in some former Soviet Union countries where former state-sanctioned churches are attempting to re-establish and even strengthen their prior (to the advent of the Soviet Union) positions. Sometimes minority religious groups can become pawns in such efforts, especially if politicians are willing to form alliances with former state-approved churches for their own purposes. This has happened in Russia (Shterin and Richardson 1998, 2000), where laws and have been passed limiting religious freedom for minority faiths, and the court system has been used as well in efforts to exert control over such groups (Richardson and Shterin 1999; Shterin and Richardson 2002). Such control efforts using the legal system have usually met with success at the trial court level, but the Russian Constitutional Court has issued several rulings in recent years suggesting that minority faiths have found some significant defenders in that country as well. Similar efforts to promote former dominant churches are also under way in other former Soviet countries, with mixed success so far (see Shanda 1999 for one example from Hungary).

In Western Europe the situation is also quite complex, with, as has been mentioned, neighboring countries taking vastly different approaches to dealing with minority faiths. Germany, France, and Belgium have taken a rather hard line, with France being the most strident in its anti-cult actions (Dasi 2001; Richardson and Introvigne 2001). Germany and Belgium appear to be ameliorating their social control efforts somewhat, bringing them closer to those of Italy, Switzerland, England, The Netherlands, and Scandinavian countries (see Seiwert 1999; Schoen 2001; Deneaux 2002; Krannenborg 1994; Barker 2001; Geertz and Rothstein 2001; and Introvigne 2001). The Western European situation is complicated by a perception among some, particularly in France, that NRMs are an American product and thus a part of American imperialism, and therefore they represent a major threat to the French culture and way of life (Beckford 2003). This anti-Americanism has played a role in some Western European countries, adding to the social repulsion felt toward controversial NRMs in those countries. This perception, coupled with the strictly secular approach to government in France, has led to some extremely harsh (and much criticized) laws being passed as part of the effort to exert control over NRMs in that country (Introvigne and Richardson 2001; Hervieu-Leger 2001).

In other parts of the world NRMs are also encountering difficulties, as described above, some of them quite understandable in places such as Japan, with its sarin gas attacks by Aum Shinrikyō. These attacks have resulted in Aum (and other newer religious groups) having a very low status and few friends in places of power. Indeed, some who have supported the Aum during this time of crisis have suffered loss of status themselves (Reader 2000, Mullins 2001). In China extremely harsh measures have been brought to bear on many different religious groups, including especially the Falun Gong. The government's paranoia about the Falun Gong (or any other large religious movement) has caused them to use extremely harsh measures against the Falun Gong and anyone who would support them. Practitioners and supporters have lost status, sometimes dramatically, as when leaders in the Chinese Communist Party itself were found to be participants. Again, anti-Americanism seems to be playing a role, as the Falun Gong have been supported most strongly by U.S. foreign policy and American human rights groups. The intervention of "third parties" that are themselves in ill repute within China has not helped the cause of the Falun Gong.

In Australia, although there is some strong negative public opinion about some NRMs, the situation is much more calm and following a course that appears supportive of pluralism (see Hume 1995; Ireland 1999; Bouma 1999; Richardson 1995a, 2001). Although there are sometimes xenophobic tendencies among more conservative groups, in general those in positions of power officially support pluralism, thus making it clear that minority religious groups have friends in high places. The High Court in Australia has been supportive of aboriginal rights, as well (Mortesen 2000). In Singapore, the relative newness of the nation-state and the history of severe conflict between ethnic and religious groups had caused the government to act quite harshly to any efforts to proselytize (Hill 2003). Those in power in Singapore support government action of this nature and make it clear that those who would support religious groups that proselytize (mainly Protestant) are doing so at some risk.

CONCLUSIONS

The legal status of NRMs varies greatly around the globe, with some countries allowing them considerable freedom to exist and recruit new members. Other societies are much more closed to the presence and activities of NRMs, either native or foreign, for historical and political reasons. Explaining fully why these specific differences occur is beyond the scope of this brief analysis. Suffice it to say that knowledge of historical factors in the various countries, coupled with an application of theories from the sociology of law, can bring much understanding of the situation.

In closing, it is interesting to note that, particularly in some former Soviet Union countries, China, and some countries in Western Europe, at least some of the concern about NRMs derives from fears about American influence. This concern, which has contributed to efforts at social control of minority faiths, is based on growing anti-American sentiment and the general globalization of American culture. There are some ironies involved in this motivation, not the least of which is that the strongest efforts to exert control over NRMs in certain European and former Soviet countries, as well as China, are making use of a definitely American ideological product—the ideology of "brainwashing."

NOTES

1. The tragic Waco episode involving the Branch Davidians represents a major exception to the general "hands off" policy of the federal government. See Wright 1995, Tabor and Gallagher 1995, and Wessinger 2000 for thorough explanations of how this unusual event occurred. Also see Wright 2002 and Richardson 2002 for analyses of the major legal trials that occurred after the Waco tragedy.

2. It should be said that by far the vast majority of former members in these high-attrition groups (see Bird and Reimer 1983) did not file legal actions. But the small percentage of former members who did file civil actions sometimes received considerable media attention, and they were generally well received by a legal system that seemed to adopt a somewhat normative role vis-à-vis NRMs (Richardson and van Driel 1997; Richardson 2000, 2001a).

3. In civil or criminal cases against deprogrammers the brainwashing issue would be raised as support for a "necessity or choice of evils defense," by which the defendant(s) claim that since the person they were deprogramming had been "brainwashed," it was justified for them to be kidnapped and "rescued" from the "cult" (Richardson 2000: 113–114).

4. The COG, now called The Family, currently has around eight thousand members, of whom nearly five thousand are second generation (Richardson 1994).

5. The articles by Fautre, Seiwert, Swantko, and Introvigne all appear in a special issue of *Social Justice Research* edited by this writer (*Social Justice Research* 12, no. 4). In this issue there are also articles dealing with Canada, Hungary, Australia, England and Wales, and Russia, as well as other more general articles dealing with "brainwashing" claims and with experimental evidence of how bias can operate within judicial systems. Also see the April 2001 issue of *Nova Religio*, which has a special focus on NRMs and their legal and political context around the world.

6. An example of such legislation that can be considered discriminatory on its face would be statutory hierarchies of religious groups that allow more privileges from some groups and less for others. Sometimes such arrangements, which are prevalent in European countries, may have three or four levels of privilege defined in law. See Durham 2001 and Richardson 2001a for a discussion of such hierarchies.

7. A more powerful religious group might seek special privileges through a "concordant" made with the government, allowing the church to offer religious instructions in a public school system, or having special access to those in the military or in prisons. Special tax privileges is another prominent area of special treatment for preferred religious groups. The Greek Orthodox Church has even succeeded in having proselytizing made a criminal offense in Greece, a provision that has caused considerable international concern and has resulted in significant losses in the European Court of Human Rights (Evans 2001; Richardson 1995d).

REFERENCES

Anthony, D. 1990. "Religious Movements and Brainwashing Litigation: Evaluating Key Testimony." In *In Gods We Trust* ed. T. Robbins and D. Anthony, 295–344. New Brunswick, N.J.: Transaction Books.

———. 1999. "Pseudoscience and Minority Religions: An Evaluation of the Brainwashing Theories of Jean-Marie Abgrall." *Social Justice Research* 12: 421–456.

Anthony, D., and T. Robbins. 1992. "Law, Social Science, and the 'Brainwashing' Exception to the First Amendment." *Behavioral Sciences and the Law* 10: 5–30.

Anthony, D., and T. Robbins. 1995. "Negligence, Coercion, and the Protection of Religious Belief." *Journal of Church and State* 37: 509–537.

———. 1998. "Negligence, Coercion, and the Protection of Religious Belief." *Journal of Church and State* 37: 509–527.

Barker, E. 1995. "Plus ca change." *Social Compass* 42: 165–180.

———. 2001. "General Overview of the Cult Scene in Great Britain." *Nova Religion* 4: 235–240.

Beckford, J. A. 1985. *Cult Controversies: The Societal Response to New Religious Movements.* London: Tavistock.

———. 2003. " 'Lacicite': 'Dystopia' and the Reaction to New Religious Movements in France." In *Regulating Religion: Case Studies from Around the Globe* ed. J. T. Richardson. New York: Kluwer.

Bird, F., and W. Reimer. 1983. "Participation Rates in New Religious Movements and Para-Religious Movements." *Journal for the Scientific Study of Religion* 21: 1–14.

Black, D. 1976. *The Behavior of Law.* New York: Academic Press.

———. 1999. *The Social Structure of Right and Wrong.* New York: Academic Press.

Black, D., and M. P. Baumgartner. 1999. "Toward a Theory of the Third Party." In *The Social Structure of Right and Wrong* ed. D. Black, 95–124. New York: Academic Press.

Bouma, G. 1999. "Social Justice Issues in Management of Religious Diversity in Australia." *Social Justice Research* 12: 283–296.

Bromley, D. 1983. "Conservatorships and Deprogramming: Legal and Political Prospects." In *The Brainwashing/Deprogramming Controversy* ed. D. Bromley and J. Richardson, 267–294. New York: Edwin Mellen Press.

Carter, Lewis. 1990. *Charisma and Control in Rajneeshpuram.* New York: Cambridge University Press.

Crumper, P. 2001. "The Public Manifestations of Religion or Belief: Challenges for a Multi-Faith Society in the Twenty-First Century." In *Law and Religion* ed. R. O'Dair and A. Lewis, 311–328. New York: Oxford University Press.

Dasi, M. 2001. "Religious Freedom and NRMs in Europe." *ISKCON Communications Journal* 8: 65–78.

Denaux, A. 2002. "The Attitude of Belgium Authorities toward New Religious Movements." *Brigham Young University Law Review* 2002, no. 2: 101–130.

Deutscher Bundestag. 1998. "Final Report of the Enquete Commission on 'So-Called Sects and Psychogroups.' " Trans. W. Fehlberg and M. Ulloa-Fehlberg. Bonn: Deutscher Bundestag.

Durham, C. 1999. "Freedom of Religion or Belief: Laws Affecting the Structuring of Religious Communities." OSCE/ODIHR Background Paper 1999/4.

———. 2001. "The Emerging Legal Environment Faced by Smaller Religious Communities in Central and Eastern Europe." Presented at CESNUR/INFORM Conference, London School of Economics, April.

Edleman, B., and J. T. Richardson. 2002. "Falun Gong and the Law: Development of Legal Social Control in China." *Nova Religio* 6, no. 2: 312–331.

Evans, C. 2001. *Freedom of Religion under the European Convention on Human Rights.* New York: Oxford University Press.

Faust, D., and J. Ziskin. 1988. "The Expert Witness in Psychology and Psychiatry." *Science* 241: 31–37.

Fautre, W. 1999. "Belgium's Anti-Sect War." *Social Justice Research* 12: 377–392.

Flinn, F. 1987. "Criminalizing Conversion: The Legislative Assault on New Religions." In *Crime, Values, and Religion* ed. J. Day and W. Laufer, 153–192. Norwood, N.J.: Ablex.

Geertz, A. W., and M. Rothstein. 2001. "Religious Minorities and New Religious Movements in Denmark." *Nova Religio* 4: 298–309.

Ginsburg, G. P., and J. T. Richardson. 1998. " 'Brainwashing' Evidence in Light of *Daubert.*" In *Law and Science* ed. H. Reece, 265–288. Oxford: Oxford University Press.

Gunn, T. J. 1996. "Adjudicating Rights of Conscience under the European Convention on Human Rights." In *Religious Rights in Global Perspective: Legal Perspectives* ed. J. van der Vyver and J. Witte, 305–330. The Hague: M. Nijhoff.

Guttman, J. 1985. "The Legislative Assault on New Religions." In *Cults, Culture, and the Law* ed. T. Robbins, W. Shepherd, and J. McBride, 101–110. Chico, Calif.: Scholars Press.

Hervieu-Leger, D. 2001. "France's Obsession with the 'Sectarian Threat.' " *Nova Religio* 4: 249–257.

Hill, M. 2003. "The Rehabilitation and Regulation of Religion in Singapore." In *Regulating Religion: Case Studies from Around the Globe* ed. J. T. Richardson. New York: Kluwer.

Hume, L. 1995. "Witchcraft and the Law in Australia." *Journal of Church and State* 37: 135–150.

Introvigne, M. 1998. "Blacklisting or Greenlisting? A European Perspective on the New Cult Wars." *Nova Religio* 2: 16–23.

———. 1999. "Holy Mountains and Anti-Cult Ecology: The Campaign Against the Aumists in France." *Social Justice Research* 12: 365–376.

———. 2001. "Italy's Surprisingly Favorable Environment for Religious Minorities." *Nova Religio* 4: 275–280.

Introvigne, M., and J. G. Melton. 1996. *Pour en finir avec les sectes.* Milan: CESNUR.

Introvigne, M., and J. T. Richardson. 2001. "Western Europe, Postmodernity, and the Shadow of the French Revolution: A Response to Soper and Robbins." *Journal for the Scientific Study of Religion* 40: 181–185.

Ireland, R. 1999. "Religious Diversity in the New Australian Democracy." *Australian Religious Studies Review* 12: 94–110.

James, G. 1986. "Brainwashing: The Myth and the Actuality." *Thought: A Review of Culture and Idea* 61: 241–257.

Kilbourne, B., and J. T. Richardson. 1984. "Psychotherapy and New Religions in a Pluralistic Society." *American Psychologist* 39: 237.

Kisala, R., and M. Mullins. 2001. *Religion and Social Crisis in Japan: Understanding Japanese Society through the Aum Affair.* New York: St. Martin's.

Krannenborg, R. 1994. "The Anti-Cult Movement in the Netherlands: An Unsuccessful Affair." In *Anti-Cult Movements in Cross-Cultural Perspective* ed. A. Shupe and D. Bromley, 221–236. New York: Garland.

Kurokawa, T. 1999. "Mind Control and New Religions." *SYZYGY* 8: 77–84.

Lemoult, J. 1983. "Deprogramming Members of Religious Sects." In *The Brainwashing/Deprogramming Controversy* ed. D. Bromley and J. Richardson, 234–257. New York: Edwin Mellen Press.

Lewis, J., ed. 1999. "Aum Shinrikyo and Human Rights." *SYZYGY* 8 (special issue).

Lewis, J., and J. G. Melton. 1994. *Sex, Slander, and Salvation: Investigating The Family/Children of God.* Stanford, Calif.: Center for Academic Publications.

Mickler, Mike. 1994. "The Anti-Cult Movement in Japan." In *Anti-Cult Movements in Cross-Cultural Perspective* ed. A. Shupe and D. Bromley, 255–274. New York: Garland.

Mortensen, Reid. 2000. "Interpreting a Sacred Landscape: Aboriginal Religion and Law in Australia in the 1990s." In *La religion en droit comparé à l'aube du 21 siècle,* ed. E. Caparros & L. Christians, 281–306. Brussels, Belgium: Bruylant.

Mullins, M. 2001. "The Legal and Political Fallout of the 'Aum Affair.' " In *Religion and Social Crisis in Japan* ed. R. Kisala and M. Mullins, 71–88. London: St. Martin's.

Palmer, S., and C. Hardman. 1999. *Children in New Religions.* New Brunswick, N.J.: Rutgers University Press.

Pfeifer, J. 1999. "Perceptual Biases and Mock Juror Decision-Making: Minority Religions in Court." *Social Justice Research* 12: 409–420.

Reader, I. 2000. "Scholarship, Aum Shinrikyo, and Academic Integrity." *Nova Religio* 3: 368–382.

Regan, R. J. 1986. "Regulating Cult Activities: The Limits of Religious Freedom." *Thought: A Review of Culture and Idea* 61: 185–196.

Richardson, J. T. 1985. "The 'Deformation' of New Religions: Impacts of Societal and Organizational Factors." In *Cults, Culture, and the Law,* ed. T. Robbins, W. Shepherd, and J. McBride, 163–176. Chico, Calif.: Scholars Press.

———. 1986. "Consumer Protection and Deviant Religion: A Case Study." *Review of Religious Research* 28: 168–179.

———. 1991. "Cult/Brainwashing Cases and the Freedom of Religion." *Journal of Church and State* 33: 55–74.

———. 1993a. "Religiosity as Deviance: Anti-Religious Bias in the DSM." *Deviant Behavior* 14: 1–20.

———. 1993b. "A Social Psychological Critique of Brainwashing Claims about Recruitment to New Religions." In *Handbook of Cults and Sects in America* ed. J. Hadden and D. Bromley, 75–97. Greenwich, Conn.: JAI Press.

———. 1994. "Update on 'The Family': Organizational Change and Development in a Controversial New religious Group." In *Sex, Sin, and Slander* ed. J. Lewis and J. G. Melton, 27–40. Stanford, Calif.: Center for Academic Publication.

———. 1995a. "Clinical and Personality Assessment of Participants in New Religions." *International Journal for the Psychology of Religion* 5: 145–170.

———. 1995b. "Legal Status of Minority Religions in the United States." *Social Compass* 42: 249–264.

———. 1995c. "Minority Religions ('Cults') and the Law: Comparisons of the United States, Europe, and Australia." *University of Queensland Law Journal* 18: 183–207.

———. 1995d. "Minority Religions, Religious Freedom, and the Pan-European Political and Judicial Institutions." *Journal of Church and State* 37: 39–60.

———. 1996. " 'Brainwashing' Claims and Minority Religions Outside the United States: Cultural Diffusion of a Questionable Legal Concept in the Legal Arena." *Brigham Young University Law Review* 1996: 873–904.

———. 1997. "Sociology and the New Religions: 'Brainwashing,' the Courts, and Religious Freedom." In *Witnessing for Sociology* ed. P. Jenkins and S. Kroll-Smith, 115–137. New York: Praeger.

———. 1998a. "The Accidental Expert." *Nova Religio* 2: 31–43.

———. 1998b. "Law and Minority Religions: 'Positive' and 'Negative' Uses of the Legal System." *Nova Religio* 2: 93–107.

———. 1999a. "The Religious Freedom Restoration Act: A Short-Lived Experiment in Religious Freedom." In *Religion and Law in the Global Village* ed. D. Guinn, C. Barrigar, and K. Young, 142–164. Atlanta: Scholars Press.

———. 1999b. "Social Control of New Religions: From 'Brainwashing' Claims to Child

Sex Abuse Accusations." In *Children in New Religions* ed. S. Palmer and C. Hardman, 172–186. New Brunswick, N.J.: Rutgers University Press.

———. 2000. "Discretion and Discrimination in Legal Cases Involving Controversial Religious Groups and Allegations of Ritual Abuse." In *Law and Religion* ed. R. Ahdar. Aldershot, U.K.: Ashgate.

———. 2001a. "Law, Social Control, and Minority Religions." In *Frontier Religions in Public Space* ed. P. Cote, 139–168. Ottawa: University of Ottawa Press.

———. 2001b. "New Religions in Australia: Public Menace or Societal Salvation?" *Nova Religio* 4: 258–265.

———. 2002. " 'Showtime' in Texas: Social Production of the Branch Davidian Trials." *Nova Religio* 5: 152–170.

Richardson, J. T., and B. van Driel. 1994. "New Religions in Europe: A Comparison of Developments and Reactions in England, France, Germany, and The Netherlands." In *Anti-Cult Movements in Cross-Cultural Perspective* ed. A. Shupe and D. Bromley, 129–170. New York: Garland.

———. 1997. "Journalists' Attitudes toward New Religious Movements." *Review of Religious Research* 39: 116–136.

Richardson, J. T., and B. Edleman. 2002. "Social Control of Minority Religions in Japan and China: Legal and Historical Comparisons." In *Minority Religions and Church-State Relations* ed. D. Davis. Waco: Baylor University Press.

Richardson, J. T., and M. Introvigne. 2001. " 'Brainwashing' Theories in European Parliamentary and Administrative Reports on 'Cults and Sects.' " *Journal for the Scientific Study of Religion* 40: 143–168.

Richardson, J. T., and B. Kilbourne. 1983. "Classical and Contemporary Applications of Brainwashing Models: A Comparison and Critique." In *The Brainwashing/Deprogramming Controversy* ed. D. Bromley and J. Richardson, 29–46. New York: Edwin Mellen Press.

Richardson, J. T., and M. Shterin. 1999. "Minority Religions and Social Justice in Russian Courts: An Analysis of Recent Cases." *Social Justice Research* 12: 393–408.

Robbins, T. 2001. "Combating 'Cults' and 'Brainwashing' in the United States and Western Europe: A Comment on Richardson and Introvigne's Report." *Journal for the Scientific Study of Religion* 40: 169–175.

———. 1998. "Objectivity, Advocacy, and Animosity." *Nova Religio* 2: 24–30.

Robbins, T., D. Anthony, and J. McCarthy. 1983. "Legitimating Repression." In *The Brainwashing/Deprogramming Controversy* ed. D. Bromley and J. Richardson, 319–328. New York: Edwin Mellen Press.

Saliba, J. 1993. "The New Religions and Mental Health." In *Handbook of Cults and Sects in America* ed. J. Hadden and D. Bromley, 99–113. Greenwich, Conn.: JAI Press.

Schoen, B. 2001. "New Religions in Germany: The Publicity of the Public Square." *Nova Religio* 4: 266–274.

Seiwert, H. 1999. "The German Enquete Commission on Sects: Political Conflicts and Compromises." *Social Justice Research* 12: 323–340.

Shanda, B. 1999. "Freedom of Religion and Minority Religions in Hungary." *Social Justice Research* 12: 297–314.

Shterin, M., and J. T. Richardson. 1998. "Local Laws on Religion in Russia: Precursors of Russia's National Law." *Journal of Church and State* 40: 319–341.

———. 2000. "Effects of the Western Anti-Cult Movement on Development of Laws

Concerning Religion in Post-Communist Russia." *Journal of Church and State* 42: 247–272.

———. 2002. "The *Yakunin v. Dworkin* Trial and the Emerging Religious Pluralism in Russia." *Religion in Eastern Europe* 22: 1–38.

Shupe, A., and D. Bromley. 1980. *The New Vigilantes: Anti-Cultists and the New Religions* Beverly Hills, Calif.: Sage.

———. 1994. *Anti-Cult Movements in Cross-Cultural Perspective.* New York: Garland.

Soper, C. 2001. "Tribal Instinct and Religious Persecution: Why Do West European States Behave So Badly?" *Journal for the Scientific Study of Religion* 40: 177–180.

Stark, R. 1996. *The Rise of Christianity.* Princeton, N.J.: Princeton University Press.

Swantko, J. 1999. "The Twelve Tribes Communities, the Anti-Cult Movement, and Government Response." *Social Justice Research* 12: 341–364.

Tabor, J., and Gallagher E. 1995. *Why Waco?* Berkeley: University of California Press.

Wessinger, C. 2002. *How the Millennium Comes Violently.* New York: Seven Bridges Press.

———, ed. 2000. *Millennialism, Persecution, and Violence: Historical Cases.* Syracuse, N.Y.: Syracuse University Press, 2000.

Wright, S. 1995. *Armageddon in Waco.* Chicago: University of Chicago Press.

———. 2002. "Justice Denied: The Waco Civil Trial." *Nova Religio* 5: 143–151.

CHAPTER 8

THE NORTH AMERICAN ANTI-CULT MOVEMENT

Vicissitudes of Success and Failure

ANSON SHUPE

DAVID G. BROMLEY

SUSAN E. DARNELL

THROUGHOUT North American history, new religious movements (NRMs) have emerged consistently, stimulating oppositional hostility and even repression from the general public, various levels of government, and more institutionalized religious competitors (Bromley and Shupe 1989). Indeed, as Shupe and Bromley (1979) suggested about earlier controversies concerning the Unification Church, and as Jenkins (2000) more recently asserted about conflict in America's ongoing pluralistic experiment, the twin social movement phenomena "cult (NRM) and anticult (ACM) movements" go hand-in-hand. Most research on NRMs and other unconventional religions, whether from a variety of religious perspectives (Fuss 1998; Melton 1990) or a social science perspective (see, e.g., Bromley and Hadden 1993; Saliba 1990), suggests both that these movements gradually mature and that few succeed in attaining the goals articulated in their ideologies. More commonly, movements experience mixed successes and failures and manage to do no more than carve out a modest niche within the religious economy. Likewise, what little recent research has been conducted on the ACM indicates that the ACM, like the movements it opposes, has encountered developmental problems that it has been unable to resolve (Shupe 1985; Shupe and Bromley 1987; Shupe and Darnell 2003 forthcoming).

There is an enormous body of theory and research on the organization of social movements. However, the ACM is a particular kind of social movement; it is a countermovement, which means that it derives its organizational purpose from the existence of other movements. There is much less theory and research on countermovements than the movements to which they respond (Mottl 1980). The sociological problem is to understand how the ACM operated as an exemplar or this type of movement. While it is now well documented that ACM history is replete with radical acts and actors (Shupe and Bromley 1980; Shupe and Darnell 2002; Shupe and Darnell forthcoming), we argue that the most useful sociological perspective on the ACM can be gained by analyzing it in terms of an internal countermovement structure/economy and an external alliance network.

By countermovement structure we refer to an integrated network of roles (organization) and an integrated symbolic system (ideology) that constitute the countermovement form. The key roles within the ACM include members (rank-and-file organization participants), functionaries (organization leaders), restorative agents (deprogrammers/exit counselors, therapists), experts (attorneys and therapists), and apostates (former members who disaffiliated from NRMs and affiliated with the ACM). The basic format of the ACM ideology as it was initially developed is that a new and dangerous social problem has emerged (cults); that the problem is unrecognized, is growing rapidly, and presents a clear and present danger to society; and that remedial action to recover and treat compromised individuals (deprogramming/counseling) and to counter the groups themselves (regulatory measures) is imperative.

The countermovement economy consists of a primary medium of exchange and a primary transactional mechanism. In the case of the ACM, the primary medium of exchange is cultists (the persons, information about them, services to them, and control over them). The primary transactional mechanism is information exchanged for referrals (voluntary or coercive) or donations. The concept of economy therefore does not involve simply finances, although money is obviously a critical resource. Rather, it also involves a moral element as cultists constitute a social category about which remedial action, including coercive referrals (deprogramming), is mandated. Together the medium of exchange and transactional mechanism constitute the countermovement's internal logic, connecting the constituent elements and the countermovement as a whole.

The alliance network refers to the set of organizations and institutions that significantly impact or are impacted by the countermovement structure and economy. As a movement organized to counter cultic groups, the ACM necessarily attempted to legitimate and undertake actions that had consequences outside its own boundaries. Such actions required that the ACM gain the overt support or at least neutralize the opposition of external groups interested in and capable of accepting or resisting them. Legal status for organizational units, which conveys legitimacy and financial advantages, and acceptance of countermovement ideology as knowledge are particularly critical forms of alliance. Allies need not be active coalitional partners, therefore, but rather must simply be engaged in sufficiently parallel lines of action that they implicitly or explicitly accord the countermovement legitimacy and allow it to be effective in conducting its mission. Legitimacy and effectiveness are the broadest indices of organizational success and failure.

Our argument with respect to the development of the countermovement structure and economy is as follows. NRMs emerged as protest movements in the West in response to a pervasive structural crisis (Bellah 1976; Glock 1976; Cox 1977), and the ACM quickly arose in direct reaction to NRMs (Shupe and Bromley 1980, 1985; Shupe and Darnell forthcoming; Melton 1999). In order to counter NRMs, the ACM attempted to create a structure and economy that would function both to coordinate the identification and processing of cultists within the component units of this countermovement and to coordinate ACM interests with external organizations. This required an ideology that would override the NRMs' claim to religious legitimacy and an organizational structure that effectively redirected the loyalties of NRM members and disempowered NRM organizations. The ACM attempted to accomplish this objective by (1) developing a cult/mind control ideology that identified a set of subversive groups and practices and (2) erecting an organizational network that accumulated cases, investigated and sorted groups, provided services, and exercised controls.

By creating its ideology and organizational network, the ACM essentially created cultists. The ideology designated groups and practices against which claims could be made, and the organizational network created operational procedures for processing those claims. This countermovement structure served as the basis for a countermovement economy in which cultists were the primary medium of exchange. Because the various components of the ACM network developed independently, the countermovement was a loosely integrated network of roles that converged around exchanges related to cultists rather than a single formal organization.

The intractable problem that the ACM faced was to create a countermovement structure that could simultaneously integrate internal activity and integrate with the organization and ideology of institutions with which it needed alliances.

We trace the process of ACM development through three stages: emergent, expansion/consolidation, and domestic accommodation/international expansion. The *emergent stage* from the late 1960s to the end of the 1970s, witnessed the initial construction of the countermovement structure and economy, most notably its mind control ideology. During the *expansion/consolidation stage* of the 1980s, national-level organization was achieved and the countermovement structure and economy were fully developed. The *domestic accommodation/ international expansion stage* that began in the early 1990s has been one in which the ACM has lost its most visible and radical organizational unit. The result has been that movement rhetoric and action has moderated, although the ACM contributed to the implementation of radical control measures in Europe.

THE EMERGENT STAGE

The emergent stage began in the mid- to late 1960s when a number of groups, such as the Children of God (now the Family), the Unification Church, and Hare Krishna, began to attract countercultural, idealistic young adults (Bromley and Shupe 1979). The distraught families of these recruits, disappointed that their offsprings' life trajectories were seemingly moving away from traditional educations, conventional families of procreation, and mainstream employment, reacted by organizing themselves in search of answers and redress. Most of the key elements of the countermovement structure (organization, ideology) and economy (the patterning of transactions integrating the organizational network) were established during the emergent stage, and there were several initiatives to build alliances with state and federal governmental units. The end of the emergent stage is marked by three developments: massive defections from NRMs in the latter half of the 1970s by affiliates who only briefly experimented with membership (Barker 1984); failure of the murder-suicides by the Peoples Temple to produce governmental mobilization against cults (Shupe, Bromley, and Breschel 1989), and the ACM's inability to devise grounds for legally extracting affiliates from NRMs. All three developments led the ACM to reassess its countermovement strategy.

The most immediate problem confronting distraught families of NRM converts was to provide a label for the troubles they were confronting that could serve as the basis for legitimation. To invoke C. Wright Mills's insightful phrase, the problem was converting private troubles into public issues. The affiliation of young adults with religious movements was not presumptively a social problem. The ACM sought to construct a public issue through its cult/ mind control ideology. "Cult" already had a long history as a pejorative term utilized by conservative Christian groups to identify theologically heretical churches (e.g., Martin 1977; Shupe, Bromley, and Oliver 1994). In the secular ACM model, cults were also pseudoreligious groups, but the negative appellation attached to putatively subversive recruitment/control techniques. Indeed, the ACM went to great lengths to assert that religious beliefs were not at issue in order to avoid constitutional proscriptions on constraint of free exercise. Initially identifying the cult problem was facilitated by the fact that the ACM defined cults in terms of the small number of groups that shared in common a communal lifestyle and public proselytization. The concept of mind control was more problematic. The movement began with a motley and often inconsistent set of explanations, improper diet, drugging, and hypnosis but fairly quickly began to draw on post–Korean War brainwashing research as the foundation of its ideology (Richardson 1983).

The cult/mind control model provided the countermovement with an important legitimation resource. It offered a paradigm of unusual behavior that (1) attached no stigma to either the families or the cultists, who became victims; (2) offered the veneer of scientific legitimation; (3) linked together a set of otherwise apparently disparate groups; (4) created the basis for retrieving NRM affiliates; and (5) potentially circumvented the facts that the groups at issue claimed religious status and the affiliates were overwhelmingly legal adults. The cult concept allowed the ACM to identify cultists; the mind control concept created the informational base that the ACM used in counseling families and coordinating with the media and government agencies.

The major components of the countermovement structure and economy were established during this period, albeit often in elemental form. These components included formation of a decentralized organization network, a two-tiered organizational structure, services for cultists, the production of apostates, and an information-referral exchange base.

The ACM began with the individual, localized efforts of family members of recruits to the Children of God, which initially was located in the western United States, and led to the formation of FREECOG. Soon thereafter, the rapid growth of the Hare Krishna, the Unification Church, and a number of other new groups expanded and diversified the ranks of aggrieved families, but FREECOG was initially resistant to broadening its organizational focus to incorporate other groups. The result was the formation of literally dozens of regional ACM organizations that functioned primarily as information and support groups. These organizations operated as nonprofit, educational associations (although most did not achieve tax-exempt status) with an information-donation–based economy. Beset by a network of weak, local organizations and NRMs that were well financed and nationally organized, ACM leaders made several attempts at forming a national confederation, but these foundered over disagreements on fund-raising, fund dispersal, and local autonomy. In 1974 representatives from a number of ACM groups met and did form a national organization, the Citizens Freedom Foundation (CFF). However, it was not until the early 1980s that CFF funded a national director position (Coates 1994: 96). During the intervening years various components of the ACM developed independently, leading to a decentralized ACM network linked by information/referral exchanges.

Fledgling ACM groups developed a simple two-tier organization structure, members and functionaries, that is characteristic of many voluntary associations.

ACM members were almost all relatives of current and former NRM members. Membership turnover was high because loyalty was limited as members' primary objective was simply recovering a wayward family member. During this stage organization functionaries typically were crusading rank-and-file members who assumed leadership by investing the enormous time and energy required to keep this type of voluntary association operating. The resulting burnout produced considerable turnover in both membership and functionary ranks, which limited ACM size and strength.

The first restorative agents also appeared during this stage in the form of both deprogrammers and therapists. In fact, deprogramming and ACM organizations emerged almost simultaneously. The practice of deprogramming was devised as a technique that putatively reversed the effects of cultic programming (mind control). During the early years most deprogrammings involved some measure of coercion as deprogrammers abducted and forcibly confined NRM members, requiring them to listen to mind control theory, negative literature and media presentations, and testimonials from apostate members (Bromley 1988a). The success rates for deprogramming were high, particularly for more recent affiliates, and these successes provided one of the most important means by which the ACM bolstered the legitimacy of its ideology and demonstrated effectiveness in providing the service families wanted most, recovery of the NRM affiliate (Bromley 1988a). For a number of years CFF actively and publicly promoted deprogramming, and there probably were several thousand deprogrammings during this stage. While deprogramming was a very lucrative vocation for a time, entrepreurial deprogrammers were not formally connected to ACM organizations but rather functioned as entrepreneurs who were employed directly by families usually on the basis of a referral from an ACM organization. The independence of deprogrammers therefore also contributed significantly to the development of an ACM network based on an information-referral exchange, with referrals from deprogrammers taking the form of apostates.

As an adjunct to deprogramming, therapeutic services of various types emerged to help former cultists recover from the deleterious effects of mind control. In addition to private therapy, formal rehabilitation centers were established to provide facilities where cultists could be deprogrammed and reintegrated into conventional society under supervision. One of the most prominent of these was the Freedom of Thought Foundation (FTF), founded jointly by an attorney and deprogrammer in 1976. Like deprogramming, rehabilitation centers created the potential for generating financial resources for the ACM. Also like deprogramming, rehabilitation services developed independently of ACM organizations and linked to those organizations through the emerging information-referral system. Rehabilitation as a complement to deprogramming declined rather rapidly as opposition to deprogramming mounted. FTF operated only a few years before being forced to close in the face of a wave of legal injunctions and lawsuits.

The final element of the countermovement structure that appeared during this stage was the apostate role. Apostates were critical to the legitimation of the ACM because they provided the eyewitness testimony of legal and moral violations in which cults and their leaders allegedly engaged (Bromley 1998). In many cases apostates had been deprogrammed, and some went on to become deprogrammers themselves. Apostates became a critical ACM resource. They appeared at ACM conferences where their testimonials were offered as legitimation for ACM ideology and where they could participate in support groups and informational workshops. They were particularly effective in generating atrocity stories that became an increasing staple of media accounts by the mid-1970s (Bromley, Shupe, and Ventimiglia 1979). Apostates influenced public opinion by authoring books, delivering public lectures, assisting in deprogrammings, appearing in court cases, and testifying at legislative hearings where cults were excoriated. Apostates were also useful in deprogrammings where deprogrammees could be confronted by peers who recounted stories of their own personal victimization at the hands of a cult. And so while apostates often were not ACM functionaries, their careers were often rather tightly connected to the ACM and most generally involved testimonials in return for referrals.

The ACM was successful in creating an elemental countermovement and economy within just a few years. However, if the ACM was to function as a private regulatory agency with a capacity to combat cults and recover cultists, some type of alliance with governmental agencies was necessary. During this stage the greatest effort was expended on legitimating deprogramming, and for the first few years the alliance with government functionaries was quite informal and ad hoc. Deprogrammers and family members were able to enlist the support of local authorities on a case-by-case basis by rehearsing cult/mind control ideology. Sympathetic authorities often treated the confrontations as family disputes involving unruly juveniles and did not contest the use of force. However, within a few years NRMs and civil liberties groups began to contest the abductions in court. Thereupon a more formal alliance was needed. The problem the ACM faced was finding a means of enlisting state support for custody of adults professing a voluntary religious affiliation. The mechanism the ACM discovered was court-ordered conservatorships that traditionally had been used to allow families to assume legal control of aging relatives with diminshed mental capacity. Appeals for conservatorships in ACM cases were based on assertions of diminished capacity as a result of cultic mind control. While families and deprogrammers were successful in locating sympathetic judges for a time, NRMs soon began contesting conservatorships. One pivotal case in California, *Katz v. Superior Court*, involved five adult members of the Unification Church (dubbed the "Faithful Five") who contested a conservatorship order that would have allowed parents to place them in a deprogramming center. The trial judge awarded custody to the parents, but the decision was overturned on appeal, and the conservatorship strategy quickly disintegrated thereafter (Bromley and Robbins 1992).

The ACM sought formal governmental intervention against NRMs as organizations in a range of states through the 1970s, but the result invariably was legislative hearings at which cults were castigated by ACM sympathizers rather than substantive legislation that would empower the ACM or deliver governmental sanctions. There was comparable activity at the national level where then Senator Robert Dole held public hearings in 1976 and again in 1979 after the murder-suicides at Jonestown. When even the horrific events at Jonestown failed to translate into governmental initiatives, the ACM began to recognize that a direct alliance with state and federal government units was unlikely. The ACM came close to establishing sanctioning power in New York when a sympathetic legislator introduced a bill to amend the penal code to include as offense "promoting a pseudo-religious cult." The bill was vetoed in 1978 after passing both legislative houses. By the end of the decade it became evident that if the ACM was to perform a regulatory function, a new strategy was required.

In sum, the broad outlines of the countermovement structure and economy had appeared by the end of the 1970s, and the ACM undertook several initiatives to forge alliances with governmental agencies. Certainly the most striking and enduring success of the ACM during this stage was the construction of its cult/mind control ideology, which transformed affiliation with NRMs from a private problem to a public issue and legitimated the ACM's extreme claims and actions. The ideology served as the basis for dispensing information to families, media, and government agencies. Major components of countermovement organization also were established, most notably restorative agents and apostates, but cohesive national organization eluded the ACM during these years. Because restorative agents and apostates both developed independently of local and regional ACM organizations, the countermovement economy developed as a loosely coupled network integrated by a system of information/referral/donation exchanges. Deprogramming was a key element of the countermovement structure and economy as it provided legitimation of ACM ideology, a flow of apostates to ACM organizations, and an effective response to family demands. However, the ACM was unable to develop an alliance with governmental agencies that would create legal auspices for deprogramming. The tension between the ACM's internal structure and economy and its relationships with external institutions is reflected in the fact that deprogramming was an integral part of the ACM's internal economy and its relationship with families of cultists but also violated ACM organizations' self-presentation as educational associations. As a result, the ACM was forced to disavow deprogramming publicly while continuing the practice clandestinely. Over the next several years the ACM sought to implement a new strategy that would resolve this contradiction.

THE EXPANSION/CONSOLIDATION STAGE

During the expansion/consolidation stage, which encompassed the 1980s, all of the elements of the countermovement structure and economy were fully developed, and the ACM was at the height of its influence. This stage began with several significant developments. The ACM established a national organizational presence at the beginning of the decade, coordinating the various elements of the countermovement. Disaffiliations from NRMs that began in the late 1970s became a massive exodus as most affiliates concluded that the movements did not constitute viable long-term lifestyle alternatives. ACM ideology shifted to account for these "walkaways," and the large number of former members provided the ACM with a pool from which to recruit. This stage ended at the close of the decade when several legal cases were settled in such a way that it became clear that the ACM's current strategy for combating cults would not be successful.

A key development in the countermovement structure during the expansion/consolidation stage was the establishment of national-level organizations. By the turn of the decade CFF had received tax-exempt status as an educational trust (Citizens Freedom Foundation-Information Services), and many of the 1970s local and regional ACM groups had simply collapsed. Obtaining tax-exempt status constituted a major victory for CFF as it both increased the probability of donations and allowed the organization to retain all of those revenues. It also created organizational vulnerability as CFF was obligated to operate as an educational organization. One ACM functionary described the major national ACM organization as a "national consumer protection organization to educate the public about what they called spiritual frauds or destructive cults" (Coates 1994: 94). This mission rested uneasily with its continuing involvement in deprogramming. A second national organization, the American Family Foundation (AFF), began as a CFF affiliate but became an independent entity in 1979. AFF and CFF developed somewhat different missions, although the overlap in their membership and leadership indicates a close alliance (Shupe and Darnell forthcoming). AFF became a think tank and information clearinghouse, holding annual meetings at which anticult-oriented research was reported and publishing the *Cultic Studies Journal* as a means of creating scientific legitimation for the ACM. CFF, which changed its name to the Cult Awareness Network (CAN) in 1986, rapidly became the public face of the ACM. With the demise of many local ACM groups and the increased visibility of CAN, the number of inquiries to which it responded grew over the next decade from 5,000 to 16,000 annually (Coates 1994).

The prominence of CAN meant that requests for information were now most likely to be received by the new national organization, and this information became central to the countermovement economy. In most cases the exchanges involved information about a cultist and a donation in return for information about the cult and its brainwashing practices. As CAN received inquiries, each could be added to its database. The inquiry/response database produced information about a new group demonstrating the pervasiveness of cultism, additional information about a group already being tracked, a higher case count confirming the seriousness of the cult problem, and the basis for memberships and charitable donations appeals. Responses to inquiries typically took the form of information packets of various kinds that were sent to inquirers in return for a donation, which became a primary source of revenue for CAN. Information packets were also sold to local affiliates, which bought them at a reduced rate and then distributed them in response to inquiries they received. CAN also used the information it received as the basis for referrals to ACM-connected deprogrammers, experts offering therapeutic or litigation services, recovery and rehabilitation services, or journalists. In return for information, ACM service providers exchanged sanctioning of cults, reintegration of former cultists with families, legitimation of ACM ideology, and apostate testimony. Journalists hopefully responded with sympathetic coverage of the ACM mission.

Both AFF and CAN continued to rely on a membership base composed of small donors, newsletter subscribers, family members of NRM affiliates, and former NRM members. However, the 1980s witnessed the emergence of both a more broadly based membership (lawyers, clergy, mental health professionals, and social scientists) and functionaries, paid staff, and professional managers. CFF (CAN), which had drawn up plans for a national director several years earlier, finally made the first appointment in 1980. While the addition of professional and paid staff created greater organizational stability, it also increased operating costs. ACM organizations, and CAN in particular, continued to contain costs by relying heavily on volunteers to handle the enormous increase in day-to-day inquiries from family members and the media. AFF established a modest but viable economic base from the outset by relying on journal subscriptions, payment for information packets, and conference subscriptions, as well as donations for income. Both organizations, however, continued to face fiscal challenges, a problem that CAN attempted to address by soliciting donations for referrals.

The other major development in ACM structure was the expanded importance of experts and apostates. These roles became more central as the ACM shifted its strategy in response to the massive exodus of NRM members and the increased resistance to coercive deprogramming. The new ACM strategy was to bring civil suits with NRMs and/or individual leaders as defendants.[2] By contrast with coercive deprogramming, civil actions did not require an alliance with the state; the courts were to function simply as neutral arbiters of claims brought by private parties. Typically making generic claims of intentional infliction of emotional distress, these suits offered a new source of legitimation for the ACM's brainwashing ideology. Civil suits also potentially created the twin consequences of potentially bankrupting NRMs and generating funding that would support at least certain elements of the ACM network. This strategy required a more prominent role for attorney and therapy experts who could secure fees for initiating cases, providing courtroom testimony, and dispensing therapeutic services. Apostates also played a decisive role, as it was information provided by them to either therapists or the court that constituted the basis for legal action. Former members who were potential plaintiffs came to the attention of ACM organizations, and ACM officials could then refer those individuals to the appropriate attorneys and therapists.

The civil suit strategy was quite successful for several years. There was a series of high profile cases in which former members requested jury trials on charges of intentional infliction of emotional distress. These cases featured ACM-affiliated experts who testified to the use of mind control practices by the defendant group that resulted in a variety of debilitating psychological conditions. For example, psychologist Margaret Singer, one of the most prominent ACM experts, testified in over three dozen such cases by the end of the decade. Singer developed a version of mind control theory (Anthony 1990; Bromley 1983) that proved very convincing in jury trials. As one observer commented, "Singer's testimony in civil suits based on her brainwashing argument may constitute all by itself the most effective tactic of the anticult movement" (Anthony 1990: 299). These cases brought the ACM publicity, the opportunity to attack NRMs directly, and financial resources for experts (although not for the national organizations). However, while the ACM scored a number of victories at the trial court level, the most common pattern was plaintiff victory in the trial but reversal or reduction of penalties at the appellate level.

Among the most significant cases that led to the demise of civil suits based on mind control testimony were *Robin George vs. ISKCON*, in which former member Robin George sued Hare Krishna, and *Molko and Leal v. Holy Spirit Association*, in which two former Unificationists sued the Unification Church. In the Molko and Leal case the plaintiffs alleged that they had been deceptively recruited and subjected to mind control. The testimony of ACM experts was rejected by the trial court, and an appeals court concluded that the expert opinions in the case lacked scientific basis. The California Supreme Court reinstated the suits for infliction of emotional distress and fraud, but the case was finally settled out of court in 1989 (Biermans 1988: 200–203). In the George case, a former member of Hare Krishna brought suit against the group on several grounds, including infliction of mental distress (Bromley 1988b). In the 1983 trial the plaintiffs were awarded over $32 million, a sum reduced to under $10 million by the trial judge. Following several appeals the mind control–related charges were dismissed by a Los Angeles court, and the suit was finally settled in 1993. The definitive case on the admissibility of mind control testimony was *U.S. v. Fishman*, a 1989 criminal case in a federal court, in which the defendant argued that crimes he had committed were the result of the debilitating influence of his membership in a cult. Based on reports submitted to the court, the judge ruled against allowing mind control testimony on the basis that it did not possess scientific standing.

The professionalization of the ACM was accompanied by a broad-based effort to reconceptualize mind control theory so that it would pass muster with the judiciary and professional associations that adjudicated the standards for knowledge as well as account for "walkaways" and address the growing opposition to mind control theories from NRM scholars. The AFF's *Cultic Studies Journal* was a major forum for ACM-oriented research. However, ACM-connected scholars developed a variety of mind control theories rather than coalescing around a single theory, which complicated acceptance of the theory in professional and judicial forums (Conway and Siegelman 1982; Ofshe and Singer 1986; Singer and Ofshe 1990; Hochman 1990; Sirkin and Wynne 1990). For example, Conway and Siegelman (1982) developed an "information disease" theory that attributes affiliation to a cybernetic trauma that compromises normal cognitive functioning; Ofshe and Singer (1986) identified different types of thought reform techniques, with the most destructive being a current form that attacks one's "core sense of being"; Sirkin and Wynne (1990) developed the concept of inappropriate types of social relationships, which they termed a "relational disorder." More problematic for the ACM was the fact that numerous social scientists who were studying NRMs and the NRM-ACM conflict challenged the entire range of mind control theories (e.g., Barker 1984; Beckford 1985; Robbins 1988; Richardson 1983; Bromley and Richardson 1983; Bromley and Shupe 1981).

In a campaign to gain professional legitimacy, ACM-connected psychologists sought the support of the American Psychological Association for mind control ideology. In 1983 a task force, the Deceptive and Indirect Methods of Persuasion and Control (DIMPAC), was established to report to the APA's Board of Social and Ethical Responsibility (BSERP). ACM members dominated the task force. When a report was submitted three years later, BSERP concluded that it lacked scientific rigor and rejected it. At the same time, NRM scholars were mobilizing professional sociology and religion associations to oppose mind control testimony, serving as expert witnesses in court cases and assisting in the preparation of amicus brief filings in key cases. However, ACM activists were successful in gaining the inclusion in *DSM-III* (the *Diagnostic and Statistical Manual* used by clinicians in making diagnoses of mental disorders) new language that made reference to cult-induced disorders and revised atypical dissociative disorders to include mind control as a cause (Richardson 1993). Overall, the effort to revamp ACM ideology was never completely successful, although it was more successful in popular than scientific culture. For example, around the turn of the decade apostate NRM members produced a number of popular books (film versions of several were later produced) in which mind control was offered as an explanation of their NRM affiliations (Durham 1981; Edwards 1979; Elkins 1980; Kemperman 1981; Swatland and Swatland 1982; Underwood and Underwood 1979; Wood 1979).

The increasing importance of professionals in the ACM and of gaining a professional legitimation base was also reflected in a campaign to move restorative agents in a more professionally compatible direction. Deprogramming activities were particularly problematic in this regard. There had been a string of cases during the 1970s in which deprogrammers had used excessive force, abducted the wrong individual, attempted to deprogram mature adults with rather conventional religious affiliations, or been prosecuted for failed deprogrammings. During the 1980s there were revelations of deprogrammers taking drugs during deprogrammings and having sexual relations with deprogrammees. In the face of the stigma created for the ACM by such practices and by criminal prosecution of deprogrammers, during the 1980s there was a concerted effort to redirect restorative agents. One of the key developments was the transition from coercive deprogramming to exit counseling, with the latter referring to voluntary deprogramings in which the individual agreed to be present in the situation. As two ACM representatives described the distinction, "exit counseling refers to a voluntary intensive, time-limited, contractual educational process that emphasizes the respectful sharing of information with cultists" (Langone and Martin n.d.: 7). Attempting to stake out an identity as professionals, exit counselors prepared a code of ethics for "cult interventionist" behavior, statements on their relationship to established mental health professions and disciplines, and even addressed practical issues such as appropriate fee scales for degreed versus nondegreed practitioners. By 1988 a Statement of Purpose was issued by a newly formed Exit Counselors Group; a resolution was passed prohibiting drug use and sex with clients. While not all restorative agents submitted to the new guidelines, by 1990 few in the ACM wanted to be identified as a deprogrammer.

While the shift from deprogramming to exit counseling contributed to a more professional image within the ACM and reduced legal liabilities, it did not entirely resolve the problem. The frequency of deprogamming declined precipitously, but it did continue surreptitiously for ideological and financial reasons despite CAN's public pronouncements to the contrary. CAN in particular faced persistent financial problems, and one solution to these problems was arranging a referral for contribution exchange with both exit counselors and deprogrammers. Exit counselors and deprogrammers made contributions to CAN in exchange for referrals, or families made donations directly to CAN so that the fees could not be directly traced to them (Shupe and Darnell forthcoming). A special unit within CAN, the National Resource Development and Economic Council, was formed in the mid-1980s and made regular contributions to its parent body. According to Shupe and Darnell, CAN derived as much as one-third of its revenues from returns from exit counselors and deprogrammers who were the recipients of case referrals.

In sum, in contrast to the prior stage in which the primary ACM achievement was broad popular acceptance of mind control ideology while organizational units remained fragmented, in this stage national organizations were established but ideological legitimation eroded. Nonetheless, the countermovement structure and economy were fully developed and operative during this stage. With the establishment of national organizations, the ACM became a much more visible presence. The increased flow of inquiries from families created the information base that CAN in particular needed to coordinate the information/referral/donation economy. The civil suit strategy tied the ACM network together effectively for a number of years. CAN functionaries provided referrals to restorative agents, experts orchestrated litigation, apostates offered personal testimony, and restorative agents produced apostates. However, the civil suit strategy ultimately faltered, and the ACM was unable to produce professional or judicial legitimation for its mind control ideology. The ACM strategy, as CAN pursued it, contained an intractable contradiction. CAN organized itself as a tax-exempt, educational organization, but coercive referrals remained an integral part of the countermovement economy that produced internal legitimation, an effective response to family needs, and a source of revenue (Shupe, Moxon, and Darnell 2000). Public renunciation of deprogramming and covert referrals concealed but did not resolve this contradiction. CAN's inability to resolve this contradiction proved decisive during the next decade.

The Domestic Accommodation/ International Expansion Stage

The domestic accommodation/international expansion stage of the ACM began around 1990 and continues through the present. The most significant events that marked the beginning of this stage were conflicts with one of the largest NRMs, the Church of Scientology—although the implications of those conflicts was not evident at the time—and growing connections between the American and European anticult organizations. The unexpected series of violent episodes involving NRMs in Japan, Europe, and North America also changed the ACM's fortunes, particularly in Europe. The primary developments that it now appears will shape the future of the North American ACM are the extent to which its accommodation initiative progresses and its role in European efforts to regulate NRMs, although paradoxically these two potential developments would lead the countermovement in opposite directions.

The 1990s did not initially appear to be a particularly eventful time for the ACM. The countermovement was stymied in certain key respects, as it had been unable to legitimate its mind control ideology in professional or judicial arenas or find legal auspices for deprogramming. These were major setbacks for the ACM, as they sharply limited its ability to extricate individual NRM affiliates or to build alliances with governmental agencies. At the same time, the ACM had achieved a high level of public visibility and widespread public acceptance of its ideology, built a minority position within the academic community coordinated through AFF, expanded voluntary exit counseling in order to service families, and continued to surreptitiously support deprogrammings through referrals by CAN functionaries. The ACM's internal economy remained based on information/referral/donation exchanges. Further, as CAN's visibility increased, dialogue between American and European anticult functionaries increased. There had long been ACM organizations in a number of European countries, but their size and influence was limited (Shupe and Bromley 1994). Creating an international coalition of anticult organizations held the potential for increasing the influence of the ACM as well as matching the international-level organization of the largest NRMs.

The North American–European ACM connections assumed new significance in the aftermath of the 1994 Solar Temple murder-suicides. There was a series of violent episodes through the 1990s—the Branch Davidian murder-suicides at Mount Carmel outside of Waco in 1993, the Solar Temple murder-suicides in Switzerland and Canada in 1994, the Aum Shinrikyō murders in Tokyo in 1995, the Heaven's Gate collective suicide in California in 1997, and the Uganda murder-suicides involving the Movement for the Restoration of the Ten Commandments in 2000. While this series of events did not significantly alter the NRM-ACM conflict in North America, the Solar Temple episode had a dramatic impact in Europe, and in France and Germany in particular. A number of American ACM experts and functionaries consulted with European governments, and the ACM's mind control ideology became a key component of reports and legislation (e.g., Davis, 2000; Shupe and Darnell 2001; Shterin and Richardson 2000; Richardson 1996).

The primary French ACM organization, the Association pour la Défense de la Familie et de l'Individual (ADFI), was able to form a coalition with elements of the French government. A parliamentary committee and ADFI produced a report in 1996 that identified 172 *sectes* (cults) operating in France that had become a source of concern, based on allegations of what was termed "mental manipulation" (the equivalent of mind control in the United States). In 1998 an office, the Mission Interministérielle de lutte les sectes (the Interministerial Commission to Make War on the Sects) was established to monitor and control sects. Specific sanctions were sought over selected groups, but all 172 groups were compelled to fill out extensive reports on their financial dealings. Subsequently, the commission proposed legislation to criminalize "mental manipulation." However, the expanded governmental powers have not translated to date into a visible increase in prosecution of religious groups. In Germany the controversy centered on the

Church of Scientology, which the government had refused to recognize as a religious organization. In 1996, the Bundestag established an Inquiry Committee to examine "sects" and "psychogroups." Contrary to prevailing expectations, however, the 1998 commission report concluded that the great majority of new religions did not pose a serious problem and called upon the government to cease using derogatory labels such as "cult" and "sect." Even in the case of the Church of Scientology, official observation was discontinued after two years. In both France and Germany a coalition of churches, religious liberty and human rights organizations, and religion scholars was instrumental in blunting the anticult initiatives, with the result that once again a potential ACM-governmental alliance proved elusive.

While the ACM structure and economy appeared to be stable, the contradiction that had plagued the countermovement throughout its history rather suddenly came to pose a major threat. Since its inception the ACM had focused its opposition on different NRMs as those movements gained size and visibility. By the early 1990s the Church of Scientology was experiencing mixed fortunes. The church had become one of the largest NRMs in North America and Europe and had attained legal recognition in several nations, most notably acceptance as a tax-exempt organization by the IRS in 1993 after two decades of conflict. At the same time, Scientology had developed a reputation as one of the most powerful and belligerent NRMs, as perhaps most visibly demonstrated in a *Time* cover story about the church titled "The Church of Greed" (Behar 1991). Given the visibility and controversy in which Scientology was involved, it became a rather obvious ACM target; Scientology responded with a vitriolic campaign against the ACM, publicly referring to it as a "hate group" (Freedom 1991). As the conflict progressed, members of Scientology exploited the contradictions inherent in the ACM structure and economy. First, a number of Scientologists attempted to join CAN and attend conferences. When they were denied admittance, these individuals brought civil suits against CAN on grounds of religious discrimination by a nonprofit, tax-exempt voluntary association. At one point CAN was the target of several dozen such suits, which placed the organization in dire financial condition. Second, the church became aware of an unsuccessful coercive deprogramming of Jason Scott, an adult member of the Life Tabernacle Church, a branch of the United Pentecostal Church International. The deprogramming occurred in 1992 when Scott's mother hired deprogrammers based on a referral by a CAN volunteer worker. Ironically, at its 1993 annual conference the CAN Board unanimously passed a resolution disavowing any "illegal or involuntary act," as a means of distancing itself from coercive deprogramming and deviant practices that were occurring in exit counseling cases. Seizing the opportunity presented by the failed deprogramming, a Scientology attorney offered Scott legal representation. The trial resulted in a verdict against CAN that awarded Scott $1,000,000 in punitive

damages and $875,000 in actual damages (upheld on appeal). The judgment bank-
rupted CAN, and in 1996 the organization closed and its assets were sold at
auction.

The destruction of CAN eliminated the linchpin of the ACM economy as the
information and referral dispensing function was disrupted. ACM activists responded to the demise of CAN by founding a replacement organization, the Leo
J. Ryan Foundation (named for the congressman killed at Jonestown), but it has
not achieved the visibility or influence of its predecessor.

In the wake of CAN's demise, therefore, AFF became the dominant ACM
organization in North America. AFF responded to the new situation by opening
lines of communication with NRM scholars. In the late 1990s members of social
science societies studying religion and AFF began participating in one another's
annual meetings (Lattin 2000). Representatives of the two camps also undertook
a book project in which proponents exchanged views on the mind control issue
(Zablocki and Robbins 2001). Some NRM scholars softened their stance toward
the ACM, referring to it as the "cult awareness movement" rather than the "anticult movement" (Barker 2002). In a major statement, one of the leading AFF
functionaries has distanced from the traditional mind control arguments (asserting simply that some groups harm some people under some circumstances) and
from stereotypical depiction of cults (acknowledging that groups vary enormously
and the scientific and political issues are complex). The moderation of the ACM
position has opened up the potential for ACM-NRM scholar dialogue as a number
of NRM scholars have established interests in issues such as child/member abuse
(Jacobs 1989; Rochford 1998) and violence (Hall, Schuyler, and Trinh 2000; Wessinger 1999; Bromley and Melton 2002).

In sum, the Domestic Accommodation/International Expansion stage proved
to be a decisive moment in ACM history. It appeared that the ACM structure
and economy could continue to function despite problems in gaining legitimacy
for its ideology and legally sanctioned means for retrieving cultists. And the potential for an international coalition with European ACMs and governments
seemed within reach. However, anticult momentum across Europe gradually de-
celerated. More significantly for the North American ACM, the contradiction
between CAN's status as an educational organization and its public renunciation/
covert continuation of deprogramming created a fatal vulnerability for that organization. There is no shortage of irony in this outcome. CAN was undone by
the same kind of civil suit strategy it had employed against NRMs, in a case
involving the same kind of coercive practices it accused cults of employing, and
with the result that its name and assets were purchased by members of one of its
most bitter enemies. The demise of CAN undermined the carefully built infor-
mation/referral/donation economy that had been the basis for ACM integration.
AFF subsequently became the dominant ACM organization and pursued a more
moderate course that opened up the possibility of greater academic legitimacy

and a mission built around counseling and support groups for NRM adherents who were the victims of abusive practices.

SUMMARY AND CONCLUSIONS

Using the example of the ACM, we have argued that a productive means of analyzing social movements of all kinds is in terms of a structure (organization and ideology), economy (medium of exchange and transactional mechanisms), and alliance network (external units accepting the countermovement structure and economy). Establishing and maintaining a structure, economy, and alliance network yield legitimacy and effectiveness, two broad indicators of movement success.

The ACM developed through three distinct stages that are demarcated by significant events that shaped its structure, economy, and alliance network. During the emergent stage the ACM developed the major components of its structure and economy, but it was much more successful in constructing ideology than organization. The viability of its alliance network fluctuated but had deteriorated by the end of the decade. The domestic expansion/consolidation stage was marked by the reverse pattern. National-level organization was achieved, but the legitimacy of ACM ideology was seriously challenged. Nonetheless, during this stage the ACM's structure and economy were fully developed, and for several years it was able to create an alliance with the judicial system, at least to the extent that its experts were permitted to offer testimony based on mind control ideology. The domestic accommodation/international expansion stage witnessed the kind of anticult-governmental alliance in Europe that the American ACM had hoped to cultivate domestically, although the ultimate impact of that alliance remains uncertain. In the U.S. the contradiction between CAN's status as a tax-exempt, educational association and its participation in coercive referrals as part of its information/referral/donation economy left the organization legally vulnerable. CAN's demise left AFF as the dominant ACM organization and shifted the ACM in a more moderate direction. This shift moves the ACM toward "denominational" status as one of many groups addressing individual abuse and victimization.

REFERENCES

Anthony, Dick. 1990. "Religious Movements and Brainwashing Litigation: Evaluating Key Testimony." In *In Gods We Trust*, ed. Thomas Robbins and Dick Anthony. New Brunswick, N.J.: Transaction.

Anthony, Dick, and Thomas Robbins. 1981. "Culture Crisis and Contemporary Religion." In *In Gods We Trust*, ed. Thomas Robbins and Dick Anthony. New Brunswick, N.J.: Transaction.

Barker, Eileen. 1984. *The Making of a Moonie: Choice or Brainwashing?* Oxford: Basil Blackwell.

————. 2002. "Watching for Violence: A Comparative Analysis of the Roles of Five Types of Cult-Watching Groups." In *Cults, Religion, and Violence*, ed. David G. Bromley and J. Gordon Melton. New York: Oxford University Press.

Beckford, James. 1985. *Cult Controversies: The Societal Response to the New Religious Movements*. London: Tavistock.

Behar, Richard. 1991. "Scientology: The Thriving Cult of Greed and Power." *Time* (May 6): 50–57.

Bellah, Robert. 1976. "New Religious Consciousness and the Crisis in Modernity." In *The New Religious Consciousness*, ed. Charles Y. Glock and Robert Bellah. Berkeley: University of California Press.

Biermans, John T. 1988. *The Odyssey of New Religions Today*. Lewiston, N.Y.: Edwin Mellen Press.

Bromley, David. 1983. "Conservatorships and Deprogramming: Legal and Political Prospects." In *The Brainwashing/Deprogramming Controversy*, ed. David G. Bromley and James T. Richardson. Lewiston, N.Y.: Edwin Mellen Press.

————. 1988a. "Deprogramming as a Mode of Exit from New Religious Movements: The Case of the Unificationist Movement." In *Falling From the Faith*, ed. David G. Bromley. Newbury Park, Calif.: Sage.

————. 1988b. "ISKCON and the Anti-Cult Movement." In *Krishna Consciousness in the West*, ed. David G. Bromley and Larry Shinn. Lewisburg, Pa.: Bucknell University Press.

————, ed. 1998. *The Politics of Religious Apostasy: The Role of Apostates in the Transformation of Religious Movements*. Westport, Conn.: Praeger.

Bromley, David G., and J. Gordon Melton, eds. 2002. *Cults, Religion, and Violence*. Cambridge: Cambridge University Press.

Bromley, David G., and Jeffrey K. Hadden, eds. 1993. *The Handbook on Cults and Sects in America*. Parts A and B. Vol. 3, Religion and the Social Order series. Greenwich, Conn.: JAI Press.

Bromley, David G., and James T. Richardson, eds. 1983. *The Brainwashing/Deprogramming Controversy*. Lewiston, N.Y.: Edwin Mellen Press.

Bromley, David G., and Thomas Robbins. 1992. "The Role of Government in Regulating New and Unconventional Religions." In *Governmental Monitoring of Religion*, ed. James Wood. Waco, Tex.: Baylor University Press.

Bromley, David G., and Anson D. Shupe Jr. 1979. *Moonies in America: Cult, Church, and Crusade*. Beverly Hills, Calif.: Sage.

————. 1981. *Strange Gods: The Great American Cult Scare*. Boston: Beacon Press.

————. 1989. "Public Reaction against New Religious Movements." In *Cults and New Religious Movements,* ed. Marc Galanter. Washington: American Psychiatric Association.

Bromley, David G., Anson D. Shupe, and Joseph C. Ventimiglia. 1979. "Atrocity Tales, the Unification Church, and the Social Construction of Evil." *Journal of Communication* 29: 42–53.

Coates, Priscilla. 1994. "The History of the Cult Awareness Network." In *Anti-Cult Movements in Cross-Cultural Perspective,* ed. Anson Shupe and David G. Bromley. New York: Garland.

Conway, Flo, and Jim Siegelman. 1982. "Information Disease: Have the Cults Created a New Mental Illness?" *Science Digest* (January): 86–92.

Cox, Harvey. 1977. *Turning East: The Promise and Peril of the New Orientalism.* New York: Simon and Schuster.

Davis, Derek H., ed. 2000. *Religious Liberty in Northern Europe in the Twenty-First Century.* Waco, Tex.: Baylor University (J. M. Dawson Institute of Church-State Studies).

Durham, Deanna. 1981. *Life among the Moonies: Three Years in the Unification Church.* Plainfield, N.J.: Logos International.

Edwards, Christopher. 1979. *Crazy for God.* Englewood Cliffs, N.J.: Prentice-Hall.

Elkins, Chris. 1980. *Heavenly Deception.* Wheaton, Ill.: Tyndale House.

Freedom Magazine. 1991. "Exposing the Criminal Clique Called 'CAN': Disclosure of Criminality and Perversions Rock Anti-Religious Hate Group." *Freedom Magazine* (October): 28–32.

Fuss, Michael A., ed. 1998. *Rethinking New Religious Movements.* Rome: Research Center on Cultures and Religion, Pontifical Gregorian University.

Glock, Charles. 1976. "Consciousness among Contemporary Youth: An Interpretation." In *The New Religious Consciousness,* ed. Charles Glock and Robert Bellah. Berkeley: University of California Press.

Hall, John, Philip Schuyler, and Salvaine Trinh. 2000. *Apocalypse Observed.* New York: Routledge.

Hochman, J. 1990. "Miracle, Mystery, and Authority: The Triangle of Cult Indoctrination." *Psychiatric Annals* 20: 179–187.

Jacobs, Janet. 1989. *Divine Disenchantment.* Bloomington: Indiana University Press.

Jenkins, Philip. 2000. *Mystics and Messiahs: Cults and the New Religions in American History.* New York: Oxford University Press.

Kemperman, Steve. 1981. *Lord of the Second Advent.* Ventura, Calif.: Regal Books.

Langone, Michael D. n.d. "The Two 'Camps' of Cultic Studies: Time for a Dialogue." Unpublished paper. Bonita Springs, Fla.: American Family Foundation.

Langone, Michael, and Paul Martin. n.d. "Exit Counseling and Ethics: Clarifying the Confusion." Unpublished manuscript in Cult Awareness Network Box #230 entitled "Deprogramming," located in the New Religions Collection at Davidson Library, University of California at Santa Barbara.

Lattin, Don. 2000. "Combatants in Cult War Attempt Reconciliation: Peacemaking Conference Is Held Near Seattle." *San Francisco Chronicle* (May 1).

Martin, Walter. 1977. *The Kingdom of the Cults.* Minneapolis: Bethany Fellowship.

Melton, J. Gordon, ed. 1990. *The Evangelical Anti-Cult Movement: Christian Counter-Cult Literature.* New York: Garland.

————. 1999. "Anti-Cultists in the United States: An Historical Perspective." In *New Religious Movements: Challenge and Response,* ed. Bryan Wilson and Jamie Cresswell. London: Routledge.

Mottl, Tahi. 1980. "The Analysis of Countermovements." *Social Problems* 27: 620–635.

Ofshe, Richard, and Margaret Singer. 1986. "Attacks on Peripheral versus Central Elements of Self and the Impact of Thought Reforming Techniques." *Cultic Studies Journal* 3: 3–24.

Richardson, James. 1983. "The Brainwashing/Deprogramming Controversy: An Introduction." In *The Brainwashing/Deprogramming Controversy,* ed. David G. Bromley and James T. Richardson. Lewiston, N.Y.: Edwin Mellen Press.

Richardson, James T. 1993. "Religiosity as Deviance: Negative Religious Bias in the Use and Misuse of the DMS." *Deviant Behavior* 14: 1–21.

————. 1996. " 'Brainwashing' Claims and Minority Religions Outside the United States: Cultural Diffusion of a Questionable Concept in the Legal Arena." *Brigham Young University Law Review* 4: 873–904.

Robbins, Thomas. 1988. *Cults, Converts, and Charisma.* Beverly Hills, Calif.: Sage.

Rochford, E. Burke, Jr. 1998. "Child Abuse in the Hare Krishna Movement: 1971–1986." *ISKCON Communications Journal* 6: 43–69.

Saliba, John A. 1990. *Social Science and the Cults: An Annotated Bibliography.* New York: Garland.

Shterin, Marat S., and James T. Richardson. 2000. "Effects of the Western Anti-Cult Movement on Development of Laws Concerning Religion in Post-Communist Russia." *Journal of Church and State* 42: 247–271.

Shupe, Anson. 1985. "The Routinization of Conflict in the Modern Cult/Anticult Controversy." *Nebraska Humanist* 8: 26–39.

Shupe, Jr., Anson D., and David G. Bromley. 1979. "The Moonies and the Anti-Cultists: Movement and Countermovement in Conflict." *Sociological Analysis* 40: 325–334.

————. 1980. *The New Vigilantes.* Beverly Hills, Calif.: Sage.

————, eds. 1985. *A Documentary History of the Anti-Cult Movement.* Arlington: Center for Social Research, University of Texas at Arlington.

————. 1987. "The Future of the Anticult Movement." In *The Future of New Religious Movements,* ed. David G. Bromley and Phillip E. Hammond. Macon, Ga.: Mercer University Press.

————, eds. 1994. *Anti-Cult Movements in Cross-Cultural Perspective.* New York: Garland.

Shupe, Anson, David G. Bromley, and Edward Breschel. 1989. "The Legacy of Jonestown and the Development of the Anti-Cult Movement." In *Jonestown: A Ten Year Retrospective,* ed. Rebecca Moore and Fielding McGehee. Lewiston, N.Y.: Edwin Mellen Press.

Shupe, Anson, David G. Bromley, and Donna Oliver. 1984. *The Anti-Cult Movement in America: A Bibliographic and Historical Survey.* New York: Garland.

Shupe, Anson, and Susan E. Darnell. 2001. "Agents of Discord: The North American–European ACM Connection." Paper presented at the international conference titled "The Spiritual Supermarket. Religious Pluralism and Globalization in the 21st Century: The Expanding European Union and Beyond." London: London School of Economics.

————. 2002. "Field Notes: Issues of Access to Primary Anticult Documents: The Cult Awareness Network." *Nova Religio* (Spring).

————. 2003. *Agents of Discord: Deprogramming, Pseudo Science, and the American Anticult Movement.* Forthcoming.

Shupe, Anson, Kendrick Moxon, and Susan E. Darnell. 2000. "CAN, We Hardly Knew Ye: Sex, Drugs, Deprogrammers' Kickbacks, and Corporate Crime in the (Old) Cult Awareness Network." Paper presented at the 2000 meeting of the Society for the Scientific Study of Religion, Houston, Tex.

Singer, Margaret, and Richard Ofshe. 1990. "Thought Reform Programs and the Production of Psychiatric Casualties." *Psychiatric Annals* 20: 188–193.

Sirkin, Mark, and Lyman Wynne. 1990. "Cult Involvement as Relational Disorder." *Psychiatric Annals* 20: 199–203.

Swatland, Susan, and Anne Swatland. 1982. *Escape from the Moonies.* London: New English Library.

Tipton, Steven M. 1982. *Getting Saved from the Sixties.* Berkeley: University of California Press.

Underwood, Barbara, and Betty Underwood. 1979. *Hostage to Heaven.* New York: Clarkson N. Potter.

Wessinger, Catherine. 1999. *How the Millennium Comes Violently.* Chappaqua, N.Y.: Seven Bridges Press.

Wood, Allen Tate. 1979. *Moonstruck: A Memoir of My Life in a Cult.* New York: William Morrow.

Zablocki, Benjamin, and Thomas Robbins, eds. 2001. *Misunderstanding Cults.* Toronto: University of Toronto Press.

CHAPTER 9

SOMETHING PECULIAR ABOUT FRANCE

Anti-Cult Campaigns in Western Europe and French Religious Exceptionalism

MASSIMO INTROVIGNE

ANTI-CULT CAMPAIGNS IN WESTERN EUROPE

"Sects" and "cults" are often quintessential targets of moral panics (Jenkins 1996: 158; Introvigne 2000). Moral panics usually have some objective basis. Nobody would deny that some new religious movements have been guilty of criminal activities, ranging from cases of fraud to the horrors of the Solar Temple. The real problem, however, is prevalence, rather than existence. Most scholars of new religious movements would subscribe to the conclusion of the 1998 Swiss federal report on Scientology that "the immense majority of these groups ["sects" or "cults"] represents neither a danger to their members nor to the State" (La Scientologie en Suisse 1998: 132–133). Few scholars, on the other hand, would agree with the French (Assemblée Nationale 1996) or Belgian (Chambre des Représentants de Belgique 1997) parliamentary reports that listed dozens of groups—from Mormons to Quakers and Baha'is—as "sects" or "cults" actually, or potentially, dangerous.

Moral panics start with a basis in reality but escalate through exaggeration when comments appropriate to particular incidents are generalized. This happened in the United States after Jonestown (in 1978) and is currently evident in Europe following the Solar Temple murders and suicides (in 1994, 1995, and 1997), especially as demonstrated by so many official reports on new religions, or "cults and sects." It is in the escalation, rather than the creation, of moral panics that moral entrepreneurs with vested interests enter the picture. They include different anti-cult movements, some of which currently receive considerable public support in some European countries.

Within this context, some European parliamentary and other official reports generated in the wake of the Solar Temple incidents have adopted an interpretive model that offers a virtual guarantee of inflating, rather than deflating, moral panics. James Richardson and I (2001) have proposed a distinction between "Type I" and "Type II" official documents on "cults" generated by Western European institutions after the Solar Temple incidents. "Type I" official documents, which include the French reports (Assemblée Nationale 1996 and 1999), the Belgian report (Chambre des Représentants de Belgique 1997), large parts of the Canton of Geneva report (Audit sur les dérives sectaries 1997) and of the same Canton's report on brainwashing (Commission pénale sur les dérives sectaries 1999), the deliberations of the French Prime Minister's Observatory of Sects (Observatoire Interministériel sur les Sectes 1998) and of its successor, the Mission to Fight Against Sects (MILS 2000 and following yearly reports) all adopt a four-stage interpretive model, described as follows:

1. *Cults or Sects Are Not Religions.* First, the model claims that some minority religious groups are not really religions but something else: namely, "cults" and "sects." The two words are used almost interchangeably in Europe, with the word equivalent to "sect" (e.g., *secte* in French, *setta* in Italian, or *sekte* in German) being the most derogatory in several languages. Because religious liberty is recognized in Western Europe as a value often constitutionally safeguarded (including by international treaties and declarations), the best way to discriminate against a religious minority is to argue that it is not religious at all (Dillon and Richardson 1994; Barker 1996; Introvigne 1999b). As sociologist Larry Greil says, religion is "a cultural resource over which competing interest groups may vie. From this perspective, religion is not an entity but a claim made by certain groups and—in some cases—contested by others to the right of privileges associated in a given society with the religious label" (Greil 1996: 48).

2. *Brainwashing and Mind Control.* Second, since religion is usually defined as an exercise of free will, it is argued that a nonreligion can be joined only under some sort of coercion, which is quite often couched in brainwashing-like terms. The hypnotic paradigm used against Mormonism, the Shakers, and other groups by nineteenth-century countercultists (Miller 1983) resurfaced—after the Cold War had conveniently supplied the metaphor of "brainwashing"—in the 1970s "cult wars" in the United States and elsewhere (Robbins and Anthony 1982; Anthony, Robbins, and McCarthy 1983; Richardson and Kilbourne 1983; Introvigne 2002). By the end of the 1980s, the first crude theories of brainwashing had been largely debunked among English-speaking scholars (Barker 1984; Anthony 1990, 1996; Richardson 1993, 1996), although neo-brainwashing theories have been proposed more recently, and the situation could change. However, these crude brainwashing theories continue to inform Type I reports done by European governmental agencies (see Anthony 1999, especially).

3. *Apostates.* Third, because brainwashing theories are the object of considerable scholarly criticism, the model requires discrimination in terms of sources and narratives. The French and Belgian reports make little or no use of scholarly sources. The Belgian report explicitly states that it is aware of scholarly objections against the mind control model, but it has made the "ethical" choice of preferring the actual accounts of victims. By "victims," the Belgian Commission means people usually defined by social scientists as "apostates," i.e., former members who have become active opponents of the group they left, and who develop "accounts" of their involvement that cast their former group in a negative light (Richardson, Van der Lans, and Derks 1986; Bromley 1998). The prevalence of apostates among former members is certainly no more than 10 or 20 percent, depending on the movement (Solomon 1981; Lewis 1986, 1989; Introvigne 1999a). Most ex-members usually are not interested in joining a crusade against the group they have left, but the model usually regards apostates as adequate representatives of the total larger category of former members.

4. *Anti-Cult Organizations.* "Cults" or "sects," we are told, are not religions because they apply brainwashing techniques, whereas religions by their very nature are "free" and people may join or leave them at will. We know that "cults" and "sects" use brainwashing because we have the testimonies of their "victims" (i.e., apostates). We know that apostates are representative of the groups' general membership because they are hand-picked by reliable watchdog organizations, groups referred to by scholars as "anti-cult" (Shupe and Bromley 1994). Anti-cult organizations, prominent in all Type I reports, are, we are told, more reliable than academics

because the former, unlike the latter, have "practical" experience actually working with the "victims."

This four-stage model plays an important role in perpetuating the moral panic about cults and sects, and is rather strictly adhered to in official documents and institutions throughout French-speaking Europe. Of particular note in all these Type I reports is the lynchpin role played by brainwashing-type theories. Without this ideological device, the reports would be considerably weaker in both claims and recommendations.

Scholarly criticism directed against Type I reports (see Introvigne and Melton 1996) seems to have exerted some influence in other countries. We have seen Type II reports published in 1998 by the German Parliament (Deutscher Bunderstag—13. Wahlperiode 1998), the Italian Ministry of Home Affairs (Ministero dell'Interno 1998), the Swiss Canton of Ticino (Dipartimento delle Istituzioni, Repubblica e Cantone del Ticino 1998), a governmental Swedish Commission (1998) that investigated new religious movements and, in 1999, by the Council of Europe (Council of Europe—Committee on Legal Affairs and Human Rights 1999) and by a commission of the Swiss Parliament (Commission de gestion du Conseil National 1999). We would include the general part on "sects" of the Swiss report on Scientology in the larger Type II category, as well as the Berger report presented to, but not adopted by, the European Parliament (European Parliament, Committee on Civil Liberties and Internal Affairs 1997). These reports differ from each other and are subject to considerable debate and criticism, but they do not apply the same Type I model and they concentrate more attention on academic findings. For example, they generally acknowledge that:

1. It is extremely difficult to define such terms as "cult" and "sect," or "religion," and it may not be the province of secular states to attempt such definitions.
2. Although there is concern that some religious movements may exert excessive psychological pressures on their members, it is generally understood that there is no agreement among scholars on the definition of "brainwashing" or "mind control."
3. Militant ex-members are not viewed as the only reliable source of information about the groups. Those who report positive experiences should also be heard (the Swedish report notes that "the great majority of members of new religious movements derive positive experiences from their membership" [1998:§ 1.6]), as well as scholars.
4. Private anti-cult organizations may perform a legitimate function but, as the Canton of Ticino report puts it, the governments should not support them to the point of "cooperating in spreading prejudices" or even a sort of "anti-cult terrorism" (terrorismo antisetta).

Type II reports represent more acceptance of scholarly work when compared with Type I reports and prove that cooler tempers can prevail. Although Type II reports are still uncertain concerning the use of brainwashing/mind control metaphors, and most contain suggestions that problems remain in the area of recruitment and retention techniques, these reports are leading to a sober public discussion of "cult" issues in countries such as Germany or Switzerland (or, at least, most Swiss Cantons). Type II reports have also influenced Belgium, a country where the local "Observatory of Harmful Sects," quite surprisingly, is increasingly distancing itself from its French counterpart and exerting a moderating influence. France (in close cooperation, in several international fora, with China and Russia) remains the only staunch defender of the anti-cult attitude of the Type I reports in Western Europe, now embodied in the French anti-cult law of May 30, 2001; its position is followed only in certain French-speaking Cantons of Switzerland, and even there not without political resistance. The question of why a French exceptionalism manifests itself on the cult issue is, as a consequence, crucial for an understanding of the whole European cult/sect controversy.

French Exceptionalism

Why, exactly, is France different from its European neighbors on the issue of cults (known in France as *les sectes*)? In 2001, French sociologist Danièle Hervieu-Léger published an important book, *La Religion en miettes ou la question des sectes*, in which she addressed the question of why a governmental anti-cult crusade is being promoted in France and not in other countries. Discussing this book is, in my opinion, crucial in order to answer the question about French exceptionalism; Hervieu-Léger's theories on Europe, secularization, and "cults" play at any rate a central role in contemporary Western European sociology of religion (see Davie 2000). Hervieu-Léger is not what, in certain quarters, would be called a "cult apologist." She has, in fact, never participated in international academic protests against the anti-cult activities of the French government, and she confirms in the book that, in her opinion, some governmental cult-watching is acceptable. However, the French anti-cult law passed in 2001 has found in Hervieu-Léger a critic, and she now acknowledges that the question of cults has been "overdramatized" in France (61), and that political measures are taken based on faulty information grounded on the vested interests of private anti-cult organizations, on former members, and on the controversial notion of brainwashing (61–65). Although there is some interesting (and, within the French context, quite new) criticism of all this, Hervieu-Léger's main aim is to explain why France, a notoriously contentious country, exhibits such a suspicious unanimity in politics and the media, when it comes to cults or *sectes*. Hers is a long book, not only in pages; it discusses other issues as well and, in order to do it justice, the book has to be considered within the framework of the author's previous works. Since this is impossible here, I will confine my remarks to a discussion of three main answers to the question, Why in France?, which Hervieu-Léger presents in her latest book.

First, Hervieu-Léger reminds us that France, since the Revolution and before it in the eighteenth century, has had a somewhat unique antireligious tradition. Of course, anticlericalism and secular humanism are international phenomena, but the French brand has its own specific peculiarities. Religious belief in general is regarded as "intrinsically incompatible with reason and individual autonomy" and "should be eradicated from human minds." This wish, or dream, explains what the French sociologist calls "an angry and radical (although, today, less often explicitly manifested) hostility to any kind of religious belief in general" (22, with a quote from Pierre Bouretz). This tradition is not only about limiting the social influence of religion, but also about being persuaded that extirpating religious belief is both desirable and possible. I would add to Hervieu-Léger's remarks that French *laïcité active* (somewhat different from Anglo-American secular humanism, and transmitted to new generations through the French public school system, a bastion of *laïcité*) manifests itself in a number of different ways, obvious to the French but more difficult for other nations to understand. First, it is regarded in France as politically correct to pay at least lip service to *laïcité*, even if one does not agree with it entirely. In a general election in France, almost all candidates competing for the top offices tend to reaffirm their commitment to *laïcité*, and it would be exceptional to hear them voicing any kind of religious comment or appeals to God or Christianity. Without even mentioning the United States, in the period before the 2001 Italian general election, both candidates proclaimed themselves to be Catholic and visited bishops and cardinals during their electoral tours, notwithstanding the fact that one is divorced while the other started his political career as a militant anticlerical and only recently returned to Catholicism (after being considered for national political office). Second, if (as I believe) popular culture is a mirror of national prejudices, then the French and the British both love detective stories; a comparison, thus, between Sherlock Holmes, or the heroes of Edgar Wallace (1875–1932), and Arsène Lupin, the gentleman-thief created in France by Maurice Leblanc (1864–1941), might be quite instructive. All these characters quite often find themselves very close to death (if only to survive at the last minute, ready for yet another episode). Wallace's characters quite often pray, and Holmes, whose author was a lapsed Catholic turned Spiritualist, took comfort in a higher good and a vague spirituality. Lupin (no doubt, quite strangely for readers in nations with no strong nationalist traditions) often waits for what he thinks is his imminent death with patriotic thoughts on *la République* and *la France*. And, if we want to include comics, then the national French hero, Asterix, is nothing less than a Gallic hero fiercely defending the autonomy of his French village against Julius Caesar and his Roman gods and lifestyle. The metaphor (France resisting Rome) is almost too obvious. Third, such anti-religious feelings find, in France, a philosophical justification in the distinction made between "freedom of belief" and "freedom of religion." Freedom of belief is construed as the freedom to reach autonomous individual conclusions about religion (or atheism) devoid of any external constraints. Recently, brainwashing (or "mental manipulation") has offered a convenient metaphor for these external constraints, but the controversy was there long before. When, at the beginning of the twentieth century, the very anticlerical French government of Émile Combes (1835–1921) dissolved the majority of both male and female Catholic religious orders, compelling several monks and nuns either to go home or leave France altogether, it proclaimed that it was protecting their "freedom of conscience" against the institutional freedom of the religious orders and the Catholic Church. The same applies to cults.

At the Supplemental Meeting on Freedom of Religion, held by the Organization for Security and Cooperation in Europe (OSCE) in Vienna on March 22, 1999, the secretary of the French governmental Mission to Fight Cults, Denis Barthélemy, answering criticism in the OSCE reports introducing the discussion on religious pluralism, explained the French position in a particularly interesting way. He stated that "religious liberty" and "freedom of belief" are two different concepts and that they may indeed conflict. "Religious liberty" (a "collective liberty" for churches and movements) may be limited for the sake of "freedom of belief," the "individual liberty" of thinking and believing without "constraints" external to the individual conscience. France will protect its people against any "constraints" to the formation of their individual "belief," Barthélemy concluded, adding that not only children but adults are "in need of protection" in this respect. Protecting individuals against groups may look like a legitimate option within the framework of a general acceptance of personal freedom. However, Barthélemy's speech implied that the individual citizen's freedom to form his or her belief "freely" shall be protected if necessary *against this citizen's wish*, precisely because—being subject to brainwashing or mind control—he or she merely *thinks* that he or she has accepted a belief freely, when such is in fact not the case. The ostensibly liberal reference to "freedom of belief" hides the quintessentially reactionary presupposition that the government knows better than its adult citizens "in need of protection" where their real freedom and best interests lie.

The second element of Hervieu-Léger's model is one that most observers of the French cult scare may have overlooked. *Laïcité*, she says, not only became an essential part of the French national *ethos* and culture; it also became embodied in the French legal system. For a few years, some French Revolution leaders really believed that religion could simply be destroyed in France. Napoleon I (1769–1821), however, knew only too well that this was impossible, not because he was less antireligious than his predecessors, but because he was more realistic. He also wanted to conquer Europe and realized that he could not achieve that by diverting resources to fighting pockets of Catholic resistance against religious persecution at home. Accordingly, he created a French model of a State-controlled church. Paradoxically, while Napoleon's model was designed to protect the State from the influence of the Catholic Church, at the same time he conceived religion in general as being based on the Catholic model. The Catholic Church was granted a certain degree of liberty and simultaneously placed under a system of State control. The ideal of Napoleon and his successors was to have a territorialized control based on the Catholic system of dioceses and parishes, with a *préfet de police* behind each bishop and a local chief of the *Gendarmerie* behind each parish priest. In the long run the system worked, particularly after the Catholic Church, having resisted it for decades, found it convenient to comply, under the guise of the *ralliement* policy inaugurated by Pope Leo XIII (1810–1903). Hervieu-Léger notes that, particularly after the *ralliement*, the Catholic Church agreed to perform "police work" in France on behalf of the State (p. 27). France was so predominantly Catholic that it was felt that if any bizarre or potentially dangerous form of religion were to arise, then it would likely do so within the Catholic fold. In this case the "police" function afforded to bishops and parish priests would be to take repressive action in advance of the State.

How the system worked has been confirmed by several scholarly studies surrounding the apparitions of the Virgin Mary and subsequent pilgrimages to Lourdes and La Salette, both events potentially disruptive of *laïcité* and the French model. Recent studies show that, in fact, only a minority of extreme anticlericals gave any serious consideration to suppressing the shrines or the pilgrimages. Instead, the model was put to work precisely in order to control them, and the Catholic hierarchy often cooperated in repressing potentially antigovernmental interpretations of the Marian apparitions, or political oppositional activity at the shrines (see, on Lourdes, Norman 1999; on La Salette, Angelier and Langlois 2000). These scholarly works are fascinating in that they show how peculiarly French the system was and how it had extended into unexpected areas. When a new shrine was built at La Salette, for instance, the local bishop had to deal with regulations which allowed the construction of new churches but which dictated that a governmental bureaucracy, stretching from the local *préfet* to Paris, controlled not only when and where they were built, but also by which architect and in which architectural style (see Leniaud 2000). Controlling Catholicism meant controlling religion in France; Napoleon himself, however, also took care of the most significant minorities, trying to fit them into a structure modeled originally on the Roman Catholic Church, with its dioceses and parishes. This was comparatively easy with French Protestants. It was less easy, however, with Jews, but Napoleon ultimately succeeded in promoting the creation of that peculiar French institution, the Jewish Concistory, a sort of "Jewish Church" or "a Judaism reconstructed in order to fit an organizational model basically patterned after the Catholic Church" (Hervieu-Léger 2000: 223). Today, notes Hervieu-Léger, French ministers of internal affairs have tried to create a similar "Moslem Church" and "often start their speeches, quite significantly, by denying that they are "regarding themselves as Napoleon" (Hervieu-Léger 2001: 25). In short, the French model *may* accommodate other religions, but only insofar as they fit into a model patterned after the Roman Catholic Church, while offering, in turn, some sort of *ralliement*—a guarantee of their loyalty to the Republic and a promise not to explicitly fight *laïcité*.

The third part of Hervieu-Léger's argument moves from a comparison of France and Italy. The French often regard Italy's tolerance of religious minorities and "cults" or *sectes* as somewhat "surprising" (34). After all, Italy went through (post-1870) a long season of institutionalized anticlericalism patterned after its French counterpart and took similar measures to control religion. The difference, Hervieu-Léger suggests, is that in Italy active Roman Catholics still constitute a significant portion (in fact, more than a third) of the total population, while they constitute less than 10 percent of the population in France, and in general the Catholic Church and its culture still appear to be very strong. This is not the case in France, where Catholicism is becoming "culturally devoid of significance" (35), thus generating anxious reactions from both Church and State. Although the French model was institutionally anti-Catholic, it also relied heavily on the deal it had made with the Catholic Church to keep religion under careful scrutiny and to quickly detect and suppress any anti-institutional religious fringes. The current crisis in the French Catholic Church means that it is no longer able to perform its "police" function, and the State is becoming increasingly concerned about being able to effectively control a newly deregulated religious market; hence, its curious reaction against cults. In a country like Italy, on the other hand, it is the Catholic Church's strength that helps the State feel confident that the religious situation, in general, is under control and that the novel minorities are no real threat.

Although many other factors could be presented, by following Hervieu-Léger we take what might be an important step toward explaining why an anti-cult governmental crusade is being promoted in France rather than elsewhere in Western Europe. Hervieu-Léger seems to confirm the point of view expressed by James Richardson and myself (2001), which sees *laïcité* as more important than the established churches' " fear of competition in explaining the French scare. Hervieu-Léger notes that the French Catholic Church is divided on the question of *sectes*. While the National Conference of French Catholic Bishops is mostly critical of the anti-cult laws and campaigns (fearing that, through the use of the brainwashing argument, they may easily extend to Catholic movements and institutions), there are individual priests, nuns, and bishops who cooperate quite cheerfully with the anti-cult enterprise. Their presence, however, does not make them leaders of the anti-cult movement, and the Catholic hierarchy is more active in putting brakes on the national anti-cult crusades than in adding fuel to the fire. The impression is that, ultimately, what the Catholic Church does in France will not be crucially relevant in orienting the government's choices.

If, following Hervieu-Léger, we are right in thinking that the French anti-cult scare is a direct consequence of the peculiar French public organization of religion (and of its current crisis), it should follow that it will not be easy to export it abroad. Officers of the official French anti-cult institutions have tried to act as international missionaries, but with mixed degrees of success. So far, only the Swiss Canton of Geneva seems prepared, to some extent, to follow suit. Belgium passed a French-like parliamentary report on cults or sects in 1997, but—as mentioned earlier—its Observatory of Harmful Sects is progressively adopting a much more moderate attitude than its French counterpart, as evidenced by its declared willingness to cooperate with international scholars. In the United States, even those anti-cultists who regard themselves as secular humanists are not sure whether they should support the French measures. After all, as Hervieu-Léger notes, the American separation was aimed at protecting religion (and, occasionally, irreligion) from the State, while in France separation is aimed at protecting the State from religion (31). Russia and China may claim to find a model in France for their repression of minority religions, but this is a purely rhetorical argument since their motivations are obviously different.

Finally, we may ask whether this historical investigation helps us predict what will happen in the future, and whether international human rights and religious liberty watchdogs may persuade France to back away from its present predicament. Although she is also willing to defend some of her government's activities against international (particularly American) criticism, this is a question Hervieu-Léger considers. First, she is encouraged by the category recently established by the governmental Mission to Fight Cults of "absolute cults" (*sectes absolues*, typified by Scientology and a few others) and the dozens of other *sectes* listed as such in the parliamentary reports of 1996 and 1999. Perhaps, she implies, the government will gradually focus on the absolute cults and leave the others alone. Perhaps, but the point here is that the French government operates on the basis of faulty information. Hervieu-Léger acknowledges this problem and comments that this opinion is expressed not only by international "legal experts and sociologists," but also by French judges, who recently found the president of the 1999 Parliamentary Commission guilty of defamation for having called the Anthroposophical Society a *secte* on the basis of parliamentary reports in which, according to the French judges, "the research done does not appear to be serious" (48–49; the decision was later modified on appeal). Lack of serious scholarly investigation of new religious movements is a real problem in France, where scholars have been systematically discouraged from entering this field. Why should a research work which "does not appear to be serious" be regarded as more reliable when it relates to "absolute cults"? In fact, Hervieu-Léger occasionally relies on faulty information about these groups. She writes, for instance, that Scientology is not entitled to tax exemption in Italy (190). This, however, is a misinterpretation of the *Bellei* decision of the Italian Supreme Court (December 16, 1999–February 23, 2000), which regarded as nonreligious the services offered by Narconon, a Scientology-related organization, to drug addicts. As such, these services are not tax exempt, but the tax exemption and the religious nature of the auditing services offered by the Church of Scientology (a different legal entity with respect to Narconon) had been recognized by previous Supreme Court decisions and not revoked by *Bellei*. In pointing out this factual mistake, I am not trying to be pedantic. What is interesting, is that the misinterpretation of *Bellei* is found in statements by the French governmental Mission to Fight Cults (in turn relying on Internet postings by French anti-cultists). That this kind of inaccurate information can find its way into scholarly works of the highest class confirms that the problem of obtaining reliable information about cults is serious indeed in France.

Hervieu-Léger also predicts that globalization will have consequences for France. She regards as naïve those French officers who are persuaded that they can convert other countries to their anti-cult gospel. It is more probable, partly as a result of international litigation in forums such as the European Court of Human Rights, that France will have to adapt its idiosyncratic peculiarities about religion to a globalized scenario. Hervieu-Léger thinks, and also hopes, that France will not be compelled to surrender its peculiarities entirely and (like many other French authors and political figures) is clearly not in favor of an internationalization of the American model. On the other hand, with the exception, perhaps, of "absolute cults," she hopes that society-rejecting, unpopular, and "strange" novel religions may be accommodated in a France ready to discard its model of State-controlled religion, which leans too heavily on the Roman Catholic model. Hervieu-Léger believes that no French government will accept an Americanized religious laissez-faire in the foreseeable future, but it will have to discard the model of control based on Catholicism if it wants to avoid accusations of discrimination. Hervieu-Léger proposes that the State become not less, but (to a certain extent) more (or more truly) secular, inter alia, by creating a "High Council of *Laïcité*." How effective such measures would be, I do not know, but the comments are interesting insofar as they show that foreign criticism (particularly from the United States) generates an immediate nationalist (and anti-American) reaction in the French media and governmental agencies, but it may have a certain influence on French views in the long run.

There is, however, one factor not mentioned by Hervieu-Léger that may be equally crucial in the fate of the cult wars in France. Both government and the media rely on preinterpreted information and on *narratives* before making their comments or political choices. In other countries, the anti-cult narrative on the new religious movements is in competition with an academic narrative (in the United Kingdom and in Italy, the information circulated respectively by INFORM and CESNUR certainly plays a significant role), while in France, this competition of narratives is virtually nonexistent. The overwhelming bulk of the information available on groups labeled as cults comes from anti-cult sources (occasionally, and to a much more limited extent, from Christian counter-cult literature). The situation is somewhat circular: French scholars, although very capable of general commentaries, are reluctant to engage in fieldwork and produce monographic studies of controversial movements in the face of the prevalence of the anti-cult narratives, which would brand them as "cult apologists" (a label, it should be added, carrying much more danger for a scholar's career and access to publishing houses in France than in the United Kingdom, Italy, or the United States: see comments by Duval [2002], whose book is one of the few monographic studies published after the beginning of the official anti-cult campaign in 1996). Conversely, until competing scholarly narratives are produced, anti-cult narratives will maintain their virtual monopoly. Circular problems are notoriously impervious to any form of quick fix. However, the narratives market is, in turn, being increasingly globalized, and European and international networks, offering reliable and independent information on minority religions, will eventually create international resources, which it would be ever more difficult for the French media and authorities to ignore. It is in this perspective that international scholars may in time be able to contribute, at least indirectly, to the creation in France of the more flexible attitude which is slowly prevailing in other Western European countries.

REFERENCES

Angelier, François and Claude Langlois, eds. 2000. *La Salette: Apocalypse, pèlerinage et literature (1856–1996)*. Grenoble: Jérôme Millon.

Anthony, Dick. 1990. "Religious Movements and Brainwashing Litigation: Evaluating Key Testimony." In *In Gods We Trust*, ed. Thomas Robbins and Dick Anthony, 295–344. New Brunswick, N.J.: Transaction.

———. 1996. "Brainwashing and Totalitarian Influence: An Exploration of Admissibility Criteria for Testimony in Brainwashing Trials." Ph.D. diss. Berkeley, Calif.: Graduate Theological Union.

———. 1999. "Pseudoscience and Minority Religions: An Evaluation of the Brainwashing Theories of Jean-Marie Abgrall." *Social Justice Research* 12: 421–456.

Anthony, Dick, Tom Robbins, and James McCarthy. 1983. "Legitimating Repression." In *The Brainwashing/Deprogramming Controversy*, ed. David Bromley and James Richardson, 319–328. Lewiston, N.Y.: Edwin Mellen Press.

Assemblée Nationale. 1996. *Les Sectes en France. Rapport fait au nom de la Commission d'Enquête sur les sectes (document n. 2468).* Paris: Les Documents d'Information de l'Assemblée Nationale.

————. 1999. *Rapport fait au nom de la Commission d'Enquête sur la situation financière, patrimoniale et fiscale des sectes, ainsi que sur leurs activités économiques et leurs relations avec les milieux économiques et financiers (document n. 1687).* Paris: Les Documents d'Information de l'Assemblée Nationale.

Audit sur les dérives sectaires. Rapport du groupe d'experts genevois au Département de la Justice et Police et des Transports du Canton de Genève. 1997. Geneva: Editions Suzanne Hurter.

Barker, Eileen. 1984. *The Making of a Moonie: Brainwashing or Choice?* Oxford: Basil Blackwell.

————. 1996. "But Is It a Genuine Religion?" In *Between Sacred and Secular: Research and Theory on Quasi-Religion,* ed. Larry Greil and Thomas Robbins, 97–109. Greenwich, Conn.: JAI Press.

Barthélemy, Denis. 1999. Intervention of the French Delegation at the OSCE Supplementary Meeting on Freedom of Religion, Vienna, March 22.

Bromley, David G. 1998. *The Politics of Religious Apostasy: The Role of Apostates in the Transformation of Religious Movements.* Westport, Conn.: Praeger.

Chambre des Représentants de Belgique. 1997. *Enquête parlementaire visant à élaborer une politique en vue de lutter contre les pratiques illégales des sectes et les dangers qu'elles représentent pour la société et pour les personnes, particulièrement les mineurs d'âge. Rapport fait au nom de la Commission d'Enquête,* 2 vols. Brussels: Chambre des Représentants de Belgique.

Commission de gestion du conseil national. 1999. *"Sectes" ou mouvements endoctrinants en Suisse. La nécessité de l'action de l'Etat ou: vers une politique fédérale en matière de "sectes." Rapport de la Commission de gestion du Conseil national du 1 er juillet 1999.* Bern: Commission de gestion du conseil national.

Commission pénale sur les dérives sectaires. 1999. *Rapport de la Commission pénale sur les dérives sectaires sur la question de la manipulation mentale.* Geneva: Commission pénale sur les dérives sectaires.

Council of Europe—Committee on Legal Affairs and Human Rights. 1999. *Illegal Activities of Sects: Report (Doc. 8373).* Strasbourg: Council of Europe.

Davie, Grace. 2000. *Religion in Modern Europe: A Memory Mutates.* Oxford: Oxford University Press.

Deutscher Bundestag—13. Wahlperiode. 1998. *Endbericht der Enquete-Kommission "Sogenannte Sekten und Psychogruppen."* Bonn: Deutscher Bundestag.

Dillon, Jane, and James T. Richardson. 1994. "The 'Cult' Concept: A Politics of Representation Analysis." *SYZYGY: Journal of Alternative Religion and Culture* 3: 185–197.

Dipartimento delle Istituzioni, Repubblica e Cantone del Ticino. 1998. *Interrogazioni sulle sette religiose.* Bellinzona: Dipartimento delle Istituzioni, Repubblica e Cantone del Ticino.

Duval, Maurice. 2002. *Un Ethnoloque au Mandarom. Enquête à l'intérieur d'une.* Paris: Presses Universitaires de France.

European Parliament, Committee on Civil Liberties and Internal Affairs. 1997. *Draft Resolution on Cults in the European Union.* Brussels/Strasbourg: European Parliament.

Greil, Arthur L. 1996. "Sacred Claims: The 'Cult Controversy' as a Struggle Over the

Right to the Religious Label." In *The Issue of Authenticity in the Study of Religions*, ed. David Bromley and Lewis Carter, 46–63. Greenwich, Conn.: JAI Press.

Hervieu-Léger, Danièle. 2000. *Le Pèlerin et le converti. La religion en mouvement.* Paris: Flammarion.

———. 2001. *La Religion en miettes ou la question des sectes.* Paris: Calmann-Lévy.

Introvigne, Massimo. 1999a. "Defectors, Ordinary Leave-Takers, and Apostates: A Quantitative Study of Former Members of New Acropolis in France." *Nova Religio* 3: 83–99.

———. 1999b. "Religion as Claim: Social and Legal Controversies." In *The Pragmatics of Defining Religion: Contexts, Concepts and Contests,* ed. Jan G. Platvoet and Arie L. Molendijk, 41–72. Leiden: Brill.

———. 2000. "Moral Panics and Anti-Cult Terrorism in Western Europe." *Terrorism and Political Violence* 12: 47–59.

———. 2002. *Il lavaggio del cervello: realtà o mito?* Leumann (Torino): Elledici.

Introvigne, Massimo, and J. Gordon Melton, eds. 1996. *Pour en finir avec les sectes. Le débat sur le rapport de la commission parlementaire.* 3rd ed. Paris: Dervy.

Jenkins, Philip. 1996. *Pedophiles and Priests: Anatomy of a Contemporary Crisis.* New York: Oxford University Press.

La Scientologie en Suisse. Rapport préparé à l'intention de la Commission Consultative en matière de protection de l'État. 1998. Bern: Département Fédéral de Justice et de Police.

Leniaud, Jean-Michel. 2000. "La basilique de La Salette: l'achat du terrain, la construction, l'érection de la chapelle en basilique mineure." In *La Salette: Apocalypse, pèlerinage et literature (1856–1996),* ed. François Angelier and Claude Langlois, 135–153. Grenoble: Jérôme Millon.

Lewis, James R. 1986. "Reconstructing the 'Cult' Experience." *Sociological Analysis* 47: 151–159.

———. 1989. "Apostates and the Legitimation of Repression: Some Historical and Empirical Perspectives on the Cult Controversy." *Sociological Analysis* 49: 386–396.

Miller, Donald. 1983. "Deprogramming in Historical Perspective." In *The Brainwashing/Deprogramming Controversy,* ed. David Bromley and James Richardson, 15–28. New Brunswick, N.J.: Transaction.

MILS (*Mission Interministérielle de Lutte contre les Sectes*). 2000. *Rapport d'activité.* Paris: MILS.

Ministero dell'Interno, Dipartimento della Pubblica Sicurezza—Direzione Centrale Polizia di Prevenzione. 1998. *Sette religiose e nuovi movimenti magici in Italia.* Rome: Ministero dell'Interno.

Norman, Ruth. 1999. *Lourdes: Body and Spirit in the Secular Age.* New York: Viking.

Observatoire Interministériel sur les Sectes. 1997. *Rapport annuel 1997.* Paris: La Documentation Française 1998.

Richardson, James T. 1993. "A Social Psychological Critique of 'Brainwashing' Claims about Recruitment to New Religions." In *The Handbook of Cults and Sects in America* (vol. 3, part B of "Religion and the Social Order"), ed. Jeffrey Hadden and David Bromley, 75–93. Greenwich, Conn.: JAI Press.

———. 1996. " 'Brainwashing' Claims and Minority Religions Outside the United States: Cultural Diffusion of a Questionable Legal Concept." *Brigham Young University Law Review* 1996: 873–904.

Richardson, James T., and Massimo Introvigne. 2001. " 'Brainwashing Theories' in Euro-
    pean Parliamentary and Administrative Reports on 'Cults' and 'Sects.' " *Journal for
    the Scientific Study of Religion* 40, no. 2 (June): 143–168.
Richardson, James T., and Brock Kilbourne. 1983. "Classical and Contemporary Uses of
    Brainwashing Models: A Comparison and Critique." In *The Brainwashing/Depro-
    gramming Controversy,* ed. David Bromley and James Richardson, 29–46. Lewiston,
    N.Y.: Edwin Mellen Press.
Richardson, James T., Jan van der Lans, and Frans Derks. 1986. "Leaving and Labelling:
    Coerced and Voluntary Disaffiliation for Religious Social Movements." *Research in
    Social Movements, Conflict, and Change* 9: 97–126.
Robbins, Thomas, and Dick Anthony. 1982. "Deprogramming, Brainwashing, and the
    Medicalization of Deviant Religion." *Social Problems* 29: 283–297.
Shupe, Anson, and David Bromley, eds. 1994. *Anti-Cult Movements in Cross-Cultural
    Perspective.* New York: Garland.
Solomon, Trudy. 1981. "Integrating the Moonie Experience: A Survey of Ex-Members of
    the Unification Church." In *In Gods We Trust: New Patterns of Religious Pluralism
    in America,* ed. Thomas Robbins and Dick Anthony, 275–294. Princeton, N.J.: Rut-
    gers University Press.
Swedish Commission. 1998. *In Good Faith. Society and the New Religious Movements* (Of-
    ficial English-language summary). Stockholm: Norstedts Tryckeri AB.

CHAPTER 10

....

SATANISM AND
RITUAL ABUSE

....

PHILIP JENKINS

FRINGE religions and cults have often caused widespread fears in American history, but in terms of the seriousness of charges, no cult scare has really come close to the anti-Satanism movement that peaked between about 1985 and 1992. In these years, the Satanic danger was the subject of countless reports in the news media, sensational books, and television movies. Customers scanning the shelves of bookstores could find (supposedly) true-life accounts of Satanic misdeeds in books with titles like *The Ultimate Evil, Unspeakable Acts, Cults That Kill*, or *The Devil's Web: Who Is Stalking Your Children for Satan?* A reputable publisher offered what was ostensibly a serious professional manual titled *Treating Survivors of Satanist Abuse*. Patrons could also explore these themes in novels by popular writers like Andrew Vachss and Andrew Greeley.[1] In one of the highest rated television programs of 1988, journalist Geraldo Rivera claimed to "expose Satan's Underground" in the United States. Viewers of this and other programs (broadcast on Halloween) were told that North American Satanism existed as a secret religion, almost a complete alternative society, perhaps millions strong. The hypothetical Satanic religion had existed for centuries, both in Europe and the U.S., and Satanic practices were often passed on through particular families. Covertly, Satanists were very well represented in positions of power, in government, law enforcement, media, education, and the churches.

The clandestine power of the Satanic churches had long permitted them to prevent investigations of their nefarious deeds, but in the 1980s enough details

came to light to suggest a harrowing picture. The religion revolved around seasonal festivals at which human beings were sacrificed, both adults and infants,
amid scenes of staggering sexual depravity and perversion. The number of victims
who perished each year might run to fifty thousand or more in the United States
alone. One of the individuals most often presented as an expert on this cult
activity was a retired FBI agent, who declared that

> I have been told it is a common occurrence for these groups to kidnap their
> victims (usually infants and young children) from hospitals, orphanages, shop-
> ping centers and off the streets. I have been informed that Satanists have been
> successful in their attempts to influence the Boy Scouts. I can say that there is
> a network of these people across the country who are very active, they have
> their own rest and relaxation farm, they are in contact with each other, it ties
> in loosely to the drug operation, it ties into motorcycle gangs and it goes on
> and on. They have their own people who specialize in surveillances and pho-
> tography, and in assassinations.

In 1985, authorities in Lucas County, Ohio, embarked on a massive excavation
of what was believed to be the cemetery of a local Satanic sacrifice cult, where
over fifty bodies were reputedly buried. Needless to say, nothing out of the ordinary was found.[2]

Apart from their homicidal activities, Satanic rings were supposedly en-
trenched in schools and kindergartens across the nation. Children in these settings
were frequently subjected to extreme sexual abuse, including the forced consumption of urine, feces, and blood. These practices were so often discussed in
the media and professional studies that they acquired their own acronym, SRA,
for Satanic Ritual Abuse. Around the world, thousands of individuals were accused in abuse cases said to involve SRA elements, and many were imprisoned—
though no cult activity was ever proven in court.

Although little more than a decade has passed since these events, it seems
astonishing that the Satanic Panic achieved anything like the impact it did, or
that dissenting voices were so rarely heard. Not only were the specific charges so
wildly, insanely improbable, but there is real doubt if any of the movements
reportedly involved even existed. Now the United States does indeed have Satanic
groups like the Church of Satan and the Temple of Set, but anti-Satanic critics
were at pains to point out that these legal overt movements were not the ones
involved in ritual murder and ritual abuse. (The critics had no alternative to
discretion, if they were not to be sued out of existence). The real culprits, we were
told, were clandestine networks of "cult Satanists," which do not exist and never
have. This particular cult scare therefore differed from all others in that it was
wholly built upon rumor and speculation. With whatever justification, critics may
detest new or fringe religions like Scientology, the Unification Church, or even
Aum Shinrikyō, but at least these groups clearly exist and can operate openly.

There are, however, simply no Cult Satanists of the sort identified in the late 1980s.[3]

This chapter therefore differs significantly from the others in this book, but some common themes do emerge. For all its hysterical exaggeration, the Satanism scare illustrates many of the themes commonly found in the rhetoric so often directed at new and fringe religions, especially in its emphasis on protecting endangered children. Also, this example shows how information about new religions is shaped (however inaccurately) through popular culture and the mass media: these cultural manifestations can affect both anti-cult movements and often the religious adherents themselves. Though there are no Cult Satanists, media stereotypes have proved attractive to many individuals who try and portray themselves in what is presumed to be the proper Satanic mold. And finally, in understanding popular images of new religions, fears can be just as important as objective reality. So the proverb is wrong: there can be a very great deal of smoke without any fire whatever.

THE ORIGINS OF SATANISM

In the 1980s, it was common to claim that the supposed Satanic religion dated back centuries. This is true only to the extent that we can indeed go back many centuries to find the images and stereotypes that would eventually be combined into the modern anti-Satanic mythology. We find several separate currents, which would be brought together in relatively modern times, but especially during the Romantic and Decadent movements of the nineteenth century. At every stage, we find that the supposed religion of Satanism is an artificial, literary, and intellectual concoction, a purely bookish product of relatively recent times.

We can trace three major ideas that would ultimately intertwine to invent modern Satanism, though in their day, each strand was wholly unrelated to the other. These elements are, respectively, ritual magic, the Black Mass, and the witches' Sabbat.

Ritual Magic

Ever since the earliest civilizations, magicians and necromancers have tried to control the forces of nature, often by summoning angelic or demonic forces. We know that in the European Middle Ages, there was a lively clandestine subculture of sorcerers, and magic texts (grimoires) survive in abundance.[4] The activities of ritual magic are well documented, for instance, in the autobiography of Benevenuto Cellini, who records how, in sixteenth-century Rome, he encountered someone who "cultivated the black art. We went together to the Coliseum; and there the priest, having arrayed himself in necromancer's robes, began to describe circles on the earth with the finest ceremonies that can be imagined. I must say that he had made us bring precious perfumes and fire, and also drugs of fetid odour." The ceremony "lasted more than an hour and a half; when several legions appeared, and the Coliseum was all full of devils."[5]

The greatest English work on ritual magic is Francis Barrett's *The Magus* (1801), which instructs, among other things, "the method of raising evil or familiar spirits by a circle; likewise the souls and shadows of the dead."[6] The tradition drew heavily on the Jewish Qabala, so that many of the mystical names of power they employed are nothing more than standard Hebrew titles for the divine. Sometimes, rituals involved not just summoning a demon but signing a pact with him: the most famous legend in this genre concerns the German magician Faust.

This all certainly sounds "Satanic," but it differs massively from the modern stereotype. This is not any kind of church or organized religion—there are no hierarchies or initiations, no ritual calendar. There is no sexual element, and children are never mentioned, much less abused. The magus works alone or in tiny groups of skilled specialists: there are no "covens," no mass congregations. And followers certainly were not numerous, comprising some kind of an alternative religion.

The Black Mass

Closer to our recent model is the kind of magic that existed in some Catholic European nations during the seventeenth and eighteenth centuries, when we first hear of the "Black Mass." This parody of the Catholic ritual was celebrated by a defrocked priest, who used a naked woman for his altar and who sacrificed living creatures, including children. Incidents of this sort are recorded, notably during the great "Affair of the Poisons," which was one of the greatest scandals in seventeenth-century France.

Apparently, aristocrats and courtiers involved themselves in these secret activities to seek hidden knowledge, or to win the favor of the king. It is anybody's guess how far police investigations were recording actual behaviors, or if they were merely accumulating sensational charges to discredit powerful courtiers, perhaps in the interests of some rival faction.[7] This is what had happened in France during the fourteenth century, when the authorities used widespread torture to force members of the Knights Templar to confess to all manner of fictitious crimes, including devil worship. Also, even if the allegations of the 1670s were correct, this still would not prove the existence of any kind of alternative religion. There is no suggestion of anything like the ritual calendar attributed to modern Satanists, with their great holy days like May Eve (April 30), Halloween, and the rest.

The Witches' Sabbat

Ritual magic did exist (and still does); the Black Mass probably did occur; but the most important element of the Satanic synthesis was wholly mythical. Though witches' Sabbats were recorded so frequently in early modern Europe, it is all but certain that they never really took place. Witchcraft certainly did exist: through history, people have tried to use magic to affect themselves and their neighbors, and sometimes that meant placing curses. Only in the fourteenth century, however, did European churches and secular regimes begin to seek out witches as part of an alternative secret religion, in which believers were organized into secret cells called covens, usually thirteen strong. These groups held regular gatherings on great seasonal festivals, the Sabbats. Contrary to much speculation about the meaning of this word, this is simply the common term for "Sabbath." Its usage reflects the idea that Jews and witches both in their separate ways followed deviant anti-Christian religions, both worshiped the devil and the Antichrist, and both victimized Christian children in their rites.

Reading contemporary accounts of the Sabbats, we can see that we have here the precise origins of the modern anti-Satanic mythology. According to a French work published in 1612, Satan was present personally at these events.

> On his right sits the queen of the Sabbath, and kneeling before them a witch
> presents a child she has abducted. Partaking of the Sabbat feast are witches and
> demons; only the meat of corpses, hanged men, hearts of unbaptized children,
> and unclean animals never eaten by Christians are eaten. At the extreme right,
> poor witches who dare not approach the high ceremonies watch the festivities.
> After the banquet, the devils lead their neighbors beneath an accursed tree
> where, forming a ring facing alternately inward and outward, the company
> dance in the most indecent manner possible. A group of noble lords and ladies
> mingle with rich and powerful witches who are disguised or masked to avoid
> recognition and who conduct the important business of the Sabbat. During the
> Sabbat, witches arrive on pitchforks and broomsticks, or on goats with their
> children whom they will present to Satan.[8]

We note here the key idea of child murder, and of clandestine elite believers. Satanists do what they do because they are deliberately inverting and mocking all customarily accepted behavior.

Most early modern Europeans probably believed that Sabbats did occur, and hundreds of thousands of persons were executed for these crimes between, say, 1350 and 1700. The problem here is that every one of these stories about the Sabbat was obtained under torture and represented a response to leading questions placed by witch-hunters. We can prove this because, fortunately, we have a kind of control group in the form of nations like England, which did not permit judicial torture. English courts executed thousands of witches, though nothing like the numbers in continental Europe, but never once do we hear of English covens, ritual calendars, or Sabbats. All these elements do, however, appear in their full phantasmagoric splendor when we observe neighboring nations that did torture suspects, namely France and Scotland. However influential, the Sabbat stories are bogus. Accused witches may, on occasion, have cast spells or even tried to curse neighbors, but they were never part of an organized religion.

ROMANTICS AND DECADENTS

When modern-day Americans describe Cult Satanism, they are drawing on these three elements, which in earlier ages were so distinct as to represent almost different worlds. Ritual magic was a matter for clergy and academics, the Black Mass for aristocrats and courtiers, witchcraft for peasants. How, then, did the different components come together to form such a synthesis? How, historically, did the Sabbat merge with the Black Mass, magicians with witches?

We can understand this process in terms of the interests and obsessions of the nineteenth century. Once the witch trials were safely consigned to history (the last witch to be legally executed in Europe suffered death in Switzerland in 1775), it was possible to reexamine them through the Romantic lens, and to transform the elderly social outcasts of the witch trials into heroic and glamorous figures. At the start of the nineteenth century, Goya was painting his famous pictures of witches and demons gathered at the Sabbat. In 1808, Goethe's *Faust* brought the great ritual magician to the witches' Sabbat supposedly held in Germany's Harz mountains on April 30—that is, May Eve, or Walpurgis Night. Witches and devil worshipers were beginning to form a nodding literary acquaintance.

But the real fascination with witchcraft and Satanism was chiefly a product of French Romantics, particularly during the 1850s and 1860s. In this era, renowned historians like Jules Michelet suggested that witchcraft had been a real phenomenon, a kind of peasant social protest against feudal oppression, and thus a true alternate religion.[9] Intellectuals built on this theme with their own cultivation of diabolism as a revolt against social conformity, bourgeois morality, and

industrial ugliness. In the 1860s, the poems of Charles Baudelaire show a fascination with the devilish, most famously in his liturgy, the Litanies of Satan. This
was also the time of a full-scale occult revival led by English ritual magician
Bulwer Lytton and his French counterpart Eliphas Lévi. In these years, too, the
pioneering American occultist Paschal Beverly Randolph integrated a strong sexual
element into his rituals. From the 1880s, ritual magic was revived through the
London-based Order of the Golden Dawn, which is basically the source for most
modern occultism. In the 1890s—that great age of "Decadence" and medieval
revivalism—some occultists were exploring the darker aspects of the magical tradition. The Black Mass achieved a literary revival among the decadents of late-
nineteenth-century France, and an extensive account of such an event in contemporary Paris appeared in J.-K. Huysmans's novel *La-Bas* (Down There).

By the turn of the century, too, Golden Dawn alumnus Aleister Crowley was
experimenting with magical rituals that involved extensive sex practices, drugs,
and animal sacrifice. While he denied to the last that he was a Satanist or that
he ever engaged in any kind of Black Mass, we have certainly moved close to the
common stereotype of what Satanists are meant to do. Contemporary legends
about Crowley's excesses certainly shaped views of the occult. In 1930, Charles
Williams's novel *War in Heaven* depicted a clique of devil worshipers who attempt
to sacrifice a child in order to win control of the Holy Grail.

Crowleyan followers were operating in North America by the First World
War, and lodges of his OTO (Ordo Templi Orientis) appeared in the U.S. and
Canada. In the next generation, one of the most important would be rocket
scientist Jack Parsons, who became a highly active ritual magic practitioner in
southern California in the 1930s and 1940s. Like his mentor, Parsons was also
deeply involved in sex magic and was fascinated by the dark side of the occult,
the Left-hand path: in 1945, he was said to be "enamored with witchcraft, the
houmfort, Voodoo." Even so, we are still far removed from the modern Satanism
myth. Parsons and his like were never part of an organized underground church,
they never operated in anything resembling covens, they ignored the ritual calendar supposedly characteristic of the witches' Sabbats, and, like Crowley, they
would certainly have denied a belief in "Satanism": Satan, they would have said,
is a Christian obsession. They did not commit acts of violence, much less human
sacrifice. Nor did children (or nonconsenting adults) feature in their sexual practices.[10]

To understand how witchcraft merged with ritual magic, we have to step back
from the actual practitioners and look instead at the antiquarians and academics.
During the 1890s, scholars pursued the notion that the witch trials had in fact
revealed the existence of an authentic clandestine religious movement, a "witch-
cult," which genuinely did engage in the worship of a rival deity, perhaps Satan.
In 1893, pioneering feminist Matilda Gage proposed that the witch-cult really had
existed and had maintained an ancient woman-oriented fertility cult. A few years

later, folklorist Charles Godfrey Leland asserted not only that a witch-cult existed, but that he had actually interviewed some of its members. Talking to Italian peasants, Leland claimed to have discovered a surviving pagan religion that dated back to pre-Roman times.[11]

Also influential was the work of anthropologist Sir James Frazer, whose book *The Golden Bough* first appeared in 1890. Frazer claimed that fertility cults represented a universal primal religion that practiced regular human sacrifices, and these ideas had an enduring impact on both elite and popular culture. One influential disciple was Margaret Murray, whose 1921 book *The Witch Cult* in Western Europe popularized the concept of widespread secret religions. Murray argued that the witch-hunters of the sixteenth and seventeenth centuries had exposed an authentic goddess-worshiping Old Religion, and the witch-hunters were reporting no more than the sober truth when they told of cells (covens), each comprising thirteen members. Each coven was headed by a disguised leader bearing some title such as the Devil or the Black Man, and the groups met in periodic assemblies known as Sabbats. The orgiastic rituals of the Sabbat were really fertility rites. Also accurate, according to Murray, were accounts of the witches' calendar, which preserved ancient agricultural cycles, with key dates like Halloween and May Eve.

Satan Comes to America

By the 1920s, all the ideas necessary for the invention of modern Satanism were in place, waiting to be synthesized. The elements can be summarized like this:

- Witchcraft had really existed as an authentic ancient religion that worshiped the devil. The witch-cult really was a devil-cult.
- There really had been Sabbats, with rituals involving blood sacrifice and extensive sexuality. They might even have involved the ritual killing of children or adults.
- Witchcraft really had been structured into covens, and there was a genuine hierarchy.
- Witchcraft was intimately connected with Satanism, Black Magic, and the Black Mass.

The question unanswered by Gage, Michelet, and Murray was just when the old witch-cult had perished. In 1700? With the coming of industry? Or—and this was the key issue—might it still be thriving underground in the modern world? By the 1920s, tales of witches and Black Masses were appearing in popular culture, in fantasy and horror fiction, and an American translation of *La-Bas* appeared in 1924. In 1914, the *New York World* published one of the first American accounts of a "Black Mass," when it reported on one of Crowley's London rituals held in London.[12] In every case, though, these stories were given an exotic setting, because everyone knew that such things simply did not happen in the United States. Within a few years, however, this opinion changed fundamentally, due to the influence of one now forgotten novel, Herbert S. Gorman's thriller *The Place Called Dagon* (1927). This book portrays a secret cult in a western Massachusetts town populated by descendants of refugees from Salem, still practicing a witch-craft religion that is almost identical to the modern image of Cult Satanism. Gorman is anything but a well-remembered writer today. He was primarily a literary biographer best known for two major biographies of James Joyce.

However, his career had two other main aspects, both of which would be crucial for our present purposes. First, he was thoroughly familiar with the thought of late-nineteenth-century France, which meant that he could draw on French speculations concerning the Black Mass. Second, Gorman worked exten-sively on American writers like Longfellow and Hawthorne, and it was in 1927— the same year as *The Place Called Dagon*—that Gorman also published his bi-ography, *Hawthorne: A Study in Solitude*. The Hawthorne link is critical, since that writer too was deeply interested in New England witch persecutions, and his story "Young Goodman Brown" could be read as describing a genuine witch-cult, a group of real American devil worshipers. What Gorman did was to bring that idea into the twentieth century, and to take the utterly unprecedented step of presenting an occult or Satanic theme in contemporary America.[13]

The Place Called Dagon seems quite commonplace today in its theme of secret witch-cults and sacrificial rings. Yet in his time, Gorman's work was radically innovative. For Gorman, the Salem witches were part of "a secret and blasphe-mous order that met all over the world, that they were divided into covens or parishes, that they each had their leader in the shape of a Black Man who rep-resented the devil, and that they attempted to practice magic." Surviving the persecution, some of the Salem magicians fled to Dagon, where they raised the great altar of the Devil Stone. In modern times, Jeffrey Westcott, a charismatic leader, "re-instituted witch meetings, formed a coven here, and made himself the ruling Black Man. . . . These people lead two lives, and one of them is the surface life that we see going on about us. The other is the secret life that centers about the place called Dagon."[14]

The book finds its climax in chapter 10, when after long anticipation, we observe the secret rituals at Dagon, at which Asmodeus is invoked in what is essentially a Black Mass, complete with the attempted sacrifice of a woman.[15] The people cry, "Enter into us Asmodeus! Enter into your heritage! Were we not sold to you by the bond of blood by Salem Village two hundred and thirty years ago? In the deep forest you accepted us and made a pact with us. We forsook all other gods but you for you were the eternal will of man. Though we have slept for generations, the ancient pact still holds." Throughout this section, we have an amazingly complex portrayal of neopaganism, or at least paganism as it could be imagined by a bookish writer of the 1920s. Virtually every allegation about real-life American Satanism, particularly during the great scare of the 1980s and 1990s, can be located in this one novel, and especially in this particular chapter.

Gorman's novel had an enormous impact on other fantasy writers, especially the group who published regularly in *Weird Tales*, authors like H. P. Lovecraft, Robert Bloch, and Henry Kuttner. Through the 1950s, the *Weird Tales* school created a familiar image of secret blood cults in the American countryside, communities following Satanic witch-cults with rituals dating back centuries. In England, too, a similar synthesis occurred between the various worlds of witchcraft, ritual magic, and the Black Mass diabolism. The main activist here was the popular thriller writer Dennis Wheatley, whose much-imitated book *The Devil Rides Out* appeared in 1934. I do not know if he had read Gorman, but his approach is so similar that I think he must have. Since both he and Gorman also worked extensively on late-nineteenth-century France, it is inconceivable that Wheatley did not know Gorman's other writings. Whatever the nature of the borrowings, Wheatley too presented a detailed picture of something like Cult Satanism—which he now called Black Magic. For Wheatley, too, evil magicians do not work alone, as in tradition: they have followers who gather in covens at the great seasonal meetings, or Sabbats. He depicts a clique of aristocratic witches/Satanists who meet at an English country house and then organize a Sabbat in the best seventeenth-century French or German tradition, complete with a sexual orgy, child sacrifice, and cannibalism. The date, of course, is May Eve.

By the 1930s, the literary creation of Satanism was well advanced, and it was beginning to have a wider social impact. Throughout this decade, the news media were reporting regularly on alleged instances of human sacrifice in American cities. Law enforcement agencies began to explore possible "cult" interpretations when they were faced with unsolved serial murder cases. They thought that there really could be Satanic rings in Cleveland or Philadelphia. Just how commonplace the language of cults and human sacrifice had become is suggested by the abundance of references in popular culture in these years. In 1939, Raymond Chandler's *The Big Sleep* features a joking reference that seems to fit much better into the Satanism scare of the 1980s than the New Deal years. When asked to explain a bloody crime scene, detective Philip Marlowe suggests sardonically that maybe "Geiger was running a cult and made blood sacrifices in front of that totem pole."

In his 1947 novel *The Scarf*, Robert Bloch depicts a sensationalistic California journalist urging a colleague to write a book on a recent serial murder case: "People like to read about it. Look at the way those true detective magazines sell. Sex crimes. Blood. Everybody wants to know. . . . Ever hear about the ritual murders we had out here? The devil worshipers? They cut up a kid." By 1956, on no known evidence, *Newsweek* declared that some forty groups in southern California alone "devote themselves to the celebration of the Satanic Mass."[16]

POPULARIZATION, 1965–1980

Most of the ideas that emerged during the recent Satanism scare were well established before the Second World War. Having said this, a number of new factors ensured that the problem would attract much wider publicity in the last quarter of the twentieth century. One was that, from the 1960s onward, there were for the first time public above-ground groups that were avowedly Satanist. The best known was Anton LaVey's Church of Satan, founded on Walpurgis Night 1966, and explicitly based on the Romantic rediscovery of the Black Mass. This was never a major movement and never sought a wide public, but the image of a Satanic church was influential and spawned a number of offshoots and imitators.[17] Some, like the Temple of Set, were close to La Vey's original model, others were Crowleyan, and one intriguing group, the Church of the Process, evolved from an environment close to Scientology.[18] These groups were also significant because it made it easier for anti-Satanic theorists to justify their claims of an authentic menace. Much the same function was served by the rising wave of neopagan and Wiccan movements, which included some of the familiar elements of the old witchcraft stereotypes: they did follow the seasonal festivals, and some of their rituals featured nudity and sometimes sexual activity. Though Wiccans often tire of proclaiming that they are not Satanists, they were sufficiently close to the popular image to justify concern in some anti-cult circles.

Also new during the late 1960s was a genuine surge of popular interest in all aspects of the occult, including witchcraft and Satanism. Much of this derived from the United Kingdom, where Dennis Wheatley's successive novels on Satanism had always been popular, and where an influential film of *The Devil Rides Out* appeared in 1968. Over the next few years, occult and even Satanic themes permeated rock music and would later become influential in heavy metal. Led Zeppelin used romantic pagan imagery, with ideas of stone circles and Viking human sacrifice, while a popular pioneering heavy metal group took the name Black Sabbath. One minor rock group, Black Widow, drew heavily on Wheatley Satanism for its songs and performed imitation Black Magic rituals on stage.[19]

The occult became a familiar theme on the fringe of the hippy subculture, and this connection would later popularize notions about clandestine Satanic activity. One key part of this package was the notion of ritual murder or human sacrifice, theories that emerged from journalistic speculations about the cult environment of Charles Manson. In 1971 Ed Sanders's book *The Family* placed Manson in the context of the numerous occult and mystical movements then flourishing in northern California.

One story linked Manson to the Church of the Process, a connection that the group would staunchly contest in the courts: Sanders "alludes to the existence of a sort of modern Thuggee or Satanic underground, in which he claims The Process to have been a central organizing factor." Since Sanders's book was such a major contribution to anti-Satanic theory, it is important to realize that the author was not a sober social scientist, but a fairly eccentric activist and Beat poet, and it pays to realize that much of *The Family* reads like it was written with tongue in cheek. Sanders often indulges in considerable irony in order to parody the sensationalistic press exposés of the Manson clan. How exactly are we to take the portentous closing words of the book: "And only when all these evil affairs are known and exposed can the curse of ritual sacrifice, Helter Skelter and Satanism be removed from the coasts and mountains and deserts of California"?[20]

THE PANIC OF THE 1980S

All that really remained to be added to form the full-blooded Satanism of the panic years was the notion of a special threat of children, and in fact that requires some explanation. Though children were said to be killed and/or eaten during both the Sabbat and the Black Mass, such charges had not surfaced too often during the literary accounts of the twentieth century. This may reflect the rather lower emphasis placed on crimes against children at various times in this period, or else there simply was not the slightest authentic evidence linking the occult to offenses against the young. From the 1970s, however, social sensibilities changed dramatically, with a radically new emphasis on child protection as an urgent social need. It was in 1977 that the term "child abuse" acquired its special modern meaning of sexual acts committed against the young, and over the following years there was an outpouring of exposés about child murder, child pornography, and kidnaping. Elsewhere, I have called the decade after 1977 the era of America's "child abuse revolution."[21]

It is in this context that we must see the new interest in the extreme physical and sexual maltreatment said to be inflicted upon children in cult groups. The massacre of children at Jonestown in 1978 excited the interest of police officers and journalists who would later become important writers on Satanism and other cult activities. Kenneth Wooden's 1981 book, *Children of Jonestown*, pioneered the notion of cults "ritualistically abusing" young people and even suggests that "babies, born into cults, their births unregistered, are reported to have died of unnatural causes and to have been buried in secrecy, like pets."[22] Wooden's position as a television reporter and producer gave him a unique platform from which to disseminate his concept of cult abuses. In 1980, the key book *Michelle Remembers* drew attention to the developing idea of ritualized child abuse and explicitly suggested that the cults involved were Satanic in nature. The pseudonymous Michelle described memories that she claimed to have recalled during therapy in the late 1970s. In these sessions, she reported sexual atrocities inflicted on her as a child in Vancouver in the early 1950s.

This text would shape all subsequent narratives of ritual child abuse and legitimized the theory that traumatic events could lie dormant until resurfacing during therapy. This would be the basis of the "recovered memory" movement of the late 1980s, in which people so often claimed to recollect victimization at the hands of cults. (*Michelle Remembers* itself must be treated with great skepticism, not least because literally all the charges involved seem drawn from accounts of West African secret societies in the 1950s, imported to Canada.)[23]

The various strands of speculation—about Satanism, cult violence, and ritual abuse—merged as a result of one of the most notorious criminal cases of the decade, the mass abuse case at the McMartin preschool in southern California, which was first reported in the media in 1984. According to prosecutors, hundreds of small children attending this school had been sexually abused by a ring of teachers, often in ritualistic settings involving robes, pentacles, and church altars. One ten-year-old child told a court "how he and other children were taken to a church where he said adults wearing masks and black robes danced and moaned." Though the McMartin case is now generally recognized as spurious, this affair generated fears that Satanic rings lurked behind the walls of preschools and daycare institutions across the country. There would be many subsequent investigations, and a number of equally unfounded criminal charges, with the most outrageous instances occurring at Bakersfield (California), Jordan (Minnesota), Edenton (North Carolina), Martensville (Canada), and Wenatchee (Washington).[24]

The origins of the ritual abuse scare have been analyzed so extensively over the last few years that the affair needs only brief discussion here. In each case, the affair generally began with a limited and plausible allegation that a small number of children had been abused, often in a preschool or kindergarten setting. In the ensuing investigation, interrogation of child "victims" produced evidence that far more abuse had occurred, until reports and rumors implicated dozens of local residents in sex rings. Specific charges were based on statements that therapists derived from impressionable small children, who responded to repeated leading questions by generating answers designed to please their interrogators.

Lacking knowledge of sexual matters, they concocted the most shocking acts available to their imaginations, which would explain the tales of teachers forcing pupils to engage in or observe toilet functions.

As therapists became familiar with accounts of stars, circles, and robes, they incorporated "ritualistic" elements into subsequent questioning, where suggestions were easily confirmed. Psychological findings seemed corroborated by speculative types of pediatric examination which were believed to prove that many child witnesses had been subjected to anal and genital rape. Unfortunately, these techniques are also likely to produce large numbers of false positives, on the strength of symptoms that have a quite normal and noncriminal interpretation. Flawed therapeutic evidence was then taken over wholesale by local prosecutors, who employed it as a literally correct account drawn forth by skilled behavioral science investigators and used the material as the basis for their florid indictments. And ritual abuse was born.

Ideas about SRA were disseminated through networks of professional seminars which targeted therapists, youth workers, and police officers, and which all presented a broadly similar account of a vast Satanic danger. Not surprisingly, these seminars tended to provoke the discovery of yet more new ritualistic cases, and encouraged agencies to impose "Satanic" interpretations where they would not have dreamed of doing such a thing in the past. By the late 1980s, U.S.-style Satanic investigations and SRA charges were surfacing in the United Kingdom, Australia, Canada, South Africa, and The Netherlands—everywhere, in fact, where American therapeutic and criminological literature was read.

Charges that children were being abused in these ritualistic circumstances won support from an improbably large and diverse coalition of interest groups, who would normally have had next to nothing in common: one study notes that the idea found adherents among "social workers, therapists, physicians, victimology researchers, police, criminal prosecutors, fundamentalist Christians, ambitious politicians, anti-pornography activists, feminists, and the media."[25] The coalition between fundamentalists and feminists seems odd but possesses a definite logic.

Fundamentalists had much to gain from proving the charges, which demonstrated their basic point about the upsurge of evil as the world approached the End Times. For feminists, meanwhile, much of their mobilization since the 1960s had focused on the issue of rape and sexual assault, and a cardinal belief was that victims must be believed at all costs. This was just as true of children as of adult women. However the allegations of abuse had been obtained, it was vital to accept them, and the phrase "Believe the Children" became a war cry of the era.

By the mid-1980s, the panic was reaching full force. In addition to the general area of ritual abuse, several related issues now came to light.

Breeders and Survivors

One of the oldest themes in anti-cult movements is that of defectors or apostates, people who claim a special authority to expose a suspect movement because they knew it from within, and reveal its darkest secrets.

The best-known example may be Maria Monk, who revealed what were alleged to be the sexual atrocities allegedly committed in nineteenth-century Catholic convents. Since the Satanic movement was (reputedly) so uniquely lethal, defectors who claimed to have escaped from this cult commonly bore the title of "survivor." One of the first was evangelical Mike Warnke, whose 1972 book *The Satan Seller* claimed to reveal his experiences as a Satanic high priest in the California hippy world of the 1960s. In fact, all the claims made by the book have been challenged, and the work is regarded as highly suspect. At least, though, Warnke depicted a plausible social setting and makes no claims that automatically stretch credulity.

Far different are the numerous "survivor" titles which grew out of the *Michelle Remembers* phenomenon. These works claim to be the autobiographies of women who were raised in cults, severely abused in their youth, and in later life forced to bear babies for the cult to sacrifice. This last idea, of cult women as "breeders," has been a strikingly common theme both in survivor stories and instances of recovered memory. Among the best known of survivor accounts are books by Lauren Stratford (*Satan's Underground*) and Judith Spencer (*Suffer the Child* and *Satan's High Priest*). Spencer's books are all the more important because they appeared from mainstream publishing houses and were presented in the form of a serious psychiatric study. Stratford, meanwhile, was a powerful witness on a number of the television exposés of the era.[26]

The charges made by these alleged survivors are remarkable. If we are to believe her, the "Jenny" described by Spencer grew up in an atmosphere that was literally hellish. Initiated into her mother's cult at the age of five, "the rhythms of Satan worship permeated her childhood." She "stood boldly to see other dogs, and then cats, chickens, squirrels, rabbits and goats killed. She watched the amputation of fingers and nipples, and sometimes, penises." The religious life described here suggests a large and influential cult, with frequent rituals including as the centerpiece a classical Black Mass.[27]

In none of the cases can the "survivor" stories be verified, and where they can be tested, they fall apart. Lauren Stratford's claims were dismantled by a notable exposé in the evangelical magazine *Cornerstone*. *Cornerstone* noted Stratford's numerous contradictions and generally suggested a consistent pattern of wild fantasies on her part. Even her accounts of her parents and siblings have been subject to kaleidoscopic changes over the years. Her claims of abuse had similarly changed frequently over time, and a Satanism element had only appeared as a claim as late as 1985, in the aftermath of the McMartin case. Of the most dramatic charge, about "breeding" and sacrificing three children, the story noted that she had variously claimed: "she's sterile/ had two children killed in snuff films/ three children killed, two in snuff films, one in Satanic ritual/ says she had children during teenage years/ her twenties/ lived two years in a breeder ware-house. In reality, no evidence she was ever pregnant." The article's most remark-able conclusion was neither that the charges were unsupported, nor that they frequently contradicted known events; it was that virtually no outlet for these claims had undertaken any serious verification. "The most stunning element . . . is that no one even checked out the main details."[28]

Precisely the same problems affect the countless cases of "cult survivors" who surface during recovered memory therapy and whose claims are, simply, incred-ible. The charges presupposed a far-reaching conspiratorial network. SRA advo-cates were suggesting that child sacrifice is a daily event in North America, that a clandestine alternative religion exists undetected, and that its agents have infil-trated schools, kindergartens, churches, and police departments; that women reg-ularly bear babies for sacrifice; and that all these phenomena have occurred sys-tematically in American society for decades, perhaps back to the seventeenth century. Nor had these mass atrocities come to light before the 1980s. A typical survivor claimed that she had as a child been the victim of a cult led by the "town leaders, business-people and church officials" of "an upper middle class town in the Midwest" in the mid- or late 1930s. The pseudonymous Annette was "abused in rituals that included sexual abuse, torture, murder, photography and systematic brainwashing through drugs and electric shock." By the age of twelve, she was a "breeder," bearing children for the cult to sacrifice.

Though her account is published as authentic in the massively popular re-covery text *The Courage to Heal*, the bible of the incest survivor movement, the story stretches credibility to the limit and beyond. I reiterate, there simply is no evidence for any authentic Satanic groups in the United States before the 1960s: so just who was committing these horrors?[29]

Teenage Satanism

At the height of the Satanism crisis, media and law enforcement spent almost as much time warning of a danger to teenagers as they did to small children. Among the charges commonly made were that teenagers were turning to Satanic cults in significant numbers because of constant exposure to dangerous occult ideas through films, rock music, and role-playing games. In his 1988 television special, Geraldo Rivera claimed that "it is teenagers who are most likely to fall under the spell of this jungle of dark violent emotions called Satanism, and in some cases to be driven to committing terrible deeds—There is no doubt that teenage Satanic activity in this country is increasing dramatically."[30]

It should be said here that, unlike ritual abuse, teenage Satanism does exist. Over the last thirty years or so, many young people have affected Satanic dress and symbols, in part because this seems the most effective way of shocking jaded communities. One might ask how else one could mount a teenage rebellion against baby boomers who themselves grew up in a culture of sex, drugs, and rock and roll. Whether teen Satanism can be described as a new religious movement is open to some debate, because it has so few of the aspects of a religion, no hierarchy, no membership system, no structure, not even a network connecting regions or neighborhoods. It tends to exist as a rhetorical style, supported by common adherence to favored books, films, and rock music. In many cases, "membership" involves little more than listening to particular albums, wearing black, and purchasing a copy of Anton LaVey's *Satanic Bible*. Since adherence is so casual, assessing numbers involved is next to impossible.

This picture is utterly different from the sinister image offered in the late 1980s, with its threatening image of a slippery slope. The commonplace view during the great scare was that occult dabbling would inexorably lead to serious cult involvement. Young people would graduate from mere "self-styled Satanists" to become Religious Satanists or even Cult Satanists, the most pernicious group of all. The consequences, it was alleged, might include violence and gang activity, suicide, and homicide, and this last notion was substantiated by well-publicized cases of teenagers murdering friends or family members. The prime exhibits in this account were killers like Sean Sellers and Pete Roland, both of whom were widely discussed in books and television specials, and both did indeed claim to have killed for Satan.

But we should be very cautious about accepting such claims. By definition, multiple killers are not normal people, and they might have odd motivations for their acts. In fact, it is quite common for acts of violence to have as their goal some imagined religious motive, such as a response to a divine commandment. Receiving orders from supernatural forces is a common manifestation of paranoid schizophrenia, a condition believed to be present in a number of multiple homicide cases. In many such cases, offenders receive orders from what they perceived to be the Christian God, and this is the norm in the vast majority of such delusions. The number of murders attributed to divine command is many times greater than those blamed on Satan. On the other hand, it would surely be unacceptable to describe such actions as "Christian ritual killings" or "biblical sacrifices." These were the work of disturbed individuals whose psychiatric conditions chanced to be expressed in the language and rhetoric of a belief system widespread in their particular social background. Disturbed individuals might well claim to be acting in the name of Satan with no more plausibility than another might kill in the cause of Christ or Allah.

The problems with the "teenage Satanism" theory are evident from a cele-brated case that occurred in West Memphis, Arkansas, in 1993, when three small boys were found murdered and mutilated. Police arrested three local teenagers for the crime, which was widely said to be Satanic in nature. Here at last, it seemed, we had the classic example of a Satanic serial murder ring, perhaps even Cult Satanists at work. This view of the case might have become orthodoxy, had the affair not become the subject of two major television documentaries broadcast by HBO under the general title of *Paradise Lost*. These documentaries showed beyond any reasonable doubt that the teenagers had been falsely accused and had suffered mightily because of their presumed Satanism, which had led them to Death Row. In brief, the group made themselves unpopular by wearing black and listening to heavy metal music. One boy who had taken the name "Damien" was supposed to be imitating the Antichrist figure in *The Omen* film series, though in reality he was just expressing his devotion for the Catholic saint of that name. The case of the "West Memphis Three" remains open, as one of the most egre-gious miscarriages of justice resulting from the Satanic scare.[31]

The Panic Collapses, 1992–1995

Despite years of allegation and investigation, no cases validating the ritual abuse menace could be produced by the early 1990s, raising questions about the whole portrayal of the supposed menace. The federal government itself did much to damp down the most extreme speculations. Crucially, the FBI's leading investi-gator of sex ring cases was Kenneth Lanning, who remained severely skeptical of allegations about "occult crime," so that media sources exploring the validity of the ritual charges would soon encounter this critical source. In 1994, a study of ritual crime allegations sponsored by the National Center on Child Abuse and Neglect discredited virtually all charges. In a massive survey of psychologists, social workers, prosecutors, and police departments, researchers found a very few cases where "lone perpetrators or couples" had employed ritualistic trappings to intim-idate children and perhaps to add a bizarre thrill to sexual activities. However, in not one out of twelve thousand incidents investigated was there the slightest hint of "a well-organized intergenerational Satanic cult who sexually molested and tortured children in their homes or schools for years and committed a series of murders." The same conclusion emerged from a comparable investigation of the mushrooming SRA cases in Great Britain.[32]

The failure of the McMartin trials in 1990 initiated a general media reaction against ritual abuse cases, as well as of mass abuse cases that lacked an overt ritualistic element. Between 1990 and 1994, pieces debunking the whole SRA notion appeared in many major newspapers and magazines. And while publishers continued to issue the sculpted fantasies of ritual abuse "survivors," there were also critical studies like with titles like *Abuse of Innocence* (on the McMartin case) and *Satanic Panic*.[33] The landmark in this field was the comprehensive demolition of the SRA idea by Debbie Nathan and Michael Snedeker in their 1995 book *Satan's Silence*.

The visual media were equally hostile. From about 1987, most network news programs and news magazines turned decisively against the Satanic charges, partly in embarrassed reaction to the extravagance of tabloid documentaries and talk shows. Through the early 1990s, mass abuse prosecutions were attacked in segments on all the major television news magazine shows, which produced psychological evidence showing how easily leading questions could be used to get children to make wholly false statements. The same news outlets presented regular exposés of the highly dubious means by which therapists generated so-called recovered memories of cult abuse.

Sometimes, therapists involved were well-intentioned zealots, but a few seemed motivated by crude financial motives, basically trying to convince people that they were sick and abused in order to prolong their treatment and thus maximize insurance payments. Attacks on therapists and anti-cult theorists reached flood proportions by 1993–1994. By 1995, criticisms of the ritual abuse idea achieved a still wider audience through the television docudrama *Indictment*, which portrayed the incompetent prosecutorial work and media hysteria in the McMartin case.[34]

A media consensus now viewed the McMartin case and its clones as "witch-hunts," a peculiarly apt term given the occult nature of many of the charges. The term gained popularity from the Arthur Miller play *The Crucible*, which showed how alleged witches became scapegoats for the fears and repressions of the Salem community. Also implied in the usage was the networking mechanism by which charges were disseminated: a presupposition of guilt permitted flimsy or ludicrous charges to adhere to one suspect, proving that grave evil was present in the community. In this paranoid environment, the slightest unorthodoxy or misbehavior was taken as a sign of membership in the conspiracy, and proof of guilt was readily forthcoming from witnesses whose credibility would not normally be entertained, including children and the mentally unstable. Originating among isolated critics of the mass abuse prosecutions during the mid-1980s, the evocative terms "witch-hunt" and "Salem" now became the standard description of such affairs.

While the Satanic Panic can be taken as beginning with the publicity over the McMartin charges, no single comparable event marks its end. A convenient turning point is marked by the child abuse care that got under way in 1994 in the town of Wenatchee, Washington, a case that initially threatened to become a witch-hunt as grotesque as any of the previous decade. Yet it did not, since on this occasion media expectations were utterly different. The sources used to interpret the Wenatchee events were not the anti-cult theorists who might have appeared some years earlier, but skeptical investigative reporters like Debbie Nathan and Dorothy Rabinowitz. From the time the affair reached national attention in 1995, it was assumed that such allegations could only reflect the malice or incompetence of investigators engaged in a "witch hunt." A revised media atmosphere cannot but affect the decision of future prosecutors contemplating similar "mass" charges. Nobody wants to bear the stigma of "another McMartin," a new witch hunt.

Another highly suggestive incident occurred in April 1999, or rather, did not occur. When two disturbed students launched a shooting rampage at Columbine high school in Littleton, Colorado, the news media floated many stories suggesting perverse and conspiratorial motives or the crime. Perhaps (they suggested) the event was inspired by Nazism, because the attack occurred on Hitler's birthday; maybe the two were part of a secret cultish gang called the Trenchcoat Mafia; they particularly targeted Christian students for execution. The word that did not appear, however, was one that would certainly have been in the forefront a decade previously, namely "Satanism." Superficially, a "Satanic" explanation could have fitted so many aspects of the crime, including the conspiratorial atmosphere that surrounded the attackers and their apparent anti-Christianity. The media had, however, learned the lesson that Satanic charges were no longer viewed with any seriousness, and "experts" who treated them seriously should be regarded as cranks. It would be too optimistic to believe that the Satanic Scare has vanished entirely, but at least this particular virulent phase has now subsided. And at least in mainstream discourse, the ritual abuse idea is extinct.[35]

NOTES

1. Maury Terry, *The Ultimate Evil* (New York: Bantam, 1987); Jan Hollingsworth, *Unspeakable Acts* (Chicago: Congdon and Weed, 1986); Larry Kahaner, *Cults That Kill* (New York: Warner, 1988); Pat Pulling, *The Devil's Web: Who Is Stalking Your Children for Satan?* (Lafayette, La.: Huntington House, 1989); Carl A. Raschke, *Painted Black* (San Francisco: Harper and Row, 1990); Andrew Vachss, *Sacrifice* (London: Macmillan, 1991); Andrew Greeley, *Fall from Grace* (New York: G. P. Putnam, 1993); Valerie Sinason, ed., *Treating Survivors of Satanist Abuse* (London: Routledge, 1994). For statements of the "Satanic danger," see, for instance, James R. Noblitt and Pamela Sue Perskin, *Cult and Ritual Abuse* (Westport, Conn.: Praeger, 1995); Colin Ross, *Satanic Ritual Abuse* (Toronto: University of Toronto Press, 1995); Linda Blood, *The New Satanists* (New York: Warner, 1994); Stephen A. Kent, "Deviant Scripturalism and Ritual Satanic Abuse" (two-part article), *Religion* 23 (1993): 229 and 24 (1994): 355; Jerry Johnston, *The Edge of Evil*

(Dallas: Word, 1989); Bob Larson, *Satanism* (Nashville: Thomas Nelson, 1989); Bob Larson, *In the Name of Satan* (Nashville: Thomas Nelson, 1996).

2. The FBI agent is Ted Gunderson. These quotes are taken from Alan Peterson, ed., *The American Focus on Satanic Crime*, vol. 1 (South Orange, N.J.: American Focus, 1988); and from the Geraldo Rivera special *Devil Worship: Exposing Satan's Underground*.

3. For critical views of the Satanic panic, see James Richardson, David Bromley and Joel Best, eds., *The Satanism Scare* (Hawthorne, N.Y.: Aldine de Gruyter, 1991); Robert D. Hicks, *In Pursuit of Satan* (New York: Prometheus Books, 1991); Jeffrey S. Victor, *Satanic Panic* (Chicago: Open Court, 1993); Richard Ofshe and Ethan Watters, *Making Monsters* (New York: Charles Scribner's, 1994); Lawrence Wright, *Remembering Satan* (New York: Knopf, 1994); Debbie Nathan and Michael Snedeker, *Satan's Silence* (New York: Basic, 1995); Philip Jenkins, *Moral Panic* (New Haven: Yale University Press, 1998) and *Mystics and Messiahs* (New York: Oxford University Press, 2000); Bill Ellis, *Raising the Devil* (Louisville: University Press of Kentucky, 2000).

4. The Penn State Press has an important series of texts under the general title "Magic in History," published in 1998. These titles include: Richard Kieckhefer, *Forbidden Rites*; Claire Fanger, *Conjuring Spirits*; Elizabeth M. Butler, *Ritual Magic* and *The Fortunes of Faust*. See also the trilogy by Jeffrey Burton Russell, all published by Cornell University Press: *Satan* (1981), *Lucifer* (1984), and *Mephistopheles* (1986).

5. Benvenuto Cellini, *The Autobiography of Benvenuto Cellini* (London: Penguin, 1998).

6. Francis Barrett, *The Magus* (London: Lackington Allen, 1801), ii, 99.

7. Frances Mossiker, *The Affair of the Poisons* (New York: Knopf, 1969).

8. Caption to illustration in Pierre de Lancre, *Tableau de l'Inconstance des Mauvaises Anges* (1612), in *Man Myth and Magic*; Carlo Ginzburg, *Ecstasies* (New York: Pantheon, 1991).

9. Jules Michelet, *Satanism and Witchcraft* (New York: Citadel Press, 1946).

10. John Carter, *Sex and Rockets* (Venice, Calif.: Feral House, 2000).

11. Matilda Joslyn Gage, *Woman, Church and State* (Chicago: C. H. Kerr, 1893); Charles Godfrey Leland, *Aradia, or, The Gospel of the Witches* (London: D. Nutt, 1899).

12. Jenkins, *Mystics and Messiahs*, 135–148.

13. Herbert S. Gorman, *The Place Called Dagon* (New York: George H. Doran, 1927); Gorman's other writings included *The Procession of Masks* (1923; reprint, Freeport, N.Y.: Books for Libraries Press, 1969); *James Joyce, His First Forty Years* (Folcroft, Pa.: Folcroft Library Editions, 1971); *Hawthorne: A Study in Solitude* (New York: Doran, 1927); *The Incredible Marquis, Alexandre Dumas* (New York: Farrar and Rinehart, 1929); *James Joyce* (New York: Farrar and Rinehart, 1939); *James Joyce, a Definitive Biography* (London: John Lane, 1941); *Brave General* (New York: Farrar and Rinehart, 1942); *The Wine of San Lorenzo* (New York: Farrar and Rinehart, 1945); *A Victorian American* (Port Washington, N.Y.: Kennikat Press, 1967).

14. Gorman, *The Place Called Dagon*, 221, 229.

15. Ibid., 270–297.

16. Robert Bloch, *The Scarf* (New York: Dial Press, 1947); Jenkins, *Mystics and Messiahs*, 141–145.

17. Blanche Barton, *Secret Life of a Satanist* (Los Angeles: Feral House, 1992).

18. Arthur Lyons, *Satan Wants You* (New York: Mysterious Press, 1988); Terry, *The Ultimate Evil*.

19. Didrik Søderlind, *Lords of Chaos* (Los Angeles: Feral House 1998).

20. Ed Sanders, *The Family* (London: Panther, 1972), 348.

21. Jenkins, *Moral Panic*, 118–144.

22. Kenneth Wooden, *The Children of Jonestown* (New York: McGraw-Hill, 1981), 205.

23. Michelle Smith and Lawrence Pazder, *Michelle Remembers* (New York: Congdon and Lattes, 1980); Philip Jenkins and Daniel Maier-Katkin, "Occult Survivors," in James T. Richardson, Joel Best and David Bromley, eds., *The Satanism Scare* (Hawthorne, N.Y.: Aldine De Gruyter, 1991), 127–144.

24. Nathan and Snedeker, *Satan's Silence*.

25. Ibid., 5. For the international context of the SRA idea, see Richard Guilliatt, *Talk of the Devil* (Melbourne, Australia: Text, 1996); Judy Steed, *Our Little Secret* (Toronto: Vintage Canada, 1995); Philip Jenkins, *Intimate Enemies* (Hawthorne, N.Y.: Aldine de Gruyter 1992); Tim Tate, *Children for the Devil* (London: Methuen, 1991); Andrew Boyd, *Blasphemous Rumors* (London: Fount, 1991); Kevin Marron, *Ritual Abuse* (Toronto: Seal, 1988).

26. For survivor memoirs, see Jeanne M. Lorena and Paula Levy, eds., *Breaking Ritual Silence* (Trout and Sons, 1998); Judith Spencer, *Satan's High Priest* (New York: Pocket Books 1998); Laura Buchanan, *Satan's Child* (Minneapolis: Compcare, 1994); Gail Carr Feldman, *Lessons in Evil, Lessons from the Light* (New York: Crown, 1993); Judith Spencer, *Suffer the Child* (New York: Pocket 1989); Lauren Stratford, *Satan's Underground* (Eugene, Ore.: Harvest House, 1988); Jenkins and Maier-Katkin, "Occult Survivors."

27. Spencer, *Suffer the Child*, 14–15.

28. Bob Passantino, Gretchen Passantino, and Jon Trott, "Satan's Sideshow," *Cornerstone* 18, no. 90 (1989): 23–28.

29. Annette's tale is quoted in Ellen Bass and Laura Davis, *The Courage to Heal* (New York: Harper and Row, 1988), 417.

30. "Devil Worship: Exposing Satan's Underground," October 31, 1988.

31. A large collection of relevant materials can be found at the Web site of the group's supporters, at http://www.wm3.org/.

32. Gail S. Goodman, *Characteristics and Sources of Allegations of Ritualistic Child Abuse* (Washington: GPO, 1995); J. S. LaFontaine, *Speak of the Devil* (New York: Cambridge University Press, 1998).

33. Paul Eberle and Shirley Eberle, *Abuse of Innocence* (Amherst, N.Y.: Prometheus, 1993).

34. Jenkins, *Moral Panic*, 164–188, and *Mystics and Messiahs*, 208–215.

35. Though so-called survivors still exist, and books sympathetic to SRA continue to appear. See the discussion in Sara Scott, *The Politics and Experience of Ritual Abuse* (Philadelphia: Open University Press, 2001).

CHAPTER 11

CONVERSION AND "BRAINWASHING" IN NEW RELIGIOUS MOVEMENTS

DICK ANTHONY

THOMAS ROBBINS

A substantial amount of research has transpired regarding patterns of conversion to "alternative religions" or "new religious movements" (NRMs).[1] A disproportionate amount of this research and related theorizing has concerned the assertion that recruitment to certain "cults" has been essentially involuntary in the sense that powerful techniques of "brainwashing," "mind control," or "coercive persuasion" have rendered the processes of conversion and commitment psychologically coercive and nonconsensual, notwithstanding its formally voluntary status (Clark 1976, 1979; Ofshe and Singer 1986; Verdier 1980). Although various forms of the mind control thesis have received support from self-proclaimed "cult experts," most scholars who have actually done research on the topic view their results as contradicting the thesis (Anthony 2001; Anthony and Robbins 1994; Barker 1984; Bromley 2002; Richardson 1993).

This chapter will focus primarily on the issue of involuntary conversion of the "brainwashing thesis." In addition to summarizing research on the topic, we will also present a theoretical critique that will identify its cultural significance.

A supporter of the brainwashing thesis notes that "brainwashing" entails "a useful though scientifically imprecise concept which refers to an array of complex phenomena resulting in the impairment of the individual's cognitive and social functioning" (Enroth 1984: 141). According to Enroth, scientists and scholars have discovered

> extremist cults' recruitment and indoctrination procedures that effectively in-
> duce behavioral and attitudinal changes in new recruits. Such changes are usu-
> ally described as relatively sudden and dramatic, resulting in diminished per-
> sonal autonomy, increased dependency and the assumption of a new identity.
> Psychospiritual conditioning mechanisms used by cults have reportedly affected
> members' ability to remember, to concentrate, and to fully exercise indepen-
> dent judgment. Members are subjected to intense indoctrination pressures
> which include the manipulation of commitment mechanisms so that new re-
> cruits assume a posture of rigid loyalty and unquestioning obedience to the
> leadership. (Enroth 1985: 141)

In this connection, the present writers have earlier identified what they view as a flawed *extrinsic model* of conversion to controversial movements (Anthony and Robbins 1998). "There appears to be an operative model in which alleged cultist psychological coercion is viewed as fully equivalent to physical constraint such that the 'psychologically coerced' individual is as unambiguously under someone else's control as is a physical captive":

> Basic elements of the model include: (1) a notion of total subjugation of victim
> who loses the ability to exercise *free will;* (2) a rejection of the idea that con-
> verts are attracted to cults by virtue of motivations and orientations that ren-
> der them predisposed to be attracted to a particular type of movement (to the
> extent that such *predisposing motives* are acknowledged, they tend to be down-
> played or trivialized and denied independent variable status); (3) an emphasis
> on alleged *hypnotic processes* and induced trance states and their consequences
> in terms of suggestibility, dissociation and disorientation; (4) an assertion with
> regard to the processes of *conditioning* or other allegedly deterministic influence
> processes ... which supposedly overwhelm free will; (5) a specification of im-
> paired cognition or patterns of *defective thought* that allegedly result from con-
> ditioning, hyper-emotionality and/or trance states; (6) the hypnotic conditioning-
> indoctrination process is seen as operating to implant *false ideas* in a victim's
> mind; (7) finally, brainwashing is seen as producing a *false sense* or cultic iden-
> tity which is superimposed on one's authentic identity. (Anthony and Robbins
> 1996: 11)

Brainwashing claims thus entail a model of conversion/commitment in which there is an overwhelming preponderance of extrinsic or external forces (as opposed to intrinsic or authentic self-related forces) which determine religious

choices. In effect, what is being maintained is that "brainwashed" religious choices are *irrational*, that is, based on emotion, instinct, debilitation, and automatic conditioning rather than on reason and conscious consideration. As one eminent psychiatrist once maintained, conversion to "cults" does not entail a true conversion but rather a "pseudo-conversion" that involves "unthinking participation in group activities, a schedule designed to deprive followers of sleep and a conditioned reflex which is reinforced by group interaction" (West 1975: 2). Other formulations involve references to "disorientation," "hypnotic trance," "snapping," and so on.[2] In effect, conventional utilitarian individualism and instrumental rationality are being prioritized at the expense of intuition, epiphany, mystical gnosis, and intense emotion by the crusaders against cultic brainwashing. Choices based on nonrational factors such as emotion, intuition, or ineffable mystical experiences are implicitly derogated as regressive primitive responses.

Finally, it should be noted that cult/brainwashing theory often tends to posit the emergence of a *false self* which cultic conditioning and mind control is said to superimpose on the authentic, developmental self of the convert. Thus one psychiatrist distinguishes between the "original" personality of cultists that has developed gradually through normal processes of socialization and maturation, and the artificially "imposed" cognitive and behavioral patterns suddenly induced by the intensive regimens of the cult (Clark 1976: 2–3).

HISTORICAL BACKGROUND

Today the notion of "conversion" generally tends to connote some kind of *group switching*—for example, a Catholic becoming a Pentecostal/Protestant or someone from a Christian or Jewish background becoming involved in an NRM. Historically, however, "conversion" has more often connoted a transformation of self that may not necessarily entail group switching—for example, a nominal adherent undergoes an experiential transformation which intensifies his fervor and commitment to a faith to which he was previously weakly connected. Conversion thus entails a shift in the centrality of a "master status" for one's self-system (Snow and Machalek 1984). A latent or dormant religious self becomes manifest.

Religious conversion can be seen as the achievement of a new (religious) self. In this sense conversion is partly convergent with "brainwashing," which also entails the acquisition of a new albeit putatively false and inauthentic self. Both concepts, conversion and brainwashing, can thus be linked to what has been called "self-estrangement theory" (Brian 1987). Since the "Axial Age" of very roughly 1000 B.C.E. to 1000 C.E., the great salvation religions have had as their core conception a duality of "true" versus "false" self. As Weber (1946) notes, all historical salvation religions have shared a notion of a false phenomenal or natural self that the convert must transcend upon pain or some sort of torment, suffering, or endless malaise.[3] The devotee of a salvation religion is urged to achieve a "new self" which is often seen to embody values that challenge the instrumental, utilitarian, or legalistic rationality which Jesus in the New Testament attributes to the Pharisees and scribes. The main spiritual currents of self-estrangement theory have thus rejected utilitarian instrumental rationality in favor of irrational or nonrational experience amounting to an engagement with the latent self at a deeper level.

A number of seminal conceptualizations of the stages of sociocultural and religious evolution in the world (Bellah 1970; Weber 1946) and in the United States (Hammond 1992) have highlighted the increasing structural differentiation of sociocultural spheres (including a growing "separation of church and state") and a consequent accentuation of individual autonomy and of the capability and significance of social and religious *choice*. Transition points between the stages of development have often witnessed the emergence of dynamic and controversial religious movements whose prophets have formulated new conceptions of religious identity and spiritual self-transformation. Such movements have tended to develop in a milieu pervaded by anomie while an institutionalized cultural pattern is dissolving. These transition points accentuate religious conflict and controversy.

Medieval society and its official Church ("Christendom") entailed an "organic social ethic" (Bellah 1970; Weber 1946) which blunted the power of Christianity as a radical salvation religion. Salvation was grounded in a sacramental system and was not considered problematic for conforming participants. Powerful self-transformation and emotional intensity were not absolutely required. Some of the dissident, reform, or pietist movements which emerged during the transition to capitalist modernity have been called "religions of the heart," focusing on inner spiritual apotheosis and repudiating conventional selves unconcerned with radical salvation (Campbell 1991). Many of these movements initially developed as reforming or "enthusiastic" currents within either Catholicism or an established Protestant Church (Knox 1950); however, they were stigmatized as heresies or otherwise odious aberrations and more or less compelled to elaborate their own distinctive doctrines and organizations—hence assimilation to such groups became a form of religious "switching" or conversion to a new independent church or sect. Inconclusive "wars of religion" raged and led ultimately to support for "toleration" and for the notion of a "separation of church and state" in terms of governmental neutrality among competing faiths.

According to Phillip Hammond (1992), American religious history has evolved through three "disestablishments" in which autonomy, status, legitimacy, and opportunity have been continuously extended beyond white Protestant Christians and even conventional churches and synagogues, as socioeconomic and cultural constraints on religious diversity as well as lifestyle options have dissipated. Expressive individualism pervades "postmodern" American culture. Personal autonomy has been more or less sacralized. There are extensive choices, and what was aberrant yesterday may appear at least marginally legitimate today (e.g., exotic gurus). Opponents of deviant religions are thus compelled to frame their indictment in terms of the norm of personal autonomy, which "mind controlling" cults are said to be violating and thereby committing the cardinal sin of anti-individualism (Beckford 1995). The debate thus centers around who is really contravening individualism: cults practicing "coercive persuasion" or crusaders against cults working through the courts to impose various disabilities on disvalued sects and on those devotees who insist upon maintaining a stigmatized commitment (Anthony, et al. 2002; Robbins 1979).

Contemporary disabilities impinging upon deviant religiotherapeutic movements and their persisting adherents are often not crushing, but pending a fourth "disestablishment" they are tangible and serious. Bracketing physical violence, which has involved only a tiny proportion of alternative religions,[4] the disabilities reportedly imposed on their members by cults more or less depend for their validity on the brainwashing concept (or alleged overpowering psychological coercion in a formally voluntary context) and its application to alternative religions, which we will evaluate below.

In general, we consider the conflict between alternative religions and their "anticult" adversaries to be essentially a *religious conflict*. The "anticult movement" (AM) can be viewed as a sort of revitalization movement for conventional instrumental rationality and utilitarian individualism. The autonomy and individualism which cults are accused by the AM of destroying are not what might be termed "expressive individualism"; that is, true autonomy cannot from the standpoint of the AM be grounded in transcendental experiences, ecstatic or mystical states of consciousness, or intense emotions. Rather, such experiences are interpreted in terms of dangerous hypnotic trances, pathological dissociative states, infantile regression, depersonalization, and manipulated emotional excess that supposedly erodes personal autonomy and superimposes an artificial group identity on the victim's authentic ego. Conflicts over cults thus entail fundamental value conflicts and are more akin to earlier "religious wars" than to a polarity of objective psychological science exposing induced psychopathology.

Let us briefly restate the foregoing discussion. "Conversion" as well as "brainwashing" are generally seen as involving the emergence (or recovery) of a religious self that is discontinuous with preconversion personal or group identity. However, from a (particular) religious standpoint, this is really a good rather than a bad thing. Both "cultic" and "anticult" perspectives are subvarieties of pervasive "self-estrangement theory."

"Cult" leaders and their followers, who are viewed by critics as alienating new converts from their natural or authentic selves, likely view themselves as facilitating converts' recovery of their primordial religious selves from their epiphenomenal material and culturally conditioned selves. As we show below, the anticult brainwashing viewpoint, insofar as it is formulated precisely enough to make its empirical claims testable, has tended to be disconfirmed by research. What the anticult perspective boils down to after such empirical disconfirmation is a pseudoscientific, all-embracing value perspective or ideology. Shorn of its scientific pretensions, the anticult ideology is a fundamentalistic, arguably totalistic, version of the modernist worldview that targets competing worldviews as, in effect, tools of the devil.

To conceal its character as an intolerant, arguably totalitarian rationale for the all-embracing truth claims of the modernist worldview, spokespersons for the anticult ideology have employed two interrelated rhetorical strategies. As Shapiro (1983) notes, defenders of coercive (abductive) deprogramming tended in the 1970s and early 1980s to imply that, rather than developing a new religious self (which might possess a claim to religious freedom), brainwashed cult indoctrinees—sometimes overtly typified as "robots" and "zombies"—inhabited the limbo of not really having a self. They were pathologically "depersonalized," "dissociated," "regressed to psychological infancy," and so on (Clark 1976).

This argument was often not made fully explicit and is now somewhat outmoded, having been associated with the controversy surrounding the extreme anticult measure of coercive deprogramming. The broader and more significant anticult argument has entailed the proposition that the converts' acquisition of a different religious self has been *involuntary*. The convert's "born-again" or otherwise new spiritual self has been coercively "imposed" through brainwashing/mind control procedures, which are intrinsically nonconsensual and operate insidiously to destroy or obviate free will.

Most of the remainder of this chapter will critically evaluate this claim (and to a degree the related psychopathological claim) with respect to several areas: (1) the claimed theoretical basis in the prestigious foundational work on Maoist "thought reform" by Robert Lifton and Edgar Schein; (2) research on recent 'new religious movements'; (3) research on the personalities of converts to NRMs; and (4) research on hypnosis. If the extreme model cannot withstand critical scrutiny, than the social conflict between alternative religions and their most vociferous and legally activist critics remains essentially a value conflict which the First Amendment guarantee of religious freedom forbids the state to regulate. Despite their pseudoscientific pretensions, then, the assertions of the anticult ideology do not in general warrant coercive state intervention aimed at counteracting the allegedly objectionable internal milieu of exotic sects.

EVALUATING THE BRAINWASHING MODEL

The authors of a review on the sociology of conversion note that, "the 'brain-washing' or 'coercive persuasion' model is the most popular explanation of conversion [to NRMs] outside of sociological circles. The basic thesis is that conversion is the product of devious and specifiable forces acting upon unsuspecting and therefore vulnerable individuals" (Snow and Machalek 1984: 178–179). The brainwashing or mind control explanation for conversion to deviant movements "has gained considerable currency among the public" in part because "it provides a convenient and 'sensible' account for those who are otherwise at a loss to explain why individuals are attracted to 'deviant' and 'menacing' groups" (Snow and Machalek 1984: 179). One crusading clinician maintains that, "today's [cultic] thought reform programs are sophisticated, subtle and insidious, creating a psychological bond that in many ways is far more powerful than gun-at-the-head methods of influence" (Singer 1994: 3–4). Scholars who have conducted research on NRMs have tended toward skepticism regarding such demonological accounts (Barker 1984, 1986; Richardson 1993).

As noted above, brainwashing theories represent an extreme form of an *extrinsic model* in which a presumptively *passive* convert is overwhelmed by dynamic overpowering stimuli and converted to ideas and to a self-conception which would previously have been highly distasteful to the convert. As noted in an influential social psychology text, in brainwashing "the subject is assumed to be passive, without choice or freedom of will to escape his or her brain being laundered" (Zimbardo et al. 1977: 190).[5] In brainwashing, "a unitary entity, agency or procedure" is seen to regularly produce quick and effective results in transforming attitudes, behavior, and identity. In contrast, "when a number of factors over a long period of time affect some people but not others, the 'impact' is evaluated more in terms of dispositional properties of targeted individuals (their personal traits) than in the power of their techniques . . . even when the impact on particular people may be substantial" (Zimbardo et al. 1977: 190–191).

Although there are some valid components of the 'mind control' stereotype—authoritarian movements, manipulative leaders, zealous devotees, and groups with violent proclivities—there may also be substantial distortions and exaggerations. In this paper, we have delineated key elements of the brainwashing model, or rather the *extrinsic* or externalist model of conversion to extreme apocalyptic movements in which the recruitment, mobilization, and transformation of members is seen as totally instigated and controlled by sinister techniques of persuasion and intrinsic (e.g., personality, predispositional) factors are deemed insignificant. Below we will question this model both in terms of its posited pedigree in the foundational work of Robert Lifton on ideological totalism and Maoist thought reform, and in terms of its compatibility with recent research on marginal religious movements and the personalities of their members, as well as research on hypnosis. In terms of an alternative approach we will posit an interaction between certain "totalist" movements and ideologies on the one hand, and certain predisposing configurations of individual personal identity which are further distorted and extrapolated in a militant totalist milieu in which there may also (rarely) be a mobilization for violent acts. Finally, we will consider what kinds of movements and worldviews are most likely to elicit the support of certain predisposed individuals and to facilitate their development of a "contrast identity" in which an idealized self-concept is combined with projection of negativity onto outsiders and scapegoats, a pattern which may have some implications for possible violence and authoritarian control.

FOUNDATIONAL THINKERS AND THE EXTRINSIC MODEL

In the context of the "Cold War," an extreme, extrinsic brainwashing model was formulated and popularized by Edward Hunter, a journalist and publicist for the CIA (1951, 1960). Hunter claimed that brainwashing represented a devastatingly effective psychotechnology of extrinsic psychic coercion which could transform a victim into a kind of robot or zombie through the use of Pavlovian conditioning, hypnotic trances, and other means. "The intent is to change a mind radically so that its owner becomes a living puppet—a human robot—without the atrocity being visible . . . with new beliefs and new thought processes inserted into a captive body" (Hunter 1960: 309). The brainwashing process is said to entail the use of "hypnotism, drugs and cunning pressures that plague the body and do not necessarily require marked violence" (Hunter 1951: 11). Physical coercion is sometimes present, but it is not a necessary feature of the brainwashing or "brain-changing" process as Hunter conceptualizes it. Brain-changers are able to induce the false beliefs and memories in their victims (Hunter 1951: 10–11). Other early writers (dealing largely with Stalinist or Maoist indoctrination) conceptualized brainwashing in terms of the use of trance states to induce a primitive and regressive mental state in which an individual exhibits heightened suggestibility such that he or she can more easily be programmed by scientific (e.g., Pavlovian) conditioning methods (Farber et al. 1957). One early writer actually claimed to identify parallels between Pavlov's conditioning experiences with dogs and early revivalist conversions to Methodism (Sargent 1951, 1974).

Although the extrinsic brainwashing model has often been attacked in terms of its applicability to "new religious movements," it has been assumed to be an accurate portrait of the Korean War POW situation that played such a vital role in the development of the model. This is not the case, however; for example, a much cited article, published in 1956, which reviewed much of the existing Korean POW data, concluded that those prisoners who went beyond forced compliance and embraced the ideas of their captors were initially somewhat sympathetic to those beliefs (Hinkle and Wolff 1956).

In cases in the 1980s experts testifying against "cults" often cited the prestigious foundational work of Robert Lifton (1961) and Edgar Schein (1961) on "coercive persuasion" and "thought reform" as establishing the theoretical basis for their testimony. In 1988, the California Supreme Court in a key opinion appeared to accept the notion that Schein and Lifton affirmed that "brainwashing exists and is remarkably effective,"[6] although in 1990 a federal court perceived greater ambiguity regarding the foundational texts (Anthony and Robbins 1992). In the review essay on the sociology of conversion quoted above, the authors cite Schein and Lifton as sources of the brainwashing model (Snow and Machalek 1984).

In our view, the views of Schein and Lifton are actually significantly at variance with the thoroughly extrinsic Cold War model. Although they clearly affirm a manipulative process aimed at producing false confessions and conversions, their views have been distorted to the effect that they are wrongly said to affirm a highly effective coercive psychological process which is equivalent to physical imprisonment and in which individual predispositions, premotives and personality patterns play no vital role.

In this chapter, we will be primarily concerned with the view of Robert Lifton, because it is more fully developed, and the subtle interactions he delineates between a totalistic milieu and certain personality-identity patterns are, in our view, particularly significant in terms of understanding conversions to contemporary totalist movements. Nevertheless, one of the present writers has previously shown that the findings from Schein's study of Korean POWs and Maoist indoctrination undermine the extreme extrinsic model in a number of respects (Anthony 1990). Thus, Schein considered that the Chinese program of POW indoctrination was a relative failure given the resources allocated (Schein 1964; Anthony 1990). Unlike the clinicians and other "experts," Schein considered physical imprisonment such a vital element of communist psychological coercion that he built it into his definition of "coercive persuasion."[7] Though physically debilitated, POWs were mentally alert and rational while being subjected to thought reform and did not exhibit defective thought patterns (Schein 1961: 202–203, 238–239); moreover, he suggests that the popular image of "brainwashing" as entailing "extensive self-delusion and excessive distortion . . . is a false one" (1961: 239; Anthony 1990: 312). Schein also downplays the role of hypnotic trance disorientation and dissociative states in coercive persuasion, which is really intended "to produce ideological and behavioral changes in a fully conscious, intact individual" (Schein 1959: Anthony 1990: 316). Finally, Schein rejects both the term "brainwashing" and the assumption that communist ideas were initially alien and antithetical to all American POWs in Korea (1961: 18, 202).

In his pioneering work, *Chinese Thought Reform and the Psychology of Totalism*, Robert Lifton (1961: 419–437) sets forth a "complex set of psychological themes," including "Milieu Control," "Mystical Manipulation," "Demand for Purity," "Sacred Science," "Loading the Language," "Doctrine Over Person," and "The Dispensing of Existence." The development of totalistic commitments in individuals (or personal conversions to totalism), and, indeed, the crystallization of a totalist milieu, entails a process of interaction between individual proclivities and ideologies. Thus, the key term, *ideological totalism*, is meant "to suggest the coming together of an immoderate ideology with equally immoderate character traits—an extremist meeting round of people and ideas" (1961: 419). Lifton's view appears to suggest that Weberian term, which Lifton doesn't employ: *elective affinity*. Each of the eight psycho-ideological themes of totalism "mobilizes certain individual emotional tendencies, mostly of a polarizing nature." Nevertheless, "psychological theme, philosophical rationale and polarized individual tendencies are *interdependent;* they require rather than directly cause, each other" (1961: 422; our emphasis).

Although there are definitely ideological and institutional qualities of totalism, "the degree of totalism depends greatly upon factors in our personal history: early lack of trust, extreme environmental chaos, total domination by a parent or parent-representative, intolerable burdens of guilt and severe crises of identity . . . an early sense of confusion and dislocation, or an early experience of extremely intense family milieu control can produce later a complete intolerance for dislocation and confusion, and a longing for the reinstatement of milieu control" (Lifton 1961: 436). While one might get the impression from some recent writings on "cults" that an individual must be brainwashed qua deeply disoriented, dissociated, literally deluded, and totally conditioned to adhere to a totalistic movement, Lifton notes that "ideological totalism itself may offer a man an intense peak experience: a sense of transcending all that is ordinary and prosaic, of freeing himself from the encumbrances of human ambivalence, of entering a sphere of truth, reality, trust and sincerity beyond any he had ever known or imagined" (1961: 435).[8]

It is important to realize that the overwhelming majority of Lifton's Western subjects, who had undergone Chinese thought reform, exhibited only *behavioral compliance* under physical duress and threats; communist thought reform obtained from each subject "the extraction of an incriminating personal confession because it made this confession a requirement for survival" (1961: 150). Very few subjects, principally "Miss Darrow" and "Father Simon," exhibited significant (but not total) alternation of their convictions in the direction of Maoism. The quasi-conversion experiences of these subjects are analyzed in depth by Lifton, but the analysis deals rather extensively with their preconversion personalities, past history, emotional strains, and identity problems, which are viewed as indispensable factors.

Each Westerner who underwent thought reform "tended to be influenced to the degree that his identity, whatever it may have been, could be undermined through the self-deprecating effects of guilt and shame. This susceptibility in turn depended upon his balance between flexibility and totalism and their special significance for his character structure" (1961: 150).

One of the "apparent converts," Miss Darrow possessed a "negative identity." For Miss Darrow, "the usual problems of guilt about parents and biological identity were intensified." She was unable to open letters from home because of the guilt they stimulated, and she "found herself preoccupied with her 'badness' as a daughter" (1961: 129). Also significant was the fact that "an element of totalism—a tendency toward all or nothing emotional alignments—seems ever-present in Miss Darrow, working against some of the more moderate aspirations of her liberalism" (1961: 129). Maoist thought reform "exploited each of these aspects of her negative identity, made conscious what was previously latent, and built into grotesque dimensions what had previously been held in balance" (1961: 130).

The personality of Father Simon, "the Converted Jesuit," possessed an even more prominent totalist streak than that of Miss Darrow. "As the conscientious enthusiast, he had shown a tendency to embrace totally a series of influences—Catholicism, American know-how, Chinese life and then Chinese communism" (1961: 219). Alternating phases of defiance and conversion with respect to each strong influence he encountered, Father Simon both sought and feared "total unity with an all-powerful force." "Whether defying or converting, his was an all or nothing approach." Simon "sought trust and intimacy on absolute terms. For him both conversion and defiance were attempts to ward off inner feelings of aloneness, weakness and helplessness" (1961: 219–220). "This authoritarian priest shared with the liberal missionary's daughter [Darrow] psychological traits characteristic for the apparent convert: strong susceptibility to guilt, confusion of identity, and most important of all, a long-standing pattern of totalism" (1961: 218).[9] Thus, by implication the impact of the manipulative thought reform process on Lifton's partially converted subjects was not really psychologically involuntary but rather was based on the dynamic interaction of the authoritarian ideology and a predisposing longing for surrender to a totalistic worldview.[10]

At this point, it is important to note that one of Lifton's mentors was the psychoanalyst Erik Erikson, from whom Lifton got his conception of totalism (Erikson 1954), as well as theories of negative and polarized identities which permeate Lifton's analyses of the conversions and other responses of his subjects.

Erikson's paper on "Wholeness and Totality" (1954) represented an early attempt to formulate a general model of authoritarianism—a general psychology of totalism which would be applicable to persons attracted to fascist and communist movements, as well as other totalistic groups. Some persons, Erikson maintains, develop a kind of totalistic or proto-totalistic syndrome which bears some relationship to an inadequate resolution of the tensions of the oedipal developmental stage of childhood. Persons with certain psychological conflicts may develop a self-concept which is polarized between unrealistically positive and negative self-images competing for domination in the person's self-definition. Totalitarian movements appeal to such persons by reinforcing a narcissistically grandiose self-conception and providing a collective foundation for the projection of elements of the polarized negative self-image onto a scapegoated contrast group.

Erikson maintains that a personality embodying "wholeness" is characterized by open and fluid boundaries. Moral principles and other differentiations of reality constructed by the ego take the form of somewhat ambiguous continua rather than sharp and dichotomous polarities. In contrast, the totalistic organization of the personality entails an emphasis on an absolute boundary between the person and the exterior social environment. The person feels fundamentally separate from the outside world. A sense of relationship is attained by forming intense negative and positive identifications with crudely dichotomized parts of the person and of social reality. Moral and ideological principles are internalized as absolutes. Impulses, fantasies, behaviors, and opinions not fully consistent with positive identifications are denied and dissociated. But this rigid organization tends to be unstable, in part because split-off parts of the psyche may continue to seek expression and threaten the unrealistic and dualistic definition of acceptable selfhood (Erikson 1954).

Like the authors of the famous volume *The Authoritarian Personality* (Adorno et al. 1950), Erikson maintains that persons with unconscious guilt tend to possess a "negative external conscience" that renders them prone to transferring responsibility for their beliefs and actions to authoritarian hierarchies legitimated by absolutist ideologies and to the projection of anger and guilt onto demonized outgroups.[11]

It is well-known that Erikson (1956) broadened and extended the received psychoanalytic scheme of individual psychosexual development, replacing the tripartite childhood model with eight developmental stages extending through adulthood. Favorable vs. unfavorable resolutions of the polarity which dominates each stage determine whether a wholistic or totalistic personality pattern evolves. The initial stage features the antimony of *basic trust vs. mistrust*. The emergence of "Basic Mistrust" patterned by recurrent disruptions of an infant's sense of ontological security can produce "total rage" accompanied by fantasies of total control over the sources of nurturance and consequent apocalyptic-totalist proclivities. Religious worldviews may confer meaning qua metaphysic reality on Basic Mistrust via symbols of ultimate evil, although religious rituals can help facilitate a collective restitution of trust.

Resolutions of the polarities of other stages, particularly the Third, Oedipal (or built vs. initiative) phase, which may produce a punitive super-ego or negative conscience, also contribute to the contingent emergence of totalistic rigidity in individuals. In his article "Wholeness and Totality," Erikson places special emphasis on the adolescent/postadolescent context of the "identity crisis" and the threat of *identity/role diffusion*, which develops when a young person cannot integrate emergent adult responsibilities with a childhood sense of self in order to evolve a coherent picture or image of himself/herself as a continuous, unitary individual. A temptation for persons who experience difficulties in this respect is to effect a "total immersion in a synthetic identity" through totalistic participation in a movement affirming extreme nationalism, racism, or class consciousness and thematizing a "collective condemnation of a totally stereotyped enemy" (Erikson 1954: 170).

In Erikson's view, an adolescent in the throes of identity confusion may, to avoid remaining "a contradictory bundle of identity fragments," adopt a "negative identity" (1954: 169). A youth will thus undergo an "almost willful" total realignment in which the polarized-punitive self, the characteristic legacy of unresolved oedipal tension, undergoes a sudden reversal in which a formerly condemned "bad self" is consciously affirmed as one's true identity. Youth who affirm negative identities frequently act out through drugs, crime, promiscuities, and involvement in delinquent subcultures or countercultures. An alternative (or subsequent) strategy entails reorienting the negative identity into a contrast identity (our term) through a transvaluation in which participation in some sort of radical or esoteric subculture is redefined as totally good while the exterior mainstream is condemned as evil. Erikson sees radical leftist or rightist political groups helping to crystallize contrast identities by giving their rebellion a "stamp of universal righteousness within a black and white ideology" (1954: 169).

Lacking "inner wholeness," some persons who are predisposed to totalism develop a self-concept which is polarized between a good self and a bad self. Involvement in a totalistic group with an absolutist, Manichean worldview and a charismatic leader creates a basis for affirming the pure idealized self in terms of a strong identification with the noble virtues of the movement, its vital truth, and its heroic leader, while incompatible or rejected feelings and weaknesses are projected onto demonized scapegoats—for example, Jews, Reds, homosexuals, bourgeoisie, nonbelievers. Thus, through totalistic commitment, an internally fragmented person may evade both identity confusion and an oppressive negative conscience.

THE HYPNOSIS FACTOR

What is it that supposedly overwhelms the will and dispositions of converts and propels them into psychological imprisonment? Emphases on hypnosis, trances, and dissociation appear to be almost ubiquitous in clinical anticult formulations in the 1980s through 1990 (cf. Singer and Ofshe 1990). Thus, according to the one clinician, "a naïve or deceived subject who is passing through or has been caused to enter a susceptible state of mind" is subjected to "highly programmed behavioral control techniques . . . in a controlled environment" such that "the subject's attention is narrowed and focused to the point of becoming a trance." The trance state "is maintained during several sleep periods until it becomes an independent structure." A "continued state of dissociation" is thus sustained, with resulting drastic personality alteration (Clark 1976: 280).

"At the core of Scientology's influence," maintains sociologist Richard Ofshe, in a court document, is its (putatively therapeutic) *auditing* process. "At the heart of the auditing procedure is the use of hypnosis," which "is important because it is used within Scientology to deceive clients and cause them to believe that they are able to accomplish para-normal feats and regain memories of past life experiences. . . . The fantasies that are induced through hypnosis have the quality of seeming more real that most memories" (Ofshe 1989: 7). A bit of a *Manchurian Candidate* theme appears in the comments of a clinician who states that, in cults, "many individuals are hypnotized. Many individuals are objects of hypnosis and autohypnosis where certain phrases and words will trigger a certain kind of thought pattern within the individual" (Benson 1977: 234). Cult recruiters are alleged to systematically employ hypnotists' techniques (Miller 1986).

As we have noted, theories of cultic brainwashing often allege that hypnotic rituals (such as Scientology's "auditing" procedures) are integral to cultic mind control (Abgrall 1999a, 1999b see also Anthony 1990, 1999; Martin 1993; Singer 1983; Singer and Lalich 1995). Nevertheless, as Anthony (1999: 444) has noted, there is in fact a scientific consensus that "hypnosis is not an effective technique for causing people to engage involuntarily in behavior that is immoral, illegal, or against their own self-interest" (see also Barber 1961; Conn 1982; Fromm and Shor 1979: 6–12; Orne 1961–1962; Spanos 1996). Anthony (1999: 444) continues:

> This is one of the most well-researched questions in the history of hypnosis research, and it is the consensus of informed scientific opinion that hypnosis cannot be used effectively for overwhelming free will or for substituting the will of the hypnotist for the will of the hypnotized . . . the idea that hypnosis could be used to impose a false personality on another and establish long-lasting control over their whole lifestyle is so far fetched that it is found only in popular science fiction on the topic of brainwashing such as the book *The Manchurian Candidate* (Condon, 1958). Indeed the idea that participating in a

new religion changes one's basic personality is itself unsupported by empirical research. (See Paloutzian, Richardson, and Rambo 1999.)

An additional important line of research regarding hypnosis suggests that there is no method of definitively determining whether someone is "hypnotized." From this standpoint hypnosis is really a socially collaborative situation which does not distinctively differ from various other collaborative situations (Anthony 1999; Barber 1969; Gauld 1992; Kirsch 1995). The "hypnotic trance" is really somewhat of a myth and the state of consciousness of a person under hypnosis is not clearly empirically distinguishable from normal consciousness. Therefore the claim that a given pattern of social influence is actually based on hypnosis is not provable. Thus, Anthony (1999: 447) concludes that, "with respect to the [scientific] criteria of falsifiability, there is no scientifically accurate way of disconfirming the claim that [particular] social influence is based on hypnosis. Consequently . . . [the] contention that Scientology auditing is a form of hypnosis is unfalsifiable and results in irrefutable allegations," which should not be viewed as an acceptable basis for legal evidence. Anthony (1999: 446–451) also demonstrates that concepts of conditioning, infantile regression, and addiction, which also crop up in anticult formulations (Abgrall 1999a, 1999b; Martin 1993; Zablocki 1998), do not meet scientific standards of falsifiability, at least in terms of their dubious applications to patterns of commitment in religious movements.

CONTEMPORARY RESEARCH ON RECRUITMENT

It is clear from the foregoing that, at the very least, Robert Lifton's foundational analysis of conversion to totalism is at variance with application of an extreme model of brainwashing to contemporary "cults"—most principally regarding the denial of a dynamic role for individual predispositions and preconversion psychological currents. Hypnosis has also been overhyped as a coercive vehicle. There is no inescapable omnipotent psychotechnology which renders individual predilections irrelevant.

Looking at more recent issues, there exists a body of research on kinds of persons who participate in new and unconventional spiritual movements or are attracted to such groups. The research appears to indicate that such individuals are not randomly chosen from the population (or even from the young adult population) but rather manifest certain attributes of personal background and orientation which tend to be correlates of participation and attraction. Some of the pertinent data comes from the Bay Area survey study of a random sample of hundreds of individuals in the early 1970s.

In his volume *The Consciousness Reformation* (1976), Robert Wuthnow reports that certain value orientations or varieties of perceived "locus of causation" of outcomes in human affairs appear to be correlated with expressions of interest in three "Eastern" religious groups—Yoga, Zen, and Hare Krishna. Two "traditional" orientations, *theistic* (divine intervention determines our fate) and *individualistic* (individual character and will determine our fate) are negatively correlated with favorable dispositions toward Eastern mystical groups. Significantly more attracted to such groups are individuals who score high on two nontraditional or modernistic orientations: a *social science* orientation in which sociological and psychological factors are seen as shaping human destiny, and a *mystical* orientation which grounds the locus of causation in human affairs in wholistic conceptions of the universe, intuitive or transrational states of consciousness, etc. The implication here is that persons may be self-selected into nontraditional groups in part because they support or are attracted to the values and orientations these groups espouse.

In a follow-up volume, *Experimentation in American Religion* (1978), Wuthnow deals not only with expressed attraction to Eastern religions but also with actual participation in such groups. Wuthnow finds that both attraction to and actual participation in the four Eastern groupings are predicted by four constructed, multi-indicated variables which are distinct from each other and operate additively and cumulatively to make a substantial difference. The variables are *exposure* to novel religions, which entails a measure of cultural sophistication or cosmopolitanism, as well as claims to awareness of such groups; *legitimacy*, which entails liberal attitudes on social issues and support for sexual experimentation, homosexuality, abortion, etc.; *opportunity* for social experimentation, which involves factors such as being single, youth, geographic mobility, and career mobility; and finally, *motivation*, which entails measures denoting the lack of a sense of the meaning and purpose in life, dissatisfaction with one's sex life, unsettling financial vicissitudes, and a lack of stable work or work plans. Among persons with high scores on the variables of exposure, legitimacy, and opportunity, seven-eighths express attraction to unorthodox Eastern groups and half admit to having participated in such groups. As few as 5 percent express attraction to these groups among persons with very low scores on the key variable, while as many as 87 percent of high scorers express favorable dispositions toward the groups.

The "motivational" variable, which appears in part to embody a factor of sexual-relational-economic *stress*, does not by itself much increase the likelihood of either favorable attitudes or actual involvement. Only when the cognitive foundations of attraction to new mystical currents have been established by cultural sophistication, opportunity, and legitimating orientations toward modernistic social experimentation does the probability of participation substantially increase. Thus, stress and related "vulnerability" and "suggestibility" does not by itself lead persons to become involved in nontraditional "cults" unless such stress is accompanied by attitudes supportive of spiritual innovation.

Further support for this proposition derives from a careful study which entailed questionnaires administered to a probabilistic sample of 1,000 high schools in the San Francisco Bay area in 1980 (Zimbardo and Hartley 1985). Although published in what is generally considered an "anticult" journal, the authors affirm that "in the past, fascination with the 'psychology of persuasion' and the surprising effectiveness of their [cults'] recruitment techniques, has paradoxically led to a narrowness of focus and, consequently, to a neglect of the *interaction* that takes place between recruiter and prospective recruit" (1985: 93; emphasis in the original). They suggest that, contrary to the "prototype of passive vulnerability" on the part of the recruit to controversial religious movements, "the target of a cult recruiter may be a seeker of engagement. His or her needs, values, knowledge and personal experiences may impel movement toward selection of or contact with certain kinds of recruiters" (ibid.).

Fifty-four percent of the sample had had at least one prior contact with a cult or cult recruiter and "more than half of the students surveyed were receptive to attending a cult function if invited to one, whether or not they had prior contact" (1985: 139). A majority of students who had not been approached by a cult recruiter expressed at least some interest in having contact with a cult activity. The researchers wanted to know if it is "possible to identify a set of characteristics that predict which individuals will be contacted by a cult recruiter, and if contacted, which of these students will reject or be receptive to further inducements for affiliation with a cult" (1985: 109).

Of those who had contact with a cult, 70 percent reported never having any thought about joining a cult, 2 percent had thought about joining but never would, 1 percent were presently contemplating joining a cult, and 3 percent said they were currently members of a cult group. "It is interesting to observe that more of those students who had no contact with a cult recruiter were receptive to an invitation [to attend a cult function] than were those who had been approached (60 percent vs. 45 percent, $p = <.01$)" (1985: 111). The fact that subjects were less predisposed to accept contact if they had prior contact could indicate that initial contact does not enhance suggestibility and that, by implication, the willingness of a majority of subjects to consider contact represents authentic, meaningful predispositions rather than "vulnerability." Can cults be potent "brainwashing" agencies if contact with them turns many people off?

Some of the predictor variables which influence whether members of the total sample have had prior contact with a cult appear to indicate that initial contact is not random but reflects definite predispositions—"seekership"—on the part of the subjects. Students who perceive a cult as having a *positive purpose* as opposed to being basically exploitative or mercenary, etc., are more likely to have had contact. Students who identify a given group as a cult are more likely to have had contact with it, that is, their contact did not deceive them. Persons who believe in the value or necessity of having exposures to differing views are more likely to have had contact, as are students who have a more favorable view of the prototypical cult member. Persons whose fathers have a higher occupational status are more likely to have had more contact (cultural sophistication?). Persons with contact tend to get poorer grades than noncontacters, which may relate to alienation and thus to Wuthnow's "legitimacy" factor. Finally, persons who have made contact tend to engage in more religious and spiritual practices than persons who have not had contact. "It is reasonable to conclude that those students who are contacted by cult members differ in systematic ways from those not approached." But the differences are subtle and "more a matter of degree than of a qualitative nature" (1985: 170).

Another set of variables predicts greater openness to accepting a future invitation to a cult function among the subsample of 523 students who had previously had contact with a cult, and for those 389 who had not been approached. "Engaging in spiritual, religious or mystical practices predisposes students to be more open to cult invitations," but only among persons who had not been previously approached (1985: 124). Although persons who had previous contact with a cult recruiter were less likely to be open to future contact, there are varying and divergent evaluations of the behavior, manner, and self-presentation of the recruiter. "What 'works' for some targeted students works against developing favorable attitudes in others" (1985: 127). Persons who perceive the recruiter more positively are more receptive to further contact, as in the case when they perceive the group's purposes less negatively. Among persons who had been contacted, receptivity to further contact was enhanced if the initial contact had been via the recruiter's "private channels" (e.g., a cult function) rather than in public spaces, such as on campus. Familiarity with spiritual terminology such as "cosmic consciousness" or "meditation" is positively related to willingness to attend a cult function, but only among persons not previously approached. Persons whose contact with a cult recruiter did not take place in a family setting are more open to further contact. In the view of the present writers, some of these variables seem to represent "seeker" variables and "choice" behavior rather than mere "vulnerability" or "suggestibility"—for example, persons who went to a cult site or function (private channels) are more favorable to future contact than persons sought out by recruiters at school or in their homes ("familial" settings). "Contacted students who would consider/accept [future contact] are *not* necessarily uninformed students with poor grades, shy, poor or gullible. They have lots of media exposure, know what cults are, engage in a moderate amount of religious practices, and are undogmatic about being exposed to contrary views" (1985: 141; emphasis in original).

In general, Zimbardo and Hartley are impressed with the large proportion of persons who would be receptive to attending a cult function if invited, notwith-standing the milieu of highly negative media treatments of cults and their own negative evaluations of cults and recruiters. "This is one reason why the subject of a cult recruitment attempt should not be viewed as a passive target over-whelmed by coercively compelling 'mind control tactics' " (1985: 139).

The supposition that conversion to (even relatively authoritarian and totalist) movements tends to reflect an interaction of individual predispositions with the properties—including ideational and valuative properties—of the movement, re-ceives further support from an acclaimed study by Eileen Barker (1984) of 1,017 prospective "Moonies" who began a series of indoctrination seminars run by the controversial Unification Church in London in 1979.[12] Barker's comparisons in-volve a sample of persons who went through the 21-day tri-seminar indoctrination program and then actually joined the Church, plus a sample of "nonjoiners" who completed the indoctrination process but did not join, a sample of "leavers" who joined but shortly left, and a control sample matched to the original seminarians on demographic variables. On the basis of her additional qualitative research, Barker estimates that about 1 out of 100 persons who are approached "on the street" agree to attend the seminars. Thus the control sample presumably consists of persons, the overwhelming majority of whom would refuse to come to the initial 3-day seminar, and their characteristics can be compared to those of initial attendees.[13]

A profile of the Moonie and how she or he differs from others emerges from Barker's tabulations and her interviews with indoctrinees and their relatives. "Moonies tend to have come from what could be called conventional and highly 'respectable' homes in which traditional values of family life, morality and 'de-cency' were upheld—or at least in which it was generally acknowledged that they ought to be upheld" (Barker 1984: 211). It also appeared that Moonist converts had a substantially greater exposure to organized religion (e.g., early church at-tendance) than had either the control group or the nonjoiners and the "leavers" (who joined but shortly left), "although these latter groups still had considerably more exposure than the rest of the population." Barker suggests "that Moonies are people who had been prepared for religious answers to problems" (1984: 213).

Moonists tend to be fairly well educated but to have, after childhood, "re-defined themselves as no longer being a willing part of the educational system, even though, objectively speaking, they may still have been in it" (1984: 216). There is a hint here of *alienation* evocative of Wuthnow's "legitimacy" and motivation variables, which enables the individual to feel free to engage in innovation, ex-perimentation, or extremism. Yet, politically, Moonies are more likely to be con-servative and less likely to be socialist than members of the control group, with leavers being intermediate. Finally, persons who joined the movement are more likely than the control group to claim to have been actively idealistic in terms of actively seeking to "improve the world" at the time they began the first seminar, with nonjoiners intermediate but leavers even more idealistic than members. A similar pattern emerges with respect to the ideal of "understanding God."

To summarize, there do appear to be significant differences between joiners and nonjoiners, joiners and leavers, and between neophyte seminarians and controls. But this finding, in combination with the findings of Wuthnow and Zimbardo-Hartley, does not fully discredit the extrinsic model. Predispositional patterns may make some persons more likely to visit a group or start seminars than others, yet it may still be claimed that once one enters the indoctrinational setting, the "conversion" one may experience is totally determined by extrinsic manipulations and psychotechnology. It will be recalled that in their text on social influence Zimbardo et al. (1977: 190) state that in the brainwashing model, indoctrinees are assumed to be totally passive and all transformation can thus be attributed to a single agency which, by providing a specified input, can elicit "a big, quick, reliable output in most people" over a limited time period. It is in this respect that Barker's data is particularly striking.

Barker maintains that any conversion situation is likely to be influenced in varying degrees by a number of factors (or ensembles of factors), including the preconvert's *dispositions* which he or she brings to the situation, the broader *social context*, the positive *appeal of the movement* (e.g., its ideals), and the actual *immediate indoctrination process*, in this case the Unificationist seminars. These factors interact, but with different relative significance, to shape an individual transformation. Barker typologizes a number of conversion patterns in which these factors are differentially weighted to produce a convert. In chemico-biological *brain control, physical control* entailing physical captivity, and *mental coercion*, the immediate, intensive indoctrination process will necessarily become the key independent variable and will overshadow other contributions. There are also two kinds of induced *suggestibility* (biological and psychological) which are really weaker forms of brain control and mind control, in which the immediate indoctrination has a lesser but still paramount weight. However, its significance is much less in two other situations: where unsatisfied persons are "pushed" to join the movement as a refuge from society and where they are "pulled" in by the perceived utopian promise of the movement.

Barker's English data, plus her review of data compiled by psychiatrist Marc Galanter (1980, 1989) from his study of a Moonist indoctrination center in Los Angeles, allow the researcher to conclude that, of those prospective recruits who visit a Unification center, no more than 0.005 percent will be associated with the movement two years later. If the number of persons attending an introductory 2-day workshop is taken as 100 percent, then 29–30 percent will attend the follow-up 7-day workshop, 17–18 percent will attend the 21-day workshop, and 8–9 percent will join the Church as a full-time member, living in a Unification Church center and working full time for the movement (Barker 1984: 246–248). Galanter's study of 104 potential converts stops here, but out of Barker's sample of 1,017 persons at a London center, only 5 percent were full-time members after a year, and 4 percent were full-time members after two years.

It appears, then, that very few potential converts are converted and about half of the converted drop out by two years. This fact, as well as indications arising from interview, observational, and questionnaire data that individuals responded differently to the seminars, allow Barker to reject those formulations such as "brain control" or induced suggestibility, which *presuppose the overwhelming efficaciousness of the immediate indoctrinational environment*. Barker's analysis also indicates that those persons who might appear most suggestible—isolated, drifting, unhappy young adults—tended either not to join or to join temporarily. Persisting converts compare favorably with "the ones that got away" on various measures of psychological stability. Barker analyzes deceptive and manipulative elements in the indoctrinational process, but she concludes that most recruits make their affiliative decision voluntarily. The persuasive stimuli presented by indoctrinators acts differently on different persons; thus, according to the criteria of Zimbardo et al., brainwashing is not occurring.

Barker's findings are partly compatible with the findings of Saul Levine, a Toronto psychiatrist, who studied several hundred young persons who had made "radical departures" from their families and other conventional institutions through involvement in radical and close-knit social, religious and political movements (Levine 1984a, 1984b).[14] Levine finds that more than 90 percent of such departures "end in a return home within two years," and "virtually all joiners eventually abandon their groups . . . they resume their previous lives and find gratification in the middle-class world they had totally abjured. In short, they use their radical departures to grow up." Levine's analysis is clearly convergent with Erikson's conceptualization of the adolescent "identity crisis," in which adolescents and young persons must wrestle with the problem of achieving a sense of "wholeness" and "inner identity," an awareness of who he or she fundamentally is as a person relative to social institutions and roles beyond one's family of origin. Lacking the unconditional love provided by parents in childhood and having to abandon unconditional faith in parental guidance, young persons "find they cannot proceed into adulthood without the love and faith that typify childhood." When problems arise regarding compensatory intimate relations with friends and lovers, a radical departure may provide the basis for a more extreme process of reconstructing love, faith, and identity through a seeming absolute commitment to belief systems which often "closely match the ideals of the joiner's family" (1984b: 25). Becoming disenchanted with the radical group and disaffiliating also contributes to the consolidation of a sense of personal autonomy and identity.

Levine discusses a multistage recruitment process through which some individuals are drawn into radical groups while others are in effect screened out as unsuitable. Though often somewhat manipulative, the process is viewed as fundamentally voluntary. Levine estimates that only 5 out of 100 individuals who are initially approached by recruiters make an actual site visit, and out of every 500 who are approached, only 1 person actually joins. "If recruitment techniques are so sinister," asks Levine, "why do they so rarely work?" (1984b: 27).

The Barker and Levine studies indicate that alternative religions exhibit a substantial *voluntary turnover*. Extensive research by sociologists of religion supports this conclusion.[15] High-demand groups such as the Unification Church and Hare Krishna have been like revolving doors through which recruits have been moving in and out. This has not always been apparent. In the 1970s and early 1980s concerned citizens, journalists, and social scientists focused largely on converts entering strange cults; and "few were aware of a steady stream of disaffected members exiting these movements by the back door . . . popular conceptions of brainwashing most likely precluded any suspicion of mass voluntary defections" (Wright and Ebaugh 1993: 118).

A number of studies indicate that leavers are more likely to fiercely recriminate against the groups from which they have emerged and to allege that they were "brainwashed" if they have been forcibly removed from a group and if they had substantial contact with "anticult" networks and associated processes such as deprogramming, rehabilitation, exit counseling, ex-member support groups, and so on.[16] Other ex-members who leave groups voluntarily and do not have substantial contact with anticult networks tend to be less recriminatory and less likely to express the highly stereotyped ideology centered around mind control claims.

Finally, there is solid evidence that persons who have been involved in a particular controversial totalist movement are likely to have been involved in other, (often more than one) esoteric movements—that is, to have developing "conversion careers" (Richardson 1978). In his acclaimed study of converts to the Unification Church, Galanter found that 90 percent of the Moonies in his study had been involved in another new religious movement (1989: 57).

PERSONALITY DYNAMICS

The preceding sections have discredited the extreme extrinsic model and have enhanced the plausibility of alternative models (Anthony and Robbins 1994, 1996) that envision the commitment of devotees to austere, totalistic sects arising from an interaction of individual totalist proclivities and group properties, including ideology, leadership, and indoctrination. Sectarian devotees are not helpless, brainwashed "cult victims," although they may sometimes belong to highly authoritarian and somewhat manipulative movements which aspire to discipline and control their adherents.

Over two decades ago, Anthony (1979–1980) identified various positive consequences associated with joining alternative religious movements in the 1960s and 1970s. Prosocial, functional, and adaptive consequences included the rehabilitation of drug users, rewarding interpersonal relationships, renewed vocational commitment, suicide prevention, relief from depression and anxiety, psychological integration, etc.

In effect, the model which implicitly or explicitly informed these observations was a *deprivation model* in which anomie related to moral ambiguity or lack of "deep" interpersonal relations produces psychic distress, which in turn leads to an alienation from the conventional and a willingness to experiment with social innovations and heterodox movements. In some of these movements, converts do find, at least temporarily, relief from distress (Galanter 1989) or spiritual and communal gratification, although sometimes these rewards incur various and significant costs. We presently incline toward a variant of this model grounded in Erik Erikson's posited sequence for youth confronted with impending identity diffusion, who initially develop negative identities often associated with social alienation and acting out and may become involved in totalist movements which encourage the emergence of extropunitive *contrast identities* (our term). Such individuals come to define themselves largely in terms of what they stridently reject ("contrast symbols") such that they provisionally heal fragmentation of the ego by identifying with an idealized (often ideologically grounded) self-image and projecting negativity and inadequacy onto scapegoats whose demonization is related to the movement's ideology (Anthony and Robbins, 1995). In this way absolutist sects both selectively recruit predisposed individuals and further encourage and intensify their dispositions through social reinforcement and socialization patterns congruent with movements' beliefs and goals.[17] As Lifton has emphasized, what transpires is a pattern of *interaction* between individual personalities and movements. (In contrast, the extrinsic model posits a movement-created, totally ego-alien "false self" which is simply "imposed" on the hapless convert.)

Contrast identities, as the authors have noted elsewhere, are often linked to groups whose worldviews we have previously designated *exemplary dualism*, an apocalyptic motif "in which contemporary sociopolitical or socioreligious forces are viewed as exemplifying absolute contrast categories in terms of not only moral virtue but also of eschatology and the millennial destiny of humankind" (Robbins and Anthony 1995: 242). The motif was originally applied by the authors to the symbolic universe of the Unification Church, and a student in one of Dick Anthony's seminars subsequently published an application to Jim Jones and the ill-fated Peoples Temple (Jones 1989). The contrast identities of devotees become anchored in the extreme dualist worldview of movements, which regard certain putatively wicked and antagonistic outsiders as embodying demonic, world historical forces: for example, the Papacy is the "Whore of Babylon," the Tsar is Antichrist, the New Age–Occult milieu is Satan's instrument to destroy the Church. More generally, exemplary dualism might be applied to social movements which depend for their morale on sharp contrasts with groups and cultures outside the movement. Group members define themselves in opposition to such "contrast symbols" and thereby gain a sense of purpose, wholeness, and meaningful commitment, as well as a conviction of personal righteousness and purity. Troubled persons with fragmented egos and "negative identities" are likely converts who experience temporary relief from anxiety or depression.

In Galanter's (1989 [1999]) important study of converts to the Unification Church in the 1980s, there did appear to be a lot of troubled or alienated young persons: only a fraction of those who began college graduated. "A sizeable portion (39 percent) felt they had experienced serious emotional difficulties in the past," which had led 30 percent to seek professional help and 6 percent to be hospitalized. Sixty-five percent had used marijuana on a daily basis and 14 percent had used heroin (Galanter 1989: 34–35, 38–60). They had high levels of self-reported psychological distress (compared to a matched control sample) which, however, declined significantly over the course of conversion, while drug use also declined very markedly. The decline in feeling of psychological distress was directly proportional to the degree of cohesiveness they felt toward the group (1989: 35), which did, however, make losing faith in the beliefs or contemplating disaffiliation somewhat stressful. The "relief effect" or decline in psychic distress was correlated with the individual's variable feeling of solidarity with the group and with acceptance of group beliefs. The "relief effect" is thus mediated by the affiliative attitudes of social cohesiveness and shared beliefs—that is, by both social and cognitive modalities.

It is possible to question the (essentially self-reported) relief effect or at least to not take it entirely at face value. Converts affirm a sense of well-being, and they are less likely to make such a claim before they join; yet there is a rather high defection rate. In any case, as one review essayist notes, there is little evidence that merely becoming committed to the group has really resolved Galanter's respondents' personality conflict. "The 'relief effect' could be temporary and/or superficial (Saliba 1993: 107).

A different perspective comes from sociologist Robert Simmonds (1978), who poses the question "conversion or addiction." Personality inventories administered to 96 members of a "Jesus Movement" group in the early 1970s yielded a profile of highly anxious individuals who were very dependent upon external authority. Like Galanter's Moonies, the subjects reported high levels of drug use and other deviance despite "relatively affluent" middle-class backgrounds. The subjects expressed happiness and strong satisfaction with their involvement in what appeared to be a rather authoritarian and regimented communal sect with a strong fundamentalist belief system, as well as a commitment to "serving the Lord." The questionnaires were readministered two and a half months later after the subjects had undergone an intensive resocialization in the movement's leadership training program. Symptomatic behavior such as drug use had declined markedly, but there did not appear to be much change with respect to underlying character problems. Simmonds infers that the devotees were essentially "switching addictions" and that conversion to the Jesus movement did not involve significant personality change. Instead, the subjects had found a secure and stable authoritarian setting to facilitate "a continuation of the same basic psychological patterns had by these people before they joined the group" (1978: 127).

We will now briefly look at some communal "Eastern" mystical groups which one might expect to be rather different from the fundamentalist "Jesus movement" converts or Moonies. Richardson (1995) reviews several studies involving the administration of personality inventories to followers of the late, controversial Shree Bhagawan Rajneesh in Oregon. The "Rajneeshees" were generally older than the typical Moonies or most other "cultists" (even the fairly recent converts). They were very highly educated, often creative, social service professionals, affluent, over 50 percent female, and with backgrounds which often entailed involvements in other unconventional spiritual and therapeutic groups (Latkin et al. 1987). They reported fairly high levels of life satisfaction and low levels of perceived stress. Their perceived level of social support was slightly higher and the report of recent depressive symptoms was lower than normative population baselines. Scores on public and private anxiety and private self-consciousness scales indicated introspective persons less concerned with others' opinions of them. They perceived themselves to be in control of their destinies. They had strong self-concepts with, however, suggestion of a predilection toward antinomianism (i.e., "norm-doubting" types predominated over "norm-favoring" types). The overall profile seems to undercut the plausibility of an extrinsic model of psychologically coerced induction; however, it has been noted that the imbalance of personality types in terms of too many antinomian types may have contributed to the demise of the Rajneeshpuram community in Oregon (Sundberg et al. 1992), which more or less self-destructed after an escalating sequence of conflict with neighbors and state authorities culminating in violence directed by subleaders (particularly Ma Sheela, who was criminally prosecuted and imprisoned) and the guru's deportation (Carter 1990).

Personality measures administered after the traumatic forced departure of the guru showed a marked rise in the depression scores, which went from below to above the baseline for the general population. Perhaps subjects' earlier happiness had been precarious in the sense that it required integration into a close-knit group and could not survive the apparent disconfirmation of the group's expectations embodied by the triumphs of the group's adversaries. (There may thus be hazards in happiness, stability, and psychic integration grounded in movement participation.) It is worth noting that some critical (but not stereotyped anticult) works on Rajneesh's movement and its doomed Oregon settlement suggest that the attitudes of members and particularly of the inner circle of leadership were redolent of elitism, antinomianism, contempt for outsiders and for persons and groups blocking the expansion of the Oregon community, violent proclivities, contrast identities and "paranoid" concern for internal security, and rigid boundary maintenance (Carter 1990; Fitzgerald 1991; Milne 1986).

Similarly, there is substantial critical literature on the Hare Krishna sect, which is now in decline in the United States. A celebrated study by two journalists, which uncovered the story behind two murders of devotees (one guru ultimately went to prison), also reveals abundant evidence of spiritual elitism, antinomianism, intense contempt for "Karmis" (nondevotees enmeshed in Karmic entanglements who are said to live to kill and rape and hate devotees), paranoia, and anticipation of violent conflicts ahead (Huber and Gruson 1990).[18]

There is a particularly sizeable corpus of personality studies of Krishna devotees, recently reviewed by Richardson (1995). To very briefly summarize, there is strong evidence of selectivity for certain character traits and a tendency for acculturation in the group to reinforce elements selected for in the recruitment process (Weiss and Mendoza 1990). The evidence for selection for certain personality types, as well as the absence of serious psychopathology undermines the relevance of extrinsic brainwashing and induced pathology models. There were the usual reports (Ross 1983) of persons from privileged backgrounds becoming involved in deviant behavior, identity crises, rejection of parental authority, and generalized spiritual seeking prior to conversion, followed by dramatic declines in drug use and social alienation, plus self-reports of satisfaction (Poling and Kenny 1986).

Certain interesting results arise, however, from the administration of instruments such as the MMPI, the (Jungian) Myers-Briggs Inventory, the Rokeach Dogmatism Scale, and other personality measures. In one study, 93 devotees appeared to be markedly homogenous in terms of a character type described as sensate-oriented, pleasure-seeking, but anxious about a perceived recurrent danger of falling victim to an endless pursuit of sense gratification. Such persons were particularly attracted to a regimented sect which combines puritanical rejection of a range of intoxicants and strict regulation of sex behavior with ecstatic spiritual practices such as rhythmic, repetitive chanting. Thus, sense pleasure is rejected on the mundane level but accepted on the transcendent level (Poling and Kenny 1986: 108). Adherents also tended toward dogmatic thinking and intolerance regarding the beliefs and lifestyles of others (1986: 135). An additional study found devotees scoring high on *compulsivity*: they have a strong need for order (males' scores are significantly higher than normal range). Devotees also score high on social conformity and emotional stability and low on trust (but scores were within the normal range). Richardson (1995: 15–16) notes the agreement of the Weiss-Comrey and the Poling-Kenny studies with respect to dogmatic thinking, judgmental constraints on latent impulsivity, and rigidity in certain areas, as well as the absence of serious pathology.

AUTHORITARIANISM AND TOTALISM

It is suggestive that certain interrelated traits seem to show up in a number of studies in which personality inventories were administered to participants in close-knit, disciplined, clearly bounded communal sects which demand behavioral conformity and adherence to distinctive beliefs from the devotees. Although configurations vary from group to group, the observed traits relate somewhat to the *authoritarian personality*, particularly as reconstructed by Bob Altemeyer. Altemeyer (1988) redefines authoritarianism in terms of three key components: *conventionalization* (social conformity, strong support for normative ideas); *authoritarian submission* (deference to hierarchical superiors and authorities, dependency on authoritarian leadership and decision-making); and *authoritarian aggression* (extropunitiveness and hostility directed against minorities and toward socially designated objects of scorn).

As we have seen, there is suggestive, though perhaps not conclusive, evidence that elements linked to the personality variables of authoritarianism dogmatism characterize the devotees of some of the controversial, structurally authoritarian, and "totalistic" religious movements of cults—although little direct research has been done on "authoritarian personalities" among controversial cults.[19] On the other hand, a number of studies have produced correlations between authoritarianism or dogmatism and Protestant fundamentalism, and between both authoritarianism and dogmatism and varieties of social prejudice and scapegoating (Altemeyer 1981, 1988).[20]

Below, we very tentatively suggest nine characteristics which appear to be shared by authoritarian personalities, fundamentalists, and authoritarian cults such as Hare Krishna, the Unification Church, etc. (see also Anthony and Robbins 1995).

1. *Separatism*, or the heightened sensitivity and tension regarding group boundaries. This may be equivalent to "authoritarian aggression" and involves rejection and punitive attitudes toward deviants, minorities, and outsiders.

2. *Theocratic leanings,* or willingness to see a future utopian state enforce moral and ideological preferences at the expense of pluralism or church-state separation.

3. *Authoritarian submission,* involving dependency on and deference to strong leaders.

4. *Conventionalism and conformity* (there are conspicuous exceptions, however, in terms of egregiously antinomian groups).

5. *Evangelism,* or concern with proselytization (there may be exceptions here in terms of groups which have isolated themselves in such a way as to inhibit outreach—such groups may be particularly volatile).

6. *Apocalypticism/Millennarianism,* or a heightened expectation of imminent, cataclysmic transformation of material and social reality.

7. *Coercive tendencies* in terms of either punitive reactions to dissidence and diversity within the group or willingness to have a utopian state suppress dissidents.

8. *Consequentialism* in terms of perceiving moral virtue or ideological correctness as producing tangible rewards for believers.

9. *Strong beliefs* and use of doctrinal correctness as a criterion of acceptance.

THIRD-STAGE BRAINWASHING FORMULATIONS

The previous sections of this chapter have demonstrated that the theory of coercive conversion embodied in brainwashing formulations has been disconfirmed both with respect to the original research on Communist thought reform and by a substantial body of research on new religious movements or cults. We earlier published an analysis of the history of brainwashing formulations in both settings, which we refer to as "first phase" and "second phase" brainwashing formulations (Anthony and Robbins 1995). In an attempt to surmount the definitive disconfirmations of these earlier stages, We also describe a third phase of brainwashing formulations that have recently arisen.

In order to understand this recent stage, it is important to realize that neither of the earlier phases were used as a basis for methodologically sound scientific research. The original brainwashing explanation of Communist influence was developed by the American CIA as a social weapon in a propaganda/disinformation program. It was intended to undermine the authenticity of Communist influence in the Cold War era by interpreting it as the result of a sinister psychotechnology.

The primary use of second-phase brainwashing arguments has been as an ideological rationale for practical actions by families and the courts to counteract the influence of new religions, by explaining conversions as resulting from coercive influence. (The plausibility of the cultic brainwashing argument has always been based upon its claimed foundation in research on Communist thought reform rather than research on new religions.) In many civil lawsuits against new religions, anticult experts have used the cultic brainwashing theory as a basis for testimony, arguing that ex-members had joined a new religion against their will and as a result were owed compensation because of alleged emotional damages. From the mid-1970s to the mid-1990s, cultic brainwashing testimony and legal actions were often successful in punishing and even crippling new religions as the result of the imposition of large compensatory and punitive damages, sometimes as high as $20–30 million and sometimes forcing a new religion into bankruptcy and even dissolution. Largely because of concern over the effects upon new religions' civil liberties, scholars began to conduct substantial research evaluating the coercive conversion idea. As we have seen, most of this research challenged the cultic brainwashing idea.

In addition, Anthony published a sequence of articles and book chapters (some of which were coauthored by Robbins) demonstrating the lack of congruence between cultic brainwashing formulations and its claimed theoretical foundation of research on Communist thought reform. These articles also demonstrated scientific and constitutional problems in the admission of cultic brainwashing testimony, as well as defects in the legal reasoning that construed the cultic brainwashing theory as a basis for legal actions against NRMs.

Professional associations (the American Psychology Association, the American Sociological Association, and the Society for the Scientific Study of Religion) submitted a series of amicus curiae briefs in the appeals of legal decisions based upon cultic brainwashing testimony, arguing that such testimony was inadmissible because of the body of research disconfirming it and because of its inconsistency with its claimed theoretical foundation and conflicts with constitutional and scientific standards of admissibility. Anthony has used the arguments developed in these articles as the basis for his consultation and expert testimony in over forty legal cases since the early 1980s. His forensic activities have been largely successful in limiting the effect of or excluding brainwashing testimony from admissibility in these cases.[21] As a result, cultic brainwashing theory and the legal cases built upon it have been generally discredited and marginalized in the U.S.

In the wake of such reversals, a new stage of brainwashing arguments has emerged, the most prominent of which are the so-called exit costs interpretations, developed largely by Benjamen Zablocki and Steven Kent. Anthony (2001) published a detailed critique of formulations based upon the exit costs interpretation.

We include a précis of this critique here because the exit costs argument claims to reinterpret the brainwashing idea in a way that rescues its scientific plausibility from the criticisms it has received. The basic exit costs interpretation argues that brainwashing is a theory of coercive commitment to groups and their ideology rather than a theory of coercive conversion to groups. In other words, according to Zablocki and Kent, the processes that psychologically imprison NRM members occur after they have made a superficial conversion to the group, rather than causing that conversion in the first place.

Zablocki's Argument

In his recent articles, Zablocki claims that brainwashing is a valid scientific concept that has been supported by considerable research of both upon Communist coercive persuasion and coercive influence tactics in new religions or cults (1997: 104–107). He acknowledges, however, that brainwashing is is widely regarded in sociology and psychology as being without scientific foundation (1997: 96–97; 1998: 217) and says that many scholars in those disciplines regard it as an evaluative rather than a scientific concept.

He contends that this pejorative view is based upon a misunderstanding of brainwashing's true nature and of the validly scientific research supporting it (1997: 100). According to Zablocki, such misunderstanding was brought about by the use of a distorted caricature of the concept, the development of which was motivated by legal and pecuniary goals rather than by an honest concern with the scientific understanding of the phenomenon (1997: 100–101). He claims that his recent articles straighten out this misperception and restore the concept to its proper scientific status (1997: 102, 106).

According to Zablocki, the primary ideologically motivated misinterpretation of the scientific brainwashing concept is that it has to do with illicit recruitment mechanisms, when it is actually a concept concerning influence processes which bring about addictive commitments to worldviews to which the targets of brainwashing have already been converted. He states:

> Popular usage has come to imply that brainwashing has something to do with recruitment mechanisms when, on the contrary, it has mostly to do with socio-emotional exit costs. An examination of any of the foundational literature makes it very clear that what these researchers were attempting to explain was the persistence of ideological conversion after the stimulus was removed, not how subjects were initially hooked into the ideology. (1997: 100)

In his recent brainwashing articles, Zablocki refers to his approach as "exit cost analysis," and in the subtitle to his 1998 article he calls it "new approach to the scientific study of brainwashing." (His claim that his approach is new is somewhat confusing, since he also claims that it is well known that exit cost analysis has always been the primary theme of validly scientific brainwashing theory and research.) Zablocki claims that his formulation has identified the moderate and scientifically testable essence of the brainwashing paradigm (1997: 106), as opposed to the caricature of the brainwashing model which has been misused for ideological and legal purposes.

In a footnote to the above passage Zablocki identifies the "foundational literature" of the brainwashing concept referred to therein as the 1961 books by Robert Lifton and Edgar Schein, in which they reported their research upon Communist thought reform in China around the time of the Korean War. These books are normally claimed as the primary theoretical foundation for anticult brainwashing testimony in legal trials. Thus, a primary burden of Zablock's approach would seem to be that he make good on his claim that his interpretation of this foundational literature—that is, Lifton's and Schein's 1961 books—is different from the epistemologically spurious version used in legal trials.

Brainwashing as Exit Costs in the Foundational Literature

The novel feature of Zablocki's version of the CIA model, is the surprising claim that Lifton's and Schein's research on thought reform did not demonstrate involuntary conversion of its victims to a new Communist worldview, but rather *the coercive intensification of commitment to a Communist worldview to which the victims of thought reform were already committed.* None of Schein's or Lifton's subjects were Communists before they were subjected to thought reform in the sense of having adopted, provisionally or otherwise, the Communist worldview. What could Zablocki possibly mean when it is central to his formulation of a brainwashing argument?

Could he be implying that because their Western subjects were imprisoned in Communist thought reform prisons, and Lifton's Chinese subjects were living within a Communist society, these conditions were somehow equivalent to their having provisionally adopted a Communist worldview, and thus that they had already been "hooked into the ideology" before being subjected to thought reform? How does that follow? None of their subjects had adopted a Communist worldview before they were subjected to thought reform. (This is particularly obvious with their Western subjects, who were imprisoned during the thought reform process; if they were already seeing the world through the lens of Communist ideology, why would they need to be imprisoned in order for them to undergo thought reform?)

Elsewhere Zablocki seems to be saying that Lifton's and Schein's subjects were already Communists prior to thought reform in the sense of already having joined a Communist organization. He states:

> Brainwashing may be defined as a set of transactions between a charismatically led collectivity and an isolated agent of the collectivity with the goal of transforming the agent into a deployable agent. In the terminology I am using here, there exist three levels of affiliation in such collectivities: recruits, agents, and deployable agents. A recruit is a person who is considering membership in the group and perhaps is also being courted by the group. An agent is a person who has already made the commitment to become a member of the group and accept its goals. A deployable agent is a person who has internalized the group's goals to such an extent that he or she can be counted on with high probability to act so as to implement those goals even when free of direct surveillance and even when those goals run counter to the individual's personal goals.
> The target of brainwashing is always an individual who has already joined the group. (1998: 221)

It seems clear that Zablocki is claiming that brainwashing is only used with respect to people who have already adopted an alternative worldview—that is, "agents" or "ordinary members," "who have already joined the group" but who have not yet become so-called "deployable agents." Is Zablocki contending that Schein's and Lifton's subjects had already joined Communist groups because they were in Communist prisons or living in a Communist society? That doesn't follow, either. None of their subjects ever joined Communist organizations, either before or after they were subjected to thought reform.

Anthony demonstrates (2001) that none of Lifton's or Schein's subjects ever became recruits, agents, or deployable agents of Communism by adopting Communist worldviews or joining Communist organizations, even after they had been subjected to thought reform. None had trouble repudiating any degree of interest they may have had in Communism after they left the thought reform environment; the only exit costs they encountered were the difficulty of getting out of prison. Zablocki's definition of "new" exit costs in brainwashing does not hold up.

Pre-Motives

It would seem that Zablocki's insistence that Lifton's and Schein's subjects were Communists (recruits or agents) before being brainwashed involves a strained analogy between Communist imprisonment and becoming a member of a new religion. This analogy doesn't hold up. Imprisonment does not indicate that a person has adopted a worldview or joined a group, whereas those who voluntarily become members of new religions have accepted, at least provisionally, the world-view of the group they have joined.

Zablocki's insistence that brainwashing consists of coercive change in *level of commitment* to totalistic ideology, rather than coercive *conversion* to totalistic ideology in the first place, is all the more puzzling when other passages are taken into account in which he seems to define brainwashing as coercive conversion to a new worldview (see 1997: 104–105; 1971: 239, 243–246, 251–252, 257, 282; 1980: 7–10, 357 and throughout).

It seems likely that Zablocki's tactical ambiguity on this key aspect of his theory can be explained by his attempt to evade the implications of the body of research on both Communist indoctrination practices and NRMs, which challenged the contention of both first-and second-stage brainwashing formulations that brainwashing produces, purely through extrinsic techniques of influence, involuntary conversion to a new worldview.

Research has rather conclusively established that the "invasion of the body snatchers" view of conversion to NRMs is inaccurate. The research demonstrates that the overwhelming majority of converts to NRMs (including most plaintiffs in brainwashing trials) fit a "seeker" profile of people who were disillusioned with mainstream worldviews and were actively searching for alternative worldviews prior to their conversion to NRMs. Clearly, if brainwashing perspectives were to survive such voluminous disconfirmations, and the repeated findings by the courts that cultic brainwashing testimony could not be allowed because of its lack of scientific support, some revision of the involuntary conversion aspect of the CIA brainwashing model was necessary.

According to Zablocki and other theorists, brainwashing consists of overwhelming or irresistible "extrinsic" influence to which the inner qualities of the person are irrelevant, as opposed to normal "intrinsic" influence, resulting from an interaction between the inner characteristics of the person and outside influence. (For a book-length analysis of the difference between extrinsic and intrinsic psychological paradigms of influence and motivation, see Pervin 1984. For a discussion of the application of this distinction to brainwashing versus totalitarian approaches to social influence, see Anthony 1996: 221–225.)

Zablocki repeatedly claims that the brainwashing paradigm does not take into account individual differences between people who are being exposed to brainwashing in accounting for how such influence occurs or which person will be successfully brainwashed. He states, "It is situational and relational factors rather than predispositions that help us to predict this [successful brainwashing] phenomenon" (Zablocki 1998: 225; see also Zablocki 1998: 222, 235; 1993; 83–84; 1997: 101; Singer and Lalich 1995: 15–20).

The extrinsic-influence character of brainwashing formulations is essential to establish that such influence is "involuntary." Sociologists have demonstrated that contemporary postmodern (pluralistic, multicultural) society is characterized by a focus upon individual autonomy as the prime determinant of authentic personhood. Unreflective conformity is the mark of the inauthentic or "false" self (Winnicott 1960).

In order to be a genuine person in the contemporary, multicultural society, individuals are expected to independently reflect upon and consciously choose their own identities and worldviews from among the pluralistic mixture of alternatives with which they are presented. Consequently, if a person is viewed as having passively accepted an identity and worldview without evaluating it in relation to their own distinctive characteristics and organic development of authentic personhood, he/she is viewed as not being a "real" or authentic person. However, in practice all of us choose our identities, worldviews, and lifestyles as a result of a indeterminate mixture of outside influence and inner reflection and choice. Thus most of us are unsure of the degree to which we are conformists or authentic "self-actualizers."

One function of the brainwashing myth may be that it provides its believers with a line at which social influence overwhelms inner authenticity. By doing so this myth creates for its believers a definition of false personhood, thus creating a stereotype by contrast with which they can reaffirm their own supposedly authentic personhood. Unfortunately, this aspect of the paradigm has been disconfirmed by three important sources of data: research on conversion to Communist and other totalitarian political ideologies; research upon conversion to alternative religions; and statements by brainwashing theorists about the intrinsic motivation for joining new religions.

The question of whether internal motivation for joining new religions is an important predictor of who responds favorably to proselytization has been repeatedly answered in the affirmative by the same anticult brainwashing authors who elsewhere (often in the same publications in which they also deny it) claim that conversion and commitment are solely determined by extrinsic influence. The types of preexisting motivation for joining new religions affirmed by brainwashing theorists fall into two broad categories: 1) alienation or anomie relative to mainstream values and social institutions, resulting in a pattern of "seeking" for nontraditional alternatives; 2) family dysfunction combined with character logical predispositions to respond favorably to totalitarian ideologies (see, e.g., Halperin 1987).

Virtually all brainwashing authors describe widespread social change since the 1960s as resulting in widespread alienation or anomie, which in turn motivates young people to seek and join nontraditional religions. Such authors seem not to realize that accounting for responsiveness to proselytization in this way essentially negates the claim that people involuntarily join new religions primarily for extrinsic reasons. Obviously, even in periods of social turmoil, not all members of society are equally alienated from traditional values and institutions. Alienation, therefore, differs in degree from person and person, and the more alienated are more apt to seek alternative worldviews and institutions.

Zablocki's recent brainwashing articles are theoretical and speculative rather than based on research on new religions. He claims, however, to base his brainwashing theory upon research on minority religions and communes that he conducted and described in earlier books (Zablocki 1971, 1980). Both of these books adopt *the social change producing individual differences in anomie/alienation* view of why particular people are more likely to join new religions (1971; 1980).

Indeed, in *Alienation and Charisma* (1980), alienation is one of the two master concepts (the other being charisma) by which he organizes his data. In this book, alienation is clearly treated as a motive which predisposes individuals to be influenced by charismatic social movements, with higher levels of alienation predisposing individuals to choose more authoritarian movements or, in Zablocki's current terminology, "cults." (In his basic thesis, alienation is cured by involvement in a charismatic social movement, with more extreme degrees of alienation requiring more authoritarian and extreme forms of charismatic organization for its cure.)

Thus Zablocki is, as the author of these earlier publications, a proponent of what he now labels the "seekership conjecture" school of new religions scholarship (1998: 234–236), a theoretical orientation that he now sees as conflicting with his current brainwashing perspective. In one of the theoretically incoherent and self-contradictory twists characteristic of his brainwashing articles, he claims that his earlier works are actually the empirical basis for his new brainwashing formulation. (He also self-contradictorily affirms the *anomie equals seekership* idea in his recent brainwashing articles [1997; 1990]).

Interestingly, in footnote 43 in the seekership section of his 1998 article, which lists a number of publications that Zablocki considers to be reputable scientific instances of the seekership conjecture, he lists Robert Lifton's 1968 article, "Protean Man," as one of the examples. In this article, Lifton views *proteanism*, that is, anomic, relativistic cultural tendencies and the confused and ambiguous self-concepts that result from them, as the source of motives for conversion to alternative religious movements. (In his later books on new religious movements [1993: 10–11 and throughout; 1999: 5, 236–238], Lifton uses the proteanism concept as a master concept, along with totalism, to explain preexisting motives—for example, "seekership" as an explanation for why people convert to new religions and totalistic, fundamentalistic, Christian sects [1993: 177–187].) Thus, Zablocki appears to be acknowledging Lifton as a proponent of the seekership explanation of conversion to new religions, whereas elsewhere he views Lifton's work as the primary theoretical foundation for the brainwashing explanation which he regards as contradictory to the seekership explanation.

These indications that Zablocki both repudiates and embraces what he refers to as the seekership explanation for conversion to new religions are further examples of the theoretical incoherence of his brainwashing formulation, a trait that Anthony, in his critique of Zablocki's exit costs argument, calls *tactical ambiguity*.

Disorientation, Defective Thought, Suggestibility, and the False Self

The following are the individual elements or hypotheses within Zablocki's definition of his supposedly "new approach to the scientific study of brainwashing." (Below, we evaluate the relationship of these individual elements/hypotheses to the theoretical foundation which Zablocki contends supports their role in brainwashing.)

1. Absence of premotives. People who join new religions cults are not seeking alternatives to mainstream worldviews prior to their membership in the new group.
2. Disorientation. New religions or cults induce irrational altered states of consciousness as the core technique in seducing people into giving up their existing worldview. (Zablocki refers to this primitive state of consciousness as disorientation; other brainwashing theorists have referred to it as hypnosis, dissociation, trance, etc., but there is no meaningful distinction between these terms for primitive consciousness as they are used by brainwashing theorists; they are functional synonyms within the brainwashing worldview.)
3. Defective cognition. In the disoriented state essential to brainwashing, the person has a significantly reduced cognitive capacity to evaluate the truth or falsity of the worldviews with which he or she is confronted.
4. Suggestibility. As a result of externally induced disorientation and defective cognitive capacity, the victim of brainwashing is highly "suggestible"— that is, prone to accept as her/his own ideas and worldviews which are recommended to her/him by the person or organization that has induced the defective cognitive state.
5. Coercive or involuntary imposition of a defective or false worldview. The above sequence of criteria of brainwashing results in the involuntary imposition of a defective or false worldview which anyone in a rational state of mind would have rejected.
6. Coercive imposition of a false self. As a result of the brainwashing process, the person manifests a pseudoidentity, or shadow self, which has been involuntarily imposed upon him/her by brainwashing.
7. Deployable agency. The involuntarily imposed false self and defective worldview persist after the brainwashing process has been completed,

and as a result the brainwashed person retains his commitment to the new self and worldview even when he or she is not in direct contact with the group doing the brainwashing.

8. Exit costs. It is extremely difficult for the person to later repudiate his new worldview and false self-conception because he no longer has the capacity to rationally evaluate these choices.

All of these hypotheses were aspects of the original, generally discredited CIA brainwashing model that Zablocki claims to be replacing with his new approach. As we shall see, all of them were disconfirmed by generally accepted research on Communist thought reform, including the research Zablocki claims supplies the primary theoretical foundation of his formulation. Basically, Zablocki's statement of the CIA brainwashing theory conflicts with generally accepted research on Communist thought reform in the same ways as did second-stage perspectives, but he has added a new level of tactical ambiguity to his argument.

At its core, Zablocki's publications on brainwashing affirm the same characteristics of allegedly involuntary influence as did first-and second-stage brainwashing formulations—for example, those of Hunter, Singer, and Ofshe. For instance, he asserts that disorientation and a suspension of critical rationality are essential to the brainwashing process. He states:

> The core hypothesis is that, under certain circumstances, an individual can be subject to persuasive influences so overwhelming that they actually restructure one's core beliefs and worldview and profoundly modify one's self-conception. The sort of persuasion posited by the brainwashing conjecture is aimed at somewhat different goals than the sort of persuasion practiced by bullies or by salesman and teachers. . . . The more radical sort of persuasion posited by the brainwashing conjecture utilizes extreme stress and disorientation along with ideological enticement to create a conversion experience that persists for some time after the stress and pressure have been removed. . . . To be considered brainwashing this process must result in (a) effects that persist for a significant amount of time after the orchestrated manipulative stimuli are removed and (b) an accompanying dread of disaffiliation which makes it extremely difficult for the subject to even contemplate life apart from the group. (Zablocki 1997: 104–105; our emphasis)

The reader may recognize the same altered states/suggestibility/overwhelmed will concept that constituted the essence of the CIA brainwashing theory described above and is typically used as the primary basis for cultic brainwashing legal suits.

The "profoundly modified self" Zablocki refers to as characteristic of brainwashing is essentially the same as the false self or "pseudoidentity" which Singer (1995: 60, 61, 77–79), West and Martin (1994), and other brainwashing theorists regard as an essential aspect of brainwashing. The new identity is viewed as false because it is imposed wholly by extrinsic influence and thus is discontinuous with the preexisting values and self-conception of the person. (In psychoanalysis, "ego-dystonic" refers to distortions of rational thought processes, e.g., delusions, hallucinations, obsessive thoughts, or compulsive behaviors, produced by eruptions of primitive unconscious materials into consciousness.)

Zablocki discusses the false self imposed by brainwashing, which he refers to as a "shadow self" (1998: 223, 226, 244). He states:

> The result of this [brainwashing] process, when successful, is to make the individual a deployable agent of the charismatic authority. This is not merely commitment but a form of commitment that does not depend on continuous surveillance by the group. A rational choice perspective on the brainwashing model conceives of this process as a fundamental restructuring of the self through a reorganization of preferences. We are talking about change on a deep although not necessarily permanent level. . . . This "doubling" or creation of a shadow self is something that I have often observed but cannot pretend to understand on more than a metaphoric level. (1998: 223)[22]

At a later point, Zablocki states: "In these terms, brainwashing can be operationalized as an influence process orchestrated toward the goal of charismatic addiction. . . . The identification stage creates the biochemical alignment and the rebirth stage creates the fully addicted shadow self" (1998: 244).

As Zablocki has stated in his definition of brainwashing, in his view the cult is able to overwhelm—and replace with a shadow self—the preexisting authentic self of the person only by inducing an altered, primitive state of consciousness in which the person is unable to resist indoctrination. Zablocki refers to this alleged state of primitive consciousness as "disorientation." This is one of several terms used by brainwashing theorists to refer to this allegedly primitive state of consciousness induced by brainwashing techniques; the other most common ones are "hypnosis" and "dissociation."

It is important to realize that neither disorientation, as Zablocki uses the term, nor any of the other terms that brainwashing theorists commonly use—trance, hypnosis, disorientation, loose cognition, etc.—are defined specifically enough to differentiate them from each other nor from normal consciousness. (For instance, Zablocki doesn't provide a definition for his use of the term "disorientation," nor does he supply any citation of scientific research or other literature which could explain what scientific meaning he intends by the term.)[23] These terms thus are functionally equivalent as used by brainwashing theorists and are, in effect, synonyms.[24]

Elsewhere, Zablocki elaborates upon the disoriented state which he considers to be the core of the brainwashing process. He states that those in the throes of brainwashing are, at times, so disoriented that they appear to resemble zombies or robots: glassy eyes, inability to complete sentences, and fixed eerie smiles are characteristics of disoriented people under randomly varying levels of psychological stress. "I, myself, happened to witness an entire building full of several hundred highly disoriented Moonies, and it is not an experience that I will ever be able to forget. These people, though gentle and harmless, were frightening in their disjointed affect and loose cognition" (1998: 232). In this passage, in addition to an extreme level of disorientation resembling that of "zombies or robots," Zablocki refers to the "loose cognition" he believes to be characteristic of those in the process of being brainwashed. He elaborates later on the "loose cognition" and suspension of critical rationality, which he regards as essential to the brainwashing process (1998: 241–244). He states:

> My argument is that this transition to the biological [essential to brainwashing] involves both *a suspension of incredulity* and an addictive orientation to the alternation of arousal and comfort comparable to the mother-infant attachment. . . .
> At the cognitive level this relationship [between the charismatic cult and its brainwashed victim] involves the *suspension of left-brain criticism of right-brain beliefs such that the beliefs are uncritically and enthusiastically adopted. . . . By preventing even low-level testing of the consequences of our convictions, the [brainwashed] individual is able rapidly to be convinced of a changing flow of beliefs, accepted uncritically.* (1998: 241–242; our emphasis)[25]

This passage defines the "suggestibility" which Hunter and other brainwashing theorists contend results from the inducement of a primitive state of consciousness in brainwashing. As should be clear from our discussion, the notion that brainwashing uses the induction of a primitive state of consciousness and a resulting inability to resist indoctrination, leading to an addictive or compulsive attachment to a new worldview and a false self, is the heart of the first-stage CIA brainwashing paradigm. (In Zablocki's formulation, the conversion to the new worldview is regarded as involuntary and compulsive because it follows from the absence of even "low-level testing of the consequences of our convictions" and thus the new worldview is "accepted uncritically.")

Disconfirmation of the Primitive Consciousness Hypothesis

As we discussed, Zablocki claims to base his brainwashing formulation upon research on Communist thought reform at the time of the Korean War, particularly the research of Schein and Lifton. Contrary to his claims that such research supports his formulation, however, with its central proposition that brainwashing results from the induction of a primitive state of defective cognition and resulting suggestibility, these researchers found that such Communist influence did not result from diminished cognitive competence. Schein states:

> There is always a certain amount of distortion, sharpening, leveling, and false logic in the beliefs and attitudes which other people acquire. Because people are ambivalent on many issues it is easy to play up some "facts" and play down others when our value position or feeling changes. Coercive persuasion

is no more or less of such distortion than other kinds of influence, but our popular image of "brainwashing" suggests that somehow the process consists of extensive self-delusion and excessive distortion. We feel that this image is a false one: it is based on our lack of familiarity with or knowledge about the process and the fact that so much publicity was given to the political influence which resulted in a few cases. (Schein 1961: 239)

In addition, Schein found that Communist coercive persuasion did not result from the induction of hypnosis or other forms of dissociation. He states:

Given these considerations, it is difficult to see how Meerloo and Huxley can be so sure of the effectiveness of brainwashing and of their interpretation of it as a process based on hypnosis and Pavlovian psychology. The chief problem with the hypnotic interpretation [of Communist coercive persuasion] is that the relationship between hypnotist and subject is to a large degree a voluntary one, whereas the coercive element in persuasive persuasion is paramount (forcing the individual into a situation in which he must, in order to survive physically and psychologically, expose himself to persuasive attempts). A second problem is that as yet we do not have an adequate theoretical explanation for the effects seen under hypnosis, and hence there is little to be gained by using it as an explanatory concept. Third, and most important, all hypnotic situations that I know of involve the deliberate creation of a state resembling sleep or dissociation. *The essence of coercive persuasion, on the other hand, is to produce ideological and behavioral changes in a fully conscious, mentally intact individual.* (Schein 1959: 437; our emphasis)

Such statements indicate that cultic brainwashing formulations, such as Zablocki's, that highly resemble the CIA mind control theory on the issue of whether brainwashing is based upon the induction of primitive states of consciousness explicitly contradict their claimed theoretical/empirical foundation of generally accepted research on Communist thought reform.

BRAINWASHING VS. TOTALITARIAN INFLUENCE: SUMMARY OF EMPIRICAL CONFLICTS

As we have shown, the CIA brainwashing model provides the claimed theoretical foundation for all statements of brainwashing theory, including cultic brainwashing formulations such as Zablocki's. Consequently, Zablocki's cultic brainwashing theory, like the earlier second-stage statements of cultic brainwashing theory is contradicted by its own claimed theoretical foundation. Anthony (1990) demonstrated that eight variables differentiated Singer and Ofshe's second-stage brainwashing theory from Schein's and Lifton's research. Anthony (2001) demonstrated the same conflicts between Zablocki's approach and generally accepted research on Communist thought reform, and this article has demonstrated similar conflicts between all brainwashing formulations, including Zablocki's, and a large body of contemporary research on NRMs.

As Anthony (1990) argued, Schein's and Lifton's research on Communist indoctrination practices disconfirmed the CIA model with respect to eight variables. These are as follows.

1. Conversion. None of Schein's and Lifton's subjects became committed to Communist worldviews as a result of the thought reform program. Only two of Lifton's 40 subjects and only one or two of Schein's 15 subjects emerged from the thought reform process expressing sympathy for Communism, and none of them actually became Communists. Communist coercive persuasion produced behavioral compliance but not belief in Communist ideology (Lifton 1961: 117, 248–249; Schein 1958: 332; 1961: 157–166; 1973: 295).

2. Predisposing motives. Those subjects who were at all influenced by Communist indoctrination practices were predisposed before they were subjected to them (Lifton 1961: 130; Schein 1961: 104–110, 140–156; 1973: 295).

3. Physical coercion. Communist indoctrination practices produced involuntary influence only in that subjects were forced to participate through extreme physical coercion (Lifton 1961: 13; 1976: 327–328; Schein 1959: 43726; 1961: 125–127).

4. Continuity with normal social influence. The nonphysical techniques of influence utilized in Communist thought reform are common in normal social influence situations (Lifton 1961: 438–461; Schein 1961: 269–282; 1962: 90–97; 1964: 331–351).

5. Conditioning. No distinctive conditioning procedures were utilized in Communist coercive persuasion (Schein 1959: 437–438; 1973: 284–285; Biderman 1962: 550).

6. Psychophysiological stress/debilitation. The extreme physically based stress and debilitation to which imprisoned thought reform victims were subjected did not cause involuntary commitment to Communist worldviews (Hinkle and Wolff 1956; Lifton 1961: 117, 248–249; Schein 1958: 332; 1961: 157–166; 1973: 295). Moreover, no comparable practices are present in new religious movements (Anthony 1990: 309–311).

7. Deception/defective thought. Victims of Communist thought reform did not become committed to Communism as a result of deception or defective thought (Schein 1961: 202–203, 238–39).

8. Dissociation/hypnosis/suggestibility. Those subjected to thought reform did not become hyper-suggestible as a result of altered states of consciousness—hypnosis, dissociation, disorientation, and so on (Schein 1959: 457; Biderman 1962: 550).

The primary basis for Zablocki's exit costs third-stage brainwashing perspective is this: the research of Lifton and Schein had demonstrated that Communist thought reform could bring about a conversion to the Communism worldview that (1) did not result from predisposing motives to respond favorably to Communist ideology; (2) resulted from disorientation, suppression of critical thought, hyper-suggestibility, and the resulting inability to resist propaganda advocating an alternative worldview; (3) persisted once the thought reform process had been completed; (4) was difficult for the convert to Communism to repudiate even when he or she desired to do so.

As Anthony demonstrated (1990, 1996, 2001), however, all of these propositions were disconfirmed by Schein's and Lifton's research. None of their subjects became Communists at any point, and only a very small number showed any degree of increased sympathy for Communist ideas. Those few who became more sympathetic to Communism did so because of predisposing motives to respond favorably to Communist ideology rather than because of a disoriented state, decreased cognitive ability, hyper-suggestibility, or a resulting inability to resist ideas to which they were not naturally attracted. Furthermore, there was no evidence that those subjects felt trapped or mentally imprisoned by their sympathy for some Communist ideas.

It would seem that, like Singer and Ofshe's account of the brainwashing paradigm, Zablocki's "exit costs" brainwashing theory conflicts in fundamental ways with its claimed theoretical and empirical foundation of generally accepted research on Communist thought reform. If there is any scientific support for Zablocki's brainwashing perspective, it would have to come from other sources.

In our discussion of the history of the conversion concept, we showed that in Western history the concept typically has been interpreted as the transformation of person's identity to a form that embodies a deeper commitment to a religious worldview to which he was already superficially committed. It is only in relatively recent times that conversion has been seen as necessarily involving switching to a different religious worldview or organizational commitment.

The "conversion" or "born again" experience, common in Western religious history from English and American puritanism to contemporary American revivals such as the ones conducted by Billy Graham, has typically not involved religious switching in the sense assumed by some versions of cultic brainwashing theory. Adopting a new worldview and changing one's religious affiliation may or may not be as aspect of religious conversion, but it is the adoption of a "new" self and a "new" more religiously committed way of life that is the essence of conversion concept.

Zablocki's reinterpretation of the brainwashing concept as a coercively imposed transformation of identity and a dramatically enhanced degree of commitment to a preexisting religious worldview is compatible with conversion in this traditional sense. In terms of the scientific evaluation of the brainwashing idea, it is not significant whether such coercive conversion to a different self and a deeper level of commitment to a religious worldview is conceptualized as occurring at the beginning of an an attachment to a religious worldview or coercively imposed after the initial commitment to the worldview has already begun. In either case, this transformation involves "conversion" in the sense of a religiously significant self-transformation.

The key issue here is whether the transformation of self and commitment (to a new or to a preexisting worldview) has been coercively imposed in a way that contradicts the free will of the individual, and whether that claim of coercive influence has been confirmed by scientific research. As we have shown, in its major dimensions and empirical claims, Zablocki's exit costs formulation is the same as the earlier versions of brainwashing theory that he claims to repudiate as unscientific. Zablocki's formulation, like all other brainwashing formulations, is essentially a minor, cosmetically altered version of the same basic theory. That core brainwashing theory has been conclusively disconfirmed in all of the realms in which it has been scientifically evaluated.

CONCLUSION

This essay has achieved its purpose if it has raised some doubts about the simplistic brainwashing model of participation in new religions or other social movements and has suggested a more nuanced, interactive model. Those who undergo a conversion tend to be seekers who experiment with the transformation of the self to a deeper and more religiously committed form.

Notwithstanding some groups' deception and manipulation in their self-presentation, there is generally some "elective affinity" between the group and the recruit, and this commences a process of interaction in which certain types of individuals and certain types of groups jointly create a religious milieu. The group may strongly influence the devotee and play a necessary but not sufficient condition in the nature of his/her conversion to a new self, but devotees also influence the evolution of groups, even when a group attracts many unstable persons or when participants' orientations entail an expectation of strong, charismatic leadership.

Recruits frequently defect when they perceive that a group does not meet their needs, is ideologically or otherwise in congruent with their predispositions, or is evolving in a problematic direction. The selectivity of potential recruits and potential defectors would appear to limit the application of the extrinsic model. Moreover, contrary to the exit costs' interpretation, members of relatively totalitarian groups are more apt to defect than members of more democratic groups. This would seem to indicate that so-called cults have lower rather than higher exit costs when compared to more democratic groups. There appears to be little evidence that people are confined in totalistic groups against their will or that the "new self" resulting from a conversion experience in such groups is imposed in a way that is independent of the nature of their preconversion selves.

This essay has a subtext. The realities of recruitment, defection, and authoritarianism in even totalistic "cults" cannot fully explain the fixation of the anticult movement on the use of "mind control" and allied constructs to characterize or stigmatize conversion/commitment processes in "cults." Elsewhere we have documented a latent or concealed concern with the content of cultic beliefs on the part of the fiercest critics of "destructive cults" (Anthony 1990; Anthony and Robbins 1996). As noted, through various "disestablishments" (Hammond 1992) American culture and religion have evolved in a direction in which personal autonomy, religious diversity, and lifestyle choices have continually expanded. The proliferation of esoteric movements may reflect the emergence of a new postmodern cultural stage.

The authors believe that the anticult movement is a kind of revitalization movement for a modern (as opposed to postmodern) culture in which there has been considerable spiritual diversity yet less than the current disorientating explosion, with its challenge to the dominant utilitarian individualist ethos. An additional dimension of the mind control fixation is related to the problematic quality of autonomy in the postmodern world, in which an expansion of apparent diversity and choice coexists with both a cultural celebration of individualism and latent anxieties over hidden threats to personal autonomy emanating from mass advertising, state surveillance, new technology, the "iron cage" of bureaucratic rationalism, currents of fanaticism, and so on. As James Beckford suggested in *Cult Controversies* (1985), the symbolic and social issues raised by controversies over cults may ultimately be more significant than the movements themselves.

NOTES

1. For summaries of conversion research in the 1970s and 1980s, see Snow and Machalek 1984 and Robbins 1988: 63–99. See also Machalek and Snow 1993 and Richardson 1993. For an overview of cult/brainwashing discourse, see Dawson 1998: 102–127. See also Zablocki and Robbins 2001 for several papers representing different perspectives on cult/brainwashing issues.

2. See particularly Flo Conway and Jim Siegelman's popular volume *Snapping: America's Epidemic of Mass Personality Change* (1978; 2d ed., 1986).

3. Political and therapeutic ideologies such as Marxism and Freudian psychoanalysis may also qualify as varieties of self-estrangement theory.

4. On suicidal/homicidal collective violence associated with alternative religions, see Robbins and Palmer 1997, Dawson 1998: 128–157, Hall et al. 2000, Wessinger 2000, Richardson 2001, Anthony et al. 2002. It is not the view of the present writers that there are no objectionable, disruptive or even pathological and dangerous elements associated with some deviant religious movements (cf. Anthony et al. 1991; Robbins 1997, 2002).

5. Conversion has often been thought of as something that happens to or is done to a more or less passive recipient, e.g., Saint Paul being converted by a divine voice on the road to Damascus. Richardson (1985, 1993) argues that conversion is often a dynamic active endeavor on the part of the convert and particularly with regard to converts to new movements.

6. Majority opinion of Judge Stanley Mosk et al., *David Molko and Tracy Leal vs. the Holy Spirit for the Unification of World Christianity*. 762 p. 2d 46 (Cal. 1988), p. 52.

7. Schein (1961: 125–127). Elsewhere Schein (1959) has suggested that elements of coercive persuasion may be found in many conventional institutions such as reputable religious orders, college fraternities, etc. This latter view expands the coercive persuasion idea beyond the setting of physical constraint but still affords little basis for separating "cults" from other institutions as distinctively coercive, i.e., coercive persuasion becomes nearly ubiquitous. See Anthony and Robbins 1992.

8. Lifton employs the term "brainwashing" a number of times in his book (1961), but generally puts the term in quotation marks. Moreover, he demystifies the term, rejecting "an image of 'brainwashing' as an all-powerful, irresistible, unfathomable and magical method of achieving total control over the human mind." Such misleading and sensational usage "makes the word a rallying point for fear, resentment, urges toward submission. Justification for failure, irresponsible, accusation and for a wide gamut of emotional extremism" (1961: 4). We would argue that Lifton is not really writing in the brainwashing tradition of Sargent, Meerloo (1956), and others. He has been interpreted in this connection in part because of the Cold War context and partly because of the harsh conditions that the Chinese officials imposed on the subjects he describes.

9. Darrow and Simon were particularly predisposed or susceptible to manipulation by totalitarian captors because, as Lifton notes, they lacked the strong beliefs and integrative totalist center of their fellow captive, fundamentalist Bishop Barker. Darrow and Simon thus "responded very strongly to the opportunity to merge with the Chinese

people," and through their embrace of new values and their evident "sincerity," cope with their guilt feelings. "Both achieved a greater harmony with their prison environment than with any they had previously known" (Lifton 1961: 218).

10. This is not to say that the brutal treatment of their subjects by the Chinese communists wasn't atrocious or didn't "cause" the conversions by compelling subjects to remain accessible to their captors. Theorists in the crusade against cults maintain that *deception* employed by some cult recruiters (which appears to us as basically a foot-in-the-door tactic) is the functional equivalent of the raw physical constraint employed by totalitarian officials in initially bringing and keeping subjects in an indoctrination setting (Delgado 1977). It has also been claimed that the subtle and purely psychological (i.e., nonphysical) persuasive methods of cults more potent and destructive than the crude tactics of communist totalitarians (Ofshe and Singer 1986). Of course, the use of physical coercion may well reduce the amount of authentic, persisting orientational shift (as opposed to short-term behavioral compliance), but simply because nonphysically coercive methods may be more effective than crude constraint doesn't mean that "subtle" nonphysically coercive methods are more involuntarist.

11. It is worth noting that *The Authoritarian Personality* (Adorno et al. 1950) represents, in part the culmination of an initially European tradition of theorizing about the appeal of racism that involved scholars such as Hannah, Arendt, William Reich, and Erich Fromm. As the Cold War developed and concern shifted from fascism to communism the focus of inquiry shifted from the types of persons who are attracted to totalitarianism to the manipulative indoctrination methods employed by sinister communist regimes to remold followers (Anthony and Robbins 1984). See Erikson 1942 for an early contribution to the original European tradition of inquiry into the appeal of totalism that anticipates some of the ideas developed here.

12. Dr. Barker's book (1984) received the Distinguished Book Award from the Society for the Scientific Study of Religion. In the late 1970s and early 1980s, the Unification Church ("Moonies") was in its heyday and was generally considered the most controversial and stigmatized "destructive cult."

13. Barker's analysis of the on-site intensive indoctrination process really picks up where Zimbardo and Hartley's discussion of preliminary contacts with cult recruiters leaves off.

14. Levine (1984ab) claims to have heavily studied fifteen groups and several hundred individuals. These are part of a larger group of about a thousand individuals who, as a therapist and consultant, he has had some contact with (or with their relative). The 1970s and 1980s may have been the heyday of youth culture alternative religions.

15. See Reimer and Reimer 1982, Bromley 1987, Wright 1988, Rochford et al. 1989, and Wright and Ebaugh 1993.

16. See Solomon 1981, Wright 1984, and Lewis 1986.

17. This pattern is evident in a study of a racist Christian Identity Group (Young 1990). "Identity members engage in self-idealization" (1990: 150) and project defects and weaknesses onto outsiders. "To perceive oneself as pure, impure feelings and impulses must be projected into a world where they become embodied in others" (Young 1990: 157). The racist leader legitimates recruits' existing pent-up hostility and directs it toward designated ideological scapegoats. "As a transitional object, the cult leader helps members express hostile impulses . . . when the cult leader initiates an antisocial act. . . . Cult leaders become free to act in a guiltless and violent way" (1990: 157). See also

Wright and Wright 1980, an important theoretical piece on leaders of solidarity groups as parental surrogates and "transitional objects."

18. For evidence of elitism, paranoia, and conspiracy theories in the Church of Scientology, see (surprisingly) *The Scientology Handbook* (1994), an official publication based on the writings of founder L. Ron Hubbard. For discussions of elitism, volatility, and antinomianism in various groups, see Anthony, Eckard, and Wilber (88).

19. In an unpublished but provocative study (Jones et al.), a Hare Krishna sample scored the highest among eleven samples of (mainly but not entirely unconventional) religious groups to whom was administered a revised authoritarianism (F. Scale) measure in Berkeley in 1980 under the supervision of R. Nevitt Sanford, one of the original coauthors of *The Authoritarian Personality* (Adorno et al. 1950).

20. The "Dogmatism" construct and "D" scale were developed by Milton Rokeach in attempt to refine the earlier "Authoritarian Personality" construct into a pure measure of cognitive style.

21. Anthony's approach has served as the primary basis for legal briefs (motions in limine, summary judgment motions, appeal briefs) designed to convince judges to exclude cultic brainwashing testimony because of the unscientific character of the brainwashing formulations upon which it is based. (As a legal consultant and expert witness Anthony has both testified against the scientific standing of cultic brainwashing testimony and has also helped lawyers in applying this approach to the legal issues and facts of specific cases.)

See Anthony 1990 for the original statement of the argument that has become the primary basis for legal briefs and testimony arguing the unscientific character of cultic brainwashing testimony; see Anthony 1996, 2000; and Anthony and Robbins 1992, 1995a, for elaborations of this basic argument and descriptions of its effects upon cultic brainwashing legal cases.

22. On 223 Zablocki quotes Lifton as arguing that cults produce "doubling" in their converts. The quote from Lifton is the following: "Intense milieu control can contribute to a dramatic change of identity which I call 'doubling': the formation of a second self which lives side by side with the former one, often for a considerable period of time" (Lifton 1991: 2). I am not sure what Lifton intended his readers to understand by this statement, but he could not accurately be claiming, as Zablocki interprets him as claiming, that his "doubling" concept is equivalent to the brainwashing notion of a false or shadow self. Lifton developed the concept of *doubling*, by which he meant the simultaneous existence of two radically dissimilar selves in the same person, which would express themselves in contradictory manners in different social contexts, to account for the behavior of Nazi doctors who engaged in inhumane medical research in their Nazi professional context but who were during the same period humane and decent individuals with their families (Lifton 1986; 1987: 195–208).

Doubling as Lifton defines it may be seen as an extreme example of the very different interpersonal styles which people in modern industrialized nations express in their professional and their personal lives. In the former they may be highly competitive (and metaphorically bloodthirsty) capitalists whereas in the personal context they may be humane and loving. The differences in ethical and interpersonal character of the same people in the economic vs. the personal spheres in a much remarked upon characteristic of modern societies which has served as a central organizing principle of major sociological theories, e.g., those of Parsons and Habermas.

On the other hand, Zablocki's and other brainwashing theorists conception of the false or shadow self, is very different than the concept of doubling in that it involves the notion of a new but inauthentic self which replaces the original and authentic self rather than living side by side with it at the same time in the same person. If the brain-washed person as described by Zablocki, Singer, and other cult brainwashing theorists were characterized by doubling they should be able to move smoothly back and forth between the cult and the pre-cult or familial contexts without apparent difficulty. But Zablocki and his cohort describe the brainwashed person as being unable to this except with great difficulty. See, for instance, Zablocki's discussion of what he refers to as the "shadow self imbued with the cult ideology" (1998: 236, 237). See also West and Martin, 1994.

Doubling as Lifton defines it, no matter how extreme, could not reasonably be in-terpreted as implying the involuntary, compulsive or addictive attachment to a false self that Zablocki imputes to it. According to Lifton, doubling is the normal means by which people choose to engage in immoral activity. As such it is voluntarily chosen by the person rather than being imposed upon him/her by an external agent or institution. In addressing the involuntariness issue relative to the doubling concept, Lifton says: "In sum, doubling is the psychological means by which one invokes the evil potential of the self. That evil is neither inherent in the self nor foreign to it. To live out the doubling and call forth the evil is a moral choice for which one is responsible, whatever the level of consciousness involved. By means of doubling, Nazi doctors made a Faustian choice for evil: in the process of doubling, in fact, lies an overall key to human evil" (1986: 423, 424; Lifton repeats the same quote in his 1987 article: 201).

23. Disorientation has an accepted and well-defined scientific meaning in only in two interrelated scientific field, i.e., psychiatry and neurology. In those fields, disorienta-tion refers only to the specific lack of awareness of one's identity, the time and date, and one's geographical location. See Campbell 1981: 180, 434. See also *Webster's Un-abridged Dictionary* (1996), s.v. "disorient": "*Psychiatry.* to cause to lose perception of time, place or one's personal identify." In these definitions, personal identity refers only to literal awareness of one's name and of one's status as a specific psychological/physical entity with a specific physical and social history. It does not refer to the subtler and more controversial discontinuities in selfhood that are alleged to be a consequence of brainwashing. Testing for "orientation" with respect to personal identity, place, and time is generally the first test conducted in a standard psychiatric interview of mental status exam. Disorientation in this sense is considered to indicate that the patient is suffering from a neurological rather than a psychological disorder, e.g., one of the senile demen-tias, or a toxic brain conditioned induced by drugs or physical disease.

In defining brainwashing as a process that is accomplished primarily by means of disorientation, Zablocki appears to be giving the disorientation term a more meta-phorical and less precise meaning than its scientific meaning in psychiatry, as a way of disputing the allegedly transcendent or mystical character of the altered states of con-sciousness in which religious influence often occurs. In this less precise form, however, disorientation is an evaluative rather than a scientific term, as it is unfalsifiable. That is, thus used, the term has no clear operational definition such that its presence could be disconfirmed in research on the conversion process. In discussing this issue with Za-blocki, he was unable to provide me with a precise scientific definition for his usage such that its absence in a specific instance could be empirically determined, and he questioned whether the term has the restricted meaning in psychiatry which I have specified above. However, he was unable to provide me with a citation to any other well-accepted and falsifiable usage in psychiatry or any other science.

As I have indicated, in psychiatry or neurology, lack of orientation with respect to person place and time is considered to be diagnostic or some form of organic brain dysfunction, as opposed to the sorts of mental disease that have social environmental and psychodynamic causes. In the latter part of his 1998 article, Zablocki claims that brainwashing has an organic basis (neuroendocrinological or neurophysiological) and is thus distinguishable from other forms of social influence on this basis. In using the term disorientation rather than hypnosis or trance, Zablocki may have been implying this speculative organic basis for brainwashing. As I will discuss below, he bases his hopes that the brainwashing concept will some day be falsifiable on the assumption that it has a distinctively organic basis. However, as he admits in that section, he cannot provide any scientific or empirically falsifiable basis for this speculation, and his vague and unfalsifiable use of the disorientation term seems consistent with this admission.

24. Zablocki does supply a scientific citation for his use of the term "hypnotic suggestibility," which he uses as an apparent synonym for the meaning he gives to the disorientation term in the passages quoted above. On page 237 of his 1998 brainwashing article he claims that Orne's 1972 article reports research that demonstrates that people "can be hypnotized to do things against their will." As I will discuss below, however, Orne's article demonstrates findings which are exactly the opposite of the conclusion that Zablocki imputes to it: that is, Orne's research demonstrated that *hypnosis cannot be used to get people to do things against their will.* In Zablocki's case as is typical for brainwashing theorists, the terms for primitive consciousness viewed as essential for brainwashing are either so vaguely defined that they unfalsifiable, or when they are defined through a claimed basis in scientific research, that research is typically misinterpreted, as with Zablocki's and other brainwashing theorists' claim that the brainwashing thesis is based upon Lifton's and Schein's research.

Orne has done some interesting experimental work on the extent to which subjects can be hypnotized to do things against their will.

25. In his 1980 book Zablocki describes the disorientation and cognitive deficiency which he believes to be characteristic of the imposition of the brainwashed state thusly: "The *cognitive disorder* associated with type 5, or absolute, charisma is submissiveness. The common manifestations of this among cult members, *the glassy eyes, the hollow beaming smile,* are too well known to need examples here. As many accounts of cult experiences have indicated (e.g., Edwards 1979), *these exaggerated symptoms of extreme cognitive submissiveness (turning off the mind)* are a conditioned response, among cult members, to any challenge to the absolute truth of the cult reality" (Zablocki 1980: 332, emphasis mine). On the next page Zablocki describes the transition of a group from being a legitimate Christian group to a brainwashed cult: "It was at this time also that *the glassy-eyed, frozen smile look* began to appear on the faces of the Waystation members. In terms of our model this was a symptom of a crisis of *self-estrangement.* A sense of legitimate total commitment to the charismatic leader had given way *to an artificial forced total commitment, maintained only through adherence to the mind-emptying discipline of submissiveness*" (Zablocki 1980: 333, emphasis mine). In his 1998 article Zablocki acknowledges that research has demonstrated that such disorientation and defective cognition are not characteristic of allegedly brainwashed member so so-called cults (pg.

232), but he attempts to get around this by claiming that these qualities are only essential characteristics of cult converts during the process of brainwashing rather than after they have been successfully brainwashed. "The popular association of brainwashing with zombie or robot states comes out of a confusion between the physical characteristics of people *going through* the brainwashing process and the characteristics of those who have completed the process" (232, emphasis in the original). In his earlier book however, he appears to be saying that such cognitive defects are continuing characteristics of cult members, i.e., "an artificial forced total commitment, maintained only through adherence to the mind-emptying discipline of submissiveness." It is likely that this shift (from viewing disorientation and extreme cognitive defects as essential to the ongoing maintenance of brainwashed "forced total commitment" to the cult, to viewing disorientation and extreme cognitive defects as characteristic only of the process of brainwashing but not of continuing commitment to the cult), is an example of tactical ambiguity in the face of disconfirming evidence.

26. Schein states: "The coercive element in coercive persuasion is paramount (forcing the individual into a situation in which he must, in order to survive physically and psychologically, expose himself to persuasive attempts)" (1959: 437).

REFERENCES

Abgrall, Jean-Marie. 1990. *Rapport Sur L'Eglise de Scientology: Les Techniques de la Scientology, La Doctrine Dianetique de la, Leurs Consequences Medico-legals.* Submitted in Criminal Prosecution for Fraud, Case No. 90: 6119074, Higher Court of Marseilles.
———. 1996. *La Mechanique des Sectes.* Paris: Documents Payot.
———. 1999a. *L'Apocalypse: Gourus de l'an 2000.* Paris: Calmann-Levy.
———. 1999b. *Soul Snatchers: The Mechanism of Cults* (translation of *La Mechanique des Sectes*). New York: Algora.
Adorno, Thedore, Else Frenkel-Brunswick, Daniel Levinson, and R. Nevitt Sanford. 1950. *The Authoritarian Personality.* New York: Norton.
Altemeyer, Bob. 1981. *Right-Wing Authoritarianism.* Winnipeg: University of Manitoba Press.
———. 1988. *Enemies of Freedom.* New York: Jossey-Bass.
Anthony, Dick. 1979–1980. "The Fact Pattern Behind the Deprogramming Controversy." *New York Review of Law and Social Change* 9, no. 1: 73–90.
———. 1990. "Religious Movements and Brainwashing Litigation: Evaluating Key Testimony." In *In Gods We Trust*, ed. Thomas Robbins and Dick Anthony. New Brunswick, N.J.: Transaction.
———. 1996. *Brainwashing and Totalitarian Influence: An Exploration of Admissibility. Criteria for Testimony in Brainwashing Trials.* Ann Arbor: UMI Dissertation Services.
———. 1999. "Pseudoscience and Minority Religions: An Evaluation of the Brainwashing Theories of J. M. Abgrall." *Social Justice Research* 12, no. 4 (December): 421–456.
———. 2001. "Tactical Ambiguity and Brainwashing Formulations: Science or Pseudoscience." In B. Zablocki and T. Robbins, *Misunderstanding Cults*, 215–317. Toronto: Toronto University Press.

Anthony, Dick, and Thomas Robbins. 1992. "Law, Social Science and the 'Brainwashing' Exception to the First Amendment." *Behavioral Sciences and the Law* 10: 5–30.

———. 1994. "Brainwashing and Totalitarian Influence." In *Encyclopedia of Human Behavior*, ed. V. S. Ramchandran. San Diego: Academic Press.

———. 1995. "Negligence, Coercion and the Protection of Religious Belief." *Journal of Church and State* 37: 509–536.

———. 1996. "Religious Totalism, Violence and Exemplary Dualism." In *Millennialism and Violence*, ed. M. Barkun. London: Frank Cass.

Anthony, Dick, Thomas Robbins, and Steven Barrie-Anthony. 2002. "Cult and Anticult Totalism." *Terrorism and Political Violence* 14, no. 1 (Spring): 211–242.

Barber, T. X. 1961. "Antisocial and Criminal Acts Induced by Hypnosis: A Review of Experimental and Clinical Findings." *Archives of General Psychiatry* 5.

———. 1969. *Hypnosis: A Scientific Approach.* New York: Litton.

Barker, Eileen. 1984. *The Making of a Moonie: Choice or Brainwashing?* New York: Blackwell.

———. 1986. "Cult and Anticult Since Jonestown." *Annual Review of Sociology.*

———. 1989. *New Religious Movements.* London: HMSO.

Beckford, James. 1995. *Cult Controversies: The Societal Response to New Religious Movements.* London: Tavistock.

———. 1999. "Max Weber and World-Denying Love." *Journal of the American Academy of Religion* 67, no. 2: 277–304.

Bellah, Robert. 1970. *Beyond Belief.* New York: Harper and Row.

Benson, Dr. Samuel. 1977. Testimony of Dr. Samuel Benson, *Katz v. Superior Court.* 73 Cal. App. 3d 952141 Cal. Rptr., 234.

Biderman, A. 1962. "The Image of Brainwashing." *Public Opinion Quarterly* 26: 547–563.

Bird, Fred, and William Reimer. 1982. "Participation Rates in New Religious Movements." *Journal for the Scientific Study of Religion* 21, no. 1: 1–14.

Brian, Fay. 1987. *Critical Social Science.* Ithaca, N.Y.: Cornell University Press.

Bromley, David. 1988. *Falling from the Faith.* Newbury Park, Calif.: Sage.

———. 2002. "Dramatic Denouements." In David Bromley and J. G. Melton, eds., *Cults, Religion and Violence*, 11–41. Cambridge: Cambridge University Press.

Campbell, Ted. 1991. *The Religion of the Heart: A Study of European Religious Life in the Seventeenth and Eighteenth Centuries.* Columbia, S.C.: University of South Carolina Press.

Carter, Lewis. 1990. *Charisma and Control in Rajneeshpuram.* Cambridge: Cambridge University Press.

Clark, John. 1976. "Investigating the Effects of Some Religious Cults on the Health and Welfare of Their Converts." Testimony to the Special Investigating Committee of the Vermont Senate.

———. 1979. "Cults." *Journal of the American Medical Association* 242, no. 3: 279–281.

Condon, Richard. 1958. *The Manchurian Candidate.* New York: McGraw-Hill.

Conn, J. 1982. "The Myth of Coercion Under Hypnosis." In *Eriksonian Approaches to Hypnosis and Psychotherapy*, ed. J. Zeig, 357–368. New York: Brunner-Mazel.

Conway, Flo, and Jim Siegelman. 1978. *Snapping: America's Epidemic of Mass Personality Change.* Philadelphia: J. B. Lippincott.

Dawson, Lorne. 1998. *Comprehending Cults: The Sociology of New Religious Movements.* New York: Oxford University Press.

Delgado, Richard. 1977. "Religious Totalism." *South California Law Review* 51: 1–99.

Enroth, Ronald. 1984. "Brainwashing." In *Baker Encyclopedia of Psychology*, D. G. Benner. Grand Rapids, Mich.: Baker Book House.

Erikson, Erik. 1942. "Hitler's Imagery and German Youth." *Psychiatry* 5: 475–593.

———. 1954. "Wholeness and Totality: A Psychiatric Contribution." In *Totalitarianism*, ed. C. J. Friederich. Cambridge: Harvard University Press.

———. 1956. "The Problem of Ego Identity." *Journal of the Psychoanalytic Association* 4: 56–121.

Farber, I. E., H. F. Harlow, and L. J. West. 1957. "Brainwashing, Conditioning, and the DDD Syndrome." *Sociometry* 29: 271–285.

Fitzgerald, Frances. 1991. *Cities on a Hill: A Journey through Contemporary American Cultures*. New York: Touchstone/Simon and Schuster.

Fromm, E., and R. Shor. 1979. *Hypnosis: Developments in Research and New Perspectives*. New York: Aldine.

Galanter, Marc. 1980. "Psychological Induction into the Large Group: Findings from a Modern Religious Sect." *American Journal of Psychiatry* 137, no. 12.

———. 1989. *Cults: Faith, Healing and Coercion*. New York: Oxford University Press.

Gauld, A. 1992. *A History of Hypnotism*. Cambridge: Cambridge University Press.

Hall, John, Philip Schuyer, and Salvaine Trinh. 2000. *Apocalypse Observed: Religion Movements and Violence in Europe, N. America and Japan*. New York: Routledge.

Halperin, David. 1987. "Psychoanalysis and Cult Affiliation: Clinical Perspectives." *Cultic Studies Journal* 4, no. 1 (Spring–Summer).

Hammond, Phillip. 1992. *Religion and Personal Autonomy: The Third Disestablishment and America*. Columbia: University of South Carolina Press.

Hinkle, Lawrence and Harold Wolff. 1956. "Communist Interrogation and the indoctrination of 'Enemies of the State.'" *AMA Archives of Neurological Psychology* 76: 117–127.

Huber, John, and Lindsey Gruson. 1990. *Monkey on a Stick: Murder, Madness, and the Hare Krishnas*. New York: Onyx/Penguin.

Hunter, Edward. 1951. *Brainwashing in Red China*. New York: Vanguard.

———. 1960. *Brainwashing: From Pavlov to Powers*. New York: Bookmaster.

Jones, Constance. 1989. "Exemplary Dualism and Authoritarianism in Jonestown." In *New Religions, Mass Suicide and the Peoples Temple*, ed. Rebecca Moore and Fielding McGehee, 209–230. Lewiston, N.Y.: Edwin Mellen Press.

Jones, Constance, Paul Schwartz, and James McBridge. 1981. "Empirical Indicators of Authoritarianism in Religious Groups." Unpublished report.

Kirsch, I. 1995. Foreword to *Hypnosis: A Scientific Approach*, by T. X. Barber. New York: Jason Aronson.

Knox, Ronald. 1950. *Enthusiasm: A Chapter in the History of Religion*. London: Oxford University Press.

Latkin, Carl, Richard Littman, and Normal Sundberg. 1987. "Who Lives in Utopia: A Brief Report on the Rajneeshpuram Research Project." *Sociological Analysis* 48, no. 1.

Lewis, James. 1986. "Reconstructing the 'Cult' Experience." *Sociological Analysis* 47, no. 2: 151–159.

Lewis, James, and David Bromley. 1988. "Cult 'Information Disease': A Misattribution of Cause?" *Journal for the Scientific Study of Religion* 26, no. 1: 508–522.

Levine, Saul. 1984a. *Radical Departures: Desperate Detours to Growing Up*. London: Harcourt, Brace and Jovanovich.

———. 1984b. "Radical Departures." *Psychology Today* 18, no. 8: 20–29.

Lifton, Robert. 1961. *Chinese Thought Reform and the Psychology of Totalism*. New York: Norton.

———. 1968. "Protean Man." *Partisan Review* 35: 13–27.

———. 1993. *The Protean Self: Human Resilience in an Age of Fragmentation*. New York: Basic Books.

———. 1999. *Destroying the World to Save It: Aum Shinrikyo, Apocalyptic Violence, and the New Global Terrorism*. New York: Holt.

Machalak, Richard, and David Snow. 1993. "Conversion to New Religious Movements." In *The Handbook of Cults and Sects in America, Religious and the Social Order*, ed. D. Bromley and J. Hadden, part 3B. Greenwich, Conn.: JAI Press.

Martin, Paul. 1993. "Post-Cult Recovery: Assessment and Rehabilitation." In *Recovery from Cults*, ed. M. Langone, 201–231. New York: Norton.

Meerloo, Joost. 1956. *The Rape of the Mind: The Psychology of Thought Control, Menticide, and Brainwashing*. Cleveland: World Publishing.

Miller, Jesse. 1986. "The Utilization of Hypnotic Techniques in Religious Conversions." *Cultic Studies Journal* 3: 243–250.

Milne, Hugh. 1986. *Bhagawan: God That Failed*. New York: Caliban Books/St. Martin's.

Ofshe, Richard. 1989. "Report Regarding Mr. Steven Fishman." Submitted for Court Case *U.S. v. Fishman,* 743 F. Supp. (N.D. Cal. 90).

Ofshe, Richard, and Margaret Singer. 1986. "Attacks on Peripheral vs. Central Elements of the Self and the Impact of Thought Reform Techniques." *Cultic Studies Journal* 3: 2–24.

Orne, Martin. 1961. "The Potential Uses of Hypnosis in Interrogation." In *The Manipulation of Human Behavior*, ed. A. Biderman, H. Zimmer. New York: Wiley.

———. 1962. "Antisocial Behavior and Hypnosis." In *Hypnosis: Current Problems*, ed. G. Estabrooks. New York: Harper and Row.

Paloutzian, R., J. Richardson, and L. Rambo. 1999. "Religious Conversion and Personality Change." *Journal of Personality* 67: 1047–1049.

Poling, T., and J. Kenney. 1986. *The Hare Krishna Character Type*. Lewiston, N.Y.: Edwin Mellen Press.

Richardson, James. 1978. *Conversion Careers: In and Out of the New Religions*. Beverly Hills, Calif.: Sage.

———. 1985. "The Active vs. the Passive Convert: Paradigm Conflict in Conversion/ Recruitment Research." *Journal for the Scientific Study of Religion* 24, no. 2: 163–179.

———. 1993. "A Social Psychological Critique of 'Brainwashing' Claims About Recruitment to New Religions." In *The Handbook of Sects and Cults in America, Religion and the Social Order*, ed. D. Bromley and J. Hadden, part 3B, 75–98. Greenwich, Conn.: JAI Press.

———. 1995. "Clinical and Personality Assessments of Participants in New Religions." *International Journal for the Psychology of Religion* 5, no. 3: 145–170.

———. 2001. "Minority Religions and the Context of Violence." *Terrorism and Political Violence* 13, no. 1 (Spring): 103–133.

Robbins, Thomas. 1979. "Cults and the Therapeutic State." *Social Policy* (May/June): 42–46.

Robbins, Thomas, and Dick Anthony. 1995. "Sects and Violence." In *Armageddon in Waco*, ed. S. Wright, 236–259. Chicago: University of Chicago Press.

Robbins, Thomas, and Susan Palmer, eds. 1997. *Millennium, Messiahs, and Mayhem.* New York: Routledge.

Rocheford, E. Burke, Sheryl Purvis, and Nemer Estman. 1993. "New Religions, Mental Health and Social Control." *Research in the Social Sciences of Religion* 1: 67–82.

Rokeach, Milton. 1960. *The Open and Closed Mind.* New York: Basic Books.

Ross, Michael. 1983. "Clinical Profiles of Hare Krishna Devotees." *American Journal of Psychiatry* 140: 416–420.

Saliba, John. 1993. "The New Religions and Mental Health." In *The Handbook of Sects and Cults in America, Religion and the Social Order*, ed. D. Bromley and J. Hadden, part 3B, 99–103. Greenwich, Conn.: JAI Press.

Sargent, William. 1951. "The Mechanism of Conversion." *British Medical Journal* 2: 311–316.

———. 1957. *Battle for the Human Mind.* London: Heineman.

———. 1974. *The Mind Possessed: A Physiology of Possession, Mysticism and Faith Healing.* Philadelphia: Lippincott.

Schein, Edgar. 1958. "The Chinese Indoctrination Program for Prisoners of War: A Study of Attempted 'Brainwashing.' " In *Readings in Social Psychology*, ed. E. Maccoby et al. New York: Holt.

———. 1959. "Brainwashing and the Totalitarianization of Modern Societies." *World Politics* 2: 430–441.

———. 1961. *Coercive Persuasion.* New York: Norton.

———. 1964. "Management Development as a Process of Influence." In H. Leavitt and L. Pondy, eds., *Readings in Managerial Psychology.* Chicago: University of Chicago Press.

Scientology Handbook. 1994. Los Angeles: Bridge Publications.

Shapiro, Robert. 1983. "Of Robots, Persons and the Protection of Religious Beliefs." *Southern California Law Review* 6: 1277–1308.

Simmonds, Robert. 1978. "Conversion or Addiction?" In *Conversion Careers*, ed. J. Richardson. Beverly Hills, Calif.: Sage.

Singer, Margaret. 1983. *Testimony in Robin and Maria George v. Int. Society for Krishna Consciousness of Cal. et al.* Orange County Superior Court.

———. 1994. "Thought Reform Exists: Organized, Programmatic Influence." *Cult Observer* 17, no. 4.

Singer, Margaret, and L. J. West. 1980. "Cults, Quacks, and Non-Professional Psychotherapies." In *Comprehensive Textbook of Psychiatry III*, ed. H. Kaplan and B. Saddock. Baltimore: Wilkins and Wilkins.

Singer, Margaret, and Richard Ofshe. 1990. "Thought Reform Programs and the Production of Psychiatric Casualties." *Psychiatric Annuals* 20, no. 4: 188–193.

Singer, Margaret, and Janja Lalich. 1995. *Cults in Our Midst: The Hidden Menace in Our Everyday Lives.* San Francisco: Jossey-Bass.

Snow, David, and Robert Machalek. 1984. "The Sociology of Conversion." *Annual Review of Sociology* 10: 167–190.

Solomon, Trudy. 1981. "Integrating the 'Moonie' Experience: A Study of Ex-Member of the Unification Church." In *In Gods We Trust*, ed. Thomas Robbins and Dick Anthony. New Brunswick, N.J.: Transaction.

Spanos, Nikos. 1996. "Multiple Identities and False Memories: A Sociocognitive Perspective." Washington: American Psychological Association.

Sundberg, Norman, Carl Latkin, Richard Littman, and Richard Hagan. 1992. "Personality in a Richard Commune." *Journal of Personality Assessment* 55: 7–17.

Verdier, Paul. 1980. *Brainwashing and the Cults.* N. Hollywood, Calif · Wilshire.

Weber, Max. 1946. *From Max Weber: Essays in Sociology.* Trans. H. H. Gerth and C. W. Mills. New York: Oxford University Press.

Weiss, A., and A. Mendoza. 1900. "Effects of Acculturation into Hare Krishna on Mental Health and Personality." *Journal for the Scientific Study of Religion* 29: 173–184.

Wessinger, Catherine. 2000. *How the Millennium Comes Violently.* New York: Seven Bridges Press.

West, Louis, and Paul Martin. 1994. "Pseudo-Identity and the Treatment of Personality Change in Victims of Captivity and Cults." In S. Lynne and J. Rhine, eds., *Dissociation: Clinical and Theoretical Perspectives.* New York: Guilford.

West, L. J. 1975. "In Defense of Deprogramming" (pamphlet). Arlington, Tex.: International Foundation for Individual Freedom.

Winnicott, D. 1960. "Ego Distortion in Terms of True and False Self." In *The Maturational Process and the Facilitating Environment,* 15–20. London: Routledge.

Wright, F., and P. Wright. 1980. "The Charismatic Leader and the Violent Surrogate Family." *Annals of the New York Academy of Science* 347: 66–76.

Wright, Stuart. 1987. *Leaving Cults: The Dynamics of Defection.* Washington: Society for the Scientific Study of Religion.

Wright, Stuart, and Helen Ebaugh. 1993. "Leaving New Religions." In *The Handbook of Cults and Sects in America, Religion and the Social Order,* ed. D. Bromley and J. Hadden, 117–138. Greenwich, Conn.: JAI Press.

Wuthnow, Robert. 1976. *The Consciousness Reformation.* Berkeley: University of California Press.

———. 1978. *Experimentation in American Religion.* Berkeley: University of California Press.

Young, Thomas. 1990. "Cult Violence and the Identity Movement." *Cultic Studies Journal* 7, no. 2: 150–157.

Zablocki, Benjamin. 1971. *The Joyful Community,* Baltimore: Penguin.

———. 1980. *Alienation and Charisma: A Study of Contemporary Communes.* New York: Free Press.

———. 1993. "Rational Models of Charismatic Influence." In S. Lynne and J. Rhine, eds., *Essays in Honor of James S. Coleman.* Westport, Conn.: Praeger.

———. 1997. "The Blacklisting of a Concept: The Strange History of the Brainwashing Conjecture in the Sociology of Religion." *Nova Religio* 1: 96–112.

———. 1998. "Exit Cost Analysis: A New Approach to the Scientific Study of Brainwashing." *Nova Religio* 2, no. 1: 216–249.

Zablocki, Benjamin, and Thomas Robbins. 2001. *Misunderstanding Cults: Searching for Objectivity in a Contested Field.* Toronto: Toronto University Press.

Zimbardo, Phillip, Ebbe Ebbesen, and Christian Masloch. 1977. *Influencing Attitudes and Changing Behaviors.* Reading, Mass.: Addison-Wesley.

Zimbardo, Phillip, and Cynthia Hartley. 1985. "Cults Go to High School." *Cultic Studies Journal* 2: 91–147.

CHAPTER 12

LEAVING THE FOLD

Disaffiliating from New Religious Movements

DAVID G. BROMLEY

CONVERSION has been the dominant topic of theory and research in the study of new religious movements (NRMs). The outpouring of research on conversion is attributable to two factors. The appearance and growth of NRMs challenged the widespread expectation among social scientists that the contemporary social order was becoming ever more secular in nature. This challenge was even more direct because the primary constituency for NRMs has been the middle-class young adults who were expected to constitute the leading edge of secularization. Conversion also became a focus of scholarly interest as a result of allegations that NRM memberships were not the product of authentic conversions but rather pseudoconversions produced by "brainwashing" programs administered by NRM leaders. The intellectual and public policy controversies surrounding NRMs have spawned a large number of theoretical models and field studies on NRM recruitment practices beginning in the 1970s (Saliba 1990; Snow 1984).

Research and theorizing on the process of exiting NRMs began a few years later when scholars discovered that NRM membership size was not increasing as rapidly as expected in light of recruitment successes. Indeed, none of the largest, most visible and most controversial movements that launched the study of NRMs—the Unificationist movement, The Family, Hare Krishna—attained a total membership of more than a few thousand members despite vigorous recruitment programs. Researchers quickly resolved this apparent anomaly when they observed that individuals were leaving NRMs at rates at least as high as the rates at which they were joining (Barker 1984, 1988; Galanter 1980). This discovery triggered a new body of theory and research on the exiting process. The observation that the rates of joining and leaving NRMs were both high made it evident that the traditional conceptualization of conversion as a major moment of spiritual transformation that permanently reoriented individual thought and action was not useful in interpreting the experiences of many NRM members. It also led to the conclusion that the processes of joining and leaving NRMs are equally significant in understanding their developmental histories. Since members' relationships to movements generally do not conform to the traditional concept of conversion, I argue that it is more productive to employ the term "affiliation." The corresponding term for deconversion is "disaffiliation." These concepts will be employed through the remainder of this chapter (Bromley 1991).

There has in fact been a broad reassessment of conversion as applied to NRMs. In interpreting individual transformations that do occur, some scholars have emphasized the adoption of a symbolic identity (Snow 1984) while others have emphasized movement role playing (Bromley and Shupe 1979a, 1979b, 1986). Distinctions have been drawn between different types of conversions. For example, Lofland and Skonovd (1981) have distinguished intellectual conversion, which involves a gradual cognitive acceptance of movement ideology; mystical conversion, which resembles the traditional conception of conversion as an instantaneous, spontaneous event; revivalist conversions, in which there is intense social pressure to make an immediate personal commitment; affective conversions, which evolve out of forming personal relationships with movement members; and experimental conversion, which entails gradual individual exploration of movement membership. Travisano (1970) has contrasted "alternation," a more transitory change that does not involve permanent transformation with conversion. Straus (1979) explores the joint influence of group and neophyte in producing what is termed a conversion. There has also been an often contentious intellectual and political debate over the "brainwashing" thesis, which finds a more significant sociological basis in the balance of structure and agency in producing personal transformation (Bromley and Richardson 1983; Zablocki and Robbins 2001).

The theory, research, and debate over affiliation/disaffiliation has yielded several conclusions. First, the extent to which affiliation involves a behavioral or identity change varies by individual and at different points in the affiliation process. This fact is often obscured since many movements prescribe role behavior, new affiliates typically adopt normative role behavior, and appropriate role behavior creates the appearance of identity change. Second, the extent of individual initiative and group influence in the affiliation varies by movement, within different components of the same movement, and within the same movement over time. Generalizations about the balance of individual/group determinacy are therefore problematic, which is one reason that the highly deterministic brain-washing thesis has been heavily criticized as a viable explanation for NRM membership. Third, if there are many types of conversion, then it appears that it is not a single phenomenon but rather a common destination that may be reached by diverse social paths. Finally, whatever personal transformations may occur during the affiliation process, they are not highly predictive of later behavior since most individuals ultimately disaffiliate.

These conclusions cumulate to the empirical reality that NRM membership is extremely variegated at any moment in time. Some individuals are in the process of affiliating while others are disaffiliating; some are experiencing profound personal transformations while others are simply experimenting. Since affiliation-disaffiliation is a continuum along which individuals are arrayed on several dimensions, it follows that individuals may disaffiliate at any point along that continuum. For purposes of the present analysis, I assume that individuals have formed at least a moderately strong connection to a movement on some dimension. Given that assumption, there are two basic questions to be addressed: (1) what are the factors that precipitate and contribute to disaffiliation, and (2) what are the identifiable phases of the disaffiliation process.

Factors Precipitating
Movement Disaffiliation

For individuals who developed a longer-term relationship and a higher level of involvement in their respective movements, three major issues giving rise to disaffiliation can be identified: disruption of internal solidarity, destabilization of leadership and authority, and problems in organizational development.

During their initial period of mobilization, NRMs typically seek to direct all of members' time and energy to the movement cause and to reduce competing demands on members' time and energy by creating strong organizational boundaries. Disruption of internal solidarity therefore can have major impact on members' commitment. One common cause of internal solidarity erosion is individual disconnection from the group. For example, individuals may be sent on missions of various types that isolate the person for extended periods of time. In the early history of Heaven's Gate, movement leaders sent a number of couples on missions that separated them from the group. Virtually all of those couples drifted away from the movement (Balch 1985). The Unificationist movement created a "pio-neer" program that required one or two individuals to establish movement pres-ence in remote locations, sometimes on other continents, with similar results (Bromley and Shupe 1979: 180–184). Another source of solidarity erosion has been employment of members outside the movement. Both the Hare Krishna move-ment and the Love Family encountered severe economic problems that forced them to require members to earn incomes to support the movement (Rochford 1984; Balch 1985). There were several consequences. Individuals had an opportu-nity to experience an alternative lifestyle each day, financial resources made em-ployed members less dependent on the group, and possession of financial re-sources created divisive inequality within the group. In the case of The Family, the practice of "flirty fishing" by The Family did directly not produce defections, but the movement discontinued the practice before defections occurred when the women involved began living increasingly separate lives and possessed consider-able power within the movement by virtue of generating economic resources (Chancellor 2000).

Charismatic leaders often embody the movements; adherents regard their re-lationship to the leader as highly personal, and it is difficult for them to conceive of the movement apart from the leader. Under these conditions, changes in the level of charismatic authority can impact member commitment. Two types of change are particularly important—claims to additional charismatic authority and erosion of charismatic authority. While leaders occasionally have diminished their own charismatic authority, by far the more frequent case has been a claim to enhanced authority requiring additional sacrifice by disciples. When Branch Dav-idian leader David Koresh announced that he was creating the House of David, through which he would father children with married women in the movement to create a new spiritual lineage, a number of couples complied. However, some couples resisted and ultimately disaffiliated when they concluded that their non-compliance meant they would no longer be accepted within the movement. There was a similar development within the Solar Temple when movement leaders began organizing marriages of members and met with resistance. Charismatic leaders have also engaged in actions that members regarded as betrayal or corruption of basic movement doctrines. Sexual indulgence by the leader when members are called upon to remain celibate has been particularly common. Jacobs (1989) re-counts numerous instances in which charismatic leaders not only falsely claimed to be celibate but also told multiple romantic partners that they were the only objects of affection.

A number of longstanding members of the Unificationist movement defected in disillusionment following the publication of an exposé book by Nansook Hong (1998), one of Reverend Moon's daughters-in-law. She revealed that Moon had a sexual relationship out of marriage earlier in his life and also detailed an imperious

Moon household and physical abuse at the hands of Moon's son. Similarly, there was widespread defection in the Divine Light Mission following the guru Maharaj Ji's announcement that he was going to marry his secretary.

Finally, movements face developmental problems that have both collective and individual impact. One problem is failed prophecy. NRMs typically begin with a vision of world transformation and prophetic revelations about how and when that transformation will transpire. There are numerous cases of movements that have engaged in specific endtime predictions only to experience prophetic failure. While the evidence indicates that failed predictions are not fatal to movements (Miller 1991), they frequently are accompanied by defections. The leaders of Heaven's Gate, Ti and Do, announced that they were heavenly messengers who would be murdered and then ascend to Heaven in a spacecraft. Their "demonstration" would prove that death could be overcome. Ti and Do issued a "final statement" indicating that the demonstration was imminent. When the demonstration failed to occur while members were literally camping out with winter coming on, over half of the membership disaffiliated. In the case of the Branch Davidians, one of the movement's early leaders, Florence Houteff, announced that she had discovered the biblical code contained in the Book of Revelation through which the timing of the second coming could be known. She then proclaimed April 22, 1959, as the date for the establishment of the Kingdom of God. Between 500 and 1,000 believers responded by selling their homes and possessions and moving to Waco for the expected transformation. In the wake of prophetic failure, all but about 50 members disaffiliated.

Although not as dramatic, long-term failure of NRMs to progress toward stable organizations that provide viable lifestyles for members also produces discouragement and disaffiliation. While the Krishnas did create a network of temples, the Unificationists a corporate conglomerate, and The Family an international network of homes that gave those movements substance and stability, all three movements had fewer adult members at the beginning of the new millennium than they did in the 1970s. Members sacrificed their personal and family lives for extended periods to help build the movements. This led to a variety of problems; unauthorized romantic relationships resulted in individuals being expelled from the movements, or individuals simply left those movements to pursue a more conventional family lifestyle. Some of these disaffiliations were doubly problematic for the movements as the disaffiliation of one individual led either to the disaffiliation of their partner or split loyalties among partners that resulted in contentious child custody disputes. An inability to develop meaningful employment within movements likewise led members to seek more conventional careers outside the movement. The result in those cases has been that some individuals have migrated to the margins of the movements while others have gradually disaffiliated as they became financially independent.

THE DISAFFILIATION PROCESS

The disaffiliation process differs from affiliation in several important respects. Disaffiliation is not as coordinated as affiliation; many movements have rituals associated with affiliation and membership while few have rituals through which individuals disaffiliate. Where rituals do exist, they involve efforts to recover members who are deviating from movement norms. In some cases movements do have formal expulsion rituals, but these involve relatively few individuals. The affiliation-disaffiliation process also is not symmetrical in that there are no organizations independent of NRMs actively promoting affiliation, while the anti-cult movement has served as an agent in directly and indirectly promoting disaffiliation (Shupe and Bromley 1980). The presence of the anti-cult movement has led to two distinctive features of NRM disaffiliation—ritually orchestrated exits (deprogramming/exit counseling) and support for oppositional roles for former members (apostates). Further, disaffiliation is likely to occur over an extended period of time for those individuals who attain a strong affiliative link to the movement. Members develop strong identity, marital, community, occupational, financial, and spiritual ties to the movement. Particularly for higher-demand movements, the movement may come to constitute a member's entire social world. Under these conditions, leave-taking can pose a daunting challenge. Finally, just as the affiliation process may not lead to long-term, committed membership, disaffiliation may not result in a complete severance of a relationship with a movement. Barker (1998) has pointed out that individual members may opt for more marginal roles in the movement or may be moved into more marginal roles by the movement.

Disaffiliation from NRMs typically involves several phases: individual disinvolvement, during which the member harbors but does not publicly express growing disaffection; organizational disinvolvement, which involves more public expression of disaffection and some open tension between member and movement; a precipitating event or series of events which make it clear to the member and/or movement that conflicts are unlikely to be resolved; separation, the point when an individual crosses the boundary from member to former member; and post-disaffiliation readjustment. A small number of former NRM members have extended their movement careers in a countermovement capacity as deprogrammers/exit counselors or apostates.

The recruitment successes that many NRMs achieved early in their histories indicates the positive attraction of their ideologies and of the promise of their alternative lifestyles; the fact that the vast majority of affiliates chose to leave after a brief experimentation with life in these groups indicates an equally strong negative reaction to the realities of movement membership. The experience of many longer-term members reflects this same ambivalence. Put simply, most members have doubts episodically or continuously. Expression of doubt in groups engaged in intense organizational mobilization is problematic, however, and movement leaders employ a variety of tactics for suppressing dissent. For their part, affiliates often are engaged in what they regard as a spiritual struggle in which they seek to overcome doubts and hence may be reluctant to publicly express misgivings. As a result, it is not uncommon for individual affiliates to feel that they are the only ones questioning their faith when in fact such feelings are quite prevalent. As Skonovd (1983) has pointed out, affiliates therefore typically deal with initial reservations through techniques such as repression, rationalization, redefinition, or relocation.

Given the constraints on public expression of doubt, individual disinvolvement (private distancing, limiting emotional investment) is likely to precede organizational disinvolvement. The first visible expression of a troubled relationship therefore is likely to take the form of cues such as altering dress and appearance, eschewing insider movement language, reading unapproved literature, privately sharing concerns with trusted friends, or expanding relationships with outsiders (family members, friends, former members). The movement is likely to respond by redoubling its efforts to reintegrate the wayward member, either through positive or negative sanctions. Movement reintegration efforts may be countered by external parties, particularly family members, once a member's doubts become public.

It is commonplace for individuals in the process of disaffiliation to go through a process of withdrawal and reintegration, sometimes on several occasions. Some attempt to resolve conflicts by finding a different niche within the movement. Barker (1998) distinguishes between "peripheral" and "marginal" members. The former gain the movement's blessing to move to a new organizational or geographic location, accept a lesser status, or become part-time members. By contrast, marginal members continue to dispute some movement beliefs or practices but continue to act and be treated as core members. This role, of course, evokes considerably more tension and leaves individuals in a much more ambiguous position within the movement. At the same time, marginal members avoid pressures to defect and the stigma and identity reconstruction problems that may accompany disaffiliation.

If tensions continue and cannot be resolved, a moment ensues when the individual and/or the movement determine that continued affiliation is not acceptable even if the costs of exiting are high. The precipitating event that moves the individual across the insider-outsider boundary is often trivial from an outsider perspective. It may involve the reemergence of a conflict that has recurred many times or a minor conflict that symbolizes in microcosm the larger issues that have been at the root of the affiliate's disaffection. Whatever its nature, the precipitating event produces the necessary resolve and energy to undertake an organizational boundary crossing.

For individuals deeply connected to an NRM, the transition period following exit is likely to be one of emotional turbulence. Former members routinely experience continuing ambivalence about their exit decision and sometimes a sense of personal failure and loss of community. In the case of high-demand NRMs with a totalistic environment, the problems of adjusting to a conventional environment may require considerable time and effort. However, as former members resume conventional lives, the problems they face gradually moderate. The high turnover in NRM membership has resulted in the formation of former-member support groups, and some individuals use these groups to ease their transition back into conventional roles.

Most former members appear disposed to put their movement experiences behind them. However, some former members have taken on roles in support groups, as apostates, or as deprogrammers/exit-counselors (Shupe and Bromley 1980; Bromley 1998a, 1998b). Former-member support groups historically have been rather loosely organized, ephemeral organizations; with the advent of the Internet, they may simply consist of Web sites, e-mail list serves, and chat rooms. Some groups have focused on a single movement while others have been concerned with a broad array of NRMs. The stance they assume toward the movements with which they are concerned has varied from neutral, in which case the negative experiences of the individual are addressed without a cult/brainwashing template, to hostile, in which case the core assumption is that the movement is directly and primarily responsible for any personal trauma (Barker 1998; Rothbaum 1980). Since their life spans are relatively short, support groups have offered few opportunities for developing long-term oppositional career roles.

The longer-term effects of the transition out of NRMs vary considerably. While studies of NRM members indicate that most former members have positive or neutral assessments of their NRM experiences (Lewis and Bromley 1987; Solomon 1983; Wright 1987), members who experienced manipulation and abuse and those who were deprogrammed are particularly likely to express negative sentiments. There are numerous reports in the NRM literature of exploitation and abuse of movement members. Examples of documented incidents include the sexual abuse of children in the Hare Krishna movement (Rochford 1998) and the Family (Chancellor 2000), spiritual and sexual exploitation of female adherents by movement leaders in a variety of groups (Jacobs 1989), and homicide in Aum Shinrikyō (Reader 2000) and the Solar Temple (Introvigne 1999; Mayer 1999). There have been numerous types of economic violations, as well. These kinds of cases have resulted in profound disillusionment on the part of victims, reverberations through remaining movement membership, and public reports that have increased hostility toward NRMs generally (Hong 1998; Muster 1996).

New Directions in Disaffiliation Theory and Research

There is now a substantial body of theory and research on both affiliation and disaffiliation. However, there are a number of problems and limitations in the work that has been done on these processes. In order for work in this area to progress, two major issues need to be addressed: an integrated theory of the complete affiliation-disaffiliation process should be developed, and theoretical recognition should be given to the diverse types of disaffiliation (as well as affiliation) that empirically occur (Richardson, Van der Lans, and Derks 1986).

It is not surprising that studies tend to be of either affiliation or disaffiliation, rather than the entire sequence. Most research on these processes involves participant observation, and the time scale of either process normally exceeds the length of the study. Nonetheless, both the theory and research on affiliation and disaffiliation lead to the conclusion that these are logically counterpart processes that should be analyzed empirically and theoretically as phases of a single process (Levine and Moreland 1985). The case of NRMs is particularly instructive since the vast majority of individuals ever affiliated with an NRM have traversed the entire process and because a number of NRMs create environments in which powerful transformative experiences may occur. I have argued elsewhere that the affiliation-disaffiliation sequence can be conceptualized in terms of a series of phases: preaffiliation contact, affiliation, organizational involvement, individual involvement, membership, individual disinvolvement, organizational disinvolvement, disaffiliation, and post-disaffiliation adjustment (Bromley 1991, 1997).

The disaffiliation sequence has been outlined above. For affiliation, comparable phases would be as follows. Preaffiliation begins with movement-recruit contact and is a period during which there is some type of interaction between recruit and movement that stops short of a formal relationship. The affiliation phase commences when the individual crosses the movement-society boundary and assumes a formal status, however tenuous, within the movement. From this point on, affiliates are involved to varying degrees in two processes—organizational involvement and individual involvement. Organizational involvement refers to role performances through which affiliates engage in social behavior and present a social identity to others that is consistent with organizational prescriptions and proscriptions. Individual involvement refers to subjective performances through which affiliates engage in personal intentionality construction and present a personal identity to themselves consistent with organizational prescriptions and proscriptions. Both individual and group initiatives may move affiliates toward greater organizational and/or individual involvement. Transformative rituals are particularly important in this process. Membership involves equilibration of some combination of organizational and individual involvement sufficient that affiliates continue and the group accepts their participation.

To argue that affiliation and disaffiliation are most productively viewed as a single sequence is not to imply that the sequence is completely symmetrical, however. For example, affiliates are more likely to become involved in movements before experiencing identity changes while disaffiliates are more likely to experience the reverse. Too, there are few organized external proponents of affiliation while there are well-organized oppositional groups that promote disaffiliation.

Use of the affiliation and disaffiliation concepts also has implications for the role of the traditional concept of conversion in theorizing about movement-member relationships. I am arguing that conversion is a special case of organizational and individual involvement and that it may or may not occur in any particular case of affiliation. Conversion has two related but independent referents. One is to the process of convergence of organizational individual involvement such that individual and group do not perceive any distinction between social and subjective performances or between social and personal identity. Converts thus experience what Turner (1978) refers to as a convergence of role and person and assume what Swanson (1978) terms an "agentic" (as opposed to an instrumental) orientation toward the group. However, the empirical research on affiliation clearly indicates that affiliates may reach and sustain a position of membership in most circumstances without any dramatic transformative events. Of course, whether or not most individuals experience dramatic transformations, conversion narratives and conformity to the expectations of convert status are critical to the stability and solidarity of NRMs. The other referent is political. Conversion is a designation that legitimates the affiliate-movement relationship. By designating themselves as converts, affiliates are indicating public acceptance of movement ideology and organization in orienting their behavior. The movement is indicating its acceptance of the affiliate as a legitimate member and its expectation of conformity to organizational ideology and norms. To the extent that external parties, including social scientists, are involved, use of the term "conversion" indicates acceptance of the change of loyalties as religiously privileged conduct.

Theory and research on disaffiliation has focused almost exclusively on individual exiting by first-generation, lower-ranking members in which the member makes the exit decision. However, disaffiliation is much more diverse, and other forms of disaffiliation need to be integrated into theoretical models and research findings. There are a number of alternative conditions under which disaffiliation occurs that may have far-reaching consequences for the movement: collective disaffiliation, single or multiple expulsions by the movement, forcible extraction by outsiders, second-generation disaffiliations, and disaffiliations by high-ranking members.

Disaffiliation sometimes involves a large number of individuals independently exiting at the same time or an organized group exiting in response to conditions within the movement. A relatively uncoordinated collective exit occurred in The Family in response to a demand by movement leaders for a higher level of commitment to the movement. In some Family homes members had lost personal dedication to the movement's goals and lifestyle, which resulted in an overall decline in morale and motivation. Under the new policy, Shakeup 2000, members were informed that they could choose between core member status and a less committed affiliate member status if they chose to remain within the movement. A significant number of members chose to leave the movement entirely rather than accept a lower status. A comparable episode occurred in Heaven's Gate in 1975–1976. Movement leaders, Ti and Do, consciously attempted to build commitment within the group by increasing demands on members. Individuals were required to conform to dress and grooming requirements, give up drugs and sex, and struggle to rise above other personal attachments in order to prepare for life at the Next Level. Ti and Do literally drew a line on the ground and asked those who wanted to stay to cross over it. In the face of this call for personal asceticism, movement membership plummeted. Noncoordinated disaffiliations usually do not produce hostile defections, but in some cases they have had a substantial impact on movement membership, particularly where a succession of incidents occur. By contrast, an organized collective exit occurred in the Peoples Temple in 1973 when a group of youthful members, referred to as the "gang of eight," left the movement over allegations of racist practices by Jim Jones and Jones's version of socialism. This conflict in turn led two influential movement members, Jeannie and Al Mills, to challenge Jim Jones's authority. The Mills were defeated in the ensuing conflict and thereafter lost a position of trust within the movement. They subsequently left the Peoples Temple and became outspoken public critics of the movement. Collective exits are important because they are likely to involve highly visible conflict and have the potential for producing open divisions within the movement, other defections, or even schism.

There have been a number of cases of expulsion of members or demotions in status that have led directly to leave-taking. In the Hare Krishna movement a Governing Board Commission was established, following the death of the movement's founder, consisting of gurus that Prabupada had initiated. Several of those gurus were expelled from the movement during the 1980s. One was accused of illegal drug use and sexual exploitation of female devotees; another was charged with illicit drug use. The single most public scandal involved Bhaktipada, spiritual leader of the New Vrindaban community. He and other members of the New Vrindaban community were charged with child abuse and murder and were expelled from the movement. The impact on the movement was substantial, as the movement was tainted by the scandal and New Vrindaban was one of the largest, most financially successful communities. The Church of Scientology established the Guardians Office in 1966 to defend what the church regarded as hostile ex-

ternal attacks. The Guardians Office subsequently began intimidating church critics, using a variety of unethical and illegal means. A number of Scientologists
were criminally prosecuted for these activities. The church subsequently stripped
those individuals convicted and otherwise implicated in these activities of their
organizational positions. Some members who were organizationally marginalized
became involved in open conflict with the church and ultimately left. Several of
these leave takers subsequently became part of the network of church opponents
(Atack 1990). In The Family, the movement's leader, Moses David Berg, became
increasingly dissatisfied with abusive practices by high-ranking leaders, as well as
challenges to his charismatic leadership. In 1978 he adopted a radical solution to
these problems in the form of the "Re-organization Nationalization Revolution"
(RNR), removing 300 leaders from their positions and ordering them into the
streets as ordinary disciples. Several inner-circle leaders, including Berg's oldest
daughter, left the movement. Berg's daughter went on to write a book condemning the movement and charging Berg with sexual abuse (Davis 1984). Disaffiliation
involving demotion and expulsion is likely to have real political repercussions for
a movement, as those former members are much more likely to harbor grievances
against the movement.

It is clear that all disaffiliations are not equal; leave-taking by higher-ranking
members can have great impact on a movement. If these individuals are influential, their departure may change the movement's direction. For example, John
Campbell and Dr. John Winter were two early influential supporters of L. Ron
Hubbard as he developed Dianetics, and both served on the executive board of
the Hubbard Dianetic Research Foundation. When practitioners began reporting
experiences from past lives during therapy, Hubbard legitimated these reports and
soon developed the spiritually based Church of Scientology. Both Campbell and
Winter vigorously opposed these ideological and organizational developments and
subsequently left the movement. Their departure solidified Hubbard's control of
the movement, increased his charismatic authority, and eliminated opposition to
shifting the movement in a more spiritual direction. Influential individuals who
disaffiliate possess insider information and may ally with external control agencies
following exit. In the case of Branch Davidian leader David Koresh's initiative to
create a new spiritual lineage by fathering children with women in the movement,
one of those affected was Marc Breault, a core Koresh supporter. Breault and his
new bride were among those who demurred and finally left the movement after
concluding that their resistance would make it impossible for them to remain on
acceptable terms. Breault possessed knowledge that Koresh was initiating sexual
relationships with underage girls in the movement and was able to mobilize other
movement members, the media, and government agencies to investigate the Davidians. Breault played a key role in initiating the investigatory process that ultimately led to the confrontation between the Davidians and federal agents at
Mount Carmel.

There is very limited research on second-generation NRM members to date (Palmer and Hardman 1999). This issue is important for two reasons. First, NRMs initially grew exclusively through recruitment, but virtually none of the movements has been able to sustain membership growth through proselytization, as disaffiliation rates have remained high. Therefore, growth through procreation has become increasingly crucial to the survival of a number of groups. The available evidence suggests that movements vary considerably in their ability to retain second-generation members. Among the NRMs, the Hare Krishna has faced serious alienation problems because leaders placed higher priority on achieving movement objectives than childrearing and because of the widespread abuse of children in child care facilities. By contrast, The Family has been much more successful in retaining second-generation members by integrating them fully into their communities and providing them with opportunities to participate in shaping the future of the movement. Second, the causes and dynamics of first- and second-generation disaffiliation differ markedly (O'Dea 1983). Second-generation members are not converts but rather are socialized into their traditions through childhood, do not experience the trials and tribulations common for first-generation members, and are not targets of anti-cult groups to the same extent. For second-generation members, affiliation and disaffiliation patterns are likely to more closely resemble those of established churches.

Finally, externally precipitated disaffiliation has been significant for many NRMs both because movements became more closed and defensive in response but also because they have lent legitimacy to allegations of cultic brainwashing (Bromley and Richardson 1983; Zablocki and Robbins 2001). Externally precipitated disaffiliation began during the 1970s as forcible deprogramming. There probably were several thousand deprogrammings of NRM members during the 1970s and 1980s, with high-profile groups like the Unificationist movement being frequent targets (Bromley 1988). Judicial resistance to coercive deprogramming led to the development of exit counseling, a process premised on the voluntary participation by the individual being counseled. The two processes share a highly ritualized format that involves attempts to discredit the movement and challenge the affiliate's volition. Both coercive deprogramming and voluntary exit counseling have yielded high rates of disaffiliation and a high probability of ex-members with a hostile stance toward their former movements. Individuals who have undergone deprogramming or exit counseling frequently have reported emotional difficulties in making a transition back to conventional society, which anti-cult groups have attributed to the lingering effects of cultic brainwashing. However, several studies have suggested that it was the deprogramming ritual rather than prior discontent that resulted in both the post-disaffiliation adjustment problems and the hostile stance toward disaffiliate's former movements (Lewis and Bromley 1987; Solomon 1983; Wright 1987, 1988).

CONCLUSIONS

The study of disaffiliation from NRMs emerged as a significant issue when NRM scholars recognized that most movements were unable to retain the loyalty of those individuals they recruited. In the work that has been done since, there is considerable agreement on the causes of exiting NRMs and the process whereby exiting occurs. However, most of the theory and research to date has focused on individual member exits. I have argued that, in order for theory and research on the exiting process to progress, two developments are necessary. It is important to integrate work on the exit process with the much larger body of work on the entry process. I have suggested that the terms "affiliation" and "disaffiliation" be employed to conceptualize the total sequence from initial contact with a movement to final separation. In this model conversion would become a special type of relationship that may or may not occur. I have also suggested that a number of different types of disaffiliation be identified and their consequences for movements be explored more thoroughly. Both of these initiatives would approach disaffiliation, and its counterpart process of affiliation, from a more political stance that does not conceptually privilege relationships with movements simply because they make claims to religious status.

REFERENCES

Arnott, Dave. 1999. *Corporate Cults: The Insidious Lure of the All-Consuming Organization.* New York: American Management Association.

Atack, Jon. 1990. *A Piece of Blue Sky: Scientology and L. Ron Hubbard Exposed.* New York: Carol Publishing.

Balch, Robert. 1982. "Bo and Peep: A Study of the Origins of Messianic Leadership." In *Millennialism and Charisma,* ed. Roy Wallis. Belfast, Northern Ireland: Queen's University Press.

————. 1985. "When the Light Goes Out, Darkness Comes: A Study of Defection from a Totalistic Cult." In *Religious Movements: Genesis, Exodus, and Numbers,* ed. Rodney Stark. New York: Paragon House.

Barker, Eileen. 1984. *The Making of a Moonie: Choice or Brainwashing?* Oxford: Basil Blackwell.

————. 1988. "Defection from the Unification Church: Some Statistics and Distinctions." In *Falling from the Faith: Causes and Consequences of Religious Apostasy,* ed. David G. Bromley. Newbury Park, Calif.: Sage.

————. 1998. "Standing at the Cross-Roads: The Politics of Marginality in 'Subversive Organizations.'" In *The Politics of Religious Apostasy: The Role of Apostates in the*

Transformation of Religious Movements, ed. David G. Bromley. Westport, Conn.: Praeger.

————. 2002. "Watching for Violence: A Comparative Analysis of the Roles of Five Types of Cult-Watching Groups." In *Cults, Religion, and Violence,* ed. David G. Bromley and J. Gordon Melton. Cambridge: Cambridge University Press.

Bromley, David G. 1988. "Deprogramming as a Mode of Exit from New Religious Movements: The Case of the Unificationist Movement." In *Falling from the Faith,* ed. David G. Bromley. Newbury Park, Calif.: Sage.

————. 1991. "Unraveling Religious Disaffiliation: The Meaning and Significance of Falling from the Faith." *Counseling and Values* 36: 164–185.

————. 1997. "The Process of Exiting New Religious Movements." In *Leaving Patterns of Religious Life: Cross Cultural Perspectives,* ed. William Shaffir and Motti Bar Lev. Greenwich, Conn.: Association for the Sociology of Religion and JAI Press.

————, ed. 1998a. *The Politics of Religious Apostasy: The Role of Apostates in the Transformation of Religious Movements.* Westport, Conn.: Praeger.

————. 1998b. "The Social Construction of Contested Exit Roles: Defectors, Whistleblowers, and Apostates." In *The Politics of Religious Apostasy: The Role of Apostates in the Transformation of Religious Movements,* ed. David G. Bromley. Westport, Conn.: Praeger.

Bromley, David G., and James T. Richardson, eds. 1983. *The Brainwashing/Deprogramming Controversy.* Lewiston, N.Y.: Edwin Mellen.

Bromley, David G., and Anson D. Shupe. 1979a. "Just a Few Years Seem Like a Lifetime: A Role Theory Approach to Participation in New Religious Movements." In *Research in Social Movements, Conflicts, and Change,* ed. Louis Kriesberg. Greenwich, Conn.: JAI Press.

————. 1979b. *Moonies in America: Cult, Church and Crusade.* Beverly Hills, Calif.: Sage.

————. 1986. "Affiliation and Disaffiliation: A Role-Theory Interpretation of Joining and Leaving New Religious Movements." *Thought: A Review of Culture and Idea* 61: 197–211.

Bromley, David G., Anson D. Shupe, and Joseph C. Ventimiglia. 1979. "Atrocity Tales, the Unification Church, and the Social Construction of Evil." *Journal of Communication* 29: 42–53.

Chancellor, James. 2000. *Life in the Family: An Oral History of the Children of God.* Syracuse, N.Y.: University of Syracuse Press.

Davis, Deborah. 1984. *The Children of God.* Grand Rapids, Mich.: Zondervan.

Galanter, Marc. 1980. "Psychological Induction into the Large Group: Findings from a Modern Religious Sect." *American Journal of Psychiatry* 137: 1574–1579.

Hong, Nansook. 1998. *In the Shadow of the Moons.* New York: Little, Brown.

Introvigne, Massimo. 1999. "The Magic of Death: The Suicide of the Solar Temple." In *Millennialism, Persecution and Violence: Historical Cases,* ed. Catherine Wessinger. Syracuse: Syracuse University Press.

Jacobs, Janet. 1989. *Divine Disenchantment.* Bloomington: Indiana University Press.

Levine, John, and Richard Moreland. 1985. "Innovation and Socialization in Small Groups." In *Perspectives on Minority Influence,* ed. Serge Moscovici, Gabriel Mugny, and Eddy Van Avermaet, 143–169. Cambridge: Cambridge University Press.

Lewis, James, and David Bromley. 1987. "The Cult Withdrawal Syndrome: A Case of Misattribution of Cause?" *Journal for the Scientific Study of Religion* 26: 508–522.

Lofland, John, and Norman Skonovd. 1981. "Conversion Motifs." *Journal for the Scientific Study of Religion* 20: 373–385.

Lofland, John, and Rodney Stark. 1965. "Becoming a World-Saver: A Theory of Religious Conversion." *American Sociological Review* 30: 862–874.

Mayer, Jean François. 1999. " 'Our Terrestrial Journey Is Coming to an End': The Last Voyage of the Solar Temple." *Nova Religio: The Journal of Alternative and Emergent Religions* 2: 172–196.

Miller, Timothy, ed. 1991. *When Prophets Die: The Postcharismatic Fate of New Religious Movements.* Albany: State University of New York Press.

Muster, Nori. 1996. *Betrayal of the Spirit: My Life in the Hare Krishna Movement.* Urbana: University of Illinois Press.

O'Dea, Thomas. 1983. *The Sociology of Religion.* Englewood Cliffs, N.J.: Prentice-Hall.

Palmer, Susan, and Charlotte Hardman, eds. 1999. *Children in New Religions.* New Brunswick, N.J.: Rutgers University Press.

Reader, Ian. 2000. *Religious Violence in Contemporary Japan: The Case of Aum Shinrikyô.* Richmond, Surrey, England: Curzon Press; Honolulu: University of Hawaii Press.

Richardson, J., J. van der Lans, and Frans Derks. 1986. "Leaving and Labeling: Voluntary and Coerced Disaffiliation from Religious Social Movements." *Research in Social Movements, Conflicts and Change* 9: 97–126.

Rochford, E. Burke, Jr. 1984. *Hare Krishna in America.* New Brunswick, N.J.: Rutgers University Press.

———. 1998. "Child Abuse in the Hare Krishna Movement: 1971–1986." *ISKCON Communications Journal* 6: 43–69.

Rothbaum, Susan. 1980. "Between Two World: Issues of Separation and Identity after Leaving a Religious Community." In *Falling from the Faith: Causes and Consequences of Religious Apostasy,* ed. David G. Bromley. Newbury Park, Calif.: Sage.

Saliba, John A. 1990. *Social Science and the Cults: An Annotated Bibliography.* New York: Garland.

Shupe, Anson, and David G. Bromley. 1980. *The New Vigilantes.* Beverly Hills, Calif.: Sage.

Skonovd, Norman. 1983. "Leaving the Cultic Milieu." In *The Brainwashing/Deprogramming Controversy,* ed. David G. Bromley and James T. Richardson. New York: Edwin Mellen.

Snow, David. 1984. "The Sociology of Conversion." *Annual Review of Sociology* 10: 167–190.

Solomon, Trudy. 1983. "Integrating the 'Moonie' Experience: Social Psychology Applied." In *The Brainwashing/Deprogramming Controversy,* ed. David G. Bromley and James T. Richardson. New York: Edwin Mellen.

Straus, Roger. 1979. "Religious Conversion as a Personal and Collective Accomplishment." *Sociological Analysis* 40: 158–165.

Swanson, Guy. 1978. "Trance and Possession: Studies on Charismatic Influence." *Review of Religious Research* 19: 253–278.

Travisano, Richardson V. 1970. "Alternation and Conversion as Qualitatively Different Transformations." In *Social Psychology through Symbolic Interaction,* ed. Gregory Stone and Harold Faberman. Waltham, Mass.: Ginn-Blaisdell.

Turner, Ralph. 1978. "The Role and the Person." *American Journal of Sociology* 84: 1–23.

Wright, Stuart. 1987. *Leaving Cults: The Dynamics of Defection.* Washington: Society for the Scientific Study of Religion.

————. 1988. "Leaving New Religious Movements: Issues, Theory, and Research." In *Falling from the Faith: Causes and Consequences of Religious Apostasy,* ed. David G. Bromley. Newbury Park, Calif.: Sage.

Zablocki, Benjamin, and Thomas Robbins, eds. 2001. *Misunderstanding Cults.* Toronto: University of Toronto Press.

PART III

SOCIAL AND PSYCHOLOGICAL DIMENSIONS

CHAPTER 13

PSYCHOLOGY AND THE NEW RELIGIOUS MOVEMENTS

JOHN A. SALIBA

FOR over a quarter of a century the psychological study of new religious movements has figured prominently in debates not only in the psychological disciplines, but also in sociology and religious studies. Scholars from different disciplinary fields have discussed at length—in the context of the brainwashing controversy—the mental and emotional states of those who join these movements, remain members, or have left and still bear the scars inflicted allegedly by their involvement. Moreover, the issue of whether new religious movements are a serious threat to public health has often made headlines in newspapers and magazines, determined the kind of counseling given to ex-members and parents of those who have remained members, and been the subject of debates in lawsuits.

THE PSYCHOLOGICAL/PSYCHIATRIC STUDY OF RELIGION AND NEW RELIGIOUS MOVEMENTS

The psychological evaluation of new religious movements must be seen in the context of the history of the psychological study of religion (cf. Gorsuch 1988). When the examination of religion from a psychological standpoint emerged in the early twentieth century, the few scholars who pursued research in the area tended to stress religious experience rather than religious belief and ritual. By the 1920s religion was already being criticized as an irrational and inhibitory burden on the individual. Freud's works on religion, which dominated both psychology and psychiatry for decades, looked on religion as a neurosis, a kind of wish-fulfilling illusion that had to be dealt with in therapy. While there has been a gradual revival in the psychological study of religion since the 1950s (cf. Collins 1994), the views of Freud and, later, of the behavioral school, created a hostile attitude toward religion that, to some degree, still persists. Religion was neglected by most psychologists, was ignored in the teaching of psychology, and played a minor role in counseling and therapy (cf. Wulff 2001, esp. 19–20).

The topic of religion was practically omitted even in introductory psychology texts. If mentioned at all, it was likely to be included in sections that referred to mental illnesses. It is certainly not surprising that psychological evaluations of new religious movements, where intense experience and commitment are encouraged, have been largely negative.

It is this negative attitude to religion which has been portrayed in the *Diagnostic and Statistical Manual of Mental Diseases* until its third edition, published by the American Psychiatric Association in 1987.[1] This edition, for example, regarded cultic beliefs and lifestyles as causes of mental illness and as obstacles to the development of a healthy personality. Leaders of cults and other fringe religions are said to have paranoid personalities (American Psychiatric Association 1987: 338). Trance states and altered states of consciousness are viewed as indicators of dissociative disorders (1987: 277), while magical thinking and ecstatic states are said to be signs of immaturity and indications of serious personality weaknesses (1987: 401). *DSM-III* still favored the brainwashing theory of conversion as an explanation of why people join and remain within new religious movements.

Recent approaches to the psychology of religion[2] in general may be, in part at least, responsible for the obvious changes regarding new religions in *DSM-IV* (American Psychiatric Association 1994). Among the many areas being explored by psychologists are religious development, religious experience, the dynamics of religious behavior, and the therapeutic effects of religion (cf. Luckoff et al. 1996: 232). Rather than treating religion as having a consistently negative effect on human behavior and functioning, many psychologists are now looking at religion as an independent variable that can have positive as well as negative effects on human personality.

DSM-IV mirrors, to some extent, this changing attitude toward religion. For a start, *DSM-IV*, unlike *DSM-III*, is sensitive to cultural diversity and thus makes it easier to look more positively on the influx and attractiveness of Eastern religious practices that have made it to the West since the late 1960s. *DSM-IV* states that a "cross-cultural perspective is particularly important in the evaluation of Dissociative Disorders because dissociative states are a common and accepted expression of cultural or religious experience in many societies. Dissociation should not be considered inherently pathological and often does not lead to significant stress, impairment, or self-seeking behavior" (American Psychiatric Association 1994: 477). Though it includes trance as a dissociative disorder, *DSM-IV* adds that this disorder "should not be considered in individuals who enter trance and possession states voluntarily and without distress in the context of cultural and religious practices that are broadly accepted by the person's cultural group. Such voluntary and nonpathological states are common and constitute the overwhelming majority of trance states encountered cross-culturally" (1994: 727). This new approach to trance behavior is particularly useful because many meditative practices[3] (like mantra chanting), notwithstanding the abundant research to the contrary (cf. Shear 2001), have routinely been interpreted as psychological mechanisms to "brainwash" the mind, as tools to mind control, as subtle ways to manipulate the emotions, or as harmful practices causing serious forms of dissociation.

Probably the most innovative initiative in *DSM-IV* is the introduction of a diagnostic category, namely religious and spiritual problems that need counseling but are not indicative of any mental disorder (1994: 685). Under "religious problems" are included change of denomination or conversion to new religion, intensification of beliefs and practices, loss or questioning of faith, guilt, and cults (which are a special case of the conversion experience); while under "spiritual problems" one finds mystical experience, near-death experience, spiritual emergence, meditation, terminal illness, and addiction. *DSM-IV* does make a distinction between psychopathology and religious/spiritual problems and lays the ground for further research in the area.

The distinction made in *DSM-IV* had been discussed for a while in psychological literature. Greenberg and Witztum (1991), for example, had already argued in favor of distinguishing between religious and spiritual problems and psychopathology and pointed out that those who are burdened by religious or spiritual difficulties are in need of advice and counseling and should not be treated as if they suffered from one of the psychological or mental illnesses that traditional psychiatric manuals deal with. The difficulty is that sometimes there is an overlap between religious and/or spiritual problems and mental or psychotic disorders that might contain religious or mystical elements. The therapist is thus called upon to determine, among other things, whether religion is the cause of the problem or its outcome.

Some psychologists have attempted to clarify and expand on the new *DSM-IV* category of religious and spiritual problems. Luckoff et al. (1996), for instance, discuss the difference between milder and more severe cases of spiritual emergences. The former, they argue, should not be treated as mental disorders; the latter, however, may indicate psychopathology, since they disrupt one's psychological and social functioning. Battista (1996) also stresses the fact that spiritual awakenings and crises are not the same as psychotic states. He further distinguishes between "true transformative spirituality" and "false defensive spirituality." The former is not an indication of mental or psychological illness, but the latter may be a sign of masochistic tendencies that require therapy. And more recently, Turner et al. (1998) explore the distinction between religion and spirituality, assess the different kinds of religious and spiritual problems, and point to ways in which these might be distinguished from mental disorders. When dealing with cults, they admit that some cults can be destructive, but they note that the generalization that cults are detrimental to one's mental health is "doubtful."

DSM-IV leads to a different approach to the role played by health professionals when they are called on to understand religions (both old and new) and treat mental and psychological states associated with religious beliefs and practices. But it also raises a number of still unresolved issues. It might appear easy to determine, especially in a specific case of religious conversion, whether there are indications of some psychopathology that preceded or followed the individual's commitment. However, Sparr and Ferguson's (2000: 110) efforts to explore "the relationship between traumatic events and moral, spiritual and religious issues" point to some of the difficulties that therapists are bound to encounter in dealing with their patients. And in spite of the distinctions between religion and spirituality and between religious crises and pathological cases, the line separating deep religious commitment and pathology remains undefined. Moreover, the realization that religion forms a key role in the formation of one's personality and that diverse religious beliefs and practices should be seriously taken into consideration raises another question—namely, what qualifications a therapist must have to be able to make a correct diagnosis between a religious or spiritual problem that is "normal" and one that is the product or cause of deeper psychological or mental issues. Some scholars (cf., e.g., Luckoff et al. 1996: 245) have raised the question of whether psychologists are equipped to deal with religious and spiritual problems.

The issues therapists encounter when treating religious patients have been recognized for some time. Greenberg and Witztum (1991: 554) suggest three guidelines that should help therapists in their work: "(1) cooperation with the patient's spiritual mentor to reduce the patient's resistance, (2) examination of the therapist's own religious attitudes to modify countertransferential feelings, (3) acquisition of knowledge about the patient's religion to facilitate interviewing, and help distinguish belief from delusion, and ritual from compulsion."

These guidelines were formulated in the context of patients from orthodox Jewish backgrounds, yet they could be easily and profitably applied when dealing with members of new religious movements.

CURRENT PSYCHOLOGY STUDIES ON NEW RELIGIOUS MOVEMENTS

In spite of these promising initiatives of *DSM-IV* and the changing attitudes in the psychological and psychiatric studies on new religions, evaluations of new religious movements have been mixed. In fact, many studies of new religious movements still tend to be negative. They frequently refer to the movements as malevolent and destructive cults or totalistic groups that demand hyper-compliance and use coercive power and undue authority. They still subscribe to the view, which has been common among most psychologists over the last few decades, that cults use brainwashing, hypnosis, thought reform, coercive persuasion, or indoctrination (cf., e.g., Lilliston and Shepherd 1999: 123–125).

Negative in-depth studies of individual groups are rare. Gerald Alper (1994), for instance, argues that cult members lose their freedom. In his opinion the groups they belong to use excessive control, seduction, and manipulation to maintain their members, who are indoctrinated in cult belief and practices. Alper, however, bases his assessment on only three cult members, one from each of three groups. He takes them as typical members of all cults without outlining his reasons for so doing. In like manner, Colin Wilson (2000) examines many self-styled messiahs, including Sabbatai Sevi, Jim Jones, David Koresh, and Rudolph Steiner, and maintains that the serial killer and the manic messiah have similar problems; namely, they are driven by power and sex beyond the normal limits that are, however, never clearly defined. Other psychiatrists depict the leaders of the new religious movements as authoritarian personalities that exert undue influence on their followers (Feuerstein 1991) or that suffer from schizophrenia (Storr 1996). Arthur Deikman (1994) tries to uncover patterns in the behavior of the members of new religions. He lists the following features common to these groups: compliance with the group, dependence of a leader, devaluation of outsiders, and avoidance of dissent. Seduction, coercion, corruption, and regression are the patterns of cult behavior. Deikman concludes that members would be healthier if they returned to their former way of life, avoided the danger of cult thinking, and found a better way to security and meaning. The problems with Deikman's generalizations is that many of the negative features he lists can be found among many groups that are not usually considered to be cults and that the negative patterns of cult behavior may be applicable to only a relatively small number of new religions. None of the mentioned writers seem to have studied in some depth the beliefs and practices of the religious groups they investigated. Further, they make little or no effort to see the leaders of the new movements in their historical and cultural contexts, much less in the broader context of the sociocultural and religious changes taking place in Western society.

Several more thorough studies of one particular religious and/or psychological group reach similar negative conclusions. Hanna Hyams (1998) did some therapeutic work with ex-members of the Order of the Solar Temple who had survived the mass suicide of the leaders and most members of the group.[4] She thinks that members of new religious movements suffer from "dissociation," which is usually defined as a condition in which "a coordinated set of activities, thoughts, attitudes or emotions becomes separated from the rest of the person's personality and functions independently" (Reber 1985: 208). After briefly outlining the diagnosis, stages, and manifestations of dissociation, Hyams applies the various expressions of dissociation to members of new religious movements. She diagnosed the survivors of the Solar Temple as suffering from trauma and psychosis and concluded that this "trauma was experienced as a repetition of their childhood traumatic abuse" (Hyams 1998: 239). She does not even theorize that the trauma may have been partly caused by the mass suicide and is a direct result of the survivors' grief and disappointment. She further generalizes about the behavior of all sect or cult leaders (including those of Aum Shinrikyô, the Unification Church, Jehovah's Witnesses, Rajneeshpuram, and Scientology), which are lumped to together in spite of the many differences in their beliefs, practices, and ways they operate. "These leaders," she states, "elicit in dissociated persons the projections of the ideal, mythical good-father/mother, heightening dissociation through memories of old, repetitious abuse, lack, and loneliness" (1998: 239). In other words, members who join new religious movements had prior psychological problems which are exacerbated by their involvement. Those who are attracted to new religions are vulnerable. They are burdened with guilt and shame and have unsatisfied emotional needs, all of which are exploited by cult leaders and members to the detriment of their new converts.

Other studies of individual groups have reached similar conclusions regarding the effects of cult membership. Marybeth Ayella (1998) explored a self-styled therapeutic group, the Center for Feeling Therapy, and concluded that in this group both authority and influence are abused to control individuals and that, consequently, the lives of those who join it can be damaged forever. No attempt is made to explore what benefits members might possibly gain or to test the mental and psychological states of those who remain members. Roger Dean (1992), in his studies of the Moonies, is more thorough. He starts by giving an analysis of Unification Church philosophy and theology. Though he avoids making the common accusations leveled at the Moonies, he still describes them as individuals who are emotionally immature and who thus need to be under a strict authority that supplies them with simple answers for life's many difficulties. Moonies, he concludes, are religious seekers and social nonconformists. One is left with the following two impressions: the Unification Church attracts individuals who are emotionally immature and/or unstable, and involvement in the movement fosters immaturity and is therefore unhealthy. Indirectly, Dean's analysis leads to the conclusion that some of these "negative" qualities might also be present in traditional religions.

Most of the pejorative evaluations of new religious movements are based on studies on ex-members who obviously needed therapy.[5] Studies of current members have tended to yield quite different results (cf. Saliba 1996; Lilliston and Shepherd 1999). Among the groups whose active members have been psychologically tested are ISKCON, The Family (formerly known as the Children of God), Rajneeshpuram, and the Church Universal and Triumphant. Studies of members of Rajneeshpuram provide an excellent example not only of the mental and psychological state of its members, but also of the difficulties encountered in psychological studies in general. Because of the rather eclectic nature of this group and the negative publicity of their peculiar lifestyle, a brief review of the psychological studies that have been made of its members will illustrate some of the typical issues involved in the psychological study of all new religious movements.

The Psychology of the Followers
of Bhagwan Rajneesh

Psychological studies of the followers of Bhagwan Rajneesh (1931–1990)[6] date from the early 1980s. The first three articles on the movement appeared in the *Journal of Humanistic Psychology*, which, together with the *Journal of Transpersonal Psychology*, has the reputation of treating religious matters more benignly than the more established psychological journals. Two of the articles, those by Swami Prem Amitabh (1982) and Swami Deva Amrito (1984), were written by psychologists who had joined the movement. The third, by William T. Drennen (1983), was written by a sympathizer who never became a follower of Rajneesh. All three writers treat the movement basically as a kind of therapy rather than a religion, and they all relate its methods to the fields of humanistic and transpersonal psychology and to the various alternative therapies that started to achieve notoriety by the late 1960s and early 1970s. Amrito's article doesn't say much about Rajneesh therapy but treats it as a kind of supertherapy that transcends all other therapeutic treatments by making the individual go deeper in self-analysis and by aiming at a kind of super-consciousness. Amitabh's article provides more information on the therapy itself and on some of its effects. He describes the goal of this therapy as self-actualization and an increase in awareness. He claims that it causes "people to become aware of and confront directly their deeply conditioned resistances to change" (Amitabh 1982: 27), leads the individual to achieve a more integrated, mature personality, breaks down fear and repression, and is conducive to greater self-acceptance. Drennan stresses that Rajneesh wanted his followers "to become fully conscious in the 'here and now'" and to be able, for instance, to unite human sexuality with spirituality. He expands on the male/female dichotomy that Bhagwan tried to eliminate. He does, however, express some reservations. He thinks that "Bhagwan has mixed up the adult ego state with the 'sick' adaptive child state" (Drennen 1983: 88) and disagrees with the way Bhagwan "denigrates the mind (ego) as a major hindrance, a computer without any creativity, a sick computer out of touch with or suppressing feelings (valued as more authentic)" (1983: 94).

The problem with these studies is that they tend to describe the authors' feelings toward and experiences with the Bhagwan method. No attempt is made to explain what methodology is used. In fact, one is left with the impression that these essays are nothing but self-reports or biographical accounts. No standardized psychological tests are employed. Studies of this nature seem to assume that the results of the Rajneesh therapy are generally beneficial.

A much more reliable study, conducted in the late 1980s and early 1990s, is that of Latkin et al. (1987) who administered several standard psychological tests to, and/or conducted interviews with, over 200 Rajneesh followers. Latkin (1989) explores the gender roles in Rajneeshpuram and found that, though "both men and women described their ideal partner as androgenous," strict equality of the sexes did not exist. While there were certainly gender transformations in the commune, it is not clear whether this had a positive effect on the psychological and mental health of its members. Latkin (1990a, 1990b) also explores the "self-concept" of the commune members and finds that they had a higher self-esteem and a lower social anxiety and public self-consciousness than the general population. He concludes that Rajneesh members do not conform to the general notion that those who join new religious movements are easily persuaded or gullible. In yet another study (Sundberg et al. 1990) members scored high on independence and flexibility and were strongly "norm-doubting." But, otherwise, they fell within the normal range of both psychological and mental well-being. Latkin (1993) further examines the mental health of members who relocated after the commune disbanded and found few signs of psychopathology. He concludes that their communal lifestyle and belief system enhanced their coping abilities when they had to leave the commune and rejoin the general population.

Latkin et al. (1993) concede that there are problems with studying an experimental community like Rajneeshpuram. Yet their results led to the conclusion that there are no solid grounds for labeling Rajneeshpuram's members as mentally sick nor for claiming that membership in the group inevitably caused or aggravated mental or psychological illness.

A relatively minor study of Rajneesh followers conducted in Germany in the mid-1980s (cf. Kraus 1999: 270–273) examined five ex-members and twenty members of the movement. The aim of the study was to explore the psychological benefits offered by membership, to examine the conversion processes and the factors connected with conversion, and to determine the interpersonal problems members had before conversion. It was concluded that one-third of the group "had depressive personality structures that were disguised by euphoric moods," while another third or so "displayed hysterical personality structure" (1999: 271). The rest were described as "psychologically inconspicuous." The conversion experiences of most Rajneesh sannyasins were judged to be "processes of transferences." None of these members seemed to have been psychologically healthy since their conversions stemmed from narcissistic dysfunctions with or without stern and rigorous superegos, or from hysterical or depressive tendencies, or from psychosomatic complaints. The tendency toward narcissism was also detected by Sundberg et al. (1992). In psychiatry primary narcissism is described as "the early stage of development when libido is overly invested in the self or the ego, or, more simply, in the body" (Reber 1985: 462) and is considered normal. Yet if it persists in adulthood it is classified as a neurosis. Hence one can conclude that, since most German members of Rajneeshpuram were adults, the majority suffered from "narcissistic neurosis."

Issues and Prospects in the Psychological Study of New Religious Movements

The conflicting results of psychological and psychiatric studies on new religious movements are well summarized by Jodi Aronoff et al., who claim to have made "the first critical review of research that addresses the question of whether cult membership is psychologically harmful" (2000: 91). They reach the following conclusions:

1. Though many cult members report some psychopathology prior to conversion, the majority do not. Aronoff and his coresearchers find these studies unreliable because of the lack of comparison groups and psychological records that predate conversion to a new religious movement.

2. Many members of new religions seem to be psychologically as healthy and well adjusted as the general population. Aronoff et al. are not convinced by these studies. Referring specifically to the work of Galanter (1980) on the members of the Unification Church, of Weiss and Comrey (1987) on the Hare Krishnas, and of Sundberg et al. (1990) on members of Rajneeshpuram, they conclude (2000: 107–108): "These findings need to be interpreted with caution, given the conformity pressures on current cult members as well as the numerous methodological shortcomings noted above, including the lack of standardized measures, the failure to use comparison groups, and sampling and reporting biases."

3. Former cult members indicate that they suffer from significant psychological symptoms. Though some ex-members seem to be psychologically healthy, the majority exhibit serious pathology.

All of these conclusions are debatable. The reservations expressed are equally applicable to those studies that reach negative conclusions on the effects of new religions on their members. While psychological records before entry into a religious movement are rare, it should be noted that family backgrounds can be checked and used to assess whether family disfunctions are indicative of mental illness or psychological weakness in those who join new religions. And while there are limitations to the reliability of studies of cult members, particularly with regard to sampling methods, it is simply incorrect to state that standardized methods have not been employed. Most of the studies criticized by Aronoff et al. used such tests. Moreover, the majority of those who are no longer members of new religious movements have simply not been tested, and any speculation about their psychological state is bound to be determined by preconceived hypotheses of the effects of cult membership. Besides, many of the negative results were reached from studying cult members who were forcibly persuaded to return to their former belief system and lifestyle. Without denying that membership can cause or aggravate psychological problems, it is equally legitimate to theorize that forceful deprogramming can have similar results.

The disagreements between psychiatrists and psychologists on the mental and psychological state of those who join new religious and on the impact membership has on their mental health point to several unresolved issues.

1. The psychological study of new religious movements is the study of individuals, and hence the researcher must determine and choose the subjects of his or her investigation. Several groups can be distinguished: (a) current members who may or may not need therapy; (b) ex-members who have left on their own and who apparently do not need therapy; (c) ex-members who have left on their own and opted for therapeutic intervention; and (d) ex-members who were forced or pressured to leave and brought to therapy by their parents or guardians. It appears that the studies made so far lead to different conclusions on the effects cult membership has on mental health, depending largely on which of the groups is the focus of one's research.

2. Secondly, one must determine the methods to be used. What kind of psychological testing is to be applied? And should interviews form part of the process of evaluation? Marybeth Ayella's outline (1990) of the difficulties sociologists encounter in the study of new religious movements are shared, to some degree, by psychologists and psychiatrists. Access to the group; the level of members' participation, control, and involvement in the research; and the influence the leaders of the group might have on the sampling methods and interviews are but a few of the issues that cannot be easily resolved. While it is possible to draw up psychological profiles of cult members and ex-members, it is harder to determine the cause of individuals' present psychological or mental state. Thus, for example, if a member or ex-member of a new religious group is found to suffer from some form of dissociation, how does one conclude that the cause of the dissociation is involvement in the group? He or she could have been suffering from the problem before entry into the group and membership could have made it worse or alleviated it. Psychological studies and test results of individuals before they joined a new religion are simply not available, except maybe in a minority of cases.

3. The assumptions adopted by psychiatrists and psychologists in their research are likely to influence both the method used and the outcome. *DSM-IV* seems to have provided some norms. Thus, for example, *DSM-IV* rules out a general negative view of religion and encourages researchers to take sociocultural conditions into consideration. Further, *DSM-IV* suggests that knowledge of religion and of the particular religious group (including new ones) being studied is a requirement. Unfortunately many of the negative conclusions on the effects of cult membership give little indication that the researchers had explored, much less understood, the belief system of the individuals they were studying. The training of mental health care providers to recognize and deal with religious or spiritual problems needs to be addressed.

For the foreseeable future, psychologists and psychiatrists will still figure prominently in the study of new religions. Their research will make a greater contribution to the assessment of the effects of new religious movements on their members if the following areas of exploration are given greater attention.

1. The first need is for some concentrated efforts to deal with the issues described above. How does one reconcile, for instance, the contradictory conclusions exemplified by the many works referred to in this essay?

2. Given the relatively large number of new religions, full-length, in-depth studies of particular groups are rare. More groups need to be studied before any general conclusions can be drawn on the psychological effects on those who join or leave them.

3. Ways must be found to resolve both the theoretical and methodological differences that characterize psychological studies of members of new religions. One must avoid generalizing on the mental and psychological states of ex-cult members who have been brought to the psychiatrist's office in obvious need of therapeutic help or of cult members who have adjusted to their new lifestyle. Access must be gained to larger samples of those who have left with no apparent psychological harm.

4. Further work needs to be done to develop the new label of "religious or spiritual problem" mentioned in *DSM IV* and to apply this category to members and ex-members of new religious movements.

5. The application of standard testing methods needs to be pursued more uniformly and consistently. Latkin (1995: 177), commenting on Richardson's review (1995) of psychological literature on new religious movements, observes that "future studies must use more sensitive measures to assess attitude and behavioral change, social and personal networks of new members, and organizational lifestyles." Thus it is also possible that new tests must be designed that are more suitable for exploring the psychology of members and ex-members of new religious movements and for applying the new category of "spiritual or religious problem."

The distinction introduced by *DSM-IV* between religious and spiritual problems and psychopathology suggests that a different and more innovative psychological approach to the understanding of new religious movements is required. Galanter (1996: 289–290), who prefers the label "charismatic groups," applies the systems theory to understand new religious movements and to evaluate the psychological health of their members. He thinks that the common terminology used in psychopatholgy is problematic for at least two reasons: "In the first place, it was developed as a typology of mental illness rather than of social adaption. Charismatic group experience, however, is essentially normal in certain contexts. . . . The nomenclature was also developed specifically to describe the phenomena of individual behavior, whereas the zealous group's phenomena here must be understood in relation to the demand characteristics of a group context." Taking into consideration the new category introduced by *DSM-IV* and Galanter's incisive remarks, one wonders whether some serious rethinking needs to be done in the way most psychologists and psychiatrists have approached, both theoretically and methodologically, the majority of new religious movements.

NOTES

1. For a critical evaluation of the treatment of religion in *DSM-III*, see Richardson 1993.

2. For recent attempts to discuss the relationship between psychology of religion and to resolve some of the conflicts between the two, see, for example, Jonte-Pace and Jones 2001.

3. A brief survey of psychological studies on meditation can be found in Saliba 1993: 104–106.

4. For a concise profile of this new religious movement see Sloan 1999.

5. One must add that the negative evaluations of cults and their members, formulated in the mid-1970s, are still routinely repeated with little refinement. See, for examples, Singer 1995; Langone 1993, 2001; and Shields and Carter 2001.

6. For a profile of "Rajneeshism" see Skane 1999.

REFERENCES

Alper, Gerald. 1994. *The Puppeteers: Studies in Obsessive Control.* Lanham, Md.: International Scholars Publications.

American Psychiatric Association. 1987. *Diagnostic and Statistical Manual of Mental Disorders.* 3d ed. Washington: American Psychiatric Association.

———. 1994. *Diagnostic and Statistical Manual of Mental Disorders.* 4th ed. Washington: American Psychiatric Association.

Amitabh, Swami Prem. 1982. "Shree Rajneesh Ashram: A Provocative Community." *Journal of Humanistic Psychology* 22.1: 19–42.

Amrito, Swami Deva. 1984. "Rajneesh Therapy." *Journal of Humanistic Psychology* 24.1: 115–118.

Aronoff, Jodi, Steven Jay Lynn, and Peter Malinoski. 2000. "Are Cultic Environments Psychologically Harmful?" *Clinical Psychology Review* 20: 91–111.

Ayella, Marybeth. 1990. " 'They Must Be Crazy': Some Difficulties in Researching 'Cults.' " *American Behavioral Scientist* 33: 562–577.

———. 1998. *Insane Therapy: Portrait of a Psychotherapy Cult.* Philadelphia: Temple University Press.

Battista, John R. 1996. "Offensive Spirituality and Spiritual Defenses." In *Textbook of*

Transpersonal Psychiatry and Psychology, ed. Bruce W. Scotton, Alan B. Chisen, and John R. Battista, 250–260. New York: Basic Books.

Collins, G. R. 1994. "Religion and Psychology." In *Encyclopedia of Psychology,* ed. Raymond J. Corsini, vol. 3, pp. 300–302. New York: Wiley and Sons.

Dean, Roger. 1992. *Moonies: A Psychological Analysis of the Unification Church.* New York: Garland.

Deikman, Arthur. 1994. *The Wrong Way Home: Uncovering the Patterns of Cult Behavior in American Society.* Boston: Beacon.

Drennen, William T. 1983. "Rajneeshpuram: Hound Dogs with a Scent." *Journal of Humanistic Psychology* 23.3: 82–100.

Feuerstein, Georg. 1991. *Holy Madness: The Shock Tactics and Radical Teachings of Crazy-Wise Adepts, Holy People, and Rascal Gurus.* New York: Paragon.

Gallanter, Marc. 1980. "Psychological Induction into the Large Group: Findings from a Modern Religious Sect." *American Journal of Psychiatry* 137: 1574–1579.

———. 1996. "Cults and Charismatic Group Psychology." In *Religion and the Clinical Practice of Psychology,* ed. Edwards P. Schfranske, 269–296. Washington: American Psychological Association.

Gorsuch, Richard L. 1988. "Psychology of Religion." *Annual Review of Psychology* 39: 201–221.

Greenberg, David, and Eliezer Witztum. 1991. "Problems in the Treatment of Religious Patients." *American Journal of Psychotherapy* 44: 554–565.

Hyams, Hanna. 1998. "Dissociation: Definition, Diagnosis, Manifestations, and Therapy, with Special Reference to Cults/Sects." *Transactional Analysis Journal* 28: 234–243.

Jonte-Pace, Diane, and William B. Jones, eds. 2001. *Religion and Psychology: Mapping the Terrain. Contemporary Dialogues, Future Prospects.* New York: Routledge.

Kraus, Daniel. 1999. "Psychological Studies of New Religious Movements: Findings from German-Speaking Countries." *International Journal for the Psychology of Religion* 9.4: 263–281.

Langone, Michael. 2001. "Cults, Psychological Manipulation and Society: International Perspectives—An Overview." *Cultic Studies Journal* 18: 1–12.

Langone, Michael, ed. 1993. *Recovery from Cults: Help for Victims of Psychological and Spiritual Abuse.* New York: Norton.

Latkin, Carl A. 1989. "Gender Roles in the Experimental Community: Rajneesh-puram." *Sex Roles* 21: 629–652.

———. 1990a. "The Self-Concept of Rajneeshpuram Commune Members." *Journal for the Scientific Study of Religion* 29: 91–98.

———. 1990b. "Self-Consciousness in Members of a New Religious Movement: The Rajneeshees." *Journal of Social Psychology* 130: 557–558.

———. 1993. "Coping with the Fall: The Mental Health of Former Members of the Rajneeshpuram Commune." *International Journal for the Psychology of Religion* 3: 97–109.

———. 1995. "New Directions in Applying Psychological Theory to the Study of New Religions." *International Journal for the Psychology of Religion* 5: 177–180.

Latkin, Carl. A., Richard A. Hagan, Richard A. Littman, and Norman D. Sundberg. 1987. "Who Lives in Utopia: A Brief Research Report on the Rajneeshee Project." *Sociological Analysis* 48: 73–81.

Latkin, Carl. A., Richard A. Littman, Norman D. Sundberg, and Richard A. Hagan. 1993. "Pitfalls and Pratfalls in Research on an Experimental Community: Lessons in Integrating Theory and Practice from the Rajneeshpuram Research Project." *Journal of Community Psychology* 21: 35–48.

Lilliston, Lawrence, and Gary Shepherd. 1999. "New Religious Movement and Mental Health." In *New Religious Movements: Challenge and Response,* ed. Bryan Wilson and Jamie Cresswell. New York: Routledge.

Luckoff, David, Francis G. Lu, and Robert Turner. 1996. "Diagnosis: A Transpersonal Clinical Approach to Religious and Spiritual Problems." In *Textbook of Transpersonal Psychiatry and Psychology,* ed. Bruce W. Scotton, Alan B. Chisen, and John R. Battista, 231–249. New York: Basic Books.

Reber, Auther S. 1985. *Dictionary of Psychology.* New York: Penguin Books.

Richardson, James T. 1993. "Religiosity as Deviance: Negative Religious Bias in and Misuse of the DSM-III." *Deviant Behavior: An Interdisciplinary Journal* 14: 1–21.

———. 1995. "Clinical and Personality Assessment of Participants in New Religions." *International Journal for the Psychology of Religion* 5: 145–170.

Saliba, John A. 1993. "The New Religions and Mental Health." In *Religion and the Social Order: The Handbook on Cults and Sects in America,* ed. David G. Bromley and Jeffrey K. Hadden, vol. 3, part B, pp. 99–113. Greenwich, Conn.: Jai Press.

———. 1996. *Understanding the New Religious Movements.* Grand Rapids, Mich.: Eerdmans.

Shear, Jonathan. 2001. "Experimental Studies of Meditation and Consciousness." In *Religion and Psychology: Mapping the Terrain. Contemporary Dialogues, Future Prospects,* ed. Diane Jonte-Pace and William B. Parsons, 280–294. New York: Routledge.

Shields, Leland E., and F. Jeri Carter. 2001. "Healing Experiences with Unhealthy Spiritual Groups and Cults: Treatment Using Myths and Folk Tales." *Cultic Studies Journal* 18: 109–139.

Singer, Margaret. 1995. *Cults in Our Midst.* San Francisco: Jossey-Bass.

Skane, Elizabeth. 1999. "Osho (or Rajneeshism)." http://religiousmovements.lib.virginia.edu//nrms

Sloan, Jennifer. 1999. "Order of the Solar Temple." http://religiousmovements.lib.virginia.edu//nrms

Sparr, Landy F., and John F. Ferguson. 2000. "Moral and Spiritual Issues Following Traumatization." In *Psychiatry and Religion: The Convergence of Mind and Spirit,* ed. James K. Boehnlein, 71–83. Washington: American Psychiatric Press.

Storr, Anthony. 1996. *Feet of Clay: Saints, Sinners, and Madmen: A Study of Gurus.* New York: Free Press.

Sundberg, Norman D., Marion S. Goldman, Nathan J. Rotter, and Douglas A. Smyth. 1992. "Personality and Spirituality: Comparative TATs of High-Achieving Rajneeshees." *Journal of Personalty Assessment* 59.2: 326–339.

Sundberg, Norman D., Carl A. Latkin, Richard A., Littman, and Richard A. Hagan. 1990. "Personality in a Religious Commune: CPIs in Rajneesh-puram." *Journal of Personality Assessment* 55.1–2: 7–17.

Turner, Robert P., David Luckoff, Ruth Tiffany Barnhouse, and Francis G. Lu. 1998. "Religious or Spiritual Problem: A Culturally Sensitive Diagnostic Category in DSM-IV." *Journal of Nervous and Mental Disease* 180: 435–444.

Weiss, A. S., and Comrey, A. L. 1987. "Personality Characteristics of Hare Krishnas." *Journal of Personality Assessment* 51: 399–413.

Wilson, Colin. 2000. *The Devil's Party: A History of Charlatan Messiahs.* London: Virgin.

Wulff, David M. 2001. "Psychology of Religion: An Overview." In *Religion and Psychology: Mapping the Terrain. Contemporary Dialogues, Future Prospects,* ed. Diane Jonte-Pace and William B. Parsons, 15–29. New York: Routledge.

CHAPTER 14

MILLENNIALISM

RICHARD LANDES

TYPES OF MILLENNIALISM
AND APOCALYPTICISM

LITERALLY, millennialism refers to the belief, expressed in the book of *Revelation*, that Christ will establish a one-thousand-year reign of the saints on earth before the Last Judgment. More broadly defined, millennialists expect a time of supernatural peace and abundance *here on earth*. It is a form of *social* mysticism in which, the time come, believers horizontally organize (collective mysticism) to bring about the new age (social body) in which the spirit of divinity flows like milk and honey. At its origins, millennialism offers a concrete version of the fundamental eschatological belief that at the "end of time," God will judge the living and the (resurrected) dead and reward some while punishing the rest. This belief in an ultimate divine justice has provided the solution to the problem of *theodicy* for countless generations of believers suffering hardship and oppression, and has, therefore, had immense appeal for commoners in every age. Whereas the name comes from the thousand-year period of perfection, in fact the key factor concerns the *earthly* nature of the coming "new world." Whether it is of a duration of forty years or four thousand, the radical transformation necessarily means an end to the current institutions of power and, therefore, gives all millennial beliefs a revolutionary quality that has made them unwelcome to those in positions of authority. In alternative terms, millennialism represents a meme—the advent of a time of collective human perfection—that is programmed to sweep through entire cultures with an infectious enthusiasm (Lynch 1996).

The key issue in terms of millennialism's impact on society, however, is the matter of timing. As long as the day of redemption is not yet come, millennial hopes console the suffering and inspire patience (Revelation 13:10) and political quiescence, and have a profoundly conservative influence. Secret societies can exist for extended periods invisible to both the historian and the political elites of the time while awaiting the "moment." But driven by a sense of imminence, believers can become disruptive, even engaging in revolutionary efforts to overthrow so-ciopolitical order in an attempt to bring about the kingdom of "peace" for the meek and the defenseless. This *apocalyptic millennialism* constitutes a powerful and volatile mixture, fascinating the hearts and minds of people throughout the ages. No matter how often the apocalyptic beliefs have been proven wrong (until present, always), no matter how often the millennial efforts to establish God's kingdom on earth have led not to heaven on earth but disastrous destruction in defeat and equally disastrous totalitarianism in victory, apocalyptic expectations repeatedly revive. From the failed Jewish revolts against Rome that led to hundreds of thousands of deaths and slavery (3 B.C.E., 66–70, 132–135) to the temporarily successful Taiping Rebellion (1850s) and Nazi *tausandjähriger Reich*, which led, in both cases, to the death of tens of *millions* of people, to the successful Marxist revolutions of the twentieth century, which "purged" almost 100 million people in the middle decades of the last century, such movements have a tendency to submit to and engage in staggering violence and destruction (Mendel 1992, 2000). And yet, for all the costly failures, the appeal remains and generation after gen-eration finds devotees in search of the chimerical kingdom.

But most of the time, millennial beliefs remain dormant. In these normative states, millennialism tends to play the narcotic role that Marx attributed to all religion. It convinces believers to accept passively the current status quo, despite the clear dominance of darkness and evil in the political relationships between men (violence, enslavement, oppression, betrayal). Since all this will rapidly pass away when the time has come, slaves should, in the meantime, obey their masters and not seek to rectify the world, to usurp God's role. During these lengthy periods of "normal time," elites will often propagate nonapocalyptic millennial ideals as a form of comfort to those at the lower reaches of the social hierarchy. Of course such beliefs, for all their value as conservative religious forces, neces-sarily create tensions over the eventual advent of this profoundly subversive future. Certain cultures developed a tradition of "dating the end," in which a specific future moment, often the end of the century or the millennium, became a widely accepted apocalyptic expectation, creating a kind of "balloon mortgage" for cer-tain dates (Mujadded tradition in Islam for the end of the century, sabbatical millennium in Judaism and Christianity for the end of the millennium).

Historians, however, tend to detect the presence of such beliefs only when the millenarian faithful enter *apocalyptic* time. Then the sense of imminence dra-matically changes behavioral patterns, liberates hopes, and galvanizes believers to participate in the great transformation. *Apocalyptic* material—references to people preaching either the "end of the world" or the coming "day of Judgment"—often comes from outsiders and does not necessarily inform us on the millennial vision of an ultimate goal, but primarily about the timing and nature of the transformation that leads us from this evil world to the world to come, whether millennial or celestial. On occasion such collective apocalyptic behavior makes a profound impression on the larger society (sometimes, if briefly, sweeping the whole society up in its expectations). In such cases, the composers of texts describing these events will record its presence most often *ex post defecto* (from after the disappointment), either with hostile descriptions or efforts to distance themselves from the now-falsified prophecies.

Despite an unblemished record of failure in predicting the advent of the millennium, apocalyptic millennialism has shown astounding resilience over the last three millennia. This seems to derive primarily from the immense psychological rewards these beliefs offer. Those who embrace them find themselves at the center of the ultimate universal drama, and their every act has cosmic significance. Moreover, they can almost taste the fulfillment of their burning desire to see justice done—the good lavishly rewarded, the evil savagely punished. And on those (relatively) rare apocalyptic occasions, believers become convinced that the times of this great apocalyptic transformation and the advent of a promised world have dawned. Apocalyptic believers become semiotically aroused (even semiotically promiscuous), finding cosmic messages in the smallest incident, in every coincidence: all the universe exists to give them messages about the nature of cosmic time now unfolding and their role at the heart of the drama. Such arousal, precisely because it believes that the future will be radically discontinuous with the present, liberates believers from any earthly inhibitions. With the rules about to change, no fear of future consequences (except from a judging deity) restrains the conscience of apocalyptic actors. In James Scott's (1992) terms, hidden transcripts burst to the surface. Without fear of future punishment by those who now hold power, a wide range of repressed feelings—sexual, passionate, violent—burst forth. Such a combination proves irresistible to many. Apocalyptic hope for the millennium *possesses* believers (Desroche 1979).

SCHOLARSHIP ON MILLENNIAL PHENOMENA

Recognition of millennialism as a significant issue began in conjunction with the field of NRMs, in the postwar period, initially as a result of anthropological studies of the cargo cults of the Pacific southwest. One could actually argue that James

Mooney's study of the late-nineteenth-century Native Americans, *Ghost Dance* (1973), marks the dawn of modern anthropology and serves as the prototypical study of NRMs and millennial phenomena. The observations of modern researchers working either on exotic cultures (Burridge 1969; Whitehead 2000) or on the sociology of apocalyptic groups in the U.S. (Festinger et al. 1956, 1964) inspired historians to review the historical record and detect, by homology, the presence of charismatic millennial preachers who, with an apocalyptic discourse, gathered brief but vast crowds of devoted followers (Hall 2000). In tracing the lineage of these movements in the medieval period and the inquisitorial mechanisms of the Church hierarchy in opposition, Norman Cohn (1959) drew a dramatically different history of the West, linking millennialism both to the appearance of egalitarian revolutionary traditions and to Communist and Nazi totalitarianism, theses that met with considerable opposition.

Over the last generation, the field has grown significantly, and major studies have emerged, some examining in detail famous millennial incidents such as the Canudos community in late-nineteenth-century Brazil (Levine 1992), the Taiping of mid-nineteenth-century China (Spence 1996), or the global Jewish messianic movement around Shabbetai Zvi in the mid–seventeenth century (Scholem 1975); some reconsidering major incidents of the modern period in terms of millennialism such as the English Civil War (Hill 1993), American Revolution (Bloch 1985), modern science (Noble 1998), and Nazism (Rhode 1980); and some more broadly arguing that apocalyptic millennialism lies at the heart of many if not all great religious movements (La Barre 1970; Desroche 1979; Mendel 1992, 2000). Cohn's work on millennialism has created a cottage industry of studies of millennialism in the Middle Ages, especially around the figure of Joachim of Fiore, whose millennial exegesis of history foreseeing a new age that would come about through the transformation of vast numbers of individual souls from within seems to have profoundly affected the great religious movements of the thirteenth and fourteenth centuries, especially the various currents of Franciscan thought and action (Reeves 1977; McGinn 1979, 1994; Lerner 1976, 2000). Some medievalists have argued that millennialism played a role even in the supposed period of dormancy (400–1100), including the year 1000 (Fried 1989; Landes 1988), but that has not yet achieved acceptance in early medieval historiography, especially among French medievalists who spilled a good deal of ink at the approach of 2000 denying any apocalyptic expectations around 1000 (Barthélemy 1999; Gouguenheim 1999). The advent of 2000 brought out a plethora of books on the millennium, some of which represent good broad syntheses (Thompson 1996, 1999; Wojcik 1997; Weber 1999; Katz and Popkin 1998; Abanes 1999), others broad treatments of particular fields (Graziano 1999 on Latin American millennialism, Noble 1998 on science and technology). A significant number of edited volumes offer a wide range of studies (Lincoln 1985; Andrews et al. 1987; Verbeke et al. 1988; Bull 1995; S. Cook 1995; Stozier and Flynn 1997; Schafer and Cohen 1998; Kleinhenz and LeMoine

1999; Vessey et al. 1999; Baumgarten 2000; Wessinger 2000; Robbins and Palmer 1997; Whitehead 2000; Amanat and Bernhardsson 2002). The bibliography of millennial studies, already enormous at the beginning of the 1990s (Daniels 1992), has continued to expand exponentially.

Nonetheless, the broader field of historiography, and the overall interpretations of the course of civilizations, has not progressed beyond the general perspectives outlined by the positivist historians of the last third of the nineteenth century. These historians, emphasizing the importance of factual evidence and "objectivity" in reconstructing "what actually happened," and preferring rational to psychological analyses, dismissed poorly documented and irrational millennialism as a minor theme in Western history, acknowledging at most a brief appearance during early Christian history, vanishing by the end of the fourth century until Joachim of Fiore in the late twelfth century (Reeves 1977; McGinn 1979, 1994), and playing at best a secondary role thereafter. There is, as a result, virtually no room in the "grand narratives" for millennialism as a contributing factor to the course of Western history. Similar struggles have taken place within the historiographical traditions of East Asian history and of the history of Judaism and Islam. In each case, while some historians argued that evidence indicated a pervasive and central role for millennialism within the larger culture, the larger historical community considered the phenomenon marginal if not irrelevant.

As among medieval historians, some modern historians have examined the role of millennialism in major episodes of their period, with the most thoroughly documented analysis in Christopher Hill's (1993) extensive examination of the millennial currents of the English Civil War and a similar perspective in Denis Crouzet's (1996) work on the French wars of religion. Almost every field of Western historiography has produced studies of millennial themes and movements, including analyses of the French and American Revolutions (Schwartz 1990; Bloch 1985), and among millennial scholars there is little question that both Nazism and Communism represent secular millennial movements (Rhodes 1980; Mendel 1992, 2000; Wessinger 2000). Mainstream historians, however, remain more skeptical and reluctant to identify movements as millennial even when they themselves use that rhetoric (*tausendjähriger Reich*), by cleaving to Aristotelian analytic categories. As strange as the formulation that "Nazism is not millennial because it is secular, and millennialism religious" may strike the social scientist familiar with millennial dynamics, it has inhibited most modern historians from considering Nazism as a millennial movement. Thus, just as anthropologists and sociologists began to realize the importance of millennial thinking in the NRMs they observe, they can find little guidance from the writings of the historical profession; and, conversely, historians have proved enduringly reluctant to absorb the analytic and historical lessons of the emerging field of millennial studies.

Millennialism, on the other hand, represents a major area of research for NRM scholars, whose early and foundational focus on new movements highlighted the importance of apocalyptic rhetoric in the origins of many successful NRMs, and the millennial themes that undergird this arousing discourse (O'Leary 1994). Attuned to the rapid mutations that religious movements go through during the early phases of their development, and the strong apocalyptic content of much of the earliest discourse (Hall 2000), they have little difficulty identifying the dynamic similarities in, say, Taiping millennialism, Nazism, and Maoism, and classing them as a type of millennial phenomenon (Wessinger 2000). Work addressed to questions of religious violence invariably must deal with millennialism, since in certain forms (active, cataclysmic, apocalyptic) it represents one of the most volatile and destructive religious phenomena recorded (Wessinger 2000; Robbins and Palmer 1997). The value of interdisciplinary work became especially visible recently when, as a result of the Waco crisis, a scholar trained to read Dead Sea Scrolls studied the biblical exegesis of Vernon Howell (David Koresh) and detected the same semiotic arousal in both men (Tabor and Gallagher 1995). Unfortunately, the poor state of *historical* scholarship on millennialism has encouraged NRM scholars to focus on the modern situation, reluctant as they understandably might be to tell ancient historians how to interpret things like the early Jesus movement, Zealotry, and Montanism.

And yet, at the dawn of the first global era in recorded history, we are faced with the phenomenon of NRMs the world over, many triggered, intensified, and apocalypticized by the encroachments of capital markets whose acidic impact penetrates deep into indigenous cultures (Burridge 1969; Lanternari 1963; Adas 1977; Whitehead 2000). The role of millennialism in such responses forms one of the leitmotivs of modernization and the wide range of reactions it provokes. At present, the most widespread and dangerous millennial activity in the world comes from Islam, where various elements of a largely antimodern resurgence (Islamism) have renewed the early vision of Islam as a battle of the true believers fighting to extend the world of submission to Islam: *Dar al Islam*—the realm of submission/ peace—versus. *Dar al Harb*—the realm of the sword/war (see below).

Anthropologists and sociologists have rapidly recognized the importance of millennial (perfect world) and apocalyptic (now) themes in the early stages of new religious movements, and still more their prominence in successful religious movements like the Mormons, the Seventh-Day Adventists, and Jehovah's Witnesses (Penton (1985). Already by 1990, the literature in millennial studies was enormous (Daniels 1992). In addition to these products of various religious revivals that have periodically swept the U.S., larger and more mainstream Protestant denominations manifest pervasive millennial elements, most notably the "premillennial dispensationalism" of modern "Fundamentalism" (Couch 1996). Indeed, the postwar period (the second half of the twentieth century) has proved a breeding ground for apocalyptic and millennial themes in wide ranges of American and Western culture, especially under the cloud of nuclear destruction (Boyer 1992), from the politically oriented militias and Aryan Christians (Barkun 1994,

1996; Lamy 1996; Berlet 2000); to the religious sects like Aum Shinrikyō (Lifton 1999; Mullins 1997; Reader 2000), Solar Temple (Hall and Schuyler, Mayer 2000), and Heaven's Gate (Introvigne 2000); to New Age groups like the Urantians and Raelians (Palmer 1997).

For some analysts, the 1960s, with its communal movement, its radical egalitarian politics, and its capacious interest in other religions, represents a global wave of millennial enthusiasm beginning among the baby boomers of the West and spreading, by the late 1960s to countries around the world (Hall 1978; Mendel 1992, 2000; Schwartz 1999). Among the most prominent aspects of this millennial culture, which, while "fringe," has become extensively diffused by popular media, are global conspiracy theories and UFO lore. In a sense UFOs offer a "secular" and technological apocalyptic millennium, in which the extraterrestrials are redeeming saviors (postmodern cargo cults), or bearers of apocalyptic destruction, or the inaugurators of the reign of the Antichrist (UFO conspiracy theories). The advent of the World Wide Web has generated new groups and intensified the contact between them (Brasher 1998). Such developments offer deeply ambiguous prognoses; millennialism offers both peaceful and progressive forms (Wessinger 2000) and a deeply disturbing embrace of coercive and violent dreams of dominion (Quinby 1994). Understanding the intimate dance that unites them in such a volatile and creative mix produces profound insights (Mendel 1992, 2000).

The pervasiveness of millennialism in the Western world, with its embedded biblical theologies and its technology-invigorated variants, has sometimes blinded scholars to its presence in the rest of the world. Many cultures have indigenous millennial traditions that, when combined with Western ones, can produce a kaleidoscope of variations, as in Latin America with everything from Marian visionary communities to Rastafarians (Graziano 1999; Salter 2000). Anthropologists have, perhaps first among all modern scholars, detected and chronicled the behavior of millennial movements in tribal cultures, often rapidly provoked by contact with modern Western culture. Many indigenous movements of tribal and peasant societies, often anti-imperialist in nature, take on the full range of characteristics of millennialism (Lanternari 1963; Adas 1977). In the Western hemisphere, for example, native populations produced a wide range of millennial movements, from the *Gaiwiio* of Handsome Lake, ca. 1800 (Wallace 1976) to the *Ghost Dance* of the prophet Wovoka in the 1890s (Pesantubbee 2000). In the Pacific southwest, the twentieth century has seen the emergence of "Cargo Cults," which, responding to the arrival of cargo planes (especially during World War II), believed that by carrying out the proper rituals, they could bring the "cargo" from the great bird in the sky (Burridge 1969; Stewart and Strathern 1997). Modern UFO cults, many of which have strong millennial elements, represent a kind of postmodern cargo cult: whether the coming aliens will help us transform our world into paths of peace or enslave us to carry out their rapacious will, the result of their advent and the nature of their cargo marks an apocalyptic transformation of the world (Wojcik 1997). The global conspiracy—whether benevolent or (more often) maleficent—that characterizes so much of UFO thought represents a classic delineation of the *already/not yet* of apocalyptic time: "They have landed but they are not yet public" corresponds exactly to "Antichrist is born, but not yet reached his manhood" (Barkun 1974, 1994, 1996).

The non-Western array of millennial phenomena often displays the kinds of magical thinking that includes bullet-proof vests (Ghost Dance, Boxers) and cattle-killing (Xhosa), as well as more aggressively revolutionary movements (Mau Mau, al-Qaeda). Indeed, millennialism constitutes one of the most creative—and often one of the most violent—ways in which more traditional or tribal cultures respond to the dissolution of their own bonds as the result of contact with the West. From such observations one can safely predict that the ongoing wave of globalization now under way will produce a wide range of millennial manifestations that could potentially take on the kinds of global proportions that millennial memes are constructed to achieve. In fact, at the time of this writing, two major candidates for apocalyptic millennialism that may have global impact have become clearly visible to the practiced eye: an apparently modernizing movement—Falun Gong (Ownby 2002)—and a, at this stage, still violently antimodern one—Islamism (D. Cook 1996).

Notably, both of these "turn of the millennium" millennial phenomena come in cultures with a long and largely unnoticed millennial tradition. Islam, as a "religion of revelation," began as an apocalyptic movement anticipating the "Day of Judgment" (Cook and Crone 1976; Bashear 1973; D. Cook 1996). The global political vision of Islam—the spheres of the sword and of submission (Dar al Harb and Dar al Islam)—represents the (unintended) imperial results of these millennial jihads. Dhimmi status for those who refuse to convert constitutes a classic case of religious *apartheid* (Bat Ye'or), the "normal time" consequence of failed millennial expectations. Apocalyptic expectation of Al Kiyama (Day of Resurrection) remained a perpetual possibility. In particular, the Mujaddid tradition, which foresees a "renewer" at every century turn (A.H.), appears to constitute—already at the approach of the first "century" marker in 719 C.E.—a form of apocalyptic messianic expectation in the coming of the hidden Mahdi (D. Cook 1996; Bashear 1973). At the approach of 1000 A.H. (1591–1592 C.E.), for example, some of the most powerful representatives of a hierarchical millennialism formed Islamic empires in India (Moghuls), Persia (Saffavids), and the Eastern Mediterranean (Ottomans). In particular, Suleiman the Magnificent and Akhbar, the Moghul ruler of India, rose to their exceptional positions of authority on the basis of a reforming millennialism (Fleischer 2004; Amanat; and Bernhadsson 2002). Similarly, breakaway movements like the Baha'i arise from demotic currents of Islamic millennialism activated by apocalyptic time and an apocalyptic prophet— the Bab—who can so identify and galvanize believers.

At certain times, the apocalyptic atmosphere heats up in more than one of the monotheistic traditions, mostly according to the principle that "one person's messiah is another's Antichrist/Dajjal." Historians need to identify such moments and analyze the dynamics more carefully, like the early eleventh century or the sixteenth century in the Mediterranean. In 1009 c.e., for example, the Fatimid Calif of Cairo, Al Hakim, partly in response to the advent of the year 400 A.H., partly in response to a nova that astronomers all over the world spotted in 1006, and partly in response to the renewed Christian interest in Jerusalem at the advent of 1000, destroyed the Holy Sepulcher and other Christian churches and forced Christians to convert. This set off a wave of pogroms against the Jews in Western Europe, where the millennial expectations around 1000 were most acute (Eastern Christians used an Annus Mundi calendar, and Latin Christians used *Anno Domini*), triggering apocalyptic expectations among the Jews. Similarly, at the approach of the Christian year 7000 (1492–1508) and the Muslim year 1000 (1591/2), both cultures reached so high a pitch of millennial discourse that ambassadors used prophetic texts to make alliances (Fleischer). Right now in Africa, a conflict of this type is taking shape that pits two millennial movements with demonizing discourses at their core (Hackett 2003).

Many of the Islamic millennial moments, no matter how important a demotic dimension they had at an early stage, eventually settled into imperial hierarchies. In the Christian West, however, stimulated by the printing press, more demotic millennial principles continued to eat away at the legitimacy and control of these hierarchies, contributing eventually to both democratic revolutions and industrial transformation (Puritanism vs. the English monarchy). Contact with the modern West over the last three centuries has created extremely difficult conditions for these empires, which largely operated according to hierarchical principles at clear odds with the egalitarian notions of *isonomia*, characteristic of Western political modernity and, in the case with Islam, also characteristic of the demotic trends within their own religion (*Ulama*). Much of the rhetoric of Islamism is egalitarian and socially concerned with the poor and dispossessed.

The repeated failures, both military and economic, of the Muslim countries in the face of modern Western successes have set up a long-term sense of decline and defeat. Imperial conquests encroached upon regions once ruled by Islam, intensified the corruption of the Arab world with the oil money channeled directly to elites, and produced a defiant nationalism among Jews who returned to Zion, establishing beachheads of modern secularism and a religious challenge—a Dhimmi people in revolt against subjection—in the heart of Dar al Islam. The first clear response to the challenge of modernity was Arab nationalism, a secular, socialist ideology that rapidly foundered into authoritarian and proto-totalitarian political states (Ba'ath party in Iran and Iraq). Islamism consists of a religious backlash to both Arab (secular) nationalism and Western modern cultures, a broad range of fervent antimodern revivalists, often modeled, whether acknowledged or not, on Protestant antimodern fundamentalism. It has important demotic ideological elements (which closely resemble those of early Arab national-ism), but also equally important authoritarian tendencies that threaten to discard the demotic for the totalitarian (Taliban). Given the cultural framework of Islam-ism (aggressive Quranic exegesis, authoritarian teaching and rule, stratified honor cultures), we find a proliferation of the most virulent aspects of antimodernism—conspiracism, apocalyptic violence, genocidal urges. For Islamists, the "big pic-ture" behind their local efforts at religious rigor reconstitutes the early millennial dream of Islam—all the world either converted or reduced to subject (Dhimmi) status.

By far the most powerful nonmonotheistic millennial tradition is found in Buddhism, with the Pure Land traditions and the expectation of the Matreya Buddha, a kind of messianic final incarnation of the Buddha. Early Chinese im-perialism around the turn of the common era deployed important themes from hierarchical millennialism—the salvation of political unity (Ownby 1999, 2002)—and many subsequent expressions of Chinese millennialism have favored the hi-erarchical, even if they began with demotic aspirations like the White Lotus so-cieties (Naquin). Especially strong in China, but evident in Korea, Japan, Vietnam, and Burma, millennial strains of Buddhism have given birth, in the aftermath of disappointment and defeat, to secret societies, martial arts monastic traditions, and occasionally powerful popular movements, one of which toppled the Mongol dynasty in the fourteenth century and another of which, the Taiping (Great Peace), almost toppled the Qing dynasty in the mid–nineteenth century (Spence 1996; Lowe 2002). By the time the Taiping, itself a mixture of native Buddhist and imported Christian millennialism, had been suppressed, 20–35 million people were dead. The Boxer rebellion of the late nineteenth century again demonstrated the power of millennial beliefs, whether generated by a formal theology (White Lotus) or the cultural dynamics of nativist resistance (Cohen 1997), especially the char-acteristic magical belief, shared by the Ghost Dancers of North America and the Kartelite Cults of Africa, that certain incantations could render the believer in-vulnerable to bullets (La Barre 1970).

The limitless violence of some millennial movements, no matter how peaceful, progressive, or voluntary they are at the beginning, cannot be underestimated. The Taiping (Great Peace) left tens of millions dead, as did the secular explosions of mid–twentieth century. Perhaps the most disturbing development in this sense comes from Aum Shinrikyō, the Japanese cult that tried to trigger a massive loss of life in order to "save the world by destroying it." The presence of apocalyptic technology of mass destruction has greatly increased the ability of even small (and immature) millennial groups to pursue an option of active catastrophic violence, thus posing an intolerable threat to the larger culture in which they grow. The violence of Islamic movements, something that has accelerated impressively since the (relatively) peaceful Iranian revolution (1979 C.E. or 1400 A.H.), and largely in the framework of the Arab-Israeli conflict, has taken suicidal violence to new and disturbingly popular heights (Al Aqsa intifada, 9/11 bombings) and has a strong apocalyptic dimension (D. Cook 1996).

All these remarks suggest that, at the dawn of the first genuinely global era, millennialism will play an increasingly prominent role in many of the patterns of adjustment and resistance, and we need an extensive analysis of the conditions under which millennial movements shift from peaceful to violent and vice versa, identifying ways in which the host culture can interact with them to encourage the latter and avoid the former. One might go so far as to define a key element of modernity as a shift from the default position of governments to wipe out millennial movements (Romans and Jesus, Protestant/Catholic alliance against Anabaptists) to a more modulated one in which millennial movements could find more peaceful and constructive ways to return from their apocalyptic origins to "normal" time. The problems in developing such relations came painfully to the fore in the 1990s in the U.S. with the Waco catastrophe and its fallout, leading law enforcement circles to at last consult with NRM scholars on these issues (Megiddo Report).

Arthur Mendel's reflections on tautological millennialism (transformational apocalyptic, demotic millennial) offer the beginnings of a psychological and ideological reflection which, combined with the reflections of NRM scholars on assaulted, fragile, and revolutionary groups (Wessinger 2000; Kaplan 2003) offers a crucial starting point. Any effective policy approach must understand that it deals with a moving target, movements that are immensely protean in apocalyptic time and surprisingly responsive to contacts with the supposedly rejected outside world. The efforts of the Chinese Communist government to throttle Falun Gong, as well as the failure of the Arab governments to confront Islamism, represent the two poles of policy failure in this vital arena. These problems become all the more acute under conditions when a media technology developed in the West precisely at a time when governments were learning to tolerate.

But such "enlightened" approaches among law enforcement at the approach of 2000, however halting and preliminary in places like the U.S. and Israel, do not even characterize all Western governments. The French government led a number of European countries (Italy, Germany) in legislating aggressively against NRMs (Introvigne 2000), and the Chinese have eagerly sought the French model as justification for their policies. Still more troubling, the spread of both "human rights" rhetoric and media technology around the world has fundamentally changed the nature and impact of religious discourse and interaction in other cultures, and has created a potentially violent mix of NRMs that use both the freedom guaranteed by new laws and the amplifying capacities offered by the new technology to aggressively press an intolerant agenda (Hackett 2003). The problems inherent in such issues, so prominently visible in the case of Islamism (e.g., the religious-political instability of Saudi Arabia) presents the scholarly community with enormous challenges in addressing millennialism, the most political of all new religious movements. The disorientation of the press in thinking about the challenge of Islamism ("political or religious?") merely illustrates how preliminary our culture's understanding of these forces remains into the third millennium C.E.

One of the most evident and consequential conclusions of the first major round of millennial scholarship, most prominently addressed by the NRM community in immediately current terms, concerns the role of mutual tolerance in allowing a larger culture to both contain and integrate the millennial movements it generates. The "agreement" between governments and millennial NRMs to a peaceful resolution depends on a larger cultural commitment to mutual tolerance. Millennial NRMs, with their far more urgent and cosmic agenda, tend to exploit the language of tolerance until they can take over, a pattern Nietzsche identified with *ressentiment* (*Genealogy of Morals*) and which the increasingly intolerant behavior of the "Christian" Roman empire illustrated so disturbingly (Gibbon, *Decline and Fall of the Roman Empire*, ch. 28). A recent study of the wars of (millennial) religion that exploded in Europe as a result of the printing press's empowerment of NRMs (the "Protestant" "Reformation") concluded that religious tolerance was primarily a "loser's creed," that winners rapidly dismissed their prior commitments to tolerance as irrelevant once God had given them the power to carry out his task (Grell and Scribner 1996). In this sense, the American constitution represents the first time in the history of Christian millennialism that tolerance became a winner's creed, a fruitful accord whose rich legacy continues to play out. We scholars are both the grateful beneficiaries of and contributors to this rare development.

But the past, as Burke reminded Paine, has ballast, inertial force. Paradigms, no matter how faulty in dealing with reality, still carry emotional weight. Long after anomalies need addressing, they can still inspire scholars to ignore the inconsistencies of an approach that should make more sense. As a historian, I may be unfairly critical of my field, but my sense is that we are the worst offenders, the slowest to pay attention to millennialism as a historical factor. As a result, NRM scholarship remains largely a field about current religious movements, and its insights have fallen on inexcusably barren soil among historians of late Antiquity, especially the history of early Christianity. The consequences blight both fields and leave us in a state of discontinuity in our understanding of how we as a culture reached this stage of our millennial developments, and in our ability to think about millennial developments in other cultures. The remainder of this chapter, therefore, offers my contribution to a remedy to this situation. I will first suggest elements of an agenda for millennial/NRM studies and then address some methodological and definitional issues.

MILLENNIALISM: METHODS
AND TYPOLOGIES

Millennial studies argues that the rare explicit mentions of millennial movements that appear in a hostile documentation are almost all composed *ex post defecto* (after the disappointment/failure) and need to be treated as the tip of an iceberg that includes vastly more oral discourse than ever reaches written form, and a radically different attitude toward the prophecy on the part of contemporaries before its failure (Landes 1996a). Millennial scholarship calls for a counter-intuitive correction on two points: First, historians must try and imagine a phase *before* the failure, when enthusiasts vocalized far more extravagant (millennial) hopes and found a receptive audience even, as our sources complain, among educated clergy. Second, they must ponder the nature of their written medium and its ability to register the phenomenon in question. Without such preliminary work, historians resemble a nuclear scientist who dismisses the trail left by sub-atomic particles as too insubstantial to consider.

The ability to follow millennialism through its various and protean stages as it takes off in apocalyptic time and reenters with a profoundly ambiguous relationship to "normal" time gives an appreciation for the multiple forms that millennialism can take. A number of scholars have offered valuable typologies to capture some of this variability (O'Leary 1994; Wessinger 2000), each emphasizing the importance of viewing the categories as continua, and the ability of movements, under various conditions to move from one end to the other, often at startling speed. This speed reflects the inherent extremism and instability of apocalyptic beliefs: while almost all positions constitute some combination of the two extremes, the more extreme, the more coherent the position. Apocalyptic emotions despise compromise and even-handedness: "Because you are neither hot nor cold, but lukewarm, I spew you out!" (Revelations 3: 15).

Here I'd like to offer the reflections of a historian on the kinds of categories and terms that may help us grasp this elusive phenomenon. I suggest we think in terms of three major graphs: eschatological, millennial, and apocalyptic, each with two axes/continua.

Eschatology (from *eschaton* = end) concerns the collective salvation that comes to mankind at the end of time in a spectacular, all-embracing resolution to the problem of evil in the world. Eschatology focuses on a Day of (Last) Judgment, the prophetic "Day of the Lord" when the living and the (resurrected) dead pass before the heavenly throne. The first major axis here concerns whether this final redemption occurs on a celestial plane or a material one. On the celestial one, earth has passed away and rewards and punishments are meted out in heaven and hell; on the earthly one, the saved enjoy their rewards in the flesh, on earth (i.e., millennialism). Given the necessary intervention by a divine force in order to achieve the former, its social function tends to be conservative (pie in the sky bye and bye). Indeed, when Marx and others criticized religion as the opiate of the masses, they were thinking specifically of the kind of resignation and lack of commitment to "this-worldly" concerns that this celestial eschatology encourages. On the other hand, when the redemption occurs on the embodied plane, i.e., millennialism, the belief can have revolutionary implications since it views this world as ruled by forces of corruption and evil and anticipates a time when the now dominant forces will disappear and those now oppressed will have their day in the sun. Ironically, Marx, one of the great millennial thinkers of Western history, despised his religious lineage.

The second axis concerns the basis of salvation. Here the poles go from moral to credal. At one extreme, salvation comes exclusively to those who earn it by how they relate to their fellow man, expressed in the formula "the righteous among the gentiles have a place in the world to come" (Maimonides). In the more extreme cases of this belief (secular humanism), membership in a religious community guarantees nothing and indeed may impede genuinely moral behavior because it tends toward zealotry and intolerance. On the other end of the continuum, salvation comes to those who embrace a specific faith or credal formula, or are members of a specifically defined "in-group." Here we find a denominational solidarity that overrides moral concerns (including a capacity for violence against outsiders), as well as a claim to monopoly of the faith on salvation. Most credal eschatologies do not eliminate moral concerns entirely: those who do evil and do not repent will be punished on Judgment Day, but only those who are within the faith community can be saved, and repentance consists of submission or return to that community (modern Christian fundamentalism, Islamism): "No salvation outside the Church."

Millennialism: Along one axis, millennial beliefs tend to bifurcate between *hierarchical* and *demotic* poles, and on the other, between *restorative* or *progressive* visions of the new world. At one end of the first axis we find imperial, authoritarian visions of a messianic kingdom ruled over by a just (if severe and even ruthless) imperial figure, who will conquer the forces of chaos and impose "true" order on society. In monotheistic traditions, this millennialism adopts iconic political formulas in which an earthly order imitates the heavenly, and the earthly ruler imitates the divine in his relationship to the ruled: "One God, one king (ruler/rule), one religion." Many world conquerors have used some variant of millennial "savior" imagery to bolster their rule (Cyrus, Alexander, Augustus, Constantine), as have great reformers (Akhenaten, Herod, Charlemagne). In the Muslim and Christian "Middle Ages" these imperial uses of millennial imagery proliferated, leaving a great trail of empires that soon splintered into parts, often creating "national" or monarchical sub-kingdoms (Fowden 1993). The spokesmen for these millennial endeavors used a rhetoric of control, conceived of the final battle as one between order and chaos, and favored legal hierarchies of privilege and power. Because it found considerable favor among reforming elites, especially the clerical circles that produce and preserve so much of our documentation before the printing press, this imperial tradition has left the most pronounced literary trace and is, hence, easiest for the historian to track.

At the other end of this axis lies the demotic millennial tendency that envisages an egalitarian world where dominion of man over man ceases from the world. Here the monotheistic formulas insist on a radical discontinuity between heaven and earth, "no king but God," and "God is too great for any one religion." The anti-imperial, anti-authoritarian demotic vision sees the forces of evil as oppressive empires (e.g., Daniel 7–12) and foresees redemption in the victory of holy anarchy, where all live by the same law (*isonomia*) and manual labor is dignified. It looks forward to a time when men would beat the instruments of war and domination into instruments of peace and prosperity; each one sitting under his own tree, enjoying the fruits of honest labor undisturbed (Isaiah 2: 1–3; Micah 4: 1–4). This "world to come" marks the end of the rapacious aristocracy (lion and wolf will lie down with the lamb) and beginnings of the peace of manual laborer (lamb gets up the next morning). Perhaps no idea in the ancient world, where the dominion of aristocratic empires spread to almost every area of cultivated land, held more subversive connotations (Baumgarten 1997). In its modern secular forms—socialism, in which the state withers away and workers live at peace with each other—these demotic millennial projects continue to inspire fervor, hostility, and anxiety.

The second axis opposes visions of the millennium in terms of a return to an original purity, or in terms of a new and unprecedented society. Traditionally conservative forces tend to romanticize a lost past, and there seems to be a high correlation between hierarchy and restorative millennialism. In the Middle Ages, the notion of a once and future messianic emperor (Arthur, Charlemagne, Frederick I and II) reflects this restorative nostalgia for an empire that never was. Nonetheless, restorative visions that harken back to a time of primitive simplicity can carry powerful demotic messages (Ghost Dance, Islamism). Progressive notions, ones that view the coming perfection as unprecedented, represent one of the more protean notions in the millennial arsenal and have inspired many of the "modernizing" movements of the past thousand years, including various utopian and communal experiments. Historians have long noted the unusual prominence of the idea of progress in Western culture, and millennialism has unquestionably contributed importantly to this anomalous presence (Manuel and Manuel1979).

Apocalypticism: In apocalyptic scenarios we find two major polarities. The first distinguishes between catastrophic scenarios of rapid and vast devastation (Revelation 6–19), and transformative ones of equally vast, but generally slower, voluntary conversions (Isaiah 2:2–4). The former generally involves great violence and suffering, the *tribulation* of the Christian premillennialists, the "birthpangs" of the messianic Jews; while the latter is more peaceful, invoking images of healing and unfolding. These two are not mutually exclusive since many scenarios call for an initial destruction followed by a transformation, and often one can consider a movement transformational when it has "merely" (in its own perception) already passed the period of tribulation. The second axis here concerns the role of humans in bringing about this apocalyptic transformation. Passive scenarios give God all the work (and glory) and tend to encourage political and even social passivity. Such scenarios will foster strong ascetic activities and, in some cases, preaching aimed at preparing listeners for the cosmically important news of the coming of the Day. "Repent, for the kingdom of heaven is at hand." The opposite extreme places the operative deeds in the hands of a redeemed community of faithful who, either as God's agents or in "his" absence, build the millennium. Secular apocalyptic movements are almost always active, even virulently so, since there is no divine force to anticipate, no divine force upon which to depend.

The distinction between "apocalyptic" and "millennial" is conceptually critical. Most historians and anthropologists (Cohn 1961, 1970, 1999; Talmon 1932, 1970; Wessinger 2000) think of millennial as including the apocalyptic sense of imminence. But this lack of distinction disguises crucial factors: apocalyptic, for example, can prove and consistently has proven, to be wrong. Apocalyptic beliefs by their very nature flame brightly and pass rapidly; the briefer the anticipated time between present and transformation, the brighter the flame and more rapid its disappointment. And the vast majority of narratives about apocalyptic millennial movements tend to be written ex post facto—from the perspective of after the disappointment. Millennial beliefs in a coming age, however, are not subject to disconfirmation and tend to mutate rather than vanish under the pressures of disappointment. The historical evidence suggests that millennialism continues to exist and work in less visible and spectacular forms even when not activated by apocalyptic hopes and fears, and in order to understand the phenomenon in its broader social context, especially in terms of its longer-term impact on the societies in which such movements occur, we need to distinguish various kinds and processes of millennialism. The role of the sabbatical millennium in carrying millennialism through the long Augustinian twilight of the early Middle Ages (400–1200) can only be understood in terms of nonapocalyptic variants of the more spectacular, familiar, and ephemeral episodes (Landes 1988). To understand that, whatever the explicit denials, various religious traditions contain deeply embedded millennial commitments and that postapocalyptic NRMs preserve these traditions in less public forms helps us understand why millennialism is a phenomenon of the *longue durée* and apocalyptic episodes are perennial.

For example, we can term what Wessinger calls "progressive millennialism" as gradual, transformative, active apocalyptic anticipation of a coming demotic millennium; and current Christian premillennial dispensationalism as catastrophic passive apocalyptic anticipation of a sudden demotic millennium. This refinement of categories can help both identify some of the resonances between what would seem radically different millennial movements (Jewish Zionists and premillennial Christians; Aryan Christians, neo-Nazis, and Islamic Jihad), as well as help us follow the transformations in a millennial movement as it goes from apocalyptic take-off, through varied, often hostile interactions with the larger culture, and into its *post defectum* reentry (Bolsheviks, Maoists, Khmer Rouge). Thus a movement that begins with a transformative and rapid apocalyptic scenario leading to a demotic millennium (e.g., Anabaptists) can, in response to a widespread experience of persecution (Wessinger's "assaulted" community), turn more sudden (prophecy of the New Jerusalem in 1533 at Münster) and, under the pressure cooker of a date passed and an open defiance of the surrounding culture (Münster, 1534–1535), become violently hierarchical and authoritarian (Middlefort 1999).

Here we find the genealogy of totalitarianism (Cohn 1961, 1970, 1999; Mendel 1992, 2000). Indeed, authoritarian, imperialist monotheism remains one of the worst and most dangerous tendencies of men in power, certain that they are God's agents, carving the promised land out of a coerced body social (Quinby 1994; Berlet 2000). With these analytic categories in mind, and the methodological awareness of the documentary bias in favor of hostile authors writing ex post facto, let us turn to the earliest periods of millennial activity in Western history (ancient, early medieval) and reexamine them.

AGENDA FOR FUTURE RESEARCH

Integrate historical and contemporary perspectives: To develop a method for analyzing both oral and written data that integrates the historical *longue durée* with the anthropological and sociological insight into the apocalyptic moment. On the one hand, the latter brings to historians the dynamics that documents almost never record and thus permits the reconstruction of key, if invisible, initial segments of the process; on the other hand, the former brings to social scientists a sense of how many of these movements play out in the longer run, and how they have contributed to the development of the societies in which these later, now contemporary movements appear. One might, in this context, identify key moments in Western history when we find a rapid and widespread proliferation of new religious movements (not all necessarily millennial). Some of the more prominent such moments in Western history might include

- Y0K (first two centuries C.E.) in the eastern Mediterranean: the proliferation of "sign prophets," "Eastern cults," philosophic schools, and monastic, rabbinic, apostolic, and gnostic communities.
- Y6K (500 C.E., then again 800 C.E.): the spread of popular messianic prophets, the response of imperial millennialism (the last emperor).
- Y1K (eleventh and twelfth centuries) in Western Europe: the appearance of new lay and clerical religious movements during the "high" Middle Ages; many eventually persecuted as heresies.
- The thirteenth century in Western Europe: the proliferation a new religious communities (Beguines, Humiliati), orders (Franciscan, Dominican), and heresies (Waldensians, Cathars).
- Protestant Reformation (sixteenth century): the print-enhanced religious turmoil triggered by Luther and steeped in apocalyptic rhetoric.
- Y2K (dawn of the global era): media-enhanced religious turmoil occurring on an unprecedented scale, with unprecedented connections between cultures the world over.

In the process of reexamining the historical record for the West, both NRM and millennial studies scholars will find significant new kinds of material and documentation to work with, and at the same time will help historians understand the world of oral discourse that lies behind the literate artifacts that the social dynamics of composition and the partially aleatory dynamics of document preservation have cast upon its literate shores.

Systematize the nature of comparison and discuss millennial causation. In order to examine the remarkable similarities between apocalyptic movements over both temporal and cultural boundaries, we need to discuss the nature of the comparisons. This involves a great deal of supple thinking, in which the lumpers (connecting wide-ranging phenomena) and the splitters (insisting on the unique nature of each incident) need to go beyond agreeing to disagree. Similarly, scholars have shown considerable reluctance to attribute any significant role to religious forces (a kind of residual Marxism in which one only acknowledges the narcotic effects), especially a religious force that almost always, by the time it reaches our attention, has gone through disappointment. The remarkably protean and creative properties of millennialism, despite the ephemeral nature of the apocalyptic stage, demand consideration in any discussion of causative factors in cultural change, whether it be toward violence, acculturation, economic activity, institutional reform, NRMs, etc. For NRM scholarship this means above all investigating how often apocalyptic expectations and millennial hopes play an important role in the earliest stages of the movements they study, and developing techniques for detecting the role of denial in testimony given ex post facto by believers who could not possibly attribute error to their founding prophets.

Integration of psychological research into millennial and NRM studies: Interestingly, a phenomenon similar to the divorce between NRM and historical studies also characterizes the lack of connection between millennial studies and cognitive dissonance studies in psychology. Cognitive psychologists have developed the insights of Festinger and his colleagues (1956, 1964) into a major field of valuable research, but they rarely mention apocalyptic expectation (something already true about Festinger's book, which followed *When Prophecy Fails, Cognitive Dissonance*. So one of the major intellectual challenges for millennial studies and NRM studies to pursue in the next generation also involves bringing psychologists and historians into the discussion, much to the enrichment of all the disciplines involved. More generally, historians, anthropologists, NRM scholars, sociologists, and social psychologists need to exchange their findings in creative rather than territorial ways.

Gender studies and millennialism: One of the most important approaches to understanding millennialism may emerge from gender studies. On one level, the very style of millennial discourse and action seems gendered, with the most destructive and coercive forms taking on clearly recognizable traits of testosteronic aggression, of an honor culture driven to apocalyptic rage by a perceived and unbearable shame (Quinby 1994). The Nazis at the middle of the twentieth century, and the Arab and Muslim anti-Zionists at the turn of the new millennium, represent the most dangerous exponents of a narcissistic male aggression amplified and channeled by an active catastrophic apocalyptic vision (Rhodes 1980; Cook 2004). On another hand, transformative apocalyptic and demotic millennialism in some of their more radical forms involve a complete renunciation of the male drive for triumphalist dominion (turn the other cheek, Lamentations 3:30; Matthew 5:39). These forms often feature women in prominent positions of charismatic authority, and it may well be that the earliest moments when commoner women have a prominent public role comes in transformative apocalyptic time when, like Thiota in Mainz in 847–848 C.E., they can literally take over a city for a brief moment (Landes 1999). The return of normal time regularly brings an effort to control these once holy, now disorderly impulses from inspired women (Juster 1994, 1999), and the study of these dynamics represents a major dimension of millennial studies that aims at peaceful and socially creative resolutions to the immense energy such movements unleash (Palmer 1997; Brasher 1998; Brasher and Quinby 1997; Keller 1996).

Conspiracy theory: Perhaps the most consistent element of the most dangerous millennial currents is conspiracy theory. These future victim narratives justify obsession with violent "defense" by projecting the worst instincts of the believer onto an imagined enemy (as Hitler screamed about the Jews plotting to enslave mankind, he planned precisely that), and justifying a dualistic world of the paranoid imperative: "exterminate or be exterminated." The cognitive appeal of conspiracy narratives reflects two major desires: 1) to find narrative coherence in a chaotic world one does not control—everything, including previously unnoticed details, now "makes sense"; and 2) to deal with the cognitive dissonance of the formerly dominant in modern conditions where they no longer dominate, and yet remain free to express their beliefs and (largely) to run their lives—this is all a trick, an illusion of freedom meant to set up a still more depraved servitude. The antimodern dimension of these issues suggests that conspiracism will accompany like a shadow the spread of modernity, thriving in the toxic wake of the cultural turmoil that the new "freedoms" of "free market" cultures (goods and ideas) create. The prominence of conspiracist themes in popular culture, the enormous exposure that the World Wide Web gives to otherwise isolated conspiracy theories, and the huge increase of justified concerns about the destructive and pervasive impact of modernization and globalization explain the vigor and improvisational quality that conspiracy theories displayed in the 1990s (Barkun 1974, 1994, 1996). Conspiracism represents one of the most difficult issues for scholars to deal with because of the enormous intellectual energy that conspiracy theorists put into their arguments, making it nearly impossible to keep track and argue against them. And yet conspiracies do exist (if only, primarily, to cover up incompetence rather than to implement impossibly competent plots to enslave mankind); and dismissing the concerns of these people as "paranoid" not only intensifies their fears, but also fails to notice what they point out about the anxieties of modernity (Berlet 2000; Strozier and Flynn 1997).

Policy issues: This is perhaps the most active of the areas of NRM work, especially since Waco and the FBI's decision to develop a working group between agents and scholars (Jensen 1999; Kaplan 2003). But neither the initial successes nor the failures should blind us to the immensity of the task. The culture of law enforcement and that of academia lie far apart, and the directions matters take in the future depend not only on events but on the degree of trust and maturity we can develop between these two different styles of analysis and action. Scholars will greatly increase their effectiveness if they develop the tools and curricula necessary to communicate effectively and anticipate the needs of law enforcement communities in many different cultures. In this way, far more contributors can play a role than those whom various agencies feel comfortable consulting and learning from directly. The preparedness of the scholarly community to contribute to a peaceful and productive interaction between millennial NRMs and the larger (now global) culture taking shape depends on our tactful honesty not only with government agencies, but also within our own disciplines and intellectual communities. The ideological and political agendas that underlie many of the approaches to the field do not undermine the insights that come from these approaches, but they may prevent further development. This is perhaps most important right now in terms of the relationship between the American Muslim community and American law enforcement: one cannot imagine a relationship fraught with more danger of crossed signals.

Antisemitism: One of the constant elements of both Christian and Muslim apocalyptic belief and behavior concerns the Jews. This dates back to the birth moments of both religions, when they first broke off from an apocalyptic Jewish expectation and, insisting that their founder had transformed all previous teachings (a characteristic of totalistic, supersessionist, apocalyptic claims) and that salvation came from a "conversion" to the new, true faith, found the persistence of Jews to be a disturbing reminder of the persistence of "normal time." As each of these movements became more hierarchical and authoritarian, they added to this distaste for Jews a fear that Jewish apocalyptic and millennial beliefs would now undermine their newly established religions in precisely the ways they had imagined they undermined Judaism. Thus moments like the advent of a triumphalist monotheism (our physical victory proves the correctness of our claims—a version of "might makes right") tends to intensify hostility to Jews. Nonetheless, periods of demotic and transformative apocalyptic expectation tend to bring out an unusual philo-Judaism, especially notable among Christians in the last half-millennium, primarily among Protestants and liberal revolutionaries. This, however, can rapidly transform into violent anti-Judaism in a scapegoating response to disappointment—if only the Jews had converted, Jesus would have returned (Landes 1996b; Gow 1995). Modernity, in the minds of its founders, should have put an end to anti-semitism when it in fact produced even more virulent forms. The prominence of Jews, either openly identified or lurking in the background of most antimodern conspiracy theories (*Protocols of the Elders of Zion*) reflects the immensely close ties between antimodernism, anti-semitism, and active, catastrophic apocalyptic beliefs. We overlook the pervasiveness of all three of these themes among Arab and Muslim anti-Zionists and anti-Western ideologues at our own peril.

REFERENCES

Abanes, Richard. 1999. *End Time Visions: The Doomsday Obsession.*) New York: Broadman & Holman.

Adas, Michael. 1977. *Prophets of Rebellion: Millenarian Protest Movements against the European Colonial Order.* Cambridge: Cambridge University Press.

Ajami, Fouad. 1981. *The Arab Predicament: Arab Political Thought and Practice since 1967.* Cambridge: Cambridge University Press.

Amanat, Abbas, and Magnus Bernhardsson. 2002. *Imagining the End: Visions of Apocalypse from the Ancient Middle East to Modern America.* New York: I. B. Tauris & Co.

Andrews, V., R. Bosnak, and K. W. Goodwin. 1987. *Facing Apocalypse.* Dallas: Spring Publications.

Barkun, Michael, 1974. *Disaster and the Millennium.* New Haven, Conn.: Yale University Press.

———. 1994. *Religion and the Racist Right: The Origins of the Christian Identity Movement.* Chapel Hill: University of North Carolina Press.

———. 1996. *Millennialism and Violence.* New York: Frank Cass and Co.

Barthélemy, Dominique. 1999. *L'an mil et la paix de Dieu.* Paris: Fayard.

Bashear, Suliman. 1973. "Muslim Apocalypses and the Hour." *Israel Oriental Studies* 13: 75–99.

Baumgarten, Al. 1997. *The Flourishing of Sects in the Maccabean Era: An Interpretation.* Leiden: Brill.

Berlet, Chip, and Matthew Lyons. 2000. *Right-Wing Populism in America.* New York: Guilford Press.

Bloch, Ruth. 1985. *Visionary Republic: Millennial Themes in American Thought, 1756–1800.* New York: Cambridge University Press.

Boyer, Paul. 1992. *When Time Shall Be No More: Prophecy Belief in Modern American Culture.* Cambridge: Harvard University Press.

Brasher, Brenda. 1998. *Godly Women: Fundamentalism and Female Power.* New Brunswick, N.J.: Rutgers University Press.

———. 2001. *Give Me That Online Religion.* San Francisco: Jossey Bass.

Brasher, Brenda and Lee Quinby, eds. 1997. *Engendering the Millennium.* Boston: *Journal of Millennial Studies* 2: 1 (http://www.mille.org/publications/summer99.html).

Bull, Malcolm. 1995. *Apocalypse Theory and the Ends of the World.* Oxford: Blackwell.

Burridge, Kenelm. 1969. *New Heaven, New Earth: A Study of Millenarian Activities.* New York: Schocken.

Cohen, Paul. 1997. *History in Three Keys: The Boxers as Event, Experience, and Myth.* New York: Columbia University Press.

Cohn, Norman. 1961. *The Pursuit of the Millennium: Revolutionary Millenarians and Mystical Anarchists of the Middle Ages.* New York: Oxford University Press.

———. 1993. *Cosmos, Chaos and the World to Come: The Ancient Roots of Apocalyptic Faith.* New Haven, Conn.: Yale University Press.

———. 1996. *Warrant for Genocide: The Myth of the Jewish World Conspiracy and the Protocols of the Elders of Zion.* London: Serif.

Cook, David. 1996. "Muslim Apocalyptic and *Jihad.*" *Jerusalem Studies in Arabic and Islam* 20: 66–104.

———. 2004. *Struggle in the Path of God: Understanding Jihad in Theory and Practice.* Berkeley: University of California Press.

Cook, Michael, and Patricia Crone. 1976. *Hagarism: The Making of the Islamic World.* Cambridge: Cambridge University Press.

Cook, Stephen. 1995. *Countdown to 2000: Essays on Apocalypticism.* New York: *Union Seminary Quarterly Review* 49.

Couch, Mal. 1996. *Dictionary of Pre-Millennial Theology.* Grand Rapids: Kregel.

Crouzet, Denis. 1996. *La genèse de la réforme française, 1520–1562.* Paris: SEDES.

Daniels, Ted. 1992. *Millennialism: An International Bibliography.* New York: Garland.

Desroche, Henri. 1979. *The Sociology of Hope.* Trans. Carol Martin-Sperry. London: Routledge & Kegan Paul.

Emmerson, Richard K., and Bernard McGinn. 1992. *The Apocalypse in the Middle Ages.* Ithaca, N.Y.: Cornell University Press.

Festinger, Leon. 1957. *A Theory of Cognitive Dissonance.* Evanston, Ill.: Row, Peterson.

Festinger, Leon, et al. 1964. *When Prophecy Fails.* New York: Harper Torchbooks.

Fleischer, Cornell H., ed. 2004. *The Cambridge History of Turkey.* Vol. 2: *The Ottoman Empire as a World Power.* Cambridge: Cambridge University Press.

Fowden, Garth. 1993. *From Empire to Commonwealth: Consequences of Monotheism in Late Antiquity.* Princeton, N.J.: Princeton University Press.

Fried, Johannes. 1989. "Endzeiterwartung um die Jahrtausendwende." *Deutsches Archiv für Erforschung des Mittelalters* 45.2: 385–473.

Gorenberg, Gershom. 2000. *The End of Days: Fundamentalism and the Struggle for the Temple Mount.* New York: Basic Books.

Gouguenheim, Sylvain. 1999. *Les fausses terreurs de l'an mil: Peur de la fin du monde ou profondissement de la foi?* Paris: Picard.

Gow, Andrew. 1995. *The Red Jews: Antisemitism in an Apocalyptic Age, 1200–1600.* Leiden: Brill.

Graziano, Frank. 1999. *The Millennial New World.* New York: Oxford University Press.

Grell, Ole Peter, and Bob Scribner. 1996. *Tolerance and Intolerance in the European Reformation.* Cambridge: Cambridge University Press.

Hackett, Rosalind. 2003. *Challenges of the New Media Order to Freedom of Religion and Belief, Freedom of Expression and Group Rights.* Cambridge: Harvard University Press.

Hall, John. 1978. *The Ways Out: Utopian Communal Groups in an Age of Babylon* London: Routledge and Kegan Paul.

Hall, John, Sylvaine Trinh, and Philip Schuyler. 2000. *Apocalypse Observed: Religious Movements and Violence in North America, Europe, and Japan.* New York: Routledge.

Hill, Christopher. 1993. *The English Bible and the Seventeenth-Century Revolution.* London: Penguin.

Introvigne, Massimo. 2000. "The Magic of Death: Suicides of the Solar Temple." In *Millennialism, Persecution and Violence: Historical Cases,* ed. Catherine Wessinger, 138–57. Syracuse, N.Y.: Syracuse University Press.

Jensen, Karl. 1999. "Law Enforcement and the Millennialist Vision: A Behavioral Approach." *Law Enforcement Bulletin.*

Juster, Susan. 1994. *Disorderly Women: Sexual Politics and Evangelicalism in Revolutionary New England.* New York: Cornell University Press.

————. 1999. "Demagogues and Mystagogues? Gender and the Language of Prophecy in the Age of Democratic Revolution." *American Historical Review* 104.5: 1560–81.

Kaplan, Jeffrey, ed. 2003. *Millennial Violence, Past, Present and Future.* Special Edition of *Terrorism and Political Violence* 14, no. 11.

Katz, David, and Richard Popkin. 1998. *Messianic Revolution: Radical Religious Politics to the End of the Second Millennium.* New York: Hill and Wang.

Keller, Catherine. 1996. *Apocalypse Now and Then: A Feminist Guide to the End of the World.* Boston: Beacon.

Kleinhenz, Christopher, and Fannie LeMoine. 1999. *Fearful Hope: Approaching the New Millennium.* Madison: University of Wisconsin Press.

La Barre, Weston. 1970. *Ghost Dance: The Origins of Religion.* Garden City, N.Y.: Doubleday.

Lamy, Philip. 1996. *Millennium Rage: Survivalists, White Supremacists, and the Doomsday Prophecy.* New York: Plenum Press.

Landes, Richard. 1988. "Lest the Millennium Be Fulfilled: Apocalyptic Expectations and the Pattern of Western Chronography, 100–800 C.E." In *The Use and Abuse of Eschatology in the Middle Ages,* ed. W.D.F. Verbeke, D. Verhelst, and A. Welkenhysen, Medievalia Lovaniensia ser. 1, studia 15, pp. 137–211. Leuven: Leuven University Press.

———. 1995. *Relics, Apocalypse, and the Deceits of History: Ademar of Chabannes, 989–1034.* Cambridge: Harvard University Press.

———. 1996a. "The Massacres of 1010: On the Origins of Popular Anti-Jewish Violence in Western Europe." In *From Witness to Witchcraft: Jews and Judaism in Medieval Christian Thought,* ed. Jeremy Cohen, 79–112. Wolfenbüttel: Wolfenbüttler Mittelalterlichen-Studien.

———. 1996b. "Owls, Roosters, and Apocalyptic Time: A Historical Method for Reading a Refractory Documentation." *Union Seminary Quarterly Review* 49: 165–85.

———. 1999. "Women, Millennialism, and Modernity: A Contribution to Gender Studies." *Engendering the Millennium; Special Issue of the Journal of Millennial Studies* 2, no. 1.

———. 2000. *Encyclopedia of Millennialism and Millennial Movements,* ed. Richard Landes. New York: Berkshire Reference Works; Routledge.

Lanternari, Vittorio. 1963. *Religions of the Oppressed: A Study of Modern Messianic Cults.* New York: Knopf.

Lerner, Robert E. 1976. "Refreshment of the Saints: The Time After Antichrist as a Station for Earthly Progress in Medieval Thought." *Traditio* 32: 99–144.

———. 2001. *The Feast of Saint Abraham: Medieval Millenarians and the Jews.* Philadelphia: University of Pennsylvania Press.

Levine, Robert. 1992. *Vale of Tears: Revisiting the Canudos Massacre in Northeastern Brazil, 1893–1897.* Berkeley: University of California Press.

Lifton, Robert J. 1999. *Destroying the World to Save It: Aum Shinrikyō, Apocalyptic Violence, and the New Global Terrorism.* New York: Metropolitan Books.

Lincoln, Bruce. 1985. *Religion, Rebellion, and Revolution.* New York: Saint Martin's Press.

Lowe, Robert. 2000. "Western Millennial Ideology Goes East: The Taiping Revolution and Mao's Great Leap Forward." In *Millennialism, Persecution and Violence: Historical Cases,* ed. Catherine Wessinger, 220–40. Syracuse, N.Y.: Syracuse University Press.

Lynch, Aaron. 1996. *Thought Contagion: How Belief Spreads through Society.* New York: Basic Books.

McGinn, Bernard. 1979. *Visions of the End: Apocalyptic Traditions in the Middle Ages.* New York: Columbia University Press.

———. 1994. *Antichrist: Two Thousand Years of the Human Fascination with Evil.* New York: HarperCollins.

Manuel, Frank E., and Fritzie P. Manuel. 1979. *Utopian Thought in the Western World.* Cambridge: Harvard University Press.

Mendel, Arthur. 2000. *Vision and Violence.* Ann Arbor: University of Michigan Press.

Middlefort, Eric. 1999. "Madness and the Millennium at Münster, 1534–1535." In *Fearful Hope: Approaching the New Millennium,* ed. Christopher Kleinhenz and Fannie LeMoine, 115–34. Madison: University of Wisconsin Press.

Mooney, James E. 1973. *The Ghost Dance: Religion and Wounded Knee.* New York: Dover.

Mullins, Mark R. 1997. "Aum Shin Rikyo as an Apocalyptic Movement." In *Millennium, Messiahs, and Mayhem,* ed. Thomas Robbins and Susan J. Palmer, 313–24. New York: Routledge.

Naquin, Susan. 1976. *Millenarian Rebellion in China: The Eight Trigrams Uprising of 1813.* New Haven, Conn.: Yale University Press.

Noble, David. 1998. *The Religion of Technology: The Divinity of Man and the Spirit of Invention.* New York: Knopf.

O'Leary, Stephen. 1994. *Arguing the Apocalypse: A Theory of Millennial Rhetoric.* New York: Oxford University Press.

Ownby, David. 1999. "Chinese Millenarian Traditions: The Formative Age." *American Historical Review* 104.5: 1513–30.

———. 2002. *Falun Gong and China's Future.* New York: Rowman & Littlefield.

Palmer, Susan. 1997. *Moon Sisters, Krishna Mothers, Rajneesh Lovers: Women's Roles in New Religions Women and Gender in North American Religions.* Syracuse, N.Y.: Syracuse University Press.

Penton, M. James. 1985. *Apocalypse Delayed: The Story of Jehovah's Witnesses.* Toronto: University of Toronto Press.

Pesantubbee, Micheline. 1997. "From Vision to Violence: The Wounded Knee Massacre." In *Millennium, Messiahs, and Mayhem,* ed. Thomas Robbins and Susan J. Palmer, 62–81. New York: Routledge.

Protocols of the Elders of Zion. First published through the agency of the Tzarist secret police in 1904 in Russian; translated into English by Victor Marsden, 1920.

Quinby, Lee. 1994. *Anti-Apocalypse: Exercises in Genealogical Criticism.* Minneapolis: University of Minnesota Press.

———. 1999. *Millennial Seduction: A Skeptic Confronts Apocalyptic Culture.* Ithaca, N.Y.: Cornell University Press.

Reader, Ian. 2000. "Aum Shinrikyo, Millennialism and the Legitimation of Violence." In *Millennialism, Persecution and Violence: Historical Cases,* ed. Catherine Wessinger, 158–82. Syracuse, N.Y.: Syracuse University Press.

Reeves, Marjorie. 1977. *Joachim of Fiore and the Prophetic Future.* New York: Harper & Row.

Rhodes, James. 1980. *The Hitler Movement: A Modern Millenarian Revolution.* Stanford, Calif.: Hoover Institution Press.

Robbins, Thomas and Susan J. Palmer, eds. 1997. *Millennium, Messiahs, and Mayhem: Contemporary Apocalyptic Movements.* New York: Routledge.

Salter, Richard C. 1997. "Shooting Dreads on Sight: Violence, Persecution, Millennialism, and Dominica's Dread Act." In *Millennium, Messiahs, and Mayhem: Contemporary Apocalyptic Movements,* ed. Thomas Robbins and Susan J. Palmer, 101–118. New York: Routledge.

Schafer, Peter, and Mark Cohen. 1998. *Toward the Millennium: Messianic Expectations from the Bible to Waco Studies in the History of Religions, 77.* Leiden: Brill.

Scholem, Gershom. 1975. *Sabbatai Zevi: The Mystical Messiah.* Princeton: Princeton University Press.

Schwartz, Hillel. 1990. *Century's End: An Orientation Manual Toward the Year 2000.* New York: Doubleday.

Scott, James C. 1992. *Domination and the Arts of Resistance.* New Haven, Conn.: Yale University Press.

Spence, Jonathan. 1996. *God's Chinese Son: The Taiping Heavenly Kingdom of Hong Xiu-quan.* New York: Norton.

Stewart, Pamela J., and Andrew Strathern, eds. 1997. *Millennial Markers.* Townsville, Australia: James Cook University, Centre for Pacific Studies.

Strozier, Charles, and Michael Flynn, eds. 1997. *The Year 2000: Essays on the End.* New York: New York University Press.

Tabor, James D., and Eugene V. Gallagher. 1995. *Why Waco?: Cults and the Battle for Religious Freedom in America.* Berkeley: University of California Press.

Talmon, Jacob. 1970. *The Origins of Totalitarian Democracy.* London: Sphere Books.

Thompson, Damian. 1999. *The End of Time: Faith and Fear in the Shadow of the Millennium.* London: Sinclair Stevenson.

Verbeke, W., D. Verhelst, and A. Welkenhuysen. 1988. *The Use and Abuse of Eschatology in the Middle Ages.* Louvain: Catholic University Press.

Vessey, M., K. Pollmann, and A. Fitzgerald. 1999. *History, Apocalypse, and the Secular Imagination: New Essays on Augustine's* City of God. Bowling Green, Ohio: Philosophy Documentation Center.

Wallace, Anthony. 1970a. *Culture and Personality.* New York: Random House.

———. 1970b. *The Death and Rebirth of the Seneca.* New York: Knopf.

Weber, Eugen. 1999. *Apocalypses: Prophecies, Cults, and Millennial Beliefs through the Ages.* Cambridge: Harvard University Press.

Wessinger, Catherine, ed. 2000. *Millennialism, Persecution and Violence: Historical Cases.* Syracuse, N.Y.: Syracuse University Press.

Whitehead, Neil. 2000. *Millennial Countdown in New Guinea.* Durham, N.C.: Duke University Press.

Williams, Ann, ed. 1967. *Prophecy and Millenarianism: Essays in Honour of Marjorie Reeves.* Essex: Longman.

Wilson, Bryan R. 1980. *Patterns of Sectarianism.* London: Heinemann.

Wojcik, Daniel. 1997. *The End of the World as We Know It: Faith, Fatalism, and Apocalypse in America.* New York: New York University Press.

CHAPTER 15

THE MYTHIC DIMENSIONS OF NEW RELIGIOUS MOVEMENTS

Function, Reality Construction, and Process

DIANA G. TUMMINIA
R. GEORGE KIRKPATRICK

THROUGH our own research of several relatively new spiritual groups (Wiccans, American Zen, ISKCON, MSIA, Unarius, and New Age enclaves), we have come to appreciate the intricate interpretive worlds being socially constructed using incipient mythological frameworks.[1] As adherents of these groups spoke to us about their experiences, they constructed narratives about themselves and about the world using their mythological meaning systems. Our intrigue with these encounters made us question the role mythology played in social construction of reality within new religious movements (NRMs). We have, over the past few decades, noticed the enormous amount of NRM mythmaking taking place, some of it truly original but most borrowed, blended, and reinvented from other traditions. This chapter deals with certain theoretical perspectives and empirical examples that help examine the varied mythologies of these newer spiritual in-novations. Because of the general stigma placed upon the newer cosmologies as problematic unrealities, intellectuals and the educated public-at-large have not fully explored NRM mythology for its more basic functioning aspects.

What is a myth? In contrast to ubiquitous beliefs, core myths present sacred narratives that usually include venerated characters whose actions lead to the present state of spiritual affairs that must be addressed through the group's action. Many wrongly view NRM myths as accomplished facts, rather than considering them as embedded in and part of the emergent social processes found in the day-to-day interaction within a group (Turner and Killian 1987). Some myths remain fixed, while others, according to the nature of the group, function as key interpretive procedures of a fluid improvised nature.

Finding a workable definition for myth has proved daunting for mythologists. Ponderous paragraph-length definitions with chapter-long explanations appear to be the norm, as seen in Doty (1986), Murray (1962), and Honko (1984). According to Honko, four definitional criteria exist: 1) myths are transmitted in narrative form, 2) myths convey informational content, 3)myths function as models of worldviews, 4) myths occur in context, usually associated with ritual reenactments. By contrast, Dundes (1984) simply defined myth as a sacred narrative. Indeed, the original Greek *mythos* meant sacred words and oral stories. Eliade (1957/1959) referred to them as hierophanies, or sacred stories.[2]

To illustrate the mythological dimension, let us first consider the example of one group. The Church of Scientology professes an interesting origin myth. Zellner (1995: 108) explains Hubbard's thetan (soul) origin narrative:

> According to Hubbard, 75 million years ago the earth, then called Teegeeack, was part of a 76-planet galactic confederation ruled a tyrant called Xenu (pronounced Zeenew). To solidify his power and control the population, Xenu gathered his officers and told them to capture beings of all shapes and sizes living within the confederation and freeze in an alcohol and glycol compound. Billions of these frozen creatures were then transported to earth in aircraft that resembled DC-8s and were thrown into volcanoes.
>
> To add to the woes of these creatures, hydrogen bombs were dropped on them. Their souls (called thetans) were then captured by Xenu's forces and implanted with religion, sexual perversions, and other weaknesses to remove the memory of what Xenu had done to them . . . Overthrown soon after the mission was accomplished, Xenu was taken to a mountain and put into a wire cage, where he remains today.

Scientology advocates many levels of auditing and training to enable people to remove their implants to become "clear." Like Scientology, most NRM groups possess any number of imaginative mythic tales that warrant further examination; these venerated tales undergird group action and interpretations of reality.

WHY IS MYTHOLOGY UNDERANALYZED?

New religious movements have created a wealth of mythical stories that frame perception for a variety of adherents, yet the social processes involved in the use of mythology have been underanalyzed. The reasons for this lack of focus on the subject stem from the difficulty of defining the breadth of the field, social concerns with other aspects of NRMs, and the general prejudice against the types of internal logic employed within these groups. Too numerous to name and to reference in one chapter, these spiritual groups vary in terms of origins, types of social organization, and sorts of leaders and followers, as well as the kinds of interpretive universes created in the mix (Melton 1999; Glock and Bellah 1976; Freedland 1972). Research on the NRMs has exploded, although it has barely kept pace with the rapid emergence of such groups and the diversity of their activities (Lewis 1998a). Melton (1999) states that common characteristics of NRMs remain difficult to define because of the range of beliefs and practices, and that these groups manifest theological divergences by operating apart from the religious mainstream. NRM practices can range from nontheist organized traditions like American Zen (Preston 1988) to mail-order occult divination, from the pseudosecularized quasi-therapeutic (Stone 1984; Tumminia 1995) to a paucity of messianic millenarianism (Lewis 1999; Landes 2000), and from entrepreneurial marketing of New Age channelers (Brown 1997; Bowen 2002) to the much-touted vibrations of the Hare Krishna mantra (Rockford 1985). The social distance from the religious mainstream allows for new myths to flourish.

The public often dismisses the new mythological systems as nonsensical, while researchers struggle to explain the extensive diversity of beliefs. A significant amount of NRM literature remains devoted to the cult and brainwashing debate (Bromley and Richardson 1983; Robbins and Anthony 1989), while other research tracks recruitment-commitment issues and the details of the problematic nature of the groups themselves (Robbins 1988). This focus on the social problem aspect of NRMs steers us further away from the social constructed validity of the new mythology. Some ethnographic work allows us an insider's view of everyday life in new religions (Balch and Taylor 1978; Luhrmann 1989: Griffin 2000; Vega 2001), while other literature attempts to explain the complicated and sometimes implausible practices of NRMs (Wallis 1977; Snow and Machalek 1982; Saliba 1995; Tumminia 1998; Lewis 1998b). However, research on *how* members use myth remains sketchy and worthy of further investigation.

The collective mythology of new religious movements conceptualizes the interactions of the physical and the spiritual worlds in phantasmagorically dissimilar ways, yet most, if not all, create magico-religious stories that organize reality for their practitioners. In the rush to scrutinize, researchers often push aside the analysis of the newly created (or synthesized) mythology to privilege other foci of analysis, and so myths remain somewhat obscured by being included in the larger analytical category of unconventional beliefs. Ideology, creeds, and assumptions about the nature of reality are part of the general character of NRM belief, but mythic stories go further because they justify the beliefs themselves.

The mythology of NRMs must contend with the generalized stigma of being just another form of kooky inanity. The curious may value this recent rise in mythic material for its astonishing breadth of invention and its surprising variety of apologetic fabrication. Even so, contemporary NRM mythology may still seem unimportant given the lack of contextual relevance. In common parlance, myth denotes a false idea, a notion even subscribed to by some researchers. Critics often label new religious movements as cults, subjecting them further to the cultic stereotype (Dillon and Richardson 1994; Lewis 1994), an image of a valueless misguided human belief system and that of a social problem. However, social scientists who taken more objective view have a unique opportunity to witness NRM myth-making in progress, a glimpse into the unfolding process of social reality creation.

GENERAL PERSPECTIVES ON MYTH

We are not suggesting that all NRM myths or myth generation processes are alike. Further, a systematic classification of the new cosmologies has yet to be done, making any generalizations purely speculative. Nevertheless, a step toward the understanding of these varied discursive universes would be to place some analysis within the study of myth. Older anthropological works (Malinowski 1954; Lévi-Strauss 1963; Doty 1986) tended to emphasize the importance of different levels of mythological belief as master blueprints for experiential reality, a perspective that has been somewhat lacking of late. Bronislaw Malinowski (1954; Doty 1986) emphatically placed myth in the context of its respective society, where it infused culture and social organization with meaning. Drawing on his work in Melanesia, Malinowski instructed us to look at myth in everyday life. In essence, he asked us to look at the ways myth permeated and ordered a shared reality. Malinowski (1954: 100–101; Doty 1986) is often quoted as referring to myth as "not merely a story told, but a reality lived"; he saw myth among the "savages" as an alive "hard-worked cultural force," rather than an "idle tale." This passage from Malinowski's (1954: 100–101) essay, "Myth in Primitive Psychology" extorts us to value living belief:

> The forms of myth which come to us from classical antiquity and from the
> ancient sacred books of the East and other similar sources have come down to

us without the context of a living faith, without the possibility of obtaining comments from true believers, without the concomitant knowledge of social organization, their practiced morals, and their popular customs, at least without the full information which the modern fieldworker can easily obtain.

An earlier thinker, Edward B. Tylor, influenced many generations of mythographers (Kardiner and Preble 1961). In *Primitive Culture* (1871), Tylor theorized that the childlike animistic myths of simple societies led to the development of later, more advanced forms of religion. Despite his linear social-evolutionary theory, we have benefited from his impetus, because Tylor urged the collection of myths from indigenous cultures, thus sparking the cross-cultural views of myth we have today. Tylor also influenced Frazer. Most scholars (Malinowski 1954; Kirk 1970; Doty 1986; Vecsey 1991) have named Sir James Frazer's *Golden Bough* (1951) as the pivotal work in the modern study of mythography. The first two volumes appeared in 1890, and subsequently it was enlarged to twelve volumes from 1911 to 1915. Looking for recurring themes as many mythologists do, Frazer believed that all myths were initially related to the images of fertility and nature. Frazer's nature hypothesis countered Max Müeller's previous speculation that celestial imagery formed the only basis for myth. With the wealth of mythic narratives that have been recorded since the nineteenth century, we can safely say that myths employ all manner of culturally bound symbols to convey meaning and to preserve cognitive categories. Curiously, some NRMs have awakened animistic narratives long thought to be the activity of so-called primitive peoples.[3]

Later thinkers building on Tylor and Frazer emphasized how myth was related to social function. Emile Durkheim (1938/1966; 1915/1965), of course, saw myths as collective representations of the over-arching beliefs that fostered social solidarity in a society. Durkheim recognized the interactive nature of myth, symbol, and ritual. The functionalists, like Claude Lévi-Strauss and Bronislaw Malinowski, looked at myth in terms of the interpretive work it did for the society as a whole (Malinowski 1954; Lévi-Strauss 1963; Doty 1986; Strenski 1992). In their view, myth served to cement the pieces of the social fabric and to charter social organization with its beliefs and practices. Both formal and informal rituals based on mythic stories drive NRMs. Some groups, like Hare Krishna, have the textbook example of the myth-ritual link, while others, like Scientology, have adopted quasi-psychological processes that structure interaction. Stark (2001: 619) disputes this functionalist perspective, asserting that religions and rituals may not sustain the proverbial moral order unless they are based on "morally concerned gods." Presumably, these gods are defined in myth.

Other thinkers have shaped our thinking about myth; however, they have been criticized for their lack of knowledge about cultural anthropology, social structure, and social organization (Dudley 1977). The often-cited Mircea Eliade (1949/1954; 1957/1959) focused principally upon cosmogonic, or creation/origin, myths. He stressed that myths organize a culturally specific perception of time.

By experiencing myths as true stories through ritual reenactment (Eliade 1957/ 1959), we escape linear or historic time via narratives of sacred time, or *illud tempus*. Employing the reasoning that myths fashioned their own definition of time and space, Eliade contended that they also created sacred histories of the origins of all things. Mythically speaking, these cosmic beginnings set in motion divine journeys, wherein all that was created ultimately returns. Some myths, like the Hindu stories of Brahma, fit his grand model, while others do not. For example, the Iroquois myth of the Great Peacemaker, Deganaweda, chartered the origin of social cooperation for the Six Nation Confederacy, but it is not a myth concerning a sacred return to a source of creation (Vecsey 1991).

Many myths involve violent plots. Freud (1950) presumed that the ostensible irrationality of myth originated from the unconscious, with its storehouse of repressed fears and anxieties. René Girard (1977) drew on Freudian ideas in analyzing the origins of myth and ritual. Girard placed the central act of ritual sacrifice at the source of religious narratives, a theme that Eliade (1957/1959: 51) referred to as "tragic blood-drenched cosmogonies." Pointing to what he called a surrogate-victim mechanism, Girard believed in the cathartic function of sacrifice. Girard related the plethora of myths that tell of the murder of one character by another. He insisted that "the objective of ritual is the proper reenactment of the surrogate-victim mechanism; its function is to perpetuate a way to keep violence out of the community" (1977: 92). The older sacred stories of Passover and the Crucifixion fit this description, as do some NRM myths like that of Scientology and those of the Unarius Academy of Science, which we will discuss later.

Mythologist Joseph Campbell captured the popular imagination by stressing the pleasures of exploring mythic narratives (Doty 1986; Polkinghorne 1988). He preferred to emphasize the psychological purposes of myth in terms of its evocative storytelling power. Campbell saw myths as tales of self-discovery, harboring universal messages. As explained in The *Hero with a Thousand Faces* (1968), the psychological function of myth is exemplified by the monomyth, a synthesis of various tales into a typified story. The archetypal hero leaves home and embarks on a quest, which calls upon inner strength and courage. He crosses into the unknown and performs difficult tasks such as slaying a monster. The hero returns, transformed, to his community. The narrative of departure, initiation, and return of the monomythic hero has been linked to universal themes of symbolic death and rebirth. In NRMs, we see the creation of numerous heroes in the form of new gods and charismatic leaders who are considered divine. In addition, New Age healers, Neo-pagans, and pop psychologists alike use myth for its therapeutic symbolism, with one example being Jean Shinoda Bolen, who wrote *Goddesses in Everywoman: A New Psychology of Women* (1985). In the case of the alternative NRM theme of feminine divinity, seekers have sought out the heroine with the thousand faces in tales of goddesses, amazons, and female nature spirits.

An obvious criticism of Campbell's heroes says that they were chosen without regard to their social and historic context. For example, he equated the Hindu god, Krishna, with the Greek hero, Jason, whose stories are retold for quite different purposes in the respective cultures. We might ask ourselves if Dorothy's trip to Oz would qualify as a modern heroic monomyth. Surely it would, but so far as we know her story has not sparked widespread religious activity. Still, who can deny the intrigue of a tale well told? And who among us has not seen reflections of ourselves in such stories? Mythic stories can reflect the psychological process of selfhood, or making sense out of life's journey.

Since the days of early anthropologists we have been left with a weighty legacy in terms of myth. Contemporary scholars (Doty 1986; Dudley 1977) have, however, criticized attempts to attribute universality to thematic structures or to psychological and social functions. They have preferred to recognize the different contexts in which myths occur, conceding as Doty did (1986; 55) to the "polyfunctionality" of myth. In sum, myths can operate differently within a single culture and from culture to culture, but their importance as interpretive frameworks cannot be denied. Some propositions about functionality still prove useful. Summarizing recurrent themes, Honko (1984) listed twelve services mythology performed. Myths serve as sources for cognitive categories, forms of symbolic expression, projections of the subconscious, integrated worldviews, charters of behavior, legitimations of social institutions, indicators of social relevance, mirrors of culture and social structure, historic markers, religious communication, religious genre, and mediums for structure.

How much myth operates in NRMs in the functional sense is still open to debate and further research. Newer sociological analysis tends to avoid using the terms "myth" and "sacred narratives" partly because the cult stereotype tells us that NRM worldviews express needlessly bizarre tales unworthy of comment. Moving away from the more functional analyses, social constructionist theorists point to a parallel explanation of NRM meaning systems. Although writing from a different paradigm, Berger (1967, 1970) implies as much with his notion of the sacred canopy, a sacred objectification of socially constructed, overarching meaning used to define reality from any given spiritual or related mundane activity. Belief systems demand social validation to thrive and to endure. Under the sacred canopy what would normally be absurd is sustained as reasonable through plausibility structures, networks of believers who bound together through their commitment to the shared discourse and who validate belief (Berger 1967; Snow and Machalek 1982). Building on the work of Erving Goffman, Snow, et al. (1986) refer back to the problems of alternative perception and micromobilization with their idea of frame alignment. Further, Benford and Snow (2000) analyze interpretive schemata in new social movements as experiential meaning in constituted reality. In essence, whether approaching the subject through the idea of socially constructed worldviews (Berger 1967) or frame analysis (Goffman 1974) as an organizer of experience, NRMs contain a variety of interpretive frameworks based on beliefs intertwined with mythic stories experienced as authentic explanations for what is real.

Although it is difficult to generalize given the existence of so many different types of groups, the diverse corpus of NRM mythology addresses age-old concerns about understanding the human condition, and it defines the nature of reality for believers (Bednarowski 1989). In that sense, there is nothing new about new religions. Through mythological worldviews, they instruct practitioners on proper conduct in relation to the universal riddles of meaningful existence, like how to manage emotions in suffering and how to behave in regard to the meaning of death. Mythic stories verbalize what is good and what is evil while also defining the use of personal power or one's submission to the community. These stories articulate the individual's place in a mythopoeic existence, in addition to providing a therapeutic course of action in which to seek comfort and healing.

NOT MERELY A STORY TOLD, BUT A REALITY LIVED

Malinowski (1954, 100–101) refers to myth as "not merely a story told, but a reality lived." As fieldworkers in a small sample of NRM groups, we experienced radical shifts in cognitive and emotional territory when we visited the various groups. Each group obviously had its own belief system substantiated in different degrees by sacred stories. Sustained interaction with informants hinged upon our learning the right kind of questions to ask, and our satisfaction with the progress of the research entailed being able to record and to interpret responses in a way that resonated relatively close to the member's notion of reality.

A case in point is our investigation of the Unarius Academy of Science, a millenarian psychotherapeutic, flying-saucer organization (Tumminia 1995; Tumminia and Kirkpatrick 1995; Kirkpatrick and Tumminia 1989, 1992b). Unarius presented a convoluted discourse of past-life "memories" mixed with pseudoscientific verbiage about energy oscillations, a worldview difficult for outsiders to understand. Most outsiders, including researchers, who asked us to explain the sociological aspects of Unarius characterized their written material as gibberish. We contended that the Unarian reality was cohesive and coherent, if one understood their mythology. Unarian mythology consists of an elaborate pastiche of borrowed and improvised themes invented since 1954, most of which reveal the divinity of its leadership, a common theme in many NRMs.

Unarian mythology borrowed from the cultic milieu myths about Atlantis,

Lemuria, and ascended masters only to combine them with rumored sightings of flying saucers.[4] Through psychic revelations and channeling, Unarian founders Ernest and Ruth Norman described their own spiritual origins and their linage of authority.[5] Mrs. Norman claimed over fifty incarnations, ranging from archangels and Space Brothers who lived millions years ago to numerous historic figures in earth's history. What is instructive about Unarian myth-making is that it was accomplished in a gradual process that included the full participation of the committed members. Unarians recognized the so-called truth about Mr. and Mrs. Norman only if they experienced somatic reactions, visions, dreams, or what Unarius calls "inspired messages." Members described their experiences, which were transcribed and put into book form. Each incarnation story wove an elaborate account of betrayal, violence, and redemption that sprang from the improvised statements Unarians made in their past-life therapy classes.

What we called mythic stories Unarians called "true stories." Unarians know they are true because they have experienced them as real. Various followers produced "memories" of those times when they interacted with Mr. and Mrs. Norman in past lives. Members usually described the "memories" as painful, some of them resulting in illnesses that lasted for days or weeks. For example, one origin myth involves the story of Dalos, an incarnation of Ruth Norman as a Pleiadian scientist who traveled to Tyron in order to save the planet and its people. During a period when Mrs. Norman went to the hospital, her followers met in class at the Academy where they confessed to have tortured her in this previous lifetime. They referred to this "fact" as they tried to remember what role they played in the torment. Some Unarian members wept during their testimonials, experiencing both the guilt of their supposed acts and the relief of being released from past-life karma through their contrition.

Unarian mythology (Tumminia 1995) purports stories of a cosmic origin, the fall from grace, the separation from the divine source, and the promise of cosmic return. For over a decade, Unarius touted the promised arrival of Space Brothers in 2001. Several researchers have trained their eyes on the event at Unarius in anticipation of yet another failed prophecy, a not uncommon occurrence in NRM circles. What other observers may not catch is the way Unarian members are presently dealing with this disconfirmation. Some Unarians are now reporting that they are reliving the time when they tried to kill Osiris and Isis.

This makes little sense to anyone who does not understand Unarian myth. According to Unarius, thousands of years ago Ernest and Ruth Norman incarnated as Osiris and Isis. They came from Atlantis to set up the Egyptian civilization by teaching the Unarius Science. Set, who was the reincarnation of an Unarian student, Antares, plotted to kill the divine couple. Set (Antares) enlisted the aid of other Unarians now enrolled as members of the Academy. When the spaceships came to take the couple back to the planet Aries, Set and his followers killed Osiris and Isis (Ernest and Ruth Norman). In the Unarian way of thinking, present-day members are now reliving their past-life guilt over the murder, a deed that prevented the landing of the saucers then and now.

In the case of Unarius, we observed both the process of mythmaking and its functional usage. Mythmaking emerged from a collective process of improvisation of stories with meaning between leaders and followers. The common meaning system held people together. Followers testified to the heroic and exalted spiritual nature of their leaders. The mythic stories explained the cohesive nature of the social bonds that supposedly went back millions of years. As Unarians repeated their recovered memories, they used the mythic themes idiosyncratic to their group. As a reality lived, myths explained the truth of Unarian experience from the invisibility of the space fleet to the manifestation of illness or joy. Members engaged in their socially constructed reality using their sacred narratives as reasonable and logical interpretations of what is so.

Self-Exploration, Values, and Ritual through Myth

People use mythological images and stories to express their own value systems, especially in NRMs where belief manipulates relatively freely chosen imagery in contrast to inherited religion. Newer forms of magical spirituality foster more of the imaginative-impulse self without the context of rigid rules or hierarchical submission (Tumminia 1987). Even so, when people establish communities around such values myth takes ritualistic form. In the past two decades, we have observed and researched some of the phenomena associated with American witches (Wiccans), feminist witches, and a variety of Neo-Pagans (Kirkpatrick, Rainy, and Rubi 1986; Tumminia 1987). Taking some of its mythology from Gerald Gardner's notions of the old religion and Doreen Valiente's focus on the Goddess (Guiley 1992), witchcraft developed several free-floating practices and some basic traditions, most without authoritarian structures that valued individual expression and creativity. Later generations of practitioners brought more innovations with a measure of popular appeal, the effects of which we see today where knowledge about magical spirituality can be had in mainstream bookstores, on college campuses, or through Internet access. Nature symbolism used in the service of self-expression and wish-fulfillment marks the magical improvisations of Neo-paganism the latter half of the twentieth century (Kirkpatrick, Rainy, and Rubi 1986; Guiley 1992; Jorgensen and Russell 1999). This magical mythos emphasizes being in the world rather than being saved from the world. We, like other researchers (Griffin 1995, 2000), have noticed the extensive use of mythic symbolism in ritual, sense-making, and psychological self-examination, especially among feminist witches.

The emphasis on female images and feminine principles in feminist spirituality distinguishes itself from most other forms of mythology. Part of the shift away from male-centered symbolism rests upon the idea that female reasoning differs because it strives for continuity and connection (Griffin 1995). The general understanding suggests that woman rewrite myths or reinterpret mythic lessons in order to create positive role models for themselves and future generations. Once stripped of their patriarchal significance, female archetypes will then shed their older connotations of passivity, subservience, and stigmatized irrationality. Griffin (1995) argues that feminist witches critique conventional religions for their emphasis on hierarchy and dominance in general and women specifically, taking seriously the challenge to create alternatives. Witches link women's oppression, environmental degradation, and sometimes exploitation of animals to notions of sociopolitical male domination reflected in masculine-centered divinities. Additionally, they critique patriarchal religions because they stress lineal intellectual constructs and suppression of the body (like mortification of the flesh), concepts that devalue corporal experience and expression that is not in the service of instrumentality. In feminist spirituality and the related feminist witchcraft, practitioners become active, creative mythmakers both in communal sense-making and in their own individual experience.

Feminist spirituality inspired a whole literary genre that helped spread the ideology. Some of the mythmaking in this vein came from keynoting writers like Starhawk, Marija Gimbutas, and Jean Shinoda Bolen. Merlin Stone's *When God Was a Woman* (1976) popularized the idea of feminine deity, and Margot Adler's *Drawing Down the Moon* (1986) presented a virtual how-to-manual of witchcraft. Charlene Spretnak's *Politics of Feminist Spirituality* (1982) collected cutting-edge essays in the political ramifications of goddess religion, as did many others. As previously stated, seekers of feminine divinity explored myths from all cultures for images of goddesses, female warriors, and nature spirits—the heroine with a thousand faces, so to speak. Collections of mythology—for instance, Merlin Stone's *Ancient Mirrors of Womanhood* (1984)—served as instruments in the ideological toolbox of exploring selfhood. Hungry for symbols from the shifted paradigm, cultural feminists and feminist witches rearticulated mythological imagery to reflect their contemporary value system.

Griffin (1995) asserts that adherents consciously use mythopoeic images in ritual to re-create an ethos of revision of power, authority, sexuality, and social relations. Drawing on her fieldwork, she further suggests that women experience the embodiment of the Goddess through ritual as they sometimes use the names of goddesses to represent themselves during ceremonies. The three aspects of the Goddess—Maiden, Mother, and Crone—drive the symbolism of many rituals. For example, Griffin describes a ritual circle of women who call in the Crone goddesses to be present, images used to confront the stereotype of aging women. Typical rituals address the moon time, or the menstrual period, and they can also be used at menopause in keeping with the notion that women are part of nature itself. Thus ritual enactment allows believers to live the very myths they use as ideology.

Leader as Hero, Holy One, and Myth

A definite strain of NRM mythmaking derives from the hero worship and great deference paid toward group leaders. Groups often develop as much mythology about their leaders as they do about the whole cosmos itself. Guru deference exists in many NRMs that pattern themselves on Eastern mysticism. Followers of gurus visualize themselves being in an intimate, if not all-consuming, relationship with their teachers as all-knowing guides and representatives of God. A case in point is MSIA, or the Movement of Spiritual Inner Awareness (Lewis 1998b), which calls itself an ecumenical church. Believers chant "Ani-Hu" (or secret chants for the initiated) to clear karma. MSIA's theology of cosmic return, which concerns the journey of the soul back to God, comes borrowed and adapted from Eckankar and the Sant Mat tradition of India. Sant Mat implies a formless God without divine personage myths like those of Hinduism or Buddhism. Borrowing further, MSIA teaches that the Light guides its activities with the help of Christ and the Holy Spirit; it mentions, although does not dwell upon, the actions of the negative force, called Kal. Christ and the Holy Spirit are rarely represented pictorially, and MSIA presents no mythic imagery of the negative force. MSIA's theology collects and celebrates various traditions from Zen Buddhism to the "trainings" of the Human Potential Movement. Truly eclectic in its orientation, MSIA sometimes hosts a Jewish Seder for its members at Passover, although not without the briefest references to Christ or the Light.

Despite being publicly criticized by ex-members (Lewis 1998b), most MSIA members literally adore their leader, declaring how much they love "J-R." The group's leader, John-Roger (J-R), is said to possess the Mystical Traveler Preceptor Consciousness. According to MSIA, Travelers have come throughout the ages as renowned religious personages or other men of stature, but this Traveler is different, possessing more abilities and spiritual dispensations than others. The Traveler acts as the Wayshower home to God; his spiritual presence can manifest in the form of a purple light, a phenomenon members attest to seeing. Jokingly, John-Roger calls himself the Garbage Man, meaning that he can take karma away from his devotees as an act of grace. Part clown, part professor, and part saint, John-Roger's persona generally speaks of the need to be loved and to love. John-Roger's seminars and discourses include symbolic material from major religions, as well as New Age sentiment, in a mythic collage of universal wisdom, but the Traveler remains the primary unitary symbol for the group. John-Roger's spiritual credentials stem from the notion that his consciousness contains John the Beloved, the favorite apostle of Jesus Christ. Charmed by their charismatic perception, adherents invest energy into being noticed by him, getting a hug from him, and being called on to ask questions. One can easily hear dozens of statements, like "If it wasn't for J-R, I wouldn't be here [meaning, I would not be alive]" at any MSIA event. MSIA members exchange stories about J-R and his ability to heal them with his love in an act of modern, unconscious mythmaking. The church has thousands of tape and video recordings of his talks and travels, which can keep his legend alive long after his body dies. If the organization survives, the myth of John-Roger will live on as long as it serves as a working symbol of MSIA's spiritual authority and power.

In the late 1980s, John-Roger passed on the keys of Traveler Consciousness to his named successor, John Morton. After more than a decade at the helm of MSIA, John Morton plays a vital part, but John-Roger still holds the spotlight, having issued more publications and tape recordings in his name. Older initiates focus their attention on the elder Traveler, accounting for their devotion by referencing his sense of humor and Preceptor status. Older initiates also cite the length of the association with John-Roger with their preferential focus. We would speculate that John-Roger's legendary living status will lead to further mythmaking, which will probably become more evident after the charismatic crisis of his eventual passing. MSIA is a good example of NRM mythmaking because it shows how some groups borrow, but still they invent their own mythology. Furthermore, it illustrates how leaders become symbolic, mythological images that hold groups together.

CONCLUSION

New religious movements use mythology to create interpretive worlds for adherents to traverse in much the same ways that the cosmologies of older religions do. They often fashion narratives about the spiritual origins of humans and sometimes venture promises of cosmic return. Myths articulate our charters for appropriate behavior, common values, and the nature of reality itself. Such sacred narratives function to substantiate the importance of group action and interaction as they explain the reasons for routine activities, as well as formal ceremonies. Myth lives as an active imaginative force when it becomes the vehicle for processing new images and meaning, giving form to nascent belief.

Believers use mythological imagery and stories in order to experience what their group assigns as important for them to experience. Stories can take the most implausible forms, but they remain reasonable and logical within the living collective agreement of group meaning. In addition to shaping an ongoing group reality, a mythos guides one's interpretation of oneself, because myth symbolically articulates a person's selfhood within the context of the definitions and images the group supplies. Myths, especially in NRMs, are not entirely fixed because they often reflect the unfolding process of reality construction taking place with leaders and followers in reference to the outside world.

Using our fieldwork experiences, we ventured three examples of how myth works in the Unarius Academy of Science, feminist witchcraft, and the Movement of Spiritual Inner Awareness. In all examples we observed myth as an active process of explaining reality and as a continually evolving meaning system. Unarius showed how mythic stories were created within the group around the channeled revelations of the group leaders. In response to their leaders, members experienced psychosomatic symptoms that supposedly proved the validity of the stories. Moreover, Unarians explained away the failure of their prophecy by referencing their myth of Isis and Osiris. In the case of feminist witches, we see a mythology that largely formed over the past fifty years, which blossomed within the cultural feminist political argument against patriarchal religion. Feminine myth, ritual, and symbol emerged as a way to celebrate collective and individual power. Feminist witches actively choose mythic symbolism from any cultural tradition, and they reinvent it to reflect their own value systems. They admittedly use symbols of feminine divinity or power as images of self. As for the example of MSIA, here as in the Unarius, the group borrowed some of its cosmological stories and theology, but it also assembled its cohesive symbolism around stories of leadership in an unfolding process of mythmaking that will probably continue for decades.

Although the recognition of NRM myth as an important focus of study has yet to receive the fullest consideration, students and researchers can find the study of how new groups use mythology fascinating territory. Because of the overabundance of groups and diversity of mythology, the field remains wide open to further investigation. Students, fieldworkers, and other researchers have yet to record and analyze all the ways NRMs construct their own realities within the social space of their belief systems.

NOTES

1. *Wicca* means "witch," and it refers to our research on American Neo-Pagan witchcraft and feminist witches. ISKCON stands for the International Society for Krishna Consciousness, or the Hare Krishna Movement. MSIA applies to the Church of the Movement of Spiritual Inner Awareness, based in Los Angeles. Unarius (Universal Articulate Interdimensional Understanding of Science) is short for the Unarius Academy of Science, a flying-saucer and past-life therapy educational group in San Diego.

2. This simple definition stands with one proviso. The concept of sacred is not universal; thus we are left with another imperfect definition. Malinowski (1954) and others have repeatedly criticized Durkheim's division between sacred and profane because of the fact that many societies categorized all experiences as sacred or magical, without providing the cognitive categories for a separate profane sphere of reality. Postmodern myths may indeed prove themselves to reside entirely within the profane sphere of experience, so our sacred and profane definition must stand as qualified.

3. The early thinkers obviously did not see NRMs coming as they predicted the disappearance of less "rational" types of worship. Sociologist Max Weber (Ritzer 1999, Griffin 1995) predicted a further rationalization of all aspects of society, including religion, with the advent of science, capitalist growth, and bureaucratization of the public sphere. Weber contended through his disenchantment of the world thesis that magical and animistic notions would be displaced. Far from irrelevant in contemporary society, animistic myths enliven and propel many of the new groups into radical departures from mainstream religions. An interesting aspect of some NRMs emerged with extensive of use of animistic imaginary in channeling and in rituals. Animistic myth abounds in New Age groups, UFOists, Neo-Pagans, and African-influenced religions. African-influenced, Yoruba-derived practices, like Voudon (voodoo) and Santeria (Vega 2001), have a longer historical tradition of drawing on indigenous themes with animistic imagery. Their mythology involves the orishas, originally African nature spirits, and their workings in the world. Such practitioners use simple magical charms and spells, as well as partaking in ceremonies of spirit possession. Voudon and Santeria survived hundreds of years of cultural repression, only to resurface as newly recognized religions.

4. Tales of extraterrestrial contact represent a strong theme in American folklore and modern myth (Jung 1959; Lewis 1995, 2000), created on the one hand by rumor and popular culture, and on the other hand by more serious spiritual seekers. Contact through channeling sprouted in part from the roots of American spiritualist influence (Kirkpatrick and Tumminia 1989; Lewis 2000). Newly fashioned cosmologies increasing employ technological and scientist themes in animistic frameworks with advent of UFO religions, like Aetherius, Chen Tao, or Raelians (Lewis 1995, 2000; Landes 2000). Kirkpatrick and Tumminia (1989) called this fusion of magical thinking with technological imagery "techno-animism."

5. The animistic practice of channeling (Brown 1997) spirit voices gave rise to numerous practitioners, launching their spiritual careers and countless groups. Groups like Unarius, Urantia, and the Ramtha School of Enlightenment got their starts from channeled messages (Landes 2000). Channeling, which is fairly common in New Age and some UFO groups, provides a perfect conduit for the introduction and mainte-

nance of mythic stories. If believers can be found, a mythology can be born. Not all channeling practices look alike as techniques vary from mild trance states to ecstatic spirit possessions, but as a nonrational means of constructing reality channeling has been successful in capturing the attention of some segments of the NRM audience.

REFERENCES

Adler, Margot. 1986. *Drawing Down the Moon.* Boston: Beacon Press.

Balch, Robert W., and David Taylor. 1978. "Seekers and Saucers: The Role of the Cultic Milieu in Joining a UFO Cult." Pp. 43–65 in *Conversion Careers,* ed. James T. Richardson. Beverly Hills, Calif.: Sage.

Bednarowski, Mary Farrell. 1989. *New Religions and the Theological Imagination in America.* Bloomington: Indiana University Press.

Benford, Robert D., and David A. Snow. 2000. "Framing Processes and Social Movements: An Overview and Assessment." *Annual Review of Sociology* 26: 611–639.

Berger, Peter. 1967. *The Sacred Canopy: Elements of Sociological Theory of Religion.* Garden City, N.Y.: Doubleday.

———. 1970. *A Rumor of Angels: Modern Society and the Rediscovery of the Supernatural.* Garden City, N.Y.: Doubleday.

Bolen, Jean Shinoda. 1985. *Goddesses in Everywoman: A New Psychology of Women.* New York: Harper Colophon.

Bowen, John R. 2002. *Religions in Practice: An Approach to the Anthropology of Religion.* Boston: Allyn and Bacon.

Bromley, David G., and James T. Richardson, eds. 1983. *The Brainwashing/Deprogramming Controversy: Sociological, Psychological, Legal and Historical Perspectives.* New York: Edward Mellen Press.

Brown, Michael F. 1997. *The Channeling Zone.* Cambridge: Harvard University Press.

Campbell, Joseph. 1968. *The Hero with a Thousand Faces.* 2nd ed. Princeton, N.J.: Princeton University Press.

Dillon, Jane, and James Richardson. 1994. "The 'Cult' Concept: A Politics of Representational Analysis." *Syzygy* 3(3–4): 185–197.

Doty, William G. 1986. *Mythography: The Study of Myth and Rituals.* University: University of Alabama Press.

Dudley, Guilford, III. 1977. *Religion on Trial: Mircea Eliade and His Critics.* Philadelphia: Temple University Press.

Dundes, Alan, ed. 1984. *Sacred Narrative: Readings in the Theory of Myth.* Berkeley: University of California Press.

Durkheim, Emile. 1965 [1915]. *The Elementary Forms of Religious Life.* Trans. Joseph Ward Swain. New York: Free Press.

———. 1966 [1938]. *The Rules of the Sociological Method.* 8th ed. Trans. Sarah A. Solovay and John H. Mueller. New York: Free Press.

Eliade, Mircea. 1954. *The Myth of the Eternal Return: Or, Cosmos and History.* Trans. Willard R. Trask. Princeton, N.J.: Princeton University Press.

————. 1959. *The Sacred and the Profane: The Nature of Religion.* Trans. Willard R. Trask. New York: Harcourt, Brace, and World, Inc.

Frazer, James George. 1951 [1900]. *The Golden Bough: A Study in Magic and Religions.* 2d ed. New York: Macmillan.

Freedland, Nat. 1972. *The Occult Explosion.* New York: G. P. Putnam's Sons.

Freud, Sigmund. 1950. *Totem and Taboo: Some Points of Agreement between the Mental Lives of Savages and Neurotics.* New York: Norton.

Girard, Rene. 1977. *Violence and the Sacred.* Baltimore: Johns Hopkins University Press.

Glock, Charles Y., and Robert N. Bellah, eds. 1976. *The New Religious Consciousness.* Berkeley: University of California Press.

Goffman, Erving. 1974. *Frame Analysis: An Essay on the Organization of Experience.* New York: Harper Colophon.

Griffin, Wendy, ed. 2000. *Daughters of the Goddess: Studies of Identity, Healing, and Empowerment.* Walnut Creek, Calif.: Alta Mira Press.

————. 1995. "The Embodied Goddess: Feminist Witchcraft and Female Divinity." *Sociology of Religion* 56(1): 35–49.

Guiley, Rosemary Ellen. 1992. "Witchcraft as Goddess Worship." Pp. 411–424 in *The Feminist Companion to Mythology*, ed. Carolyne Larrington. London: Pandora.

Honko, Lauri. 1984. "The Problem of Defining Myth." Pp. 41–52 in *Sacred Narrative: Readings in the Theory of Myth*, ed. Alan Dundes. Berkeley: University of California Press.

Jorgenson, Danny L., and Scott E. Russell. 1999. "American Neopaganism: The Participants' Social Identities." *Journal for the Scientific Study of Religion* 38(3): 325–338.

Jung, C. G. 1959. *Flying Saucers: A Modern Myth of Things Seen in the Skies.* Trans. R.F.C. Hull. New York: Harcourt, Brace and Company.

Kardiner, Abram., and Edward Preble. 1961. *They Studied Man.* New York: Mentor Books.

Kirk, G. S. 1970. *Myth: Its Meaning and Functions in Ancient and Other Cultures.* Berkeley: University of California Press.

Kirkpatrick, R. George, Richard Rainy, and Kathryn Rubi. 1986. "An Empirical Study of Wiccan Religion in Postindustrial Society." *Free Inquiry in Creative Sociology* 14(1): 33–38.

Kirkpatrick, R. George, and Diana Tumminia. 1989. "A Case Study of a Southern Californian Flying Saucer Cult." Paper presented to the annual meeting of the American Sociological Association, San Francisco, August.

————. 1992a. "California Space Goddess: The Mystagogue in a Flying Saucer Group." Pp. 299–311 in *Twentieth-Century World Religious Movements in Neo-Weberian Perspective*, ed. William H. Swatos, Jr. Lewiston, N.Y.: Edwin Mellen.

————. 1992b. "Space Magic, Techno-Animism, and the Cult of the Goddess in a Southern Californian UFO Contactee Group: A Case Study of Millenarianism." *Syzygy: Journal of Alternative Religion and Culture* 1(2): 159–72.

Landes, Richard, ed. 2000. *Encyclopedia of Millennialism and Millennial Movements.* New York: Routledge.

Lévi-Strauss, Claude. 1963. *Totemism.* Trans. Rodney Needham. Boston: Beacon Press.

Lewis, James R. 1994. "The 'Cult' Stereotype as an Ideological Resource in Social Conflicts: A Case Study of the Movement of Inner Awareness." *Syzygy* 3(1–2): 23–37.

————, ed. 1995. *The Gods Have Landed: New Religions from Other Worlds.* Albany: State University of New York Press.

————, ed. 1998a. *Cults in America: A Reference Handbook.* Santa Barbara, Calif.: ABC-CLIO.

————. 1998b. *Seeking the Light.* Los Angeles: Mandeville Press.

————. 1999. *Peculiar Prophets: A Biographical Dictionary of New Religions.* St. Paul, Minn.: Paragon House.

————, ed. 2000. *UFOs and Popular Cult: An Encyclopedia of Contemporary Myth.* Santa Barbara, Calif.: ABC-CLIO.

Luhrmann, Tanya M. 1989. *Persuasions of the Witch's Craft.* Cambridge: Harvard University Press.

Malinowski, Bronislaw. 1954. *Magic, Science and Religion and Other Essays.* Garden City, N.Y.: Anchor Books.

Melton, J. Gordon. 1999. "The Rise of the Study of New Religions." Paper presented at the CESNUR Meetings at Bryn Athyn, Pa.

Murray, Henry A. 1962. "Definitions of Myth." Pp. 7–37 in *The Making of Myth,* ed. Richard M. Ohmann. New York: G. P. Putnam's Sons.

Polkinghorne, Donald E. 1988. *Narrative Knowing and the Human Sciences.* Albany: State University of New York Press.

Preston, David L. 1988. *The Social Organization of Zen Practice.* Cambridge: Cambridge University Press.

Ritzer, George. 1999. *Enchanting a Disenchanted World: Revolutionizing the Means of Consumption.* Thousand Oaks, Calif.: Pine Forge.

Robbins, Thomas. 1988. *Cults, Converts, and Charisma: The Sociology of New Religious Movements.* London: Sage.

Robbins, Thomas, and Dick Anthony, eds. 1989. *In Gods We Trust: New Patterns of Religious Pluralism.* New Brunswick, N.J.: Transaction Press.

Rockford, E. Burke, Jr. 1985. *Hare Krishna in America.* New Brunswick, N.J.: Rutgers University Press.

Saliba, John A. 1995. *Understanding New Religious Movements.* Grand Rapids: William B. Erdmans.

Snow, David A., and Richard Machalek. 1982. "On the Presumed Fragility of Unconventional Beliefs." *Journal for the Scientific Study of Religion* 21(1): 15–26.

Snow, David A., E. Burke Rochford, Steven K. Worden, and Robert Benford. 1986. "Frame Alignment Processes, Micromobilization, and Movement Participation." *American Sociological Review* 45: 787–801.

Spretnak, Charlene, ed. 1982. *The Politics of Feminist Spirituality.* New York: Anchor Press.

Stark, Rodney. 2001. "Gods, Rituals, and the Moral Order." *Journal for the Scientific Study of Religion* 40(4): 619–636.

Stone, Donald. 1976. "The Human Potential Movement." Pp. 93–115 in *The New Religious Consciousness,* ed. Charles Y. Glock and Robert N. Bellah. Berkeley: University of California Press.

Stone, Merlin. 1976. *When God Was a Woman.* San Diego: Harcourt Brace Jovanovich.

————. 1984. *Ancient Mirrors of Womanhood: A Treasury of Goddess and Heroine Lore from Around the World.* Boston: Beacon Press.

Strenski, Ivan, ed. 1992. *Malinowski and the Work of Myth.* Princeton, N.J.: Princeton University Press.

Tumminia, Diana. 1987. *The Sacred Self: A Social-Psychological Study of Religious Self-Identity and the Case of Hare Krishna.* Master's thesis, San Diego State University.

———. 1995. *Brothers from the Sky: Myth and Reality in a Flying Saucer Group.* Ph.D. diss., UCLA.

———. 1998. "How Prophecy Never Fails." *Sociology of Religion* 59(2): 157–170.

Tumminia, Diana, and R. George Kirkpatrick. 1995. "Unarius: Emergent Aspects of an American Flying Saucer Group." Pp. 85–104 in *The Gods Have Landed: New Religions from Other Worlds,* ed. James R. Lewis. Albany: State University of New York Press.

Turner, Ralph H., and Lewis M. Killian. 1987. *Collective Behavior.* Englewood Cliffs, N.J.: Prentice Hall.

Vecsey, Christopher. 1991. *Imagine Ourselves Richly: Mythic Narratives of North American Indians.* New York: HarperCollins.

Vega, Marta Moreno. 2001. *Altar of My Soul: The Living Traditions of Santeria.* New York: One World/Ballantine.

Wallis, Roy. 1977. *The Road to Total Freedom: A Sociological Analysis of Scientology.* New York: Columbia University Press.

Zellner, William W. 1995. *Countercultures: A Sociological Analysis.* New York: St. Martin's.

CHAPTER 16

WOMEN IN NEW RELIGIOUS MOVEMENTS

SUSAN J. PALMER

WOMEN's presence in new religions, often dismissed as "cults," is an intriguing topic for study. It raises questions concerning gender equality, sexual exploitation, and the future of the nuclear family.

Depending on what new religion becomes the object of study, one can argue that NRMs are regressive enclaves of patriarchal power (the Black Hebrews) or utopian experiments in matriarchy (the Brahmakumaris or the Rajneesh Foundation in the mid-1980s). As for sexual exploitation, one could point to the recent scandals involving Hindu swamis (Satchitananda of Integral Yoga, and Shyam of Kulu), whose female disciples complained of "spiritual incest" with their supposedly celibate enlightened gurus. On the other hand, some "cults" have been criticized for forcing women to renounce their sexuality. Margaret Singer, a proponent of the brainwashing theory, claims that Unificationist women stop menstruating. Then there is the example of Dianic Wiccans, who exclude men from their circle and celebrate same-sex eroticism.

The radical and experimental nature of women's roles in new religions raises anxieties about the future of the family. Rosabeth Moss Kanter, in her 1972 study of communal groups (intentional societies), argues that "successful" communes (lasting 25 years or more) enhance their members' commitment to the leader and the collective by demanding the renunciation of family ties. This theory offers an insight into why so many communal groups reject monogamy in favor of celibacy, polygamy, or "free love"—and also explains why communal religions tend to raise fears that they pose a threat to the sanctity of the family.

New religions are forums of experimentation in gender and new patterns of governance, where we find an abundance of female messiahs, mediums, and prophetesses. In North America we have outstanding examples. The famous channeler, JZ Knight, presides over the Ramtha School of Enlightenment near Seattle and voluntarily enters a trance state so that Ramtha, an "entity" from ancient India, can expound his radical gnostic philosophy and conduct workshops where Ramtha's students cultivate shamanistic powers. One can also find striking examples of feminine charisma in Canada, such as Quebec's Marie-Paule Giguere, revered as the reincarnation of the Virgin at the end of time by Catholic priests and nuns disillusioned in the wake of Vatican II.

Women's charisma on the margins of religion must be understood within the context of our North American history and culture, as the consequence of recent, rapid changes that have affected the structure of the family and the mainstream churches. These changes include the impact of secularization and modernization on traditional religion and family life. New religions seem to provide the useful social function of offering forums for experimentation in gender roles and fictive family life that are fueled by utopian visions of the future or by spiritual revelations regarding male-female relations.

There have been attempts by scholars to divide new religions into two categories: the "neopatriarchal" and the "feminist." They point to bastions of neoconservative family life, insisting that women's place is in the home (e.g., the Lubavitch, the Aryan Nations, Mormon Fundamentalists), or to radical matriarchies that reject marriage and chidbearing. The opposite extreme can be found in la Mission de l'Esprit Saint, whose founder, Eugene Richer, Third Person in the Trinity in Flesh, blessed the wombs of women so they could become breeders of a new, sinless race of Enfants de Dieux. Women who failed to give birth once a year would be publically reprimanded in front of the congregation. When Richer died, his successor, Gustav Robitaille, preached the most egregiously misogynistic doctrines to be found in NRM literature.

Searching for cases of "feminist" NRMs, we might choose the Raelian Religion, whose founder, Rael, claims that extraterrestrials created the human race from their own DNA. Raelians are advised *not* to give birth, but to acknowledge extraterrestrials as their creators and to cultivate their sensuality in the hope of being cloned in the Age of Apocalypse. Rael has recently created an Order of Pink Angels, young women who are to save themselves for the advent of the aliens ("Elohim") to become their companions and ambassadors, when they descend in their spaceships sometime before the year 2035 to endow their "creations" with their advanced scientific knowledge.

But a close look suggests that the real situation is more complex. Contemporary new religions are often incongruous syncretisms of what is old-fashioned and what is futuristic; ultramontane Catholicism merges seamlessly with gnostic heresies; patriarchy and matriarchy waltz together in strange new steps. Quebec's mystical pope of the Apostles of Infinite Love ordains women as priests and elevates the Virgin to a place in the Trinity. Farrakhan's Nation of Islam requires women to wear the veil and sit separately in the mosques, and train to be good, faithful wives and mothers, but it also encourages their educational and professional development. "Cults" are frequently portrayed in anti-cult literature as a backlash against contemporary feminism, resulting in domestic enslavement in patriarchal enclaves or in degrading sexual experiments at the hands of charismatic prophets. There are plenty of testimonials of women ex-members who indeed regret their investments in demanding spiritual movements. News reports since Jonestown advertise the destructive trajectories in the histories of certain NRMs. However, a broad knowledge of contemporary marginal religions indicates that women's participation in them is by no means a pathological nor tragic phenomenon. I would argue that the remarkable variety of women's roles, the sheer complexity and richness of their experiences in the new religions, cannot be reduced to an anti-cult, journalistic stereotype. To be truly just, one must assess each group, if not each female member, as a unique case.

If one brings a sociological perspective to the problem, one can argue that new religious communal experiments do not occur in a vacuum, and as strange as many of these patterns of sexuality are, the motives which shape them do not necessarily originate exclusively from the "charismatic cult leader's" dark psyche but are influenced by the countercultural experimentation and reshaping of gender roles that is an ongoing process in the larger society.

The notion that NRMs serve a special function in society as laboratories of social and sexual experimentation has been explored by Foster (1981), Wagner (1985), Melton and Moore (1982), and others. Warren Lewis (1982: 191) writes that "new religions in the history of the American people have served at least one particular function: they have allowed the nation to explore, work out, and relieve deep cultural needs . . . to solve within [their] laboratories . . . some more general cultural problem."

A useful typology for studying women's roles in NRMs is the model of sex identity originally formulated by Sister Prudence Allen (1987: 294). Her three types bear some affinity to Rosemary Reuther's typology of eschatological, liberal, and romantic feminist reactions to patriarchal anthropologies in Christian history that speak of woman's original equality in the image of God, restored in Christ Reuther (1983: 199).

A Typology of Sex Identity into NRMs

The three conceptualizations of sex identity found in NRMs are sex complementarity, sex polarity, and sex unity. This tripart typology has two variables, equality and difference. I have adapted this typology to apply to new religions (see Palmer 1994).

Sex complementarity sees the sexes as gifted with quite different emotional, psychological, and spiritual qualities. It stresses the necessity of marriage as a union between two incomplete halves of the same soul, so that a balanced and harmonious being can emerge. Marriage often continues into the spirit or celestial worlds, ritual marriage between the living and beings in the spiritual realm is often practiced, and marriage and procreation may be a path to personal salvation and a step in ushering in the new millennium. One often finds a dual or androgynous godhead in these groups.

Sex polarity proposes that women and men are spiritually distinct and separate, but insists that men and women should not unite and are inessential or irrelevant to the other's salvation. Inequality is the order of the day, since one sex is perceived as purer, more intelligent, or closer to God at the expense of the other. It is (of course) men who are usually held to be the superior sex, but some NRMs besides the Rajneesh—the Raelians, Dianic Wiccans, and the Brahmakumaris, for example—view women as superior to men. Fears of spiritual pollution justify sexual segregation. In some NRMs the sexes are permitted to engage in limited, tightly controlled relationships as a necessary phase in the individual's spiritual development or to contribute children to the group.

Sex unity regards the physical body as a superficial layer of false identity obscuring the immortal, sexless spirit. Groups espousing sex unity might dress unisex and foster androgynous social personas; or they might play-act traditional sex roles while maintaining an inner detachment from the role. In neoshamanic groups or neognostic groups there is often the notion that letting go of one's attachment to the body and gender is a necessary prelude to realizing one's godhood or infinite power. Sex unity groups often view gender as something that can be chosen or changed; through elective surgery for Raelians, through reincarnation or conscious rebirth for Scientologists, and through metamorphosis into a higher androgynous being for Heaven's Gate members.

These types are not necessarily found in their "pure" form; mixtures of two types are frequent (as in the Children of God, which embraced procreation and free love, and yet has always encouraged and facilitated women's equal involvement in leadership). Longitudinal studies of a group's history can show a transition from one type to another. For example, both the Hare Krishna and the Rajneesh movements have shown a recent trend toward discarding their sex polarity views in favor of sex complementarity values that tend to foster more conventional, stable relationships between the sexes.

It could be stated that in new religions one finds that women's role is simple and more clearly defined than in our larger, pluralistic society. This simplicity and clarity is acheived by emphasizing one role (or sometimes two) while deemphasizing or rejecting other roles.

The role of "lover" is a highly valued role for women disciples of Rajneesh/Osho and also of Raelian women, who define themselves as "lovers" and reject the marriage contract and tend to postpone or reject motherhood. Rajneesh women tend to reject the role of wife and mother. To be a devoted disciple or "lover of Bhagwan" in the 1980s required living in the commune, where women and men were encouraged to engage in short-term, pluralistic heterosexual love affairs. This expressed an ideal of communal sharing and equality in love, where touching and erotic emotions were conduits for Bhagwan's "energy" that flowed through the charismatic community, propelling the individual toward enlightenment.

Disciples of Bhagwan referred to themselves as "lovers of Bhagwan." The spiritual quest and the feelings of charisma evoked by the master's presence are linked to sexual desire and romantic love. Rajneesh, as the "enlightened one," is "beyond sex" and is perceived as male in relation to the disciple who surrenders to him and receives his energy in the initiation ritual of *sannyas*. In Rajneesh's system, women are regarded as spiritually superior to men (see *A New Vision of Women's Liberation* 1987).

In Rajneesh's India ashram, a core group referred to as the "power ladies" held the executive offices. At the height of the communal experiment, in the city of Rajneeshpuram in Oregon (1983–1986), women held over 80 percent of leadership positions (Braun 1984). These leaders were called "moms" or "supermoms," and the authority structure has been dubbed the "ma-archy" by the press. An interesting experiment in role reversal was tried out in the commune. Men were described as "soft" or "beautiful" and encouraged to develop feminine qualities, whereas women were referred to approvingly as "strong" and "dynamic." Gender-based work roles were exchanged during the building of Rajneesh's utopian city, Rajneeshpuram. Women drove earth-moving equipment while the men took charge of the children brought in by single parents and supervised the kitchen. Unisex fashions, perfume, and earrings were shared by both sexes, as were bathroomns and bedrooms.

Rajneesh predicted a "New Age of Woman" that would be characterized by ecological harmony, technological advancement, strict birth control, and meditative consciousness.The Rajneesh movement has always strongly discouraged procreation. Rajneesh recommended "twenty years absolute birth control" due to the overpopulation of the planet. In order to acheive enlightenment, it was advisable to stay unattached and childless in order to "give birth to oneself." During its four-year existence, Rajneeshpuram did not witness the birth of a single baby among its 4,000-odd sexually active residents. In the Poona ashram sterilization operations were a common practice among the leaders, particularly for men, since the operation was less invasive for them.

Rael, the messianic founder-prophet of the Raelian Movement International ("Raelian Religion" in the U.S.), preaches the "sex unity" view of gender—that is, men and women possess identical abilities. He compares them to "biological robots" that are programmed to give the other pleasure. Since cloning will soon be possible, reproduction through sexual intercourse is considered outmoded, and for Raelians the purpose of sex is pleasure. Sex is a panacea for man's violent impulses (Rael urges his male followers to be more like women, for the "Age of Apocalypse is the age of women!") and a way to promote world peace. Sexual pleasure stimulates the growth of new brain cells and is even a technique of meditation in which one might establish telepathic contact with the Elohim. Homosexuals are welcomed and prominent in the Raelian community and Raelians participate in international gay marches every year.

Thus, for Raelian women, their charismatic, meaningful role is that of lover or playmate. Women attend the meetings dressed in a sexy, seductive fashion, and the legal marriage contract is considered to be inimicable to love. Motherhood and parenthood are by no means prohibited, but they are deemphasized since the planet is overpopulated.

Raelian women participate in all levels of leadership in the movement's hierarchy, which is patterned after the Catholic Church. Rael is the equivalent of the Pope, supported by a five-tiered pyramid called the "Structure"—of Bishops, Priests, Animators, Assistant Animators, and Probationers. The Raelians' "laity" are just plain Raelians who have been baptized but who don't necessarily pay their 10 percent tithing or observe the dietary rules (no recreational drugs, alchohol, or caffeine), and whose attendance at the monthly meetings may be occasional. Since men outnumber women in the Raelian movement, women are still a minority in the Structure, but they have gained a stronger presence in the last five years. Recently Rael created a woman's auxiliary organization in the Raelian Religion, the Order of Rael's Angels.

Rael announced in July 1998 that he had received a revelation from the Elohim to found a special women's caucus or religious order called the Order of Rael's Angels, which has become a women's caucus in the Raelian Religion. The purpose was to "gather young women who consciously wish to put their inner and outer beauty at the service of their Creators and of their Prophets, when we [the extraterrestrials] arrive at the Embassy." Within this order, there are the Pink Angels and the White Angels. They can be distinguished by the pink or white feathers appended to their necklaces, and the number of feathers denotes their rank. Rael's Angels have two aims: to take care of Rael and the other 39 prophets (when they return), attending to their comfort, dietary needs, and general well-being; and to spread the message to women outside the movement. The Pink Angels have a more specialized role—to prepare themselves to be companions and lovers for the Elohim and prophets when they arrive. To prepare for the aliens' advent, the Pink Angels must take vows of celibacy.

Raelian women appear to fit the sex unity model, since autonomy is a virtue, leadership is free of gender bias, and women, men, and gays explore their sexual preferences independently in working toward self-realization. But it could be argued that the Angels suggest a return to the sex complementarity model, as women are cultivating uniquely "feminine" qualities so as to be ready to complement the extraterrestrials when they land (the Raelian equivalent of marriage to spirits).

What is the larger social significance of these new, radical and religiously defined roles for women? Presumably, very few of them will achieve the majority status and respectability of the Church of Latter-day Saints, which has arguably had an impact on mainstream family patterns. And what is the secret of their evident appeal for contemporary women?

The "cult experience" actually appears *less* significant (or at least less threatening to mainstream religions) when one considers the well-documented fact that they exhibit a high dropout rate. Sociologists have consistently found that between 80 and 90 percent of members participate in these movements for one, two, or three years—and then leave. The theory that NRMs provide experiences analogous to those found in traditional rites of passage has been convincingly argued by a number of scholars (Melton and Moore 1982; Levine 1984; Palmer 1994).

But the "cult experience" may appear *more* significant within the context of our culture if one considers the possibility that these radical religions are fulfilling a function similar to tribal or traditional rites of passage. Modern women voluntarily participate in these new religious rites of initiation in order to heal past wounds or in a quest for interior psychological growth. Some might judge them to be "brainwashed," but it could also be argued they are expoiting the resources of the group for their own ends.

A recurring theme found in the rhetoric of new religions, whether the prophet preaches sex unity, complementarity, or polarity, is the notion of the androgyne. Women and men, whether they practice celibacy, free love, or monogamy, set aside their individuality and strive to build a common group identity, to experience "communion" (Kanter 1972) with the opposite sex, and to merge into an undifferentiated whole. Hierarchical relationships and social status are repudiated while these initiates embrace symbols of totality, the presexual simplicity of childhood, or the harmony of androgyny. Thus, new religious movements might be described as protective retreats where women can recapture a sense of innocence and wonder and slowly recapitulate the stages of their own sexual and social development. The strange phenomenon of a modern woman who chooses to inhabit the stylized roles of a new religion, whether she becomes a sexually expressive Rael's Angel or a soberly dressed "sister" in the Nation of Islam or a celibate shaven-headed "classmate" in Heaven's Gate, might best be understood as the age-old quest for the ecstatic experience and spiritual epiphanies through the ritual passage.

REFERENCES

Aidala, Angele. 1985. "Social Change, Gender Roles, and New Religious Movements." *Sociological Analysis* 46(3): 287–314.

Allen, Prudence. 1987. "Two Medieval Views of Woman's Identity." *Studies in Religion* 16: 21–36.

Barker, Eileen. 1984. *The Making of a Moonie: Choice or Brainwashing?* New York: Basil Blackwell.

Foster, Lawrence. 1981. *Religion and Sexuality: Three American Communal Experiments of the Nineteenth Century.* New York: Oxford University Press.

Kanter, Rosabeth Moss. 1972. *Commitment and Community: Communes and Utopias in Sociological Perspective.* Cambridge, Mass.: Harvard University Press.

Lewis, Warren. 1982. "Coming Again: How Society Functions through its New Religions." In *New Religious Movements: A Perspective for Understanding Society,* ed. Eileen Barker, 191–215. Lewiston, N.Y.: Edwin Mellen.

Levine, Saul. 1984. *Radical Departures: Desperate Detours in Growing Up.* Toronto: Harcourt, Brace, Jovanovich.

Melton, J. Gordon, and Robert L. Moore. 1982. *The Cult Exerience: Responding to the New Religious Pluralism.* New York: Pilgrim.

Palmer, Susan J. 1994. *Moon Sisters, Krishna Mothers, Rajneesh Lovers: Women's Roles in New Religions.* Syracuse, N.Y.: Syracuse University Press.

Rajneesh, Bhagwan Shree. 1987. *A New Vision of Women's Liberation.* Poona, India: Rebel Press.

Reuther, Rosemary. 1983. *Sexism and God Talk.* Boston: Beacon.

Rich, Adrienne. 1976. *Of Woman Born.* New York: Norton.

Wagner, Jon. 1982. *Sex Roles in Contemporary Communes.* Bloomington: Indiana University Press.

CHILDREN IN NEW RELIGIOUS MOVEMENTS

CHARLOTTE E. HARDMAN

IN the U.S., Canada, the United Kingdom, and much of the rest of Europe, the period since the 1950s has been one in which the mainstream Christian churches have seen a decline in numbers. There is little argument that the U.S., Canada, and the U.K. are increasingly secular and multicultural. At the same time they have seen the rise of numerous organizations, a massive and in some senses compensatory growth in the number of practitioners of alternative, often eclectic, often non-Christian new religions. Some are Hindu, some Buddhist, some Islamic, some Earth religions; many are a mixture of elements from several traditions, including the Human Potential Movement. First in the U.S., and now in the U.K., to a lesser degree, we have also seen the increase in fundamentalist movements. In spite of the secular ambience with the decline in mainstream religions, there is still a percentage—possibly increasing—of the populations in the U.S., the U.K., and Canada, for whom religion is utterly serious.[1] Belonging to a new religion or a fundamentalist religion, a communally based religion, a millennialist religion, or an individually inspired religion involves commitment and strong beliefs about the nature of the world and the importance of the direction and shape of the lives of those involved. The "dropouts" who joined NRMs from the late 1960s and 1970s lived life as an ideal, to help transform the world—whether through self-improvement, missionary work, or radical lifestyles. They chose to reject the materialism, values, and lifestyle of the mainstream and took control of their lives in a particular way (deviating often from the "right" way their parents would have chosen for them). They found new and powerful directions for themselves. But what about the next generation? This chapter examines this question. The arrival of the second generation has had an enormous impact on new religious movements, and new issues and debates have arisen—about the future of their children, the movements themselves, and the direction the movements should take.

It was a surprise, when I was looking for material on children in new religious movements in the early 1990s, to find first little had been written on this fast-growing group of individuals. By the 1990s the percentage of children and young people in the movements was increasing; in some groups there are now more second-generation members than first generation. In The Family, which averages six children per family, the first generation is now a minority.[2] The increasing number of children had implications in terms of the maturity, responsibilities, and goals of the parents: now they had less mobility, and they had to be more realistic and less idealistic. There were economic implications, and they had to educate the incoming generations. The "dropouts" were now responsible for the lives and futures of numerous children. Yet this is still a little researched domain. In 1999 *Children in New Religions* (Palmer and Hardman 1999) looked at four key areas of interest—the enormous impact that children have on a young movement, how movements socialize their children, what issues of religious freedom arise as a result, and how children in NRMs construct meaning.

The main aim of the chapter is to outline the main issues and debates that have arisen surrounding "kids in cults" and to demonstrate how the vast majority of the literature upon which most people's understanding of children in new religious movements has been constructed remains focused on three key themes, which have preoccupied the public and academics alike. The first part of the chapter puts our understanding of children in NRMs in perspective, pointing out the historical and cross-cultural relativity of the concept of the child. The second part looks at the research and media interest in children in NRMs, which have concentrated on child abuse, including mental and sexual abuse and neglect; child socialization and education; child custody cases and "the best interests of the child." I will outline the key arguments in each of these three areas. In conclusion, the chapter argues that, the focus on the scandals involving children in NRMs draws attention away from developing wider research on the ways in which children develop spiritually, how they gain meaning and order from the religious and cultural patterns in which they live, and what they think about religion and spirituality, whether growing up in new religious movements or the mainstream.

"Child" and "Childhood" in Historical and Social Perspective

Compared to the scarcity of literature on children in NRMs, there is a burgeoning literature on children and "childhood" in mainstream society.[3] Much of it underlines the extent to which childhood is a cultural, economic, and social construction. Since the publication of Ariès's book *Centuries of Childhood* in 1962 numerous articles have been written on the historical development of childhood and the impact of culture and society on its formation. For Ariès the concept of childhood began in the mid–eighteenth century. Prior to this, according to him, there was no such thing as the modern "awareness" (*sentiment*) of what distinguishes children from adults, and hence there was no separation of the worlds of child and adult. "The idea of childhood did not exist. Children were miniature adults. This is not, however, to suggest that children were neglected, forsaken or despised. The idea of childhood is not to be confused with affection for children" (1962: 125). Whether or not Ariès's interpretation is correct, and some historians disagree, what his work achieved is an important emphasis on the extent to which childhood varies according to particular time or place;[4] he thereby greatly heightened awareness of the relativity of childhood.

In terms of this chapter, an emphasis on the relativity of childhood is significant for two reasons. First, it suggests that to appreciate and assess the way children are treated in any new religion, it is essential to explore the context in which children are being raised and the context of any one child-rearing practice. The concept of childhood needs to be understood, as well as the existing power structure of that NRM, along with an understanding of the kind of rules and regulations about children, their attitudes toward children's behavior, restrictions on activities and play, and the adults' expectations of children's responses to authority. This is not to say that relativism should reign supreme, but simply that judgment should be suspended until the context is fully appreciated. Freedom to raise one's children according to one's beliefs is part of religious freedom. In English and U.S. law a parent still has the right to determine his or her child's religion. The apparent preposterousness of someone else's way of raising children is simply related to our own beliefs and prejudices. This can have an impact on decisions in courts, as Anthony Bradney (1993, 1999) and Michael Homer (1999) describe, when parents divorce and the quality of parenting is assessed.

The second significance of Ariès's work lies in highlighting how recent is the "modern" view of childhood and the nuclear family. This influences our own, often unconscious, bias about what is "right" when looking at children in NRMs. This is particularly pertinent when looking at communal movements reacting against contemporary Western society. Though "modern" conceptions are often inconsistent, the concept of childhood is one that has assimilated various myths and ideologies, "imaginative projections" which can be seen to have influenced popular views of children. There are several features of this modern conception of childhood. Ariès (1962) highlighted as particularly modern the separation of children from adults both in play and work. This is seen as the ideal: children should have their own space and play, their own books and toys; children should be allowed their innocence, should not have to "work", should be listened to; they are morally good. If children help their parents with housework in the West it must be as a helper and without responsibility. If the work has some significance in the wider society parents may be considered negligent or exploitative. The modern view is that no one expects children to behave like adults. Our perspective is dominated by the idea that children should develop into *autonomous, separated persons*, but as children they should be protected and their desires should be heard. They should have toys. Indeed in some areas there is an obsession with childhood as manifest in the proliferation of toys, media, and consumer culture. But there are contradictions. On the one hand, children are being given more rights. They now have civil rights (see the United Nations Convention on the Rights of the Child): in English law the Children's Act of 1989 means that welfare agencies must take into account the "best interests of the child" and the wishes and desires of children as individuals. Children's rights are not judged in terms of age but in terms of children's capacity to understand their situation and to form their own opinions. On the other hand, children are increasingly restricted, being "at risk" from the dangers and demands of modern society, which some argue is depriving them of a childhood.

As a whole, then, Western society has become particularly indulgent of children and child focused. This modern view tends to influence popular and media views about children. The view of the separateness of children in the West has its theoretical base in developmental psychology: children are seen as going through different "stages." The work of Piaget and Freud defined children in terms of stages and therefore in terms of their lack of capacities, skills, and powers and what is required to develop those capacities. The works and findings of these "fathers" are now being questioned by developmental psychologists. They argue, for example, that Piaget's conviction that the asocial and nonlogical features of children's thinking were supplanted by rationality and objectivity led him to overstate young children's naiveté and to underestimate their rate of progress (see Harris 1989; Harris 2000; Wellman and Gelman 1998). In spite of the fact that their findings reveal that children develop rational and objective capacities much earlier than Piaget claimed, the modern view of children has not been seriously challenged in academia.

There is rejection of the this view of children in those new religious movements which maintain the virtues of "traditional" parenting techniques, adopting practices which don't fit in with the indulgence of children or their separation from adulthood or ideas about developmental stages. The mainstream is not always nonjudgmental about "alternative childhoods," and those parents wanting their children to exist within the framework of what they conceive childhood should be—when, for example, children of Jehovah's Witnesses don't celebrate birthdays or Christmas or when children in The Family preach on the streets or distribute literature, or when Mennonite children are discouraged from fantasy.[5] Disagreements over how to raise children are "more fundamental and significant than previous discussions have recognized" (Bartkowski and Ellison 1995: 22). Moreover, there is very little research investigating the role of religion in child development, the volume by Rosengren, Johnson, and Harris (2000) being an exception. Whereas different forms of child-rearing in Africa or among American Indians are appreciated as being based in another culture, this is not always the attitude when dealing with alternative attitudes to children in new religious groups. In the U.K. and the U.S. legal decisions about children in religious groups are supposed to be impartial about religion (according to the First Amendment in the U.S. and in the U.K. since the Children's Act of 1989), yet religion has been a factor in some custody disputes. Bradney argues that presentations by lawyers in cases involving NRMs need to be attempts to educate judges (1999: 216).

CHILD ABUSE

One of the key areas of local knowledge or themes that have so far constructed our understanding and misunderstanding of children in NRMs may be loosely described as "child abuse," including mental, sexual, and physical abuse, as well as neglect. Spurred on by Jonestown in 1978, accusations of child abuse within new religions have gradually gained momentum as accusations about coercive persuasion, or "brainwashing," as it is popularly called, have met with more opposition, stronger academic arguments, and less success in the courts (see Bromley and Richardson 1983; Barker 1984; Anthony 1990; Richardson 1999a, 1999b). The notion of mind control was finally defeated in the 1990s in the courts in the U.S.[6] As Richardson remarked (1999a: 172), child abuse became the "ultimate weapon" in attempts to control new religious movements.

In 1980 West and Singer promoted the notion that the very character of the cult organization and its lifestyle, with its stereotyped totalitarian cult leader's control over members, was conducive to child abuse and neglect, with little to restrain the cult leader from any whimsical ideas about child-rearing that might occur to him or her. The anti-cult argument went like this: since all cult parents are obsessed with personal salvation or creating a heaven on earth, since these parents have become dependent on the leader, since their ability to think critically and independently is prohibited, and since they work in exploitative working conditions with little time for family, children are simply "an imposition upon their emotionally fragile, dependent parents," all of which tends to "lead toward a path of child abuse, for the cultist parent is regressed and unable to cope with the parenting demands and need of children" (Moos 1993: 12). From this view "cult children" are raised in organizations predisposed toward abusive practices.

Marcia Rudin (1982: 8) has written,

> How are children treated in these authoritarian groups often physically isolated from the world? There are mushrooming reports that children are separated from parents and siblings, receive inadequate or no medical care sometimes even at the moment of birth, may not have their births recorded or receive inoculations, get inadequate or no schooling at all, live in crowded and unsanitary conditions, suffer from improper diets which can damage their physical and mental growth, are subject to sexual abuse, and undergo harsh discipline and physical abuse so severe it has in a few cases led to death.

We see here the kind of concern about child abuse and the way in which it was and is typically expressed. There is little need to explore in depth any particular NRM to see whether child abuse is occurring. Information from ex-members about the totalitarian nature and lifestyle of the organization is sufficient. If a group can be defined as a "destructive cult" (Shapiro in Robbins 1988: 143) or an "extreme cult" (Enroth 1977), detailed evaluations of the religious group are not needed to make allegations of child abuse. The work of Michael Langone (1985) and John Clark (1981) gives some of the more sophisticated formulations of the criteria for determining whether a group is a "destructive cult." The definitions are, however, as Robbins (1988) points out, highly psychological[7] and could apply to any grouping such as any family or monastic group or commune. Furthermore, it is ex-members that the anti-cult considers the "experts" in terms of evaluating the nature of any NRM. Some would argue that this reliance on ex-members is misguided, ignoring research on apostasy and "deprogramming," which has shown that ex-members may have a resentment against the religious group they have left particularly if they have to face the reconstruction of a new life, career, and family outside of the group (see Bromley 1988). Information from disgruntled or even distressed ex-members or members should be dealt with carefully. The difficulty for both the child in an NRM of reporting sex abuse and for officials dealing with reports of suspected abuse is discussed by Malcarne and Burchard (1992: 77) "If a cult member were to report suspicions of child abuse/neglect to state officials, it would likely be a cult member who was dissatisfied or disillusioned with the cult—and in these cases, the motivation of the member (or ex-member) would certainly be questionable. Other possible reporters would be nonmembers who were relatives of member children, and whose motivations would also be open to question." Caution in such matters has not always been heeded by the anti-cult movement.

The kind of generalizations about the second generation in "cults" does unfortunately still constitute a popular view, and one that appears most often in the media. Moreover, the negative stereotype can support, and of course often is supported by, reference to cases in which children have either tragically died in considerable numbers (as at Jonestown in 1978, or in Uganda in 2000 with the deaths of members of the Movement for the Restoration of the Ten Commandments of God) or in individual cases of violence, such as the often mentioned 1983 House of Judah case, in which corporal punishment led to a boy's death (Singer 1996: 254). Children have also been abused. And they have died because their parents believed that spiritual healing could cure their child's illness; criminal charges against those parents has increased with the increase in governmental roles in protecting children. In the U.S. adults can either seek medical attention to deal with a physical disorder or they can use faith healing or alternative medicine. If a child dies from not seeking medical attention, however, parents can face criminal charges. Concern about the welfare of children has at times overridden concern about parental rights and freedom of religion (see Richardson and Dewitt 1992: 558).[8] In the U.K. there is a law that requires parents, if their child's condition does not improve after 72 hours of nonmedical treatment, to seek medical help.[9] Christian Science is an obvious example of a group that has come under criticism for promoting faith healing and neglecting children in need of medical attention. In the U.S. since 1983 and a new federal child abuse regulation defining failure to provide medical care as child neglect, criminal charges have been brought against some Christian Science parents whose children have died after spiritual healing (Richardson and Dewitt 1992: 551). In 1993 Douglass Lundman was awarded damages of over $5 million (reduced to $1.5 on appeal), after his son died from a diabetic coma, against the Church, his Christian Science exwife, and her new husband.

Some children, as we have seen from the case in the House of Judah, have also suffered from severe corporal punishment. However, no evidence has as yet been produced to show that children in new religious movements are more likely to be harmed than children in other institutions or mainstream society. The Institute for the Study of American Religion carried out a survey in 1986 exploring the reports of child abuse in cults and concluded that beliefs about corporal punishment and strict discipline could lead to violent tendencies in the control of children. But the survey also concluded that such behavior "did not come from the major nonconventional religions (that is, those identified as cults in the public mind) but from conservative evangelical Christian groups" (Melton 1986: 255, 258).

Part of the problem is the one of relativity; child-rearing methods, and with them appropriate forms of discipline, vary according to culture and time. At one time James Dobson's book *Dare to Discipline* (1970) was fashionable. It is still used by some evangelical Christians, and some Christian NRMs such as The Family, who see children as sinners by nature in the sense that the infant is fallible and naturally selfish and has to learn to love. Sinners-by-nature children need strong boundaries; they need to be taught self-discipline and self-control. Dobson's attitude that "permissiveness has not just been a failure; it's been a disaster!" advocates caring but also strict disciplining of children, including corporal punishment. This is very different from the more liberal attitudes of the later childcare experts Dr. Spock (1988) or the "modern" Penelope Leach (1989), who are supported by liberal, secular, and New Age parents who view children as innocent, vulnerable, and in need of the love of parents who should steer away from confrontation. Here, parents are urged to appreciate the unique nature of each child, view situations from their point of view, and offer an "open future," tolerating diversity in adult ways of life. No doubt the question of whether parents should be restricted from hitting their children will increasingly become an issue between religious conservatives and liberals. In the past two decades countries have in general become more liberal. Laws were passed to abolish spanking in British state schools in 1986 and in privately funded schools in 1998; it is still permitted in some states in the U.S. Nowhere is it allowed in Scandinavia.[10]

This more liberal legal framework has made it harder for those NRMs advocating strict discipline, particularly if they openly support corporal punishment. Whereas they believe it is in the children's best interests sometimes even to "break the will" of the child (Greven 1991), others consider this behavior abusive. This has led to some accusations and investigations, the most notorious being the Community in Island Pond in Vermont, a fundamentalist Christian sect, which was the object of controversy in the 1980s (see Robertson 1994; Palmer and Hardman 1999; Malcarne and Burchard 1992). The community was raided and more than 100 adults and 112 children were arrested. Though all were released, the techniques for the allegations of abuse, as Robertson (1994) points out, were seen to work for the anti-cult movement, the raids made headline news, which highlighted the allegations of abuse and barely mentioned. The same pattern can be seen in the raids worldwide on The Family: front page news as the allegedly abused children were dragged from their parents in nighttime raids, with scarcely a mention of their return after no abuse could be found in any of the children, in any of the six countries. Some of the officials' treatment of the children in The Family might, on the other hand, be seen to constitute abuse (see Oliver 1994). Over 190 children in 1992 were taken away by social services in Australia from parents who were members of The Family, but within a few days all were returned. A few of the key anti-cult figures who instigated some of these raids (Rick Ross, for example) also used child abuse allegations against David Koresh and the Branch Davidians. Attitudes toward Koresh and his group were heavily influenced by the media allegations of child physical abuse first publicized by the *Waco Tribune-Herald* and then circulated in the national media (Ellison and Bartkowski 1995: 120). Apostate claims of child physical abuse and extreme corporal punishment were taken at face value by the media and by officials, even though, as Ellison and Bartkowski elaborate, there was plenty of room for skepticism (ibid.: 121–126). Marc Breault, an ex-member and key informant, was jealous of or horrified by Koresh and became a "cult buster," working to bring Koresh down with atrocity tales, mostly rumors, nightmares, and anticipated events which went as far as suggesting human sacrifices (Hall 1995: 213–214). Justification for the ATF (Arms, Tobacco, and Firearms) attack and the later FBI siege and fatal assault was child abuse (see Lewis 1994: 159–164) even though "the Justice Department publicly acknowledged that they had no solid evidence of child abuse—only *speculation* by mental health professions who had been studying Koresh from a distance ... [and] two allegations of child abuse by disgruntled former members" (1994: 161).[11]

So children have been taken away from their parents and their NRM families. Modern democracy commands the right to tell parents how to raise their children, but at what point should the state take children away? Unfortunately, the anti-cult movement has grasped the growing sensitivity about children as a new weapon that can be used in their fight against new religions. The state is being persuaded to intervene on the basis of accusations and what amounts to misleading information from the anti-cult movement about lesser-known religious groups. Unfortunately, there is still little other information on children in these groups for the state to go on.

In spite of evidence, as we have seen above (Melton 1986), that children are no more at risk in nonconventional religious groups, some authors and "experts" on children and cults argue that it is the very nature of the cultic and authoritarian groups, their "psychological dynamics," that gives them "the capacity to harm children physically and psychologically" (Langone 1993: 327). Langone is convinced of the problem in "cults." Confessing that "scientific research on child abuse in cultic groups is almost nonexistent ... [and] the connection between a group's practices and child abuse is not always clear (ibid.), Langone nevertheless argues,

> Their absolutist ideology provides a rationalization for child abuse. Their limited interaction with members of mainstream society (for example members don't visit doctors, children attend group-run schools) tends to close off the normal means by which authorities learn about child abuse and neglect. Their religious nature magnifies their capacity to avoid the scrutiny because they can invoke the First Amendment in order to curtail investigative efforts. For these reasons, raising the question of child abuse and cults is not analogous, as some have suggested, to asking about child abuse and Episcopalians, or Catholics, or

Baptists. The social structure and psychological dynamics of mainstream religions simply do not incline them toward child abuse and neglect as do the
structures and dynamics of cultic groups.

So, according to Langone, Catholics and Baptists are different *kinds* of organizations. Yet ironically this book was written at the same time as the Catholic sex
abuse scandals in the U.S. were emerging in the media. With this, the realization
that abusive behavior in hierarchies of abusive power can exist in mainstream
churches just as much, if not more than, elsewhere was given concrete evidence.
Pedophile priests such as James Porter and David Holley "have preyed upon
literally hundreds of young victims" (Shupe 1998: 5). In Ireland monk Brendan
Smyth "had sexually molested uncounted numbers of minors" since he was reas-
signed to new positions each time his sexual activities became known. He had
access to children in orphanages and schools (Sipe in Shupe 1998: 133). In 1993,
the year Langone is writing about "cultic groups," the Catholic Church was attempting to protect Smyth from prosecution and itself from scandal "stances so
traditional in Irish church-state politics—where bishops could control the courts
and the media" (Shupe 1998: 135). Shupe argues that clergy malfeasance should
be seen as part of *elite deviance* "defined by Simon and Eitzen as constituting
illegal and unethical acts committed by persons in the highest corporate and
political strata of society" because most churches and denominations have corporate status. Though the Catholic Church has tried to separate individual abuse
from any connection with the social structure or practices of the Church, research
suggests that there may be problems when the total economic structure and power
of a group which rests on male, unmarried clergy.

Of course, the accusations against Catholic clergy and against new religious
movements should be seen in a wider context (see Shupe 1995). There is growing
awareness of the problem of sexual abuse in the work place and in therapy (Rutter
1990), and especially of the particularly complex relationship between gender, age,
power, and spirituality. The relationship of guru and disciple is a particularly
sensitive one and can have an abusive impact on children, as well as women, but
it is not a necessary result. Puttick (1999: 102) describes the master-disciple relationship as "that profound experience that fueled the Rajneesh/Osho movement"
but also argues elsewhere (1995: 29) that "there is little evidence of sexual exploitation of female disciples by Osho" and notes (1999: 102) that in the second
generation children "accept Osho as their master, but in a more relaxed, less
devotional way than the adults, and . . . less as an authority figure." Problems of
authority and misuse of power did arise, however, in the International Society for
Krishna Consciousness (ISKCON), which faced a scandal after the death of Pra-
bhupda in the time of the problems of the post-1977 guru succession (see Rochford 1998). ISKCON also had problems in the early years: young celibate men
were put in charge of minors in the Gurukula schools and, with little experience
with children, had full responsibility for their lives and their education. In the

early years members had ambitious ideas about creating pure devotees in the second generation who would not have to confront the kind of difficulties their parents faced. The live-in schools were aimed to produce such children. In the first five years of the experiment concerns about some of the children arose. The young teachers were idealistic and highly motivated but untrained and over-worked, with little understanding of children's needs. Allegations were made that some of them had misused their power, in terms of either physical or sexual abuse. In response, ISKCON prosecuted the teachers who were abusing children and introduced Michelle Elliot's Kidscape scheme to the second generation, giving children knowledge of what constitutes abuse and how to deal with it (Sita 1992 INFORM Seminar). Moreover, increasingly children are sent to day schools and local schools (see Rochford 1999). As with the Catholic Church, for ISKCON the total economic structure and power of a group which rested on male, unmarried males was in some cases problematic.

Allegations of child abuse have been made among the Jehovah's Witnesses and the Bruderhof. In these groups the power and authority of male "elders" with the responsibility to protect the Church has in some cases led to pedophiles being returned to families in which they abused the children (Ian Cousins was jailed for five years). It is alleged (BBC *Panorama* July 2002) that the Kingdom Hall has a database of over 23,700 names of sex offenders, and sex offenders are still dealt with by the church elders rather than the police. One Jehovah's Witness in Canada who reported a case of child sex abuse in the church received in return investi-gations into his financial affairs and every attempt to ostracize him and his family from the Church. As in the case of the Catholic Church, these are abuses of power which rely on religious authority to maintain the status quo rather than accept that there is a problem. The prohibitions on dealing with outsiders, and the preference to deal with the problem from within to avoid harming the religion, have led to extensive problems of child abuse in the Jehovah's Witnesses and the Catholic Church.

The NRMs that have been most heavily targeted in terms of child abuse allegations leading to extensive investigations are The Family (Formerly the Chil-dren of God), the Branch Davidians, the Northeast Kingdom community, and the Church Universal and Triumphant (Lewis and Melton 1994a). Debates about and research on allegations of child abuse or neglect in NRMs can be found in in-formative books and articles (Ellison and Bartkowski 1995. Wright 1995; J. Lewis and Melton 1994a and 1994b), in the description of cases where child abuse laws have been applied to one religious group (Malcarne and Burchard 1992; Palmer and Hardman 1999 on the Island Pond; Richardson 1999 on The Family; Ellison and Bartkowski 1995 and Lewis 1994 on the Branch Davidians), and on legal cases in which religious beliefs impact the medical care or education of children (Brad-ney 1993, 1999. Richardson and Dewitt 1992).

CHILD CUSTODY

Many of the child abuse allegations which jump-started the raids on, for example, the Branch Davidians at Waco, the Church Universal and Triumphant (CUT), the Island Pond, and The Family came to the fore in child custody cases. And it is custody cases that have further stereotyped the popular picture of what is happening to children in new religions. Accusations about NRMs shifted from the theory of "brainwashing" to more insidious allegations of child abuse or neglect. In the U.S. the decline of the influence of Margaret Singer and Richard Ofshe as "expert witnesses" in the courts (Lewis 2001: 90–92) and the death of mind control or brainwashing as a theory which could be used against NRMs came in the 1990s. The American Psychological Association had rejected Singer and her colleagues' attempt to legitimize the mind control theory in 1987. In 1990 the ruling in the *U.S. v. Fishman* case finally disqualified Singer and Ofshe from testifying as expert witnesses in other cases. Instead, accusations against NRMs in court now focus on the children.

Marriage breakdowns occur in all religious groups, but when one member of the couple belongs to a new religion, this can be used by the other to gain custody or reduce access. When one partner disagrees with the child-rearing, educational system, or religious techniques of the NRM or is simply no longer a member and disapproves of the religion, children become the focus of the legal battle. In some cases (Homer 1999: 187), children have become "pawns in the ongoing struggle between alternative spiritual groups and mainline churches or secular authorities" and child custody cases are the places where new religious movements are judged. In one definitive case in the U.K., The Family lost a custody case (*Re ST*) brought to court by a grandmother. She never argued that her daughter was deficient in parenting skills: she applied for custody of the grandson simply because her daughter was a member of The Family, whose sexual experiments in the late 1970s and early 1980s gave the anti-cult movement ammunition.[12] In a 1991 case, Sahaja Yoga was brought to court—again by a grandmother. Her application for custody of her two grandchildren was to stop them from being sent to the Sahaja Yoga boarding schools in India or Rome. The main concern here was "that the children will be estranged from their cultural origins, that the education they receive is inadequate, that the children feel isolated and unhappy and that they are being inculcated with [the leader] Sri Mataji's teachings" (Coney, 1995: 117). On appeal the mother was allowed custody of her children on condition that she kept them with her at home, thereby preventing her from sending them to the Sahaja Yoga schools. This ruling was based on the court's conclusion that the mental health of the boy who had attended the school in India was "in danger and his conditions of education very severely compromised."

The difficulties for courts lie in the precarious balance between freedom of religion and the best interests of the child. My aim here is not to demonstrate how this balance is achieved in the U.S. and in Europe as well as the U.K. This is well covered by Homer (1994, 1999), Bradney (1993, 1999), and Richardson (1999). My aim is to describe one case to show that custody cases may not be the ideal place to assess the quality of parenting in any new religious group, since often the judges are as ignorant about NRMs as members of the public are. As Bradney has discussed, although courts in the U.K. are supposed to be neutral about religious matters, some parents have lost custody of their child or children "precisely because of their religion" (1993: 49).

The case I will describe involves the Church of Scientology. It was founded by L. Ron Hubbard, who initially conceived of Dianetics, mental techniques to clear the mind of unwanted memories that prevent individuals from finding their true potential. Rejected by the American Psychological Association, Hubbard transformed the packaging of his techniques into a religion. The case known as *Re B and G* (1985) concerned a Scientologist who had been looking after his two children, a girl age eight and a boy age ten, for five years and the mother, an ex-member, who sought to gain custody in 1983. The father had remarried and, according to Bradney (1993: 49), no evidence was introduced questioning the parenting of either the father or the stepmother. What is important in this case is that the judge decided in favor of the mother precisely because the father was a Scientologist. Had he not been a Scientologist "the scales would probably come down in favour of not disturbing the *status quo*" (Bradney 1993: 49). The judge described Scientology as "immoral and socially obnoxious . . . corrupt, sinister and dangerous" (Atack). Moreover, the court of appeal upheld this judgment, accepting that the beliefs of the Church were central to the case. Crucial to the judge's decision was the psychiatric evidence about Scientology presented as "expert testimony." It came from John Clark, one of the first mental health experts to criticize cults (see Clark 1979). He believes in "brainwashing" and "the unique capacity of these absolutist groups to cause harm," which he argues comes from "aggressive and skillful manipulation of a naive or deceived subject" (1979: 280).[13] The judge rejected the evidence of the Scientologists, describing them as "subjective and conditioned" (Bradney 1996: 215). He assessed the quality of the father's parenting largely on the basis of what he was told by Dr. Clark about a new religion, about which he was ignorant. He was not in possession of a range of academic material which would have put a different light on Dr. Clark's evidence and a different perspective on whether being a member of Scientology would per se affect one's parenting abilities (see, e.g., Bromley and Richardson 1983). Dr. Clark suggested that membership of Scientology amounted to a "sociopathetic illness" yet, as Richardson (1992) notes, the tests by other psychiatrists have not found any evidence of this. The evidence accepted was limited to anti-cult views about "mind control" which, as mentioned above, are not acceptable as legitimate evidence and are considered unscientific. The abilities of the father to care for his children have as much to do with his membership of Scientology as would another parent's participation in Catholicism or Hinduism. This custody case was certainly not the ideal place to assess the quality of parenting in Scientology.

SOCIALIZATION AND EDUCATION IN NRMs

With the arrival of the second generation, the parents of alternative religions have had to divert some of their attention from their radical goals to the issues of parenting.[14] Since their children did not choose to commit themselves to an alternative religion, these parents have had to decide whether to impose their own ideas and beliefs on their children. However, childhood is inevitably at least in part tied to adulthood, to the meaning-making and order of the adults, so these parents have had to work out what aspects of their own values, religion, and culture they should transmit, how far they should isolate their children from the wider society and protect them from what they themselves have rejected, how much should they insist on them accepting their ideology. Moreover, as Stark (1996) has argued, since the vitality and survival of these new religions depends in part upon retaining the second generation, many parents have had to assess the effectiveness of their attempts to transmit their ideology or consider their disinclination to indoctrinate their children. Stark argues that, to succeed, religious movements "must socialize the young sufficiently well as to minimise defection and the appeal of reduced strictness" (1996: 144). He argues that the problem for any movement must be to retain the loyalty of the second generation but not at any cost, not if the offspring push for the movement to become less strict.

What we actually find in new religions is a large variety of patterns of socialization and as varied a response from the second generation. The socialization and educational practices invariably differ from those of mainstream society since NRMs have often aimed to experiment with alternative ways of raising and educating children. Many NRMs arose as experiments for new forms of childhood, alternative kinds of families which could relieve children from what was seen as the oppression of the institution of the nuclear family. The controversial psychologist R. D. Laing was not the only person in the 1960s and 70s to view the nuclear family and established institutions of authority as the sources of personal and social problems, writing that "families, schools and churches are the slaughterhouses of our children" (1971: 102). Rajneesh denounced the family as outdated and as "the root cause of all our neurosis" (1984: 505 in Puttick 1997). The Americans Jane Pearce and her husband Paul Newton built on the psychoanalytic theories of Harry Stack Sullivan (1892–1949), viewing "the relationship of mothers to their children . . . as the cause of almost all psychopathology [and] the source of all individual's limitations. The mother [being] the first agent of repression" (Siskind 1999: 53). Other new religions have, in contrast, located social and individual problems in what they see as the permissiveness and lack of discipline in society and loss of the nuclear and extended family. As Puttick writes (1997: 129), "the conservative NRMs attempt to revive traditional, patriarchal family structures, whereas the counter-cultural movements experiment with alternative form, particularly the commune." Bainbridge notes that "American communes were self-consciously and vociferously designing alternatives to the conventional family system" (1997: 143). Janet Jacobs also sees communal NRMs as alternatives to the family and their members as "disenchanted youth in search of the ideal family" (1989: 4). The "real" family becomes the group, and all the adults within it, not just the parents, take on the responsibility of the next generation. Emphasis is placed on spiritual values, rejecting the corrupt, selfish, immoral features of modem family life, traditional education, and child-rearing. Although not necessarily as extreme as the "institutionalized allomothering" of the collective kibbutzim, in which parents partially or fully abdicated their role in socialization (Talmon-Garber 1983: 255), a relative separation between parents and children is encouraged in some groups.[15] Sometimes this leads to a tension between the needs of the collective and those of the family.[16]

In the 1960s and 1970s feminist critiques of the oppressive nature of the family simultaneously rejected all forms of authority, including schools, criticizing them as ineffective, authoritarian institutions stifling emotions and creativity, the means by which the ideology of deference to authority was passed on to children. Rudolph Steiner (1861–1925), founder of Anthroposophy, was one of the first to develop a form of education that took account of the whole human being (body, mind, spirit) that could lead to cultural renewal rather than what was seen as bigotry and destruction. His form of education can be seen in all the Waldorf schools (the first in Stuttgart, Germany, in 1919), Emerson College in Sussex, England, and others in Edinburgh, York, and Bolton and the Moray Steiner School in Scotland. A. S. Neil, who started Summerhill in 1921 as an alternative, libertarian "free school," stressed the importance of the participation of children and their freedom to choose what they learn and how they spend their time. Neil was influenced by Gurdjieff—for example, in his emphasis on absence of coercion and on pupils' responsible awareness of others' lives. His main point was that the child, rather than achievement, should be put first. All these schools are child-centred, focusing on the authority and "authenticity" of children, with the principle that curriculum should flow from the children's own interests and that adults should be friends, not authority figures. A few beacon schools in the U.S. aim for this kind of autonomous and democratic approach (e.g., Sudbury Valley school in Massachusetts).

Charles Reich (1971: 142, 143) catches the mood against schooling in his *Greening of America*: "Training in schools consists of preventing the formation of individual consciousness, taste, aesthetic standards, self-knowledge and the ability to create one's own satisfactions . . . the child is taught passivity. . . . School is intensely concerned with training students to stop thinking and start obeying." The goals of attending to the creativity and authenticity of children were confronted by John Holt (1923–1985),[17] whose view that school was the main institution creating the gulf between adults and children influenced on parents looking for radical alternatives. He argued that the education of children should be in "learning how to learn," not "learning how to be taught," and that this could only be done at home by parents, outside the school system.

This is the climate in which NRMs often chose to develop their own educational programs, which not only provided schooling for their second generation but attracted the attention of parents looking for "alternative" schools offering more emphasis on spirituality and less on external authority. For example, at the day school run by Transcendental Meditation in Skelmersdale, U.K., not all the pupils' parents are members of TM. However, all the teachers and pupils meditate. The teachers aim to create a school culture that encourages discipline from within. The view of schooling is not child-centered, as in Montessori, but aimed to be "uplifting," enhancing five fundamental principles:

- *Receptivity*—cultivating fine feelings in children
- *Intelligence*—improving the orderly functions of children's minds
- *Knowledge*—selecting and presenting children with suitable content and methods
- *Experience*—allowing children to integrate the new knowledge with their own experiences of life
- *Expressing*—ensuring that children have grasped new material by encouraging them to "tell it, say it, write it, teach it to somebody else."

As the head teacher said, "We lead them. We do not pander to them but also give them a wide choice. We always come back to the self—their consciousness." The focus is on harmony and getting rid of negativity and stress, seen as the source of all behavioral, social, or learning difficulties, through meditation, exercise, and massage. If a child is stressed, the answer is not to analyze but to balance the physiological. Analysis, or talking, is seen as merely reinforcing the bad behavior.

Other NRM schools that attract pupils from outside the movement include that of the Church of Scientology (Greenfields, which accepts a number of pupils excluded from other schools), the School of Economic Science (St. James and St. Vedant, founded 1975 in London; the teachings are derived from Vedanta and Gurdjieff), and the Ananda Marga Nursery Schools. In contrast, some have had a primary aim to school the children of their members. Osho's school (Ko Hsuan in Devon) is for children of Sannyasins from all over the world. Damanhur in Italy, has its own schools for children up to the age of fourteen (Introvigne 1999: 146), and Ananda has Living Wisdom Schools in California and Oregon. Puttick (1999) highlights the Osho movements difficulty creating a school, based on Osho's ideology of personal, social, and religious freedom from any kind of institution or authority. Their school has to give children enough knowledge to live in a complex technological society, but, consistent with Osho's ideology, the children must not lose their intuition and natural intelligence. Moreover, from the point of view of the adults involved, this is not a religious school since this would necessarily involve the negative aspects of more formal religious indoctrination. Given their ideology, and their belief in children's inner spirituality and intelligence, how can the school teach without destroying those very qualities? The school has, to some extent like the TM school, based its education on spiritual and ethical values, with a strong transpersonal dimension of meditation and techniques of humanistic psychology.

The kind of home-schooling found in groups rejecting secular schools, which are seen as lacking any spiritual education and being full of worldly temptations, are supported by all kinds of bodies: Education Now, Education Otherwise, Human Scale Education, and Accelerated Christian Education (which also runs schools) in the U.K., and the National Coalition of Alternative Community Schools, Growing Without Schooling, the Global Alliance for Transforming Education in the U.S. The influence of Maria Montessori (1970–1952) can also be seen in many of the NRMs choosing the home-schooling option, such as The Family and the Church Universal and Triumphant (Lewis 1994).

Despite the variety of socialization and child-rearing practices in NRMs, there are a few obvious key basic patterns and variations. Shaping different kinds of socialization are, first, basic ideas about the nature and concept of the "child" and the relation of "child" to the world; from an anthropological point of view these are socially constructed. As we have seen, the concept of the child is not simple. The notion of "child" embraces different concepts, such as that of "non-adult" and "offspring of parent," where the emphasis is on the status of the adult, or "autonomous developing individual," where the emphasis is on the status of the child. To explain the attitudes to children in different NRMs, researchers need to explore the relative emphasis on each of these. To what extent is emphasis placed on the status of the adults, with children seen as "not yet adult," inherently different from adults in their innocence and vulnerability, needing their love and protection? To what extent are children seen as valuable offspring, the next generation to replicate their parents? In such groups, having as many children as possible is an ideal. Are children seen as developing, yet equal and autonomous individuals, who may form their own ideals and values? What are the divisions, characteristics, or boundaries that separate children from adults?

There are here two distinct opposing concepts of the child. At one extreme is what one could call the passive concept, in which adults transmit their roles, values, and traditions to their offspring. In this view, children need protection and strong discipline from authoritarian parents. The concept is articulated by some spiritual groups as it has been by sociologists such as Durkheim and Talcott Parsons. The significant aspect of socialization is that of society shaping individuals. The emphasis is on the conformity of individuals, each one born an egotistic, asocial being, its mind a "a *tabula rasa*, very nearly" (Durkheim 1956: 72), an empty container that is trained by a social system. To some degree the malleability of the individual is such that he or she will respond to any kind of socialization. When sociologists have talked about the relationship between the individual and the group in terms of socialization, what has often been emphasized is the individual's potentiality for conformity and the learned elements of personality: "the major value-orientation patterns, . . . laid down in childhood and not on a large scale subject to drastic alteration during adult life" (Talcott Parsons 1951: 207). The concept of the passive child is inherent in the Puritan Christian concept of the child born with Original Sin and needing strict discipline to break its will, to control its proclivity to be bad. We see this concept in some mainstream religions, NRMs, and sects, most notably in Fundamentalist Christianity, Jehovah's Witnesses (see Stark and Iannaccone 1997), the Mormons (Stark 1996), Island Pond (Palmer 1999), and Branch Davidians (Ellison and Bartkowski 1995).

At the other extreme is the concept of the child as essentially active. Children within this view are meaning-makers, autonomous individuals who should be free to make their own choices, have their own will and self-determination, their own ways of exploring the world. They hold valid views which should be heard. It is society that conditions and contaminates. Rousseau's view of children as innocent and close to nature, deserving freedom to express and develop themselves, lies at this end of the spectrum. In the early 1970s there were calls for the child to be liberated, voiced for example by "radicals" or "alternative" educationalists, as we have seen above.[19] This concept characterizes those NRMs which are often labeled New Age (Heelas 1996; Melton 1992). "For the liberal the transgenerational reproducton of outlook, culture, values and tradition is acceptable so long as it is not accomplished at the expense of the child's self-determination or particular nature" (Archard 1993: 131).

The second key dimension is the group's conception of ultimate authority and power; that is, where the group views the ultimate source of authority—whether in *an external source* of authority, such as God, the Bible, Allah and the Quran, powerful beings, a divine power separate from oneself, or in *an internal source*, such as in the power of the self, in the private experience of spiritual realities, with a concept of the individual as the "ultimate locus for the determination of truth," or "epistemological individualism" as defined by Melton (1992:

7). In this case ultimate power lies in the very essence of oneself, so it is unnecessary to seek it elsewhere. These two dimensions are mapped in figure 17.1.

1. Concerns the concept of child within the group along a dimension in which *the child is active and creates reality* to the concept in which *the child is passive*
2. Concerns the spiritual ideology of the group and its concept of spiritual authority and power: the dimension of *ultimate spiritual authority lying external to the individual* or *ultimate spiritual authority lying internally.*

In Box A we find New Age children; the second generation of Rajneesh/Osho, Transcendental Meditation, est; children whose parents are involved in "the revivalist religious impulse directed toward the esoteric/metaphysical/Eastern groups and to the mystical strain in all religions" (Melton 1992: 18) believing that every person, as well society, can be transformed. We find children whose parents follow a nature religion; children of Scientologists, of the School of Economic Science, of Sai Baba; children at Findhorn, a New Age center in Scotland. The language of Findhorn has elements of theosophy, anthroposophy (Rudolph Steiner), Alice Bailey, and Christian mysticism. It combines Advaita Hindu philosophy with Pagan nature worship (Riddell 1990: 286). Both TM and Findhorn conceive of an "inner knowledge" to be attained by those who follow the path. Their parents share a monistic belief, a fundamental assumption that "all is one," emphasizing mind-body holism and the interdependence of all aspects of the cosmos, the laws of harmony and balance.[20] The model of childhood here has its focus on individ-

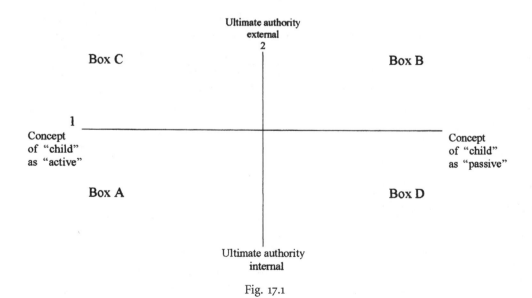

Fig. 17.1

ualism and inner potential. Based on the thinking of Carl Jung (1959) and Abraham Maslow (1968), this focus could be called the "self-realization" model. The potential of every individual is to be "the creative center of his activities and of his perceptions, more self determined . . . fully responsible, fully volitional with more 'free will' . . . more spontaneous, more expressive, more innocently behaving, more natural" (Maslow 1968: 106–107). Since self-realization is central to the model, experience and experimentation are important, whereas doctrine, unthinking obedience, and complacent acceptance or repetition are to be avoided. Children are encouraged to develop their own tastes and values, to look within and find in themselves the answers to questions. There is little need for rules because authority and responsibility lie within the children themselves. Parents I interviewed at Findhorn did not see any reason to lay down the law:

> They decide for themselves—I don't decide for them—basic morality is inside them; there are no rules, no strict rules, we all just muddle along; because we have no doctrine, there's nothing to follow—so it's all spontaneous—in the moment. We don't celebrate anything. We're in an unfolding/evolution of consciousness—life is a journey, every moment is a learning so how could we give them some static dogma?[21]

Children are empowered to challenge their elders, to "stand up for what you believe in. Rebel against that which you do not. The world is in need of change. As long as we remember that a process of love may only be created by an act of love, whatever we do is right" (Brockbank and Raymont 1993: 10). Ultimate authority lies within each person, and the concept of the child is of an autonomous individual who has self-determination.

In Box B, we find many conservative Protestants, Fundamentalist Christians, Mormons, Jehovah's Witnesses, children of Island Pond, The Family (the Children of God), the Branch Davidians, and the Unification Church (Moonies). The emphasis here is on the authority and literalness of the Bible and the hierarchical relationship between God and his creation. Many writers on conservative Protestants describe the concern for authority and obedience in all spheres (Peshkin 1986; Rose 1988; Ammerman 1987). There is an elective affinity between biblical literalism and "authority-mindedness" (Bartkowski and Ellison 1995). The authority of the Bible takes precedence over individual conscience. Children in The Family said: "The Bible is the ultimate authority"; "The Bible is more of an authority than the rest of society"; "Babies grow from milk; we grow from the Word"; "We need to read and follow the Bible and do what it says"; "When Jesus speaks to us in the Bible and tells us what to do, we should do it"; "In the New Testament the only law is love"; "The Ten Commandments were not given on a take-it-or-leave-it basis; they are to be obeyed."[22] The concept of the child is based on the belief that, though man was created innocent, through the temptation of

Satan he transgressed and fell from the Edenic happy state. Children are thus both spiritual innocents and sinners. As blessings and gifts from God, children are central to these groups. The Family write that "we consider a child to be principally and initially a spiritual entity created by God Himself. God then unites this spirit with the physical body of the forming child to become a totally new and eternal living soul, the combination of both body and spirit. A child, therefore, is an act of creation." But children are also "sinners by nature" in the sense that the infant is fallible and naturally selfish and has to learn how to love. Children are covered by their parents' faith until they can be "saved" themselves, spiritually regenerated, or "born again." "Saved" children are nevertheless vulnerable to sin and need guidance. Sinners by nature, children need strong boundaries; they need to be taught self-control and discipline. Without these, children are unhappy and insecure and develop feelings of not being loved. "If the limits and controls are lacking in the early years, a child will not only be at a loss in the later years but will also be more likely to react and rebel against any kind of control." These groups are involved in spiritual warfare. Children can be led astray by the Devil, but by developing the children's "spirit" with the Word of God, and with prayer, children can protect themselves. It is a war in which Satan and his demons are struggling to harm children. "Toys and books are carefully supervised and imaginary companions forbidden since "they are associated with the devil and it would be very bad if they had imaginary companions" (Taylor and Carlson 2000: 248). To provide the right spiritual conditions for developing the spirit, many of these groups emphasize the importance of keeping children away from mainstream society and with members of the movement in supervised environments. In this concept of the "child" there is no idea of the autonomy of children. As Coleman says (1999: 75), "to acknowledge the autonomy of different generations as makers of meaning would be to compromise the apparent internal consistency of Evangelical beliefs and practices. After all, if biblical principles are applicable across cultures, then they should also be applicable across generations."[23] In these groups the second generation's dedication to the group's goals, the children's acceptance of external authority, and the submission of their own will can explain the success in capturing the majority of its children as dedicated members. Individual ego has no place. In these communities there is no time for individuals' desires, freedom, and choice. Children learn to surrender their egos to God and community. In The Family "the cut-and-dry rule-keepers bug the teens, but if they break a rule, we just tell them to do better next time." The Family wants its children to replicate their adult parents and follow the same truth. From birth the children study, memorize, and obey the Word to gain wisdom and spiritual strength. They learn to share and be unselfish, to listen to the needs of others, and to put others first. Their sense of self, their identity, is bound up with a consistent, uniform doctrine and with the sense that they are "walking that one mile further than anyone else." Even though it might be a daily battle to follow a life of total dedication, if one knows it is the Truth, then why challenge it?

In Box C we can locate groups whose members believe in an external ultimate authority but also view the child as an active agent who should make his or her own choices, a model in which self-realization, experience, and experimentation are important. ISKCON is an example. Here we have a devotional, ecstatic (*bhakti*) Vaishnava tradition which sees "God as the doer," "the devotee obeys God," "is lost in love" (Rawlinson 1997: 103, 104). Spiritual authority is traditionally external. At the same time, children in ISKCON express their freedom to choose in various ways. One girl said, "They [parents] expect you to try and then to make up your own mind. They give you direction but not rules and regulations. You need guidance, then you can make your own decision." ISKCON teenagers were both critical and accepting of aspects of their parents' faith, wanting to hand on at least an understanding of their religion to their own children but also wanting the freedom to choose: "I want to give it to them. Then when they grow up they can reject it." Most of them said that they don't wear the traditional clothes or attend the Temple very frequently; they also don't like not associating with the other sex until married: "That's okay for Vedic times, but now you need to get to know the other sex well before you marry."

In Box D are groups which emphasize that the ultimate authority is internal yet have a passive concept of the child. Sahaja Yoga is an example. The locus of authority is within. Spontaneous union with the divine is innate and can be awakened, leading to self-realization. Central to this is awakening the *kundalini*, the dormant energy lying at the base of the spine. This is a primordial force waiting to be connected so that it may evolve to a higher stage of consciousness. Self-realized people are believed to have the power to correct imbalances in the channels and organs of the body governed by *chakras*, spiritual centers located on the central nervous system that are important in the Tantric understanding of the body. *Kundalini* can be raised by Sahaja Yoga techniques to pierce the uppermost center of psycho-spiritual consciousness—the *sahasrara chakra*—in the fontanel area of the head. Once they are self-realized, people are believed to become more aware of "vibrations," positive and negative in their environment, and mental and emotional health improves with decreased stress and increased peace and security. The fundamental assumption is that "all is one," emphasizing mind-body holism and the interdependence of all aspects of the cosmos, based on the laws of harmony and balance. Although Sri Mataji is a significant authority in Sahaja Yoga, seen as all-powerful and sacred, the ultimate authority does lie within.[24] The concept of the child is based on the view that the children born into Sahaja Yoga are "realized" from birth and from Sri Mataji's view are "hers" to be raised by her authority and "divine wisdom" (Coney 1999: 111). The children are to be passive, socialized into her particular model. Sri Mataji is ultra-prescriptive about child-rearing techniques to ensure that they are protected from the harmful vibrations they can pick up from their parents or from the "permissive" form of childhood embraced by Western society. Her aim is to socialize the children in her movement toward the definite ideal, which emphasizes the innocence, sweetness, obedience, cleanliness, and respectfulness of the child. The child "becomes everybody's property" to develop the noble qualities so that by the age of six they "respect elders, calling everybody properly, talking to them, very behaved. So after 6 years of age they are really mature, good children . . . till 5 years . . . you can beat your children in case they are not good . . . you can start telling them . . . 'behave like people with dignity, you are like a king now, you are a realized soul,' all these ideas should be pushed into their heads at that age of six . . . asking questions, by children, it should not be allowed at all till 6 years" (Sri Mataji 1986: 6–7). Coney (1999) examines how the leader's ideal effects children's lives within the movement and why it has given rise to outside criticisms. She demonstrates the problems of translating an ideal concept of the child into practical reality within a sectarian religious environment. Coney suggests that the movement has been successful in the spiritual realm. The leader's ideals have influenced the second generation's adoption of a particular kind of spirituality. The movement has not been successful in attempting to detach children from their blood kin and in trying to shelter children from the outside world.

- Stark argues that "to succeed religious movements must socialize the young sufficiently well as to minimize both defection and the appeal of reduced strictness" (1996: 144). By "reduced strictness" he means not modifying the movements in an effort to satisfy those who are discontented. Looking at the two concepts of the child and the different locations of ultimate authority, we would have to deduce, if we accept Stark's statement, that only movements with a passive concept of the child and an external source of authority (and an evangelical frame of mind) can ultimately succeed. Those with an 'active' concept of the child would not want their second generation to passively mirror the movement of their parents. For them, success might be measured not in growth rate of the parents' movement but in terms of self-realization—creativity, for example—or the growth and well-being of Nature spirituality more generally, or their children's sense of spirituality and personal growth.

CONCLUSIONS

Although the main debates about children in NRMs and child abuse, child custody cases, and the indoctrination of children have furthered our understanding of children in new religious movements, the focus on these areas to the exclusion of some others has led to a distorted picture of children in NRMs, echoing the public's misconceptions about newer religions in general. The picture is distorted because it largely highlights "problems," or scandals. From research undertaken so far, although the lives of children in most NRMs can be seen as some kind of alternative childhood, which may present some children with the challenge of being different from other children, the majority enjoy lives deviating in detail but not in quality from the lives of those whose parents are members of mainstream religions.

Children are increasingly given attention in their own right, yet little has been written about the meanings children make of their parents' religion, the role of religion in child development, or the effect parents' religion has on a child's notion of their own identity. There is also a need for a great deal more research to confront the stereotypical negative attitude to these children's lives by looking at what goes on, and by putting the models of childhood and the socialization to be found in NRMs into a wider historical and cultural perspective. NRMs are a minefield, and like most religions the majority of NRMs have both negative and positive attributes. In general, as they evolve, grow up, and have the responsibility of the second generation, the groups change—whether in response to public opinion or as a matter of course. The problem for researchers of children in NRMs is the need for constant updates. From the overview given here, it is clear that there is a growing literature on the issues of child abuse and religious freedom; we can also see the extreme diversity of the sytems of meaning in terms of which children give form, order, and direction to their lives within new religions. I have shown, However, that the key issues that have influenced the popular view of chldren in NRMs are not fundamentally different from the issues involved in raising children in mainstream religion.

A sociology and anthropology of childhood is already developing, and this is beginning to be applied to new religions. We need to recognize, first, that childhood is a social construction within the framework of any NRM; second, that there are a variety of childhoods in NRMs just as there are across cultures; third, that children are not passive vessels of the socialization process but inevitably active agents in shaping their own lives; fourth, that children's cultures in NRMs should be studied in their own right; and last, that we should consider the "best interests of the child" not only from the adults' point of view but also from the child's.[25]

NOTES

1. The American Religious Identification Survey published in 2001 at the City University of New York shows that nearly 160 million adults are Christian, 2.8 million are Jewish, 1.1 million Muslim, and 30 million secular or nonreligious.

2. Children of God worldwide statistics (1997) show that of the full-time Charter members only 33.4 percent were adults, and of the less fully committed Fellow Members only 32.2 percent were adults, which leaves infants, children, and teens constituting more than 60 percent of both groups. In contrast, in groups growing rapidly, like the Mormons, Jehovah's Witnesses, and Sôka Gakkai, the average member is still a religious convert (Stark 1996: 143).

3. See, for example, Doxiadis 1989; Cunningham 1991; Jenks 1992, 1996; James and Prout 1990; Qvortrup 1993.

4. This is also clear from the work of anthropologists such as Middleton (*From Child to Adult*).

5. Pretend play is seen as a waste of time "a potential threat to the cohesion of the group because of its association with individual freedom of expression. A general rule in Mennonite communities is that personal development must not intrude on the concerns of the group" (Taylor and Carlson 2000: 257).

6. See James Lewis 2001: 90–92 for an outline of the defeat of the anti-cultism in the courts.

7. See Langone 1993: 5.

8. Melton director of the Institute for the Study of Religion has commented that whereas in the 1900s there were many faith groups that advocated prayer instead of medicine "motivated by a backlash directed against the inroads of modern medicine," the number of groups that still advocate prayer has been dropping ever since.

9. Information from Ontario Consultants on www.religioustolerance.org.

10. Most countries and states prohibit corporal punishment but add a "not with-standing" clause which allows punishment "of reasonable intensity" in the child-parent situation (ibid.).

11. See also Homer 1999: 198, which discusses the custody battle.

12. See Lewis and Melton 1994; Williams 1998, the expose by ex-member Williams; and Family 1998, the response by the Family.

13. For a critique of Clark's model of brainwashing see Richardson and Kilbourne 1983: 36–42.

14. In understanding the patterns of children's socialization in NRMs I have inevitably been influenced by the limits of my own research on children in NRMs, which has mainly been carried out in the U.K.

15. See, for example, Gene James 1983 on the Unification Church. Also, Sri Mataji suggests that sometimes people become too attached to their families and children. Children should therefore be encouraged to call all adult Sahaja Yogis either "Auntie" or "Uncle" and accept reprimands from any of them. As Coney says (1999: 112), "Natural ties are, to an extent, . . . superseded by the primacy of the group, and the children . . . discouraged from relying too much on their parents." Osho also argues for the spiritual family: "Your real family is not your father, your mother, your brothers, your sisters, your wife, your husband, your children, Your real family is the family of a Buddha" (in Puttick 1997: 135).

16. From my own research it is clear that this tension has been the reason for defection for some members of The Family and similar conflicts exist in the Unification Church with conflicting demands of mission and family.

17. *Escape from Childhood*, The Needs and Rights of Children (Harmondsworth: Penguin, 1975).

18. See Heelas 1996: 77–80 for a description of New Age education; see also Harrison 1991.

19. In anthropology children had been overlooked and "muted," their conceptions of the world needed to be listened to (see Hardman 1973), further articulated by anthropologists (James and Prout 1993).

20. As Tipton (1982: 14) writes, "This monism constitutes the fundamental difference in cognitive orientation between the counterculture and utilitarian culture, which is predicated on philosophical realism or dualism."

21. See Hardman 1999.

22. Ibid.

23. Coleman also argues that the Word of Life's evangelical ideology "entails a partial denial of the autonomous symbolic worlds" of children and in this sense they are muted. But in respect of their spiritual potential they are empowered, sometimes having almost as much authority as adults. The ritual and verbal form of their educational and social institutions, it is argued. also act to reinforce this role adaptability and personhood ambiguity.

24. See Kalbermatten 1979, Kakar 1989, Coney 1999.

25. See Prout and James 1990, Hardman 1973.

REFERENCES

Ammerman, N. T. 1987. *Bible Believers.* New Brunswick, N.J.: Rutgers University Press.

Anthony, D. 1990. "Religious Movements and 'Brainwashing' Litigation: Evaluating Key Testimony." In *In Gods We Trust,* ed. T. Robbins and D. Anthony, 294–344. New Brunswick, N.J.: Transaction Books.

Archard, David. 1993. *Children: Rights and Childhood.* London: Routledge.

Ariès, Philippe. 1962. *Centuries of Childhood.* Harmondsworth, England: Penguin.

Atack, Jon. 1990. *A Piece of Blue Sky: Scientology, Dianetics and L. Ron Hubbard Exposed.* New York: A Lyle Stuart Book.

Bainbridge, William Sims. 1989. "The Religious Ecology of Deviance." *American Sociological Review* 54: 288–295.

———. 1997. *The Sociology of Religious Movements.* New York: Routledge.

Barker, Eileen. 1984. *The Making of a Moonie: Choice or Brainwashing?* Oxford: Basil Blackwell.

Bartkowski, J. P., and C. G. Ellison. 1995. "Divergent Models of Childrearing in Popular Manuals: Conservative Protestants vs. the Mainstream Experts." *Sociology of Religion* 56.1: 21–34.

Bradney, A. 1993. *Religions, Rights and Laws.* Leicester: Leicester University Press.

———. 1999. "Children of a Newer God." In *Children in New Religions,* ed. S. J. Palmer and C. E. Hardman. New Brunswick: New Jersey and London: Rutgers University Press.

Brockbank, J., and T. Raymont. 1993. *One Earth.* Findhorn, Scotland: Findhorn Publication.

Bromley, David G. 1988. *Falling from the Faith: Causes and Consequences of Religious Apostasy.* Newbury Park, Calif.: Sage.

Bromley, D. G., and J. T. Richardson, eds. 1983. *The Brainwashing/Deprogramming Controversy.* Lewiston, N.Y.: Edwin Mellen.

Burke Rochford, E. Jr. 1999. "Education and Collective Identity." In *Children in New Religions,* ed. S. J. Palmer and C. E. Hardman. New Brunswick, N.J.: Rutgers University Press.

Charwick, B. A., and Brent L. Top. 1993. "Religiosity and Delinquency among LDS Adolescents." *Journal for the Scientific Study of Religion* 32.1: 51–67.

Clark, J. G. 1979. "Cults." *Journal of the American Medical Association* 242: 279–281.

Clark, J. G., M. D. Langone, et al. 1981. *Destructive Cult Conversion: Theory, Research, and Treatment.* Weston, Mass.: American Family Foundation.

Coleman, Simon. 1999. "God's Children: Physical and Spiritual Growth among Evangelical Christians." In *Children in New Religions,* ed. S. J. Palmer and C. E. Hardman. New Brunswick, N.J.: Rutgers University Press.

Coney, J. 1995. "Belonging to a Global Religion: The Sociological Dimensions of International Elements in Sahaja Yoga." *Journal of Contemporary Religion* 10, no. 2: 109–120.

———. 1999. "Growing Up as Mother's Children." In *Children in New Religions,* ed. S. J. Palmer and C. E. Hardman. New Brunswick, N.J.: Rutgers University Press.

Cunningham, H. 1991. *The Children of the Poor: Representatives of Childhood since the Seventeenth Century.* Oxford: Blackwell.

Dobson, J. 1970. *Dare to Discipline.* Wheaton, Ill.: Living Books/Tyndale House.

Doxiadis, S. 1989. *Early Influences Shaping the Individual.* NATO Advanced Study Workshop. London: Plenum.

Durkheim, Emile. 1956 [1922]. *Education and Sociology.* Translation of 1922 edition by S. D. Fox. Glencoe, Ill.: Free Press.

Eckberg, D. L., and T. Jean Blocker. 1989. "Varieties of Religious Involvement and Environmental Concern." *Journal for the Scientific Study of Religion* 28: 509–517.

Ellison, C. G., and J. P. Bartkowski. 1995. "Babies Were Being Beaten." In *Armageddon in Waco,* ed. Stuart A. Wright. Chicago: University of Chicago Press.

Enroth, Ronald S. 1977. *Youth, Brainwashing and the Extremist Cults.* Grand Rapids, Mich.: Zondervan.

"The Family." 1998. Response to *Heaven's Harlots: My Fifteen Years as a Sacred Prostitute in the Children of God Cult,* by Miriam Williams. [Switzerland]: World Services.

Greven, P. 1991 *Spare the Child: The Religious Roots of Punishment and the Psychological Impact of Physical Abuse.* New York: Knopf.

Hall, John R. 1995. "Public Narratives and the Apocalyptic Sect." In *Armageddon in Waco: Critical Perspectives on the Branch Davidian Conflict,* ed. Stuart Wright. Chicago: University of Chicago Press.

Hardman, C. 1973. "Can There Be an Anthropology of Children?" *Journal of the Anthropological Society of Oxford* 4.1: 85–99.

———. 1999. "The Ethics of Children in Three New Religions." In Palmer and Hardman, *Children in New Religions,* 227–243.

Harris, P. 1989. *Children and Emotion.* Oxford: Basil Blackwell.

———. 2000. "Children's Metaphysical Questions." In *Imagining the Impossible: Magi-*

cal, Scientific, and Religious Thinking in Children, ed. K. S. Rosengren, C. N. Johnson, and P. L. Harris. Cambridge University Press.

Heelas, Paul. 1996. *The New Age Movement: The Celebration of the Self and the Sacralization of Modernity.* Oxford: Basil Blackwell.

Holt, J. 1975. *Escape from Childhood: The Needs and Rights of Children* Harmondsworth, England: Penguin.

Homer, Michael W. 1994. "New Religions and Child Custody Cases: Comparisons between the American and European Experience." In *Sex, Slander and Salvation: Investigating the Family/Children of God,* ed. J. R. Lewis and G. Melton. Stanford, Calif.: Center for Academic Publication.

————. 1999. "Freedom of Religion and the Interests of the Child." In *Children in New Religions,* ed. S. J. Palmer and C. E. Hardman. New Brunswick, N.J.: Rutgers University Press.

Introvigne, Massimo. 1999. "Damanhur: A Magical Community in Italy." In *New Religious Movements: Challenge and Response,* ed. B. Wilson and J. Cresswell. New York: Routledge.

Jacobs, J. 1989. *Divine Disenchantment: Deconverting from New Religions.* Bloomington: Indiana University Press.

James, A., and A. Prout, eds. 1990. *Constructing and Reconstructing Childhood.* Basingstoke, U.K.: Falmer Press.

James, Gene. 1983. *The Family and the Unification Church.* New York: Rose of Sharon Press.

Jenks, C. 1992. *The Sociology of Childhood: Essential Readings,* Aldershot, Gregg.

————. 1996. *Childhood.* London: Routledge.

Jung, C. G. 1959. *The Archetypes and the Collective Unconscious.* London: Routledge and Kegan Paul.

Kakar, S. 1984. *Shamans, Mystics and Doctors: A Psychological Enquiry into India and Its Healing Traditions.* London: Unwin.

Kalbermatten, G. de. 1979. *The Advent.* Bombay: The Life Eternal Trust.

Kanter, R. M. 1972. *Commitment and Community: Communes and Utopias in Sociological Perspective.* Cambridge, Mass: Harvard University Press.

Laing, R. D. 1971. *The Politics of the Family.* London: Tavistock.

Langone, M. D. 1985. "Cults, Evangelicals, and the Ethics of Social Influence Persuasions." *Cultic Studies Journal* 371–88.

————, ed. 1993. *Recovery from Cults: Help for Victims of Psychological and Spiritual Abuse.* New York: Norton.

Leach, P. 1989. *Your Baby and Your Child: From Birth to Age Five.* New York: Knopf.

Lewis, J. 1994. "Child Abuse at Waco." In *Sex, Slander and Salvation: Investigating the Family/Children of God,* ed. J. R. Lewis and G. Melton. Stanford, Calif.: Center for Academic Publication.

————. 1994. *From the Ashes Making Sense of Waco,* Lanham, Md.: Rowman & Littlefield.

————. 2001. *Odd Gods: New Religions and the Cult Controversy.* New York: Prometheus Books.

Lewis, James R., and J. G. Melton, eds. 1992. *Perspectives on the New Age.* Albany: State University of New York Press.

————. 1994a. "Church Universal and Triumphant in Scholarly Perspective." Special issue of *Syzygy: Journal of Alternative Religion and Culture.*

————. 1994b. *Sex, Slander and Salvation: Investigating the Family/Children of God.* Stanford, Calif.: Center for Academic Publication.

Malcarne, V. L., and J. D. Burchard. 1992. "Investigations of Child Abuse/Neglect Allegations in Religious Cults: A Case Study in Vermont." In *Behavioral Sciences and the Law* 10: 75–88.

Maslow, A. H. 1968. *Towards a Psychology of Being.* New York: Van Nostrand Reinhold.

Melton, G. 1986. *Report on the ISAR Survey of Cult-Related Violence.* Santa Barbara, Calif.: Institute for the Study of Religion.

————. 1992. "New Thought and the New Age." In *Perspectives on the New Age*, ed. J. R. Lewis and J. G. Melton, 15–29. Albany: State University of New York Press.

Middleton, J. 1970. *From Child to Adult: Studies in the Anthropology of Education.* New York: Natural History Press.

Moos, Kaj. 1993. *Save Our Children.* Silkeborg: Forlaget Havmaagen/Seagull Production.

Oliver, Moorman. 1994. "Today's Jackboots: The Inquisition Revisited." In *Sex, Slander and Salvation: Investigating the Family/Children of God*, ed. J. R. Lewis and G. Melton. Stanford, Calif.: Center for Academic Publication.

Palmer, S. 1994. "Heaven's Children: The Children of God's Second Generation." In *Sex, Slander and Salvation: Investigating the Family/Children of God*, ed. J. R. Lewis and G. Melton. Stanford, Calif.: Center for Academic Publication.

Palmer, Susan J., and Charlotte E. Hardman, eds. 1999. *Children in New Religions.* New Brunswick, N.J.: Rutgers University Press.

Parsons, Talcot. 1951. *The Social System.* London: Routledge and Kegan Paul.

Peshkin, A. 1986. *God's Choice.* Chicago: University of Chicago Press.

Poulter, S. M. 1989. *English Law and Ethnic Minority Customs.* London: Butterworth and Co.

Puttick, E. 1995. "Sexuality, Gender, and the Abuse of Power in the Master-Disciple Relationship: The Case of the Rajneesh Movement." *Journal of Contemporary Religion* 10.1: 29–40.

————. 1997. *Women in New Religions: In Search of Community, Sexuality, and Spiritual Power.* New York: St. Martin's.

————. 1999. "Osho Ko Hsuan School." In *Children in New Religions*, ed. S. J. Palmer and C. E. Hardman. New Brunswick, N.J.: Rutgers University Press.

Qvortrup, Jens. 1991. *Childhood as a Social Phenomenon: An Introduction to a Series of National Reports.* Eurosocial Reports no. 36. Vienna: European Centre.

Qvortrup, J. Bardy, M. G. Sgritta, and H. Wintersberger, eds. 1994. *Childhood Matters: Social Theory, Practice and Politics.* Aldershot: Avebury.

Rawlinson, Andrew. 1997. *The Book of Enlightened Masters: Western Teachers in Eastern Traditions.* Chicago: Open Court.

Reich, Charles, 1971. *The Greening of America.* Harmondsworth, England: Penguin Books.

Richardson, James T. 1999a. "Social Control of New Religions: From 'Brainwashing' Claims to Child Sex abuse Accusation." In *Children in New Religions*, ed. S. J. Palmer and C. E. Hardman. New Brunswick, N.J.: Rutgers University Press.

————. 1999b. "Law and Minority Religion." *Nova Religio* 2 (October): 3–107.

Richardson, J. T., and R. Davis. 1983. "Experiential Fundamentalism: Revisions of Orthodoxy in the Jesus Movement." *Journal of the American Academy of Religion* 51.3: 397–425.

Richardson, James T., and John Dewitt. 1992. "Christian Science Spiritual Healing, the Law, and Public Opinion." *Journal of Church and State* 34.3: 549–561.

Richardson, J., and B. Kilbourne. 1983. "Classical and Contemporary Applications of Brainwashing Models." In *The Brainwashing/Deprogramming Controversy,* ed. D. Bromley and J. Richardson, 29–45. Lewiston, N.Y.: Edwin Mellen.

Riddell, Carol. 1990. *The Findhorn Community: Creating a Human Identity for the Twenty-First Century.* Findhorn, Scotland: Findhorn Press.

Riesman, Paul. 1983. "On the Irrelevance of Child Rearing Practices for the Formation of Personality: An Analysis of Childhood, Personality and Values in Two African Communities." *Culture Medicine and Psychiatry* 7.2.

———. 1990. "The Formation of Personality on Ethnopsychology." In *Personhood and Agency: The Experience of Self and Other in African Cultures,* ed. M. Jackson and Ivan Karp. Uppsala Studies in Cultural Anthropology no. 14. Stockholm: Almquist & Wiksell International.

Robbins, T. 1988. *Cults, Converts and Charisma.* London: Sage.

Robertson, G. 1994. "Island Pond Raid Begins New Pattern." In *Sex, Slander and Salvation: Investigating the Family/Children of God,* ed. J. R. Lewis and G. Melton. Stanford, Calif.: Center for Academic Publication.

Rochford, E. Burke. 1998. "Hare Krishna Devotees and Leaders' Misconduct." In *Wolves within the Fold: Religious Leadership and Abuses of Power,* ed. Anson Shupe. New Brunswick, N.J.: Rutgers University Press.

———. 1999. "Education and Collective Identity: Public Schooling of Hare Krishna Youths." In *Children in New Religions,* ed. S. J. Palmer and C. E. Hardman. New Brunswick, N.J.: Rutgers University Press.

Rose, S. D. 1988. *Keeping Them Out of the Hands of Satan: Evangelical Schooling in America.* New York: Routledge, Chapman and Hall.

Rosengren, Karl S., Carl N. Johnson, and Paul L. Harris. 2000. *Imaging the Impossible.* Cambridge: Cambridge University Press.

Rudin, Marcia. 1982. "Elderly and Children in Religious Cults." Presented at the Citizen's Freedom Foundation Annual Conference, Arlington, Va.

Rutter, Peter. 1990. *Sex in the Forbidden Zone.* London: Mandala.

Shupe, Anson. 1995. *In the Name of All That's Holy: A Theory of Clergy Malfeasance.* Westport, Conn.: Praeger.

———, ed. 1995. *Wolves Within the Fold: Religious Leadership and Abuses of Power.* New Brunswick, N.J.: Rutgers University Press.

Singer, M. T., with J. Lalitch. 1996. *Cults in Our Midst: The Hidden Menace in Our Everyday Lives.* San Francisco: Jossey-Bass.

Siskind, Amy. 1999. "In Whose Interest? Separating Children from Mothers in the Sullivan Institute/Fourth Wall Community." In *Children in New Religions,* ed. S. J. Palmer and C. E. Hardman. New Brunswick, N.J.: Rutgers University Press.

Sita. 1992. "Children in ISKCON." Paper given at INFORM Seminar.

Spock, B. 1988. *Dr. Spock on Parenting: Sensible Advice from America's Most Trusted Child Care Expert.* New York: Simon and Schuster.

Sri Mataji. 1986. *Talk on Childcare.* Vienna, Austria, July 9.

Stark, Rodney. 1996. "Why Religious Movements Succeed or Fail." *Journal of Contemporary Religion* 11.2: 133–146.

Stark, R., and William Sims Bainbridge. 1985. *The Future of Religion: Secularization, Revival and Cult Formation.* Berkeley: University of California Press.

Stark, R., and R. Iannaccone. 1997. "Why the Jehovah's Witnesses Grow So Rapidly: A Theoretical Application." *Journal of Contemporary Religion* 12.2 (May): 133–157.

Talmon-Garber, Y. 1983. "The Family in a Revolutionary Movement: The Case of the Kibbutz in Israel." In *The Sociology of the Kibbutz: Studies of Israeli Society*, vol. 2. New Brunswick, N.J.: Transaction Books.

Taylor, M., and S. M. Carlson. 2000. "The Influence of Religious Beliefs on Parental Attitudes About Children's Fantasy." In *Imagining the Impossible: Magical, Scientific, and Religious Thinking in Children*, ed. K. S. Rosengren, C. N. Johnson, and P. L. Harris. New York: Cambridge University Press.

Tipton, S. 1982. *Getting Saved from the Sixties: Moral Meaning in Conversion and Cultural Change.* Berkeley: University of California Press.

United Nations. 1993. "The Convention of the Rights of the Child." Reprinted in *Children, Rights and the Law*, ed. P. Alston, S. Parker, and J. Seymour. New York: Oxford University Press.

Wellman, H. M., and S. Gelman. 1998. "Knowledge Acquisition in Foundational Domains." In *Handbook of Child Psychology*, ed. W. Damon, 5th ed., vol. 2: *Cognition, Perception and Language*, ed. D. Kuhn and R. S. Siegler, 523–573. New York: Wiley.

West, L. J., and Singer, M. 1980. "Cults, Quacks and Nonprofessional Psychotherapies." In *Comprehensive Textbook of Psychiatry*, ed. H. Caplan, A. Freedman, and B. Sadock, vol. 3. Baltimore: Williams and Wilkins.

Wright, S. 1995. *Armageddon in Waco: Critical Perspectives on the Branch Davidian Controversy.* Chicago: University of Chicago Press.

Zablocki, B. 1980. *Alienation and Charisma: A Study of Contemporary American Communes.* New York: Free Press.

PART IV

NEO-PAGANS, UFOS, AND OTHER HETERODOXIES

CHAPTER 18

WAITING FOR THE "BIG BEAM"

UFO Religions and "Ufological" Themes in New Religious Movements

ANDREAS GRÜNSCHLOß

By the time you receive this, we'll be gone—several dozen of us. We came from the Level Above Human in distant space and we have now exited the bodies that we were wearing for our earthly task, to return to the world from whence we came—task completed. . . . We came for the purpose of offering a doorway to the Kingdom of God at the end of this civilization, the end of this age, the end of this millen[n]ium. . . . The task was not only to bring in information about that Evolutionary Kingdom Level Above Human, but to give us the experience of working against the forces of what the human evolutionary level, at this time, has become. And while it was a good learning experience for us, it also gave all who ever received knowledge from that Kingdom an opportunity to recognize us and this information, and to even move out of the human level and into the Next Level or the Next Evolutionary Level, the "Kingdom of Heaven," the Kingdom of God.

THE passage quoted above is taken from the Heaven's Gate press release on the Internet, entitled "Heaven's Gate 'Away Team' Returns to Level Above Human in Distant Space" and dated March 22, 1997.[1] Four days later, thirty-nine ritually dressed human bodies were found in Rancho Santa Fe (near San Diego, California). In a spectacular collective suicide, the members of this apocalyptic group had decided to finally "discarnate" their bodily "vehicles" or fleshly "containers," in order to leave "this world" in expectation of a better ufological future.[2] Obviously, and contrary to many other UFO-believing groups, they did not choose to wait for a dawning millennium on this planet or for some Alien cargo to be distributed by benevolent Star Beings. Interpreting comet Hale Bopp as the decisive and final "marker" for the "last chance to evacuate Earth," they rather hoped to have their "souls" saved or beamed up to a numinous spacecraft ("My Father's Kingdom moves or travels in spacecrafts")[3] of the so-called "Higher Level," before planet Earth would finally be "recycled."

During the recent years around the turn of the millennium, a few other UFO-related religious groups made it into the media reports as well, headed internationally by the relatively well consolidated Raëlian Religion (*Religion Raëlienne*), which became hotly debated mainly because of their human cloning project Clonaid (see below). Some of these groups connect their activities internationally (e.g., Asthar Command–related groups), and others are mainly of local or at most regional significance (c.f. Fiat Lux in Germany, or Aetherius Society during their initial phase in Great Britain). Some of them are well organized and structured (like the Raëlians or Scientology), whereas others are only loosely connected and sociologically or even ritually less institutionalized (especially "esoteric" groups and "reading circles" with ufological anthropologies or eschatologies). Again, many of these groups or individual prophets have a strong emphasis on imminent apocalypticism, whereas others favor a calmer spiritual approach—mostly to "ascension" of the human soul.[4] In any case, UFO religions—or UFO-related new religious movements, generally—have indeed become an international phenomenon in contemporary industrial societies, with specific local representations in various countries of the Western world. This does not imply, however, that *all* ufologies or UFO-related groups should be regarded as "religious" in nature. From the very beginning during the last midcentury, many ufological discourses concentrated merely on cumulative research and publications about modern UFO sightings (in print and nowadays on the Web), varying in degree from strong enthusiasm to sharp criticism, but without adding an observable religious flavor. Several organizations (NICAP, CUFOS, MUFON, MUFON-CES, CENAP, GEP, and many more) serve this purpose of commenting on UFO-related issues from various such perspectives. In this respect, Jerome Clark's two-volume *UFO Encyclopedia* (2nd ed. 1997) and his shorter *UFO Book* (1998) are helpful up-to-date resources for tracing the phenomenology and history of UFO-related topics and research projects. The religious and mythic aspects are addressed more extensively in James R. Lewis's *UFOs and Popular Culture: An Encyclopedia of Contemporary Myth* (2000).[5] But there are also "borderline" cases, like Erich von Däniken and his followers in the Paleo-SETI scene. With their well-known focus on "Ancient Astronauts" they actually view themselves as rational "researchers" into humankind's historical past, but nevertheless they develop assumptions and worldview teachings with at least latent religious portents, as will be discussed below.

THE BIRTH OF MODERN
ESOTERIC UFOLOGIES

Relatively unnoticed by the wider public, a new phenomenon in modern religious history has gradually surfaced during the last fifty years: the rise of *single prophets* and more or less organized *religious groups* claiming to be in contact with—mostly humanoid—space aliens from other solar planets, other dimensions, or far remote galaxies. Shortly after the first popular North American UFO sightings in 1947 (cf. the famous Kenneth Arnold and Roswell cases),[6] several people started to receive telepathic "messages" from spiritually and technologically far advanced "star brothers," and some of them even reported personal "close encounters" with these beings and alleged flights with their interplanetary or interstellar space crafts (c.f. booklets like George Adamski's "Inside the Space Ships" or George van Tassel's "I Rode a Flying Saucer").[7]

But despite their seemingly very *modern* technological setting, the reports of such new visionary contacts with Aliens from the sky was not entirely born from heaven, so to speak. There are several earthly forerunners to these ufological revelations. One would have to recall John Ballou Newbrough with his esoteric revelations in the book *Oahspe* (1882), a grand description of the spiritual universe and its celestial angels ("ashars") who travel the skies with ethereal "ships," or, somewhat later, Charles Fort with his famous *Book of the Damned* (1919; with three follow-up volumes) reporting all kinds of strange "sightings" which had officially been "excluded" and "damned" by modern science, and propagating the general idea that "we are property" of some hidden extraterrestrial force. Fort's visionary iconoclasm inspired many writers in the science fiction and fantasy genres (e.g., H. P. Lovecraft) and popular authors like Robert Charroux[8] and Erich von Däniken, who triggered the "Ancient Astronauts" theories[9] which then started to reappear as creative neo-myths in several modern religious ufologies (e.g., Sunburst Community, Raëlian Religion). And one could actually go back as far as Lucian's (Lukianos of Samosata; ca. 120–180 C.E.) eye-twinkling "records" in his

True Stories (1974)—a collection of biting satires on the Greek utopian genre— where he relates miraculous "travels" by sailing ship to some kingdoms of the solar system and, thus, displays quite an ancient prototype for contemporary SF utopias and Star Wars scenarios up in the skies. Likewise, the mythopoetic topic of "sunken continents" and "lost worlds"[10] has also been an influential "utopian" motif for modern esoteric ufologies: Atlantis, Lemuria, or Mu are often incorporated into their mythic geography and their vision of protological or eschatological events. But probably the most important influence to the modern "contactee" version of UFO faith comes from nineteenth-century Theosophy and the various esoteric traditions following this alternative strand of Western religious history, which began as a distinct attempt of molding a new "scientific" endeavor together with a "spiritual" search for higher realms and stages of consciousness. Many central ideas (and names) from the works of Helena P. Blavatsky, Alice A. Bailey, or Guy Ballard reappear in many of the contactee revelations. Given the context of these older theosophic/esoteric traditions, therefore, much of the seemingly new religious instruction and guidance delivered by the extraterrestrial "Ascended Masters" often appears as a grand déjà vu.

To be sure, there are many interrelations between esoteric religious teachings (Theosophy, Spiritism, and other alternative religious traditions) and fantasy or science fiction literature. But a thorough historical investigation into the multifarious interrelations between alternative esoteric or even traditional theosophic sources and the various contemporary ufological teachings has not yet been done in religious studies scholarship.

Several individuals like George Adamski, George Van Tassel, Orfeo Angelucci, and Daniel Fry, who reported their extraterrestrial "contacts" back in the early fifties, can be counted among the founding "fathers" of modern religious ufologies.[11] Of course, there are some prominent founding "mothers," too, like Ruth "Uriel" Norman of the Unarius group, Gloria Lee, and some others.[12] Though located within the context of the post–World War II era, these early prophets eventually triggered a new tradition and contactee fad that continues until today. According to these early reports and "channelings," the Star People (Galactic Federation, Star Brotherhood, etc.) appear highly alarmed because of humankind's late access to the secrets of atomic energy. They approach earth in order to give spiritual advice, because a great disaster could happen with a planet's population being technologically far advanced but spiritually underdeveloped to handle their new power with care. In the end, the whole planet could be destroyed. The distinct fear of atomic energy and its abuse for war, typical of the post–World War II era, can be illustrated by the following quotation from an early "message" to contactee George Van Tassel (July 1952):[13]

> Hail to you beings of Shan [= Earth], I greet you in love and peace, my identity is Ashtar, commandant quadra sector, patrol station Schare, all projections,

all waves. Greetings, through The Council of the Seven Lights, you have been brought inspired with the inner light to help your fellow man. You are mortals and other mortals can only understand that which their fellow man can understand. The purpose of this organization is, in a sense, to save mankind from himself. Some years ago your time, your nuclear physicists penetrated the "Book of Knowledge"; they discovered how to explode the atom. Disgusting as the results have been, that this force should be used for destruction, it is not compared to that which can be. . . . Our missions are peaceful, but this condition occurred before in this solar system and the planet, Lucifer, was torn to bits. We are determined that it shall not happen again. . . . Your purpose here has been to build a receptivity that we could communicate with your planet, for by the attraction of light substances atoms, we patrol your universe. To your government and to your people and through them to all governments and all people on the planet of Shan, accept the warning as a blessing that mankind may survive. My light, we shall remain in touch here at this cone of receptivity. My love, I am Ashtar.

Not only the fear of an atomic disaster, but a correlated hope for new spiritual guidance and a widening of the (all too) human consciousness is documented in these early ufological sources. As already mentioned, a closer investigation of the "extraterrestrial" teachings, as delivered to the handful of chosen human messengers, shows striking family resemblances to already existent "earthly" strands of Theosophy or esoteric "I AM" traditions—and the same holds true for most of the later ufological channelings. For example, long before his activity as *the* Space Alien contactee of the formative period, George Adamski (1891–1965) was already interested in theosophic teachings. In 1936 he wrote a book titled *Questions and Answers by the Royal Order of Tibet: Wisdom of the Masters of the Far East*. Investigations have shown that his later and strongly ufological *Science of Life Study Course* (1964) is actually based on this early book—replacing "Royal Order of Tibet" with "Space Brothers" or "Cosmic Brotherhood" in the text.[14] Despite this and several other attempts to disenchant his alleged photographs of the famous disk-shaped "Scouts" and cigar-shaped "Motherships" or the obviously fictitious reports of his travels and conversations with humanoid extraterrestrials in the solar system,[15] the apostolic rock of contactee faith is still defended by some UFO-believers today (e.g., George Adamski Foundation). George Adamski, as well as Orfeo Angelucci with his *Secret of the Saucers* (1955), the famous "Mrs. Keech," and Norman Paulsen (see below), illustrate that the vocabulary, cosmology, anthropology, and numinous personnel of esoteric/theosophic traditions often seem to reappear simply in a modern "space age" outfit (Jerome Clark calls them "angels in space-suits"). This is true of the esoteric version of Jesus named "Sananda" or other so-called "Ascended Masters" and the "Great White Brotherhood," as well as the prominent enlightened being and star fleet commander "Ashtar" quoted above. But the spiritual teachings basically reformulate the faith patterns and common esoteric/theosophic views on reincarnation, ascension of the eternal soul, and world-and-matter-renouncing orientation to higher "spiritual" spheres and "resonating frequencies," and they often incorporate the idea of sunken continents (Atlantis, Mu) and sometimes apply Indian meditation techniques and concepts of the soul (ātman) and its gradual liberation from earthly matter.[16]

Cargoistic Hopes and Typical Millenarian Visions

Some of the extraterrestrial messages and UFO-related teachings appear apocalyptic in tone and content, and many religious UFO groups await an imminent "Big Beam" unto the Star Brothers' ships before Earth is destroyed, cleansed, or finally restored to her paradisiacal integrity. This can already be observed in the famous (and first) sociopsychological study of an early ufological group formed around "Mrs. Keech" (the pseudonym for Dorothy Martin, later head of the Association of Sananda and Sanat Kumara) in *When Prophecy Fails* (1956): Because of a giant apocalyptic "flood" the chosen few would have to be "evacuated" to another planet (Clarion or Venus) by "flying saucers," and "there they would be spiritually indoctrinated, preparatory to being sent back to earth, a cleansed and innocent earth, in order to repopulate it with good people who 'walked in the Light.' "[17] This millenarian strand of ufology has contributed much to the formation of new religious movements. For example, several loosely organized groups in varius countries of the West belong to the worldwide network of the so-called Ashtar Command.[18] Gradually replacing the early references to a nuclear holocaust or "cleansing" of earth, it is anticipated today that the cosmic "being" Earth is severely suffering from human pollution and will soon undergo a "Great Tribulation" of earthquakes, pole shifts, and floods. Before this, a great "Evacuation" and "Lift off" to the space ships is being organized by Ashtar and his celestial crew—a great event which has to be anticipated by a chosen "ground crew" of human messengers. Aboard the ships, human beings will be trained with new technologies and spiritual means in order to "ascend" to higher resonating frequencies, resulting in spiritual liberation and paranormal states of consciousness. Earth will then be turned into a perfect Garden, and the spiritually transformed will return to live in a millennium of peace, happiness, and light. The apocalyptic scenario described here is also disseminated by a variety of Ashtar-related Web sites, brochures, and books—some of them already ufological classics, like E. P. Hills, *Ashtar: In Days to Come* (1955) or "Tuella's" (Th. B. Terrel) *Project World-Evacuation* (1982). Very similar ideas are expressed by other groups, including the German Fiat Lux community of Erika "Uriella" Bertschinger Eike, the U.S. Ground Crew or Planetary Activation Organization, and many more. The idea of spiritual ascension and the hope for higher stages of consciousness is mostly blended with the advent of superior Alien "Cargo"—with incredible new technologies and ecologically harmless energies (especially so-called "free energies"). With regard to this combined vision of perfect technology and spiritual (and cosmological) perfection, many millenarian versions of UFO faith can at least partially be perceived as Western parallels to the famous Pacific "Cargo-Cults."[19] A short listing of the German Fiat Lux community's basic eschatological beliefs might serve as an illustration:[20]

> The faith of this community (with an inner circle of 135 fully initiated members and roughly 800 followers) around the "full-trance medium" Erika "Uriella" Bertschinger Eike in the southern Blackforest (near Waldshut) is syncretistic and apocalyptic in outlook, and it includes many assumptions which are typical for contemporary Western esoteric teachings (e.g., reincarnation, "ascension" of the soul, vegetarianism): Humanity is now living in the end-times; parts of earth are going to be destroyed by huge tidal waves, asteroids, volcano eruptions, earth quakes, and a terrible third World War (including Nazi-UFOs currently hidden in the Antarctic). Only one third of humanity will survive this Great Tribulation during the "three dark days." But benevolent interplanetary beings under the command of Jesus Christ will help to evacuate the chosen few in small spherical spaceships descending from giant spherical "motherships" (however, access will be denied for the spiritually unprepared). This evacuation will last for three weeks; a spiritual awakening and purification of earthly souls will take place on the motherships, and earth is going to be transformed into a new paradisiacal entity called "Amora" (with a return of the ancient sunken continents, mild climate, new fauna and flora, etc.). A millennial era of peace, harmony and unity with all creation is going to follow on Amora: Christ will return, Maria will reign, Yin and Yang will be at balance, and there will be visible contact with angels and other spiritual beings. Creative powers will prevail, new energies and solely "green" technologies are going to be employed.

In all these cases, a Golden Age is expected, and the imagery of the "perfect garden" is wed with the dream of a scientific miracle.[21] In UFO faith, there exists a remarkably consistent imagery connected with this cargoistic future which often concentrates on the paranormal. For example, in "Appeal to Earth Dwellers" ("Aufruf an die Erdbewohner", by W. and Th. Gauch-Keller), a brochure about a Swiss-German ufological mission related to Ashtar and the Ashtar Command, the so-called "New Time"—after the Great Evacuation into the millions of spaceships hovering around earth—is portrayed this way:[22]

> With the help of our Star Brothers and Sisters [Sternengeschwister] and with the newly mastered techniques of materialization, dematerialization, prognosis, etc. we will create . . . everything needed for our life. Telepathy will be every

day language, and time as we know it on earth today will no longer be valid. . . . We will not only be able to use these supernormal techniques but we will also learn how to engage in intergalactic space travel. We will master the use of free cosmic energies and we will manifest things, food, etc. by free will. Everything will be possible, when we live and act according to the cosmic/divine laws.

After the Transformation, we will live in a half-ethereal and/or ethereal body—like our Space Brothers and Sisters. Our body atoms will oscillate in such a high frequency that we will become invisible to normal physical eyes. . . .

A long era of peace, love and harmony will dawn (thousand year reign), since in this new resonating frequency wars and destructive thoughts can no longer exercise control over human minds. Any oppression of people will vanish, because these lower vibrations will cease to exist.

Obviously, the benevolent Space Brothers and Sisters function as angelic mediators and interplanetary culture heroes. When this ufological millennium breaks through after a shortened period of the Great Tribulation, its new cargo will manifest itself in completely superior technologies with special materials hitherto unknown to humankind and with a release of unknown energies of the universe. Spiritual progress, paranormal faculties, and technological advance are amalgamated into one, creation will be brought to its end, and the "Galactic Society" will be established like a "Heaven on Earth."

The ufological vision represented by Heaven's Gate is of a different kind. It is strongly millenarian in outlook, to be sure, since Earth is said to be "annihilated" or "spaded under" within a very short time, but the future is not portrayed in *cargoist* terms, nor with any "Heaven on Earth" metaphors.[23] Earth was serving as a "garden" for the cultivation and ripening of spiritual beings from the celestial level—an idea which can already be found in the "first" nineteenth-century new religion, the Church of Jesus Christ of the Latter-Day Saints (Mormons)—but Earth will now, after the visit of the "Rep[resentative]s" from the Level Above Human, be "recycled" for some other purpose. This *inner-worldly pessimism* (which has its typological predecessors in Christian *premillennialism*) is contrasted with the imminent hope for an apocalyptic "rapture" or "Big Beam" of the chosen few (cf. the paradigmatic role of the biblical "144.000"), in order to become "saved" as a *perfect new creature*[24] on a better "Higher Level." Therefore, no extraterrestrial cargo is awaited in this version of UFO faith; the focus is solely on *leaving* this apparently "unreal" and disintegrating planet—as one of the group members ("Stmody") explicitly states in their online book. "The only reality is to connect with the Reps from the only real potential future, while they visit in the present, and go out on their coattails, while the door is open. It's that simple." Accordingly, Heaven's Gate appears as quite exceptional, since most other UFO-believing groups lean to a more optimistic version of cosmology, where the "Great Tribulation" and "rapture" are often reduced to a short intermezzo, before Earth is finally restored to a millennial "paradise" or Heaven on Earth (which can thus be viewed as representing some of the topic motifs of Christian *postmillennialism*).

Some movements, on the other hand, have changed their attitude toward eschatology over time: the Californian Solar Logos Foundation (previously Sunburst Community or Brotherhood of the Sun), which was founded by Norman Paulsen, a close student of Yogananda, had strong millennial expectations in the late seventies and early eighties during their flourishing phase as one of the most successful New Age communities of that time, but the small community now seems to have resorted to a rather calm application of Paulsen's meditation technique in order to enlighten the human soul with the Solar Logos—quite similar to other common esoteric ascension programs.[25] A similar recourse to ascension and spiritual purification after a strong millenarian interplay in the late nineties can be observed in the Ground Crew and in the Planetary Activation Organization.[26] The future will show if the strongly *apocalyptic* interpretations of UFO faith are going to be less dominant after the turn of the century.

THE QUEST FOR "RELIGIOUS TECHNOLOGY" AND A "NEW SCIENCE"

Not all religious ufologies share an apocalyptic tension, but the omnipresent *combination of technological advance* (space travel, new energies, etc.) *and spiritual progress* appears to be a general character trait. Scientology, for example, has to be placed within the nonmillenarian ufological strand of modern religious history. But Scientology also shares a typical "Ancient Astonauts" myth and conceives of earthly human beings primarily as extraterrestrial spirits ("Thetans") which have now to be put on their "bridge to freedom" again—a soul conception which is paralleled by the typical ufological "star seeds" or "walk-ins" planted on this earthly "garden" for spiritual growth.[27] According to Scientology's secret mythology (contained especially in the OT III teachings), a fierce intergalactic ruler named Xenu once carried the Thetans to earth (75 million years ago). In 1977/79, L. Ron Hubbard (1911–1986) also wrote a science fiction story called *Revolt in the Stars*, where he displays this otherwise arcane story around the ancient ruler Xenu in the form of an ordinary science fiction novel (so far unpublished among his SF writings but unofficially circulating on the Internet).

It is the goal of Scientology's so-called "religious technology" to free the soul from the bonds of the physical universe. The Thetan has to be transformed into a free "Operating Thetan" (OT). A great variety of paranormal faculties will then be at his or her hands: exteriorization, telepathy, comprehensive knowledge of all "former lives" ("Whole Track" memories), astral projection, and bilocation.[28] Thus, the Thetan will gradually resume the state of "full cause over MEST" (matter, energy, space, time = the physical world). L. Ron Hubbard's most overt "mythological" writings so far publicly accessible, *Scientology—A History of Man* (1952) and *Have You Lived Before This Life?* (1960), already exhibit a grand "space opera" scenario (Hubbard's own term), and during formal "auditing"—the semitherapeutic session with the famous electronic "E-Meter"—clients are supposed to retrieve even far-reaching memories from remote interstellar times.[29] The following two illustrative passages are taken from *Have You Lived Before This Life?*:[30]

Case 38: This incident began 17,543 years ago on a "space command" post on Earth. I had the idea that I go to Mars incognito to learn how they handled disorder. The government warned me, but finally gave me unwilling assistance and transport to Mars and through the protective field of force to its surface.

On landing I was immediately surrounded and interrogated by Martian automatons [i.e., Robots] who recognized me instantly because I did not broadcast the same vibrations.

I was taken to a massive hall with insulated walls, where I was seated in front of a gray-green curtain and bombarded with invisible particles which caused confusion. Then I was immediately transferred to a cigar-shaped metal holder and whirled around rapidly to further increase my confusion. At the same time I was told that if I ever did anything or remembered any of this I'd get "zapped," that is, Hammered, again. At the end I felt I was just a little object with practically no life at all. After elementary and technical school I was given a metal body fitted with every conceivable electronic gadget and put as a solitary observer on a space outpost.

When the monotony of the robot life began to bore me I began to give all my reports a double meaning to amuse myself. Without warning my replacement arrived and I was told to join the "Reserve." When I arrived at the barracks two official automatons came out, turned me around, opened my back and began ripping out all my apparatus, the flexes from my legs, the batteries from my stomach, the computers from my body. Then they threw my empty shell of a body on a scrap heap.

I remained in the right lobe of my head, while my body rusted and disintegrated. When the head disintegrated I found myself outside the body. I hung around for a while but finally decided I could leave, and I reported back to "space command."

Case 37: Location: Planet Setus. Time: 3,750 years ago.—I started space training at seventeen years of age and when I was twenty-one years old, war broke out. I then married and left my wife with my parents and two sisters. When I was twenty-two I was given the task of destroying an enemy ship that had broken through the protective screen. During the attack my ship, a one-man attack type, was hoiled, so I pulled out of the dive, in spite of training which emphasized the danger of doing so. . . . I then became aware of a body in a spacesuit attached by a line to a damaged ship. . . . I realized that the body in question was my own, and that in pulling out of the attack I had suffered a direct hit which threw me out of the ship. . . .

[He then realized that the enemy ship had successfully bombed the town where his family lived. His life disintegrated completely after this event, and many years later he went "to an old shrine belonging to an ancient religious culture."]

I was laid on an operating table, given hypodermic injections through the corner of each eye, deep into the skull. A machine having an amber green lens was swung over my eyes and seemed to pull me into its interior. I later found that I had been fixated into a small glass-type container, then taken away. It was when I tried to follow that I realized that I was located by this jar on the shelf of the theater. . . .

I was later dumped on Earth about 1750 years B.C.—This was followed by life as a Hittite in Anatolia.

To the outside observer, such alleged recollections (reaching back to 23,000,000,000 years and more) seem to have more affinity to the phenomena of *guided fantasies* than real memories. And the end of the second story shows some parallels to H. P. Lovecraft's novel *The Shadow Out of Time* (1936). Nevertheless, Hubbard claims to have laid down a scientific proof for the reality of former lives, and it is the basic conviction of Scientology "processing" that the individual should be freed from all such traumatic "engrams" (traumatic memories), "forgetter implants," etc. on the "whole" memory "track"[31] in order to finally resume the state of a free "Operating Thetan" again.

In other esoteric ufologies, intergalactic saviors and "masters" like Ashtar, P'taah, Heraldatron, Sananda, Lord Monka, and other ufonic "Beings of Light" guarantee spiritual and technological advance; in Scientology it is Hubbard who ranks almost as a savior figure by having laid down absolutely perfect technological disclosures—a real "legacy of technology." And according to Scientology's and Hubbard's own claims, this should be compared to the Buddha and the legacy of his Dharma. In his booklet "Hymn of Asia,"[32] Hubbard explicitly toys with the role of the prophesied future Buddha ("Am I Metteyya?"), and the preface to Scientology's *Volunteer Minister's Handbook*[33] (among many other publications) describes Scientology as the direct continuation and fulfillment of the Buddha's earlier attempts at salvation. It should also be noted that because of the connections between several motifs in Hubbard's novels and specific Scientology teachings, one might perceive Scientology as one of the rare instances where science fiction (or fantasy literature generally) is related to the successful formation of a new spiritual movement.[34] Although the science fiction novels are of a different genre than the other "techno-logical" disclosures of Hubbard, they are highly appreciated by participants, and Hubbard's literary output in this realm (including the latest movie, *Battlefield Earth*) is also well promoted by the organization.

The explicit idea of "religious technology" which is so dominant in Scientology also finds many striking expressions in the British Aetherius Society of George

King (1919–1997), who is revered with many honorific titles by his followers ("Master," "Cosmic Avatar," etc.). As the group's Internet site states, "This is not a new religion. . . . It's a spiritual path to enlightenment and the cosmic evolution of mankind," and "For the first time the connection between the science of Yoga, the theology of all major religions and the mystery of the UFOs is explained."[35] For example, the ritual (and technical) accumulation and dissemination of "energy" by the group's participants is combined with an esoteric cosmology and linked with cosmic events of high impact:[36]

> As the sunspots reach their peak, the flow of energy from the Sun increases. With this increase of high vibratory energy reaching Earth must bring with it many types of subtle effects.
> This Holy Energy coming from the Sun must be in all ways good—if one can handle it, if one is prepared for such energy. However if one is not ready, it is liable have a de-stabilizing effect. Perhaps causing a similar though milder effect, as has been predicted for the coming transition to the New Age.
> We are told that as we approach the New Age, the Ionosphere will be slowly taken down. This area of our atmosphere also known to metaphysicians as the ring pass not, is responsible for protecting mankind from direct cosmic ray bombardment, which mankind as a whole is not ready for. As each 11 year cycle brings an increase of cosmic ray bombardment and as the ring pass not is slowly removed, the high frequency energy level upon Earth will continue to rise, becoming more and more noticeable, especially during periods of high sunspot activity.

During these evolutionary steps toward the "New Age," members are supposed to play a helping role (breathing practices, meditation, "auric harmonization," etc.). "Prayer energy," for example, is supposed to be "accumulated" in crystal "batteries" which can be used later to recharge certain earthly places with "good" energy for the benefit of all life on this planet.[37] As indicated above (on the group's home page), there is also a strong reception and application of Yoga exercise which is combined with the ufological cosmology and the theosophic idea of "ascended masters"; however, the outlook is not apocalyptic in tone, but rather centered on *evolutionary progress.*

"A *new* science," comprising an ultimate "synthesis" of the spiritual and the scientific, is one of the most fundamental hopes in UFO faith: something "new" is to arrive, transcending the dangerous bifurcation of spirit and matter, religion and science (this is already explicitly stated in the extraterrestrial "messages" to Howard Menger or Dan Fry and others in the early fifties).[38] In all strands of religious UFO faith, technological metaphors, tools, and explanations are continuously used for interpreting or ("magically") inducing religious results—and vice versa: traditional religious motifs (angelic beings and culture heroes, superior heavenly reigns, millenarism, etc.) can serve as hermeneutic tools for a new critical interpretation of human scientific/technological achievements. The "supernatural" is often "explained" (at least partly), and this typically "modern" *supernatural expliqué* is also the dominant trait of modern literary fantasy genres, which still toy with the transcendent but have it rather explained (away) in the end.[39] Therefore, revelation often appears technically "controlled," "explained," or "proved" by immanent tools. The television series *X-Files*'s two famous slogans, "The truth is out there" and "I want to believe," express this typical oscillation between a scientific/technological disenchantment and a religious/mythic reenchantment quite well. Religious metaphors of the paradise are amalgamated with scientific optimism; spiritual and technological perfection are molded into one. Spiritual progress can (partly) be induced by technical means—and the "cold" heavens of the modern scientific worldview are reenchanted with a return of celestial angels or culture heroes.[40] But at the same time, these apparently numinous beings from outer space are often regarded as nothing but "Ancient Astronauts."

UFOLOGICAL EUHEMERISM: THE GODS ARE "ANCIENT ASTRONAUTS"

As already indicated, and following some paradigmatic lines of Charles Fort's *Book of the Damned*, Robert Charroux (France) and especially Erich von Däniken (Switzerland) developed and disseminated the idea that "the gods of antiquity were alien astronauts—nothing else" (von Däniken 1967).[41] Similar to Euhemeros of Messana in classic antiquity, who claimed that it was nothing but ordinary men who became gradually deified because of their merits (apotheosis) and were, thus, faithfully revered as true "gods," human religions are here reconstructed as a cargo-cultlike imitation and reverence to humanoid astronauts from outer space. Instead of turning toward *eschatology*, the end times, the focus of von Däniken and his followers in the so-called "paleo-SETI" discourses (Search for Extra-Terrestrial Intelligence in ancient times) is therefore primarily on *protology*, the first time—that is, on the mythic time of "creation," the primordial "origins" of (human) life on this earth and other paradigmatic events in the past. Diverse myths, archaeological remnants, and sacred scriptures are interpreted as factual accounts of the Ancient Astronauts' interventions on Earth. Prominent themes are speculations about ancient Indian air/spaceships (*vimanas*) and nuclear weapons in the Veda, the biblical creation myth in Genesis being an echo of Alien genetic engineering, Maya remnants in the "pyramid" of Palenque as pictorial hints to extraterrestrial space flights, etc.[42] Ulrich Dopatka has compiled a (nonacademic) encyclopedia of paleo-SETI, where all these typical issues can easily be accessed in surveys with bibliographical references.[43]

The whole Paleo-SETI enterprise describes itself as an alternative kind of historical, scientific "research." In fact, it has led to local and international "research associations," like the Ancient Astronaut Society (AAS, founded in 1973), nowadays called the Archaeology, Astronautics, and SETI Research Association (AAS-RA), and running the research magazine Ancient Skies—together with its German counterpart Sagenhafte Zeiten.[44] Nevertheless, the compatibility with the self-understanding of critical interpretative science is rather small (at least, until now). Without referring with sufficient hermeneutic care to the original contexts, selected religious myths or archaeological artefacts are taken primarily at face value in order to prove the—rather normative—idea that our ancestors had contacts with superior Alien visitors and their advanced technologies. In following the thrust of Fort's books, the adherents of paleo-SETI view themselves as the spearhead of true enlightenment against narrow-minded academics and old-fashioned religionists, both being dogmatic "exclusionists." But to the student of religion, these heavily biased interpretations of ancient artefacts and texts must appear as a neo-mythic activity—indeed, as a mythic foundation of the modern worldview. Technological explanations, projected back into the past, serve as a disenchantment of old mythic accounts—that is, the supernatural is again explained in technical terms.[45] But at the same time, the myths are themselves retained as basically "true"[46]—however, only in the modern "Astronauts" sense: paleo-SETI must therefore be seen as a popular and alternative mythic "theory of religion." These "modern myths" about the alleged ancient "Astronaut Gods" reappear in contemporary Science Fiction movies like Stargate or Mission to Mars, and they are sometimes fully incorporated into contactee versions of UFO faith or other esoteric reconstructions of humanity's religious history (cf. Paulsen's Sunburst community).

The best and most prominent example here is the Raëlian Religion of Claude "Raël" Vorilhon, one of the most consolidated UFO groups internationally active today[47]—with important centers in Quebec and Geneva. In his first book, The Book Which Tells the Truth[48] (republished as part of The Message Given by Extra-Terrestrials), French-born Vorilhon related the story of his contact with a returned Ancient Astronaut named Yahwe in December 1973 on the volcanic hills near Clermont Ferrand (France).[49] The biblical interpretations disclosed to him in meetings during the following days are strikingly similar to the theories of von Däniken and Charroux published only a few years ago: Originally, the ancient extraterrestrial "Elohim" created humanity "in their image" (Gen. 1:26f) by genetic manipulation, and many other religious texts witness to similar Alien interventions on planet Earth. With Raël's election as the human contactee and final prophet for the Elohim (in Let's Welcome Our Fathers from Space, Raël indeed claims to be a direct son of Yahwe),[50] a new phase in human history has now begun. The "end time" is near when "science replaces religion." Raël also reported a spaceflight to the Elohim's planet in the follow-up booklet *Extra-Terrestrials Took Me to Their Planet*, where the Elohim are reported to live a hedonistic paradisiacal life, sustained by advanced science and technology. On Earth, too, nothing less but "eternal life" will be soon gained through genetic science: "Then, we wake up after death in a brand new body just like after a good night sleep," states the Web site of Clonaid,[51] Raël's cloning project and target of many media reports during the last few years. Since human life is nothing but a technological "product," and since there is nothing like a "soul," according to Raël's teachings, there is no problem with creating new beings according to our own image and ideals, because "man is nothing but a self-programming biological computer."[52] The gods are nothing but Ancient Astronauts; accordingly, the Raëlians conceive of themselves as an "atheistic religion like Buddhism."[53] One of the rare religious rituals is the "transmission" of the genetic code to the Elohim's giant computer up in the skies (by imposition of hands through a "guide"), in order to have access to eternal life.[54] Here again, the religious quest for eternity is met with a technological solution, and the alleged "Gods" are disenchanted with ufological Euhemerism. Nevertheless, the Elohim are still important as future culture heroes. The group plans to build a Space Embassy (originally intended for Israel but refused by the state authorities) for welcoming the Elohim on Earth, and it runs a sort of visitors center named "Ufoland" near Montreal.[55]

Together with the proposed opening of Erich von Däniken's theme park, World Mysteries,[56] in Interlaken, Switzerland, one can therefore speculate that the Ancient Astronauts myth will continue to stimulate discussions beyond the alternative bookshelves. It will be interesting to see if the second (or third) generation of PSETI followers is heading more toward critical science or toward manifest esotericism (or a consolidated philosophy); at the moment, either option can be appropriated by individuals in order to enlarge and transform (or fully transcend) the typical quasi-historical perspective on protological events.

SUMMARY AND CONCLUSIONS

Without a doubt, an important attraction of the contactee version of UFO faith is rooted in its capacity to synthesize various elements of esoteric, spiritualistic, theosophical, Indian, or Christian traditions, and to reconcile them with aspects of contemporary science, space technology, and modern cosmology—the result being a strong reenchantment of heaven with humanoid "Astronaut Gods" (von Däniken) or caring and loving "angels in space suits" (J. Clark). As G. Trompf has stated, when millenarism and cargoism are linked within the ufological vision of a spiritual and technological miracle, "the images of modern technology and scientific achievement will be retained, so that the prophesied new Order can even be articulated as the very apex of Modernity rather than (exclusively) that of a Great spiritual Return, and at times it can bear a strong ring of science fiction (or some 'science mythology') about it."[57] In certain Western contexts of economic vulnerability, sociocultural discomfort, and obscurity, these promises of new (compensatory) appropriation of power, knowledge, and control can be very attractive, the person can experience him/herself as *star seed, light worker,* or *Thetan,* located "above" mere "matter" and its intricacies, and the newborn individual is also part of an elite "ground crew." Furthermore, such a cargoistic utopia, with all its paranormal grandeur, does not appear alien to a "culture of narcissism," since it is fully compatible with the optimistic fantasies of technological evolution and increasing scientific control which are still dominant in our modern industrial societies.

Despite all their differences in detail, religious ufologies express a common theme: the search for an integral vision, a "synthesis of science and religion"— oscillating between religious interpretations of technology and technological interpretations of religion. This new ufological "unity of reality" is in accordance with the space age and modern scientific and technological worldview—with all its inherent ideas of progress, perfection, and easy utilization. But at the same time it propagates mythological reenchantments of heaven with celestial beings and reconstructs personal and cosmic life in profoundly "religious" ways (reincarnation, ascension of the soul, millennial paradise, return of the sunken continents, etc.). Obviously, it is this language of technology and of scientific "explanation" and "proof" which makes inherited religious ideas appear more plausible and compatible with the modern world. In most cases the result is an esoteric/theosophic, selective recombination and syncretistic reinterpretation of traditional religious elements in the light of an evolutionary gnosis—trying to be explicitly compatible with the modern worldview and attempting to bridge the gap between science and religion.

And there is a noticeable trend in modern religiosity to apply such ufological ideas and terms for a revision of the concept of the person or soul, and for reinterpreting eschatological or protological events. At least, these "new" traditions appear *as a typical product of postmodern Western industrial societies*, and one can assume that the paradigmatic combination of experiences in the modern technological world with traditional religious elements from different religious traditions will be an ongoing issue in the future. And since these new forms of faith are often blended together and deliberately institutionalized in "postreligious" ways, they sometimes don't fit easily into traditional concepts of religion (e.g., Scientology or PSETI discourses).

As I mentioned, not all contemporary ufologies are "religious" in nature.

Many ufological discourses focus on discussions about UFO sightings or abduction stories[58]—and some of them are very critical. The decidedly religious ufologies are often treated with special disregard by such UFO investigators (mainly because of their negative publicity),[59] and the famous photographs of alleged Alien spacecrafts by contactee George Adamski (flying saucers and cigar-shaped "motherships") have long been the target of severe criticisms, as have the stories and pictures by contactee Eduard "Billy" Meier (founder of the Swiss FIGU), who reported various UFO contacts and meetings with star people from the Pleiades (especially religious instructions by the alleged space girl Semjase). As becomes apparent—not only to the outside observer—the history of ufology is in some respect also a history of fraud and manipulation, with many mystifications and conspiracy theories. But here again, despite all technological metaphors, one can easily detect the "religious" quest for meaning, truth, and authentic revelation, especially its convincing "autopsy" and demonstrable "proof"—even in the form of fraud and alleged inspiration.

Conflict potential can appear in certain circumstances and organizational forms. Individual and collective problems may possibly arise when a movement or group defines itself in very strict antagonism to the "fallen world" (segregation of the chosen few) and with strong millennial aspirations, minimizing the relations to the socially shared world "outside." Here, the collective suicide of Heaven's Gate may mark an extreme option, since the rather cool procedures taken to finally leave this world and to "discarnate" their bodies can only be understood in the light of a very long-lasting and extensively structured reshaping of life within a thoroughly consolidated supportive enclave.[60]

In any case, given the omnipresent quest for integrating—in "alternative" ways—scientific and technological knowledge on the one hand, and religion, myth, and spirituality on the other, one can expect for our Western societies that still more individuals and groups will continue with the search for a better ufological future—or, at least, for a certain verifiable UFO-related "truth somewhere out there." In Charles Fort's famous words: "Science of today—the superstition of tomorrow. Science of tomorrow—the superstition of today."[61]

NOTES

1. This press release was not contained on all "mirror-sites," but most of the files are still accessible on the Internet: see, for example, www.heavensgatetoo.com.

2. Cf. Robert W. Balch, "Waiting for the Ships: Disillusionment and the Revitalization of Faith in Bo and Peep's UFO Cult," in *The Gods Have Landed: New Religions from Other Worlds*, ed. James R. Lewis (Albany: SUNY Press, 1995), 137–166. Balch is working on a comprehensive study of the Heaven's Gate group. See also my own article

" 'When We Enter Into My Father's Spacecraft': Cargoistic Hopes and Millenarian Cos-mologies in New Religious UFO Movements," *Marburg Journal of Religion* 3, no. 2 (Dec. 1998), available online at www.uni-marburg.de/religionswissenschaft/journal/mjr/ ufogruen.html; a slightly revised version is published in *The Encyclopedic Sourcebook of UFO Religions*, ed. J. Lewis (Amherst, N.Y.: Prometheus Books, 2002).

3. Quoted from the transcript of a videotape called "Planet about to Be Recycled—Your Only Chance to Survive: Leave with Us," on the Heaven's Gate homepage.

4. For basic orientation, see J. Gordon Melton, ed., *Encyclopedia of American Religions*, 6th ed. (Detroit: Gale, 1999), 703ff. ("Flying Saucer Groups"). A very good over-view on "religious issues" in relation with belief in UFOs is provided by John A. Saliba, "Religious Dimensions of UFO Phenomena," in Lewis, *The Gods Have Landed*, 15–64. See also my own survey, *Wenn die Götter Landen . . . : Religiöse Dimensionen des UFO-Glaubens*, EZW-Texte 153 (Berlin: EZW, 2000), and Mikael Rothstein, *UFOer og rumvæsener. Myten om de flyvende tallerkener* (Copenhagen: Nordisk Verlag, 2000).

5. James R. Lewis has edited two other valuable reference works: *The Gods Have Landed*, which includes ten helpful essays on relevant representations of UFO faith (in-cluding useful bibliographies); and *The Encyclopedic Sourcebook of UFO Religions*, which provides source material on UFO religions as well as academic essays with comments on the various groups.

6. See J. Clark's *UFO Encyclopedia* and *UFO Book* for details and bibliography.

7. Cf. J. Gordon Melton, "The Contactees: A Survey," and J. Gordon Melton and George M. Eberhart, "The Flying Saucer Contactee Movement, 1950–1994: A Bibliogra-phy," both in J. Lewis, *The Gods Have Landed*, 1–14, 251–333. No other than Carl Gustav Jung commented on the phenomenon from a psychological perspective already in 1958; cf. his *Flying Saucers: A Modern Myth of Things Seen Flying in the Sky* (German original: *Ein moderner Mythus. Von Dingen, die am Himmel gesehen werden*), in *Collected Works of C. G. Jung*, vol. 10, 307–308 (Stuttgart/Zürich, 1958; 2d ed., 1964). For an overview on research and literature, see John A. Saliba, "UFO Contactee Phenomena from a Socio-psychological Perspective: A Review," in J. Lewis, *The Gods Have Landed*, 207–250.

8. Robert Charroux, *Histoire inconnue des hommes depuis cent mille ans* (Paris: Laf-font, 1963), *Le livre des secrets trahis* (Paris: Laffont, 1965), and others.

9. Von Däniken's first best-seller was *Erinnerungen an die Zukunft. Ungelöste Rätsel der Vergangenheit* (Düsseldorf: Econ, 1986), translated as *Chariots of the Gods? Unresolved Mysteries of the Past* (New York: Berkley, 1969).

10. A classic study is Lyon Sprague De Camp, *Lost Continents: The Atlantis Theme in History, Science, and Literature* (1954; reprint, New York: Dover, 1970). Cf. A. Grün-schloß, "Lost Worlds," in *Encyclopedia of Religion and Nature* (forthcoming).

11. Cf. George Adamski (together with Desmond Leslie), *Flying Saucers Have Landed* (New York: Abelard-Schuman, 1953), George Van Tassel, *I Rode a Flying Saucer! The Mystery of the Flying Saucers Revealed* (Los Angeles: New Age, 1952); Daniel Fry, *The White Sands Incident* (Los Angeles: New Age, 1954); Orfeo Angelucci, *The Secret of the Saucers* (Amherst: Amherst Press, 955). Extensive bibliographic references for these early "contactees" are given by Melton and Eberhart in J. Lewis, *The Gods Have Landed*, esp. 259–293.

12. Cf. ibid.

13. The quote is from the Internet site (currently not operating) and e-mail corre-spondence of the Van Tassel group, "Ministry of Universal Wisdom."

14. Cf. J. G. Melton in J. Lewis, *The Gods Have Landed*, 259, and J. Clark, *The UFO Book*, 18–23; this interrelation was apparently detected by C. A. Honey, "A Need to Face Facts," *Cosmic Science Newsletter* 28 (1964): 3–8 (not seen).

15. Cf. G. Adamski, *Inside the Space Ships* (New York: Abelard-Schuman, 1955), which was apparently ghostwritten by Charlotte Blodget. I have used the 4th German edition: *Im Innern der Raumschiffe* (Gütersloh: Ventla Verlag Nachfoger, 1995).

16. A similar judgment is presented by Christopher Helland in his article "Ashtar Command" in J. Lewis, *UFOs and Popular Culture*, 37–40: "The teachings and practices of the Ashtar Command can best be viewed as a syncretism between I AM types of movements and the UFO experience. The group has attempted to incorporate the acceptance and recognition of extraterrestrial beings within a spiritual framework of teachings that recognizes the connection between ascended beings with humanity. Issues concerning the role of the Great White Brotherhood, Saint Germain, Jesus, and other ascended masters are incorporated within a belief system that regards UFO experiences and sightings as the natural progression of the spiritual development of humanity" (40).

17. L. Festinger, H. W. Riecken, and S. Schachter, *When Prophecy Fails* (Minneapolis: University of Minnesota Press, 1956), 62.

18. Cf. the entry "Ashtar" in Jerome Clark, *The UFO Encyclopedia*, vol. 1, 143ff; and Christopher Helland, "Ashtar Command," in J. Lewis, *UFOs and Popular Culture*, 37–40.

19. This analogy was already drawn by Garry Trompf, "The Cargo and the Millennium on Both Sides of the Pacific," in G. Trompf, ed., *Cargo Cults and Millenarian Movements* (Berlin: Mouton, 1990), 35–94. Cf. A. Grünschloß, "Cargo Cults," in J. Lewis, *UFOs and Popular Culture*, 60–63.

20. The following description is based on a special issue no. 76/77 of Aug./Sept. 1998 in the community's journal *Der heiße Draht* [The Hot Wire] (recently renamed *Offenbarungen* [Revelations]), with the title "Die Umwandlung" [The Transformation]; cf. A. Grünschloß, "Fiat Lux," in Chris Partridge, *Guide to New Religions, Sects, and Alternative Religions* (forthcoming), and A. Grünschloß, *Wenn die Götter landen*, 41–47.

21. Cf. G. Trompf, "The Cargo and the Millennium," 44; A. Grünschloß, " 'When We Enter Into My Father's Spacecraft,' " section 2.

22. The brochure is well known in German esoteric/ufological circles; it was published by the authors from Ostermundingen/Switzerland and disseminated through available networks. The following quote is from the 1992 edition, pp. 55–56.

23. The explicit rejection of such esoteric/New Age views concerning a dawning "Heaven on Earth" is expressed several times on the Heaven's Gate Web site (cf. "Online Book" on the group's Web site). Cf. my description in " 'When We Enter Into My Father's Spacecraft,' " section 4 ("The Heaven's Gate Group").

24. In the section "How a Member of the Kingdom of Heaven Might Appear" on the Heaven's Gate Web site, one can find a pictorial representation of such a *Homo novus*.

25. Cf. "Solar Logos Foundation," in J. G. Melton, *Encyclopedia of American Religions* (1999), 644–645; and the group's Internet URL, www.solarlogosfoundation.org. The change of millennial expectations is documented in the subsequent versions of Paulsen's autobiography, *Sunburst—Return of the Ancients* (1980), later entitled *The Christ-Consciousness* (1984ff). Cf. the revised (printed) version of A. Grünschloß, " 'When We Enter Into My Father's Spacecraft,' " in J. Lewis, *The Encyclopedic Sourcebook of UFO Religions* (Amherst, N.Y.: Prometheus Books, 2002).

26. Cf. Chr. Helland, "Ground Crew/Planetary Activation Organization," in J. Lewis, *UFOs and Popular Culture*, 140–143; A. Grünschloß, " 'When We Enter Into My Father's Spacecraft,' " section 3 ("The 'Ground Crew Project' or 'Planetary Activation Organization' "). Some of their apocalyptic pages, expecting an imminent intervention by millions of UFOs (among other cosmic events) in summer 1997, can be easily accessed on my home page at www.gwdg.de/~agruens/UFO.

27. Cf. my entry "Scientology" in J. Lewis, *UFOs and Popular Culture*, 266–268. Despite the fact that Scientology has been one of the most hotly debated new communities during the last decades, there is no all-encompassing academic publication on Scientology that could serve as a fully satisfying reference work in religious studies, doing justice to both emic *and* etic perspectives. The literature is gigantic: Among the critical publications, Jon Atack's *A Piece of Blue Sky* (Secaucus, N.Y.: Carol, 1990), and Roy Wallis, *The Road to Total Freedom* (New York: Columbia University Press, 1977), should be mentioned. Gordon Melton's *The Church of Scientology* (Torino, Italy, 2000; Salt Lake City: Signature Books, 2000) can only serve very sketchy introductory purposes. The basic self-statement by the organization itself is *What Is Scientology?* (Los Angeles: Bridge, 1998). A good annotated bibliography is presented by Marcus Frenschkowski, "L. Ron Hubbard and Scientology: An Annotated Bibliographical Survey of Primary and Selected Secondary Literature," *Marburg Journal of Religion* 4: 1 (July 1999), available online at www.uni-marburg.de/religionswissenschaft/journal/mjr/frenschkowski.html.

28. Cf. the descriptions in L. Ron Hubbard, *Scientology—A History of Man* (1952, as *What to Audit;* reprint, Los Angeles and Copenhagen, 1988), esp. 71–74. I have discussed the anthropological promise of paranormal faculties in Scientology's self-statements and advertisements in my article "Die Konstruktion des 'para-normalen' Menschen. Übermenschliche Fähigkeiten als Bestandteil religiöser Anthropologien (Fallbeispiele)," in *Menschenbild und Menschenwürde*, ed. Eilert Herms (Gütersloh: Gütersloher Verlagshaus, 2001), 497–528 (quote: 516).

29. Hubbard's *Scientology—A History of Man* is introduced as a "cold-blooded and factual account of your last sixty trillion years" (3). Hubbard's *Have You Lived Before This Life?* presents a great variety of auditing examples supporting this claim.

30. *Have You Lived Before This Life?*, 194–195 and 188 (excerpts).

31. As becomes apparent here, Scientology (and "Dianetics") has preserved the old-fashioned psychological memory theory of the 1950s/1960s, where human memory was still envisioned in analogy to magnetic tapes (with exact time "tracks").

32. L. Ron Hubbard, *Hymn of Asia: An Eastern Poem* (1965; reprint, Copenhagen: New Era, 1984), recently reissued together with audio CD (2000).

33. I have used the German translation (*Das Handbuch für den Ehrenamtlichen Geistlichen* [Copenhagen: AOSH, 1980]); the U.S. original first appeared in 1959 and was followed by several editions.

34. Another famous example would be the neo-Pagan Church of All Worlds, founded in 1962 by Tim Zell and Lance Christie (cf. *The Neo-Pagan Essence: Selected Papers from the Church of All Worlds* (Chicago, 1994), explicitly based on Robert A. Heinlein's SF-novel *Stranger in a Strange Land* (1961). Similar oscillations between mere SF-fantasies and "real" re-formations of "religion" can be observed in the *Star Trek* fan culture.

35. Cf. www.aetherius.org.

36. Cf. www.aetherius.org/NewFiles/current_cosmic_activities.html (downloaded April 2002).

37. Cf. John A. Saliba, "Aetherius Society," in J. Lewis, *UFOs and Popular Culture*, 7–10; and esp. Saliba, "The Earth Is a Dangerous Place—The World View of the Aetherius Society," *Marburg Journal of Religion* 4: 2 (Dec. 1999), for a more extensive treatment and bibliography.

38. Accordingly, on the anthropological level, one is also awaiting a "new man," a "cosmic man," a liberated being worthy of membership in the Galactic Federation, when the transformation on cosmic levels have taken place: "The by-products of decline in all doctrines and institutions based on materialism cannot be stopped any more. The effects from supra-physical levels cannot be ignored. The new type of man, the 'homo cosmicus,' is overrunning old-fashioned values, and he is building new ones with vitality, creating a transformation of the foundations in psychology, philosophy, religion, sciences and arts, etc." Karl L. Veit and Jürgen Gottsleben, *Außerirdische Raumschiffe sind gelandet: Umwälzende Ereignisse* [Extraterrestrial Spaceships Have Landed] (Gütersloh: Ventla-Verlag, 1996), 26; cf. also 14–16 ("Homo Cosmicus—Der neue Menschentyp").

39. Cf. Marco Frenschkowski, "Religionswissenschaftliche Prolegomena zu einer Theorie der Phantastik," in W. Freund, J. Lachinger, and C. Ruthner, eds., *Der Demiurg ist ein Zwitter* (München: Fink, 1999), 37–57.

40. Cf. Ernst Benz in his historical analysis of the UFO experience, *Außerirdische Welten: Von Kopernikus zu den Ufos* (Freiburg: Aurum, 2000), esp. 119–134 (1978 title: *Kosmische Bruderschaft: Die Pluralität der Welten: Zur Ideengeschichte des Ufo-Glaubens*).

41. This quote is from von Däniken's public presentation at a convention of the German UFO and IFO Study Group (DUIST), just one year before the publication of his first best-seller; the title of his talk was "Erhielten unsere Vorfahren Besuch aus dem Weltall?" ["Did our ancestors encounter visits from outer space?"], printed in *Dokumentarbericht—7. Internationaler Weltkongreß der UFO-Forscher in Mainz 1967* (Wiesbaden, 1968), 94–97 (quote: 97).

42. There is a real abundance of books on these topics—by von Däniken himself, as well as by other epigonus writers in the Paleo-SETI genre, many of them publishing only in German (Walter-Jörg Langbein, Lars Fischinger, Ulrich Dopatka, and many more). Cf. the entry "Ancient Astronauts" by Pia Andersson in J. Lewis, *UFOs and Popular Culture*, 20–25; for a good recent critical investigation into von Däniken's approach to "research" and historical "proofs," cf. Markus Pössel, *Phantastische Wissenschaft: Über Erich von Däniken und Johannes von Buttlar* (Reinbek: Rowohlt, 2000).

43. Ulrich Dopatka, *Die große Erich von Däniken Enzyklopädie: Das einzigartige Nachschlagewerk zur Prä-Astronautik* (Düsseldorf and München: Econ and List, 1997). There was also an interactive CD-ROM called *Kontakt mit dem Universum: Mysteries of the World* and published as the "official reference work of the Ancient Astronaut Society" (Taufkirchen: Magellan Intertainment, n.d.).

44. The URL is www.aas-ra.org (see also www.daniken.com). The aim of the research association is stated there in the following way: "The AAS RA is determined to prove, using scientific research methods, but in 'lay-man's terms,' as to whether or not extraterrestrials have visited Earth in the remote past."

45. This is explicitly stated by E. v. Däniken himself—e.g., in his book *Auf den Spuren der Allmächtigen* (München: Econ, 1993), where he writes in the afterword that the old religious traditions have to be "interpreted in modern fashion and made intelligent technologically" ("modern interpretiert und technisch verständlich gemacht"; p. 189); cf. also 122 ("Wie Eroberer zu Göttern wurden"). In his most "religious" book, *Erscheinun-*

gen (Düsseldorf: ⁸1974), von Däniken even develops an esoteric anthropology, where human brains are portrayed as artificially (genetically) empowered to "receive" E.T. visions and messages; this is his core explanation for all kinds of paranormal sightings and religious visions or revelations until today. This specific line of (normative-anthropological) thought was not carried on in his later works, but there are several PSETI-adherents who combine their worldview with similar contactee beliefs or an esoteric spirituality.

46. In the 1960s, both Charroux and von Däniken started with enthusiastic and paradigmatic references to Heinrich Schliemann and his *new* search for the historical "truth" of Troja behind the old mythic accounts. This combination of Fort's iconoclasm and alternative kind of "science," revealing the truth about "data" which have been overlooked and "damned" by standard academia ("dogmatic science"), and Schliemann's attempts at a layman's "archaeology" following the footsteps of mythic tales, accounts for most typical aspects in the whole PSETI endeavor.

47. See the group's URLs: www.rael.org or www.rael.de.

48. *Le livre qui dit la verité* (1973). The first English translation appeared in 1974. Together with Raël's second book, *Les extraterrestres m'ont emmené sur leur planète* (1975), it is contained in *The Message Given by Extra-Terrestrials. At Last! Science Replaces Religion.* I have used the recent German version *Das wahre Gesicht Gottes* (Fondation Raëlienne, 1998).

49. For a short review of the basic revelations, cf. George D. Cryssides, "Is God a Space Alien? The Cosmology of the Raëlian Church," *Culture and Cosmos* 4, no. 1 (Spring/ Summer 2000): 36–53; and Susan Palmer, "The Raelian Movement," in J. Lewis, *UFOs and Popular Culture*, 240–251. For an illuminating discussion focusing on the role of gender and women, see Susan Palmer, "Women in the Raelian Movement: New Religious Experiments in Gender and Authority," in J. Lewis, *The Gods Have Landed*, 105–135.

50. "The person whom you looked upon as your father was not your real father. After the explosion at Hiroshima, we decided that the time had come for us to send a new messenger on Earth. He would be the last prophet, but the first one to address mankind asking them to understand and not to believe. We then selected a woman, as we had done in the time of Jesus. The woman was taken aboard one of our ships and inseminated as we had done with the mother of Jesus. Then she was freed after we had totally erased from her memory all traces of what had happened. . . . Your real father is also the father of Jesus, and that makes you brothers. You are presently looking at your father," says Yahweh, "and I could see in Yahweh's eyes an equally great emotion and feeling of love" (113–114).

51. The URL is www.clonaid.com.

52. Cf. Raël's book *La meditation sensuelle* (Fondation Raelienne, 1980), chapter 3; I have used the German edition, *Die sinnliche Meditation* (Weiden: Rael-Bewegung, 1994), 39.

53. A recent handout on the German "Raelistische Religion" states: "The Raelian Religion, an atheistic religion like Buddhism, has 50,000 adherents in 85 countries today who discovered a spirituality based on science with the help of this philosophy" (my translation).

54. Cf. the pictures in Palmer, "The Raelian Movement" and "Women in the Raelian Movement."

55. There is also a URL: www.ufoland.com.

56. URL: www.mysterypark.chap.

57. Trompf, "The Cargo and the Millennium on Both Sides of the Pacific," 39.

58. Another ufological topic in itself is the "abductee" version of UFO faith: Inaugurated by a variety of alien abduction reports, the experiences of alien abduction and manipulation have already become a distinct genre of modern folklore. It has been tried to trace aspects of these stories back to inner-psychic, even archetypal imageries, or to topic motifs and events in traditional folklore with gnomes, dwarfs, or fairies who also played their tricks with humans: The manipulative or sometimes erotic activities of the legendary "little green men" from Mars or outer space at least seem to share several aspects of older stories about the little "green people" (dwarfs) in Europe's rural traditions. See the entries on "abduction" generally, as well as selected single abduction cases, in Jerome Clark's encyclopedia and handbook; see also the survey provided by John Whitmore, "Religious Dimensions of the UFO Abductee Experience," in J. Lewis, *The Gods Have Landed*, 65–84.

59. A good example is a German book on "UFO-sects," written by two authors who are active in PSETI genres; its apologetic, rejecting tone can be compared with Christian apologetic literature on new religious movements, since the authors want to show the silliness and the destructive impact of the contactee version of UFO faith: Lars A. Fischinger and Roland M. Horn, *UFO-Sekten* (Rastatt: Moewig, 1999).

60. Here the research conducted by Robert Balch is of high significance (see his forthcoming contribution to Lewis, *Encyclopedic Sourcebook of UFO Religions*). There was a very good TV documentary on ARTE/Germany in 1998: *Leben und Sterben der Heaven's Gate-Sekte* (original: BBC, 1998), allowing moving insights into the emic plausibility of the Heavensgaters' visions (e.g., farewell videos).

61. *The Book of the Damned* (New York: Ace, 1972), 193 (chap. 12).

REFERENCES

Selected Primary Sources

Adamski, G. 1955. *Inside the Spaceships*. New York.

Angelucci, O. M. 1955. *The Secret of the Saucers*. Amherst.

Charroux, Robert. 1963. *Histoire inconnue des hommes depuis cent mille ans*. Paris: R. Laffont.

Church of All Worlds, ed. 1994. *The Neo-Pagan Essence: Selected Papers from the Church of All Worlds*. Chicago.

Däniken, Erich von. 1968. *Erinnerungen an die Zukunft. Ungelöste Rätsel der Vergangenheit.* Düsseldorf: Econ Verlag. (English translation: *Chariots of the Gods? Unsolved Mysteries of the Past*. Trans. M. Heron. London: Souvenir Press, 1969)

———. 1974. *Erscheinungen. Phänomene, die die Welt erregen*. Düsseldorf.

Dopatka, U. 1997. *Die große Erich von Däniken Enzyklopädie. Das einzigartige Nachschlagewerk zur Prä-Astronautik*. Düsseldorf and Munich.

Fischinger, L. A. 1997. *Götter der Sterne. Bibel, Mythen und kosmische Besucher.* Weilers-
bach.

Fort, Ch. 1919. *The Book of the Damned.* New York.

———. 1923. *New Lands.* New York.

———. 1931. *Lo!* New York.

———. 1932. *Wild Talents.* New York.

Fry, D. 1954. *The White Sands Incident.* Los Angeles.

Gauch-Keller, W., and Th. Gauch-Keller. 1992. *Aufruf an die Erdbewohner. Erklärungen
zur Umwandlung des Planeten Erde und seiner Menschheit in der "Endzeit."* Oster-
mundingen, Switzerland.

Hill, E. P. 1955. *Ashtar: In Days to Come.* Los Angeles.

Hubbard, L. Ron. 1974. *Hymn of Asia: An Eastern Poem.* Los Angeles: Church of Scientology of California.

———. 1976. *The Volunteer Minister's Handbook.* Los Angeles: Church of Scientology of
California.

———. 1988 [1952]. *A History of Man [What to Audit]: A List and Description of the
Principal Incidents to Be Found in a Human Being.* Copenhagen and Los Angeles.

———. 1989 [1960]. *Have You Lived Before This Life?* Copenhagen and Los Angeles.

Langbein, W.-J. 2000. *Am Anfang war die Apokalypse. Warum wir Kinder der Astronau-
ten wurden.* Lübeck.

Lovecraft, H. P. 1936. "The Shadow Out of Time." *Astounding Stories* 17, no. 4 (June):
110–154.

Lucian. 1974. *True Story and Lucius or the Ass.* Trans. P. Turner. Bloomington: Indiana
University Press.

Newbrough, John Ballou. 1882. *Oahspe. A New Bible in the Words of Jehovih and His
Angel Ambassadors.* New York: Oahspe Publishing Association.

Paulsen, N. 1980. *Sunburst: Return of the Ancients.* Goleta, Calif. (Later editions under
the title *The Christ-Consciousness*)

Raël (Cl. Vorilhon). 1986a. *Let's Welcome Our Fathers from Space: They Created Humanity in Their Laboratories.* Tokyo.

———. 1986b. *The Message Given [to Me] by Extra-Terrestrials.* (Contains an English
version of Raël's two original books, *Le Livre qui dit la verité* [1974] and *Les extraterrestres m'ont emmené sur leur planète* [1975])

———. 1986c. *Sensual Meditation.* Tokyo.

Tuella (Th. B. Terrel). 1982. *Project: World-Evacuation.* Deming, N.Mex.

Uriellas Abenteuer mit Gott im Orden Fiat Lux! N.d. Videocassette distributed by the Fiat
Lux-Community in Ibach, Germany.

Van Tassel, George W. 1952. *I Rode a Flying Saucer! The Mystery of the Flying Saucers
Revealed.* Los Angeles: New Age Publishing Company.

Selected Secondary Sources

Atack, J. 1990. *A Piece of Blue Sky: Scientology, Dianetics, and L. Ron Hubbard Exposed.*
Secaucus, N.J.

Benz, E. 1990. *Außerirdische Welten. Von Kopernikus zu den Ufos.* Freiburg.

Clark, J. 1997. *The UFO Encyclopedia.* 2 vols. Detroit.

————. 1998. *The UFO Book: Encyclopedia of the Extraterrestrial.* Detroit.

De Camp, L. S. 1970 [1954]. *Lost Continents. The Atlantis Theme in History, Science, and Literature.* New York.

Festinger, L., H. W. Riecken, and S. Schachter. 1956. *When Prophecy Fails.* Minneapolis.

Frenschkowski, M. 1999. "L. Ron Hubbard and Scientology: An Annotated Bibliographical Survey of Primary and Selected Secondary Literature." *Marburg Journal of Religion* 4, no. 1 (July). Available online at: www.uni-marburg.de/religionswissenschaft/journal/mjr/frenschkowski.html.

Golowin, S. 1980 [1965]. *Götter der Atom-Zeit. Moderne Sagenbildung um Raumschiffe und Sternenmenschen.* Bern.

Grünschloß, A. 1998. " 'When We Enter Into My Father's Spacecraft': Cargoistic Hopes and Millenarian Cosmologies in New Religious UFO Movements." *Marburg Journal of Religion* 3, no. 2 (December). Available online at: www.uni-marburg.de/religionswissenschaft/journal/mjr/ufogruen.html.

————. 2000. *Wenn die Götter landen. Religiöse Dimensionen des UFO-Glaubens.* EZW-Texte 153. Berlin.

Jung, C. G. 1959. *Flying Saucers: A Modern Myth of Things Seen in the Skies.* London. (German original: *Ein moderner Mythus. Von Dingen, die am Himmel gesehen werden,* Zürich/Stuttgart, 1958)

Lewis, J., ed. 1995. *The Gods Have Landed: New Religions from Other Worlds.* Albany, N.Y.

————. 2000. *UFOs and Popular Culture. An Encyclopedia of Contemporary Myth.* Santa Barbara, Calif.

————. 2002. *The Encyclopedic Sourcebook of UFO Religions.* Amherst, N.Y.

Melton, J. G. 1999. *Encyclopedia of American Religions.* 6th ed. Detroit.

Rothstein, M. 2000. *UFOer og rumvæsener. Myten om de flyvende tallerkener.* Copenhagen.

Trompf, G. 1990. "The Cargo and the Millennium on Both Sides of the Pacific." In *Cargo Cults and Millenarian Movements,* ed. G. Trompf, 35–94. Berlin.

Selected Internet Sources

http://members.tripod.com/~uforelie (home page for UFOs and religion)

http://www.auditing.org/13-ot.htm (description, Operating Thetan)

www.aas-ra.org (home page, Archaeology, Astronautics, and SETI)

www.aetherius.org (home page, The Aetherius Society)

www.alien.de (German UFO-server with many interesting links)

www.daniken.com, www.mysterypark.ch (E. v. Däniken and his Mystery Park)

www.freezone.de (separatist Scientologists, with "space opera")

www.gafintl-adamski.com (home page, Adamski Foundation)

www.gwdg.de/~agruens/UFO (my own online source-material)

www.heavensgatetoo.com, www.webcoast.com/heavensgate.com, www.trancenet.org/heavensgate (mirror-sites for Heaven's Gate)

www.paoweb.org (home page, Planetary Activation Organization)

www.rael.de, www.rael.org (home pages, International Raëlian Religion). See also www.clonaid.com, www.ufoland.com

www.scientology.com (.org,.de) (home pages, Church of Scientology)
www.solarlogosfoundation.org (Solar Logos Foundation; Norman Paulsen)
www.spiritweb.org (New Age, esoteric channelings, ufology, Theosophy etc.)
www.theashtarcommand.com, www.spiritweb.org/Spirit/ashtar-command.html, www.
ashtarlightworkcenter.com, www.ashtarcommand.ws, www.ashtar.de (URLs for Ashtar and Ashtar-Command)
www.thegroundcrew.com (home page, Ground Crew)

CHAPTER 19

ESOTERICISM IN NEW RELIGIOUS MOVEMENTS

OLAV HAMMER

ON THE DEFINITIONS OF ESOTERICISM

FOR the researcher intent on surveying the topic of esotericism in new religious movements, several pitfalls present themselves. Not the least of these is the problem of arriving at a useful definition of the term "esotericism" itself. Although the adjective "esoteric" has been around since Late Antiquity, the earliest occurrence of the corresponding noun appears to be in Jacques Matter's *Histoire du gnosticisme*, published in 1828. It was popularized in the French-speaking world by Eliphas Lévi in his *Dogme et rituel de la haute magie* (1856). Its introduction in the English language is attributed to Alfred Sinnett's *Esoteric Buddhism* (1883). Although the term is a product of the nineteenth century, there are many religious currents with much older roots that in the scholarly literature are designated as esoteric. Esotericism is thus not originally a self-designation of a distinct category of religious movements, but a label applied a posteriori. And like most such labels, it does not cover an immediately definable natural kind. Esotericism is not a species of religion to be unambiguously found in the mass of empirical data, but rather a scholarly construction. That is, the term is used to designate religious phenomena that display whatever similarity a given tradition of scholarship finds interesting to highlight.[1]

Given the absence of a natural referent, it should come as no surprise that the term has been used in several more or less conflicting ways. Some definitions are pretheoretical. Among these are the many uses in texts written by self-professed esotericists. Alice Bailey, who creatively reformulated aspects of theosophy, called her own system of beliefs esoteric. She understands the term as designating a school of thought that recognizes "that behind all happenings in the world of phenomena ... exists the world of energies" (Bailey 1954: 60), that is, an underlying interplay of spiritual forces unrecognized by those who have not gained the necessary insight. As this example shows, such definitions are in part rhetorical strategies, employed to represent one's own practices and beliefs as a path leading to true insight.

Several distinct uses of the term "esotericism" can be found in the scholarly literature, and it is only with two of these that the remainder of the present article will be concerned. One usage is typological and employs the term to denote currents and religions with certain common structural features. This understanding is closely related to the dictionary definitions of the concept. These tend to center on the etymological significance of the word. The prefix *eso-* means "inner" and is generally contrasted with *exo-* or "outer." The term "esoteric" is therefore understood as an adjective describing teachings that are "intended for or understood by only a chosen few, as an inner group of disciples or initiates."[2] Esotericism in this sense can be seen as an ideal type, a form of religion that embraces the idea that access to salvific knowledge and to ritual competence is a multitiered construction. Participants in the movement consider themselves to have insights that are unavailable to outsiders. And commonly, besides the elementary insights and abilities that are afforded to any member of the movement, new and purportedly more profound levels of understanding are granted only to those who have passed further thresholds.

Another strand of scholarship takes a quite different approach and defines Western esotericism in historical and geographical terms. Thus the entry for the term in the *Encyclopedia of Religions*, by Antoine Faivre (1986: 157), does begin with the dictionary sense:

> The word esotericism has a meaning that is apparent from its etymology (Gr., esoteros, "inner"), which refers to an "interiorism," an entry into the self through a special knowledge or gnosis, in order to attain a form of enlightenment and individual salvation. This special knowledge concerns the relationships that unite us to God or to the divine world and may also include a knowledge of the mysteries inherent to God himself (in which case it is, strictly speaking, theosophy). To learn these relationships, the individual must enter, or "descend," into himself by means of an initiatory process, progressing along a path that is hierarchically structured by a series of intermediaries.

However, it is clear from the rest of Faivre's text that he does not conceive of esotericism as a typological label for any belief system with a strong element of initiation and *gnosis*, but wishes to restrict the domain of esotericism to a specific set of historically related currents in the West.

In 1992 Faivre proposed a different way of delimiting esotericism, a definition that sharpens the divide between esotericism as a term for a type of religion and as a label for a family of historically related currents (Faivre 1992a). He explicated esotericism as a mode of thought with a number of specific characteristics. Four of these characteristics are central: without the simultaneous presence of all four, the current in question would, strictly speaking, not be considered esoteric. The first of these elements is the idea of correspondences, that all parts of the universe are connected through real or symbolic links. The second is the belief that nature is living. Third is the concept of mediating symbols. The requisite insights are gained through rituals, symbols, images, or postulated spiritual beings. Finally, the concept of personal transmutation is crucial. The other three elements of the definition are not merely part of a speculative worldview, but would ideally lead to a spiritual metamorphosis.

Besides these four characteristics, Faivre identifies two others as frequently being present although not central to the definition. First is the idea of concordance, the belief that most, if not all, religious traditions are different manifestations of the same underlying essence. Second, esoteric currents may recognize a specific mode of transmission (e.g. from teacher to disciple). Although Faivre's understanding of the term is by no means the only definition of the historically related set of Western esoteric currents, many other scholars have followed his lead.

One can note that Faivre's revised definition did not significantly change the composition of the corpus of currents that the term was intended to refer to, a corpus that has been understood as related at least since the late seventeenth century (Hanegraaff forthcoming). Rather, the new definition circumscribed more clearly the boundaries of a set of currents that had long been established on more impressionistic grounds. The historical foundation of this set is a syncretistic phenomenon of the Renaissance period. A number of authors combined Christian teachings with Platonic and Neoplatonic philosophy, the Jewish kabbala, hermeticism,[3] and the traditional "occult sciences" of astrology, alchemy, and magic. Somewhat later currents of thought that present either innovative syntheses of these influences or original formulations with an air of family resemblance are also considered foundational for the understanding of Western esotericism. Among these are the current that originated in the writings of Paracelsus (1493/4–1541), and that manifested in the texts written by the German mystic Jakob Böhme (1575–1624) and his followers.

Terminological confusion may arise because the typological concept "esotericism" and the historical category "Western esotericism" overlap, but they by no means denote the same set of religions. Numerous currents within Western eso-

tericism are not esoteric in the typological sense of the word. And many movements are esoteric in the typological sense but have no historical links with the
currents of Western esotericism. Indeed, the distinction of a type of religion with
multitiered access to knowledge can be fruitfully applied to quite distinct, non-
European religious traditions (cf. Weckman 1986 and the contributions in Wolfson
1998). As Faivre (1992b: xii) notes, the word now has two meanings, of which
only one concerns him and others who study "Western esotericism" rather than
"esotericism" *tout court*.

A definition that does not refer to a set of naturally delimited objects or
elements can hardly be said to be either correct or incorrect. Any particular
method of cutting up the domain of religion will be useful for certain purposes
and less helpful for others. There are pragmatic advantages to adopting a demarcation that sets off Western esotericism as a family of historically related currents.
It directs researchers to issues such as the transmission of ideas and of the influence of one person or current upon another. It has the considerable benefit of
opening up an area of research that has been marginalized by the implicit norms
of academia. By branding magic, astrology, alchemy, and related topics as "occult"
or "irrational," entire fields of human practice have been understudied. By defining the study of Western esotericism as a subject in its own right, one can expect
this situation to be redressed. Western esotericism is thus primarily an operational
concept for scholars of Western intellectual history and other researchers with a
decidedly historical-critical approach.

However, for the scholar interested in understanding the structure and function of religions in general and new religious movements in particular, the boundary line that sets off a domain of Western esotericism from other currents is more
problematic. First, the set of present-day belief systems, religious movements, and
currents that are historically related to the defining corpus is a motley one indeed.
A list would include the Swedenborgian Church; spiritualism; Jungian spirituality;
the Theosophical Society; the Anthroposophical Society; the Church Universal and
Triumphant; the spiritual community of Damanhur, Italy; Wicca; the New Age;
the Osho movement; occultist magic; various New Thought denominations; and
several UFO religions. These are movements that diverge on just about every point
of ritual or doctrine.

Second, there are movements that by the historical definition belong to the
nonesoteric side of the line yet are in many ways structurally similar to Western
esoteric movements. Transcendental Meditation, or TM, is a religious movement
brought by Maharishi Mahesh Yogi (b. 1911) to the West (Rothstein 1996: 25–106).
Sociologically, TM resembles many New Age practices in that it attracts a large
number of people with low levels of commitment around a much smaller group
of highly committed followers. Its understanding of its own mission is quite similar to that of, for example, Anthroposophy or sectors of the New Age, by seeing
itself as a form of science and not as a religious current. Its rituals of meditation

are similar to the meditative exercises found in Western esoteric currents. For many members, the goals of meditation are phrased in terms of developing one's inner potential, just as it is in many of the techniques of the Human Potential Movement and the New Age. TM encompasses astrology and other forms of occult gnosis. Nevertheless, TM arrives at its doctrines and rituals by a creative interpretation of the Indian Advaita-Vedanta philosophy, not through a modernization of earlier Western currents, and is therefore by definition excluded from the fold of historically delimited esoteric movements.

Third, and perhaps most important, Western esotericism in the historical sense and esotericism in the typological sense not only denote somewhat different sectors of the set of human religions; they are quite different theoretical constructs. From the perspective of the philosophy of science, a basic criterion for setting up a fruitful typology of objects is that the members of a given class need to share some interesting characteristics beyond the sheer fact of fulfilling the criteria set out in the definition.[4] From the perspective of a synchronic rather than historical analysis, Western esotericism, *sensu* Faivre, is an ad hoc label and not strictly speaking a type of religion. That is, once a current has been shown to possess the four central characteristics presented by Faivre, no other structural properties follow from that fact. There would appear to be no evidence that the myths, rituals, religious objects, social formations, discursive practices, or sociopsychological mechanisms found in contemporary currents within the domain of Western esotericism display any unique and defining features.[5] Esotericism in the typological sense, on the other hand, functions as a distinguishing feature of a class of religious movements that also display other traits. Here, we shall focus on the correlation of typological esotericism and five such characteristics: social formations, rituals, purported objectives, cognitive style, and relations to mainstream society.

SOCIAL FORMATIONS

By centering on the aspect of gnosis, initiation, and access to privileged knowledge, the typological demarcation focuses on social formations, and especially on questions of hierarchy and power. Although there are dozens of ways of defining the term "religion," by most accounts religious movements elaborate their practices and beliefs around an understanding of a cosmos that comprises nonempirical agents. This understanding is codified in religious doctrines and rituals formulated by specific individuals or groups of people: the religious virtuosi, to borrow a term from Max Weber (1948: 287ff). However, the very fact that these postulated agents or forces are nonempirical implies that their existence and properties cannot be independently validated. To a considerable extent, the statements and injunctions of the religious virtuosi must be taken at face value. This gives religious social formations a specific ideological power since, to quote Bruce Lincoln (2000: 416), they "invest specific human preferences with transcendent status."

Esoteric movements present yet another angle to the question of ideological power. The simplest form of secrecy merely implies that two people share information unknown to anybody else. However, as sociologist Georg Simmel noted in his classic essay on secrecy, there also exists a form of concealment with three involved parties (1992: 421–422). In this form, secret knowledge not only defines those who are privy to it, the initiates who have access to the scarce resource. It also defines an out-group that lacks the privileged insight, by drawing boundaries between them and the in-group. The closely related concept of esotericism in religion is characteristically triadic in that it accomplishes the same separation between "Us" and "Them." Esoteric movements characteristically portray religious insight as a scarce resource. Key figures within each current will represent themselves, and will be represented by their adherents, as being in control of this resource. The degree to which one possesses the scarce resource will place any given individual on a specific rank in the social hierarchy.

The demarcation between in-and out-groups can run along lines that resemble those of the surrounding society. The in-group can be determined on the basis of social status. Some contemporary Masonic organizations count among their ranks a high proportion of individuals with an elevated social rank. Membership in such lodges need not only be a question of belonging to a spiritual fraternity; it can also create strong bonds between select members of the affluent and well-educated sectors of society. Other groups can be exclusive on grounds of gender. Some esoteric in-groups, for example in traditional Freemasonry and in Mormonism, are open to males only. Yet other movements, such as TM and Scientology, will erect boundaries against those who can ill afford to pay the fees for initiation into higher levels.

Exclusivity and social bonding are important aspects of esoteric in-groups. One set of informal interviews with candidates who had applied for membership in Masonic lodges showed that, for many, the main interest was the possibility of socializing with like-minded individuals. Only after they had been admitted did an interest in the ritualism develop (Piatigorsky 1997: 364). Nevertheless, the ideological component of social formations such as these, namely the exclusion of less privileged Others, will typically be opaque to those who sympathize with an esoteric current. In-groups have their ways of explaining why it is preferable to set apart their own group and to keep out others. A characteristic argument is that the secrets divulged and the rituals made available to the higher ranking are too spiritually powerful to be safe for the lower ranking. And, of course, this

argument actively hides the social formation of the esoteric in-group by refor-
mulating a class, gender, or economic barrier in terms of abstract ideas.

Whereas these remarks illustrate how the hierarchy of a religious organization
can mirror the inequalities of society at large, a study of the social formations of
esoteric religions can also highlight the mechanisms by which the structure of
such religious bodies is maintained over time. There is a characteristic circularity
between the beliefs, the social formations and the praxis of the higher-ranking
segments of an esoteric religious community. A ritual of initiation into restricted
insight is only meaningful within a given religious world that encompasses a
complex dogmatism, a specialized ritual vocabulary, and so forth. The mass of
arcane details that constitutes the religious worldview can only be upheld if there
is a corps of individuals who are able to allocate intellectual and other resources.
This knowledge is used as a marker of status that sets the same corps of people
off against the lower-ranking members. And in order to protect their rank, the
higher-ranking members reproduce the initiatory ritualism.

A major goal of the religious activity of those of lower rank may be to gain
access to the protected knowledge of the higher echelons. In some movements,
this upward mobility causes new titles at yet higher levels to be created. In Scientology, the highest goal used to be to reach the rank of Clear. Over the years,
new levels have been created. At the time of writing, it is possible to ascend the
ladder of initiations through steps known as Operating Thetan I to VIII. Freemasonry represents another case of the proliferation of higher degrees (see, e.g.,
Le Forestier 1987). Initiates could originally reach three degrees: Entered Apprentice, Fellow Craft, and Master Mason. The basic structure is retained by many
lodges. However, other groups confer numerous additional degrees. Thus, the
Scottish Rite has thirty degrees above the three basic ones.

RITUALS

There are different ways of marking the differential access to privileged insight
depending on the degree of structure and cohesion of various movements. In
forms of religion that are primarily consumed in the form of texts, accounts in
the media, lectures, and so forth, privileged knowledge is in fact only "mysteries
to be read about," *Lese-Mysterien* (Reitzenstein 1956: 51–53, 64). There are no high-
ranking officials who can bestow the appropriate social status on others. Instead,
the text may offer tantalizing clues that permit the reader to judge on more or
less impressionistic grounds whether a higher level of insight has been reached.

However, in structured religious organizations, ritual actions, ritual space, and ritual objects can be used to construct a set of higher ranked individuals.

Rituals that initiate members into a higher status are found in quite a few esoteric new religious movements. Thus, rituals of initiation give the neophyte access to each of the levels within Transcendental Meditation. The entry-level initiation takes place in a consecrated room.[6] The person to be initiated is instructed to bring a number of objects: fruit, flowers, a cloth handkerchief. The teacher recites a text in Sanskrit, the meaning of which is not explained to the neophyte. Published translations reveal that this text ritually places the initiate within the succession of masters and disciples that Maharishi recognizes as his own (Dahlén 1992: 229–239). Only then will the teacher reveal the mantra that the initiate shall use during his or her meditation.

The Church of Jesus Christ of Latter-day Saints (the Mormon Church) is another esoteric religion that partly constructs its hierarchy through ritualism. One of the major differences between the Mormon Church and mainstream Christian denominations is its temples (Luschin 1995; Rozsa 1995). After the construction of a temple is completed, it remains open to the public for a short time. Thereafter it is ritually declared accessible only to church members who are in possession of a temple recommend, a kind of identification document issued by the local church authorities (Tucker 1995). Temple recommends are granted only on the fulfillment of certain duties, among which are the payment of tithes and a behavior compatible with the moral code of the Mormon Church as set out in a text called the Word of Wisdom.[7] During their first visit to the temple, participants are ritually cleansed in a ritual called Endowment. In a first stage, a poncho-like cape is worn, and the individual is anointed with olive oil. Then the cape is exchanged for a garment with various symbolic patterns. Ideally, initiates will wear their garment for the remainder of their lives, as a physical correlate of their status.

Ritual objects that function as visible status signs are found in other esoteric religions as well. Scientologists who advance through the series of initiatory levels have each stage of their progress carefully documented in corresponding certificates. Specific status markers are available at the highest levels, thus, those who have attained the level of Operating Thetan VIII may wear a special bracelet with a T-shaped design on a circular background.

PURPORTED OBJECTIVES

If some individuals are ranked higher than others, and only a few people stand at the top of the ladder, the question arises: What is it like to be one of the select few? Nearly every religious movement will have hagiographic accounts of its founder or leader, describing his or her exceptional qualities. For those movements that have defined its members as belonging to several classes, there may furthermore be accounts linking the status of entire groups with purported abilities or qualities.

Some movements ascribe category labels to the recipients of higher levels of knowledge that are in fact social constructions. To be "saved," "born again," or "enlightened" is not to gain a set of empirically verifiable characteristics, but to be labeled with an attribute that only has a meaning within the specific religious context. That is, the concept of being born again is understood by the believers as a relationship between themselves and the deity, but it can be translated into empirical terms as a social status given to the individual within the religious community.

Some rewards are even more abstracted from the empirical world. Esoteric religions can project the hierarchy of the present life onto the purported destiny after death. Those who have received less of the scarce resource will be transported to a less privileged location in the hereafter. Restricted access to higher levels is thus reflected in the soteriology of the Mormon belief system (Dahl 1995). There are several different destinations for the soul after the death of the body. One's final destination is dependent not only on one's moral worth, but also on one's status within the ritual hierarchy of the church. The irrevocably wicked will go to a place referred to as outer darkness. A class of people who have transgressed to a lesser extent will pass on to the celestial kingdom. The terrestrial kingdom is reserved for honorable people who have failed to live up fully to the moral codex of Mormonism, or who had the misfortune of living in a "heathen" country and did not come to know the fullness of the gospel. Only faithful Mormons inhabit the highest three states. The three tiers of what is known as the celestial kingdom are reserved for different categories of church members. In order to achieve the very highest form of existence in the afterlife, participation in esoteric rituals known as temple endowment and temple sealing is necessary.

Many movements, however, promise rewards of a much more concrete nature to those who have gained the appropriate level. Members of Transcendental Meditation who complete the TM-Sidhi Program are thereby initiated into a level at which paranormal events are said to take place. The attempts by TM-Sidhi meditators to levitate have been widely publicized. The movement itself has ascribed the rather modest results to the as yet relatively undeveloped mental level of those who practice the technique (Rothstein 2001: 287).

Another example of a movement with spectacular empirical claims for its initiates is Scientology.[8] For years, the ultimate goal of the member was to attain the state of "clear." By following a set of courses, it was supposedly possible to achieve "Good Memory, Raised I.Q., Strong Will Power, Magnetic Personality, Amazing Vitality, Creative Imagination" (Stark and Bainbridge 1985: 266). Critics have claimed that those who reached this level did not manifest any obviously superior qualities when compared to lower-ranking members. Scientology members themselves would inevitably be confronted with the risk of disconfirmation: the realization that their own spiritual development and that of others who had reached the status of clear were quite unlike the ideals that had been presented to them. How was disconfirmation prevented? Rodney Stark and William Bainbridge (1985) point at the considerable efforts made by the Church of Scientology to avoid having members discover the gulf between their expected capacities and the considerably more mundane reality. Hubbard saw to it that the status of clear could only be conferred by his own organization. A number of other statuses, both below and above that of clear, were created. Thereby the progress from one level to the next became increasingly difficult to judge, and the ultimate goal was constantly receding. Finally, those who were on their way to reach the status of clear were isolated from contact with others who might challenge them.

Cognitive Style

According to Stark and Bainbridge (1985), the Church of Scientology would seem to have worked hard at solving the problem of disconfirmation. However, research in social and cognitive psychology suggests that it is an almost fail-safe strategy to promise followers that their skills in a variety of areas will be significantly enhanced. Esoteric religions can thus even be connected with specific cognitive strategies.

There are significant flaws in our ability to know how well we are performing and to understand how likely it is that we are accurate in our judgments. Perhaps the best illustration of this cognitive weakness is the statistically illogical tendency of the average person to believe he or she is more competent than the average human being (Dunning, Meyerowitz, and Holzberg 1989). Most people think that they are better parents and spouses than most others. Automobile drivers think they drive more safely than most others, managers believe their business skills are above average, and teachers pride themselves in didactic skills that exceed those of their peers. Furthermore, there is evidence that those who are less competent on any given task have more difficulty recognizing their true level of ability than do more competent individuals (Kruger and Dunning 1999). In experimental settings, it can also be shown that even artificially induced self-serving attributes are nearly impervious to disconfirming evidence. People who in a first phase of an experiment were made to believe that they had certain above-average interpersonal skills were not swayed by the careful debriefing procedure carried out by the researchers in the second phase of the experiment (Nisbett and Ross 1980: 176–179).

These findings can readily be extrapolated to the domain of new religious movements and offer clues to why esoteric practices that hold out tangible rewards for the initiates may be disconfirmable in theory but are rarely disconfirmed in practice. One might hypothesize that those who buy significant amounts of self-help literature or who enroll in self-improvement courses have considerable difficulties in accurately assessing their abilities. At first, their lack of skills is acutely felt. The literature that they read gradually induces a feeling of having made progress in a variety of personal areas. Although their performance may quite possibly be as paltry as before reading the books or following the course, they will come away with a deeply rooted subjective feeling of having benefited from the instruction they were given. In fact, if their level after the course is truly dismal, their tendency to overestimate their newly acquired skills will be all the greater.

Such cognitive processes may also play a role in esoteric religions that hold out promises that are strictly speaking not empirically verifiable. For an outsider, it may be obvious that there is a fundamental difference between empirical statements such as "this level of initiation gives you a higher IQ" and the attribution of nonempirical characteristics such as "this level of initiation brings you closer to enlightenment." From a logical point of view, this distinction is certainly valid. However, it is by no means certain that the heuristics involved when somebody wishes to gauge their intelligence are qualitatively distinct from those used to judge their degree of enlightenment. Normatively, a heightened IQ can only be measured by taking the appropriate tests. Informally, however, it is quite likely that such purported progress will be judged merely through subjective confirmation. And just as a quick memory search will locate instances of having behaved in a way confirming one's self-image of being more intelligent, another rough and ready search can confirm that one's behavior is coherent with some vague concept of what it means to be enlightened.

ESOTERICISM AND MAINSTREAM SOCIETY

Esotericism is a topic that fascinates surrounding society and defines the relations between religions based on initiatory knowledge and those who stand outside these movements. Several ideological movements in the post-Enlightenment West are based on the idea that other, more ancient cultures drew spiritual nourishment from sacred mysteries upheld by groups of initiates. A specific critique of modernity, often connected with political sympathies that range from the conservative to the far-right end of the spectrum, is connected with the idea that these ancient mysteries should be tapped into in order to revitalize our own society. The cultural malaise that our society is allegedly experiencing is, according to this argument, a direct result of the loss in the modern West of such initiatory insight. In the most benign versions, this historiography blames the ills of the West on the lack of guiding myths and symbols interpreted under the aegis of the more spiritually enlightened. The most malignant versions of this topos arose in German academic circles in the first decades of the twentieth century. Nazi historians of religions such as Otto Höfler projected politically expedient fantasies on the past by describing in nostalgic terms the initiatory bonding that took place in Germanic male mystery cults, in which Aryan youths were imbued with warlike virtues (Höfler 1934; for a discussion, cf. Arvidsson 2000: 225–236).

Such approving secondhand interpretations of initiatory knowledge were highly influential in the period from Romanticism to the end of the Third Reich. However, the concepts of secrecy and of elite groups of initiates have become increasingly offensive to the egalitarian sensibilities of the contemporary West. Many successful currents have adapted to this cultural shift. Thus, a few decades ago the arguably most influential forum for Jungian interpretations of religion was an elitist quasi-religious movement, the yearly Eranos conferences. A select and exclusively male group of scholars would, under ritualized forms, interpret symbols and myths in front of an audience. This audience was kept a passive recipient of the wisdom of this elite, and questions were not allowed (Hakl 2001: 101). Largely due to the influence of Joseph Campbell, Jungian religiosity today has a much more egalitarian flavor and is primarily spread through bestsellers sold in New Age and metaphysical bookshops. From the contemporary perspective, the most obvious relation between mainstream society and movements that still have a strongly esoteric structure is one of conflict. Minority religions draw criticism on many fronts, which run the gamut from skeptics who argue that the empirical claims are not valid to anti-cult organizations that present minority religions as evil organizations that brainwash their adherents. Esotericism invites further, specific forms of hostile reactions.

Outsiders may go to great lengths in order to unmask and make public the knowledge of the initiated. The movement may in turn engage in what Simmel (1992: 405) called aggressive defense, including legal action. When disclosed, the "higher knowledge" that is revealed often turns out to be something that to the outsider is either quite banal or incomprehensible. When on a couple of occasions the privileged religious knowledge of antique mystery cults was revealed to a wider audience, the contents were trivial or already well known to the public (Martin 1995: 109). In the contemporary West, the most publicizedreligious secrets to be revealed have been the documents of the higher levels of Scientology. These texts have been made public on the Internet and have generally been formulated in an arcane vocabulary that is all but unintelligible to outsiders. Less dramatically, the details of Reiki initiation rites have also been published (see, e.g., Stein 1995: 54–65, 94–104). They have shown themselves to consist of symbols that to the outsider are entirely meaningless, but that to the believer are an essential part of the instructions for how to perform a correct ritual. The privileged knowledge of an esoteric religion is thus only meaningful within the world of the religious movement itself.

The fact that the forms of knowledge a movement defines as "higher" has no value in the eyes of outsiders has led to predictable hostile responses. Critics can argue that the price, literally or figuratively speaking, of achieving a higher level can be too steep. Scientology has been repeatedly criticized for the quite considerable sums of money charged for its courses and for the allegedly dubious methods by which some members have been persuaded to gather the necessary funds to purchase the very costly higher-level courses. Although most of its writings are public, the various Operating Thetan or OT level documents are carefully protected by the Church of Scientology. Access is only permitted to members who, according to the soteriological and ritual criteria of the Church, are spiritually and ethically ready to consult this material. Fees totaling thousands of dollars are paid by some members to be allowed to read and study all eight levels of the documents.[9] Scientology has engaged in legal battles in order to prevent the public from gaining access to this material. In one particularly contentious case, a former Scientology member, Steven Fishman, was convicted of fraud. In an interview for *Time Magazine*, Fishman claimed that Scientology had pressured him to get the money to pay for courses. Scientology subsequently sued for slander. When Fishman was brought to court, he used parts of several restricted Scientology documents in his defense. These texts thereby entered the public domain and were thus freely available at the court library. The Church, in turn, had some of its members take turns reading these texts, which effectively prevented non-Scientologists from gaining access to them.

It can be argued by critics that the knowledge attained on the higher levels is entirely spurious. In Transcendental Meditation, even the entry level of becoming a meditator is associated with secret knowledge. TM instructors have routinely told initiates that the mantra disclosed during the ritual of initiation is unique to each individual, and that it must not be revealed to anybody else. As might be expected, the secret has not always been perfectly kept. One of the ways that critics have attacked TM has been to show that the mantras are in fact not unique at all, and that they are actually given to initiates according to a simple and quite mechanical system. Lists of mantras have circulated, according to which the mantra is simply determined by the gender and age of each initiate (Scott 1978).

And it can be argued that the very fact that there are secret doctrines is an affront to whatever moral and religious values the critic holds dear. Freemasonry has been subject to such criticism throughout its history. A classic accusation along these lines is Walton Hannah's *Darkness Visible*. The brunt of his argument is that the oaths of secrecy and the penalties associated with the oaths are pagan. The popularity of this argument in Christian anti-Masonic circles can be judged by the fact that this volume, first published in 1952, is at the time of writing still in print.

Judging from some of these hostile reactions, esoteric groups would seem to be minority religions that exist in a considerable amount of tension with surrounding society. Nevertheless, every religious movement also lives in symbiosis with its cultural context. The elite knowledge of the initiates will characteristically be constructed through a bricolage of culturally available myths, symbols, and rituals. The case of Scientology is, once again, instructive. Few movements have exhibited such a high degree of conflict with outsiders. Nevertheless, seen from a different angle, Scientology is entirely dependent on elements that are taken from mainstream society. Much of its doctrines are closely related to forms of popular psychology developed at roughly the same time that L. Ron Hubbard created the beginnings of what would become Scientology, that is, the 1950s. According to his theory, Dianetics, the human mind consists of two components: the analytical mind and the reactive mind. The difference between them is roughly analogous to the psychoanalytical concepts of the conscious versus unconscious mind. And as in Freud's theories, the unconscious mind contains traces of traumatic events. These are, in Hubbard's terminology, recorded as engrams.

The basic ritual of Scientology—auditing—functions as an analogy of the therapeutic session of more mainstream forms of therapy. It is by ritually removing the engrams that one can reach higher stages. The form of the auditing ritual itself is also the product of a modern age. Auditing is assisted by use of a specially designed ritual apparatus, the E-Meter. This apparatus, according to the belief system of Scientology, helps locate problem areas by detecting and displaying the state of the person being audited. Anthropologist Roy Rappaport (1999: 141–145) has described an important aspect of ritual objects: they tend to stand indexically for something intangible. Thus, what is represented by the E-Meter is something insubstantial: the ritual object displays to the participants a generally hidden quality of the person. The modernist force of this particular ritual object stems from the rhetorical ethos associated with technology: the image of objectivity and science rather than faith.

As one ascends further into the levels of Scientology, new doctrinal points are revealed. A variety of problems afflicting the human race are explained as caused by an event that took place 75 million years ago. Humanity lives in an illusion that is due to a long chain of events ultimately traceable back to a cosmic cataclysm caused by the ruler of our local part of the universe, an entity named Xenu. These esoteric doctrines are clearly influenced by science fiction themes of contemporary popular culture.

ESOTERICISM AND RELIGIOUS CHANGE

Such common denominators that unite religions that are esoteric in the typological sense of the term substantiate my claim that this use of the word "esotericism" is a fruitful one for a synchronic analysis of the form and function of religion. Of course, this does not in any way imply that a typological usage is of no interest for a scholar interested in historical processes. On the contrary, an understanding of esotericism that is both typological and informed with a sensibility to historical change opens up a comparative perspective and can generate research questions. This section will address one such topic: how does a religious praxis, traditionally built on the premise that there is a form of privileged knowledge accessible to the elect few, accommodate the changes of a surrounding culture that places increasing faith in individualism and democracy and can be deeply mistrustful of authoritative voices?

Some esoteric movements have undergone a considerable drift toward democratization. Earlier positions elaborate on the concept of spiritual initiations. According to one prevalent myth, ancient wisdom has been brought to the world due to the efforts of a handful of great initiates. Gradually, these openly elitist claims have given way to a half-hearted egalitarianism. On the one hand, it is claimed that what was once a higher form of insight is now a mode of knowledge potentially open to all. On the other hand, those who successfully claim the ability to relay information from transcendent sources remain unquestioned authorities within their respective currents. A short survey of three historically related movements, each associated with a particular period in time, illustrates how this process has taken place.[10] All three are Western esoteric movements in the historical sense. All three are to varying extents also esoteric in the typological sense.

In the 1870s and 1880s, Helena Blavatsky (1831–1891) created a vast synthesis of occult thought called Theosophy (Campbell 1980; Ellwood 1986). The doctrines of theosophy were supposedly revealed to her from a group of spiritual masters of Oriental origin. The multitiered concept of knowledge manifested itself in several ways. The hidden masters were organized in a hierarchy. The doctrines were transmitted to a very small number of people, among whom Blavatsky retained a paramount position as the prime exegete of this higher knowledge. At the same time, the esotericism was somewhat ambivalent. Blavatsky's main opus carries the fitting title *The Secret Doctrine*. Nevertheless, these purported secrets could be perused by anybody who was willing to purchase a copy of her book.

Controversies regarding the access to this superior knowledge came to plague the Theosophical Society. These problematic issues have been amply documented in specialized literature: conflicts over the leadership issue after Blavatsky's death and the concomitant fission of the society into several factions; the split between the German branch that followed Rudolf Steiner into a new organization, the

Anthroposophical Society; and the controversies that led to the expulsion of Alice Bailey from the Theosophical Society (for theosophy, see Campbell 1980; for anthroposophy, see Ahern 1984).

The founder of anthroposophy, Rudolf Steiner (1861–1925), took a decisive step toward democratization of initiatory knowledge. In his texts, the process of gaining higher insight is presented as an activity initiated by the adept himself. Not only did Steiner access esoteric wisdom, he also gave detailed instructions for would-be followers. Steiner no longer presented privileged knowledge as a unique gift, but as the fruit of correct technical procedure (see, e.g., Steiner 1997: 281–375). Nevertheless, democratization is half-hearted at best: his position within the anthroposophical movement has not been matched by a single of his disciples. The implicit goal of the anthroposophical path to knowledge would seem to be to reproduce the doctrinal statements already presented by Steiner.

Whereas theosophy and anthroposophy are structured movements, the New Age is an umbrella term for a rather amorphous collection of contemporary practices and beliefs. Any definition that tries to encompass the doctrinal contents and ritual practices of the New Age will to some extent depend on the choices of the scholar. This problem is made yet more complicated by the fact that the label "New Age" has acquired negative connotations for some of the spokespersons who by most scholarly accounts are influential in forming New Age beliefs. Wouter Hanegraaff's standard monograph on the subject circumscribes the New Age as a form of nonsectarian religiosity that emerged in the West in the mid-1970s and crystallized around a few areas of interest: channeling, healing and personal growth, New Age science, neo-paganism, and the prospect of social or personal transformation (Hanegraaff 1996: 7–19). To these might be added divination in the form of astrology, the tarot, runes, the I Ching, and other methods.

Many of these doctrines and rituals are ultimately rooted in the theosophical tradition. However, the legitimizing claims proffered by New Age spokespersons tend to differ substantially from those given by leaders of centralized movements. The amorphous and eclectic nature of the New Age is linked with the changing attitudes to privileged knowledge in the contemporary West. Spokespersons for this form of religiosity can insist that the New Age worldview is ultimately concerned with inner, personal transformation, and that there should be many different paths toward this transformation since we have different needs and have reached different stages of spiritual evolution. One of the tenets stressed in much of the New Age literature is that we should believe only what feels right to us (Heelas 1996: 21–23).

Nevertheless, this individualism in a sense masks a hidden elitism. Hanegraaff has pointed out a fundamental paradox in the New Age literature: although New Agers insist on the primacy of personal experience, the doctrines and rituals expounded in the literature are nevertheless largely based on the revelations accorded to a small number of religious virtuosi (Hanegraaff 1996: 27). Furthermore, the tendency toward individualism exists in tension with another basic New Age tenet, that of spiritual evolution. New Age doctrines stress the concept of progress and typically reckon with the existence of a host of beings that have reached a higher level of spiritual insight than ordinary humans. Some experiences would seem to be more valid than others.

There are several ways of handling the apparent contradiction between an egalitarian ethos and the belief in privileged knowledge revealed from higher sources. First, the spiritually evolved superhuman beings are generally treated with camaraderie rather than deference. Verbal exchanges with ascended masters, extraterrestrial intelligences, angels, or beings from higher spiritual planes resemble everyday conversation rather than, for example, traditional prayer. It is probably no coincidence that a best-selling New Age book of the late 1990s (by Neale Donald Walsch) bears the title *Conversations with God*. Second, the recipients of revealed knowledge are often depicted in humble terms. The spiritual entity "Ambres" is channeled by a carpenter, "Lazaris" by an insurance salesman, "Seth" by a housewife, the source of *A Course in Miracles* by a psychologist with no overt religious inclinations. Third, the ability to receive channeled messages can be portrayed as a skill available to anybody. There are even instruction manuals for those who wish to become channels (Roman and Packer 1987).

In a movement with no designated leaders, there are subtler mechanisms than the sheer exercise of authority that prevent the New Age from fragmenting into an anarchic subculture in which all doctrines and rituals are perceived as equally valid. One of the most robust findings of cognitive psychology is that any statement that one hears or reads is only likely to be accepted if it accords with the beliefs that one already holds (see, e.g., Lord, Ross, and Lepper 1979). The consequences for a rather amorphous religiosity such as the New Age are obvious. There are no censors prohibiting anybody from presenting whatever arguments and propositions they please. However, these innovations do not stand equal chances of being adopted by other people. From the insider's perspective, privileged knowledge is information that comes from the spiritually most enlightened sources. From the outsider's perspective, what is constructed as privileged knowledge in New Age circles is crucially dependent on specific social and cognitive mechanisms. The doctrines and rituals created by the most influential spokespersons of the New Age become standards of reference against which any innovations are judged. If a new book conforms with the language already in use and the ideas already prevalent in large sectors of the New Age milieu, it stands a good chance of being accepted by others. If it departs radically, the risk of being rejected increases. In this process, certain individuals function as gatekeepers. A book that influential publishers believe will conform to the expectations of a sizeable readership will be much more intensely promoted than its rivals. Thus, prominent talk-show hosts can be approached in the hope that they will endorse the book. With the appropriate marketing efforts and a bit of luck, the doctrines and rituals of this new volume can become elevated to the rank of higher knowledge for large sections of the New Age.

Only in certain sectors of the New Age does initiation into a select in-group still hold a significant place in defining privileged knowledge. One of the most characteristic New Age activities that contains initiation rituals is Reiki healing (Hammer 2001: 1–2, 139–140; Melton 2001). Since Reiki is a ritualized laying on of hands, the ability to heal through Reiki is, in theory, not a question of skill or knowledge. Reiki is said to be a universal life force for which the healer merely acts as a channel. Nevertheless, a distinct boundary is drawn between Reiki and other forms of ritualized laying on of hands. The right to call oneself a Reiki healer is passed on through a chain of masters and adepts, via a ritual of initiation. From the stage of beginner to that of master, the adept typically passes a number of clearly predefined stages. At the highest stage, the Reiki Master has the right to initiate other adepts. In this way a chain of succession has been established, going back via a Japanese-Hawaiian woman by the name of Hawayo Takata, to the semi-legendary nineteenth-century founder Mikao Usui. For the inner circle of practitioners, Reiki has the structure of a hierarchically constituted pyramid, with beginners at the bottom and the charismatic founders at the top.

In many ways, Reiki healing is a form of esoteric knowledge profoundly influenced by the characteristics of modern society. For Freemasons, the crucial precondition for gaining access to the movement was moral worth, as this concept was defined by the highest-ranking members. In associations focused on the performance of rituals of magic, knowledge of the arcana of their occult craft was paramount. What are the criteria that allow one to ascend the ladder of Reiki? The principal threshold to access the higher levels is the ability to raise the funds necessary to pay the initiation fee. In a society permeated by the ideals of the market economy, it should come as no surprise that access to esoteric knowledge can be treated like any other commodity.

NOTES

I would like to thank Wouter Hanegraaff for his many valuable comments on this text; Dag Prawitz for his helpful remarks on the philosophical issues involved in setting up criteria of classification; Olle Qvarnström for information on Transcendental Meditation; Dorthe Refslund for generously sharing her knowledge and her material on Scientology; and Mikael Rothstein for data on TM and Scientology.

1. The fact that the term "esotericism" is a scholarly construct is discussed at length in Hanegraaff 1998.

2. Quoted from *Webster's New World College Dictionary*. Among the recent literature in which esotericism is used in this sense, one finds e.g., Stroumsa 1995, Cousins 1997, and Rothstein 2001.

3. The latter is the Renaissance interpretation of certain late Hellenistic texts known as the Corpus Hermeticum, texts that gained an enormous importance by being mistakenly ascribed to an Egyptian sage from the time of Moses. For a classic discussion of Renaissance hermeticism, see Yates 1964.

4. For the philosophical aspects of classification, see, e.g., Hospers 1967: 44–47.

5. The historical definition of Western esotericism is of course one among many reflections of traditional academic politics within the study of religion, in which scholarship is built up around more or less arbitrarily defined sections of space and time. Similarly, Buddhist studies as an academic field builds on the presupposition that there are interesting common denominators between, e.g., the canonization of certain Pali texts, rituals of exorcism on Sri Lanka, sectarian schisms in Tibetan history, and the missionary efforts of D. T. Suzuki. Historically, such links of course exist; from any other perspective, this is an assumption that certainly can be problematized.

6. The description of the ritual is summarized from personal field notes.

7. The Word of Wisdom is part of one of the canonical scriptures of the Mormon church and can be found in chapter 89 of *Doctrines and Covenants*.

8. The bulk of this discussion of the esoteric nature of Scientology is a summary of Stark and Bainbridge 1985, chap. 12.

9. In view of the criticisms of Scientology, it should perhaps be noted that members can also reach many of the soteriological steps through coauditing, i.e., a process whereby auditors in training, as part of this training, carry out the auditing ritual on each other.

10. The discussion that follows is abstracted from a more detailed analysis in Hammer 2001.

REFERENCES

Ahern, Geoffrey. 1984. *Sun at Midnight: The Rudolf Steiner Movement and the Western Esoteric Tradition*. Wellingborough: Aquarian Press.

Arvidsson, Stefan. 2000. *Ariska idoler: Den indoeuropeiska mytologin som ideologi och vetenskap*. Stockholm: Brutus Östling .

Bailey, Alice. 1954. *Education in the New Age*. New York: Lucis Press.

Campbell, Bruce F. 1980. *Ancient Wisdom Revived: A History of the Theosophical Movement*. Berkeley: University of California Press.

Cousins, L. S. 1997. "Buddhism." In *A New Handbook of Living Religions*, ed. J. R. Hinnells, 369–444. Harmondsworth: Penguin.

Dahl, Larry E. 1995. "Degrees of Glory." In *The Encyclopedia of Mormonism*, ed. D. Ludlow et al. New York: Macmillan.

Dahlén, Rune. 1992. *Myter och mantra. En bok om TM och Maharishi*. Örebro: Libris.

Dunning, D., J. A. Meyerowitz, and A. D. Holzberg. 1989. "Ambiguity and Self-Evaluation: The Role of Idiosyncratic Trait Definitions in Self-Serving Assessments of Ability." *Journal of Personality and Social Psychology* 57: 1082–1090.

Ellwood, Robert. 1986. *Theosophy: A Modern Expression of the Wisdom of the Ages*. Wheaton, Ill.: Theosophical Publishing House.

Faivre, Antoine. 1986. "Esotericism." In *Encyclopedia of Religions*, ed. M. Eliade, vol. 5, 156–163. New York: Macmillan.

———. 1992a. *L'ésoterisme*. Paris: Presses universitaires de France.

———. 1992b. Introduction I. In *Modern Esoteric Spirituality*, ed. A. Faivre and J. Needleman, xi–xxii. New York: Crossroad.

Hakl, Hans Thomas. 2001. *Der verborgene Geist von Eranos. Unbekannte Begegnungen von Wissenschaft und Esoterik. Eine alternative Geistesgeschichte des 20. Jahrhunderts.* Bretten: Verlag scientia nova.

Hammer, Olav. 2001. *Claiming Knowledge: Strategies of Epistemology from Theosophy to the New Age.* Leiden: Brill.

Hanegraaff, Wouter. 1996. *New Age Religion and Western Culture: Esotericism in the Mirror of Secular Thought.* Leiden: Brill.

———. 1998. "On the Construction of 'Esoteric Traditions.' " In *Western Esotericism and the Science of Religion*, ed. A. Faivre and W. Hanegraaff, 11–61. Louvain: Peeters.

———. In press. "The Study of Western Esotericism: New Approaches to Christian and Secular Culture." In *New Approaches to the Study of Religion (Religion and Reason)*, ed. P. Antes, A. W. Geertz, and R. Warne. Berlin and New York: De Gruyter.

Hannah, Walter. 1952. *Darkness Visible.* London: Augustine Press.

Heelas, Paul. 1996. *The New Age Movement: The Celebration of the Self and the Sacralization of Modernity.* Oxford: Blackwell.

Höfler, Otto. 1934. *Kultische Geheimbünde der Germanen.* Frankfurt: Moritz Diesterweg.

Hospers, John. 1967. *An Introduction to Philosophical Analysis.* Rev. ed. London: Routledge and Kegan Paul.

Kruger, Justin, and David Dunning. 1999. "Unskilled and Unaware of It: How Difficulties in Recognizing One's Own Incompetence Lead to Inflated Self-Assessments." *Journal of Personality and Social Psychology* 77: 1121–1134.

Le Forestier, René. 1987. *La Franc-Maçonnerie templière et occultiste aux XVIIIe et XIXe siècles.* 2d ed. Paris: La Table d'Émeraude.

Lincoln, Bruce. 2000. "Culture." In *Guide to the Study of Religion*, ed. W. Braun and R. McCutcheon, 409–422. London: Cassell.

Lord, C. G., L. Ross, and M. R. Lepper. 1979. "Biased Assimilation and Attitude Polarization: The Effects of Prior Theories on Subsequently Considered Evidence." *Journal of Personality and Social Psychology* 37: 2098–2109.

Luschin, Immo. 1995. "Temples." In *The Encyclopedia of Mormonism*, ed. D. Ludlow et al. New York: Macmillan.

Martin, Luther. 1995. "Secrecy in Hellenistic Religious Communities." In *Secrecy and Concealment: Studies in the History of Mediterranean and Near Eastern Religions*, ed. H. Kippenberg and G. Stroumsa, 101–121. Leiden: Brill.

Melton, J. Gordon. 2001. "Reiki: The International Spread of a New Age Healing Movement." In *New Age Religion and Globalization*, ed. M. Rothstein, 73–93. Aarhus: Aarhus University Press.

Nisbett, Richard, and Lee Ross. 1980. *Human Inference: Strategies and Shortcomings of Social Judgment.* Englewood Cliffs, N.J.: Prentice-Hall.

Piatigorsky, Alexander. 1997. *Who's Afraid of Freemasons?: The Phenomenon of Freemasonry.* London: Harvill.

Rappaport, Roy A. 1999. *Ritual and Religion in the Making of Humanity.* Cambridge: Cambridge University Press.

Reitzenstein, Richard. 1956 [1926]. *Die hellenistischen Mysterien-religionen.* 3d ed. Darmstadt: Wissenschaftliche Buchgesellschaft.

Roman, Sanaya, and Duane Packer. 1987. *Opening to Channel: How to Connect with Your Guide.* Tiburon: H. J. Kramer.

Rothstein, Mikael. 1996. *Belief Transformations.* Aarhus: Aarhus University Press.

———. 2001. *Gud er (stadig) blå.* Copenhagen: Aschehoug.

Rozsa, Allen C. 1995. "Temple Ordinances." In *The Encyclopedia of Mormonism,* ed. D. Ludlow et al. New York: Macmillan.

Scott, R. D. 1978. *Transcendental Misconceptions.* San Diego: Bobbs-Merrill.

Simmel, Georg. 1992. *Das Geheimnis und die geheime Gesellschaft.* In *Soziologie: Untersuchungen über die Formen der Vergesellschaftung,* 383–455. Frankfurt: Suhrkamp.

Stark, Rodney, and William Bainbridge. 1985. *The Future of Religion: Secularization, Revival and Cult Formation.* Berkeley: University of California Press.

Stein, Diane. 1995. *Essential Reiki: A Complete Guide to an Ancient Healing Art.* Freedom, Calif.: Crossing Press.

Steiner, Rudolf. 1997. *An Outline of Esoteric Science.* Hudson, N.Y.: Anthroposophic Press.

Stroumsa, Guy. 1995. "From Esotericism to Mysticism in Early Christianity." In *Secrecy and Concealment: Studies in the History of Mediterranean and Near Eastern Religions,* ed. H. Kippenberg and G. Stroumsa, 289–310. Leiden: Brill.

Tucker, Robert. 1995. "Temple Recommend." In *The Encyclopedia of Mormonism,* ed. D. Ludlow et al. New York: Macmillan.

Walsch, Neale Donald. 1997. *Conversations with God: An Uncommon Dialogue.* New York: Putnam.

Weber, Max. 1948. *From Max Weber: Essays in Sociology.* Trans., ed., and intro. H. H. Gerth and C. Wright Mills. London: K. Paul, Trench, Trubner.

Weckman, George. 1986. "Secret Societies." *Encyclopedia of Religions,* ed. M. Eliade, vol. 13, 151–154. New York: Macmillan.

Wolfson, Elliot, ed. 1998. *Rending the Veil: Concealment and Secrecy in the History of Religions.* Seven Bridges: Northam.

Yates, Frances. 1964. *Giordano Bruno and the Hermetic Tradition.* Chicago: University of Chicago Press.

CHAPTER 20

THE DYNAMICS OF ALTERNATIVE SPIRITUALITY

Seekers, Networks, and "New Age"

STEVEN J. SUTCLIFFE

> The term "New Age," like the earlier terms "hippie" and "yuppie," is partly an accurate designation and partly a mass media stereotype, a symbolic canopy beneath which a very wide variety of phenomena are thrown. There is *something* going on, everyone agrees, but what?
>
> J. Simmons, *The Emerging New Age*

IN this chapter I argue that the role of "seeker" is crucial to the structural dynamics of "New Age" phenomena, helping to explain why a "New Age movement" is in practice a contradiction in terms: a conclusion borne out, I would argue, by the historical evidence.[1] The seeker role is not, however, exclusive to New Age, since popular strategies of seeking have arisen as the primary means for the articulation of an "alternative spirituality"[2] since at least the mid-nineteenth century. In any case the largely postwar career of New Age is but a comparatively recent development in a diachronic network of seekers and alternative spirituality.[3] Thus

New Age can be understood neither without the historical context of a variegated alternative spirituality (Lewis and Melton 1992; Sutcliffe and Bowman 2000) nor in isolation from the seekers who advocate it; it is best understood as a very diffuse milieu of popular practices and beliefs with unstable boundaries, goals, and personnel.

First I examine the consensus view supporting the existence of a New Age movement. Then I outline the empirical field of collective behavior—the alternative networks of beliefs and practices—that is often conflated with the New Age movement but that in fact can be shown to have predated the "New Age" trope, and will outlive it. I provide three fieldwork sketches to help argue that these networks are made up of the practices, beliefs, and oral, face-to-face exchanges of numerous individual seekers, rather than a demarcatable movement. I construct a model of seekership roles that I apply to New Age networks. The sum is that the phenomena sometimes labeled "New Age," far from being a movement, are better understood as the utilization of an *emblem*, and more recently the expression of an *idiom*, by a diffuse, burgeoning, boundary-collapsing collectivity of seekers practicing alternative spiritualities. The field thus comprises overlapping networks in time and space woven together by the crisscrossing trajectories, relationships, and exchanges of individual seekers. Thus New Age is best understood not as a movement but as a diffuse collectivity: a cluster of seekers affiliated by choice—if at all—to a particular term in a wider culture of alternative spiritual practice.

A few words are required on the trope or emblem itself. "New Age" has been used in recent decades to refer to a wide variety of phenomena from human potential groups to channeling, from alternative communities to cosmic cycles, and from positive thinking to alternative health, to mention just a few.[4] However, the emblem cannot be fully understood without exposing its apocalyptic roots and accompanying millennialistic expectations. In the modern-contemporary period these have been rehearsed, since the 1930s, in a variety of contiguous experiments that, viewed in sequence, form a more or less coherent popular ideological current. According to this ideology, humanity is on the threshold of a "New Age," an immense cultural shift analogous to the Renaissance which will dramatically augment human power and responsibility on a transnational, global scale. The main practices expressing and reinforcing this utopian ideology have been meditation, healing, channeling, and prophecy, as well as pilgrimages to geographical "power spots" such as Sedona in the U.S. and Glastonbury in England, organic and vegetarian dietary practices, and—post-1970s—a vast range of "human potential" and "personal growth" psychotherapies.[5] Historically, the chief exemplars in Anglo-American culture have been the texts—including seminal discussion of a coming New Age—and meditation groups of Alice Bailey (1880–1949); colonies like Findhorn in Scotland and the elite "esoteric syllabus" offered by George Trevelyan at Attingham Park's adult education college in England in the 1960s;

UFO groups and others of a small and eclectic nature oriented to Theosophy, occultism, and spiritualism from the 1950s into the 1960s, such as the Heralds of the New Age in New Zealand, the Universal Link in England, and the "new age subculture" in the U.S. described by Spangler (1984: 26); segments of the "hippie" or "freak" counterculture of the late 1960s and early 1970s; and, more recently, the "mind body and spirit" communities gathered at alternative/holistic healing fairs and addressed by a burgeoning popular publishing industry. According to these and related sources, the New Age is an emblem denoting an apocalyptic revelation (the preferred interpretation of the early period of usage, prior to the 1970s) or, increasingly, a gradual but profound transformation of society through a populist expansion of consciousness and cultural values (the prevailing interpretation of "late" usage, from, the early 1980s onward). In late usage there has also been a shift from subcultural and countercultural locations into popular and mainstream cultures, including entrepreneurial and corporate business practice, so that New Age is now not so much a historical prophecy as a "realized eschatology" for living in the here-and-now. In both cases a marvelous, even perfected, future is on the horizon, but achieved through very different means: in the first case largely by otherworldly, superhuman agency and, in the second by this-worldly, humanistic endeavor.[6]

NEW AGE: EXAMINING THE CONSENSUS VIEW

Meanwhile, it would be fair to say that a broad consensus regarding New Age has emerged, according to which a New Age movement (Melton 1988; Steyn 1994; York 1995; Hanegraaff 1996; Heelas 1996) exists in some shape or other. New Age has been described as a "new popular religious movement" (Melton 1988: 35) and as an umbrella term for "a remarkably fluid phenomenon" with a "loose and subtle pattern" and "certain key elements" (Steyn 1994: 6). The amorphousness of the phenomenon is stressed. Thus Hanegraaff (1996: 1) writes: "The New Age is not an organization, which could be unambiguously identified or defined on the basis of self-proclaimed leaders, official doctrines, standard religious practices, and the like." Heelas (1996: 16) also repudiates the idea of New Age being "in any sense an organised entity." York (1995: 26) questions the logical existence of a discrete self-identity—a "New Ager"—on the grounds that "adherents may 'drift' between a range of meetings, workshops, lectures or ceremonies," a point corroborated by Steyn's fieldwork (1994: xiii), which found "many of the participants

... reluctant to use the term. ... some were appalled at the idea of being labeled 'New Agers.' "

A great diversity of ideas and practices are said to inform New Age. It has been described as "a blend of pagan religions, Eastern philosophies, and occult-psychic phenomena" (York 1995: 34); as an expression of a "secularized esotericism" (Hanegraaff 1996: 520–1); and as a "highly optimistic, celebratory, utopian and spiritual form of humanism" (Heelas 1996: 28). The label has also been linked with the lifestyles of social groups as divergent as "middle-class people who had both money and status in society" (Tulloch 1993: 213) and the nomadic, post-punk "New Age travellers" in the English countryside (Lowe and Shaw 1993).

There are clearly some tensions, if not contradictions, between these accounts.[7] For present purposes I want to focus on the consensus that New Age is a bona fide movement. I will scrutinize this argument on both emic and etic counts.[8] First, emic affiliation with the term "New Age" is episodic if not—in recent years—actually in decline, and usage of the term in general has never been more than optional and elective. A good index of this is inadvertently provided by Hanegraaff's extensive literature survey: from his 111 primary source titles, only 6 actually use the term "New Age" and none mentions a "New Age movement" (Hanegraaff 1996: 525ff). Similarly, in William Bloom's reader *The New Age* only 2 out of 51 titles employ the term (1991: ix–xii) while in an even earlier activist text—*New Age Politics*—only 1 out of 200 source items carries the title (Satin 1978: 221–233). It seems remarkable that an eponymous movement should be so reluctant to disclose its identity.

A similar pattern of marginal usage characterized my fieldwork. Consider the Findhorn colony, thought by many to be "the most important New Age center on the planet" (Bloom 1991: 2). Yet a letter I received in response to my initial inquiries acknowledged the widespread perception of Findhorn as a "New Age centre" but concluded, "the general feeling here is that the 'New Age' is over."[9] And in a simple questionnaire I circulated within a residential group at Findhorn, only two out of ten participants identified themselves as New Age. Furthermore, their mode of expression was hardly unequivocal: one idiommatically described her religious exploration as "more in a 'New Age' tradition" than in her family faith; the other described himself as "New Age and still searching."[10] It should also be noted that none of the three cofounders of Findhorn chooses to identify with either New Age or a movement thereof in the titles—and most of the content—of their respective memoirs (Maclean 1980; E. Caddy 1988; P. Caddy 1996). Eileen Caddy has told me unequivocally that they did not consider themselves "part of a New Age movement."[11]

This and other evidence suggests that New Age identification and proselytization typically is and was restricted to the elective affinities of discrete groups and individuals, rather than characterizing a coherent agenda of a large and enduring collectivity, let alone an operative movement. In other words, popular choice and local circumstance dictates usage of, or affiliation to, the term. In terms of historical organizations, the Lucis Trust (Alice Bailey's organization) is perhaps the foremost example among only a few to maintain a more or less explicit New Age identity over the years; its Arcane School continues to offer the "training in new age discipleship" begun in the interwar years.[12] Findhorn, as I have indicated, is now highly equivocal, preferring now to promote itself as a "spiritual community."

Certainly some key activists have, periodically, invoked the emblem, including Peter Caddy (1917–1994) and George Trevelyan (1906–1996) in the U.K., and David Spangler (b. 1945) in the U.S. But ambiguity can be found even here. For example, Spangler writes: "I have personal doubts that there really is something called the 'New Age movement.' The New Age *idea*, yes, but a *movement*, no—at least not in any ideological, organised sense" (Spangler and Thompson 1991: 64). But if neither "ideological" nor "organised" are applicable, what realistic prime indices of a movement are left? A more recent publication of Spangler's is explicit: "There is no dogma, no orthodoxy, and essentially, no agreement on where the boundaries of the movement are and who is or is not part of it. In this sense, it is not so much a movement as a sprawl" (Spangler 1996: 34). Such emic sophistication in the matter of self-identification requires assessment (cf. Lewis 1992). As these examples demonstrate, commitment or even longer-term affiliation by seekers to New Age discourse—or any other term or emblem making the rounds of the networks—has tended to be unusual and rarely without equivocation or self-consciousness.

Let us turn now to the etic perspective on New Age. Construal in terms of a movement is immediately problematic in that New Age lacks most of the requisite sociostructural features that would viably differentiate it from other, looser types of collective behavior.[13] There is no space here to discuss the various formulations of movement that have been advanced in connection with New Age—new religious (NRM),[14] new social (NSM),[15] socioreligious,[16] cultural[17]—and certainly part of the problem is that scholars of New Age have not always fully discussed their precise usage of movement terminology.[18] But a number of common features emerge from these—and other—theorizations in which New Age is deficient. These include coordinating or umbrella organizations; a certain normative strength—and reflexive documentation—of historical tradition; a viable level of internal stability and continuity; suitable evidence of boundary and criteria of belonging by "members"; a realistic level of critical debate, social mobilization, and proselytization; and, crucially, a confident and communicable identity and goals. I would suggest that it is precisely the *absence* of most, if not all, of these sociostructural characteristics which differentiates the New Age field—that is, the various behaviors, groups, and texts associated with that label—from NRMs such as Wicca and the Osho movement, say, or other post-1960s collectivities such as feminism and environmentalism, each of which, in both general cultural terms and specific, differentiated formats, far more plausibly accommodates categorization in movement terms.

In the face of this kind of analysis, the construct 'New Age movement' does not convince. For what tends to be represented in exponents' accounts and secondary sources alike is a remarkably chameleonic collectivity capable of denying or changing its name, shifting its main foci of interests, abjuring membership and boundaries, and yet somehow persisting—according to the consensus—as a historical entity. I argue that there is no such meta-movement.[19]

PEOPLE, PRACTICES, BELIEFS: "NEW AGE" IN ACTION

But if there is, in Popperian terms, no 'falsifible' movement, there is clearly 'something going on' (Simmons 1990) of considerable cultural salience. Broad interests in healing (psychological, somatic) and meditation (discursive/nondiscursive) are prominent in this diffuse collectivity, with extraordinary diversity evident in specific systems, techniques, and prognoses. Channeling and mediumship are widespread as means to gain experience of *a*rational sources of "guidance," from the intuitional to the prophetic. Socialization typically proceeds through interpersonal transmission via relatively intimate, face-to-face encounters, structured by small groups and workshops. Popular publishing and information technology has become a significant factor in the dissemination of both ideas *and* practices, with texts like *A Course in Miracles* (Anon 1985 [1975]), *You Can Heal Your Life* (Hay 1988), and *The Celestine Prophecy* (Redfield 1994) spawning dedicated study groups, e-mail lists, and Web sites. A cluster of metavalues—holistic, vitalistic, esoteric, evolutionist—permeates the collectivity alongside popular beliefs in astrology, karma, and reincarnation.

But rather than portraying the big picture through an overview of ideas and beliefs, I offer instead three brief snapshots of the kinds of popular practice and discourse typical of contemporary alternative spirituality. These must be understood not as representative but as illustrative (and very partially at that) of what Heelas (1996: 7) calls "the thousands of different things which are going on" under the rubric of New Age.[20] They derive from my fieldwork in Scotland, but very similar accounts could be sourced in other Anglo-Americanized cultures.

In early 1995 I made several visits to meditate at the Salisbury Centre in Edinburgh, a self-styled "alternative education centre" based since 1973 in a large Georgian house with an organic garden. The weekly session was entitled "Prayer for Peace": an open, freestyle meditation, held every Friday at lunchtime for forty minutes. Afterward a simple lunch was shared. "Prayer for Peace" had run at the center, on and off, since at least the early 1980s, experiencing waves of popularity and decline. At its height, up to thirty people had gathered, although only half a dozen or so were present at the sessions I attended—English, Americans, and Scots in their twenties and thirties. We took off our shoes to meditate in a plain room with a selection of zafus and stools. The session was nondirective: when asked, the de facto leader explained that the point of the meditation was to "let the transcendental in." Several practice styles were in evidence. I followed a simple breath technique; my neighbor told me he "chanted inwardly"; another "began with a prayer." Typically meditators sat in an informal circle, facing inward, but on one occasion a visitor faced the wall, Zen style. The session was concluded with three strikes of a small bell, followed by a leisurely period of ad hoc stretching and yoga. There was a regular turnover in participants. One young man, for example, had dropped out of a university religious studies course because "it didn't make sense *writing* about Buddhism"; later he decided to move to England to follow acupuncture training. The syncretic spirituality of one center resident illustrated the culture: he combined Native American interests with Rudolf Steiner and generally pursued "whatever feels right," including leading a regular small prayer group called "Two or Three Gathered."

A more complex ritual gathering articulating a sophisticated intellectual vision was the Celtic Easter Celebration at Findhorn in Easter 1995. This was the culmination of a weeklong international gathering on "the Western Mystery tradition," very loosely defined in Findhorn literature as "one that seeks to provide direct experience and understanding of the cosmic forces which govern our lives and inform our culture with a view to creating inner and outer harmony." This tradition was said to be "highly eclectic, embracing Gnosticism, Qabala, Arthurian and Grail legends, Celtic spirituality, Renaissance ceremonial magic, alchemy, theosophy, anthroposophy, the perennial philosophy, and esoteric Judaism and Christianity." The Easter Sunday ritual in the Universal Hall—Findhorn's impressive performance building—took the form of a syncretic liturgy celebrating an evolutionary spiritual journey. It began with a slide show of astronomical phenomena, narrated by David Spangler, which came to rest on a large image of the earth in space. A prolific popular writer of grail mysteries, Caitlin Matthews, took up the tale, equating the planet with a cauldron or chalice and introducing the Goddess. Her husband, John Matthews, followed with the quest of the Knights Templar, followed by a Jewish resident who spoke on the esoteric significance of Passover (which that year coincided with Easter). An Anglican priest resident in the community then interwove themes on the blood of Christ, the water of life, and Easter lilies. At the close of each section, the narrator poured a draught of water from a jug into two chalices; to finish, the chalices were decanted into a hexagonal basin in the center of the hall. Finally, the future was invoked: children were led in by the Easter Bunny, accompanied by a folk fiddler and singing the old American gospel song with the lyrics "This little light of mine, I'm going to let it shine." The liturgy culminated with most of the gathering—130 people or so—dancing a solemn spiral dance around the Universal Hall.

My third and final snapshot illustrates popular discourse on healing, here provided by a Reiki "master" during a presentation at an alternative health fair.[21] Beginning her talk, the Reiki master stressed the universality of Reiki: it was a Japanese term, she said, translating as "universal" (*rei*) "life force energy" (*ki*). She explained that the founder, Mikao Usui, had been led to discover a "spiritual path" that transcended both Christianity and Buddhism. His technique was thus open to all, irrespective of sex, race, or creed. The "opening of the healing channels" in a Reiki treatment, she said, was an impersonal process giving direct, unmediated access to the divine. The Reiki master duly invited members of the audience to "come up for healing." A steady supply of local women in their thirties and forties took the opportunity to sit at the front, relaxed but upright, for a ten-minute session. A simple treatment was given, the Reiki master placing one hand on the top of the client's head and the other on the upper back. The hands stayed in motionless contact while she continued her exposition. Now she used illustrations from popular science to propose a model of the universe as a vibrant "energy field" rather than a collection of static "things." All entities were "wholes" with different levels of atomic vibration, she said. Reiki healing was simply a matter of "restoring the appropriate vibrationary level" to the body in question, whether person, animal, or plant. To effect this, the healer draws "energy" from the universal source, using her body as a channel. More advanced students are taught the Reiki symbols, a series of esoteric signs drawn in the air. The master also offered "energy exchanges" in which "advanced" and "master" practitioners could gather to transmit energy among themselves. Her dynamic exposition affirmed that Reiki was more than a specific healing technique. In an instruction leaflet titled "Reiki Training: A Powerful Tool for Personal Transformation," she writes, "As Reiki begins to move in and heal our whole system, it begins to move us into the next step in our evolution. It starts to work on and break through our limiting beliefs and attitudes, thus increasing our ability to take responsibility for our lives and well being." Not only a therapeutic technique but a pragmatic theology (with a hint of the millennial), Reiki was effectively presented as a self-contained spiritual package encapsulating key dispositions of alternative spirituality: it is accessible, understandable, and efficacious.

These three snapshots also usefully indicate the sociodemography of alternative spirituality. The evidence suggests this group is predominantly white, middle-class, middle-aged (thirty- to fifty-year-olds) and superiorly educated, made up of professional, managerial, arts, and entrepreneurial occupations; it is also well represented by women, typically in a ratio to men of two to one.[22]

THE SEEKER: SINGULAR, SERIAL, MULTIPLE

Crucial to the articulation of the collectivity of alternative spiritual practices sampled above is a particular role type: the seeker. Indeed, identifying and explaining the role of the seeker helps to explain why a sui generis New Age movement has always struggled (and will likely continue to struggle) to get off the ground. But let me introduce the topic of seekers and seeking through some invitations in popular publications based in the U.K.; not only do these employ the seeker/seeking trope, they also locate the tactic firmly within a wider "cultic milieu" promoting seekership as a social institution (Campbell 1972), which Roof (1999: 46ff) effectively extrapolates into a popular "quest culture."

The U.K. quarterly magazine *Kindred Spirit* first appeared in 1987, addressing itself to "seekers of truth and lovers of life."[23] A 1997 issue carried articles on faerie healing, alternative medicine, and Siberian shamanism, and included this among several hundred advertisements:

Seekers of Enlightenment Come

To receive the light of love and wisdom wherein is all knowledge. We are Reiki Masters, Crystal Therapists, Spiritual Teachers with the ability to raise you to your full potential, come drink of the waters of the ancient of ancients.[24]

Similar appeals can be found in the pages of *One Earth*, the now-defunct Findhorn magazine. Among advertisements in the summer 1994 issue was the following:

Adastra Spiritual Resource Network [Isle of Wight, England]

From our base on this magical island we can supply you with discount books, Ascension tapes and material, tarot, numerology, healing, dowsing and radionics. Also—affordable retreats/holidays, therapies, travel, translations, and much interesting information—including Cathar studies, and ethical banking. A *personal* service for spiritual seekers.[25]

Finally, *Planetary Connections*, begun in the early 1990s, is an irregular newspaper promoting "positive" news. A 1996 issue featured stories on solar energy, eco-villages, and organic agriculture, as well as a lengthy astrology article. A two-page advertising spread included the following:

Are You a Seeker?

Searching for answers to your innermost spiritual questions
* the purpose of life
* the power of love
* the meaning of death

Insights from the teachings of Alice Bailey give keys to the path of spiritual growth and loving service.[26]

Now, both emic and etic literature relating to New Age and its host networks has identified the seeker as a typical participant. Seekers are popular virtuosi able and willing to select, synthesize, and exchange an increasing diversity of cultural practices and beliefs. The role can be distinguished from traditional models of religious engagement, both folk and scholarly ("congregants," "regulars," "converts," the "lapsed"), by its expression of a self-consciously dissenting disposition.

In fact, the idea of a seeker's quest and of religious searching in general has a long pedigree in the history of religions, informing the career of Saint Augustine, the youthful wanderings of Siddhartha Gotama, and even the Exodus of the Israelites. But in alternative spirituality the notion of a spiritual quest has moved from being the prerogative of elite social groups—theologians, contemplatives, and privileged lay practitioners—to an egalitarian model. Thus whereas previously the seeker and her quest were largely the concern of specialists, alternative spirituality makes the role available to a mass audience. As Bloom (1991: xv–xvi) grandly announces, "I see the New Age phenomenon as the visible tip of the iceberg of a mass movement in which humanity is reasserting its right to explore spirituality in total freedom." Spangler (1996: 184) emphasizes the underlying populist impulse: "We are trained to listen to experts in our culture and not to ourselves. The premise of the New Age is the other way around." Seeking is thus decontextualized and democratized. Explicit declarations pervade the networks. A resident at Findhorn says, "What brought me here was a quest, a search for myself, a search for another reality."[27] A visitor describes himself as "New Age and still searching."[28] In *New Age Politics*, Satin (1978: 13) mentions his motivation to "get in touch with who *I* was and what *I* wanted from life ... a kind of inner search," while in *Heal the World*, Icke (1993: 85) writes: "It is the *seeking* which expands the mind." According to Simmons (1990: 81–82), "Each of us has his or her own path which will be unique in some respects. At any given time we must choose the sources of knowledge and experience that seem intuitively right, moving on to other books, disciplines, and scenarios when the time comes."

For analytical purposes we can differentiate three seeker role models. They articulate what I will call singular, serial, and multiple seeking tactics which are simultaneously pursued across two dimensions: the "outer" (geographical space) and the "inner" ("spiritual" experience).[29]

The singular seeker can be found across the spectrum of religions, past and present. This role type has inherited a tradition or made a decision to commit herself, or convert, to a religion, which she then pursues with reflexive devotion: that is, a self-questioning and contextual, yet fully committed, disposition. The singular seeker's commitment is likely to find reinforcement in existing kinship or community norms. Almost by definition, singular seekers are comparatively unusual in New Age circles, where eclecticism and contingency rule. When they do appear, they are typically attached to a strong, boundaried institution like Findhorn or the Lucis Trust. At the former, Eileen Caddy's meditation practice and "guidance" messages, based on what she terms "inner listening" to "the god within" (Caddy 1992), are a persuasive model. Similarly, a high level of commitment characterizes a meditation group in Scotland in which I participated during fieldwork in the mid-1990s: its core members travel from up to thirty or forty miles away once or twice a month and may also attend an annual gathering in London. One participant in this group described his involvement as "a vocation": "My journey has been from being a fairly devout Catholic to being someone who was . . . drifting a little . . . looking around. Then I hit upon the Bailey stuff."[30]

The second role type, the serial seeker, represents a fissure of the singular act of seeking: now there are plural, potentially rivalrous *foci* rather than one steady and unifying *focus*. A serial seeker has changed direction, or affiliation, more than once.[31] Adhesion to each religion or "spiritual path" may be a matter of months, years, or decades, and any number of sequential affiliations may be pursued. This mode of seeking is well illustrated by earlier generations. Consider the following U.K. New Age activists. Peter Caddy joined a neo-Rosicrucian group in the 1930s; subsequently he progressed through neo-Christian piety, UFO lore, and modern Indian mysticism. So orderly was his passage through these enthusiasms that he noted that "each major change in direction is accompanied by a change in [marital] partner" (Caddy 1996: 368). For her part, Dorothy Maclean (b. 1920) was first initiated into western Sufism, later explored various "spiritual groups" (Maclean 1980: 13) in early 1950s England, and finally made contact with nature spirits or *devas* in the Findhorn garden in the early 1960s. Another seeker (Akhurst 1992) pursued the Gurdjieff/Ouspensky "Work" in the 1960s before moving to Findhorn; he then embraced Rajneesh. Later he left the colony to follow a new guru. George Trevelyan (1906–1996)—whom Peter Caddy calls "the father of the new age in Britain" (Trevelyan 1986: 8)—enjoyed a long career in alternative education, embracing an arts and crafts apprenticeship, the Alexander Technique, and a lengthy immersion in Anthroposophy.[32] Finally, Liebie Pugh (1888?–1966), the hub of the "Universal Link" network in the 1960s, is described as "a singleminded devotee of the spiritual life" (Brooke 1976: 51) who "had travelled along or knew of most spiritual paths" (Caddy 1996: 234).

Serial seeking thus reflects confident and energetic explorations on the part of individuals alert to, and able to exploit, the dramatic growth of cultural choice in modernity. This is implicitly a model of the seeker as "the individual human acting creatively within a natural life setting in order to construct a satisfying life" (Straus 1976: 252), doing so via "creative exploitation" (ibid.: 253) of whatever resources come to hand. But seeking has also been understood as a quasi-pathological response to the removal of constraint. In this reading, the seeker is an anxious and confused individual "floundering about among religions" (Lofland and Stark 1965: 869), suffering from a "homeless mind" (Berger et al. 1981). In any case, the serial seeker is not concerned with the thrill of a "spiritual chase" but in achieving resolution and closure. The teleological thrust of serial seeking manifests as a hankering for certainty: for *the* rather than *a* "truth." This determination to complete the quest is exemplified in the poetic couplet chosen by Harry Price for the title page of his aptly named memoir, *Search for Truth* (1942): "Attempt the end, and never stand to doubt / Nothing's so hard but search will find it out."

A third role type is the multiple seeker. Unlike the tactics of the serial seeker, which proceed sequentially and diachronically, multiple seeking is a multidirectional and synchronic activity. That is, a number of religious and spiritual systems are filtered and explored more or less simultaneously. Ideas and techniques are decontextualized and reconstituted in new surroundings and adventurous juxtapositions. This practice has a particular affinity with more recent generations, and in particular the baby-boom cohort, as when Bloom (1993a: 82) remarks that "all the spiritual traditions and cosmologies are now available to us . . . and present a fantastic educational opportunity." Hence also the intensity of actress Shirley MacLaine's (1983: 363) search: "I was working with channelers, healers, and meditation; reading classics; visiting psychic centers and the like; and trying to expand and raise my own conscious awareness of dimensions . . . presently beyond our understanding." Multiple seeking is well-suited to the task of acquiring an open-ended personal "toolbox" of ideas and practices to suit and express a postmodern lifestyle. As William Bloom (1993b: 21) urges: "Spiritual practice is something that you and you alone can put together for yourself." Elsewhere he reminds the apprentice seeker that "there are a thousand different ways of exploring inner reality. Go where your intelligence and intuition lead you" (1991: xvi). The lifestyle of one respondent in a study of alternative healing practices vividly illustrates the multiple approach, as well as indicating its permeation into white-collar domestic and working routines. A typical day begins with

> a short round of yoga exercises . . . Her meals were selected for particular nutritional benefits; she used mini-meditations during her hectic moments at the office, applied acupressure and visualization to counter a headache . . . [and] employed breathing techniques and visualization at each stoplight to handle the stress of a difficult commute home. At home she used a mantra, crystal and visualization to "centre" herself during and after an argument . . . Later she had a cup of herbal tea and meditated for half an hour. (McGuire 1988: 184–185)

In contrast to serial seeking, which through its diachronic, sequential disposition is prone to inheriting and bequeathing boundaries, multiple seeking rejects closure: all is open and mutable. In a newspaper interview Shirley MacLaine remarked: "My quest in life is the most important thing. All of it is a quest and a question and none of it is answers. Every time I think I've got the answers I think it's different a week later."[33] Writer Louise Hay suggests the following affirmation:

"In the infinity of life where I am, all is perfect, whole and complete, and yet life is ever changing. There is no beginning and no end, only a constant cycling and recycling of substance and experiences" (Hay 1988: 6). Similarly, Bloom (1991: xviii) describes his own "spiritual enquiry" as "an exploration whose beginning I continually re-experience, whose end I cannot now even begin to sense." The disposition of the multiple seeker is encapsulated in the testimony of a German woman at Findhorn in her late thirties who told me: "At the moment I tend towards Eastern religions but I don't follow anything specific, I like to pick out what is true for me and follow that" (Sutcliffe 2000: 27). Not so much pilgrim's progress as pilgrim's *process*, the multiple seeker's quest is necessarily unfinished business.

I mentioned the dimensions of experience within which seeking unfolds: the "outer" (geographical space) and the "inner" (spiritual experience). The "quest" is projected both onto the world and "within" the embodied person. Most straightforwardly, seeking manifests in periodic travel and perhaps relocation according to one's "spiritual path," which might include semiregular visits to a nearby town to browse in a specialist bookshop or to attend a workshop, or it might mean a journey of several hundred miles to visit—or settle in—a location like Sedona.[34] But seeking is simultaneously mapped out reflexively in the "inner work" (Caddy 1988: 84) that transforms the organismic self into a rich, internally differentiated "institution." The books of Alice Bailey, for example, chart an immensely complex "inner" world of subtle bodies, angelic forces, and complex hierarchies of subjective relationship, while alternative healing offers a variety of esoteric models of anatomy featuring subtle forces, nodes, and conduits such as *chi, prana, kundalini,* chakras, meridians, and astral and etheric bodies.

If multiple seeking is the tactic most typical of contemporary alternative spirituality (whether or not the term "New Age" is actually invoked), then the proliferation of available "paths" suggests that one's quest has little objective beyond that of entering into the process itself: of seeking/pursuing "spiritual growth" for its own sake. Whereas singular and serial seeking entail at least minimum focus and structure, multiple seeking quickly becomes a diffuse and deregulated behavior. In contrast to the dedication of the singular seeker and the *telos* of serial seeking, the message of multiple seeking is manifestly that of absorption in the process itself. And this returns us to the much-commented-upon amorphism of New Age, for it should be clear from the evidence we have surveyed that a movement of seekers must be both a logical and an operative contradiction. This is because the exhortation to seek inevitably undermines the minimum requirements of a viable movement and yields instead a shifting aggregate of individual seekers whose wider context is not a New Age movement but dynamic networks of alternative spirituality in which New Age is merely one of a number of optional emblems and idioms for affiliation, use, and exchange. Icke (1993: 34) expresses the emic disposition unequivocally: "Beware on your spiritual journey. Listen to people, even dip into organizations here and there if it feels right. But if anyone tells you what you *must* think, or if anyone looks upon you differently because you think differently to them, it's time to go."

ALTERNATIVE NETWORKS, PAST AND PRESENT

Thus far I have argued that the role of seeker and the tactic of seeking, enacted within a broader quest culture that has increasingly shifted from the cultural margins into contemporary popular cultures, better represents the reality of the diffuse yet dynamic field of New Age practices and beliefs than does the somewhat reified notion of a New Age movement. Yet if there is no sui generis movement, then a large amorphous collectivity, insufficiently institutionalized or internally cohesive to develop singular goals or a falsifiable boundary, remains to be accounted for. Its typical fora are lectures, workshops, small groups and societies, and calendrical and ad hoc gatherings; a few dedicated buildings, including the administrative centers of groups and societies, as well as libraries, bookshops, and other commercial premises; and the open-ended networks of association—kinship, friendship, mailing lists, telephone trees, and e-mail lists and Web sites— that loosely articulate these relatively simple, but immensely flexible and resilient, cultural institutions. The resulting networks extend both synchronically (York 1995) and diachronically (Sutcliffe 2003), constituting a cultural "web" (Corrywright 2001) that both spawns its own relatively discrete enclaves and infuses a wider quest culture.

This composite notion of alternative networks and a rhizomorphic web owes much to Campbell's aforementioned model of the "cultic milieu," widely discussed in New Age studies (York 1995: 251ff; Hanegraaff 1996: 14ff). Based on the early 1970s counterculture in the U.K., Campbell's work sought to explain the many small groups of the day by reference to a wider, fecund subculture:

> Cults must exist within a milieu which, if not conducive to the maintenance of individual cults, is clearly highly conducive to the spawning of cults in general. Such a generally supportive cultic milieu is continually giving birth to new cults, absorbing the debris of the dead ones and creating new generations of cult-prone individuals to maintain the high levels of membership turnover. Thus, whereas cults are by definition a largely transitory phenomenon, the cultic milieu is, by contrast, a constant feature of society. (Campbell 1972: 121–122)

Campbell avoided periodizing this "milieu" beyond implying its encroachment into the post-1960s counterculture. However, it is possible to project it as a model back into the twentieth century as a whole and even earlier, disclosing in the process scattered genealogies of groups and seekers. For example, such broad movements as Theosophy (Campbell 1980; Washington 1993; Tingay 2000) and Spiritualism (Oppenheim 1985; Moore 1977; Hazelgrove 2000) not only provided a general pool of ideas and techniques for different constituencies of seekers to explore; they also established historical traditions that more or less directly influenced New Age spiritualities.

Consider in this regard the Bailey-Findhorn "lineage," perhaps the most influential New Age genealogy of the twentieth century.[35] Alice Bailey was a former theosophist in the U.S. who had received instruction from personal pupils of H. P. Blavatsky's (Bailey 1973: 137ff). Bailey's general career as a writer and teacher is indebted to Theosophy.[36] Her texts and ideas—seminally, the New Age emblem— were also available to serial and multiple seekers beyond her organization who were likewise prospecting for "spiritual" and "esoteric" inspiration in the period. Peter Caddy, for example, as a young man was a "voracious" reader of Theosophical literature, including "the Arcane School books by Alice Bailey" (Caddy 1996: 30). Similarly, Dorothy Maclean (1980: 50ff.) was familiar with Theosophical and Anthroposophical literature. Nevertheless Theosophy in general, and Bailey in particular, were by no means the sole influence on the Findhorn founders. Caddy and Maclean (like other mid-century seekers) were exposed to a diversity of religious beliefs in the period between the late 1920s and the mid-1950s, including the conservative Christian evangelical movement Moral Disarmament, Christian Science, the early White Eagle Lodge, a neo-Rosicrucian Order, western Sufism, eschatological ufology, and a variety of homegrown experiments in channeling, meditation, and getting "guidance" (Maclean 1980; E. Caddy 1988; P. Caddy 1996). But ideologically prominent in the mix, if in practice rarely more than *primus inter pares* in operational status, was the millennialistic emblem of a New Age, derived from Bailey's particular construction but now following a meandering career of its own.

The above example demonstrates the kind of historical vistas that can be opened up by a dynamic retrospective reading of the "cultic milieu" model. For a more contemporary mapping of the milieu, or web, consider local reticulations in Edinburgh.[37] A seeker—let's call her Jan—browsing at an alternative health fair in the city center attends two talks from a generous "taster" selection, including homoeopathy, channeling, and spiritual healing. She's sufficiently interested in the meditation talk to visit the small monthly meditation group founded in the late 1970s by the speaker; it meets in her flat and is associated with the Bailey work. The enthusiastic and friendly host lends Jan a copy of Bailey's *Discipleship in the New Age*. She reads it with fascination and considers joining the Arcane School, mentioned in the end pages, which offers "training in new age discipleship." At next month's meditation meeting, she happens to sit beside one of the regular group members who had previously lived at Findhorn and now runs a small eco-business. He invites her to a talk he's due to give at the Salisbury Centre, discussed earlier. Jan, curious as ever, attends. Before joining the small audience she peruses the notice boards in the corridors which advertise local and international groups, workshops, and gatherings, chiefly on meditation, yoga, massage, healing, and esoteric philosophies. Like the Bailey meditation group, the center hires a stall at the alternative health fair, and like Findhorn, it produces its own regular brochure of events. After the talk, Jan gets into conversation with her neighbor, a member of a local Reiki circle. She invites Jan to the next week's gathering in a flat near the university.

Historically and contemporaneously, then, the networks ceaselessly extend, collapse, and reconstitute. Although the broad collectivity of practitioners has been conflated with New Age as a discrete subculture or movement, a more realistic assessment is that "New Age" is a term episodically articulated by seekers *within* broader networks of alternative spirituality. Thus we have a diffuse collectivity of pragmatic spiritual experimentation comprising the acts in time and space of individual seekers that yet lacks sufficient complexity of organization or criteria of boundary, membership, and mobilization to constitute a bona fide (that is, falsifiable) movement. Within its nodes and social interactions the specific term or emblem "New Age" has enjoyed an occasionally dynamic but largely checkered progress. But the reticulate collectivity which regulates the networks will outlive the career of this particular emblem—"New Age"—just as surely as it preceded it, as will the broad array of popular practices, techniques, and ideas which it ceaselessly sifts, uses, and discards in the course of practicing "alternative spirituality."

PROSPECTS FOR NEW AGE STUDIES

I close this chapter with a brief assessment of future studies in the field. In recent years a fresh wave of New Age studies has emerged to challenge the consensus discussed earlier, although some of its concerns are certainly foreshadowed in the multiperspectivalism of earlier collections like Lewis and Melton (1992), the categorial analysis of Bochinger (1994), the close textual analyses in Hanegraaff (1996) and Hammer (2001a), and Heelas's (1996) engagement with cultural theory. The thematic treatment of globalization theory and New Age in Rothstein (2001) is a case in point, particularly the critiques of globalization as covert Westernization by Frisk (2001) and of New Age globalism as a neocolonial ideology promoting "spiritual imperialism" by Hanegraaff (2001) and Salamon (2001). Hammer (2001) begins to unpack hidden constraints on the content of New Age culture, *pace* practitioners' rhetoric that "all and everything" is now available for consumption.

Often characteristic of this fresh wave of studies is a more ethnographical, historical, and comparative method, applied in turn to distinctive practices, discourses, and sites. Some of these I have already cited, such as Brown (1997) on channeling, English-Lueck (1990) on holistic healing, and Ivakhiv's (2001) comparative geography of Glastonbury and Sedona. Other contributions suggesting fruitful methodological development include Danforth's (1989) comparative analysis of American firewalking and Greek folk traditions, Bloch's (1998) qualitative interviews exploring the construction of popular American spiritual discourse, Prince and Riches's (2000) comparative anthropology of New Age culture in Glastonbury, and Wood's (2003) analysis of power in local English channeling networks. These promise to be the kinds of contextualized and localized case studies the field requires to develop and diversify its theoretical concerns.

Let me propose five avenues of outstanding research to elucidate this assessment. First, we require additional ethnographies to map the richly textured heterogeneity and subtle diffusions of contemporary practices. Three interrelated areas are germane: healing practices; domestic ritual and material culture (crystals, candles, incense, dreamcatchers, domestic shrines, *feng sui*); and the dynamics of small group practice, which defines the social nuclei of alternative spirituality and also now infuses popular American religion—43 percent of Roof's (1999: 126) interview sample of baby boomers had participated in a small group of some kind.

Second, New Age studies might usefully explore methodologies from the study of popular culture in order to recover what de Certeau (1984) calls the "practice of everyday life" and J. Rose (2001: 3), in relation to reading cultures, calls a "history of audiences." Radway's (1987) analysis of female readers' variegated responses to the superficially monotone romantic fiction genre is potentially instructive here with regard to the undertheorized relationship between the *content* of popular New Age texts—such as *The Celestine Prophecy* (Redfield 1994) and the *Conversations with God* series (Walsch 1997)—and the interpretive and practical *uses* to which it is put by readers. Also relevant is contemporary oral history: for example, Summerfield's (1998) exposition of the gendered dynamics of discourse and subjectivity in women's memories of the Second World War is readily transposable to oral histories of alternative spiritualities. The simple transcripts in Akhtar and Humphries (1999) offer a lead here, as does Bloch's (1998) more sophisticated treatment.

Summerfield's gender concerns introduce a third consideration: despite a well-established ratio of women to men (two to one) in the New Age field, with plentiful evidence of women's participation as healers and channelers, we have very little sustained account of the impact of sex as a social and cultural variable, and practically nothing on particular constructions of New Age gender. In this regard New Age studies remain by and large peopled by a fuzzy collective subject. Largely absent, too, is ethnicity. Bruce (2002: 89) charges that ethnicity is "trebly absent" from New Age: minority ethnic groups are underrepresented, practitioners largely ignore the issue, and so do academics. Certainly available demographic data strongly suggest a predominantly "white" constituency of practitioners, although here again we will find local, qualitative studies helpful in nuancing and retheorizing the big picture.

Finally, there is a need to develop the preliminary studies of the salience of age cohort and generation on the transmission of New Age values and practices, such as Heelas and Seel (2002) sketch in England and Roof (1993, 1999) plots more extensively in the U.S. As I have argued elsewhere (Sutcliffe 2003: 112ff.), there is a strong correlation between the generational attitudes and mores of the "pioneers"—those active from around the mid-1930s to the mid-1960s—and the particular symbolic qualities (ascetic, transcendental, apocalyptic) of their early New Age discourse. Similarly, the more diffuse and idiomatic significations of New Age—this-worldly, therapeutic, sensual—that flourish from the 1970s onward in the wake of youth culture and counterculture correlate significantly with a "baby boom" generational profile. We need to know more about face-to-face encounters and transmissions between and within different generations of "alternative" spiritual practitioners, the auto/biographies of particular exponents in different historical periods, and the internal resistance of these vernacular cultures to attempts to mobilize and regulate them through the power of specialist cadres. In this light it would be salutary to investigate what "spiritual" values and practices (if any) baby boomers are in turn passing on to the "Generation X" or "baby buster" cohort—those born between the early 1960s and early 1980s (Beaudoin 1998; Flory and Miller 2000).

In short, a renewed and sustainable agenda for New Age studies would include additional localized ethnographies, popular cultural analyses, and closer attention to gender, ethnicity, and age cohort as mechanisms of symbolization and demographic transmission. This reinforces an important potential function of New Age studies: to connect data about alternative spirituality and religious innovation to comparative cultural studies, thereby helping to place important but neglected and often devalued strands of Anglo-American culture in proper historical and anthropological context. This is particularly germane since I would argue that, for many scholars and students of the field, the ground under our feet is, auto/biographically and culturally, coterminous with the footprint of New Age. That is, the field of practice labeled "New Age" is for many of us the vernacular religion of our own backyards and may thereby have influenced our own perspectives on religion—its study and practice—more than we allow.

NOTES

1. An earlier version of this argument appeared in the now defunct *Scottish Journal of Religious Studies* 18, no. 2 (1997) and is developed in full in Sutcliffe 2003.

2. "Alternative" by dint of its cool, even bullish, rhetoric on "organized religion" (particularly Christianity) and even "religion" in general (to which it normatively opposes the term "spirituality"): see the discussion in Sutcliffe and Bowman 2000.

3. Compare York's (1995) metaphor of the "emerging network." The singular form should not be allowed to mask a heterogenous reality of manifold networks.

4. I indicate some of these sources below: The sheer diversity of phenomena, and attendant boundary issues, is illustrated in compendia such as Melton et al. 1990, 1991, and Button and Bloom 1992.

5. For examples of these broad areas of practice see, respectively, Sutcliffe 2003: 131, English-Lueck 1990, Brown 1997, Ivakhiv 2001, Hamilton et al. 1995 and Puttick 2000.

6. I have argued this fundamental hermeneutical shift in "New Age" in greater detail in Sutcliffe 1998, 2003.

7. There have also been recurrent tensions between "New Age" and some Christian denominations (often conservative evangelicals), particularly in the U.S.: see Saliba 1999 for a summary and assessment.

8. "Emic" and "etic" denote epistemic constructs appropriate to "insider"/participant and "outsider"/comparative-analytical perspectives, respectively: see Headland 1990 and McCutcheon 1999.

9. Letter: 28.11.94; inverted commas in the original (fieldwork collection).

10. Questionnaire data from an "Experience Week" group in 1995 at Findhorn; inverted commas in the original (fieldwork collection).

11. Letter: 13.8.97 (fieldwork collection).

12. See the end paper of any Alice Bailey text: for example, *From Intellect to Intuition* (Bailey 1987 [1932]), the first of several of her books to treat the term "New Age." See also *Discipleship in the New Age*, vol. 1 (Bailey 1981 [1944]). For an extended argument on Bailey's impact on "New Age" discourse, see Sutcliffe 2003: 45–54.

13. Such as Turner and Killian's (1972) "crowd," "fads," "crazes," and "public": see Sutcliffe 2003: 208–213.

14. For examples of NRMs, see the extensive glossary in Barker 1982: 331–358.

15. For Turner and Killian (1972), the social movement is merely one of a range of forms of collective behavior: see n. 13.

16. For example, Kemp 2001.

17. Tulloch (1993: 212–213) defines New Age as "an umbrella term for a cultural movement . . . characterized by a rejection of (modern) Western-style values and culture and the promotion of a more integrated or 'holistic' approach." Cf. Hanegraaff's (1996: 517) definition in terms of "culture criticism."

18. York (1995: 237) is a notable exception.

19. In direct contrast, of course, to discrete movements *within* the wider field: Findhorn, the Lucis Trust, "Alternatives" at St. James Church, London, etc.

20. For extensive discussions of "New Age" theologies, see Bednarowski 1989, 1991, Greer 1995, Hanegraaff 1996, and Hammer 2001a. For practice-based ethnographies, see

Brown 1997 (channeling), Ivakhiv 2001 (pilgrimage) and Sutcliffe 2003 (meditation, fire-walking).

21. On Reiki and New Age, see Melton 2001.

22. See York 1995: chapter 5, Sutcliffe 1995, Rose 1998, 2001, and Heelas and Seel (2002) for U.K. data, supported by observations in Danforth (1989: 254), English-Lueck (1990: 26), Lewis (1992: 11), Steyn (1994: 27–28), Heelas (1996: 125) and McGuire (1998: 11–13). On the "baby-boom" affinities of "late" New Age, see Roof's (1993: 63) socio-biography of a typical seeker, Mollie Stone. Hanegraaff (1996: 13) classifies "New Age" discourse as "an English-American affair by any standards," while York (1995: 42) sees "New Age" as "especially an American-Canadian-British-Dutch-West German-Australian-New Zealand phenomenon." The geo-political territories included in Lewis and Melton (1992) reinforce this geopolitical footprint, although the presence of Japan and Nigeria point to interesting trends in the internationalization of "New Age," a point supported by emerging studies on "New Age" in Eastern Europe (e.g., Kubiak, n.d., on Poland). A search I conducted on the World Wide Web in August 2001, using the popular search engine Yahoo, is instructive: I found 228 entries by region under the heading "New Age: faiths and practices." Eight countries were represented: the U.S., Canada, the U.K., Australia, New Zealand, Denmark, Sweden and (curiously) Turkey. The vast majority of entries (171) was in the U.S. (California alone amounting to one third of the US total) followed by Australia (20) and the U.K. (14).

23. *Kindred Spirit* 1 (Winter 1987): 1.

24. *Kindred Spirit* 38 (Spring 1997): 73.

25. *One Earth* 14 (Summer 1994): 28.

26. *Planetary Connections* 11 (Autumn 1996): inset, p. 13.

27. Radio Scotland: "Cover Stories," 28.8.95.

28. See n. 10.

29. This typology of seekers has profited from pioneering analyses in Lofland and Stark (1965), Campbell (1972), Straus (1976), and Roof (1993). A fuller discussion is in Sutcliffe (2003).

30. Interview: 22.1.97, Stirling.

31. To allow for the possibility of the unique conversion of the singular seeker.

32. Information from obituaries of Trevelyan in U.K. newspapers: *The Guardian* (16.2.96), *The Times* (17.2.96), and *The Independent* (26.2.96), all in London.

33. "'The Force Is with Her': interview in the newspaper *Scotland on Sunday*, Edinburgh (9.3.97), "Spectrum" section, p. 3.

34. Cf. Boice's (1990) five-year passage through various international settlements including Findhorn, Auroville (India), and the Bear Tribe (North America). More reflexively skeptical, but no less culturally significant, autobiographical "quests" are narrated by McGrath (1996), Brown (1998), and Losada (2001).

35. According to Walker (1994: 287), possession "of at least one" Bailey book was essential at Findhorn in the 1970s when a "working knowledge" of her system was a "prerequisite for any serious candidate for high office." Recent evidence for the abiding influence of Bailey on Findhorn includes the practice of a daily meditation for peace using Bailey's "Great Invocation" in the wake of the attack on the World Trade Center in New York in September 2001.

36. Before her break with the Theosophical Society in the early 1920s she worked at its American headquarters, married its national secretary; published material from her

first book in the Society's journal, and taught classes on Blavatsky's *Secret Doctrine* in her early years as an independent occultist (Bailey 1973: 133). Ellwood (1995: 321) describes Bailey's approach as "eschatological Theosophy," incorporating her early—and always latent—evangelical Christian disposition.

37. Compare English-Lueck (1990) on Californian healing networks and Barker (1994: 330–332) on the London milieu.

REFERENCES

Akhtar, M., and Humphries, S. 1999. *Far Out: The Dawning of New Age Britain.* Bristol: Sansom and Co./Channel 4.

Akhurst, R. 1992. *My Life and the Findhorn Community.* Falmouth: Honey Press.

Anonymous. 1985 [1975]. *A Course in Miracles.* London: Arkana.

Bailey, A. 1973. *The Unfinished Autobiography.* New York: Lucis Publishing.

———. 1981 [1944]. *Discipleship in the New Age I.* New York: Lucis Publishing.

———. 1987 [1932]. *From Intellect to Intuition.* New York: Lucis Publishing.

Barker, E. 1994. "The New Age in Britain." In *Le Defi Magique,* ed. J.-B. Martin and F. Laplantine, vol. 1, 327–337. Lyon: Presses Universitaires de Lyon.

Barker, E., ed. 1982. *New Religious Movements: A Perspective for Understanding Society.* New York: Edwin Mellen Press.

Beaudoin, T. 1998. *Virtual Faith: The Irreverent Spiritual Quest of Generation X.* San Francisco: Jossey-Bass.

Bednarowski, M. 1989. *New Religions and the Theological Imagination in America.* Bloomington: Indiana University Press.

———. 1991. "Literature of the New Age: A Review of Representative Sources." *Religious Studies Review* 17, no. 3: 209–216.

Berger, P., et al. 1981 [1973]. *The Homeless Mind: Modernization and Consciousness.* Harmondsworth: Penguin.

Bloch, Jon P. 1998. *New Spirituality, Self, and Belonging: How New Agers and Neo-Pagans Talk about Themselves.* Westport, Conn.: Praeger.

Bloom, W., ed. 1991. *The New Age.* London: Channel Four/Rider.

———. 1993a. *First Steps: An Introduction to Spiritual Practice.* Forres: Findhorn Press.

———. 1993b. "Practical Spiritual Practice." *One Earth: The Findhorn Foundation and Community Magazine* 12: 18–21.

Bochinger, C. 1994. *"New Age" und moderne Religion: Religionswissenschaftliche Untersuchungen.* Gutersloh: Chr. Kaiser.

Boice, J. 1990. *At One with All Life: A Personal Journey in Gaian Communities.* Forres: Findhorn Press.

Brooke, A. 1976. *Towards Human Unity.* London: Mitre Press.

Brown, M. 1997. *The Channeling Zone: American Spirituality in an Anxious Age.* Cambridge: Harvard University Press.

———. 1998. *The Spiritual Tourist: A Personal Odyssey through the Outer Reaches of Belief.* London: Bloomsbury.

Bruce, S. 2002. *God Is Dead: Secularization in the West*. Oxford: Blackwell.

Button, J., and W. Bloom, eds. 1992. *The Seeker's Guide: A New Age Resource Book*. London: Aquarian Press.

Caddy, E. 1988. *Flight into Freedom*. Shaftsbury: Element.

———. 1992. *God Spoke to Me*. Forres: Findhorn Press.

Caddy, P. 1996. *In Perfect Timing: Memoirs of a Man for the New Millennium*. Forres: Findhorn Press.

Campbell, B. 1980. *Ancient Wisdom Revived: A History of the Theosophical Movement*. Berkeley and Los Angeles: University of California Press.

Campbell, C. 1972. "The Cult, the Cultic Milieu and Secularization." In *A Sociological Yearbook of Religion in Britain 5*, ed. M. Hill, 119–136. London: SCM.

Corrywright, D. 2001. "Practice prior to Doctrine: New Patterns of Relationship in Contemporary Spirituality." In *Spirituality and Society in the New Millenium*, ed. U. King, 192–205. Brighton: Sussex University Press.

Danforth, L. 1989. *Firewalking and Religious Healing: The Anastenaria of Greece and the American Firewalking Movement*. Princeton, N.J.: Princeton University Press.

de Certeau, M. 1984. *The Practice of Everyday Life*. Berkeley: University of California Press.

Ellwood, R. 1995. "Theosophy." In *America's Alternative Religions*, ed. T. Miller, 315–324. Albany, N.Y.: SUNY Press.

English-Lueck, J. 1990. *Health in the New Age: A Study in California Holistic Practices*. Albuquerque: University of New Mexico Press.

Flory, R., and D. Miller, eds. 2000. *Generation X Religion*. New York: Routledge.

Frisk, L. 2001. "Globalization or Westernization? New Age as a Contemporary Transnational Culture." In *New Age Religion and Globalization*, ed. M. Rothstein, 31–41. Aarhus: Aarhus University Press.

Greer, P. 1995. "The Aquarian Confusion: Conflicting Theologies of the New Age." *Journal of Contemporary Religion* 10, no. 2: 151–166.

Hamilton, M., et al. 1995. "Eat, Drink and Be Saved: The Spiritual Significance of Alternative Diets." *Social Compass* 42, no. 4: 497–511.

Hammer, O. 2001a. *Claiming Knowledge: Strategies of Epistemology from Theosophy to the New Age*. Leiden: Brill.

———. 2001b. "Same Message from Everywhere: The Sources of Modern Revelation." In *New Age Religion and Globalization*, ed. M. Rothstein, 42–57. Aarhus: Aarhus University Press.

Hanegraaff, W. 1996. *New Age Religion and Western Culture: Esotericism in the Mirror of Secular Thought*. Leiden: Brill.

———. 2001. "Prospects for the Globalization of New Age: Spiritual Imperialism versus Cultural Diversity." In *New Age Religion and Globalization*, ed. M. Rothstein, 15–30. Aarhus: Aarhus University Press.

Hay, L. 1988. *You Can Heal Your Life*. London: Eden Grove.

Hazelgrove, J. 2000. *Spiritualism and British Society between the Wars*. Manchester: Manchester University Press.

Headland, T., et al. 1990. *Emics and Etics: The Insider/Outsider Debate*. Newbury Park, Calif.: Sage.

Heelas, P. 1996. *The New Age Movement*. Oxford: Blackwell.

Heelas, Paul, and Benjamin Seel. Forthcoming. "An Ageing New Age?" In *Predicting Re-*

ligion: Christian, Secular and Alternative Futures, ed. G. Davie et al. Aldershot, U.K.: Ashgate.

Icke, D. 1993. *Heal the World: A Do-It-Yourself Guide to Human and Planetary Transformation.* Bath: Gateway.

Ivakhiv, A. 2001. *Claiming Sacred Ground: Pilgrims and Politics at Glastonbury and Sedona.* Bloomington: Indiana University Press.

Kemp, D. 2001. "Christaquarianism: A New Socio-Religious Movement of Postmodern Society?" *Implicit Religion* 4, no. 1: 27–40.

Kubiak, A. N.d. "New Age Made in Poland." Paper displayed at www.christaquarian.net/ (accessed August 15, 2002).

Lewis, J. 1992. "Approaches to the Study of the New Age." In Lewis and Melton, *Perspectives on the New Age,* 1–12. Albany: SUNY Press.

Lewis, J., and J. Melton, eds. 1992. *Perspectives on the New Age.* Albany: SUNY Press.

Lofland, J., and R. Stark. 1965. "Becoming a World-Saver: A Theory of Conversion to a Deviant Perspective." *American Sociology Review* 30: 862–875.

Losada, I. 2001. *The Battersea Park Road to Enlightenment.* London: Bloomsbury.

Lowe, R., and W. Shaw. 1993. *Travellers: Voices of the New Age Nomads.* London: Fourth Estate.

McGrath, M. 1996. *Motel Nirvana: Dreaming of the New Age in the American Desert.* London: Flamingo/HarperCollins.

MacLaine, S. 1983. *Out on a Limb.* London: Elm Tree Books/Hamish Hamilton.

Maclean, D. 1980. *To Hear the Angels Sing.* Forres: Findhorn.

McCutcheon, R., ed. 1999. *The Insider/Outsider Problem in the Study of Religion.* London: Cassell.

McGuire, M. 1998 [1988]. *Ritual Healing in Suburban America.* New Brunswick, N.J.: Rutgers University Press.

Melton, J. G. 1988. "A History of the New Age Movement." In *Not Necessarily the New Age,* ed. R. Basil, 35–53. Buffalo, N.Y.: Prometheus Books.

———. 2001. "Reiki: The International Spread of a New Age Healing Movement." In *New Age Religion and Globalization,* ed. M. Rothstein, 73–93. Aarhus: Aarhus University Press.

Melton, J. G., et al., eds. 1990. *New Age Encyclopedia.* Detroit: Gale.

———. 1991. *New Age Almanac.* New York: Visible Ink.

Moore, R. L. 1977. *In Search of White Crows: Spiritualism, Parapsychology and American Culture.* New York: Oxford University Press.

Oppenheim, J. 1985. *The Other World: Spiritualism and Psychical Research in England, 1850–1914.* Cambridge: Cambridge University Press.

Price, H. 1942. *Search for Truth: My Life for Psychical Research.* London: Collins.

Prince, R., and D. Riches. 2000. *The New Age in Glastonbury.* Oxford: Berghahn.

Puttick, E. 2000. "Personal Development: The Spiritualisation and Secularization of the Human Potential Movement." In *Beyond New Age,* ed. S. Sutcliffe and M. Bowman, 201–219. Edinburgh: Edinburgh University Press.

Radway, J. 1987. *Reading the Romance: Women, Patriarchy and Popular Literature.* London: Verso.

Redfield, J. 1994. *The Celestine Prophecy: An Adventure.* London: Bantam.

Roof, W. 1993. *A Generation of Seekers: The Spiritual Journeys of the Baby Boom Generation.* San Francisco: HarperCollins.

―――. 1999. *Spiritual Supermarket: Baby Boomers and the Remaking of American Religion.* Princeton, N.J.: Princeton University Press.

Rose, J. 2001. *The Intellectual Life of the British Working Classes.* New Haven, Conn.: Yale University Press.

Rose, S. 1998. "An Examination of the New Age Movement: Who Is Involved and What Constitutes Its Spirituality." *Journal of Contemporary Religion* 13, no. 1: 5–22.

―――. 2001. "New Age Women: Spearheading the Movement?" *Women's Studies* 30, no. 3: 329–50.

Rothstein, M., ed. 2001. *New Age Religion and Globalization.* Aarhus: Aarhus University Press.

Salamon, K. 2001. " 'Going Global from the Inside Out': Spiritual Globalism in the Workplace." In *New Age Religion and Globalization,* ed. M. Rothstein, 150–172. Aarhus: Aarhus University Press.

Saliba, J. 1999. *Christian Responses to the New Age Movement.* London: Chapman/Cassell.

Satin, M. 1978. *New Age Politics: Healing Self and Society.* West Vancouver, B.C.: Whitecap Books.

Simmons, J. 1990. *The Emerging New Age.* Santa Fe, N.Mex.: Bear and Co.

Spangler, D. 1984. *The Rebirth of the Sacred.* London: Gateway.

―――. 1996. *Pilgrim in Aquarius.* Forres: Findhorn Press.

Spangler, D., and W. Thompson. 1991. *Reimagination of the World: A Critique of the New Age, Science and Popular Culture.* Santa Fe, N.Mex.: Bear and Co.

Steyn, C. 1994. *Worldviews in Transition: An Investigation into the New Age Movement in South Africa.* Pretoria: University of South Africa Press.

Straus, R. 1976. "Changing Oneself: Seekers and the Creative Transformation of Life Experience." In *Doing Social Life,* ed. J. Lofland, 252–272. New York: John Wiley.

Summerfield, P. 1998. *Reconstructing Women's Wartime Lives: Discourse and Subjectivity in Oral Histories of the Second World War.* Manchester: Manchester University Press.

Sutcliffe, S. 1995. "Alternative Health Questionnaire Report." *Connections: Scotland's Voice of Alternative Health* 26: 48–49.

―――. 1998. "Between Apocalypse and Self-Realisation: 'Nature' as an Index of New Age Religiosity." In *Nature Religion Today: The Pagan Alternative in the Modern World,* ed. J. Pearson, R. Roberts, and G. Samuel. Edinburgh: Edinburgh University Press.

―――. 2000. " 'Wandering Stars': Seekers and Gurus in the Modern World." In *Beyond New Age,* ed. S. Sutcliffe and M. Bowman, 17–36. Edinburgh: Edinburgh University Press.

―――. 2003. *Children of the New Age: A History of Spiritual Practices.* London: Routledge.

Sutcliffe, S., and M. Bowman. 2000a. Introduction to *Beyond New Age,* ed. S. Sutcliffe and M. Bowman, 1–13. Edinburgh: Edinburgh University Press.

―――, eds. 2000b. *Beyond New Age: Exploring Alternative Spirituality.* Edinburgh: Edinburgh University Press.

Tingay, K. 2000. "Madame Blavatsky's Children: Theosophy and Its Heirs." In *Beyond New Age,* ed. S. Sutcliffe and M. Bowman, 37–50. Edinburgh: Edinburgh University Press.

Trevelyan, G. 1986. *Summons to a High Crusade.* Forres: Findhorn Press.

Tulloch, S., ed. 1993. *The Oxford Dictionary of New Words: A Popular Guide to Words in the News.* London: Oxford University Press.

Turner, R., and L. Killian. 1972. *Collective Behavior.* 2d ed. Englewood Cliffs, N.J.: Prentice-Hall.

Walker, A., ed. 1994. *The Kingdom Within: A Guide to the Spiritual Work of the Findhorn Community.* Forres: Findhorn Press.

Walsch, N. 1997. *Conversations with God, Book 1.* London: Hodder and Stoughton.

Washington, P. 1993. *Madame Blavatsky's Baboon: Theosophy and the Emergence of the Western Guru.* London: Secker and Warburg.

Wood, M. 2003. *Possession, Power and the New Age: Ambiguities of Authority in the Modern World.* Aldershot: Ashgate.

York, M. 1995. *The Emerging Network: A Sociology of the New Age and Neo-Pagan Movements.* Lanham, Md.: Rowman and Littlefield.

CHAPTER 21

NEW RELIGIONS IN EAST ASIA

MICHAEL PYE

THE social, political, and cultural patterns of the countries of East Asia are quite varied and, since each is extremely complex in its own right, specialists usually concentrate on just one of the countries concerned. On the other hand, the common heritage deriving from China, albeit developed in strong new ways by the recipient countries—Korea, Japan, and Vietnam—makes it interesting and valuable to consider particular subjects in a wider East Asian perspective. This applies not least to the emergence of new religious movements, which have rarely been considered in this way. Such movements, usually referred to here as new religions, have appeared at various times in all four countries and have been confronted, rejected, or digested by the powers of the day in accordance with the varying exigencies of their historical situation. At the same time some common assumptions and perspectives can be discerned, which, even if simply stated, help us to understand what is going on in particular cases. After a little more discussion of this background, I will give some introductory information about specific new religions in China, Vietnam, Korea, and Japan. In view of the large number of new religions it will only be possible to present selected examples, and even then only very briefly.

The most significant common feature of the four countries of East Asia is that over many centuries they shared, and variously developed, the written culture derived from ancient China. In the transcriptions used here, no diacritical marks are provided except for an indication of the long vowels in Japanese. Variations may also occur because of the sources used. Even today, although Korean is mainly written with its own phonetic script (*hangul*) and Vietnamese is written with an accent-laden Roman script, it is possible to see within these languages a large common stock of vocabulary. This also holds true for Japanese, in which the Chinese characters are still widely used in combination with Japanese phonetic syllabaries (*kana*). In the field of religion, one has only to think of the names of religions such as Tenrikyō (Japanese meaning "the Teaching of Heavenly Reason"), Won Bulgyo (Korean meaning "Perfect Buddhism"), or Cao Dai (Vietnamese meaning "High Palace" or, more literally, "High Platform"). Naturally such terminology carries different nuances in the different languages, just as the use of terms has shifted within Chinese itself and may vary between the People's Republic of China and Taiwan, and among widely dispersed overseas Chinese. Moreover, there has been influence in more than one direction, for some terms, though based on Chinese characters, were introduced into modern Chinese and Korean from Japanese during the nineteenth century, at a time when there was a particularly rapid linguistic development in that country to take account of the political and cultural pressure of the Western world. This applies notably to the nineteenth-century usage of a common term for religion (Japanese: *shūkyō*, Chinese: *zhongjiao*), although this has a prehistory which is usually overlooked (Pye 1994, 2002). In the internal discourse of the religions, there are common themes such as "long life," "growth," "spiritual world," "obligation(s)," "gratitude," "parent(s)," which are all based on a widely recognizable religious vocabulary and can usually be expressed with Chinese characters.

In view of these cultural and linguistic relationships, it is not surprising that typical responses to the appearance of new religions also display some recognizable similarities between the countries of East Asia. The days when China provided an immediate political model for its neighbors to adopt and follow are long past, and no attempt will be made here to summarize the historical developments of many centuries. Nowadays the political systems vary considerably. Yet even so there are certain assumptions concerning the management of religions which continue to be widely shared. First, it is regarded as quite normal that there should be more than one religion and that religions are different from each other. In other words religious pluralism is recognized as a matter of fact, and hence as a political fact. Second is the assumption that certain dominant traditions have a kind of priority. Traditionally these were the "three teachings," namely Confucianism, Buddhism, and Daoism (Taoism in the older transcription). In modern times Christianity has moved into this general category of perception, especially in China, Korea, and Vietnam, but also in Japan in spite of the fact that the numbers there have remained very small. The same is true for Islam in modern, mainland China, though on the other hand the People's Republic regards Confucianism not as a religion but as a rival ideology. In Japan Shinto remains in this dominant category, even after its separation from the state after the Second

World War. The same might be said for the reconstructed "Shamanism," which has been promoted recently as a significant feature of Korean culture. All of these dominant traditions have somehow achieved a position from which they cannot be dislodged. Third, on the other hand, is the assumption that *innovation* in religion, leading to a diversity of schools, sects, or associations, is not surprising. Indeed it seems to be widely expected when particularly gifted teachers or charismatic leaders appear. Such innovations may be regarded either as variants of the dominant traditions or, alternatively, as standing in a position of tension with them. For the political powers of the day, that is a serious question. Fourth, consequently, is the assumption that such innovatory diversity should be considered from the point of view of the general welfare of the state and the public. Can the innovatory movements be contained within known patterns, or are they likely to cause confusion and trouble? Above all, it is thought, such new religious movements or groups should not be permitted to pose a danger to the state. If anything, like the dominant traditions usually are, they should in some way be supportive of the state. Fifth is the assumption that the task of registering and regulating religions, like that of regulating currencies and calendars, is the duty of the state and its civil servants.

These assumptions all seem very evident in the countries of East Asia. Yet it should not be forgotten that while some of them may be found elsewhere, they are not universal. There are many countries where there is no official register of "religions" or of "new religions." The particular mix of assumptions about the position of well established religions and relatively new religions is different in the various countries of Europe, in India, in Indonesia, in the Americas (north and south), and in Russia, to name just a variety of interesting cases. While there are, nowadays, significant variations between the countries of East Asia, the underlying cluster of assumptions nevertheless continues to be widely shared in that region. The number of registered religious bodies in Japan is huge in comparison to the five which are officially recognized in the People's Republic of China. These are Buddhism, Daoism, Catholicism, Christianity, and Islam. ("Christianity" means Protestant Christianity in this case.) Yet the idea that the state decides which religions are to be recognized and which are not has a long history in all the countries of East Asia. So, too, does the perception that a new religion might present a threat to the established order, not only to the dominant religions but also to the political system. The matter was crystallized in a short treatise ascribed to the first ruler of the Ming dynasty (1368–1644), who decided, after having established overall military control, that it would be a good idea to regulate "the three teachings" (*sanjiao*) and associated matters such as the "network of gods and spirits," and thereby to exclude newly appearing minority religions which might upset the political order.[1]

The politicians of today, whether their perspective is socialist or capitalist, also wish to know whether any particular new religion is likely to disturb the political system they favor, or perhaps to succeed in upsetting one which they disfavor. New religions of East Asia which cannot be studied in detail without some reference to politics include Cao Dai (Vietnam), Tonghak and Tongilkyo (Korea), Taiping and Falungong (China), and Sōka Gakkai and Aum Shinrikyō (Japan). These examples are only the tip of the iceberg. Even religions which may seem to be politically quiet represent a reliable voting mass that politicians in democracies need to take into account. Independent observers, for their part, should not be taken in by simple shouts for "religious freedom," when what is really implied by some well-publicized activities is a call for political change. The negative reaction to a call for political change by members of a new religion, such as Falungong, is not simply an expression of current political power structures. It also has a historical background in the well-established East Asian idea that new religions might be a cloak for political unrest or even an attempt to topple the state. The Taiping rebellion in modern, precommunist China was a clear example of this. The role of the Cao Dai in the sequence of Vietnamese wars is also a case in point, since it even maintained its own army. In fact there are so many examples of political influence wielded by new religions that it is not surprising that governments react nervously.

A more theoretical question concerning the new religions of East Asia is whether they can properly be viewed as belonging to a particular historical period, such that a specific explanation for their emergence can be drawn from that period. Would it be right to explain the emergence of new religions in Japan, for example, by saying that in the context of the defeat of the Japanese Empire in 1945 there was a spiritual vacuum which new religions rushed to fill? While superficially attractive, such explanations cannot achieve a more general validity. This is simply because new religions have appeared at various times in history. They have arisen both in times of poverty and in times of prosperity, in times of relative peace and in times of relative instability or political insecurity, and so on. Observers of the Japanese scene used to speak of "newly arisen religions" (*shinkōshūkyō*), a term which has something of the nuance of *nouveaux riches*, only for this to be corrected by the response of the religions themselves, who felt that the term was degrading.[2] They preferred to be called "new religions." After all, some of the "new religions" had not just arisen but were by then quite well established, having their origins in the Tokugawa Period, before the onslaught of the Western powers. The term "newly arisen" is therefore usually avoided by foreign writers, even though in its English form it is not necessarily pejorative and descriptively is not entirely inappropriate. Then again, in the 1980s the existing club of new religions, some of which formed a "league" to protect their common interests, were shocked to see the emergence of yet more new religions, described by journalists and academics, without any good theoretical reason, as "new new religions" (*shinshinshūkyō*). The difficulty with all such terms is that they are inherently journalistic, by which I mean that they overemphasize the importance of a particular, current situation. Of course the particular context is important. On the other hand it is important to understand that the religious culture of East Asia has long been capable of producing innovatory forms, which in many cases turn into fully fledged new religions, at more or less any time.

CHINESE NEW RELIGIONS

Against this overall background we can appreciate the report of a Ming dynasty official in 1597, as reported by Daniel Overmyer in his fascinating account of what (in 1976) he called "dissenting sects."[3] This official argued that four kinds of people regard disorder as advantageous: the hopelessly poor, those who are by nature cruel and greedy, those who propound "heresies" such as the White Lotus Society, and political adventurers. With a heart-rending account of the poverty of the masses, the mandarin then exhorted the emperor to see to it that consumption at the top was reduced and the needs of the people met. In effect, we find here that the theory of *relative deprivation*, advanced as an explanation of the rise of "dissenting sects," was first expounded in a memorial to the throne written by an unusually perceptive and compassionate Chinese civil servant. Admittedly, a precise reading of the texts adduced by Overmyer does not document a causal argument from (a) relative deprivation to (b) the propounding of "heresies." Rather, both of these, along with lust for riches or power, were viewed as combining to produce disorder.

The White Lotus movement at the center of Overmyer's study was focused on a mantra, the original Chinese characters of which (reproduced on the dust jacket) mean "homeland of true voidness, unbegotten father and mother." From this we may deduce that, in terms of its own self-understanding, that is, from the emic point of view, this movement was neither seditious nor superstitious. The words "unbegotten father and mother," Overmyer suggests, may have had a mythical reference,[4] but they should also be understood as being complementary to "homeland of true voidness." Thus, apart from any mythical reference, the characters making up this mantra point straight to the heart of Mahayana Buddhism. As a form of rhetoric, such mantras are a little reminiscent of the political slogans current today in mainland China.

Much of the diversity in traditional Chinese religion would not be regarded by all as being provided by new religions. Should the cults focused on particular divinities such as Mazu, the popular protectress of sailors, or Guanyin, the Buddhist bodhisattva who appears in many different forms to give assistance as required and to promote the Lotus Sutra, be regarded as religions in their own right, and hence at the point of their emergence as new religions? The alternative is to see them as elements within a wider pattern of religious culture, providing options for particular providers and particular consumers. However, there was a time when these forms of devotion were new. The Mazu cult, now so popular in Taiwan, goes back to the Song Dynasty. The Guanyin cult has Indian origins but developed markedly within China when Guanyin himself was identified with a local goddess, thereby taking on the female form so popular today in China and other countries of East Asia. These examples illustrate the general propensity toward religious innovation, even though by today, especially in Taiwan and among overseas Chinese, they have simply become established as a significant part of the overall religious repertoire. Even in mainland China, the Guanyin cult is not nowadays regarded as problematic. There are two simple reasons for this. First, it is regarded as a feature of the Buddhist tradition, which is permitted. Second, the devotees of Guanyin do not advance political claims.

A major feature of specialized lay movements in China has been vegetarianism, and this has often been coupled not only with the Buddhist ideal of asceticism but also with the cultivation of longevity, which is more typical of Daoism. In Buddhism longevity is regarded as something of a diversion, since it holds the individual even longer within the ordinary cycle of birth and death. Thus such movements have not infrequently been regarded, from a Buddhist point of view, as unorthodox or heretical. From within, however, the argument has been rather that "the three teachings are one," the third teaching being Confucianism. In this way a claim to regularity and even orthodoxy could be made, even while an independent organization was being set up. However, it was precisely the existence of separate organizations which was usually regarded by the authorities as problematic, and therefore they often led to repression. Though new groups could be prohibited, prohibitions could also be lifted. An example is the religion known as Lijiao, which was first forbidden along with White Lotus sects at the beginning of the nineteenth century but in 1883 was declared to be harmless. Lijiao was even regarded quite positively because of its prohibition of alcohol and smoking, at a time when opium was a major threat to society. On the other hand, since meat-eating was permitted, the followers could take part in normal daily life without strain. In 1948 the religion is thought to have had about fifteen million followers, about half a million of them living in Tianjin. Following the Communist revolution, Lijiao has continued in Taiwan, albeit with a greatly weakened following.[5]

It should not be concluded from this that "sects" have been suppressed under Communism but freely permitted in Taiwan. A group with a considerable following known as the Way of Unity (Yiguandao) is a case in point. "Unity" in this case means something like reliable consistency or integration. It was founded effectively in the 1880s by a certain Mr. Lu, who assumed the personal name of

Zhongyi, meaning "central unity." The teaching includes the idea that Lu was the seventeenth recipient of a "celestial mandate" (*tianming*) in a complex succession including Confucius and others. Lu Zhongyi (1853–1925) was also regarded as the incarnation of the expected Maitreya Buddha (Chinese: Mi Lo Fo) and at the same time as the first patriarch of the "White Yang Epoch." In the twentieth century, under the successor leadership, the Way of Unity experienced political difficulties because it was suspected of collaborating with the Japanese invaders of China. From the Communist point of view it was regarded as "a reactionary secret society which, under the cover of religious activities, served the Japanese invaders and Kuomintang reactionaries."[6] However, it was also compelled to operate outside the law in Taiwan until 1983.[7]

The name Yiguandao has usually been translated as "the Unity Sect," but nowadays it seems more misleading than ever to use the word "sect," when Dao (Tao in the older Wade-Giles romanization) can perfectly well be translated as "Way," in line with the self-understanding of the believers themselves. Unfortunately, sinologists have long been unable to shake off the terms "sect" and "sectarianism," which reflect on the one hand the dominant interest of the political powers in China and on the other hand the continuing influence of J. J. M. de Groot's two-volume work, *Sectarianism and Religious Persecution in China: A Page in the History of Religions* (1903). In the colonial period the underlying motivation for an interest in the fate of "sectarianism" was the wider question of freedom for religious activities in the interests of Christian missions. However, the history of religions as conceived today is not required to be either colonial or neocolonial.

A major Chinese new religion in modern times was the Taiping movement, which began as a preaching organization in 1844 and ended with a military rebellion against the central government. The rebellion was put down in 1854. The meaning of the name Taiping is "great peace." This term has a long history, for the "heavenly kingdom of great peace" was the name given to an alternative government set up in north China by a rebellious movement which was active from 184 until 207 C.E. Taiping also occurs as an era name during the Song dynasty.

The nineteenth-century Taiping movement was started by Hong Xiuquan, the son of a poor Hakka family in southern China. Hong was a keen student of the classics but failed several times in the public examinations used to select civil servants. After giving up he became ill, and during the illness he experienced a vision of an old man in heaven who told him that humanity was worshiping demons instead of the creator. In the vision, Hong received a sword in order to kill demons. In later visions he met with a middle-aged man who instructed him in the methods of killing demons and to whom he referred as his elder brother. Later, on the basis of a miscellany of Protestant missionary writings provided by a cousin named Li, he identified these two figures with God the Father and with

Jesus. Hong considered himself to be a further son of God with a mission to kill demons and establish the true form of worship. Hong and Li baptized each other and Hong began a preaching career. On discovering that the "true teaching" was also being taught in Kanton (Guandong), Hong sought to join the mission, led by an American missionary. However, he was refused baptism, thus experiencing a second major rejection, and consequently returned to his own independent religious teaching.

The political turn came about as a result of an armed conflict between the Hakka, to whom Hong belonged, and another group in the region. Hong played a decisive role in the conflict and quickly found himself surrounded by his own local army. In 1851 he was proclaimed "Emperor of the Heavenly Kingdom of Great Peace," thereby becoming both the religious and the political head of the movement. In a period of weak central government, the local mandarins could do nothing. Further campaigns followed, intended to establish the new "heavenly kingdom" on a secure earthly footing. Not only considerable territory but even major cities such as Nanjing were taken over. In 1854 the threat to the central Manchu government was such that only foreign intervention was able to put a stop to it. While it lasted, the Taiping movement was a force for modernization in Chinese society. Foot-binding and prostitution were forbidden, and women's organizations were formed in parallel to those of the men. The male members were known for their long unbraided hair, avoiding the traditional "pigtail." Opium, tobacco, and alcohol were forbidden.

Against this background a few remarks may be made on the meditation movement known as Falungong, which has attracted considerable media attention in recent years. The self-presentation of this movement, in widely available pamphlets, emphasizes a meditational practice based on the symbol of the wheel (*lun*) of dharma (*fa*), which is expected not only to bring about a positive personal development but also to renew society, in particular current society in mainland China.[8] This is where the difficulties begin. The question for the Chinese government today is none other than the traditional question which has always been posed regarding separatist, innovative religious movements—namely, whether Falungong represents a social and ultimately a political threat. A relatively new feature in the situation is that this question clashes with a requirement for religious freedom (for all and any "religions"?) advanced by leading Western powers.[9] However, even this is not quite new, for the same demand was made in the nineteenth century of the countries of East Asia, with a view to opening the various countries for missionary work from the West. It is not surprising that a religion which is organized from a base in New York and which encourages its members to choose the symbolically crucial Tiananmen Square as a place to meditate arouses a suspicious and heavy response.

VIETNAM AND KOREA

It may seem strange at first sight to link Vietnam and Korea in a single section, for they are far apart and have few mutual contacts. Yet there are excellent reasons for so doing. Both Vietnam and Korea have been massively influenced over many centuries by the literary, political, and ethical culture of China. Their governmental structure was dominated by Confucianism. The Buddhist traditions of both countries are also largely Chinese derived. In this, Vietnam differs from the other countries of Southeast Asia, where Indian- or Sri-Lankan-derived Theravada traditions are dominant. In Vietnam, as in Korea, the Mahayana Pure Land and Chan traditions have been historically dominant. In both countries Daoist elements and various divinatory techniques common to East Asia have been accompanied by indigenous shamanist or spiritist practices, with ancient roots and considerable influence in modern times. Both countries underwent colonial domination during the period of Asian modernization, suffered as hot war zones during the so-called Cold War between the big powers, and are now seeking to build their own nations independently, with a strong consciousness of cultural identity. The current division of Korea into two states may be regarded as temporary, and by the time this account is published readers may already be hearing about further coordination and even integration between north and south, as in Vietnam. Of course there are and will be political differences; however, a certain convergence of economic culture is already apparent.

The most influential and fascinating case of religious innovation in modern Vietnam is without doubt the Caodai religion. The complex story of its development as an independent religion and its involvement in political events make it inseparable from the modern history of the country. Available accounts in French and English should therefore be read against this background.[10] The beginnings can be seen in the French colonial period when, in the urban context of Saigon, the practical services of Vietnamese diviners and mediums were complemented by the notion of medium-led "spiritism" then popular in France. Divine messages and revelations were eagerly awaited in informally arranged séances. Thus developed a syncretic religious counterculture which was neither traditionally Buddhist nor beholden to the new, powerful Catholic missions. It was in this context that the specific organization known as Caodai originated. In 1919 a spiritist named Nguyen Van Chieu received a message from a divinity understood to be the absolute God whose name was revealed to be Caodai, meaning "High Palace." In 1921 he was instructed in another séance to become vegetarian, and not long afterward the symbol of the single all-seeing divine eye was revealed, which later appeared over Caodai altars. Chieu himself was a respected spiritist and ascetic who impressed increasing numbers of participants in spiritist groups. The initiative to organize the new religion was taken by a different person—Le

Van Trung—and under his leadership it developed dynamically. In 1926 an official opening ceremony took place at Tay Ninh, to the northwest of Saigon. A "hierarchy" wearing newly designed robes was presented, evidently after the model of the Catholic Church, and soon afterward an impressive new center was built for liturgical purposes. In 1927 the arbitrary influence of miscellaneous séances was shaken off, and only the séances at Tay Ninh itself were regarded as normative. New revelations, for example from the spirit of Victor Hugo, were recorded in writing. Eventually they petered out. Most occurred in the 1920s, twenty-two occurred in the 1930s, and two more occurred in the 1950s. By 1928 the membership was claimed to have reached one million, though this number may have been an exaggeration for promotional purposes. Chieu's contribution continued to be honored, being described as the esoteric way of nonaction (*vo-vi*, equivalent to the well-known Chinese concept of *wu-wei*). Le Van Trung's alternative was the exoteric path of universal salvation (*pho-do*, equivalent to the Chinese Buddhist term *pu-du*, in which the *du* means to "bring across" as with a ferry over a stream).

Politically, Caodai was significant at first as a Vietnamese response to French colonial and cultural influence. Catholic missionaries were perturbed, while a number of non-Catholic French colonials were evidently intrigued and entertained by this flamboyant local alternative. In the end the sheer size of the religion caused it to be perceived as a threat. A number of Caodai personalities were banished to Madagascar in 1941, then also under French colonial control. The Caodai bishop of Phnom Penh, whose duty had been the pastoral care of the numerous Cambodian converts, returned to Vietnam and sided with the Japanese in ejecting the French from Vietnam. Following the end of the Second World War the French returned against the armed opposition of the Caodai and the Viet Minh. The French captured Tay Ninh, whereupon the Caodai forces were allowed to change sides and defend their own center and the province of Tay Ninh against the Viet Minh. When the French were finally ejected from Vietnam, in 1956, the Caodai army was integrated into a common South Vietnamese army under Ngo Dinh Diem. From these maneuvers it can be seen that Caodai was generally regarded as an independent force to be reckoned with. It was not beholden to any other political force and changed sides as was convenient. The military strength of Caodai was finally broken with the victory of the Vietcong, and since that time much of the activity of the religion has taken place, with anticommunist overtones, in the diaspora.

Caodai was appraised by the German historian of religions Friedrich Heiler as a supra-confessional religious community, the kind of thing which he regarded as offering hope for the future development of religion and the happiness of mankind. Its characterization by Frits Vos as an "eclectic" movement is more pertinent. Both the architectural symbolism and textual presentations emphasize the adoption and incorporation of elements from various religions, especially from the "three teachings" of China plus Christianity. As an eclectic and well-integrated synthesis it is by no means a general forum for interreligious activities. Rather it forms a new religion in its own right, selecting from others but by no means fully combining them.

Turning to Korea, the interaction with Western pressures and the availability of underlying Chinese-derived models provided the context for the emergence of Tonghak. The name means "Eastern Learning," as opposed to the "Western learning" (*sohak*) being heavily promoted at the time. The origins of Tonghak may be seen in the year 1860 when the thirty-seven-year-old-founder, Choe Che-U, experienced a revelation of the "Way of Heaven" (*chondo*), a term which was later taken up in the name of the successor religion Chondogyo ("the Teaching of the Way of Heaven"). The Chinese characters used to write *chondo* would be read *tiandao* in Chinese, so the close affinity with Chinese-influenced culture can easily be recognized.

The founder had been exposed to a complex pattern of religious influences, including Buddhism and Catholic Christianity (not permitted at the time). Impressed by the onward march of Western culture and colonialist expansion, he concluded that while this success was presumably based on a "mandate of heaven" (*chonmyong*, equivalent to the Chinese *tianming*, already mentioned in connection with Yiguandao above), the same mandate could also be assigned, in response, to Eastern peoples. Indeed Che-U said that his teaching was identical with that of the West, but now definitively revealed in the East. The determinative starting point for this was his belief that the heart of Chonju, the Lord of Heaven, was united with his own heart. The term "Chonju" was a challenge in two directions, for it corresponded to the term which had been selected for God by Catholic missionaries in East Asia.

The spread of the religion was controversial from the beginning. One of the practices was to provide sick people with paper amulets bearing calligraphic inscriptions. These were to be burned and the ash taken as medicine. This led to the accusation that Che-U was misleading the people, a classic Chinese reproof against minority religions. The teaching continued underground, but eventually Che-U was imprisoned and executed in Taegu in 1864. A revolt to avenge his death occurred in 1871, and though this was suppressed another occurred in 1894, leading to intervention by Chinese troops and then by Japanese troops, and to war between Japan and China. Japanese victory in 1895 led to further repression of the religion. Nevertheless the religion survived as, among other things, a focus of anti-Japanese dissent. The name was changed to Chondogyo in 1905. Today there are said to be some 700,000 followers, but many more belong to various splinter groups.[11]

In terms of sociological explanation, Tonghak may be seen as an independence movement or a revitalization movement, asserting Eastern values against powerful Western pressure. However, to present it simply as a political rebellion, as general histories such as Cordier's *Histoire Générale de la Chine et de ses Relations avec les Pays Etrangers* have done, does not do it justice.[12] The followers of Tonghak regarded their religion as a self-sufficient vehicle of revelation. In any case, Tonghak, and later Chondogyo, represented popular interests both against a Chinese-oriented government in Korea and later against the Japanese colonial power. Even today there are Koreans who, without being believers, are somehow a little bit proud of the role played by Tonghak in the modern history of a country caught between powerful neighbors.

The strong presence of Christianity in Korea, which may be explained at least partly by its function of providing an alternative to the hegemony of Japanese religious and political ideology, is the background for the emergence of Tongilkyo, literally "Unification Teaching," but widely known in English as the Unification Church. This "church" may be regarded as a Korean version of, or a Korean answer to, the relatively strong churches established by Christian missions. Key factors are the claim to overcome denominational divisions, perceived as the result of religiously irrelevant quarrels in Western history, and an emphasis on family life which corresponds to what might be called a post-Confucian, but still Confucian, mentality within Korea. The founder and leader, the Reverend Moon (after whom the media nickname "Moonies" was coined), is both charismatic and authoritarian. The charismatic aspect corresponds to an evangelical preaching style, while the authoritarian aspect derives both from his sense of religious authority and from the hierarchic concepts of Confucianism. A dramatic result of this combination is the celebration of multiple arranged marriages between believers, with much pomp and ceremony, which is believed to reinforce the values of family life. The strongest growth within Korea corresponds to the period of political polarization, when the movement profited both from anti-communism and investments in the arms industry. Strident anti-communism brought in friends in various Western countries, and the use of financial strength to support conference programs and youth programs is widely known. While the Unification Church has developed an international profile, attracting young members from many countries, its base has significant East Asian or Korean elements which are often ignored by Western commentators.

Equally internationally minded, and equally Korean, is the new religion known as Won Pulgyo (sometimes appearing as Won Bulgyo) or, in English, Won Buddhism. This religion describes itself, with considerable justification, as Buddhism, and it also describes itself with similar justification as a "new religion." This is because the founder, Pak Chung-Bin (1891–1943), having launched the movement on the basis of a deep personal experience, investigated the major religions of the world in search of parallels and concluded that his teaching was a form of Buddhism. Pak's "awakening" occurred on 28 April 1916, and he founded an association known as the Buddhist Dharma Research Association and gathered disciples around him. Pak himself came to known as the "Great Master

Sot'aesan," and since his death in 1943 the religion has been led by a series of "Prime Masters." It was Sot'aesan's successor, Chongsan, who introduced the name Won Buddhism (Won Pulgyo) in 1947. The movement has strong rationalizing and modernizing tendencies and attracts a professional and upwardly mobile membership. While theoretically a lay movement, a specialized leadership has developed which consists of married men on the one hand and a very effective order of celibate Dharma Sisters on the other. While there are temples spread throughout Korea, which in appearance are more like Presbyterian churches than like the traditional Buddhist temples of the country, the main religious center is in the city of Iksan where the current Prime Master resides. Here, too, a major university is maintained, and it is widely respected in Korea. Won Buddhism is also known for its social work in various domains. On the other hand, not being politically controversial, it has not attracted the attention of reseachers until recently.[13]

In a sense, Won Buddhism may be regarded as an impressive and influential parallel to the Unification Church. However, from the point of view of the history of religions, that is, making an assessment on the basis of perceived continuities in the constituent elements, Won Buddhism's claim to be Buddhist is probably stronger than the Unification Church's claim to be Christian. In any case, both may be regarded as extremely effectively organized Korean new religions which will continue to play a significant part in the years to come.

JAPAN

When it comes to new religions in Japan, it is hard to know where to start and even harder to know where to stop. Dozens have been listed in various general overviews and guides, with an early leading role in English played by the insightful bibliographical publications of Byron H. Earhart.[14] In Japanese, veritable guidebooks have been published, one of which has been translated into German by Johannes Laube.[15] Several of the new religions, such as Tenrikyō or Risshō Kōseikai, have become an established part of the religious scene in contemporary Japan. Politically visible religions such as Ōmoto and Sōka Gakkai have attracted particular attention, while more recently the sensational news stories surrounding Aum Shinrikyō have led to a flurry of academic activity both within and outside Japan.[16] Following the sarin gas attack on an underground railway line in March 1995, in which twelve people died and many were seriously injured, criminal charges were brought against various individuals in leadership positions in Aum Shinrikyō, and in June 2002 Niimi Tsutomu was condemned to death for his part in this act of terrorism.[17] However, it is important to pay attention to less dramatic and lesser known cases. Considerable leadership has been shown in the study of Japanese new religions by Japanese scholars. Takagi Hiroo, a sociologist at Tōyō University in Tokyo, has already been mentioned. Araki Michio[18] is an example of a scholar who takes a more historical and phenomenological approach, while others, such as Shimazono Susumu,[19] combine this with sociological considerations.

The term "new religions" is not only well established in the Japanese language but is also accepted by most of the religions themselves; some of them are even associated in a League of New Religions' (*Shinshūkyō Renmei*). The oldest Japanese religions that are today commonly designated as "new" derive from the nineteenth century—namely Kurozumikyō (founded 1814), Tenrikyō (founded 1838), and Konkōkyō (founded 1859). These three religions all appeared before the beginning of the Meiji period (from 1868), which ushered in frantic modernization in competition with the Western world. Thus, in their present healthy and well-established condition, after more than a century of eventful history, these religions are no longer new.

If the term "new religions" is restricted to religions in an early phase of development, then it may be fair to ask whether there were new religions in earlier centuries. Certainly there was much religious innovation. The question of whether vital Buddhist movements, such as Zen, Shin, and Nichirenite Buddhism in their own day (twelfth and thirteenth centuries of the Western calendar) amounted to new religions would require detailed analysis.[20] However, the question is relevant to how we view the Nichirenite Lotus Sutra movements, including Reiyūkai, Risshō Kōseikai, and Sōka Gakkai. Even if it is emphasized that these are lay Buddhist movements, in which the path of the bodhisattva is open to all without leaving "the household life," it has to be said that the ideal of monastic asceticism as the sole or even the major path to enlightenment was defnitively abrogated in the context of thirteenth-century Jōdo Shinshū. As taught by Hōnen and above all by Shinran, who renounced celibacy, the practice of the *nenbutsu* (calling on the name of Amida Buddha) opened to all who relied upon the other-power of this Buddha the possibility of being reborn in the Pure Land in the West. Nichiren, who focused his teaching on the Lotus Sutra,[21] did not himself abolish monkhood, but his emphasis on the buddha nature of all beings meant that the distinction between monk and lay were no longer important. While Nichiren's own teachings continue to command respect in the three movements, it is above all the Lotus Sutra which provides doctrinal orientation. Common to all three, and to other Nichirenite denominations, some of which also count as "new religions," according to some authorities, is the practice of reciting the *daimoku*, that is, the title of the sutra prefaced by the honorific phrase *namu*. The resultant mantra, often recited many times over, is *Namu Myōhō Renge Kyō*.

The Reiyūkai is the oldest of these movements; founded in 1925, it has some three million adherents. The founders, Kubo Kakutarō (1892–1944) and Kotani Kimi (1901–1971), emphasized the care of ancestors without personal descendants, or lost souls—or, as the Buddhist phrase has it, "buddhas without affinity" (*muen-botoke*). Shortly after the Second World War the Reiyūkai experienced a brief spell of notoriety in the press because of alleged drug use and tax irregularities. Several groups split off and organized themselves independently, including the Myōchikai and Busshogonenkai. In recent decades, however, Reiyūkai has been effectively led by Tokyo University–educated Kubo Tsugunari and his wife and offers a picture of stability. Building on the earlier idea of caring for "buddhas without affinity," it emphasizes family values and outreach to young people through various stimulating activity programs such as "Inner Trip."

Also influenced by Reiyukai were the founders Risshō Kōseikai, Naganuma Myōkō (1889–1957), and Niwano Nikkyō (1906–1999). This movement has five or six million members, depending on the counting method. Though it has no formal connection with any monastic group, its members make a point of visiting the mausoleum of Nichiren at Mount Minobu, where the headquarters of the leading Nichiren denomination (Nichirenshū) is located, and also the nearby Mount Shichimen, which is sacred to a goddess who protects the Lotus Sutra and its devotees. A distinctive practice in Risshō Kōseikai is *hōza*, which means approximately "dharma session." Believers assemble in a circle under the leadership of an experienced person and analyze various problems in their lives—for example, why a small business is not doing well, why a husband is drinking more than usual, or why children are experiencing difficulties at school or college. The analysis is based on the Buddhist model of cause and effect, with the cause usually identified as somehow residing in one's own behavior. The headquarters consist of a considerable number of large and impressive buildings in Wada-chō, Tokyo. The movement is now led by the son of the founder, Niwano Nichiko, who makes a point of being visible in various international activities.

The Sōka Gakkai was founded in approximately its present form at the end of the Second World War, when Toda Jōsei emerged from prison. He and his teacher Makiguchi Tsunesaburō had been incarcerated for not maintaining an amulet from Ise Shrine and thus failing to honor the Emperor system. Makiguchi died in prison. He had founded an association called the Academic Society for Education in the Creation of Value (Sōka Kyōiku Gakkai), but it was only gradually that the Lotus Sutra came to play an important role, emphasized especially at the time of the refoundation in 1952. "Value" was not only a general good, but came to be understood as a benefit in the present world (*genzeriyaku*). This aspect proved to be most attractive and, together with an extremely effective organization with a concerted conversion program, led to a steady and massive increase in membership. As a result, there are some 16 million members today. It may be assumed that the majority of them vote for the political party Kōmeitō ("public brightness party" or, less literally, "clean government party"), which was initially founded within the Sōka Gakkai but became formally independent in 1970. For many years the Sōka Gakkai had an institutional relationship with one of the smaller denominations in the Nichiren tradition, the Nichiren Shōshū, but this relationship eventually broke down and all ties were severed. Overseas the Sōka Gakkai is widely active in the form of Sōka Gakkai International (SGI).

Tenrikyō, the "Teaching of the Divine Reason," is one of the nineteenth-century foundations that is now firmly established. The main temple is in the city of Tenri, near Nara. The city and the railway station are named after the religion. Tenrikyō is known for its liturgical dance performances. The most central ritual (the *kagurazutome*) is only partly visible, taking place in a deepened recess in the main temple. This is the place, it is taught, where humankind was created, known in Japanese as the *jiba*. Here, too, a new day will dawn for humanity, when heavenly dew is collected on a specially built pillar that awaits it. This will open the way for a new "joyous life" (*yōkigurashi*). The pillar, which is open to the skies, is called the *kanrodai*, that is, the "stand for the heavenly dew." The number of Tenrikyō believers is reckoned to be about two million, a number of whom reside outside Japan. Both in the main temple and in the regional "churches" (*kyōkai*), the ordinary believers perform their own dance, the *te-odori* or "hand-dance," a slow, graceful movement in which various spiritual movements are enacted—for example, the brushing away of "the eight dusts" of the mind. The teaching of Tenrikyō (which a Chinese person would simply read without any difficulty as *Tianlijiao*) goes back to the experience of the foundress Nakayama Miki (1798–1887), who felt herself unexpectedly seized by a divinity named Tenri-ō-no-mikoto, or "the August King of Heavenly Wisdom" and also known among other things as "God the Parent" (Oyagami). Notice that the term "God the Parent" is gender neutral. Nowadays the city of Tenri is an important pilgrimage center which attracts the faithful from all over Japan. It also boasts a hospital, schools, a university, and a museum with a superb collection of artefacts illustrating the various phases of human culture. Perhaps not of central importance for the average Tenrikyō member, but no doubt of interest for readers of this chapter, the central library includes what is probably one of the most balanced collections in the world for the study of religions, including the history of religions East and West, and the historical development of the subject. Recently the leaders of Tenrikyō have shown an increasing interest in interreligious dialogue, accompanying the internationalization of Japanese culture in general.

Though brief, mention must also be made of Ōmoto, "Great Source," which has a prewar history of rivalry with the nationalist ideology of the state, leading to its repression with tanks, and a postwar history of peace propaganda, Esperantism, and the integration of various religions. The founding figures were Deguchi Nao (1837–1918) and Deguchi Ōnisaburō (1871–1948). The first revelation was received by Deguchi Nao in 1892. Ōmoto, sometimes known as Ōmotokyō ("the Teaching of the Great Source"), proved in fact to be a source for the emergence of other new religions of considerable importance, such as Ananaikyō (an early interfaith community), Seichō no Ie ("House of Growth"), and Sekaikyū-seikyō ("Teaching of the Salvation of the World").

As more new religions are mentioned, each with a considerable following, it will perhaps become clear that many are being left out altogether. It is with regret that I cannot give more details—for example, of the "dancing religion," Tenshō Kōtai Jingū Kyō, which began immediately at the end of the Second World War and emphasizes the dance of "non-self" (*muga*), an enthusiastic religion with superb headquarters by the architect Tange, an artist in concrete. Or consider PL Kyōdan, the Religion of Perfect Liberty (PL), with its principle that "life is art" (just the first of ten principles), its golf courses, and its artistic memorial stones for members. Or turn to the so-called "new new religions" (*shinshinshūkyō*), which have attracted more attention recently. These include Agonkyō, which has little to do with the Agon (Agama) Sutras, and the subsequent development of Aum Shinrikyō, already mentioned because of its terrorist attacks and subsequent notoriety. Another recently influential movement is Kōfuku no Kagaku ("Science of Happiness"), a businesslike religion which sells huge numbers of imaginative paperback publications by its founder. Whatever the precise derivations of these organizations, the term "new new religions" is deeply flawed from a theoretical point of view. First, it consolidates the idea that "new" religions somehow belong to a particular period, whereas in fact there have been new religions in practically all known periods of human history. Second, what term will be left for the decades to come, during which innovation is unlikely to cease? Shall we call them "new, new new religions"? Since the processes of innovation, invention, consolidation, and in some cases relative decay are evidently not bound to particular events, such as the end of a world war, any designations which tie analysis to particular decades alone will be misleading.

While a number of monographs have provided valuable studies of the better-known new religions of Japan, other religions have never been described or discussed in detail. Indeed, some are not known to the general public in Japan. A good example of such a religion, one that has between 300,000 and 400,000 members, is Ennōkyō, the "Perfectly Adapted Teaching." Based on the teaching of its almost illiterate foundress, Fukuda Chiyoko (1887–1925), who worked as a servant in a remote village in Hyōgo Prefecture, Ennōkyō draws on Buddhist and Shinto traditions to focus on family life and care for the ancestors. Members are proud of their fine headquarters, where the foundress, later leaders, and they themselves are memorialized. Regular worship is carried out before a simple curtained focus (without images) in branch churches all over Japan. The religion is uncontroversial and therefore goes largely unnoticed.[22]

Another religion which has gone largely unnoticed is Byakkō Shinkōkai, the "White Light Fellowship Association." This is a peace movement, a religion which regularly carries out an impressive liturgy for world peace, celebrating all the countries of the world which at any one time are recognized by the Japanese Foreign Office. The founder, Master Goi, was evidently a charismatic medium, his follower Saionji Masami no less so. Master Goi's excellent whistling can still be heard during the liturgy at the headquarters, Hijirigaoka in Chiba Prefecture. He still receives petitions from his followers in envelopes which, since they are ceremonially burned, should not include money. Masami-sama, as his successor is respectfully called, has called new programs into being with far-reaching titles such as "I myself am God" or "Humanity is God." Somehow this is more than a peace movement. We should also give thanks to our "guardian spirits." If we are Japanese we will rejoice that there is a special place for Japan in the salvation of the world.[23]

To conclude, consider the as yet entirely undocumented, rather secretive religion Bankeitaishisō Chiesonkyō, or simply Chiesonkyō, based in the city of Tochigi. This religion is esoteric in the correct sense of the term, for the printed materials are normally available only to members. The founder, Katō Bungo, eclectically combined elements of Confucianism and Buddhism with references to the spirit world. These were codified in a short work entitled *Chiesongaku* ("The Study of Holy Wisdom") by his successor, Katō Toshio, and published in 1979. The declared intention is to give new vitality to rituals in everyday life. This is done by practicing the "Art of Holy Wisdom" (*chiesonjutsu*).[24] Prayer is regarded as the foundation of happiness, and rituals of purification (*kiyome*) are particularly recommended. Instructions are given, for example, on the purification of one's wristwatch every morning and evening. It is quite common for the leadership of new religions in Japan to pass down through the family. However, even in 1980 Chiesonkyō seemed no longer to be thriving as it did during time of its founder. Some twenty years later, considerable irritation is shown when materials fall into the hands of nonbelievers, even when simple inquiries are not in principle unsympathetic.

CONCLUSIONS AND OUTLOOK

Even when the attitude of Chinese officialdom to minority religious movements was understanding, as in the unusual case of Lü K'un's memorial, or hostile, as it more often was, the attempts to interpret these movements were akin to modern sociology in failing to recognize the central importance of religious concepts and motivations for founders and followers. The mandarins of former centuries, some sociologists today, not to mention most politicians and most journalists, see alternative, "new" religions as deluded, misleading, or downright malevolent. They are regarded as a threat to the society. It is inevitable that innovation may appear threatening to those in established positions, and this applies no less to religious innovation than to other spheres of life. Indeed, in several of the cases the alternatives to the prevailing political and religious culture have been clear. They have challenged the cultural and ideological assumptions of the more powerful. By doing so, the new religions of East Asia have frequently played a positive role in articulating the interests of particular sections of society. In some respects they have disrupted the existing order, but in other respects they have contributed to modernization processes and provided empowerment, success, and stability for participants. Naturally the balance is varied from case to case, and the spectrum of possible effects is wide. Some religions promote greater rationality while others may seem, to the scientific mind, disconcertingly irrational. Some religions contribute to general emancipation and greater gender equality, while others reinforce traditional, hierarchic family structures. Some religions promote self-discipline and self-giving, while others promote self-interest and personal profit and enjoyment. Some religions promote internationalism and peace projects of various kinds, while others represent a haven for conservative nationalism. Indeed the pattern is in many cases baffling, for it seems that opposing tendencies may coexist within one and the same movement or organization. On closer examination a rationale for such complexities may be discovered.

In the academic study of religions, it is essential to maintain an elementary respect for the way in which believers understand themselves. It is misleading to presuppose simplistic, reductionist explanations. Instead, serious account should be taken of the self-understanding of believers and participants before attempting a full appraisal. If this is not done, misinterpretations are sure to arise.

For example, only by taking a careful look at the detail of new symbolic and ritual systems can the relationship to the major tradition or traditions upon which they draw be adequately assessed. This is particularly important for Buddhist-related movements, which, in cases such as Korea's Won Buddhism or Japan's Sōka Gakkai, may be regarded as both "Buddhist" and a "new religion." Aum Shinrikyō, on the other hand, is not Buddhist, though it has claimed to be so.

Another very delicate area is the relationship between syncretism, eclecticism, and synthesis. These theoretical or at least reflective terms should not be confused with each other or used as synonyms, as is so often the case in writing on the religions of East Asia. Eclecticism refers to the selection of materials, symbolic elements, and ritual practices from a variety of traditions. In this sense, some new religions are markedly eclectic (Caodai) and others less so (Won Buddhism). Syncretism is a feature of all religions to varying degrees and at various stages of their history. It is not a specific characteristic of new religions alone. The term "synthesis" may be used to refer to the achievement of a newly integrated religious Gestalt, whether the route to such a conclusion, itself historically temporary, was more, less, or scarcely eclectic.[25]

Since the number of new religions in East Asia is very large, especially if the full history is taken into account, it was only possible here to provide introductory information on a few selected examples, mainly well-known ones. In such a short survey, it is only possible to draw attention to the need for detailed studies. However, I hope that this will provide a springboard for further studies and reading, bearing in mind the continuities and parallels in the social and cultural experience of East Asia.

NOTES

1. For a translation and commentary on the emperor's own short treatise on the subject see Romeyn Taylor's "An Imperial Endorsement of Syncretism. Ming T'ai Tsu's Essay on the Three Teachings: Translation and Commentary," *Ming Studies* 16 (1983): 31–38.

2. The term was used, without polemical intent, by sociologist Takagi Hiroo, in his work entitled *Nihon no shinkōshūkyō* (1959), which was an important starting point in the postwar study of Japanese new religions.

3. *Folk Buddhist Religion: Dissenting Sects in Late Traditional China* (Cambridge: Harvard University Press, 1976).

4. Ibid., 238.

5. The information on Lijiao is drawn from Seiwert 1985, 183.

6. *A Chinese-English Dictionary* (Beijing: Beijing Institute of Foreign Languages, 1978), 810.

7. This information is drawn from David K. Jordan's extremely interesting chapter on the subject in his joint work with Daniel L. Overmyer entitled *The Flying Phoenix: Aspects of Chinese Sectarianism in Taiwan* (Princeton: Princeton University Press, 1986). In line with the policy of the joint work the group is referred to there, using the Wade-Giles romanisation system, as I-kuan Tao. Jordan's account includes very much valuable information based on personal observations and encounters, and indeed the whole book is to be recommended for various reasons.

8. Possibly the first academic treatment was by Hubert Seiwert in his article "Falun Gong—Eine neue religiöse Bewegung als innenpolitischer Hauptfeind der chinesischen Regierung," *Religion—Staat—Gesellschaft. Zeitschrift für Glaubensformen und Weltanschauungen* 1, no. 1 (2000): 119–144.

9. This requirement is mainly pushed by the U.S. as a means of causing difficulties for the Communist government of mainland China, but it should be noted that by no means all "Western" powers have the same arrangements for "religious freedom" and for the relations between religions and the state. There are major differences between Germany and the U.S., for example, over the treatment of Scientology, which in Germany is widely regarded as a threat to the constitution.

10. The historical information provided here is derived from Gobron 1949, Pham Cong Tac 1953, and Oliver 1976.

11. Vos 1977; Grayson 1989.

12. Cordier 1920, 4:184.

13. For an introductory account, perhaps the first in English by a nonmember, see my article "Won Buddhism as a Korean New Religion," *Numen* 49 (2002): 113–141.

14. The first edition of Earhart's bibliography *The New Religions of Japan: A Bibliography of Western-Language Materials* appeared in 1970 (Sophia University, Tokyo). It had the merit not only of drawing attention to works that appeared before and after the Second World War but also of providing an introduction to the subject in general. A second edition appeared in 1983. It will not be possible here to provide bibliographical details of the many monographs and shorter studies of particular religions.

15. This immense labor was a major service, and the result appeared as *Neureligionen: Stand ihrer Forschung in Japan. Ein Handbuch* (Wiesbaden: Harrassowitz Verlag, 1995). The Japanese original, compiled by eight editors, was entitled *Shinshūkyō kenkyūchōsa handobukku* and first appeared (in Tokyo) in 1981.

16. Outside Japan, informative analyses and discussions of Aum Shinrikyō have been provided by Ian Reader and Martin Repp (see bibliography). For a consideration of some implications of the Aum Shinrikyō case for the style and methodology of the study of religions, see my "Aum Shinrikyō: Can Religious Studies Cope?" *Religion* 26, no. 3 (1996): 261–273.

17. The time is not yet ripe to provide a full history of all these sad matters, since on the one hand some cases are still pending and on the other hand some of the rank-and-file membership has regrouped under the new name Name Aleph.

18. A specialist in the study of religions at the important, state-sponsored Tsukuba University.

19. Previously of Tsukuba University and later of the University of Tokyo, following the sociologist of religion Yanagawa Keiichi.

20. This perspective was taken very seriously in a relatively early work on the new religions of Japan by Werner Kohler entitled *Die Lotus-Lehre und die modernen Religionen in Japan* (Zürich, 1962).

21. The Lotus Sutra derives from the formative period of Mahayana Buddhism in India, approximately at the beginning of the Christian era in the Western calendar. As a religious text in Japan it is recited according to the Chinese translation of Kumarajiva and provided with various explanations in Japanese.

22. Ennōkyō is sometimes mentioned briefly in lists and guides (e.g., in Laube, *Neureligionen in Japan*). I am currently preparing a more detailed account, having frequently introduced it as a typical example of a new Japanese religion in teaching programs. My attention was first drawn to it by my wife when we were going for a walk.

23. This religion in fact provides an identity structure for Japanese persons trying to come to grips with the fact that Japan is not alone in this world but shares a history with many other states, which are duly called up in the liturgy. The peace movement profile is only part of something which in fact is considerably more complex, as I argued in an article entitled "National and International Identity in a Japanese Religion: Byakkoshinkokai," in *Identity Issues and World Religions, Selected Proceedings of the International Association for the History of Religions*, ed. V. C. Hayes (Bedford Park, S. Australia: Australian Assoc. for the Study of Religions, 1986), 234–241.

24. Art in the sense of "technique."

25. On these questions, see various articles on syncretism by the writer, especially

"Syncretism versus synthesis" in *Method and Theory in the Study of Religion* 6, no. 3 (1994): 217–229.

REFERENCES

Beijing Institute of Foreign Languages. 1978. *A Chinese-English Dictionary.* Beijing.

Center for Japanese Studies, University of Michigan. 1983. *The New Religions of Japan: A Bibliography of Western-Language Materials.* 2d ed. Ann Arbor.

Cordier, Henri. 1920. *Histoire générale de la Chine et de ses relations avec les pays étrangers.* Paris.

De Groot, J. J. M. 1903. *Sectarianism and Religious Persecution in China.* Amsterdam.

Earhart, H. Byron. 1970. *The New Religions of Japan. A Bibliography of Western-Language Materials.* Tokyo (Sophia University).

Esherick, Joseph W. 1987. *The Origins of the Boxer Uprising.* Berkeley and Los Angeles.

Franke, Otto. 1965. *Geschichte des chinesischen Reichs.* 5 vols. Berlin.

Gobron, Gabriel. 1949. *Histoire et Philosophie du Caodaïsme.* Paris.

Grayson, James Huntley. 1989. *Korea: A Religious History.* Oxford.

Hummel, Arthur W. 1943. *Eminent Chinese of the Ch'ing Period.* Washington: Government Printing Office.

Jordan, David K., and Daniel L. Overmyer. 1986. *The Flying Phoenix: Aspects of Chinese Sectarianism in Taiwan.* Princeton, N.J.: Princeton University Press.

Kohler, Werner. 1962. *Die Lotus-Lehre und und die modernen Religionen in Japan.* Zürich: Atlantis Verlag.

Laube, Johannes, ed. 1995. *Neureligionen in Japan: Stand ihrer Erforschung. Ein Handbuch.* Wiesbaden: Harrassowitz Verlag.

Murakami, Shigeyoshi. 1980. *Japanese Religion in the Modern Century.* Tokyo: University of Tokyo Press.

Oliver, Victor. 1976. *Caodai Spiritism: A Study of Religion in Vietnamese Society.* Leiden: E. J. Brill.

Overmeyer, Daniel L. 1976. *Folk Buddhist Religion: Dissenting Sects in Late Traditional China.* Cambridge: Harvard University Press.

Pham Cong Tac (Ho-Phap). 1953. *Le Caodaïsme. 3e Amnistie de Dieu en Orient.* Paris: Dervey.

Pye, Michael. 1986. "National and International Identity in a Japanese Religion: Byakko-shinkokai." In *Identity Issues and World Religions, Selected Proceedings of the International Association for the History of Religions,* ed. V. C. Hayes, 234–241. Netley, Australia.

———. 1994a. "Syncretism versus Synthesis." *Method and Theory in the Study of Religion* 6, no. 3: 217–229.

———. 1994b. "What is 'Religion' in East Asia?" In *The Notion of "Religion" in Comparative Research (Selected Proceedings of the XVI IAHR Congress),* ed. Ugo Bianchi, 115–122. Rome: "L'Erma" di Bretschneider.

———. 1996. "Aum Shinrikyo: Can Religious Studies Cope?" *Religion* 26, no. 3: 261–273.

———. 2002. "Won Buddhism as a Korean New Religion." *Numen* 49, no. 1: 113–141.

Reader, Ian. 2000. *Religious Violence in Contemporary Japan: The Case of Aum Shinrikyō*. London.

Repp, Martin. 1997. *Aum Shinrikyo. Ein Kapitel krimineller Religionsgeschichte*. Marburg.

Seiwert, Hubert. 1985. *Volksreligion und nationale Tradition in Taiwan*. Studien zur regionalen Religionsgeschichte einer chinesischen Provinz. Stuttgart: Franz Steiner Verlag.

———. 2000. "Falun Gong—Eine neue religiöse Bewegung als innenpolitischer Hauptfeind der chinesischen Regierung." *Religion—Staat—Gesellschaft. Zeitschrift für Glaubensformen und Weltanschauungen* 1, no. 1: 119–144.

Simon, Pierre J., and Ida Simon-Barouh. 1973. *Hâù Bóng. Un culte viêtnamien de possession transplanté en France*. École Pratique des Hautes Études, Cahiers de l'Homme, Nouvelle Série 13. Paris and the Hague.

Takagi, Hiroo. 1959. *Nihon no Shinkōshūkyō*. Tokyo: Iwanami Shoten.

Taylor, Romeyn. 1983. "An Imperial Endorsement of Syncretism: Ming T'ai Tsu's Essay on the Three Teachings: Translation and Commentary." *Ming Studies* 16: 31–38.

ter Haar, B. J. 1992. *The White Lotus Teachings in Chinese Religious History*. Leiden.

Vos, Frits. 1977. *Die Religionen Koreas*. Stuttgart.

Weller, Robert P. 1982. "Sectarian Religion and Political Action in China." *Modern China* 8, no. 4: 463–483.

CHAPTER 22

WITCHES, WICCANS, AND NEO-PAGANS

A Review of Current Academic Treatments of Neo-Paganism

SÍÂN LEE REID

SHELLEY TSIVIA RABINOVITCH

THE origins of the modern Neo-Pagan movement can be directly traced back to the middle of the twentieth century in England, but it draws its spiritual heritage from far earlier sources. The term "pagan" originates from the Latin word *Paganus*, meaning one who was rural rather than urban in origin. Although the main definition of the term used by dictionaries is that of a religious practitioner not of the Jewish, Christian, or Moslem faiths, a growing number of people have started to self-identify as "neo," or new, Pagans.

These new Pagans describe themselves as worshiping pre-Christian gods and goddesses, primarily with reconstructed and/or newly composed rituals. They most often describe themselves as nature-worshiping and venerating, and their cosmology includes the anthropomorphic view of the Divine in a bipartate manner: the God and the Goddesses (or gods and goddesses). Neo-Pagans often use terms including "Goddess worshiper," "witch," and "Wiccan" to describe their faith. The religion has no centralized institutional format, and numerous sects, called "traditions," have arisen since the middle of the twentieth century.

The creation and/or revival of the Celtic-based forms of Neo-Paganism is the direct result of the writings of Dr. Gerald Brosseau Gardner, a retired English civil servant, in the early 1950s. With the repeal of England's Witchcraft Act in 1951, it was no longer a crime to call oneself a witch, and Gardner wrote one book of fiction and two of nonfiction about witchcraft as a religious system. Other practitioners, such as Sibyl Leek, subsequently surfaced, claiming inherited witch ancestry after Gardner's books were published. The scholarly debate as to whether there is any proof of an unbroken lineage of witchcraft as religion prior to Gardner's books continues to this day. Although the "unbroken" claim is regarded as dubious by most serious scholars, the possibility that there were witchcraft groups prior to or contemporaneous with Gardner's group is still the ground of lively speculation.

One of the best critical evaluations of the origins of the modern Neo-Pagan movement is Ronald Hutton's *The Triumph of the Moon: A History of Modern Pagan Witchcraft* (1999). Copiously footnoted with many citations from primary sources, Hutton's work takes a critical look at the popularly held notion that Neo-Paganism in Britain continued to be practiced throughout the Christian periods of history, passed on through secret networks of Pagans.

Hutton focuses primarily on Neo-Paganism in southern England, as this is the geographic area where many traditions of witches claim their spiritual ancestry. It includes the New Forest region, so central to Gardner's legitimating narrative. As a historian, Hutton looks to textual as well as archaeological evidence in his analysis. He looks to define concepts such as "magic" and "ritual" in a manner that makes his historical analysis clear to the reader, as both words can be quite ambiguous when used by Neo-Pagans themselves.

Hutton traces the early roots of Neo-Paganism through literature such as Frazer's *Golden Bough* (1922) and Graves's *White Goddess* (1948 [1958]). Hutton mines the romantic literature of the 1800s and early 1900s in order to find threads of English paganism and/or the concepts that exist in modern Neo-Paganism. Approximately half his book looks at threads that he quite compellingly traces back in order to find precedents for many of the beliefs and practices common in Neo-Paganism today.

Hutton takes what he sees as the early building blocks of modern Neo-Pagan practice and sets up the reader for the second half of the book. Here he does modern historical research rather than mining extant texts. He interviews numerous leaders in the English Wicca communities and traces the evolution of the practice of the religion from that point on through anecdotes, interviews, and ephemera such as press clippings, flyers for gatherings, and such. One of Hutton's burning questions is whether the researcher can find a compelling and unbroken heritage for Neo-Paganism from a historical point of view. Using historical research tools, Hutton mines legend, lore, and oral tradition in order to trace the religion's evolution into a large, vibrant religious system, but he finds few traces of an unbroken heritage of paganism into early history or prehistory. *Triumph of the Moon* makes a compelling argument for the validity of the modern Pagan religions, regardless of whether they are directly descended from earlier Pagan practices.

Graham Harvey's *Listening People, Speaking Earth: Contemporary Paganism* (1997) is far less analytical in tone and more descriptive. Harvey takes great pains to illustrate various types of Neo-Pagan religious cosmology and axiology in his study. Harvey is a phenomenologist, and he uses this as his background in describing the rituals, beliefs, and worldviews that typify Neo-Pagan spirituality. He traces various beliefs practiced by Neo-Pagans in step-by-step fashion, elaborating on their festivals, traditions, and basic philosophical underpinnings. The reader has numerous types of Neo-Pagan belief systems explained, such as Goddess Worship, Druidry, Heathenry, and Wicca, along with where they are similar and where they differ.

Harvey also looks at some of the important concepts typical of many types of Neo-Pagan practice, such as magic, shamanism, and environmental awareness. The importance of nature and the natural world is highlighted in Harvey's writings as a way of explaining how modern Neo-Pagans view themselves as tied to, and identified with, nature around them. The reader is given a tour of some of the main forms of Neo-Paganism today and is shown how this group of religions functions without any centralized dogma, creed, or priesthood.

Of specific interest in *Listening People, Speaking Earth* is the manner in which Harvey shows the importance to modern Neo-Pagans of their religion's plurality of belief and practice. In the final chapter of his book, Harvey illustrates how most Neo-Pagans interact with other religions around them, as well as how other religions view Neo-Paganism. He makes a clear distinction between Satanism and Neo-Paganism and highlights how Neo-Pagans interact with Christianity, the dominant religious force around them. Harvey's book looks at the myth and reality of Neo-Paganism as a new and vibrant, lived religion.

Cynthia Eller's *Living in the Lap of the Goddess* (1993) is a study of "feminist spirituality," an area having considerable overlap with Neo-Paganism. She asserts that when "religious feminists," those trying to change traditional religions from within, became disillusioned with their project and moved toward emergent religions, their first point of contact was usually witchcraft or Neo-Paganism. Thus, much of spiritual feminism has adapted the rituals, social organization, and language of Neo-Paganism, while remaining somewhat apart from the mainstream of that movement due to their adherence to a strongly feminist agenda (1993: 49–50). Eller's observation in this regard has been borne out in other studies (Reid 2000, 2001; Rabinovitch 1992; Waldron 2001), which tend to give "Goddess spirituality" groups their own category in the typology of Neo-Paganism more generally.

Eller's approach is qualitative, relying upon numerous research approaches, including ten years of participant observation, attendance at many spiritual feminist events and gatherings, a broad and thorough reading of the movement's primary source literature, and interviews with selected spiritual feminist practitioners. Her focus is on women who have taken their sex and gender as the principal themes around which their theology and practice are constructed with a view to empowerment, which both implies and requires that the expression of feminist ideals in a spiritual framework be a fundamental appeal of her participants' religious practice. Generally, this revolves around the celebration of a Goddess and the aspects of inner divinity that reside and are expressed within women's experiences of the world. Eller's demarcation of what she defines as "feminist spirituality" is guided by several key considerations: that the movement is separatist, inasmuch as it is focused on and directed toward women; that it is centered outside of traditional religions; and that it is feminist, "believing that either women's condition or the general state of gender roles in society as we find them are unsatisfactory or need to be changed" (1993: 7).

Aside from Neo-Paganism, Eller reports that the other major influence on spiritual feminism has been the New Age movement. She notes that spiritual feminist workshops and seminars are often offered by New Age centers, and that spiritual feminists frequent New Age shops to purchase books, jewelry, and other items they use in their practice. Despite this interpenetration, Eller cautions her readers against believing that feminist spirituality is nothing more than the "women's auxiliary" of the New Age movement. Spiritual feminists have their own concerns, outside and beyond the goals of the New Age (1993: 64–65).

Eller discusses the tensions between the feminist spirituality movement and the feminist political movement. Many feminist activists view spirituality as an inappropriate and inadequate locus of praxis. Being personal, they assert, spirituality can never address the concerns and issues of women as a class. This tension began as the spiritual feminist movement gained prominence and popularity in the 1970s and peaked in the 1980s; it is much less apparent now, although the lack of overt attacks, Eller claims, should not be taken as an indication that the tensions no longer exist, but rather that they are simmering right below the surface (1993: 188–191). Eller identifies the political agenda of spiritual feminists as one that approaches the oppression of women through the ecology movement (1992: 192).

Ultimately, Eller asserts, much of the appeal of feminist spirituality can be explained by relative deprivation theory. Women, she argues, and especially white, middle-class women, despite a century of activism, still have not achieved parity with men. Having been socialized into the same aspirations and expectations as men, women find themselves without the legitimate, socially-approved means of attaining their goals. Unwilling to give up the aspirations to power and equality, women are attracted to spiritual feminism as an alternative way to attain them (1993: 212). If Eller is correct, then spiritual feminism may well be doing exactly what its critics charge—seducing women into trading the hope of real political power for a sense of spiritual power that is belied by women's actual status.

Daughters of the Goddess: Studies of Healing, Identity, and Empowerment (2000) also looks at the section of Neo-Paganism often described as "Goddess Spirituality." Editor Wendy Griffin allows the voices of both academics and practitioners alike to come through in this volume for various reasons, particularly, as she notes, to engage the discussion about objective scholarship and privileged knowledge by raising the question of the nature of understanding. This blend of the emic and etic voice makes for an engaging collection of essays which often illustrate concepts within Goddess Spirituality that might otherwise be harder to understand. Griffin points out in her introduction a particularly important issue about the entire sphere of Goddess spirituality in Neo-Paganism: most forms of Neo-Pagan practice are about the embodiment of faith and the Divine rather than reverence for the written Word, as is found in Christianity, Islam, and Judaism.

Daughters of the Goddess examines various concepts of the self and self-healing. Various studies have determined that there is a draw to Neo-Pagan practice for those who have felt disempowered by life and/or circumstance, and this volume highlights much of this in its discussions about healing and wholeness by the authors therein. The essays in this collection look at the various types of disempowerment that adherents to Goddess Spirituality view themselves as overcoming, from the dissonance between mind and body to spiritual and emotional pain attributed to patriarchal practices.

Narratives defining new images of woman are discussed, as well as how they are expressed through both writings and rituals. The issues of female identity are discussed from various points of view in the contributions, in contrast to mainstream religion, as shaped and redefined through ritual action, through artistic interpretation, and through remythologizing existing images such as Diana, Princess of Wales. *Daughters of the Goddess* takes a multidisciplinary, multivocal look at the segment of Neo-Paganism dealing directly with women's spirituality and uses it to capture a well-rounded snapshot of the creative diversity of that movement today.

Enchanted Feminism: The Reclaiming Witches of San Francisco (2002) focuses on one Neo-Pagan community—that of the Reclaiming witches. Author Jone Salmonsen self-identifies as a participant-observer in her study and discusses her topic from the points of view of both theologian and cultural anthropologist. This study looks at how the members of the Reclaiming community have created their own concept of community and, through that, create concepts of the self and the Divine.

Salmonsen points out that the Reclaiming community views the relationship between adherents and the Divine as a process, rather than as something static. She looks at the cosmology and axiology of the community in relationship to both classical theology and from a feminist perspective, uncovering some of their uniqueness. Ultimately, Salmonsen places the community within Western Esoteric traditions of belief insofar as the Reclaiming community espouses a view of the Divine as immanent rather than transcendent. She is, however, very careful to point out that their cosmology is also nonchristological, nonacademic, transcultural, and womanish, thereby making it unique when compared to the more mainstream religions of the West.

Enchanted Feminism highlights the importance of ritual in the practice of the Reclaiming community and how it is that, in their universe, the use of magic is considered the most efficacious in promoting human growth and change. Process, from the process of self-exploration to that of social change, is identified as key to the Reclaiming worldview. Most importantly, Salmonsen points out that to Reclaiming witches, the path of the Goddess is considered the single most important key to their vision of a new and revitalized society in which spirituality is unified with politics.

This volume focuses on a topic which is rarely addressed in academic material on Neo-Paganism—that of the common European religious origin backgrounds of most adherents. By doing this, Salmonsen highlights the fact that religious community building must by definition engage a dialogue involving the interconnections, complexities, and contradictions which make up human society. This volume also points out that the Reclaiming community views its spirituality as a path to be experienced rather than as a religion itself, which makes it unique within the Neo-Pagan community in general. In 1997 the Reclaiming community explicitly refused to term itself a new religion and instead agreed to continue to self-identify through its common values and worldviews, making itself notably different from most other Neo-Pagan groups. Salmonsen's study outlines some strong patterns within the Reclaiming community which can be used to analyze both other Neo-Pagan groups and other communities of faith in general.

Paul Heelas discusses Neo-Paganism in a piecemeal sort of way in *The New Age Movement* (1996). Because his focus is on the New Age, of which he believes Neo-Paganism is a small but growing part, Neo-Paganism per se does not receive a systematic or sustained treatment. Heelas believes that Neo-Paganism can be subsumed under the New Age because they share a focus on "Self-spirituality," that is, on a self that is the final moral authority in a religious practice oriented toward self-actualization. He comments that Neo-Paganism seems to be the dominant new flavor in the New Age shop, noting that his students these days tend to be more interested in witchcraft, shamanism, and earth goddesses than they are in est and other more secular human potential movements. "I think it is fair to say that paganism has become the key resource for those (increasing numbers) who have counter-cultural concerns" (1996: 88). Pagans stand out in New Age quarters because of the strength of their attraction to the environment and the frequency with which they engage in magical rituals. Where Michael York (1995) considers the New Age focus to be mostly on "self-development" while Neo-Paganism's is on "self-empowerment," Heelas does not seem to consider this sufficient cause to treat the two separately.

Heelas's strongest theoretical discussion comes out in the last two parts of his book, where he turns his analytical eye to the relationships and continuities between the New Age, modernity, and postmodernity. He frames his analysis of the New Age in terms of how it addresses both what he identifies as the "uncertainties of modernity" and the "certainties of modernity" and rejects any attempt to construct it as postmodern. Heelas considers the uncertainties of modernity to be intimately bound up with the challenges to identity construction posed by de-traditionalization. This process is associated both with the deinstitutionalization of identity—that is, the extent to which an individual is expected to construct their personal identity in a way that is not centrally informed by the mediation of factors such as class, occupation, denomination, political party, race, or nationality—and with the turn to a more expressivistic construction of personhood (1996: 141–144). He cites Peter Berger's (1974) argument that, having rejected the iron cage of determination by the capitalistic social order, many people found the liberation of "normlessness" too much to bear and found themselves allying with the secondary institutions of the counterculture.

He identifies the current state of the New Age movement as a reaction and adaptation to the conditions of modernity. A move toward postmodernity, which he considers unwise, can be seen in those segments of the New Age that have essentially reduced spirituality to a consumable lifestyle commodity. As to whether the move toward mass-consumption religiosity can be resisted by other segments of the movement, Heelas remains uncertain but cautiously optimistic.

Michael York's *The Emerging Network* (1995) is the end result of the research he did during his doctoral studies. As is the case with many dissertations that have been revised for publication, the book contains a great deal of discussion and synthesis of the insights and interpretations of other scholars, particularly those in sociology of religion. While this makes the book thought-provoking for those who are already steeped in this literature, it can make the analysis and discussion quite ponderous and difficult for the less specialized reader. Although Yorks stated aim is to examine the various church-sect typologies that appear in the academic literature, in order to see if any of them provide insight into Neo-Paganism and the New Age, this analysis, right at the end of the book, seems tangential to the more interesting discussion that precedes it about the relationships between Neo-Paganism and the New Age.

York considers both Neo-Paganism and the New Age to have emerged out of what has been called the "cultic milieu," fueled by the energy of the counterculture and with the goal of transforming the world in accordance with environmental and human potential agendas. Although they draw on many of the same ante-cedents and engage in many of the same practices, York suggests that they bring different approaches to the things they have in common. First, he notes that the New Age pursues a transcendent, metaphysical reality, while Neo-Paganism fo-cuses on an immanent locus of deity. Second, he points out that New Agers tend to think of themselves as practitioners of a new and distinct religious orientation, an awakening, while Neo-Pagans stress their connection to the past and their links, real or imagined, to earlier traditions, more of a reawakening. He also includes an informative discussion about the ambivalence, and sometimes outright hostility, with which Neo-Paganism approaches the New Age, and vice versa.

Despite the overlaps and similarities York notes between Neo-Paganism and the New Age, he treats the descriptive material he has collected on each in separate chapters, allowing his readers both to discover that difference for themselves through an immersion in York's observations, and to evaluate the claims made by each group about the other. In many places, one gets the sense that York is hiding his light under a barrel. Although it is clear from his discussion that he has synthesized some innovative insights from his material, these are often not boldly stated and get lost in York's detailed recounting of what those before him have said.

The title of Jon Bloch's 1998 book, *New Spirituality, Self and Belonging: How New Agers and Neo-Pagans Talk about Themselves,* encapsulates his focus. He shares with both Sarah Pike and Helen Berger a concern for the way in which selves are reflexively constructed within the bounds of a specific ideology, and the ways in which those who have so constructed themselves relate to and resist assimilation by the mainstream. The key issues presented by all three authors are those of identity and boundaries, sometimes discursive, sometimes physical.

Bloch, like Heelas, does not believe that there is any useful distinction to be made between Neo-Paganism and the New Age. Instead, he combines both move-ments under the label of "countercultural" or "alternative" spirituality. The culture to which it is counter is that of the "over-rationalized" mainstream in North America; the "alternative" it provides is a form of spiritual practice that minimizes formal organizational structures, hierarchy, and dogma and instead promotes self-autonomy. He notes, somewhat wryly, that the best way to get countercultural spiritualists *not* to listen to spiritual information is to present it as the one best, true way for everyone.

Bloch's research relies on in-depth interviews with countercultural spiritual-ists, half of whom he met while attending small and large-scale countercultural spiritual events, and half of whom responded to his strategically placed advertise-ments. Significantly, he notes, "Collectively, these people either knew each other or else knew many of the same people. It would not be unlikely to see them all at the same event" (1998: 13). This is perhaps why he can say so confidently that the Neo-Pagan/New Age distinction is not useful; by apparently limiting his recruitment to drop-in spiritual study groups, weekend spiritual workshops, fairs, and festivals, he has positioned himself to encounter the New Age fringe of Neo-Paganism and not the core of the movement. He also comments that most of his participants were not really concerned about what label was applied to them or to their practices. This is a direct contradiction of Michael York's finding that the people he encountered on both sides of the New Age/Neo-Pagan divide very much cared how they and their practices were labeled. We doubt that this can simply be written off as an artifact of some fundamental difference between Britain and the United States. So Bloch's observations, as interesting as many of them are, probably need to be corroborated by other work before any sweeping generalizations, including the ones he makes, are either appropriate or prudent.

His analysis of the contents of his interviews, however, is interesting on both a descriptive and theoretical level. For example, he notes the prevalence of discussion of the Goddess and the divine feminine among his subjects (1998: 69–72). He observes a difference in the way his female and male subjects frame their explanations of the role and importance of the divine feminine. He suggests that while women are inclined to speak of their relationship to the Goddess in terms of larger gender inequalities and as a means of obtaining "self-validation by having a female image of the divine with which to identify" (1998: 70), men are less likely to make reference to patriarchal social structures and tend to discuss the Goddess "more as an expressive or nurturing force that aided one's immediate self" (1998: 71). Bloch's observations about the way in which his female participants talked about the Goddess are congruent with Cynthia Eller's discussion of the Goddess as a source of empowerment for spiritual feminists. "What the goddess does for women is to give them power in their femaleness, not apart from it, to make womanhood itself a powerful quantity. It is a divine redemption of femaleness" (Eller 1993: 213).

By adopting the technique of quoting long passages from his interviews, interspersed with theoretical elaborations, Bloch makes it possible to see how his interpretations have arisen. If readers remain unpersuaded, then they have some of the data available from which to draw their own interpretations. Bloch also includes discussions about the perception of community in an environment where the self is considered the final moral and spiritual authority, the strain between scientific and spiritual explanations of reality, the ideological limitations of countercultural spirituality, and the transformation of mythology into ideology.

Tanya Luhrmann's *Persuasions of the Witch's Craft* is her study of the contemporary British magical scene. In it, she characterizes most sociocultural approaches to magic as relying on either an "intellectualist" argument, "which explained magic as based upon mistaken belief" (Tylor, Frazer), or a "symbolist" argument, "which explained away the magic by showing how it had little to do with belief" (Durkheim, Leach, Douglas) (1989: 347). These explanations, she found, were not adequate to explain the magical practices of British magicians because these people had been brought up in the scientific, progressive twentieth century and not raised in a "primitive" culture, which advocated or practiced magic as a routine matter. The apparent dissonance between magical belief and modern culture is what sparked her doctoral research, which subsequently became *Persuasions of the Witch's Craft*.

Luhrmann takes her observations of magical practitioners and turns them into a solid ethnography of modern magic in contemporary England. Her goal is to explain the manner in which magical ideas go from being alien to being accepted, and she does this with great facility, drawing upon detailed participant-observation research of the Neo-Pagan magical community in London and its environs. Luhrmann's approach to the issue of magic, treating magical practice as part of an interpretative process which acts to both nurture and explain changes in individual experience, rather than as a series of isolated goal-driven acts, is superior to the "ends-oriented" interpretation offered by more traditional social scientists inasmuch as it allows her more flexibility to answer her "classic anthropological question: why do they practice magic when, according to observers, the magic doesn't work" (1989: 4). Luhrmann's key insight is that the process through which an individual becomes magical, the magical "context," is as integral a part of the practice of magic as any ends-oriented spell.

If Neo-Pagan magic were only about ends, then repeated failures should be sufficient to delegitimize it. This is certainly the conclusion one can draw from more conventional theorists such as Stark and Bainbridge (1985). However, as Luhrmann's research makes eminently clear, repeated failure is not enough to delegitimize the practice, and indeed, magicians have developed a host of ways to turn what could be perceived as failures into successes. Magic is not a way to form a one-to-one relationship between an individual and an otherwise unattainable goal; it is an elaborate, dramatic metaphor for the relationship between an individual and the universe, and, like all metaphors, it hovers on the boundary between the figuratively and the literally true, refusing to commit itself firmly on either side.

Luhrmann describes magic as "the romantic intellectual's religion, a religion demanding no explicit belief but ripe with symbolic and experiential fruits" (1989: 341). Luhrmann's ethnography identifies as central features of magic and magical practice many of the same qualities that are highlighted by postmodern writers as characterizing the turn to the postmodern: a sense of play and irony embodied in the experience and rationalization of activity, a skepticism toward truth claims and scientific rationality, and the centrality of the interpreting individual to the nature of a truth which can only be subjective. However, although she carefully avoids labeling anything as "modern" or "postmodern," she argues that magicians have not abandoned rationality; they have expanded its bases. They have not given up on truth claims; they merely refuse to rigidly tie their behavior to the demonstrability of those claims. In this sense, they have not abandoned the "modern" enterprise; they have reinterpreted it so that its romantic elements come to the forefront.

Never Again the Burning Times (1995) is Loretta Orion's revision of her dissertation. As was the case with Michael York's work, this has left more of the common features of academic dissertations intact than was good for the book. The contextual material in this case, on the Western magical tradition, the development of British witchcraft, and the history of the witchcraze, was not only unnecessary but also distracting. Much of this material is overgeneralized and occasionally inaccurate, and the treatment she is able to give it is only superficial. Since this, and the demographic contextualization of her participants, form the first half of the book, it is not difficult to imagine that some readers would be put off before they reached Orion's main discussion.

Orion's ethnography is strong where she sticks to her main area of interest, which is Neo-Pagan approaches to health, medical, and alternative therapies. She argues that Neo-Pagans share with many others a pervasive dissatisfaction with the health care system (in the United States), but that, being out of the mainstream culture, Neo-Pagans tend to dare more than others in developing their solutions. Orion hypothesizes that by looking at the ways in which Neo-Pagans approach the issues of their own health and the health of others, we might gain insight on possible ways in which society can reduce its largely uncritical reliance on technologically expensive mainstream medicine. Because Orion was previously a nurse in the mainstream system, she brings an experience of that system into her observation of Neo-Pagan healing techniques that makes the differences between them stand out in sharp relief. One wonders, however, to what extent her findings would be replicable in a society with a socialized medical system, such as Canada's or Great Britain's.

Like Luhrmann, Orion is interested in magic, healing magic in particular. She rejects the distinction that is made between magic and prayer on the grounds of the deities invoked. Orion defines magic as "religious practice that is undertaken by individuals, alone or in concert, on their own or another's behalf to effect some change in themselves or the environment" 1995: (5). She also notes, "When individuals pray or make offerings in an effort to bring about some change in themselves or their environment—in terms of the distinction I am making—they are performing magic" (ibid.). Orion asserts that the perceived differences between magical practice in mainstream religions and magical practice in Neo-Paganism are the entirely artificial results of a value judgment arising out of prejudice against alternative belief systems.

Orion's research strategy took the form of a questionnaire, which she distributed at festivals and to which she received 189 responses, participant-observation research in two covens, and attendance at festivals and a California witch camp, among other typically Neo-Pagan activities. She recognizes that her reliance on festivals as a distribution outlet for her surveys is somewhat problematic, since not all Neo-Pagans are festival-goers, and therefore her selection had the potential to introduce significant bias into her research. Other than attempting to balance this with coven work, however, she seems to consider this an unavoidable limitation. In her final chapter, "Growing Up or Just Getting Big," Orion, like many of the authors whose books are profiled here, tries to gauge Neo-Paganism's future trajectory. Lacking a theoretical framework such as those that Heelas, Luhrmann, and Berger bring to their analyses, Orion's conclusions appear weaker, more tentative, and less convincing, even when there is some overlap in their opinions.

Magical Religion and Modern Witchcraft (1996) is a compilation of essays dealing with various aspects of Neo-Paganism, edited by James R. Lewis. One of the book's main flaws is that there is no guide to the contributors, which makes it difficult to discern where essays are emic versus etic in tone. Most of the essays are written by academics, but some are not; this differentiation would have been helpful to have.

This small problem aside, the volume is divided into five sections. The first part deals with Neo-Pagan cosmology, particularly where that worldview deals with concepts of the Goddess and/or God as compared to the larger and more familiar religions of the Western world. Chapter 2 looks at Neo-Pagan concepts of magic and ritual and how these concepts express Neo-Pagan praxis in action. Lewis points out that witches tend to stress liturgy and specific kinds of magical practice over doctrine and belief.

As with most other academic studies on Neo-Pagan witchcraft, a fair bit of the book looks at the mythic and empirical history of the religion. Lewis's volume features one essay looking at Neo-Paganism as a response to modernity, as well as pieces discussing the complex, situationally-dependent ethics found in many forms of Neo-Pagan practice.

The volume sums up with essays discussing earlier works on the religion, as well as those looking at how Neo-Paganism interacts with Christianity. One of the strong points of *Magical Religion* is the diversity of voices in the chapters: discussions are rooted in ethnography, sociology, history, and anthropology, as well as from the perspective of practicing pagans themselves.

Helen Berger's *A Community of Witches* (1999) is the product of eleven years of participant-observation work among Neo-Pagans in the Northeast United States, including the observation of one coven from its inception to its demise more than a decade later. She supplements her qualitative work with a more broadly based survey to which she received more than 2,000 responses. This book is neither a general overview nor a narrowly conceived ethnography, although the use of ethnographic material gives the book much of its texture and vibrancy.

Berger's main theoretical concern is to explore the maturation of witchcraft as a religion. She approaches this discussion as a series of ever-widening concentric circles, exploring first the magical self, then the "social cocoon" of the coven, then the Neo-Pagan community more broadly, and then the relationship between the

Neo-Pagan community and North American culture. In this way, Berger illumi-
nates how the pieces fit together—how, once people have children, it tends to
decrease their participation in the coven, leaving them to rely more on general
community events, how those events then need to alter to accommodate their
increasingly multigenerational participants, and how this in turn leads to increasing routinization, decreased radical expressivism, and a move toward greater institutionalization.

Helen Berger identifies Neo-Pagan witchcraft as a thoroughly modern movement. "Wicca . . . is a religion of late modernity rather than post-modernity. Although all of these [New Age and Neo-Pagan] religions have components of
postmodernity, they do not ultimately signify an epistemological break with Enlightenment thought" (1999: 6). She makes a compelling case for the essential
congruity of the functional values of Neo-Paganism and those of modern North
American society by emphasizing the ways in which both are products of the
application of the fundamental premises of Enlightenment thought in late modernity. "The emphasis on globalism, the belief in personal and social transformation, and the use of noninstrumental rationality place Wicca firmly within the
Enlightenment tradition" (1999: 6). The details of her analysis rely heavily on
Giddens's structuration theory and the work of James Beckford; her central point
is that Neo-Pagan witchcraft embodies the attempt to reembed moral issues
through lifestyle choices (1999: 6), a process that is undertaken by almost everyone
in modern society as the guiding role of tradition recedes. The substantive content
of both the moral issues and the lifestyle choices may not be identical with those
of the wider society, but the process is the same.

Berger also considers Wicca to be an example of the operation of what Giddens (1991) characterizes as "pure relationships." These are reflexively organized
relationships that are not anchored in or determined by the external conditions
of social or economic life, and that are sought out and maintained solely for the
benefits of the relationship itself, as experienced by the parties involved. They are
focused on intimacy and maintained through commitment and trust. Pure relationships allow for the exploration and construction of self-identity through a
process of creating shared history with selected others (Giddens 1991: 88–98). The
fluid coven and small group structure that is found throughout Wicca, Berger
asserts, is an example of the operation of an ethos of pure relationships resulting
in an amorphous constellation of "communities of choice." The congruence between what Giddens identifies as central features of late modernity and the social
forms and value orientations found in Neo-Pagan witchcraft causes Berger to
resist the idea that Wicca represents a move into the realm of the postmodern.

Berger's book is an excellent example of a scholarly work that has something
to offer both the academic community and her participants. By bracketing off
Neo-Paganism's "unusualness," taking it seriously as a legitimate product of its

cultural context, and applying to it the same concepts used in the description and analysis of other social phenomena, Berger offers her academic colleagues a fascinating example of late modern cultural innovation and adaptation, and her participants and their peers a thoughtful, serious, and grounded interpretation of how their beliefs and practices intersect and elaborate some of the leading-edge strands of social theory.

Sarah Pike's *Earthly Bodies, Magical Selves* (2000) is an analysis of the social and cultural meanings of American Neo-Pagan festivals. These festivals, often held in the summer in isolated rural locations, have become a much more prominent part of the Neo-Pagan movement over the last twenty years and are the most saturated sites of Neo-Pagan community building. This is because festivals exist as spaces set apart specifically to be Neo-Pagan, away from the watchful, often disapproving eyes of "mundania." Pike argues that it is precisely because festivals are constructed by Neo-Pagans as "safe spaces" in which to express their own senses of their identity, their relationship to others and to the natural world, that both the process and the tensions inherent in these expressions are most apparent.

Pike contextualizes the phenomenon of Neo-Pagan festivals by pointing to other historical forms of religious gathering, such as evangelical camp meetings and spiritualist conventions. She notes in a cautionary way that both of these earlier phenomena represented effervescent and "antinomian stages in emergent religious movements that later became more rigidly structured and institutionalized" (2000: 18). The potential effects of increasing levels of institutionalization in the broader Neo-Pagan movement are not followed up in Pike's analysis, although she does examine the formalization of norms that she has observed to occur over time in festival settings.

The author has taken an ethnographic and qualitative approach to her research, attending a number of different festivals, some of them regularly, over an eight-year period. The insights she has gained through her critical reflection on her own socialization to festival norms are visible in her analysis, as are those that have arisen through her extensive conversations and correspondence with others both during and between festivals. The strength of this approach lies in the way that it has allowed Pike to go beyond a simple elaboration of what Neo-Pagans say or purport to believe, into a recounting of what she has seen them do, both where their actions support their narratives and where they do not. In this way, she exposes some of the contradictions and tensions inherent in attempting to live in the perpetually "under construction" Neo-Pagan framework, within the broader context of modernity. She also examines the strategies employed by participants to address and manage dissonances and discontinuities where they occur. Her lengthy period of participant observation has given her the opportunity to experience some of the transformations that are described by others to whom she speaks. She notes, "There is a knowledge about festivals that exists only in my body, a knowledge that I gained through movement" (2000: 189). This statement, among others, indicates that Pike has successfully entered into what Maffesoli (1996) would call the "collective sensibility" of Neo-Pagan festival participants.

The chief concerns of the analysis in *Earthly Bodies, Magical Selves* are to explore the notion of boundaries and the intersection between identity and place. The construction and deconstruction of boundaries is, in Pike's estimation, essential to the transformative project of Neo-Paganism, and is also where the tensions and negotiations that take place within and between participants are most visible. She characterizes Neo-Pagan festivals as "liminal spaces," in the sense suggested by Van Gennep: loci for personal transformation which, once embodied, can then be taken out into the more rigidly structured world of "mundania." Festivals are the functional equivalent of pilgrimages, allowing participants to make a journey not only into the sacred landscape that is "nature," but also into the landscape of the self.

Continuing with the exploration of boundaries—in this case the boundary between Neo-Pagans and their mundane and sometimes hostile neighbors—Pike includes an excellent chapter on the ongoing construction of Neo-Paganism as satanic in the minds of what she terms "bible-believing Christians," and the effect that has on Neo-Pagans' constructions of themselves and of their place in American society. She also includes chapters exploring the boundaries and tensions between festival organizers and festival participants, between the needs for self-expression and the needs for community solidarity, between sexual self-expression and sexual safety, and between competing definitions of self.

Pike, like Berger, uses Giddens's ideas in reference to her observations about the construction of the self within a Neo-Pagan framework, which, she says, consists of a "non-essential, free-floating self" and a "deep self." She asserts that although Neo-Paganism might appear to be an example of extreme religious postmodernity, with its lack of fixed doctrine, its emphasis on change, its quicksilver transformations, and its trail enactments of different lives and different selves, it in fact exemplifies the process of the development of new narratives of self in late modernity that have the potential not only to illuminate the self, but also to aid in the construction of a community for the self. She writes,

> Neo-Pagans are experts on "the reflexive project of the self" as it is described by Giddens. They make the project of self-construction seem less arbitrary by sharing coherent stories about themselves that progress in a linear fashion. . . . The stories Neo-Pagans tell about their lives focus on the meaning of self and attest to the significance of individuality within the Neo-Pagan community. But these personal stories are told in order to highlight common themes and experiences that have value for most Neo-Pagans. Personal narrative works to shape a common cultural and moral universe. (2000: 224)

Like Berger then, Pike situates Neo-Paganism, through the works of Anthony Giddens, squarely in the "late modern" camp.

The Neo-Pagan community exemplifies characteristics that French theorist Michel Maffesoli (1996) ascribes to neotribes. Neotribes are unstable, open communities defined by the participants' uncoerced agreement that they share a common sentiment that gives rise to a certain ethical experience, an orientation toward proper living that may not be shared with the broader social order. This is an accurate description of the amorphous, decentralized, unregulated nature of the broad Neo-Pagan community, out of which smaller groups characterized by closer proximal relationships coalesce and dissolve, leaving the collective sentiment, which is not dependent upon any particular individual or group of individuals, intact. It also suggests that the decentralization that has been characteristic of Neo-Paganism is a fundamental part of its vitality and its ability to provide people with a sense of identity not dependent on the organizing structures of power in society. This is significant when one considers the growing push toward institutionalization coming from within the Neo-Pagan movement itself.

The increasing desire expressed by some segments of the Neo-Pagan community for the development of more formalized organizations designed to deliver "services," such as lobbying, information coordination, spiritual counseling, pagan training and education, chaplaincy, and social organizing, to the pagan community and through which they could be recognized legally as religious organizations, represents an area that is highly contested among pagans. Although most practitioners would prefer to see Neo-Pagans offered more social acceptance and legal protection, there remains a deep and abiding suspicion about whether adopting the forms of the dominant institutional order is the best way to achieve these aims.

Helen Berger sees the move toward higher levels of organization as an inevitable outcome of the increased number of adherents to the movement, the growth of information networks, the development of a professional ethic, and a greater desire for legitimacy as adherents begin to raise families in the Craft (1999: 104). Using the framework articulated by sociological theorist Anthony Giddens, she views the differentiation of expert systems to be a part of the maturation process of the Neo-Pagan movement. Loretta Orion notes the tension that exists around institutionalization but refuses to commit to an assessment of increased organization as either positive or negative. She believes that whether or not Neo-Pagans end up being welcomed as colleagues by their counterparts in more established religions, the movement will continue to grow, both in the slow, organic way exemplified by the traditional lineage coven structure, and in the more explosive, experimental manner fostered in eclectic covens and by national and regional gatherings, which will, she asserts, become more numerous (1995: 270).

We suggest that the tension that characterizes the institutionalization debates is well founded and points to the potential for a crisis of legitimation within the Neo-Pagan movement. Jürgen Habermas (1975) uses the term "legitimation crisis" to refer to a specific condition in late capitalist society in which the state must ensure capital accumulation while maintaining mass loyalty. Unfortunately, the mechanisms through which the former is accomplished can lead to the diminution of the latter, and so the former must be concealed in order for the state to maintain its legitimacy. Clearly, this state/economic orientation is not directly applicable to Neo-Paganism; however, the logic of a legitimation crisis is. The ideology through which Neo-Paganism has legitimated itself is that of individual autonomy and self-determination, which has led in turn to its existence as a decentralized neotribal religious movement existing in the sphere of the lifeworld.

Habermas characterizes the lifeworld as the realm of "culturally transmitted and linguistically organized stock of interpretative patterns" in which action and communication oriented toward mutual understanding are possible (1989: 170–171). The structural components of the lifeworld are culture, society, and personality. To the extent that these are constructed within contexts that are at least in theory negotiable among parties oriented to mutual understanding, they remain lifeworld functions, however rationalized and differentiated they become. Habermas explains,

> In the relation of culture to society, structural differentiation is to be found in the gradual uncoupling of the institutional system from worldviews; in the relation of the personality to society, it is evinced in the extension of the scope of contingency for establishing interpersonal relationships; and in the relation of culture to personality, it is manifested in the fact that the renewal of traditions depends more and more on the individuals' readiness to criticize and their ability to innovate. (1989: 181)

Structural differentiation between the components of the lifeworld is seen by Habermas to be a desirable condition, releasing the full rational potential of communicative action (1989: 180–181). Certainly in terms of the latter two points, Neo-Paganism can be seen as promoting the rationalization of the participants' lifeworlds by encouraging what Giddens characterizes as "pure relationships"—those in which one engages purely for the intrinsic rewards and satisfactions engendered by the relationship itself—and by problematizing the individual's relationship to inherited interpretations through its emphasis on personal experience as the grounding for the legitimate creation of "tradition."

Habermas also notes, however, that the lifeworld in modern societies coexists with another set of structures he names the "system." The system consists of those "increasingly autonomous organizations [that] are connected with one another via delinguistified media of communication" (1989: 189). Chief among these Habermas places the economic system, whose delinguistified medium is money, and the political order, whose delinguistified medium is power. Systemic mechanisms such as money and power must be anchored in the lifeworld by way of institutions. Where these institutions result in the logic of the systemic mechanism, which is perceived as outside of the sociocultural construction of the lifeworld, superceding the logic of communicative action in spheres where the latter has until then held sway, Habermas speaks of a "colonization of the lifeworld." Although he acknowledges that system rationalization and differentiation must proceed in concert with lifeworld rationalization and differentiation, when the former process has the effect of reducing the lifeworld, which is the source of all social patterns, to the status of "one subsystem among many," the potential for the rationality of the entire social system is compromised.

The suspicion that institutionalization will offer an anchor for the logic of systemic mechanisms such as exchange and bureaucracy in the Neo-Pagan lifeworld is the unarticulated theoretical premise underlying many of the hesitations expressed about Neo-Pagan institutions. The widely held principle that one must not accept money for instructing others in the practice of Neo-Paganism, for example, articulated first in Gardner's "Craft Laws" and subsequently adopted by many other groups of all persuasions, is one of the normative barriers erected by Neo-Pagans to prevent the wholesale commercialization of their practice, that is, its assimilation to the logic of exchange.

The perceived requirement to conform to the relevant government regulations outlining "legitimate" religious forms and practices is seen by practitioners as not only potentially restricting the organization and structure of Neo-Pagan groups, but also as having the potential to restrict the scope of dialogue oriented toward mutual understanding through the routinization of creativity and the explicit or implicit regulation of symbolically expressed discourse. To the extent that Neo-Pagan organizations are perceived to be subordinating the intersubjectively constructed and communicatively maintained discourse, upon which the movement itself is founded, to an institution conforming to either the logic of exchange or that of efficiency, they will suffer a legitimation crisis. And, since Neo-Paganism's status as a neotribe means that it possesses no sanctioning ability to coerce the disaffected into obedience, a widespread withdrawal of loyalty is destabilizing to the potential survival of the movement. In addition, the dominant cultural direction in much of the developed West seems to be toward locating religious concerns increasingly within the lifeworld and disentangling them from their existing bureaucratic structures. Moving in the opposite direction and taking Neo-Paganism from a position in which it is well adapted as a decentralized, informal affinity orientation existing within the confines of the lifeworld into a more formalized and bureaucratized structure better able to conform to systemic imperatives would seem to be maladaptive in the long term, and to hurt its chances of growing and surviving in an increasingly rationalized, some would say "postmodern," environment.

Habermas, however, does not take the presence of institutional anchors for systemic mechanisms in the lifeworld to necessarily forecast a colonization of the latter. He retains the possibility that these institutions could serve as a channel for the influence of the lifeworld on formally organized domains of action (1989: 217). In this way, the institutions offer a means to reclaim territory for the lifeworld by extending communicative logic and intersubjective value contexts into areas formerly organized solely according to their own logics. Expanding the potential base of application of the sentiment of "re-enchanting the world," which forms the core of the Neo-Pagan lifeworld and defines their "collective sensibility," into the broader society would, on the surface, seem to be a natural social project for Neo-Pagans, and certainly Bloch (1998), Berger (1999), and Eller (1993) report that many of those to whom they spoke regarded their personal transformative practices as a means through which socially transformative processes could eventually be enacted.

Maffesoli, however, implies that sentiment cannot be effectively institutionalized. It cannot reside in the role system of a bureaucracy; it must be enacted and embodied in authentic sociality, which can only be carried out between persons. Where Habermas privileges discourse oriented toward mutual understanding as the foundation of rational community, Maffesoli privileges participation in a defining sentiment that is only articulated and refined through language as the foundation for a community in which rationality is not the end goal. It is ultimately in the lifeworld that the vitality of the Neo-Paganism, Maffesoli's *puissance*, is to be found. To the extent that institutionalization would diminish the centrality of lifeworld concerns in Neo-Paganism, that institutionalization will undermine its transformative potential, and thus its long-term survival. Neo-Pagan organizations, therefore, if they are truly to serve the best interests of their communities, must resist the temptation to borrow existing structures and reflexively invent themselves according to the imperatives provided by the legitimating ideology of the Neo-Paganism itself. It remains to be seen to what extent Neo-Paganism will be able to avoid a legitimation crisis as the internal pressures to develop more formally organized subsystems increase.

REFERENCES

Berger, Helen. 1999. *A Community of Witches.* Columbia: University of South Carolina Press.

Berger, P. L., B. Berger, and H. Kellner. 1974. *The Homeless Mind: Modernization and Consciousness.* Harmondsworth, England: Penguin.

Bloch, Jon. 1998. *New Spirituality, Self and Belonging: How New Agers and Neo-Pagans Talk about Themselves.* Westport, Conn.: Praeger.

Eller, Cynthia. 1993. *Living in the Lap of the Goddess.* New York: Crossroad.

Frazer, Sir James G. 1922. *The Golden Bough.* New York: Macmillan.

Graves, Robert. 1948 [1958]. *The White Goddess.* New York: Vintage Books.

Griffin, Wendy, ed. 2000. *Daughters of the Goddess.* Thousand Oaks, Calif.: Alta Mira Press.

Habermas, Jürgen. 1975. *Legitimation Crisis.* Trans. Thomas McCarthy. Boston: Beacon Press.

———. 1989. *Jürgen Habermas on Society and Politics.* Ed. Steven Seidman. Boston: Beacon Press.

Harvey, Graham. 1997. *Listening People, Speaking Earth* (U.S. title: *Contemporary Paganism*). New York: New York University Press.

Heelas, Paul. 1996. *The New Age Movement.* Oxford: Blackwell.

Hutton, Ronald. 1999. *The Triumph of the Moon.* New York: Oxford University Press.

Lewis, James, ed. 1996. *Magical Religion and Modern Witchcraft.* Albany: SUNY Press.

Luhrmann, Tanya. 1989. *Persuasions of the Witch's Craft.* Cambridge: Harvard University Press.

Maffesoli, Michel. 1996. *The Time of the Tribes.* Trans. Don Smith. Thousand Oaks, Calif.: Sage Publications.

Orion, Loretta. 1995. *Never Again the Burning Times.* Prospect Heights, Ill.: Waveland Press.

Pike, Sarah. 2000. *Earthly Bodies, Magical Selves.* Berkeley and Los Angeles: University of California Press.

Rabinovitch, Shelley. 1992. "An Ye Harm None, Do What Ye Will": Neo-Pagans and Witches in Canada." M.A. thesis, Carleton University.

Reid, Sian. 2000. "Witch Wars: Factors Contributing to Conflict in Canadian Neopagan Communities." *Pomegranate* 11 (Feb.): 10–20.

———. 2001. "Two Souls in One Body: Ethical and Methodological Implications of Studying What You Know." *Pomegranate* 17 (Aug.): 34–39.

Salmonsen, Jone. 2002. *Enchanted Feminism: The Reclaiming Witches of San Francisco.* London: Routledge.

Waldron, David. 2001. "Postmodernism and Witchcraft Histories." *Pomegranate* 15 (Feb.): 36–44.

York, Michael. 1995. *The Emerging Network.* London: Rowman & Littlefield.

INDEX

....